W9-CMI-846

SHARING THE FRONT LINE AND THE BACK HILLS

International Protectors and Providers:
Peacekeepers, Humanitarian Aid Workers
and the Media in the Midst of Crisis

Edited by

Yael Danieli
New York, USA

Foreword by

Kofi A. Annan
Secretary-General of the United Nations

Epilogue by

Kenzo Oshima
*Under-Secretary-General for Humanitarian Affairs
and Emergency Relief Co-ordinator*

Published for and on behalf of the United Nations

BAYWOOD PUBLISHING COMPANY, INC.
AMITYVILLE, NEW YORK

Published for and on behalf of the United Nations by Baywood Publishing Company, Inc., Amityville, New York.

The views expressed in this book are those of the authors and do not necessarily reflect the views of the United Nations.

Cover Art: Ron Haviv/SABA. 07/1995 Srebrenica refugees arrive at United Nations camp after being expelled by Serbian forces.

Library of Congress Catalog Number: 2001037906
ISBN: 0-89503-000-0 (cloth)

Library of Congress Cataloging-in-Publication Data

Sharing the front line and the back hills : international protectors and providers : peacekeepers, humanitarian aid workers and the media in the midst of crisis / edited by Yael Danieli ; foreword by Kofi A. Annan.
    p. cm.
    "Published for and on behalf of the United Nations."
    Includes bibliographical references and index.
    ISBN 0-89503-263-5 (cloth)
    1. Humanitarian assistance. 2. International relief. 3. Peacekeeping forces. I. Danieli, Yael.

HV553 .S475 2001
361.2'6- -dc21

                        2001037906

Foreword

Kofi A. Annan
Secretary-General of the United Nations

Each September on Staff Day, the United Nations flag is raised in a ceremony that allows us to join together in honoring colleagues killed in the line of duty. In September 2000, we not only held that observance; just weeks earlier, I opened the Millennium Assembly by informing the assembled Heads of State and Government of the savage murder of three UN staff in West Timor. All stood for a moment of silent tribute.

Commemorations are essential, for they acknowledge the ultimate personal sacrifices of our colleagues and help heal the wounds of our losses. But they are not enough. We must also send a powerful message that we will not tolerate the increasingly frequent and deadly assaults on people who work to relieve hardship and restore peace. And we must protest just as loudly against attacks on our friends and partners in civil society, who take great risks to work side by side with us in areas of conflict and need, and in the media, whose work to inform the world about human suffering frequently puts them in great danger.

Member States of the United Nations have a responsibility for the safety and security of UN staff, and an obligation to ensure that those who attack them are promptly brought to justice. Yet less than one third of the UN's 189 Member States are parties to the 1994 Convention on the Safety of United Nations and Associated Personnel. I call upon all Member States to ratify this treaty, and to join the effort to approve a Protocol that would extend its automatic application to all UN operations and categories of personnel beyond those presently covered.

We appreciate greatly the contributions from some Member States that have enabled us to take initial steps to strengthen our efforts. But our work to provide essential security for staff cannot depend on voluntary contributions alone. Resources must be built into regular budgets.

The stories in this book bring home to us the need to create support systems that will be in place before, during, and after deployment of staff; and that will be fully sensitive not only to the physical security of those at risk, but also to their mental and emotional health. Exhausted, stressed, and inadequately supported staff cannot do their jobs effectively. They may want, and try, to tough it out, but in the final analysis, everybody is damaged. It is encouraging to know that much serious thought is being given to this matter. This book will inform and facilitate that process.

Kofi A. Annan

Contents

The book celebrates, commemorates and honors
those who put their lives on the line for others

Acknowledgments

First and foremost, I thank the contributors who brought to the book broad expertise and rich experience and those who shared their personal experiences, hearts, and wisdom through their voices. Their care and dedication joined in making the book a labor of love, and a home for today's and tomorrow's international protectors and providers.

I am deeply honored that Kofi Annan, Secretary-General of the United Nations, contributed the Foreword, and Kenzo Oshima, Under-Secretary-General for Humanitarian Affairs and Emergency Relief Co-ordinator, the Epilogue.

Katy Howe and SABA Press provided research for the cover image, and Alfredo Jaar generously shared his advice and wisdom.

Joe Sills reviewed and commented on the entire book. His continued assistance was indispensable to its realization. I am grateful to Shashi Tharoor, Interim Director of the UN's Department of Public Information, for his unfailing responsiveness and support, and to him and Edward Mortimer, Sam Daws and Annika Savill of the Executive Office of the Secretary-General for helping to navigate the bureaucratic shoals. Vladimir Lubomudrov of the External Publications Unit of the UN's Department of Public Information helped the project along from beginning to end.

Youssef Mahmoud, the Director of Africa II Division of the Department of Political Affairs and the co-author of the introduction, has been a source of clarity, creativity, and kindness.

Sue Downie helped find "protectors and providers" as the needed replacement for "interveners," and edit some of the material, with good cheer. Elizabeth Neuffer of the *Boston Globe* helped edit the media section, and more; her friendship smoothed some of the more difficult turns in the process. She and Ron Haviv of *Newsweek* opened doors to many of the journalists whose voices grace the book. Elvi Ruottinen of Gemini News Service helped as well.

John Fairbank aided with editing the data-based, Introduction and Conclusion chapters, and extended unlimited collegiality. Dorathea Halpert caringly fine-tuned some of my own language. For early helpful suggestions I thank Gillian Sorenson, UN Assistant Secretary-General for External Relations; Michael Moller of the Department of Political Affairs; David Wimhurst of the Department of Peace-Keeping Operations; Sema Gurun of the UN Staff Committee; Djoeke Van Beest of the Office of Coordination of Humanitarian Affairs; and Jean-Claude Legrand of UNICEF; Barbara Smith, Vice President of the International Rescue Committee; and Nan Buzzard of the Sphere Project. I also thank Shirley Brownell of the Department of Public Information and Marie Dimond of the UN Development Programme for coming to the rescue, and Mina Mauerstein-Bail, Linda and Paul Ares, and Kathleen Cravero for their forthrightness and friendship.

This book has been blessed with the kind of generosity that helps transcend its sometimes heart-wrenching substance and make the world a better place. I am thankful for that as well.

Introduction

Yael Danieli and Youssef Mahmoud

The number of horrifying attacks on representatives of the United Nations, relief agencies, the media, non-governmental and other organizations while on missions to alleviate and report human suffering throughout the world has escalated alarmingly. In the past, the blue UN letters and the red cross provided protection; increasingly, they designate targets.

International protectors and providers and their locally recruited colleagues have been taken hostage, tortured, and even killed. They and their families have physically and psychologically paid a very high price, both immediate and long-term, for their efforts on behalf of others. They have gone to countries and cultures not their own, often with little advance training, little support during their mission, and little or no assistance at the time of and following their (re)integration or discharge.

Who cannot but be moved by what Carlos Caceres said in his last e-mail from West Timor:

> You should see this office. Plywood on the windows, staff peering out through openings in the curtains hastily installed a few minutes ago. We are waiting for the enemy, we sit here like bait, unarmed. . . .

A few hours later, he and two of his UN colleagues were brutally murdered. And by General Romeo Dallaire's reflections after Rwanda:

> It took nearly two years to all of a sudden not being able to cope; not being able to hide it; not being able to forget it or to put it in, keep it in a drawer. I became suicidal because there was no other solution. You couldn't live with the pain and the sounds and the smell and the sights. I couldn't sleep. I couldn't stand the loudness of silence. And sometimes I wish I had lost a leg instead of having all those brain cells screwed up. You lose a leg, it's obvious, you've got therapy, all kinds of stuff. You lose your marbles; very, very difficult to explain, very difficult to gain that support that you need. But those who don't recognize it and don't go to get the help are going to be at risk to themselves and to us.

Recent decades have seen a litany of man-made and natural disasters resulting in immense suffering and misery. Violations of human rights abound. Tens of millions of refugees and internally displaced persons have cried out for help from

1

governments and international and non-governmental organizations. While the international community has made some attempts to respond to these overwhelming needs, enormous human suffering remains. In this maze of human agony, despair replaces hope and the world loses sight of the accomplishments as well as the considerable costs borne and the sacrifices made by those who are responding to the plight of the victims.

THE BOOK AND ITS VOICES

This book tells the story of the thousands of individuals who, as citizens of the world, have dedicated themselves to helping others, often with too little protection and support and at great sacrifice to themselves and their families. These are people who have worked with peacekeeping and peacebuilding missions, humanitarian workers with UN and other humanitarian and disaster relief operations, human rights defenders, journalists and other media professionals. The first goal of this book is to establish awareness of and create an appreciation for the accomplishments as well as the costs and sacrifices of these international protectors and providers. These stand in stark contrast to the acute deficits in protection and support given to them. Where failures and abdication of responsibility have occurred, such as in Somalia, Srebrenica, Rwanda, Timor or Chechnya, it draws some lessons to prevent their repetition or, at least, reduce the risk.

The second goal is to integrate issues of protection into all levels of planning, implementing and evaluating international intervention and action. The book discusses, develops, and advocates specific policies and practices that enable protectors and providers to serve effectively and safely. It reviews existing knowledge, identifies approaches that have proven useful, even in a limited way, explores and suggests future directions for the role of protectors and providers, and makes policy recommendations to relevant implementing organizations.

This book follows and will build upon two earlier related volumes published for and on behalf of the United Nations: *International Responses to Traumatic Stress: Humanitarian, Human Rights, Justice, Peace and Development Contributions, Collaborative Actions and Future Initiatives*, in 1996 [1], and *The Universal Declaration of Human Rights: Fifty Years and Beyond*, in 1999 [2]. The first described the nature of trauma, its psychological consequences, and the responses by the international community to the suffering incurred and to its prevention. The second reviewed the international human rights system and evaluated it critically from the point of view of whether it has reached the people by protecting individual human beings or averting their victimization. This book expands the initial work on the emotional responses of international humanitarian aid workers [3] and focuses specifically on international protectors and providers, those who report about traumatized people, serve them, and try to prevent (further) victimization.

Some systematic knowledge has existed about stress reactions and associated interventions primarily among military peacekeepers, both during their service and following their return. However, almost nothing comparable is known about what their civilian counterparts' experience, be it from the secretariats of organizations in the UN system, from voluntary, non-governmental organizations, or from the media. The book is the first significant effort to fill these gaps.

Following heightened coverage in the media, the security of personnel has been receiving more attention by the relevant intergovernmental bodies of the United Nations. The General Assembly at its 49th session adopted the (so far sparsely ratified) Convention on the Safety of United Nations and Associated Personnel (A/RES/49/59 of 9 December 1994) and the Declaration on the Right and Responsibility of Individuals, Groups and Organs of Society to Promote and Protect Universally Recognized Human Rights and Fundamental Freedoms (GA/RES/53/144 of 9 December 1998). The security and protection of UN personnel have been in recent years the subject of several Security Council meetings and presidential statements.

The main flaw of these conventions and declarations and other statements emerging from intergovernmental bodies remains the fact that the state in a conflict situation cannot be relied upon as the protector of international workers, given that it often cannot protect its own citizens. Multiple non-state actors, who often escape the control of central authorities and who flout international covenants and declarations, are a major hurdle in ensuring the protection of international workers.

A further goal of this book is to describe in greater detail these major initial steps taken by the various international organizations as well as their weaknesses and develop policy and practice recommendations leading to the creation of a more comprehensive support system.

The book consists of 6 Sections, subdivided into chapters according to the type of international protectors and providers (such as UN military and non-military peacekeepers and peace builders; civilian staff of the UN system; UN and national volunteers; International Federation of the Red Cross and Red Crescent; NGOs; and the media); the organizations they represent; their focus (such as women, children, and forensic work); the nature of knowledge (data-based, descriptive, and reflective experiential voices) and challenges and remedies (such as psychological, educational, legal, and political). The concluding chapter elaborates policy and program recommendations.

A special feature is the voices of the interveners themselves. These were provided by the participating organizations and individuals and are interwoven among the chapters.

The chapters present themes, points of views informed by different experiences. They include, among others, a detailed consideration of the requirements of pre-mission selection, assignment and training, support during mission, and post-mission assistance and counseling. They consider distinct problems posed by intensive, short-term involvement, usually on an emergency basis, as compared with extended assignments.

WHAT'S IN A WORD?

The initial subtitle of this book referred to protectors and providers as "international interveners." In the health professions, the choice of the word "intervention" comes naturally; it conveys the need to take urgent and sometime invasive measures to change the course of a disease and thus halt or prevent its progression. However, many colleagues working in international humanitarian and political organizations advised against the use of the word "interveners," particularly when prefaced by "international." In their view, the word conjures up unilateral and forceful interference in the affairs of other nations by powerful nations or entities who, in the guise of moral or humanitarian motives, create more problems than solutions.

Recent military and political ventures into other countries, while frequently tolerated during the cold war, have now become one of the most troubling issues on the international policy agenda and thus have given the word "interveners" a negative connotation. It also brings to the fore the international community's floundering attempts to find an appropriate response to internal conflict, having gone through counterproductive intervention in Somalia to inaction in the face of genocide in Rwanda [4].

The heated debate generated by the address of the United Nations Secretary-General to the 54th General Assembly (September 1999) [5] on sovereignty and humanitarian intervention, was pointed out as an added reason for steering clear from the word "interveners."

Others associate the word "interveners" with the hordes of competing international, non-governmental organizations which descend upon a stricken country and spend an inordinate amount of money on relief that could have been better spent on staving off the disaster. Yet others point to the media who tend to accompany military interventions and withdrawals and take interest only when deadly violence engulfs a country and massive human rights violations occur. They invariably depart when the novelty of the crisis wears off or the world's attention is drawn to more "newsworthy" events [6].

In the search for a better word than interveners, "actors" was briefly considered, only to be discarded. Finally, the phrase "international protectors and providers" was chosen to refer to all contributors to the book, including the media who provide information. Whatever their name, they are called upon to intervene because prevention has failed or did not take place in time. They intervene because the national or international entities entrusted with defending, preserving, and promoting human security are unwilling or unable to shoulder their responsibilities.

The environment in which international protectors and providers labor has changed drastically since the end of the cold war. It is a world where the core military and non-miliary threats to international peace and security no longer come exclusively from interstate violence [7]. Intra-state discord stemming from social, economic, demographic, and environmental pressures accounts for the majority of the conflicts witnessed today. In many of these states, ineffective governance and repressive or predatory practices by State and non-state actors constitute a further source of human insecurity.

In countries where internal strife has broken into open conflict and where state forces are battling armed insurgents, civilian populations are often caught in the cross fire and bear the brunt of death and destruction. In the past decade alone, internal armed conflicts have turned over 40 million people into refugees and displaced persons. The chaotic situations these conflicts create, where combatants mix with civilians, endanger not only the lives of these errant populations but also those of medical and humanitarian relief workers. In the melee, hospitals are invaded, clinics destroyed, relief convoys barred from reaching their destinations, forced military recruitment of children flourishes and women and girls are exposed to sexual and other degrading violence. Where greed for rare commodities like diamonds, rather than legitimate grievances, fuels the conflict, and where access to small arms is easy and affordable, the conflict tends to be open-ended and the human suffering visited upon the civilian population widespread and unrelenting.

This is the uncharted and hazardous environment in which international interveners—protectors and providers—and their local partners operate, often unprepared and unprotected. It is an environment where the traditional principles of humanitarian intervention (neutrality, impartiality, and consent) seem to have been fashioned for a different world populated by accountable governments and regular armies, where civilians are accidental, not prime, targets of warfare. It is a world where humanitarian assistance tends to fuel conflict dynamics and is often usurped to "sustain war economies that redistribute assets from the weak to the strong" [8].

While this book does not address directly the multiple institutional and moral quandaries protectors and providers face, it provides ample material for future reflections on the complex role they play in zones of conflict where politics and humanitarian action inexorably intersect.

REFERENCES

1. Y. Danieli, N. S. Rodley, and L. Weisaeth (eds.), *International Responses to Traumatic Stress: Humanitarian, Human Rights, Justice, Peace and Development Contributions, Collaborative Actions and Future Initiatives*, Baywood, Amityville, New York, 1999.
2. Y. Danieli, E. Stamatopoulou, and C. J. Dias (eds.), *The Universal Declaration of Human Rights: Fifty Years and Beyond*, Baywood, Amityville, New York, 1996.
3. B. Smith, I. Agger, Y. Danieli, and L. Weisaeth, Emotional Responses of International Humanitarian Aid Workers: The Contribution of Non-Governmental Organizations, in *International Responses to Traumatic Stress: Humanitarian, Human Rights, Justice, Peace and Development Contributions, Collaborative Actions and Future Initiatives*, Y. Danieli, N. S. Rodley, and L. Weisaeth (eds.), Baywood, Amityville, New York, pp. 397-423, 1996.
4. K. A. Annan, *The Question of Intervention*, published by the United Nations Department of Public Information, December 1999.
5. P. V. Jakobsen, Focus on the CNN Effect Misses the Point: The Real Media Impact on Conflict Management is Invisible and Indirect, *Journal of Peace Research, 37*:2, pp. 131-143, 2000.
6. M. J. Glennon, The New Interventionism (Getting Involved in Other Nations Conflict and Affairs), *Foreign Affairs, 78*:3, May 1999.
7. M. T. Clare, Redefining Security: The New Global Schisms, in *Approaches to Peace*, D. P. Barash (ed.), Oxford University Press, New York, pp. 52-59, 2000.
8. T. G. Weiss, Principles, Politics and Humanitarian Action, *Ethics & International Affairs, 13*, pp. 1-22, 1999.

Voices

Subject: ARE YOU STILL THERE?—REPLY
Date: 6 September 2000, 6:05 a.m.
From: Carlos Caseres

My next post needs to be in a tropical island without jungle fever and mad warriors. At this very moment, we are barricaded in the office. A militia leader was murdered last night, he was decapitated and had his heart and penis cut out. Segments of Timorese society must be some of the most violent and gory people anywhere on earth: Atambua suddenly shut down when news spread that trucks and buses full of militias were coming from Betun (my former home) to Atambua. The town suddenly deserted and all the shops were boarded up in a matter of minutes. I'm glad that a couple of weeks ago we bought rolls and rolls of barbed wire.

I was in the office when news came that a wave of violence would soon pound Atambua. We sent most of the staff home. I just heard someone on the radio saying that they are praying for us in the office. The militias are on the way and I am sure they will do their best to demolish this office. These guys act without thinking and can kill a human as easily (and painlessly) as I kill mosquitoes in my room.

You should see this office. Plywood on the windows, staff peering out through openings in the curtains hastily installed a few minutes ago. We are waiting for this enemy, we sit here like bait, unarmed, waiting for the wave to hit. I am glad to be leaving this island for three weeks. I just hope I will be able to leave tomorrow.

As I wait for the militias to do their business, I will draft the agenda for tomorrow's meeting on Kupang. The purpose of the meeting: to discuss how we are to proceed with this operation.

Carlos

I LOST MY LIFE IN KUWAIT
Kathleen Nader

I lost my life in a war zone. The air was so thick with oil fire smoke, pesticides, and radioactive dust that even after half of the oil fires were extinguished, months after I arrived, the baby's incubator filters were black after only six hours of use. The ailment that came home with me has permitted the repeated agony of being unable to use the skills that were a part of a joyful career. Each news show depicting horrible events that affect children is a reminder that I am physically unable to help where I might have in the past. So, in addition to gunfire, mines, and snipers, there are other dangers in toxic environments. Are consultants warned about these dangers? About toxic chemicals or radiation that may be present in war zones; parasites and bacteria endemic to an area for which no immunity is present in the visitor? About the dangers of exhausting oneself (and thus lowering the body's resistance) in such an environment? Do they know about the danger of providing too little assistance so that too long hours must be worked because of time constraints, the confusion in a trauma zone, false promises about equipment available and preparations made . . . ? People in war zones often need to show, tell, and demonstrate the horrors of war and the wrongs done to them. Moreover, interveners need to be briefed. Will those who go to help be warned about entering danger zones (violent or toxic) so that, when they are briefed, well meaning but naive individuals do not take them into those areas without proper protection? We learned from adolescents who testified in court that someone who had the good experience and protection of positive action during a traumatic experience can be traumatized by seeing pictures of mutilation. Will interveners be prepared for the pictures, videos, and replicas of mutilation those who have endured war want to share? . . .

I would do it all over again because of the benefits of training many local mental health professionals. I hope that they have applied their knowledge to helping the children of their nation. If I had it to do over again, I would insist upon more assistance and equipment than last time: including an air purifier.

WHY WE HAVE TO BE THERE

Christiane Amanpour
Chief International Correspondent, CNN and
Contributing Correspondent CBS 60 Minutes

Recently I have been thinking of what exactly I do for a living, this unusual introspection sparked by my new status as a mother. I have thought about how I "do danger" for a living, about how almost every working day is spent in a state of repressed fear, how survival is as thrilling and important as winning a scoop! For the past twelve years I have worked just about every major war and minor front line that has made this post-cold war period so messy. For the past *eleven* years I thought very little about personal safety, not that I did not take sensible precautions, I just did not obsess. Now that I have a one-year-old child, I obsess.

Suddenly I feel vulnerable whereas before I felt invincible.

But that is only part of the story. The most important part, the real part, is that I love what I do. I am passionately committed to covering the stories I do. I believe strongly that it is vitally important that these stories get heard: the stories of human drama and endurance, of human horror and evil, of heroism and atrocities, of fantastic success and depressing failure, of nobility and depravity that so often exist side by side. These are the stories that can give a voice to the most dispossessed and shine light into the darkest, saddest corners of our world.

What I have seen and experienced over the past 12 years has shaped my world-view and influenced my perspective of journalism and the role of journalists in society. I believe what we do in informing people makes up a vital part of our civil society. A free and independent and responsible press is a pillar of democracy. Without a properly informed citizenry you cannot have a properly functioning democracy. I believe news is a public service that everyone should have the right to access, especially in this, the information age. I believe as journalists, our words matter. We can, for better or for worse, shape the way people look at their world. During the wars I have covered, especially in Yugoslavia and Rwanda, I have seen how some journalists can be manipulated, can be used as a tool of hatred, a weapon of war. I have seen how lies and hate speech can cost lives and cause irreparable harm. But I have also seen journalists work wonders and so I will keep doing what I do, seeking stories, being there despite the risks, because I still believe that when we do our jobs properly, we can help make the world a better place.

PART I. PEACEKEEPERS

1

Peacekeepers and Peace-Builders Under Stress

Sue Downie

While most peacekeepers and peace-builders, both military and civilian, emerge from a mission with positive experiences, enhanced capabilities and greater self-confidence, some have difficulty returning to their pre-mission life. Mission stress[1] experienced by military peacekeepers is being discussed, researched, and provided for in most forward-thinking armed forces, as reported here and in the following chapter. However, until recently, civilians on peacekeeping missions received virtually no support before, during, or after a mission.

PEACE MISSIONS: FROM OBSERVING TO INSTITUTION-BUILDING

Over the past 50 years, peacekeeping has been extended beyond its original task of monitoring ceasefires and troop withdrawals (traditional peacekeeping) to include balloting, policing, administering and human rights monitoring (comprehensive peacekeeping) and, recently, to institution-building (third-generation peacekeeping). Many of the latter are also peace-building activities. Thus, peacekeepers and peace-builders include soldiers, civilian police (civpol), electoral workers, civil administrators, and human rights officers. Generally, peacekeeping missions[2] are managed by the Department of Peacekeeping Operations (DPKO) in New York. Peace missions, those without a military component, such as electoral missions, are administered by the Department of Political Affairs (DPA).

On April 1, 2001, DPKO had 15 peacekeeping missions running concurrently, engaging 33,500 troops, 1,650 military observers, 7,700 civpol, 3,600 international

---

[1] In this chapter, "stress" refers to negative stress. "Mission stress" is preferable to "operational" or "combat" stress as peacekeeping by definition does not involve combat and does involve non-military personnel.

[2] The term peacekeeping "missions" is preferable to "operations" as the latter implies "military," when second- and third-generation peacekeeping involves far more than just military components.

civilians, and 9,000 local staff, and costing \$2.5 billion[2]. Troops and civpol are provided by member states. International civilian peacekeepers are hired individually and comprise UN headquarters staff and "mission appointees," staff from other UN agencies, UN Volunteers (UNVs), and local staff (of the host country), all engaged for a specific mission.

Peacekeepers in the Field

What kind of people are suitable for peacekeeping missions? According to French journalist Patricia Tome, a civilian who has been on 10 missions, the perfect candidate must be "physically strong, mentally strong, professionally strong, emotionally strong, and be strongly passionate. If one of these requirements is missing, don't apply!" Like most peacekeepers, she found the experience immensely rewarding. Canadian welfare officer Estelle Toomey said she has yet to meet someone who was not impacted, directly or indirectly, by stress in a mission. For many peacekeepers, being on mission is a life changing experience, positively and negatively, as Australian Army nurse Bev Wright said of her time in Rwanda:

> The elastic band gets stretched but it never comes back to where it was before. You are never the same as before. Before, I was (fussy), the house had to be this way and the bills had to be paid on time. I came home and for a couple of years I didn't care if the bills didn't get paid. You become impervious to things. The most significant thing that happened in my life was Rwanda.

The first peacekeepers arriving in a mission are usually confronted with death or displacement of the local population and destruction of infrastructure, as Bev Wright recalled:

> My group arrived (in Kigali) at 3 A.M. on a very wet morning. We slept on the floor of the airport, which was all shot up, and we were told not to go outside. A terrible smell permeated everything. Think of the worst sewage you can, coupled with old blood and bodies. The taps didn't work, the toilets wouldn't flush.

In addition to the "primitive" living conditions encountered in Dili at the beginning of the East Timor mission, Alf Reina, who had served as a civilian in Cambodia and Bosnia, said a major source of conflict among staff was the lack of office furniture, communications facilities, and vehicles. "The biggest problem for me has been having to put up with incompetence, and incomprehension of our role by several colleagues who perhaps should not be here." For French TV producer Isabelle Abric it is inequity:

> I've seen people dying, seen blood, had bullets flying by, walked in mine fields. They never freaked me out. But where do we stand? I'm from a modern democracy, they're from a developing country; I'm paid a good salary, they earn zip; you go, they stay. Those are the things I would have liked to have seen a psychologist about.

[2] July 2000 to June 2001.

The "incompetence," or sub-standard capabilities of some peacekeepers is a common complaint that is demoralizing for those who are genuinely committed and hard working, and is damaging the reputation of the UN as a whole. When Svend Frederiksen was civpol commissioner in Kosovo he forced DPKO to send home 400 police officers from two developing countries who could not adequately speak English, drive a vehicle, or use a handgun.

Although a peacekeeping mission is usually not dispatched until a ceasefire between the local protagonists is agreed to, broken ceasefires and breakdown of law and order are common. Austrian captain Peter Hazard, a military observer in a contested area in central Cambodia, was one of many peacekeepers who despaired about the killings; for example, when he saw a truck carrying 15 people attacked. "It was a blood bath. It struck me because it was so useless. Why? For what? It doesn't make any sense." Even trained medics find coping with death and injury difficult. Before going to Cambodia, British Army observer Captain Richard Williams undertook combat medic training:

> Nothing quite prepares you for how horrendous injuries are, and the confusion. And we cannot understand their mentality, probably that's why it's affected all of us so much. One of the most distressing things is turning people away. But it's nice to know you make a difference. One minute you have a piece of meat on the verge of dying; a month later you see them (the person) running around, and that's very satisfying.

Trauma also impacts on the leaders, some of whom are responsible for up to 30,000 personnel. Norwegian ambassador Kai Eide was the Special Representative of the Secretary General (SRSG) in Bosnia in September 1997 when a UN helicopter crashed in a remote mountain area killing all 11 passengers:

> We had a ceremony in the cathedral in Sarajevo. I struggled like crazy for a couple of days: what should I say? After the ceremony, I drove down to the coast and walked and walked, and I don't think I said a word for a day and a half. A couple of weeks before, my daughters gave me a CD that I really liked. It took more than a year before I could listen to it again. Two and a half years later I was with my daughters at a concert with this group. They started playing that music. I was a wreck. I could not sit through it.

Nor is stress restricted to those in the field. Carina Perelli is director of the Electoral Assistance Division in the Department of Political Affairs in New York, responsible for 33 concurrent missions. "We make many decisions that cause us sleepless nights, life and death decisions, and we should have mandatory, routine debriefings for all decision makers in charge of operations in the field." Debriefings are to give information, not stigmatize those who might be stressed.

Peacekeepers are not only subjected to trauma and its aftermath but, in exceptional cases, they become the target of shootings, grenade attacks, landmines, and hostage taking. In July 1995, the Dutch battalion in Srebrenica was cut off and effectively held hostage by Bosnian Serb troops who then killed up to 7000 Muslim civilians after the Dutch were forced to evacuate. This was regarded in the Netherlands as a *national* trauma.

The UN's move into second- and third-generation peacekeeping has greatly increased the range of tasks required of peacekeepers. In Somalia in 1993, David Hurley was commanding officer of the Australian troops who provided a secure environment for humanitarian assistance in the Baidoa sector. This was initially a law and order operation, followed by elements of state-building, such as re-establishing a police force and judicial system, tasks that he and his officers had not been trained for. As he said, "My soldiers are not policemen."

Peacekeeping exposes participants to a multitude of different cultures. Those with broadly Western values find it unsettling to witness, and, in some cases, be party to, actions or attitudes that do not meet their norms. As Hurley experienced: "The UN's approach is open handed, which meant we had to sit around a table with murderers. We were not too happy about that."

PSYCHOSOCIAL ISSUES IN PEACEKEEPING

These field reports suggest that peacekeeping stressors include witnessing trauma, being the subject of attacks, interpersonal conflicts, the lack of mission amenities, the multinational dimension of peacekeeping, the frustrations of not understanding the local population, despair at preventable death, and not being able to help everyone. It could be said that mission stress falls into two categories: critical incidents and long-term exposure to abnormal circumstances that might lead to varying degrees of clinically-diagnosable Post Traumatic Stress Disorder (PTSD); and, experiences that prevent a complete reintegration after the mission.

There are the characteristic cases: The soldier who got angry every time the chef cooked pork, because it reminded him of the smell of the children's bodies he had to burn; and the police officer who could not look into his young son's eyes because they reminded him of those of the man whose intestines he had held after he was shot in the stomach.

There is the frustration of not being able to help because of UN rules: soldiers in Somalia forced to stand by and watch women being stoned almost to death for adultery, unable to intervene because the UN ordered that local customs be respected; paramedics in Rwanda unable to attend a vehicle accident in which six locals were fatally injured, lives that could have been saved if they had ignored the UN order to assist only UN personnel; and, well-armed, highly-trained soldiers in East Timor not able to seek out militia whom they know to have committed atrocities, because this was prevented by UN rules of engagement.

However, more often stressors range from the absence of paper clips and other supplies at the beginning of a mission to not being able to communicate with the local population. Stressors could be categorized as stemming from mission environment or from individuals' values. Generally, they revolve around cultural adjustment, language frustrations, sharing personal space, never being alone, boredom, feeling powerless when problems arise at home, social injustices, and civilians and military having to work with each other. How, and to what degree, someone responds to stressors depends largely on the person's own background, experiences, and values, as well as the support provided by his or her colleagues or organization. Few peacekeepers are fully prepared for the impact stressors have on them psychologically, and often they are not aware of the impact until much later. As Australian Army psychologist Martin Levey said, "People who have been able to keep a lid on emotions from one mission, on subsequent missions find that such a high level of demand rattles the lid. We are only finding out now in East Timor how difficult Cambodia was for some."

The mission environment is recognized as stressful. It might include renegade soldiers, the distant sound of artillery fire, the fear of snipers, knowing that the enemy is not always in uniform, or the possibility of driving over landmines. While commanders might be aware of these obvious stressors, generally they are less likely to identify the "little things," according to Dr. Christen Halle, Chief of DPKO's Medical Support Unit:

> The biggest stresses of peacekeeping are the day to day stresses, stresses that are not always recognized as such. You might be sitting on your bed knowing your girlfriend is a zillion miles away, and in the next bed sits a man who gets a letter from his girlfriend telling him she has found another man, and your fears are verified through another person. A political officer in Bosnia said the most stressful thing, apart from working seven days a week, was that whenever she stopped her UN car everyone queued up for something she didn't have. It might not be a chocolate or a pen, but helping get back their flat, or helping get someone out of the country. A lot of people experience what they call ungratefulness: "I give them things and they just take them. Why do I do things for these people who don't even say thank you?" It's an enormous stressor.

To a certain extent civilian and military personnel go through similar emotional experiences before, during, and after deployment, especially in terms of pre-departure separation from family and friends, acclimatizing to the mission area, and reintegration at homecoming. The main difference in their experiences is due to the fact that soldiers deploy in formed units. This provides camaraderie and a greater opportunity for debriefing with colleagues, but also means shared living and less personal freedom. Martin Levey has been debriefing military peacekeepers for the past eight years:

> No matter where soldiers go, they will be exposed to the stress of being in an operation. They will be away from their family, away from opportunities to unwind. Working in the UN system is a stressor itself; differing values and attitudes, different levels of leadership ability and military professionalism, and different commitment to the process. One has to be more tolerant of others' habits and attitudes. They are in constant contact with a small group of people with little opportunity for privacy. Boredom may be an issue.

Unless adequately briefed beforehand, many peacekeepers are unexpectedly hit by the homecoming experience, which affects almost everyone to varying degrees. Almost all aspects of life at home change during deployment. Children's relationships change, young children grow significantly in six months, neighbors move, colleagues are promoted. Relationships with partners, children, social groups, and work colleagues have to be reestablished or redefined. Some married men find it difficult to accept that their wife has become independent enough to live without them, and that the children listen to her discipline rather than his. Others return to find they are no longer in a marriage or relationship. Family and friends soon stop asking about the mission experience and, without the ability to talk with people who shared that experience they may feel isolated and lonely. They underestimate how extraordinarily tired and emotionally drained they will be at the end of a mission. Any of these can lead to frustration and to relationship problems. Some returning peacekeepers might become reclusive, angry or hostile, or adopt abnormal eating or sleep habits. Others turn to alcohol or drugs. No one knows how many commit suicide. At least four peacekeepers have committed suicide since the 1999 East Timor electoral mission. As a UNAMET officer said, "The international community has been at these (second-generation) interventions for 12 years, and still we receive nothing. And there are plenty of (mental) cases walking around out there."

Returning to work, many feel let down, bored or unfulfilled after the "high" of deployment. To relieve this, some seek community activities that help fulfill their desire to continue assisting people in need. After returning from Rwanda, for example, several Australian soldiers moved from infantry, where they felt helpless, to more caring roles in medical and police corps.

Major Suzie Rodrigue has worked on seven peacekeeping missions as a social worker, providing critical incident counseling and end-of-mission debriefings for Canadian Army personnel. She says the debriefings are a vital first step in the reintegration process, as they identify issues that peacekeepers and their families have to deal with:

> Those returning need to look at how the family has reorganized itself, then fit in slowly. For some it's overwhelming. On mission, the cooking is done for them, they don't have chores, they are used to a single's routine. One guy said, "I came out of the shower, my wife was there and I put the towel around myself!" They have to learn to get to know one another all over again because for some the mission experiences have changed priorities. They don't see the world the same way.

And, as Isabelle Abric said after 10 years on peacekeeping missions:

> When you travel all the time, you have no reference point. It's only this year that I'm living in one place that I can talk to family and friends and start thinking of having a relationship for the first time in my life. I'm doing voluntary work with (victims of) domestic violence. I could not do it before.

From 1992, Svend Frederiksen of Denmark served as a civpol commander on four Balkan missions, including as police commissioner in Bosnia, then Kosovo, and said it took more than eight weeks to get back to normal life after Kosovo:

> Leaving the mission was like going into a big, big bag of cotton. Confused. Stressed. Overworked. For the first two weeks I can't remember anything. I couldn't sleep, couldn't concentrate on anything. I was completely focused on Kosovo, trying to swallow everything (I heard).

Returning Australian military peacekeepers are most likely to identify as stressors frustrations with cultural adaptation, the bureaucratic structure they had to work within, and being trained for war then placed in peacekeeping where rules of engagement require restraint.[3] The three issues rated most highly by Australian troops 12 months after returning from Rwanda were professional jealousy, non-use of expertise gained on mission, and low job satisfaction. Comments from these peacekeepers included: "There was an attitude that we had been on holiday while they had stayed at home and done the hard work"; "I miss the positive feeling of achievement on deployment and the loss of the closeness of working as a team"; and "No one has asked me to comment on training methods and operational procedures. The organization has failed to recognize or utilize the experience I gained."[4]

The ability to cope in-mission and post-mission depends largely on services and support provided by the peacekeepers' organization. Ultimately, that organization is UN headquarters (chiefly, DPKO). Additionally, military and civpol receive support from their respective national services, and UNVs from their organization, as described in chapters 2 and 13, respectively. There is no comparable backup organization for other civilian peacekeepers.

The numerous ways of reducing stress organizationally can be placed in three categories: information, counseling, and other services.

WHAT THE UN DOES

For this chapter, a group of civilian peacekeepers were asked what they received before, during, and after deployment in terms of briefings, counseling, and debriefings. Their replies suggest that, on at least some recent and current missions, the UN had done very little to address civilians' needs:

- I have received zip. Nothing. Buckleys. Sod all, in the way of psych counseling and preparation or debriefing
- What's provided by the UN? Nothing. Zip.
- Nothing when you leave. No debriefing, no medical checks, no follow-up.
- I received a short briefing paper with a little info about the mission, living conditions, and contact numbers. I found the UN Web site quite informative on the mission, and relied on friends to fill me in.
- What advice did I get re coping? Bugger all. It's changed a bit on this mission (East Timor). We now have a staff counselor, a psychologist. It is a help to know that the UN is concerned about its staff.

There are some indications that the UN is starting to regard psychosocial issues somewhat more seriously. Both DPKO's Training Unit and Medical Support Unit were, respectively, expanded and revived in January 2000. Stress management is

---

[3] Ongoing research by Lt. Col. Linda Campbell, psychologist, Directorate of Strategic Personnel Planning and Research, Australian Defence Force, Canberra.

[4] Ongoing research by Major Stephanie Hodson, psychologist, Australian Defence Force Psychology Organisation, Sydney.

more comprehensively covered in pre-deployment briefings for military and civpol and in arrival briefings for civilian peacekeepers. A permanent New York-based stress counselor was appointed in September 2000 and is developing stress prevention policy. And stress counselors are operating in three of the current 15 peacekeeping missions, but in none of DPA's 33 missions..

Unfortunately, many peacekeepers do not receive the benefits of these changes. In addition, other areas of need are not yet covered. In particular, civilians receive comparatively little care, especially mission appointees and local staff. For example, a political officer in the East Timor electoral mission is concerned that the UN has failed to recognize local staff, especially those who were targeted by militia in the post-referendum violence. "Of all 13 staff killed not a single family has received compensation 20 months later. Their contracts ended on August 30 and they were killed a few days later. This is the UN at its best!"

1. Information: Publications, Briefings, and Training

In order to provide information dissemination, DPKO's former Training Unit, which had all but disappeared due to budgetary constraints, has been revamped, expanded, and renamed. The Training and Evaluation Service (TES) has the additional task of standardizing and evaluating peacekeeping training. Rather than train peacekeepers directly, TES trains trainers and provides advisors. TES also provides guidelines and information to member states who are responsible for training their own military and civpol units before they leave their home country and as soon as they arrive in-mission, and to field missions which are responsible for briefing civilian peacekeepers as they arrive.

As mentioned, differences in professionalism, capability, and command structure among national military contingents constitute a peacekeeping stressor. Following years of complaints that the professionalism and resources of contingents from some countries, especially less developed ones, did not meet peacekeeping standards or requirements, Secretary-General Kofi Annan directed that contingents be assessed prior to deployment. To do this, TES plans to have mobile evaluation teams visit each troop contributing country. If a contingent is not ready, it will not deploy.

Usually, before a mission begins, the military commanders from each contributing country are called to New York for two to three days of briefings. These cover the UN structure, operations of DPKO, the mandate and structure of the mission, and mission-specific issues including political, logistical, medical (especially HIV/AIDS which is a huge consideration), human rights, legal issues, and financial arrangements. The medical briefing includes a section on mission stress and is generally given by Dr. Christen Halle, an "old hand" in terms of peacekeeping experience. He tells commanders that the officer-soldier relationship has to be changed from vertical to horizontal. The senior should not expect the junior to give his or her soul; it must be also the other way around well. "Good officers and soldiers who trust each other and are willing to share emotions can cope with stress." There is no such thing as a normal reaction:

Everyone reacts according to their background and experience. You see a refugee who looks like your grandmother, then you are worse off than the man next to you who doesn't. You need to be open to that. Our experiences sometimes help us through, sometimes they hit us from some strange angle we didn't expect or understand. You need to be open to that. Peacekeepers have to relate to things that are not part of their normal life. Things that were abnormal are suddenly normal: being shot at, seeing people in stress, talking to a girl about having been raped.

With so much emphasis on military contingents, where does that leave other mission personnel: civilians (permanent staff, mission appointees, and local staff), civpol and the military observers (milobs)? The heads of components—the civilian equivalents of military commanders—are not brought to New York for pre-deployment briefings. Usually, civpol and milobs comprise much smaller units (2 to 20 personnel) from each country, and are suppose to be trained by their respective countries before arriving. But the reality is that in some current missions, a quarter at best have undergone pre-deployment peacekeeping training. In theory, civilian peacekeepers receive their induction when they arrive in the mission area, comprising two to three days of briefings. However, this is often not sufficient time, not all incoming civilians are netted and, as each mission headquarters is responsible for the briefings, the quality varies.

According to DPKO's David Wimhurst, it is mandatory that all civilians arriving in a mission attend a security briefing which typically includes background on the mission, the mandate, security precautions, local rules (don't change your money on the black market) and customs, and an introduction to the mission's security team. Local staff do not receive these briefings. John Ryan, a civilian peacekeeper since 1992 and now UN Coordinator in East Timor, believes that there has been a general improvement in preparation for field work. However, field personnel do not receive training before deployment, and it takes time to organize in-mission training. Therefore, training is usually not available to early arrivals, which is particularly important for those on their first field mission.

2. Counseling

For years, the UN hierarchy responded in an ad hoc manner to the need for stress management services in the field and resisted repeated calls to appoint a stress counselor, although DPKO had a staff counselor in 1994-95, and produced a comprehensive booklet on stress management. Through the 1990s significantly more UN staff died in the field.[5] This reflected the increase in the number of peacekeepers deployed, and the changing nature of field work where, in some cases, instead of being seen as benevolent helpers, UN workers were targeted, especially after the dissolution of the Soviet Union. A series of tragedies, including the 1998 Swiss Air crash, precipitated the hiring, in September 2000, of the UN's first staff stress

---

[5] The per capita death rate in missions has remained fairly constant, although roughly the same number died between 1948 and 1990 as between 1990 and 2000.

counselor, in the UN Security Coordinator's Office (UNSECOORD), functionally linked to DPKO.

The UNSECOORD stress counselor is responsible for providing emergency support services in response to critical incidents and developing policy for stress management and prevention for civilian peacekeepers and the UN's 150 offices around the world. The vision is to develop a psychosocial section with a team of counselors who are both field-based and at headquarters, with the emphasis on prevention.

In addition to the UNSECOORD stress counselor, DPKO has stress counselors in three of its 15 missions: East Timor (UNTAET), Kosovo (UNMIK) and Lebanon (UNIFIL). The first Staff Counseling Unit was set up in Dili, East Timor, in February 2000, to provide civpol and local and international staff individual and/or group counseling and critical incident stress defusing/debriefing (CISD), as well as stress management and coping skills; establish a training program; and, brief new arrivals. Alain Beaudoin, a Canadian psychologist on his second peacekeeping mission, says the door is open seven days a week, 24 hours a day for civilians and civpol:

> We check the living and working conditions, see what the staff morale is like, see how staff is doing leisure-wise, what are their social and sports activities. I have seen people suffering from major depressive disorder, panic attack, substance abuse, and domestic violence.

Despite efforts to the contrary, there is still a lingering sense of shame and stigma attached to mental health, especially among peacekeepers, particularly the military and "old-timers" who believe in the "tough it out" attitude.

The UN is attempting to identify ways to reduce these in-missions stressors. Measures range from ensuring military contingents are professional and that medical facilities are adequate, to providing recreational activities and satisfactory compensation.

3. Other Services and Facilities

When Dr. Christen Halle joined the peacekeeping mission in Bosnia in 1993, one of the most important considerations for his wife was the provision of adequate medical facilities there. Now, as Chief of DPKO's Medical Support Unit, he is responsible for ensuring that contributing nations provide adequate in-mission medical services. Generally, military units provide medical facilities in peacekeeping missions, but personnel on peace missions (without a military component) have to rely on local medical services. Halle says the medical contingent, which often includes doctors, surgeons, dentists, nurses, and increasingly a psychologist and/or psychiatrist, should be as good as or better than that of their own country because the situation is more demanding.

Many missions have a store, known as a PX (post exchange) where international (not local) personnel can purchase imported duty-free items, ranging from corn chips and whisky to soap and washing machines. Some missions have sports/recreation facilities. Where there are no facilities, the mission should emphasize the importance of sport and recreation for reducing stress, and help staff to create their own activities.

Feedback from the field suggests that at least three other areas should be given serious consideration by a mission:

- Adequate and timely leave, crucial in reducing stress and enhancing well-being.
- Providing means for private communications—post, phone, or e-mail—with family as a priority immediately after a mission is established.
- Adequate and equitable health and life insurance, essential for recruiting and maintaining civilians.

CONCLUSION AND RECOMMENDATIONS

The comprehensive nature of peacekeeping missions of the past decade has added to the tasks and frustrations of those in the field. While the UN and some national armies and police forces are making efforts to meet these challenges by providing briefings and debriefings before, during, and after deployment, the benefits of this have not reached all those deployed. Secondly, and significantly, very little is being done for civilian peacekeepers, before, during, and after missions. Of the civilians, local staff are the most neglected. Recommendations pertaining to military contingents are dealt with in the following chapter. Therefore, this section is limited to recommendations for civilian peacekeepers.

It may not be easy for the UN culture to change. Nevertheless, a major effort should be made to:

1. Encourage leaders, at headquarters and in the field, to appreciate the significance of mission stress, and ways of identifying and alleviating stress, and to pass this on to those under them so that it becomes part of the mission culture.
2. Include counseling and other services (such as family communications and sport/recreation facilities) at the mission planning stage, so that they are inherent in the mission, not after-thoughts.
3. Increase dissemination of information about all aspects of the mission, not only stress, at three phases: before deployment for all personnel including local staff; within missions so that personnel in one region are aware of what is happening in the mission as a whole and have a sense of inclusion and involvement; and to personnel after they leave a mission, including mission appointees and local staff.
4. Make debriefings for headquarters directors and civilians leaving the mission routine and mandatory, in order to reduce the stigma and net those who might otherwise believe they do not need debriefing.
5. Improve post-mission services for civilians, especially mission appointees who can offer considerable experience to future missions but feel alienated by the UN's lack of concern for their welfare after deployment.

In order to determine the extent of trauma or stress caused by a mission it would be necessary to have psychological benchmark testing of personnel before and after a mission. However, as unsatisfactory as it may seem, it is possible the UN is reluctant to do this as it would open the way for the UN to be sued in "mission stress" lawsuits.

Specific recommendations for improving services for civilian peacekeepers include:

1. *Personnel selection.* It is essential that DPKO and DPA develop, and enforce, criteria for selecting the most appropriate people, and that personnel be more thoroughly evaluated for mission suitability.
2. *Pre-deployment preparation* must be extended to civilians and include generic material (about the UN and peacekeeping in general) and mission-specific information and more emphasis on cultural awareness.
3. *On-arrival briefings* should be standardized by DPKO, providing generic material on peacekeeping, stress management, cultural awareness, and some mission-specific material.
4. *Managers' briefings.* Civilian heads of components should be brought to UN headquarters for pre-deployment briefings, as the military commanders are.
5. *Local staff* must be given similar briefings as international staff receive on arrival.
6. *Health services.* In order to attract and keep civilian personnel, the UN must ensure adequate medical insurance and compensation, especially for mission appointees.
7. *Sports and recreational facilities* should be built into each mission in the planning phase, and provided as soon as possible after a mission is established.
8. *R&R.* As a matter of policy, each mission should identify nearby rest and recreation locations, and provide information and facilities to encourage staff to use them.
9. *Family communications.* Regular, easily-available communication with loved ones is essential. This might require the mission to repair or reestablish physical infrastructure or install satellite communications for phone and Internet connections.
10. *Counseling.* In-mission counseling is being provided in only three of the 15 current peacekeeping missions, and no post-mission counseling is provided by the UN. It is imperative that this change.
11. *Equity.* The UN should make efforts to redress the inequity in services for, and treatment of, local staff and mission appointees compared with headquarters staff, as this generates resentment and the UN is losing experienced professionals. Member states need to recognize this as an essential investment.

Voices

AN AMBUSH IN SOMALIA

Shirley N. Brownell

Is there a day that changed your life forever? A day when you came so close to death that your life flashed before your eyes? For me, that day was November 13, 1993—a Saturday. The image, as a bullet pierced my arm, inches from my heart, was the faces of my two children back in New York, as I considered what would happen to them if I died. I emerged from that experience with a new sense of empowerment, convinced that if a bullet couldn't silence me, nothing should frighten me ever again, or stop me from accomplishing my goals. I knew, then, that I had been given the chance to live for a purpose.

THE ATTACK

I went to Africa—the land of my birth—for adventure and a chance to help make a difference in people's lives. My destination should have been Hargeisa, in break-away Somaliland. But when I reached Nairobi in mid-September, I was sent, instead, to Mogadishu as a Political Affairs Officer with the United Nations Operation in Somalia (UNOSOM).

And that was why, on a Saturday morning in November, I left my residence in south Mogadishu at 6:25 A.M., on my way to UNOSOM headquarters to prepare for the morning briefing of the Special Representative and senior officials. Twenty minutes later, I was sitting, dazed and shoeless, at the side of a dirt road, bleeding profusely from a gaping wound in my upper left arm, having flung myself from a moving vehicle as it was being commandeered by a Somali gunman. In the middle of the road lay Kai Lincoln, 23, dying from a bullet that had shattered his insides; hobbling around, with a gunshot wound in his leg and trying to take control of the situation, was Lars Andersen, our driver and security officer. A third passenger, Carole Ray, was unharmed. One of the four gunmen lay dead.

Somali gunmen, who wanted the vehicle in which we were riding, had ambushed my colleagues and me, and they were prepared to kill us to get it. Their motive: to turn it into a "technical"—a vehicle whose roof is cut off so that machine-guns can be mounted on top. Banditry, ambushes, threats to UNOSOM personnel, and inter-clan killings constituted daily life in Somalia, and we were merely the latest statistics. These were the treacherous circumstances in which civilian personnel found themselves, because the UN had been thrust into a situation where there was no peace to keep, where the security was non-existent and its staff were at the mercy of gunmen masquerading as security guards.

As the investigation of the ambush got under way, I wrote the following in my notes: "There was no way to distinguish who was Somali security and who was not. They wore no uniforms. We all assumed that if they were in UN-designated areas and were carrying weapons, they must be militiamen who had been hired by the UN for security. They carried no identification; their badges were their rifles." Thus it was that men we believed to be UNOSOM security guards—read: non-uniformed, gun-toting Somalis—were assigned to escort international staff. At a certain point along the route they abandoned us, and moments later our vehicle was surrounded by four gunmen bent on killing us.

As we waited for UN help to arrive, a beat-up, rickety bus appeared on the scene, and the sympathetic Somali driver discharged his passengers and took us to the Swedish Field Hospital at the UN compound for treatment. Kai died, despite massive transfusions of blood and valiant efforts by the medical team to save his life. I was wheeled into the room where he lay, and remember touching his cooling body from which a life, full of promise, had been so violently snatched. It was only then that I wept. I remained in the hospital for two days, returning there on November 17 for surgery to excise dead tissue and patch my wound. The doctors did the best they could, but the result was a ghastly, jagged scar with multiple suture marks and deformity of my upper left arm. Clearly, multiple-stage reconstructive surgery and months of physical therapy were in my future.

UN REACTION

Despite the many guidelines, General Assembly resolutions, Security Council condemnations, and even a Convention, the lessons of the safety and security of UN personnel in peacekeeping operations are not easily learned. Those resolutions request the Secretary-General to, among other things, ensure that adequate training in security, human rights and humanitarian law, as well as stress counseling, is provided. But I had no training in safety procedures before going off to Somalia, and I most certainly received no counseling after I was shot. My self-administered therapy was to block out the incident, make it through the flashbacks and cold sweats, and to get on with the work I had gone there to do.

The UN, as I reflect back on 1993, was totally unprepared to cope with the deaths of, and trauma to, its civilian staff, giving rise to charges of its insensitivity to loss and suffering. I received visits and comforting words from the Special Representative of the Secretary-General (SRSG) and many senior officials, but there was no mechanism in place to help me cope with the mental anguish of the attack. There was no counseling in the mission area. It was only when I reached New York, and arranged to meet with the UN Staff Counselor, Mr. Jean-Guy Morisset, that any professional help was forthcoming. Conscious of the urgent need for such a presence in peacekeeping missions, he was actively working to ensure that the personnel for peacekeeping operations included an individual who could offer counseling to staff.

In escaping from UNOSOM vehicle No. 507, I left behind my national passport containing my G-4 visa for entry into the United States, as well as my UN laissez-passer—documents which we were required to have with us at all times. I needed to get to New York to see other doctors, but in order to get there, I needed travel documents. Getting replacement documents was a nightmare all its own, and the administration's attitude was that the responsibility for doing so was mine alone. My colleagues back at Headquarters were horrified when they were told this. On one occasion, when I inquired about compensation for my injury, under Appendix D of the Staff Rules, an administration official replied, callously: "What do you want compensation for? Isn't the UN taking care of all your medical expenses?" Indeed, my medical expenses were fully covered under the Malicious Act Insurance Policy. But as far as compensation for my injury, I would have had to lose my arm entirely in order to receive full benefits under an archaic scheme whose official title is "Rules governing compensation in the event of death, injury or illness attributable to the performance of official duties on behalf of the United Nations."

What struck me as particularly tragic throughout this ordeal was that the UN administration seemed more interested in recovering its stolen vehicle—a Toyota 4 Runner—and teaching Somalis that they couldn't get away with such theft, than in showing any caring and concern about the pain, suffering, and death of its civilian staff caught up in a vicious fratricide. Over half a dozen meetings were held with different UN offices, as well as with the Somali Police, to coordinate efforts to recover the vehicle. In the end, though, no one had the stomach for a forced recovery of the vehicle, which would have required UNOSOM military support. The report on the ambush had recommended "a direct and distinctive course of action to recover all stolen UNOSOM vehicles and property." It said that bandits knew that UNOSOM was "an easy target" because the Force Command weaponry was not deployed to provide security for vehicle movement in the city. Because there had never been a military operation to recover any stolen UNOSOM vehicles, the bandits did not fear retaliation, which would lead to a surge of attacks against UNOSOM vehicles, particularly those operated by civilians.

PROTECTING THE HELPERS

When Dr. Eli Schessel, the plastic surgeon, first examined my arm in December 1993, he said, incredulously: "You went there to help those people, and this is what they did to you?" Secretary-General Kofi Annan echoed similar sentiments a year ago, after yet another attack on UN civilian staff, when he said: "What is unacceptable and really appalling is that these young men and women who go to these areas to help—to assist—then become targets. They are not at war with anyone. They went because they wanted to help, they went because they have compassion, they went because they understand the human condition and want to do whatever they can to help. It is unforgivable that these human beings would then become targets of either rebels or government forces which are at war with each other." The UN Security Coordinator, Benon Sevan, has described UN civilian staff as "soft targets" because so little protection is provided for them.

What, then, can be done to reverse this escalation of attacks on innocent UN staff? One of the recommendations in the report of our ambush was for a thorough training program, to instruct new arrivals on all security regulations and procedures. Ideally, said the investigators, a mission survival course should be conducted for all new staff members *before* deployment to the mission area, a measure that would "increase the probability of survival."

There is broad agreement that strengthened security, and training in safety and evacuation procedures, would go a long way toward protecting staff, and must be paramount in all mission-planning activities. Mr. Sevan, too, has called for tighter rules, better training, and a willingness to evacuate early as ways to improve staff safety. Resources are required to make this happen, and that's where Member States have a financial role to play. Governments also must act more decisively to protect UN staff and humanitarian workers on their territory. Ratifying the Convention on the Safety of United Nations Personnel alone is not enough.

Until recently, I seldom spoke about my experience in Somalia, even though my "mark of Zorro" serves as a constant reminder. The documents relating to that incident and its aftermath sat in a box in the corner of my office, unopened, reminders of a time I preferred to forget. But as I was packing to move to a new office, I opened the box containing medical reports, compensation papers, photographs and letters from friends, and the memories came flooding back.

I know that, with greater security, alertness and training, what happened to me in Somalia could have been prevented. At the same time, I'm realistic in acknowledging that nothing will stop senseless attacks against UN personnel by rampaging mobs, militias and other thugs who have no respect for human life, let alone human rights. But unless greater concern is given to their security, and drastic measures are taken to protect UN personnel in dangerous missions, the day will come when they will no longer be willing to risk their lives in the cause of the Organization they so nobly serve.

THE EVACUATION DILEMMA[1]

Ian Martin *

On Friday, September 3, in New York, Secretary-General Kofi Annan announced the result of the popular consultation agreed by Indonesian President Habibie after 24 years of Indonesian occupation of East Timor: 78 percent of its people had voted for independence from Indonesia. It was Saturday morning September 4 in Dili, the capital of East Timor, and, as head of the United Nations Mission in East Timor (UNAMET), which had conducted the ballot, I was simultaneously making the same announcement at a news conference. Many of the media who had intended to stay beyond the August 30 poll had left after post-ballot violence included attacks on journalists. Two UNAMET local staff had been murdered as the poll closed in Ermera and two more as violence erupted in Maliana, forcing the first withdrawal of UNAMET from one of its regional bases. Most electoral observers had left or were preparing to leave.

The vote announcement was the signal for the outbreak of violence throughout East Timor, and journalists and observers were immediate targets. Most UNAMET electoral staff had left, as planned, but civilian police (Civpol), military liaison officers (MLOs), and security officers remained in the regional offices with a few other international staff. Some local staff had taken refuge with them; many others had gone into hiding.

Just three hours after the announcement, an assault on the UNAMET compound in Liquiça began. The UN staff drove at high speed out of the compound under heavy fire from militia, police, and at least one soldier. One vehicle had at least 15 bullet holes, and bullets bounced off a shovel held by a female Civpol officer. An American Civpol officer was hit twice in the stomach. Militia were everywhere, clearly seen acting with the collusion of the Indonesian army (TNI) and police.

A UN security "Phase Three" had been declared on September 4th, and non-essential staff were evacuated to Darwin, Australia. Amid outbreaks of violence, remaining staff withdrew from regional offices to Dili. In Baucau, staff lay on the floor for two hours as Indonesian police fired automatic weapons into the UNAMET office. In most places, the militia and their allies initially refused to allow East Timorese staff to leave with UNAMET, but international staff refused to leave without them. From Baucau, the international staff were flown directly to Darwin. In the absence of Indonesian permission for the local staff to leave East Timor, they were crammed onto grossly over-crowded UN helicopters and flown to the Dili compound. If local staff had been left behind, many would have been killed. Helicopter crews flew with great skill and courage in dangerous circumstances, including being shot at.

---

[1]The author's fuller account of the evacuation of UNAMET is in I. Martin, Self-determination in East Timor: The United Nations, the ballot, and international intervention, International Peace Academy Occasional Paper, Boulder, CO: Lynne Rienner, 2001.

*The views expressed are solely those of the author and do not necessarily represent those of the United Nations.

As UNAMET withdrew to Dili, and its mobility and communications there became progressively restricted, knowledge of what was going on around the territory was limited. But UNAMET and the few journalists who remained were soon telling the world that there appeared to be a strategy to force people to move to West Timor. There was widespread burning of houses, and an unknown number of killings. The pro-independence population was the target of the violence; most had fled to the hills.

In Dili, the office of the Catholic diocese was burned and many people there killed. Several other locations where internally displaced persons (IDPs) were sheltering, including Bishop Belo's house and the ICRC compound, were attacked. Some were killed, but most were forcibly moved to West Timor. ICRC's expatriate staff were forced to leave for Darwin. In the Suai church compound, three priests and those they had been sheltering were massacred. Only after the deployment of peacekeepers would the scale of the massacres, individual killings, and rape become known.

From the day of the announcement, UNAMET staff in Dili were unable to sleep in their houses or hotel rooms, most of which were early candidates for looting and burning. In between shooting around them, they snatched sleep in their offices in the headquarters compound. Next door was a school compound, which had become a place of refuge for IDPs. Just after nightfall on September 5th, sustained automatic weapons firing close by caused the IDPs to panic. They hurled themselves and their babies over the razor wire that divided the compounds. From then on, the UNAMET compound was home to 1,500–2,000 IDPs, hundreds of local and international staff, several observers, and 20 journalists who had courageously remained in Dili.

Several UN vehicles had been shot at, and it had become impossible for UNAMET to move outside the compound without a TNI escort; when it did, it was without radio communication. Automatic weapons firing around the compound was commonplace, although most of it was shooting in the air by the police, who were supposedly protecting UNAMET. UNAMET's vehicle workshop was destroyed and with it the satellite dish that provided its main communications. Local telephones went out, as did the electricity and water supply. Fortunately, the compound—now a refugee camp with impending health risks—had its own supply of well water, but UNAMET had limited fuel for its generator. The helicopters were withdrawn to Darwin, as insurance cover became impossible. All NGOs had evacuated. The only other remaining international presence in Dili, the Australian consulate, was in a similar position to UNAMET: surrounded by shooting and protected by Indonesian troops, its power and communications failing. On September 8th the consul and most staff withdrew, leaving two military attachés to liaise with UNAMET and TNI.

On September 8th, I decided to recommend a general evacuation. It was a decision reached with extreme reluctance, in view of the commitment given to the East Timorese that UNAMET would stay beyond the ballot, and because of the situation of the IDPs in the compound. I had asked for local staff to be evacuated to Darwin. Unusual as this was, it was readily agreed in New York and Canberra, and the Secretary-General then personally obtained Indonesian consent from President Habibie. But this did not extend to the IDPs in the compound. A return to the regions was inconceivable, movement out of the compound became impossible, and conditions inside deteriorated. One hundred ninety-two Civpol, MLOs and international staff remained, and several contributing countries were questioning their continued presence. In weighing my decision, I was particularly swayed by the report from the senior MLO within the East Timor military headquarters that the TNI commander no longer had the control necessary to guarantee the protection of UNAMET. A final incident that morning entered the equation. With food and drinking water running short, a UNAMET team went to our warehouse at the port. Despite a TNI escort, they were surrounded by militia who pointed firearms at them, including to the head of a Civpol officer, and struck and damaged their vehicles. They returned empty-handed.

Some staff were horrified at the prospect of leaving behind IDPs, and immediately volunteered to remain. Staff wept as they informed representatives of the IDPs that UNAMET might be departing the next morning. New York too suggested the possibility of volunteers remaining, and I asked for a full list of those willing to stay to be drawn up.

The evacuation went ahead at dawn on September 10th. Some 80 international staff remained with the IDPs, while 110 departed with local staff and others who had been in the compound, including the last of the media, on Australian military planes to Darwin. The TNI mounted a professional operation to guard the route to the airport and escort the convoy: the martial law commander would later state that plans for the evacuation had been passed to the militia, and the TNI intercepted four truckloads of militia attempting to set an ambush for UNAMET. But while I was at the airport to see that all the East Timorese were allowed to leave, a group of militia armed with grenades, guns, and machetes, was allowed to penetrate the TNI cordon into the schoolyard next to UNAMET, and up to its front gate, where unarmed UNAMET staff confronted them. Some believed that militia might come over the wall into the main compound, and that the TNI would not provide meaningful resistance. While most of the volunteers were highly committed to staying with the IDPs, most believed it would be right to leave after the IDPs' future was resolved.

On September 11th, we and the IDPs were visited by the Security Council mission which had been sent to Indonesia. Its members had insisted that they and Defense Minister General Wiranto visit Dili, after listening with incredulity to the government in Jakarta maintaining that martial law was bringing the situation under control and international intervention was unnecessary. During that day, it became clear that the Indonesian government was going to accept international intervention. This however carried a further risk for UNAMET and the IDPs, that those TNI and militia still completing the destruction of East Timor would make them a target for their anger at the humiliation of international intervention. The only fully secure option for the IDPs was their evacuation to Australia. Prime Minister Howard agreed to this. The Security Council mission, and ultimately the Secretary-General, obtained Habibie's authorization. In the early hours of September 14th, in another operation with well-organized TNI protection, the IDPs and most of those who had stayed with them, including myself, left for the airport, and thence to Darwin. The UNAMET compound was closed, and a final brave 12 UN staff, headed by the Chief Military Liaison Officer Brigadier Rezaqul Haider, moved into the former

Australian consulate, surrounded by Indonesian troops. There they awaited the arrival of international forces.

Nothing has done more to damage the reputation of the UN than the slaughter of civilians in the presence of its armed peacekeepers in Rwanda and at Srebrenica. UNAMET had no armed peacekeepers, and had neither the means nor the mandate to protect civilians, nor itself. Yet by encouraging the East Timorese to participate in the vote, and by promising that the UN would remain after the vote, whatever the outcome, it created expectations that the UN would afford protection.

For those in East Timor, each day that passed while international intervention was under discussion was an agony, yet the Australian-led International Force in East Timor (InterFET) was mandated only 11 days after the announcement of the result, and began deploying just four days after that. This represented unprecedented speed for international action.

Two other outcomes might have occurred. UNAMET's international staff might have left behind East Timorese staff and IDPs to their fate, or the decision to remain might have resulted in international staff being killed. It was vital that the UN's commitment to the East Timorese should be fulfilled, but UNAMET had ceased to be the kind of presence that could fulfil it. The fact that all three groups in the UNAMET compound—international and local staff, and IDPs—reached safety should not conceal the impossible dilemmas that confront those responsible for security decisions. The 2000 Brahimi Report on peacekeeping [1] rightly says that if a UN operation is given a mandate to protect civilians, it must be given the specific resources to carry that out. The experience of UNAMET shows that even without such a mandate, the expectations created by a UN presence may exert pressures beyond the reasonable safety of its staff. There may be no complete way out of this protection dilemma, but it points to the need for the Security Council to be willing to authorize rapid intervention to protect civilians and UN personnel, and the contingency planning which can make it possible.

REFERENCE

1. United Nations, *Report of the Panel on United Nations Peace Operations*, A/55/305-S/2000/809, August 21, 2000.

HEAL—DON'T FORGET

Mark Quarterman

Not a day goes by when I don't think, at least fleetingly, of East Timor. I might ponder whether the UN was right to go ahead with the referendum there in 1999 when there was a strong possibility of a violent outcome (I think we were right). Or, I might examine my own behavior in East Timor as part of the mission that carried out the referendum, and measure it against standards of effectiveness, morality, and courage. Or, I think about my East Timorese friends, those who survived the post-ballot violence and those who did not.

I worked for the UN in East Timor to carry out a referendum or popular consultation in which the East Timorese were to decide whether they wanted to be part of Indonesia or independent. After they overwhelmingly chose independence, the Territory was inundated by a wave of violence that laid waste to most towns and villages and killed an unknown number of East Timorese. Pro-Indonesian militias, likely supported by the Indonesian armed forces, perpetrated these acts. Over the course of three weeks, most UN personnel, East Timorese and international, were evacuated.

The violence occurred after an intense and traumatic four-month period during which the UN Mission in East Timor (UNAMET) worked to hold the referendum in a tense and hostile atmosphere. In a few instances, militias directly attacked UN personnel. In many others, East Timorese were the victims of a campaign of intimidation that appeared designed to cause them to vote to be part of Indonesia. The overall situation caused substantial stress among UN staff, which was compounded by the short period of time available to carry out the ballot. The operation, that in the best of circumstances would take eight or nine months, had to be implemented from start to finish in four months in a location with minimal infrastructure. As a result, UNAMET staff, as a matter of course, worked seven-day weeks against a violent backdrop.

Recognizing the strain on his staff, Ian Martin, the Special Representative of the Secretary-General for the East Timor Popular Consultation, arranged for counselors to be based in East Timor for the benefit of UN personnel. They also prepared a booklet on post-traumatic stress that was provided to all UNAMET staff.

The counselors were also available after much of the mission was evacuated to Darwin, Australia. I did not take advantage of their services after I was evacuated because, in typical UN fashion, I was sent to my next assignment, representing UNAMET in Jakarta, Indonesia. However, based on reports from colleagues, I do feel that the efforts taken by the UN in the aftermath of the East Timor referendum were helpful. The evacuees also benefited from an exceptionally warm and supportive reception from the people of Darwin. After, for many of us, four months of non-stop work in a brutal environment, Darwin's welcome was a balm.

For me at least, the information provided in the counselors' booklet helped to demystify the post-evacuation experience. It was useful to know that my reactions to that experience were not unique, surprising, or misplaced. However, I know now that I would have benefited from talking to the counselors. I have learned through hard experience that one should not pretend that a traumatic experience could be shrugged off as if its effects were ephemeral. Lingering effects, of course, continue after one goes home.

On my return home, I realized that, as someone with a family, making the reentry into normal life was not a matter I could or should deal with alone. It was clear that my experience could not be confined to me alone. I had lost a lot of weight yet carried a heavy burden. I knew that I could only truly settle in at home by talking with my wife about what happened in East Timor and how I felt about it and my role there. That meant that I needed to be honest with her about continuing feelings that included anger, frustration, and sadness, as well as pride at what I considered to be a job well done. My wife's support and understanding helped to heal the wounds from the trauma of East Timor.

While I learned that I needed to talk with my wife about East Timor, I knew from previous experience that I could not burden everyone I knew with mission stories. I served as a Peace Corps volunteer in Sierra Leone from 1981-83, and was given two useful bits of advice by the Peace Corps as I was ending my service. At a close-of-service training program, I was told that I should not expect on my arrival back home that family and friends would be eager to hear lengthy accounts of my experiences. Few things are more tiresome than long stories that are only stories to the listeners. That advice saved me the disappointment of not having rapt listeners hang on every word of my tales of life in Sierra Leone. The second piece of advice was that the transition home after a powerful immersion experience could often be more difficult than the entry into that experience. That advice was borne out after my return home from the Peace Corps and was even more accurate after an extraordinary period of working on South Africa's first non-racial elections in 1994.

During that time in South Africa, I had an experience similar to that in East Timor, in that I worked around the clock against a backdrop of violence. I again felt that I was a small part of a larger, history-making event. And, after the votes were counted and Nelson Mandela inaugurated as president, I experienced a letdown. For weeks, my every waking hour was devoted to a specific task. When the task was done, the short-term reason for being disappeared. Not only did I miss the adrenalin rush of the work, I mourned the purpose going out of my life. Knowing that the post-election "hangover" and its passing were inevitable was helpful.

I know that UN mission staff have similar reactions to their experiences. I believe that the UN could more systematically prepare mission staff for powerful, intense, and often traumatic stints in missions, if only to soften their predictable effects. For me, while the effects diminish with time, the memories of people, places, and experiences linger.

2

Studies on Military Peacekeepers

Jos M. P. Weerts, Wendy White, Amy B. Adler, Carl A. Castro,
Gielt Algra, Inge Bramsen, Anja J. E. Dirkzwager,
Henk M. van der Ploeg, Maaike de Vries and Ad Zijlmans

The increasing complexity of peacekeeping missions, as described in the previous chapter, has created a need for a reorientation for military organizations. Traditional military skills are not always suited to peacekeeping. Most operations were led by two principles that are at odds with the traditional requirement of a military organization: impartiality and restraint in the use of force [1, 2].

The psychological effects of war on soldiers are well known. Early literature contains vivid descriptions of psychological distress that soldiers may experience during and after combat [3], ranging from poor adaptation after return to Post Traumatic Stress Disorder (PTSD) and other psychiatric disorders. Although the level of violence in peacekeeping is far lower than during traditional armed conflicts, there have been a significant number of combat-like incidents and casualties. The impact on soldiers shows remarkable similarities with that of traditional armed conflicts. It is well known that many veterans have problems adapting to civilian life. New Zealand studies indicate that pre- and post-deployment periods in peacekeeping are the most stressful [4, 5]. Peacekeeping presents new challenges not only to the international community, but also to national military organizations, especially their medical and psychological services. Egge, Mortensen, and Weisaeth have described peacekeeping stressors and their effects on military personnel [6].

Recently, several countries have developed specific trauma and stress support programs to decrease the distress and suffering of soldiers and their families. However, many underdeveloped countries lack the resources to support these kinds of programs. Neither the UN nor regional military organizations have a doctrine or clear policy on psychological support before, during, and after operations. Each participating country has its own responsibility. In various countries, a vast body of knowledge has been developed, based on both field experiences and on data from scientific research.

In attempting an overview of the aforementioned data, we encountered several problems. First, up to 75 percent of peacekeepers are recruited from developing countries, while western countries do most research. Secondly, much of the research into (adverse) psychological effects is done by military personnel or management units, which traditionally restrict publication of data on strengths and weaknesses [7]. Thirdly, most research is retrospective and PTSD-focused. It is difficult, therefore, to come to conclusions regarding the etiology, development, and prevention of deployment-related problems [8]. Our search found no data on civilians or civilian police, and only one study on military observers [6]. This chapter gives an overview of research and policy on psychosocial findings and assistance to military personnel and veterans, using as primary sources the Netherlands, United States, Canada and, more briefly, other countries whose fuller accounts have been described elsewhere [6, 9, 10] and concludes with recommendations.

THE NETHERLANDS

The Netherlands has a long history of involvement in peacekeeping operations, having deployed over 60,000 troops since the United Nations Interim Force in Lebanon (UNIFIL) (1979-1985) until now [11]. A general objective of Dutch defense policy is to maintain sufficient capacity for deploying four battalions concurrently for peacekeeping duties abroad. High priority is placed on early detection of symptoms and other preventive interventions.

The first assessment by psychologists at the Individual Psychological Support Division of the Royal Netherlands Army (RNLA) in 1987 of the need for psychological treatment among UNIFIL veterans estimated that between 2.5 and 10 percent of the 8700 men and women might need psychological treatment. Their most important psychological complaints were difficulties adapting to civilian life, depression, and aggressive behavior. It also showed that the closer the men were to incidents, the more were they in need of treatment. Escape from personal problems as a motive to volunteer for deployment also contributed to difficulty [12]. During deployment, many had been involved in serious incidents, witnessed acts of violence, or experienced stressful situations, including the prohibition against responding to threats and violence and discomfort and disruption of daily life. The prevalence of PTSD was estimated at 5 to 10 percent [13]. These findings were important in raising awareness that peacekeeping veterans needed special attention.

In the early1990s, the RNLA began an active follow-up approach. A questionnaire was sent to peacekeepers nine months post-mission. The results showed that 82 percent of the (ex) servicemen and women resumed normal lives and duties by themselves without problems in adaptation or coping. Nevertheless, for one third, the transition was difficult. Thirty percent reported negative changes in their personal attitude and behavior, such as somatic complaints, emotional numbing, aggression, and tensions. Three to 7 percent suffered from serious posttraumatic problems; eighteen applied for help [14].

Between 1990 and 1997, peacekeeping increasingly became a part of military routine. The experiences in Lebanon and later in Srebrenica made it clear that peacekeeping took its toll on soldiers and the army developed a comprehensive strategy for psychosocial assistance before, during, and after deployment [15].

Pre-deployment preparation includes assessing fitness for peacekeeping, education, and counseling on stress and social support.

While deployed, each battalion-size unit has a social and medical team. A psychologist advises the chain of command, conducts end-of-mission debriefings and treats personnel when necessary. Much attention is paid to family support. A home front committee, made up of partners, parents, or siblings gives support and advice. They meet before, during, and after missions, and have 24-hour access to information about relatives. Psychological debriefing takes place after each serious incident and before the soldier's return. The end-of-mission debriefing marks the beginning of the transition and provides an opportunity to educate the soldiers and to observe how they cope with the experiences of the mission.

Post-deployment, a voluntary reintegration meeting is held 8 to 10 weeks after returning to discuss adaptation to personal and professional life. The office of the Chief of Army Staff coordinates and evaluates all information during and after every mission. One study demonstrated the importance of using problem solving behavior (trying to change the situation) versus the emotional approach (changing attitudes toward the situation, avoiding, daydreaming, rationalizing). Another showed that if a commander maintained morale and team spirit at a high level, the risk of developing stress symptoms decreased. Forty percent of those held hostage considered it extremely traumatic and 7.1 suffered from serious psychological problems nine months after return [16]. Every (former) soldier receives a questionnaire six months post-mission, whose objective is to collect stress and PTSD-related data, and offer help when needed. This is now standard procedure in the armed forces, thus research into peacekeeping is continuous [17].

In 1995, due to the growing number of Dutch peacekeepers and the increasing knowledge of severe long-term psychological effects of war and violence among elderly veterans [18-20], a comprehensive study into the health care needs of peacekeeping veterans, their family members, and the health care organization [21] was conducted. The study showed that 5 percent of the veterans had a probable diagnosis of PTSD, according to the Self Rating Inventory for PTSD [22], and 21 percent one or more symptoms. Veterans of Lebanon, Bosnia (UNPROFOR 1994-95), and Cambodia (UNTAC 1992-93) had significantly higher scores than other veterans. PTSD symptoms were associated with the number and nature of stressful experiences and the appraisal of deployment. Risk factors were a lower educational level and being single [21,23]. Reporting adjustment problems in the immediate aftermath of deployment was an important predictor of PTSD symptoms [23], indicating the need for early detection. A prospective study comparing pre- and post-deployment data of Dutch soldiers in UNPROFOR, found that exposure to traumatic events was the strongest predictor of post traumatic stress symptoms. Personality traits like negativism and "psychoneuroticism" that may play a role in appraising and attributing meaning to stressful situations and choice of coping mechanisms, followed by age, also contributed to this risk [24]. For spouses and parents, the deployment is a difficult period. Though family members as a group were as healthy as the Dutch population, family members of veterans with PTSD symptoms had more PTSD symptoms themselves, as well as more sleeping problems, somatic complaints, and feelings of anxiety, depression, and anger [21].

Experiences with elderly war veterans revealed that a lack of appreciation of their efforts by society may have complicated healthy adjustment, and made giving meaning to their experiences and sacrifices particularly difficult. Younger veterans, likewise felt that their recognition from Dutch society was not adequate, as illustrated by 45 percent of the veterans agreeing with the proposition: "the media have insufficient respect for veterans" [21].

The results imply that aftercare needs depend on the degree of participation in peacekeeping, the risks experienced, and recognition of their efforts. Also, efforts by the military to prepare peacekeepers and their families, to support them during the mission and to provide aftercare might be relevant to long-term adaptation and health care needs. As peacekeepers and their families wanted a recognizable institute for mission-related problems, a Veterans' Institute for war and peacekeeping veterans [25, 26] was established, that also provides information to veterans, policy makers, clinicians, and researchers, as well as recommending new project development and research.

In 1992-93, more than 2,500 Dutch forces were deployed in Cambodia, as part of the UN Transitional Authority in Cambodia (UNTAC). A remarkably high number reported health problems, including severe fatigue, cognitive problems, and headaches, which they attributed to their service in general, to the malaria prophylaxis, and vaccinations. In 1997, a comprehensive and collaborative study into the somatic and psychological symptoms of UNTAC veterans was launched. Initial and 18-month follow-up questionnaires were sent to all Cambodia veterans [27]. In the initial postal questionnaire, 17 percent met the case definition for symptoms. For veterans who served in Rwanda and Bosnia, these percentages were 28 and 11, respectively [28]. At the 18-month follow-up, 39 percent reported partial or complete recovery, while 57 percent had the same complaints and 4 percent had become worse [29]. In a third part of this study, a distinction was made between factors precipitating the complaints and symptoms, and factors that perpetuate them. No evidence was found for a single medical or psychological precipitating factor [30]. Another study also showed that UNTAC peacekeepers had less favorable general health than the other peacekeepers, and reported fewer psychological, but more physical, health complaints. The number of UNTAC peacekeepers with a possible PTSD diagnosis was significantly lower (2 percent) than in the peacekeeper study (5 percent). Approximately 6 percent of the UNTAC peacekeepers expressed, five years following deployment, a need for health care or after care, but the proportion that wanted to talk (informally) about the mission was estimated to be much higher [31].

Soldiers deployed in central Bosnia (Lukavac) in 1994-95 suspected that their compound was chemically contaminated. 40 percent reported a deterioration of their health at two to three years after the mission, compared to 20 percent in the other Bosnia veterans. Both groups reported poor health status, compared to an equivalent group of males in the Dutch population. The Lukavac group also reported more respiratory and gastro-intestinal symptoms, fatigue, dizziness and memory and concentration problems than the other veterans. These were more common among the younger group (< 30 years), soldiers with a temporary contract, and among logistical units and units with stressful work. Further examination or treatment were considered necessary for 62 percent of symptomatic veterans. The poor health status of the Lukavac group could not be explained by stressful events. It is possible that exhaust gases from local factories, ovens, and cars led to acute respiratory symptoms in allergic or overexposed soldiers, perhaps causing chronic symptoms [32].

A summary of the data collected by the RNLA is presented in Table 1. This shows a gradual decrease in number and severity of exposure as well as symptoms. The battalion deployed in Srebrenica from January to July 1995 showed a relatively

Table 1. Exposure, Symptoms, and Assistance among
Dutch Peacekeepers, 1991-1999 [33-36]

	Early missions Aug 91-Sept 96 ($N = 5035$)	Dutchbat III (Srebrenica) ($N = 273$)	Later missions Oct 96-April 98 ($N = 2158$)	Recent missions May 98-July 99 ($N = 1517$)
Exposure and Experiences				
Witnessing agony	74.4		50.9	44.0
Gun fire (not aimed at you)	79.2		38.6	44.0
Seeing death or wounded	51.8		22.2	13.8
Rejection by local population	47.3		28.5	28.4
Personal danger	43.7		18.7	15.2
Coping, Problems, and PTSD				
PTSD, partial	20.4	29.0	14.7	13.4
PTSD, complete	4.3	8.0	2.6	2.0
Sleep disturbances	15.6	18.0	12.6	11.9
Somatic complaints	12.4	13.0	9.8	7.6
Assistance				
Contacted by telephone	27.0	40.0	16.0	13.0
Intake	8.0	15.0	3.5	2.6
Treatment Army	2.0	6.0	2.3	2.3
Treatment other	1.2	2.0	1.6	2.0

high number of soldiers and veterans with problems, and a high number who were contacted for help or who actually asked for it [33-36].

CANADA, BRITAIN, AND AUSTRALIA

Canadian military peacekeepers, 125,000 since 1947, have been involved in UN and NATO peacekeeping, peace enforcement, and humanitarian missions [37]. The tempo of missions and the concurrent downsizing of almost one third of the Canadian Forces have magnified the effects of deployment. Despite their extensive involvement in peacekeeping, studies of their needs are just beginning. As these missions have been very different from previous combat situations, the expectation of type and incidence of morbidity may have been difficult to anticipate. Rigorous preparation for a mission and proper care of peacekeepers should have a positive impact on them, their families, the organization, and the community. A recent shift in several countries' attention to deployment-related mental health issues is evidenced here by the establishment of the Operational Trauma and Stress Support Centers in Canada.

There are no published studies detailing the impact of pre-deployment preparation on Canadian peacekeepers; however, recommendations have been made for training based on reports by soldiers and mental health workers [38, 39]. Although valuable, their implementation has been inconsistent. Studies suggest that personnel selection is a primary prevention for deployment-related stress, taking into consideration personality and occupational, financial, relational, or legal stresses that exist prior to deployment [24, 40, 41]. Personality factors, such as resiliency and negativity, are limited in determining who is at risk for psychiatric morbidity. In addition, there have been a number of anecdotal reports of Canadian military members with PTSD who, with or without treatment, have successfully re-deployed. Research is required to determine the influence of gender [42], age, prior military experience, non-military trauma [43], and cultural background on an individual's risk.

Education in the history of the conflict(s), political, cultural, and ideological issues [38, 44], a "map" of the area and potential dangers (ethnic cleansing, acts of terrorism, hostage taking, combat zones), may improve the psychological and physical well-being of peacekeepers. Psychological preparation with mission and role clarity [45], stress management training [44, 46], and physical safety factors such as preparation for biological, chemical, or traditional warfare also help the soldier to adjust.

Surveys and focus groups have looked at numerous factors that might affect the soldier's experience of deployment, tolerance of stressors, or morbidity. Canadian Forces Boards of Inquiry for Somalia and Croatia [47, 48] investigated factors leading to problems during deployment, including exposures such as combat or non-combat incidents (witnessing murder, rape, destruction, poverty), and contextual stressors including length of deployment and family and marital problems. Stressors such as role conflict (the role one is trained to do conflicts with the role assigned in theater), role ambiguity (unclear assignment of duties), and overload (stress from overwhelming responsibilities), and moderating factors such as unit cohesion and leadership [40, 48, 49] have been shown to affect peacekeepers' experiences of their tour. Risk to Canadian reservist and augmented peacekeepers during deployment may be even higher depending on their integration into the unit and unit cohesion [48].

British and Canadian studies indicate that as high as 70–90 percent of soldiers in certain Bosnian missions between 1992-95 sustained direct threats such as weapons or mortar fire, being held at gun point, and sniper activity. Other exposures included mine threat, environmental toxins, hostage taking, standoff (armed face to face confrontation), body handling or body exchange, witnessing colleagues' suicide or death by accident, and sexual assault. However, witnessing ethnic cleansing, torture, rape, and mutilation of innocents such as women, children, and the elderly seems to have the most impact [40, 48, 50]. Soldiers also report that working in and around mass graves to unearth, identify, and examine bodies as possible war crimes victims is particularly distressing. Peacekeepers are often required to monitor these atrocities passively, creating a sense of impotence, helplessness, and lack of control [47, 48, 51].

Environmental conditions such as climate and geography as well as access to appropriate clothing, hygiene, accommodation, nutrition, water, and sleep may influence a soldier's experience of deployment and ability to tolerate deployment stress. Adequacy of resources such as equipment, weapons and ammunition, transportation, communication in the unit and with family, and personnel influence the soldier's perception of safety, and trust in the leadership [40].

Further study is required to clarify the controversy over the use of Critical Incident Stress Debriefing (CISD) for a single event, versus the ongoing exposures more typical of peacekeeping. Britain, Australia, and Canada are studying the impact of having a team of mental health workers with the troops throughout the deployment, versus dropping them in just prior to the end of the mission [52-54]. They become the unit's support system in theater, and in the pre- and post-deployment phases, and tend to be more readily accepted, as they are members of the unit. They are also responsible for post-deployment follow-up and referral to a mental health professional as required. These practices will improve access to care during deployment, and decrease stigma.

Many Canadian soldiers have reported inconsistent post-deployment follow-up, especially after the early tours such as Rwanda, Somalia, and Bosnia. Although many efforts have been made by the Canadian Forces to ensure this follow-up, a lack of standardization, and fear on the part of the soldier about coming forward for help, has led to the inconsistency. Some Australian formed units have kept their peacekeepers at barracks for 1–2 weeks on return to help facilitate reintegration, before allowing them to take leave. This "decompression" allows them to adjust to home and work more gradually and to unwind with colleagues with a shared experience [52]. Special attention should be given to non-married peacekeepers who may not have family support, and reservists who may have little contact with their deployed unit. Initial data from Canadian Forces trauma clinics suggest that 7 percent of those diagnosed with PTSD are reservists [51].

In retrospective studies by several countries, PTSD rates among peacekeepers vary from 2.5 percent to 20 percent depending on the tests performed and the criteria used for diagnosis [4, 46, 48, 55, 56]. Two studies recommended that to be accurate in assessing morbidity, and thus appropriate resources for care, PTSD must be redefined to reflect those with partial symptoms [48, 55].

UNITED STATES PEACEKEEPERS

Today, U.S. soldiers are deployed throughout the world on peace support operations, which entail a different combination of challenges for soldiers than does traditional combat [9]. In this section, we briefly review pre-, during, and post-deployment issues encountered by soldiers from the U.S. Army, Europe, deployed on peacekeeping missions to the Balkans, as they constitute approximately 80 percent of deployed U.S. soldiers. U.S. soldiers are deployed on peacekeeping missions as part of their active duty service, not as volunteers. They are not individually screened for selection for peacekeeping missions.

Prior to deploying on a peacekeeping mission, soldiers must attend to personal issues as well as completing necessary pre-deployment training. Soldiers preparing to deploy feel very positive about their military readiness but are usually skeptical about the utility of peacekeeping missions [57]. However, recent evidence suggests that there is a cultural shift occurring within the military, indicating that U.S. soldiers now recognize peacekeeping missions as a fundamental component of a soldier's job [57-59]. More than a third of soldiers deploying to Bosnia reported stress from not being able to complete personal business and preparing the family for their absence. Since they are away from home for a substantial time during the pre-deployment period as part of their training and equipment preparation, this compounds the impending separation. For single soldiers as well, the busy pre-deployment period does not allow adequate time to take care of personal issues.

Deployed soldiers report stress from difficulties in communication, the operational environment, and the ambiguity of the mission itself. While progress has been made in facilitating communication with loved ones back home [60], there remain difficulties in information flow between leaders and soldiers [61]. Data have clearly shown the importance of this type of communication. Soldiers deployed to Haiti on a peace support operation who were briefed on a daily basis about their mission by their leaders reported fewer physical and psychological symptoms [62].

Stress from the operational environment was reported by soldiers deployed to Kosovo, who worked more hours per day and more days per week than they did in garrison [57]. On mission, soldiers confined to the base camp for security reasons reported feelings of isolation and little opportunity to observe the contributions that the deployment made to the local population. Soldiers in Kosovo assigned to sites within the local communities reported more awareness of the contribution that the deployment made and had a more positive attitude about the mission. When soldiers actively participated in aid to the local community, they reported greater job involvement and satisfaction than those who did not [63]. Contact with the local population does, however, present problems. U.S. soldiers in Kosovo reported that despite maintenance of neutrality, local factions accused them of bias, causing apathy and resentfulness in the soldier. In addition, soldiers expressed doubt that the peacekeeping mission to the Balkans would have any lasting impact on preventing future conflicts. Not all peace support operations engender such skepticism about the specific benefits of a mission.

Although mission ambiguity has been reported as a key stressor in operations to Croatia [61], Haiti [62], and Bosnia [64], and remains a priority concern of commanders, it was not a major issue in Kosovo. Soldiers deploying to Kosovo knew the mission was indefinite, how long they would be deployed, and had clear Rules of Engagement.

Overall, soldiers report fewer physical and psychological symptoms at post-deployment than they do at mid-deployment. For Bosnia [65] and Kosovo [63] depression and physical symptoms were lower at post-deployment. Deployment experiences, and length, are important for post-deployment adjustment. It is critical to know what soldiers experienced during the mission and how it affected them. In a study of U.S. soldiers who returned from a six-month deployment to Kosovo, those who reported more incidents reported more physical and psychological symptoms, greater use of alcohol, greater use of conflict-based tactics, more days of work missed due to illness, and sleeping less than five hours a night, than soldiers who reported fewer incidents [66]. Soldiers deployed to Bosnia and Kosovo for more than four months had worse psychological health than those deployed for less than four months [67, 68]. Health measures included posttraumatic stress symptoms, depression and alcohol problems. Soldiers report high levels of job commitment at mid-deployment, reflecting the professional satisfaction they find by participating in a mission [63]. Job satisfaction declined at post-deployment, as soldiers engaged in more routine garrison duties. Despite the unique stresses of each deployment, depending on area of conflict, nations deploying and type of mission, it is expected that generalizations can be made between the Balkans research and other studies [9, 69-71] to lead to appropriate recommendations for preparation and intervention [72, 73].

DATA FROM OTHER COUNTRIES

The *Scandinavian countries* were among the first to study the psychological effects of peacekeeping on military personnel [6, 70]. A study comparing *Swedish* soldiers with and without combat experience during the Congo mission (1960-64) did not find any differences between groups in morbidity or in the incidence of "combat exhaustion." After their return, however, combat veterans were more often involved in accidents. A problematic family background and a lower education were the most important risk factors for "combat exhaustion" [74]. A study of stress symptoms among Swedish military personnel who served in UNIFIL (Lebanon), UNFICYP (Cyprus), and in the Gulf War concluded that, although the majority showed no signs of stress, factors such as primitive living conditions, climate, and worries about significant others, should be taken seriously. Those with interruption of service and high alcohol intake were at risk of developing problems later on [70]. One third of the soldiers of a Swedish I-FOR battalion (Bosnia, 1996) experienced trauma during their mission. Poor mental health afterward was related more to pre-service mental health and to a sense that a situation is coherent, manageable, and meaningful than to trauma exposure and post-trauma support. Peer support, followed by a defusing session, had a positive effect on post-service mental health, except for individuals with pre-existing poor mental health [75].

Approximately 60,000 *Norwegian* soldiers have served in UN peacekeeping missions. In 1985, a large, ongoing survey began on the nature of missions and their effects on peacekeepers. The results indicate that these veterans: are in general strong supporters of peacekeeping; have been exposed to "war-like" incidents; consider peacekeeping a useful military experience; show a change of attitude toward the conflicting parties, but remain neutral in their work; and are critical of pre-deployment training. Almost every soldier in UNIFIL had experienced a threat or an actual exchange of fire, 60 percent experienced fear of being wounded, and one or more soldiers had been taken hostage from all but one of 17 battalions. Fifteen percent of soldiers in one battalion were taken hostage. The motivation to volunteer for a UN operation has changed over the years from altruism and wish for travel, to financial benefits. This continuing study makes Norway perhaps the only country with such a complete database of its former peacekeepers [76]. Two studies of the first 26 Norwegian contingents in Lebanon [77, 78] showed that most soldiers evaluated their mission positively, that health problems equated to early repatriation, and repatriation was predicted by poor quality of home life during adolescence, negative life events before service and pronounced introverted personality. Forty-four percent of respondents reported that alcohol consumption increased during the mission due to stress [78].

Two studies in *Denmark* investigated three battalions that served in UNPROFOR (Bosnia, 1992-93) [79, 80]. These studies commented on worst and best experiences in theater, common symptoms following deployment, including arousal, re-experiencing phenomena, somatic complaints, increased alcohol consumption; and patterns of sharing their experiences on return with family and colleagues. Recommendation was made for follow-up post-deployment to evaluate delayed symptom onset, and offer group intervention to process the experience of deployment.

In 1995, the *Finnish* Ministry of Defense investigated the causes of early repatriation and the effects of UN service-related stress and morbidity [81]. Preliminary results indicate that early repatriation was associated with prior poor economic status, and a higher incidence of traumatic deaths following deployment. The prevalence of PTSD was exceptionally low in both groups, 2.7 percent in those repatriated and 1.3 percent in controls.

A *French* study described clinical observations of 40 French peacekeepers who were repatriated for psychiatric reasons from their missions in Yugoslavia and Somalia in 1992 and 1993. Three main factors contributing to the development of symptoms were: inability to counteract confrontation with danger and aggression, a permanent sense of insecurity, and the contrast between humanitarian ideals and the actual situation [82].

German soldiers entered the peacekeeping arena in Cambodia in 1992. A first study investigated stress among 450 soldiers of the medical contingent in Cambodia. Increased stress reactions immediately after return and at 18-month follow-up correlated with negativity, stresses prior to deployment, social withdrawal, and avoidance. Active problem solving, socialization, increased activity, and positive cognitive appraisal were protective against stress reactions. The prevalence of PTSD was 2 percent [83].

A second study collected data from 3,430 German soldiers who participated in UN and NATO operations in the former Yugoslavia. At follow-up, between 2 and 5 percent showed increased stress reactions, which correlated with low "sense of coherence" before deployment, low unit cohesion during the mission, deployment workload (if cohesion and unit coherence were low), and pre-existing PTSD. Peace-keepers' family members reported a need for social support [84].

Belgium has contributed almost 30,000 soldiers to peacekeeping since 1992. Participation in peacekeeping was publicly debated after the killing of 10 elite Belgian peacekeepers by Rwandan militia in 1994. This trauma led to the formation of a workgroup on psychosocial support in 1995, and since 1997 this has been a focus of discussion and research. The Department of Defense requested a first large scale study on the psychological problems of peacekeepers and their significant others, aimed at assessing the need for psychosocial support before, during, and after deploy-ment. It showed that 15–20 percent of peacekeepers experienced serious psycho-logical problems and had difficulties adapting after their return. New and young couples and families with young children appeared to be especially at risk, as well as those on their second or third long-term (four to six month) deployment [85]. The resulting recommendations were not immediately followed up by clear and consistent policy.

There have been reports or allegations of violations of standards by peace-keepers, including Belgian, Italian, and Canadian soldiers in Somalia, Dutch troops in Angola and Bosnia, and U.S. soldiers in Kosovo. The question of preserving an adequate moral standard and preventing abusive behavior or misconduct toward the local population requires special attention, in research and in policy. The Belgian Minister of Defense ordered an investigation into the causes of misbehavior, racism, and perhaps criminal acts committed by the paratroopers, and the strategy and policy response. Thirty recommendations were made, aimed at providing Belgian military personnel and their families with a solid moral and psychological framework before, during, and after deployment [86].

Another study investigated the structure of PTSD in Belgian peacekeepers and civilians who were at risk during the mass killings in Rwanda in April 1994. Five percent of the military and 15 percent of the civilians had PTSD. Many more were affected, but did not meet full PTSD criteria [87].

A *Japanese* study reported a high level of anxiety and general psychological distress among non-deployed personnel of the Japanese Self-defense Forces selected as military observers. Those actually deployed reported more physical symptoms than expected [88].

A study among *Italian* peacekeepers in Bosnia compared a deployed group with a group of military personnel stationed at their base in Italy. Those affected by stress indicated that the level of stress was high. This was associated with length of mission, lack of recreational or athletic activities during the mission, having three or more direct family members back home, and unemployment before entering military service [89].

Poland is another country with a rich experience in peacekeeping, from the Korean War to the present. In a sample of 152 former peacekeepers in Bosnia, the exposure to threatening events was widespread. Seven and three-tenths percent had PTSD, while 45.3 percent had one or more symptoms of PTSD [90].

Although the quality of these studies in terms of methodology and generalizability of the results varies widely, we can conclude that, internationally, a consistent body of knowledge is available that can be used as a basis for policy makers and professionals.

CONCLUSIONS AND RECOMMENDATIONS

While the number of peacekeeping operations has increased since 1990, during the same period most Western countries downsized significantly their armed forces. At the same time, most countries aimed to sustain capacity for several concurrent peacekeeping operations. Today, it is common practice for soldiers to be deployed several consecutive times. This puts strains on soldiers and their families, and departments of defense to retain qualified personnel. While most soldiers find peacekeeping a positive experience, a considerable number suffer from adverse effects, such as difficulties in adapting after return, serious psychological symptoms, or unexplainable somatic symptoms. Although these represent a minority among the total number of peacekeepers, in absolute numbers this group is large and should not be neglected. Findings from various studies pose serious challenges for policy, personnel management, and veteran's care. There are no data on peacekeepers from developing countries, yet these countries provide most of the troops. Recently, some countries have developed policies regarding the psychological effects of peace-keeping; however, this is not the case in the UN or NATO.

Several recommendations emerge from the studies. Promotion of good psycho-logical functioning in military personnel, as well as among veterans, must be incor-porated into regular military practice. Many countries seem to be shifting toward a mental health orientation for military personnel and veterans, accepting the psycho-logical risk of deployment. This will decrease the stigma of seeking aid in units where colleagues or supervisors are not sensitive to mental health issues.

Deployment begins with personnel selection, training, and pre-deployment preparation that should include a comprehensive health assessment, with individuals and family members, to provide early intervention if required. Adequate time must be given to take care of personal and family business. Establishing firm and reliable departure and return dates allows them to prepare for the deployment period. Providing realistic expectations of the mission stresses and training to manage them will help reduce anxiety. Briefings on the importance of the mission and the soldiers' role, and daily update briefings will help morale and to assess unit communication and effectiveness of leadership.

During deployment, quality of command and preservation of unit morale and cohesion are essential for the functioning of the unit, and psychological health and well-being. This requires providing regular communication with family members, opportunities for positive peacekeeping experiences, and ensuring good communication within the unit. Where possible, deployment should be no longer than four to six months. Monitoring of at-risk individuals and groups by caregivers throughout deployment enables identification of mental health issues and need for referral. It is highly recommended that, in addition to medical personnel and chaplains, mental health professionals are sent on mission as part of a unit. In order to increase acceptance by the troops, the alliance should begin in garrison. Pre-departure debriefings, stress counseling, and reintegration information should be provided by the mental health worker.

After deployment, soldiers need time to recover, both physically and mentally. A 6–12-month period between deployments should be a minimum. Training exercises should be scheduled only after one to three months in garrison post-deployment. All members of a deployed unit should receive a post-deployment assessment before six months after return. High-risk individuals or units who experienced traumatic incidents should be assessed for early intervention. Those with little or no unit and/or family support such as reservists, augmented personnel, temporary contract personnel, military observers, and those not married, should be given special attention. A reintegration or adaptation session with soldiers and their partners should be held at six to ten weeks post-deployment, and again at six months after return. Supporting families during this, and all phases of deployment, is crucial. Recognition and acknowledgment of achievements is also vital. Commander-led unit meetings to evaluate the mission and relate it to the soldiers' professional and personal performance can also add meaning to the mission.

Unfortunately, despite media coverage, the Secretary-General's reports on Srebrenica and Rwanda [91, 92], and peacekeepers' own accounts of their related guilt and shame, to our knowledge studies of the effects of the tragic events on them were not done. Neither could we find studies on the documented effects of other types of abuse, neglect and amoral behavior. Education regarding moral action and human rights in peacekeeping missions is crucial to preventing them from recurring.

Ongoing research to define clearly peacekeepers' needs in all phases of deployment is critical to effective peacekeeping. Prospective, longitudinal studies are required as some psychological symptoms decrease or disappear, while others become manifest, with time. Analysis of pre- and post-deployment data can reveal patterns that will increase understanding of the effects of deployment. To this purpose, each country should develop a comprehensive database with ongoing registration of medical, psychological, and social data of military personnel. Collaboration among countries, including the developing countries, to promote comparative research, will facilitate the development of further policy and program recommendations. Such research requires that military institutions open up to the public they serve, a cause par excellence.

REFERENCES

1. S. J. Stedman, The New Interventionists, *Foreign Affairs, 72*:5, pp. 1-16, 1993.
2. J. Hillen, *Blue Helmets. The Strategy of UN Military Operations,* Brassey's, Washington, London, 1998.

3. J. Shay, *Achilles in Vietnam. Combat Trauma and the Undoing of Character*, Atheneum, New York, 1994.
4. C. MacDonald, K. Chamberlain, N. Long, J. Pereira-Laird, and K. Mirfin, Mental Health, Physical Health, and Stressors Reported by New Zealand Defense Force Peacekeepers: A Longitudinal Study, *Military Medicine, 163*:7, pp. 477-481, 1998.
5. C. MacDonald, K. Chamberlain, N. Long, and K. Mirfin, Stress and Mental Health Status Associated with Peacekeeping Duty for New Zealand Defense Force Personnel, *Stress Medicine, 15*:4, pp. 235-241, 1999.
6. B. Egge, M. S. Mortensen, and L. Weisæth, Armed Conflicts. Soldiers for Peace: Ordeals and Stress. The Contribution of the United Nations Peace-Keeping Forces, in *International Responses to Traumatic Stress*, Y. Danieli, N. S. Rodley, and L. Weisæth (eds.), Baywood, Amityville, New York, 1996.
7. E. Goffman, *On the Characteristics of Total Institutions*, Proceedings of the Symposium on Preventive and Social Psychiatry, Walter Reed Army Institute of Research, Washington, D.C., April 15-17, 1957.
8. J. M. Whealin, Ch. A. Morgan, and G. Hazlett, The Role of Military Studies in Enhancing Our Understanding of PTSD, *PTSD Research Quarterly, 12*:1, pp. 1-6, 2001.
9. B. Litz, The Psychological Demands of Peacekeeping, *PTSD Clinical Quarterly, 6*:1, pp. 1-8, 1996.
10. A. Elklit, UN-Soldiers Serving in Peacekeeping Missions: A Review of Psychological After-Effects, *International Review of the Armed Forces Medical Services, 71*:10-12, pp. 197-207, 1998.
11. C. Klep and R. van Gils, *Van Korea tot Kosovo. De Nederlandse militaire deelname aan vredesoperaties sinds 1945*, SdU Uitgevers, Den Haag, 1999.
12. J. C. van der Beek, A. G. L. V. Onzevoort, and J. Verkuyl, *Nazorg ex-Unifil militairen. Een evaluatie-onderzoek naar de nazorgbehoefte van ex-Unifil militairen*, Afdeling Gedragswetenschappen van de Directie Personeel Koninklijke Landmacht, Den Haag, 1987.
13. J. P. Knoester, *Traumatische ervaringen van ex-UNIFIL militairen. Een literatuur- en dossieronderzoek*, DPKL, afdeling Gedragswetenschappen, Den Haag, 1989.
14. T. Willigenburg and N. Alkemade, *Pilot nazorg Koninklijke Landmacht*, Adeling Gedragswetenschappen en Afdeling Individuele Hulpverlening, Den Haag/Amersfoort, 1995.
15. H. W. de Swart and A. Flach, Psychologische begeleiding rond uitzendingen, *Militaire Spectator, 168*:10, pp. 542-549, 1999.
16. A. Zijlmans and A. Flach, *Nazorgonderzoek KL, nadelige gevolgen van gijzelingen tijdens crisisbeheersingsoperaties bij Nederlandse KL-militairen*. CDPO/GW-AIH, documentnr. 97-21, Den Haag, Amersfoort, 1997.
17. A. Flach, Uitzendingen als gedragswetenschappelijk onderzoeksobject in de KL, *Militaire Spectator, 167*:1, pp. 26-34, 1998.
18. I. Bramsen, *The Long-Term Psychological Adjustment of World War II Survivors in the Netherlands*, Eburon Press, Delft, 1995.
19. I. Bramsen, M. T. A. Klaarenbeek, and H. M. van der Ploeg, Militaire gevechtservaringen in de jaren 1940-1950. Klachten en gezondheidsbeleving van oorlogsveteranen vijftig jaar later, in *Veteranen in Nederland. Onderzoek naar de gevolgen van oorlogservaringen— Tweede Wereldoorlog—Politionele acties—Korea*, H. M. van der Ploeg and J. M. P. Weerts (eds.), Swets & Zeitlinger Publishers, Lisse, 1995.
20. I. Bramsen, M. T. A. Klaarenbeek, and H. M. van der Ploeg, Psychische aanpassing van oorlogsveteranen op de lange termijn. Het vervolgonderzoek onder leden van de BNMO,

in *Veteranen in Nederland. Onderzoek naar de gevolgen van oorlogservaringen—Tweede Wereldoorlog—Politionele acties—Korea*, H. M. van der Ploeg and J. M. P. Weerts (eds.), Swets & Zeitlinger Publishers, Lisse, 1995.

21. I. Bramsen, A. J. E. Dirkzwager, and H. M. van der Ploeg, *Deelname aan vredesmissies: gevolgen, opvang en nazorg*, Vrije Universiteit Amsterdam, Amsterdam, 1997.

22. J. E. Hovens, H. M. Van der Ploeg, I. Bramsen, M. T. A. Klaarenbeek, J. N. Schreuder, and V. V. Rivero, The Development of the Self-Rating Inventory for Posttraumatic Stress Disorder, *Acta Psychiatrica Scandinavica, 90*:3, pp. 172-183, 1994.

23. A. J. E. Dirkzwager, I. Bramsen, and H. M. van der Ploeg, *Factors Associated with PTSD Symptom Severity in Dutch Former Peacekeepers* (manuscript submitted).

24. I. Bramsen, A. J. E. Dirkzwager, and H. M. van der Ploeg, Pre-Deployment Personality Traits and Exposure to Trauma as Predictors of Post-Traumatic Stress Symptoms: A Prospective Study of Former Peacekeepers, *American Journal of Psychiatry, 157*:7, pp. 1115-1119, 2000.

25. Accompanying Committee Peace Keeper Study, *Participation in Peacekeeping Missions. Consequences and Short- and Long-Term After-Care*, Recommendations of the Committee Tiesinga, The Hague, 1997.

26. www.veteraneninstituut.nl

27. M. De Vries, P. M. M. B. Soetekouw, G. Bleijenberg, and J. W. M. van der Meer, Natural Course of Symptoms in Cambodia Veterans. A Follow-Up Study, *Psychological Medicine, 31*:2, pp. 331-338, 2001.

28. M. de Vries, P. M. M. B. Soetekouw, J. W. M. van der Meer, and G. Bleijenberg, Fatigue in Cambodia Veterans, *Quarterly Journal of Medicine, 93*:5, pp. 283-289, 2000.

29. P. M. M. B. Soetekouw, M. de Vries, G. Bleijenberg, and J. W. M. van der Meer, *Het Post-Cambodja klachten onderzoek fase II*, UMC, St. Radboud, Nijmegen, 2000.

30. P. M. M. B. Soetekouw, M. de Vries, L. van Bergen, J. M. D. Galema, A. Keyser, G. Bleijenberg, and J. W. M. van der Meer, Somatic Hypotheses of War Syndromes, *European Journal of Clinical Investigations, 30*:7, pp. 630-641, 2000.

31. S. C. M. van Esch, I. Bramsen, G. P. Sonnenberg, V. P. B. M. Merlijn, and H. M. van der Ploeg, *Het post-Cambodja klachten onderzoek. Het welbevinden van Cambodja-gangers en hun behoefte aan hulp en nazorg*, EMGO, Vrije Universiteit Amsterdam, 1998.

32. Y. M. Mulder and S. A. Reyneveld, *Gezondheidsonderzoek UNPROFOR. Een onderzoek onder militairen die uitgezonden zijn geweest naar Lukavac, Santici en Busovaca (Bosnië-Herzegovina) in de periode 1994-1995*, TNO, Preventie en gezondheid, Leiden, 1999.

33. A. Flach and A. Zijlmans, *Nazorgonderzoek KL, verwerkingsproblemen na uitzendingen*, CDPO/GW-AIH, documentnummer 97-21, Den Haag/Amersfoort, 1997.

34. A. Zijlmans and M. P. G. Bos-Bakx, *Nazorgonderzoek KL, uitzending, beleving en verwerking (IFOR2, SFOR1 en SFOR2)*, CDPO/GW-AIH, doumentnummer 00.32, Den Haag/Amersfoort, 2000.

35. A. Zijlmans and P. van Kuijk, *Nazorgonderzoek KL, periode SFOR3-5*, CDPO/GW-AIH (in press).

36. P. van Kuijk and A. Zijlmans, *Nazorgonderzoek KL, periode SFOR 6-7, KFOR1-2*, CDPO/GW-AIH (in press).

37. Canadian Military Web Page: www.dnd.ca/menu/Operations/pastops_e.htm

38. M. Parkes and K. Farley, *Stress in Military Operations*, Working Paper 95-2 Canadian Forces Personnel Applied Research Unit, 1995.

39. G. Shorey, *Selection and Training of Military Observers: Lessons Learned from the Naval Experience*, Maritime Command Headquarters, Halifax, 1994.

40. C. Lamerson and E. Kelloway, Towards a Model of Peacekeeping Stress: Traumatic and Contextual Influences, *Canadian Psychology, 37*:4, pp. 195-204, 1996.

41. R. Bloom, Psychological Assessment for Security Clearances, Special Access, and Sensitive Positions, *Military Medicine, 158*:9, pp. 609-613, 1993.

42. A. Norwood, R. Ursano, and F. Gabbay, Health Effects of the Stressors of Extreme Environments on Military Women, *Military Medicine, 162*:10, pp. 643-648, 1997.

43. R. Stretch, K. Knudson, and D. Durand, Effects of Premilitary and Military Trauma on the Development of Post-Traumatic Stress Disorder Symptoms in Female and Male Active Duty Soldiers, *Military Medicine, 163*:7, pp. 466-470, 1998.

44. M. Creamer, Teleconference, *February; Use of "The Lonely Planet" Books in Pre-Deployment Training for Australian Military, as well as a Field Booklet with Information on Stress Management and Coping Strategies,* 2001.

45. P. Bartone and A. Adler, *Peacekeeping Operations: Psychological Preparation,* paper presented at the U.S. Army Medical Research Unit -Europe, Heidelberg, Germany, 1995.

46. M. Deahl, M. Srinivasan, N. Jones, J. Thomas, C. Neblett, and A. Jolly, Preventing Psychological Trauma in Soldiers: The Role of Operation Stress Training and Psychological Debriefing, *British Journal of Medical Psychology, 73*(Pt 1), pp. 77-85, 2000.

47. A. English, *Creating a System for Dealing with Operational Stress in the Canadian Forces,* prepared for the Board of Inquiry-Croatia, pp. 5-6, 1999.

48. G. Passey and D. Crockett, *Psychological Consequences of Canadian UN Peacekeeping* (unpublished), 1999.

49. F. Pinch, *Lessons from Canadian Peacekeeping Experience,* unpublished report prepared for the Department of National Defense, pp. viii-xiv, 1994.

50. P. Roberts, *War in Peace: A Field Study in Bosnia of Troops in a Siege Under Fire,* presentation at the 16th Annual Meeting of the International Society for Traumatic Stress Studies, San Antonio, Texas, USA, November 16-19, 2000.

51. Preliminary data from Edmonton Garrison Operational Trauma and Stress Support Center, Canadian Department of National Defense, October 1999-February 2001.

52. M. Creamer, Teleconference re: *During—Deployment Mental Health Services Provided in E. Timor by Australian Military,* 2001.

53. C. March, *Preventing Psychological and Moral Injury in Military Service,* presentation at the 16th Annual Meeting of the International Society for Traumatic Stress Studies, San Antonio, Texas, USA, November 16-19, 2000.

54. P. Rosebush, Psychological Intervention with Military Personnel in Rwanda, *Military Medicine, 163*:8, pp. 559-563, 1998.

55. J. Pearn, Traumatic Stress Disorders: A Classification with Implications for Prevention and Management, *Military Medicine, 165*:6, pp. 434-440, 2000.

56. R. Gibson, *The Development of The Canadian Deployment Impact Scale for Assessing PTSD: A Psychometric Study,* Ph.D. dissertation, Department of Educational Psychology, University of Calgary, 1997.

57. C. A. Castro, R. V. Bienvenu, A. H. Huffman, and A. B. Adler, Soldier Dimensions and Operational Readiness in US Army Forces Deployed to Kosovo, *International Review of the Armed Forces Medical Services, 73*:10, pp. 191-199, 2000.

58. L. L. Miller, Do Soldiers Hate Peacekeeping? The Case of Preventive Diplomacy Operations in Macedonia, *Armed Forces and Society, 23*:3, pp. 415-450, 1997.

59. B. J. Reed and D. R. Segal, The Impact of Multiple Deployments on Soldiers' Peacekeeping Attitudes, Morale, and Retention, *Armed Forces and Society, 27*:1, pp. 57-78, 2000.

60. L. W. Applewhite and D. R. Segal, Telephone Use by Peacekeeping Troops in the Sinai, *Armed Forces and Society, 17*:1, pp. 117-126, 1990.

61. P. T. Bartone, A. B. Adler, and M. A. Vaitkus, Dimensions of Psychological Stress in Peacekeeping Operations, *Military Medicine, 163*:9, pp. 587-593, 1998.
62. R. R. Halverson and P. D. Bliese, Determinants of Soldier Support for Operation Uphold Democracy, *Armed Forces and Society, 23*:1, pp. 81-96, 1996.
63. A. B. Adler, C. A. Dolan, C. A. Castro, R. B. Bienvenu, and A. H. Huffman, *US Soldier Study III: Kosovo Post-Deployment.* USAMRU-E Technical Brief #00-04, US Army Medical Research Unit-Europe, Heidelberg, Germany, 2000.
64. D. R. Ritzer, S. J. Campbell, and J. N. Valentine, Human Dimensions Research during Operation Joint Guard, Bosnia, *Army Medical Department Journal, 8*:1, pp. 5-16, 1998.
65. C. A. Castro, P. T. Bartone, T. W. Britt, and A. B. Adler, *Operation Joint Endeavor (OJE): Lessons Learned for Improving Psychological Readiness,* USAMRU-E Technical Brief #98-04, US Army Medical Research Unit-Europe, Heidelberg, Germany, 1998.
66. A. B. Adler, C. A. Dolan, and C. A. Castro, *US Soldier Peacekeeping Experiences and Wellbeing After Returning From Deployment to Kosovo,* Proceedings of the 36th International Applied Military Psychology Symposium, Split, Croatia (in press).
67. C. A. Castro and A. B. Adler, The Impact of Operations Tempo on Soldier and Unit Readiness, *Parameters,* pp. 86-95, Autumn 1999.
68. A. K. Wright, A. H. Huffman, A. B. Adler, and C. A. Castro, *Redeployment Psychological Screening of 1ID Soldiers Deployed to Kosovo,* USAMRU-E Technical Brief #01-02, US Army Medical Research Unit-Europe, Heidelberg, Germany, 2001.
69. I. Johnston, *The Psychological Impact of Peacekeeping Deployment,* Proceedings of the International Military Testing Association, Edinburgh, Scotland, November 6-9, 2000.
70. T. Lundin and U. Otto, Swedish Soldiers in Peacekeeping Operations: Stress Reactions Following Missions in Congo, Lebanon, Cyprus, and Bosnia, *NCP Clinical Quarterly, 6*:1, pp. 9-15, 1996.
71. J. L. Soetters and J. H. Rovers (eds.), *The Bosnian Experience,* The Royal Netherlands Military Academy, Breda, The Netherlands, 1997.
72. B. T. Litz, L. A. King, D. W. King, S. M. Orsillo, and M. J. Friedman, Warriors as Peacekeepers: Features of the Somalia Experience and PTSD, *Journal of Consulting and Clinical Psychology, 65*:6, pp. 1001-1010, 1997.
73. T. W. Britt and A. B. Adler, Stress and Health during Medical Humanitarian Assistance Missions, *Military Medicine, 164*:4, pp. 275-279, 1999.
74. B. Kettner, Combat Strain and Subsequent Mental Health. A Follow-Up Study of Swedish Soldiers Serving in the United Nations Forces 1961-62, *Acta Psychiatrica Scandivica,* Suppl. 230, 1992.
75. G. Larsson, P.-O. Michel, and T. Lundin, Systematic Assessment of Mental Health following Various Types of Posttrauma Support, *Military Psychology, 12*:2, pp. 121-135, 2000.
76. M. H. Ness (ed.), Internasjonale operasjoner, Seminarrapport 1-6, *Forsvarets Kompetansesenter for Internasjonal Virksomhet,* Norwegian Defence International Centre, 2000/2001.
77. L. Weisæth, P. Aarhaug, L. Mehlum, and S. Larsen, The UNIFIL Study. *Positive and Negative Consequences of Service in UNIFIL Contingents I-XXVI, Report Part I, Results And Recommendations,* Norwegian Defence Command Headquarters, The Joint Medical Service, Oslo, 1993.
78. L. Mehlum, Alcohol and Stress in Norwegian United Nations Peacekeepers, *Military Medicine, 164*:10, pp. 720-724, 1999.
79. M. Bache and B. Hommelgaard, *Danske FN-Soldater. Oplevelser og stressreaktioner,* Forsvarets Center for Lederskap, 1994.

80. A. Elklit, *Strains and Afterreactions in Danish UN-Soldiers,* presentation at the First European Conference on Traumatic Stress in Emergency Services, Peacekeeping Operations and Humanitarian Aid Organisations, Sheffield, United Kingdom, March 17-20, 1996.

81. M. Ponteva, *Stress in the UN Peacekeeping Operations; The Finnish View,* paper presented at the 2nd International Conference on Human Dimensions during Military Deployments, Heidelberg, Germany, September 5-9, 2000.

82. C. Doutheau, F. Lebigot, C. Moraud, L. Crocq, L. M. Fabre, and J. D. Favre, Stress Factors and Psychopathological Reactions of UN Missions in the French Army, *International Review of the Armed Forces Medical Services, 67*:1-3, pp. 36-38, 1994.

83. W. Schüffel, B. Schade, and T. Schunk, *Belastungen und Streßreaktionen von Sanitätspersonal im humanitären Hilfseinsatz in Kambodscha,* Forschunsbericht aus der Wehrmedizin, BMVg-FBWM, 98-2 Bonn, 1998.

84. W. Schüffel, T. Schunk, and B. Schade, *Untersuchung zu Ressourcen, Belastungen und Streßreaktionen deutscher Soldaten in UN-resp. NATO-Einsätzen—Langzeitverlaufe unter gesundheitlichen Aspekten,* Forschunsbericht aus der Wehrmedizin, BMVg-FBWM 99-4, Bonn, 1999.

85. N. Wauters, *Le soutien psychosocial des militaires et leurs proches pendant les missions de longue durée à l'étranger (étude quantitative),* unpublished report, Ministry of Defense, Dept. JSP-P/C, Brussels, 1997.

86. J. Leman (ed.), *Onderzoek naar de mechanismen die kunnen leiden tot racisme bij de Belgische strijdkrachten,* Op aanvraag van de de heer Poncelet, Minister van Landsverdediging, uitgevoerd onder verantwoordelijkheid van het 'Centrum voor gelijkheid van kansen en racismebestrijding' en van het Directiecomité dat als begeleidingscel functioneert, Brussels, 1998.

87. J. Mylle, *Structures des réactions de stress posttraumatique consécutives à une catastrophe humaine délibéré,* dissertation doctorale présentée en vue de l'obtention du grade de Docteur en Psychologie, Université Catholique de Louvain, Faculté de Psychologie et des Sciences de l'Education, Louvaine-la-Neuve, 1999.

88. Y. Kodama, S. Nomura, and T. Ogasawara, Psychological Changes of Japan Self-Defense Forces Personnel during Selection and Training for the Peacekeeping Mission in the Golan Heights, *Military Medicine, 165*:9, pp. 653-655, 2000.

89. E. Ballone et al., Factors Influencing Psychological Stress Levels of Italian Peacekeepers in Bosnia, *Military Medicine, 165*:12, pp. 911-915, 2000.

90. M. Chilczuk, *Polish UN Peacekeeping Operations Veterans,* paper presented at the World Veterans Federation First International Conference on Psychosocial Consequences of War, Dubrovnik, April 26-30, 1998.

91. *The Fall of Srebrenica* (A/54/549 15 November 1999).

92. *Report of the Independent Inquiry into the Actions of the United Nations during the 1994 Genocide in Rwanda* (S/1999/1257 15 December 1999).

Voices

CAMBODIA DIARY

Mike Daly, US Army Military Observer, 1993[1]

It's difficult to describe what I'm feeling now as I prepare to go to the States on leave. I've had to suppress so much of what I feel for so long, and now that I know I'm safe, it's coming out. I didn't used to believe in delayed stress, but I do now. I've been afraid to log much of what I've seen until now. The pigs I saw eating roast persons. The body parts on trees. The look on the faces of the wounded before they died. The smell of death. The graves of the executed soldiers. The amputees. The sick children. The intense fear. The lack of sleep. The ground shaking during the massive artillery strikes. The terrible thunder of the B40s (rocket propelled grenades). The constant threat of imminent attack. The fear of driving in mined areas. The booby traps. The sound that rifle fire makes when it passes close enough to hear its whoosh. Not knowing if I would hold my wife, kids, and Mom again one more time.

The night sweats caused by intense fear. The fear of capture. The dysentery and malaria. The pressure of knowing that one wrong decision means my team, the Indonesians and the locals are dead. Performing surgery with a K-Bar (army knife). Administering drugs, hoping they'd work and not kill the patient. The blood of the dead that I can't get out of some of my uniforms. The weakness from not eating well, and drinking bad water. The longing to be in a place where people and kids aren't maimed and dying. My frustration at not being able to stop the fighting. My nightmare. My periodic uncontrollable shaking. Trying to act brave when I'm terrified. The knowledge that I'm forever changed, and wondering if I'm capable of ever being "normal" again. What's happening to me? Do the other guys who have seen and done what I do, feel the same way?

---

[1] Excerpt from diary, included in S. Downie, *Inside Peacekeeping: the UN in Cambodia and East Timor*, forthcoming.

THAT FEELING OF IMPORTANCE AND RESPECT
Major Cheryl A. Netterfield, MD, CCFP

In the spring of 1999, I was selected to deploy to Kosovo as Senior Medical Advisor for the entire Canadian Contingent. A position of tremendous responsibility, it would give me the opportunity to prove to my superiors that I was a competent leader and medical officer. Until then I was never convinced that they recognized my abilities.

From that point to the end of the tour was one of the busiest times of my life. The period before deployment was extremely stressful. There was so much to do, and my inexperience made me feel inadequately prepared. My immediate medical chain of command seemed to offer little to no support or advice.

In Kosovo I spent seven extremely demanding months. I felt completely responsible for ensuring that nothing would go wrong. I knew that I was pushing myself too hard and neglecting my own personal needs, but I wasn't able to let up. Many of the medical issues that arose were problems that I had never dealt with before and there was added pressure from the various unit commanders wanting answers to questions that I didn't have. The novelty of these medical administrative issues, along with what I thought were successful resolutions to these problems, was very empowering. I felt very important and that my superiors appreciated and respected me for the job that I did.

The extended Christmas break after arriving back in Canada was similar to any other leave in the past except for the fact that I really missed all of the people that I lived and worked with in Kosovo. As a single person, it was very lonely to come back to an empty apartment when I was used to living in a large tent with 15 other people and always had someone to talk to or confide in. I looked forward to getting back to work at my regular unit in Edmonton but once I started again, I soon realized that I was very unhappy. What should have been relaxing and relatively stress-free, I found boring and unchallenging. I was just another General Duty Medical Officer and had none of the responsibility that I did while overseas. I was no longer in charge and any change that I thought I could affect was not met with much enthusiasm. I had lost that feeling of importance and respect that I experienced in Kosovo and no one acknowledged the hard work that I had done overseas.

I eventually was posted out of this unit to Moose Jaw as a Wing Surgeon. Once again, a feeling of increased responsibility and challenge enabled me to enjoy my work. Kosovo will be both one of the toughest and most rewarding times of my life.

PART II. UN AGENCIES AND PROGRAMS

Voice

A LIFETIME OF LEARNING

Nils Arne Kastberg

The silence was palpable, touchable, and even as a new person in the area, I could feel it. I was driving the pick-up along the dusty road and my passengers traveled in silence. We had just picked up a young guerilla fighter, disguised as a woman with earrings, lipstick, and dress, but easily given away by his AK-47 machine gun and rounds of ammunition over his shoulder. The leaders had explained to him that this first white man to drive on this road in a long time was helping them return to their homes. The guerilla boy believed the war was still on, but the refugees told him that a peace agreement had been signed some days ago, and Joshua Nkomo, their leader, was part of the deal. Now they were coming back from Botswana to Matabeleland in Rhodesia, to vote for a government, for a free Zimbabwe. The boy did not seem very convinced.

We stopped a few times to ask people where landmines were, and left the road to follow a circuitous path in the bush to avoid the, potential or real, indiscriminate killers hidden below the dust. I was making mental notes of these detours, so that I would recognize the route when returning. After a while, the boy decided he would get off. Soon everyone started talking again and laughing. Expectations rose as they recognized hills, trees that had grown much larger since they left two years earlier, and health clinics that were lying in ruins, all signs showing that they were closer to "home."

Finally I was told to stop. I could see nothing other than bush. Everyone got off the pick-up. Is this where you live? It had not occurred to me, and apparently not to my passengers, that two years without maintenance, would leave their huts, *tukuls*, as small heaps on the ground. After the first minute of shock, however, they started talking again, as they unloaded bags of maize, suitcases, sports bags, rucksacks, and handbags. Many of the bags were made of green plastic sheeting that had covered the roofs of most *tukuls* in the refugee camps. All this plastic sheeting, including that lying in stores, had been converted into something useful for the return.

The leaders started searching for a piece of paper, then tore a page from a notebook and wrote something. They gave me the paper and said it was a safe-conduct in case I met more "boys," as I returned alone along the 25 miles to Tegwani Mission. I needed to quickly turn back to safer areas before it would get completely dark. I was swallowing dust, as I tried to hold back tears. It was hard to leave these families and elderly, without a roof or anything for shelter. As I drove back, though, I smiled as I read the "safe-conduct" note: "This is a friend from the United Nations

51

of the Red Cross. Let him pass, he helped us return. Signed: Refugees from Francistown." They mixed these international organizations, but they cared about their new friend.

As a very young, seconded officer from the Swedish aid and development agency, I was in my first week in Rhodesia working for UNHCR, based at Tegwani Mission which served as a reception center for returning refugees. I had the privilege of beginning immediately a career of being trained by those I was supposed to "help." As I frequently visited those who had returned, I saw them restarting their lives and witnessed their amazing survival skills. It was rewarding to see them rebuild their *tukuls*, with thorny bushes enclosing animals that they soon started getting. In this microcosm, I witnessed transition from emergency to development, as these Francistown refugees rebuilt their lives thanks to their own will, wits, and skills.

During that first week, I also learned other skills of an aid worker. Trucks continued bringing the refugees back from Botswana, a thousand at a time, every day for 25 days. But the Rhodesian "security" personnel considered the returnees as terrorists and had slowed the process to a trickle. At happy hour at the local Plumtree pub, none of the other aid workers were interested in engaging with these big boys. In the end, I played the naïve Swede: "I didn't know that all these women and children and elderly are terrorists, and that you fear them." The following morning the backlog of 4,000 was cleared and we did not have enough buses to send them all home.

As soon as I arrived at the Tegwani Mission some of the women told me that they would like some bread to go with their sadza, the porridge made of white maize. The department of Social Services said the people could do without. I thought, if this was all they asked for, why not provide it? I went to the local Plumtree bakery, where the subject of conversation was the returning "terrorists" and what they would do to their lives. I told the baker I wanted the back of the pick-up loaded every morning with loaves, each loaf inside a paper bag. After this, I never heard "terrorist" again.

What I, or UNHCR, did was necessary, but it was small compared with what the refugees did themselves. It was easy to see their skill at using the plastic sheeting, something the international community would have discarded. Not so visible was their ability to get on with and enjoy life, in the midst of what most other people would regard as misery, hardship, deprivation, or uncertainty.

It was a good first week of learning. This was so much more than just work. It needed engagement, commitment, controlling, and containing feelings. It needed respect and understanding, without condoning bad behavior. This first week has been followed by many more, accumulating into months, years and now decades, of learning.

3

Caring for Staff in UNHCR

Søren Jessen-Petersen

INTRODUCTION

A Changing Humanitarian Operational Environment

UNHCR's core mandate has not changed since 1950. The protection of refugees and the search for solutions to their problems have remained our central objectives. But the environment in which we work has changed significantly—particularly in the past decade. During the latter half of the 20th century UN Agencies, NGOs, and other humanitarian actors relied on an often tacit and unspoken agreement between all groups involved in a conflict to respect their neutrality. Humanitarian actors would be "impartial" in the delivery of assistance and were therefore perceived as "neutral." Parties would respect and consent to humanitarian action.

This situation began to deteriorate with the eruption of a series of long-simmering ethnic, religious, and other conflicts, often within States rather than between States. Many of these were characterized by intense violence committed by regular armies, militias, warlords, guerrilla, and bandit groups in which civilian populations were deliberately targeted, particularly in wars in Bosnia and Herzegovina, the Great Lakes region of Africa, Sierra Leone, Timor, and Kosovo.

Forced displacement of the "opposing group" has very often become a major objective, rather than a consequence, of these conflicts. Displacement has also grown in scale. The number of people of concern to UNHCR today is 22 million, up from 15 million in 1990 and 5 million in 1980. It has also changed in scope, with virtually no region—Europe, Africa, Asia, and Latin America—unaffected. Refugees and humanitarian workers often became deliberate targets for one side or another rather than occasional, accidental victims.

The Manipulation of Refugee Populations

Parties to conflict, including rebel movements, host countries, and other States, both within and beyond the regions directly concerned, have often made use of refugee populations in the quest to attain their political and military objectives. It is this manipulation for geopolitical purposes that often presents the greatest threat to refugee security. In such situations refugees may be held hostage by elements that are not bona fide refugees and they may also be denied access to the objective information required for making decisions about their future.

The Targeting and Intimidation of Humanitarian Personnel

More and more, the same parties to conflict expect aid organizations to care for the victims of war. At the same time, those parties have increasingly subjected humanitarian personnel to intimidation and violence with the tragic results that have been recently witnessed in locations such as Burundi, Indonesia, Guinea, and the Democratic Republic of Congo. The political, legal, and security void that exists today clearly aggravates risk to humanitarian personnel.

UNHCR's Response: A Comprehensive Security Strategy

In this dramatically changed environment, UNHCR has had to adapt its policies and operations and decided to implement a comprehensive security strategy containing measures aimed at: strengthening its emergency response capacity, operationalizing its refugee security policies, and enhancing its staff security measures.

Enhancing Staff Security

Recent attempts to enhance staff security policies and measures have focused on:

- continued support of the ratification of the International Criminal Court Statute, which stipulates that attacks on humanitarian personnel can constitute a war crime and provides for the punishment of perpetrators, including non-state actors;
- the integration of specialist security-related functions into the mainstream management of UNHCR operations;
- the introduction of security standards and procedures in the process of mission planning, budgeting, implementation, review and oversight; and
- the use of proactive rather than reactive staff security management strategies.

Staff security management is not limited to issues concerning the legal protection and physical safety of staff only. In a broader sense, it includes staff welfare and medical issues. In the world of today, UNHCR staff is exposed to operational environments characterized by insecurity and human suffering and high levels of stress and tension. Only when staff are safe, healthy, and psychologically prepared can they be expected to protect and support refugees.

In this contribution, the United Nations Joint Medical Service (JMS) and UNHCR's Staff Welfare Unit provide an overview of relevant staff welfare issues, strategies, and protocols for the support of our staff.

1. STAFF WELFARE DURING THE EARLY YEARS

During the early years, staff welfare was based on a high collegial spirit of mutual support. Occasional incidents would be taken care of on a case-by-case basis and with the absence of stressful and difficult situations, this approach was deemed feasible. It did not appear necessary to employ specialists that would provide the organization with stress management approaches. The considerable changes in UNHCR's operational environment, however, led to a rethinking of this position. The JMS, which is in charge of periodic medical examinations and consultations for UN staff members, made the first consistent observation of the psychosocial impact of adverse working conditions on UNHCR staff. During the early 1990s, it was noticed that staff members complained more often about headaches, chest pressure, digestive problems, muscle pains, extreme fatigue, sleeplessness, nightmares, and hypersensitivity to noise or smells. The frequency of hypertension, diabetes and certain types of cancer appeared to have increased. These problems seemed more frequent among those staff based in duty stations in the midst of war.

In reaction, the JMS tried to develop a network of external mental health professionals to whom colleagues could be referred. However, at that time, little awareness of post traumatic stress, especially related to war experiences, existed. Staff members were often misunderstood by the treating psychotherapists who did not understand why they wanted to continue to do the work that had put them so much at risk.

At the same time, it was difficult for staff members to admit that they were not coping psychologically. UNHCR staff, like all humanitarian aid workers, are focused on others, those in need, and not on their own concerns. They did not want to be considered vulnerable and believed that vulnerability was a sign that one should quit the job. It was like betraying the refugees. It would also be seen as betraying colleagues.

It took UNHCR a while to accept that this type of work is stressful and can be harmful to the well-being of staff unless underlying stress issues are properly addressed. With the deteriorating operational environment, however, it became obvious to the organization that the staff needed support and that this support would have to be the organization's responsibility.

Initial attempts to deal with the psychosocial effects of traumatic events were isolated; for example, ad-hoc workshops for staff in the most affected areas. The first such workshop on stress management was in 1991. In time, they became more frequent.

2. TRANSITION TO STAFF SUPPORT STRATEGIES

These initial efforts contributed toward the creation of an organizational strategy on stress management. The major challenges in doing so are the following:

Change of Culture, Values, and Beliefs

It was necessary to break the denial and to ensure that staff support was not perceived or experienced as a sanction for being weak. A number of different strategies in the area of information, education, and communication were employed, from sensitizing senior management to visits of the staff counselor and the medical staff to field locations.

Developing Capacities for Staff Support

Following the above medical observations and more frequent psychosomatic complaints, in 1994 the organization established a post of Senior Staff Welfare Officer who provided counseling services to the staff as well as psychological debriefings for individuals and/or groups. A doctor and a nurse of the JMS were trained in psychological debriefing.

In 1996, the "Peer Support Personnel Program" was launched as an additional resource. This program aimed at training volunteer staff members in identifying signs and symptoms of cumulative traumatic stress so that they could provide psychological first aid by facilitating, defusing, or simply listening to affected colleagues.

In 2000, 20 UNHCR field staff safety advisors were trained in identifying signs and symptoms of traumatic stress and in defusing stress. They helped to keep the staff welfare officers and the JMS informed about incidents in the field, thus enabling prompt action.

In order to increase their capacity and mobility, staff counselors of different UN Agencies and NGOs are presently networking and helping each other when needed. The network presently consists of about 15 counselors placed around the world.

Developing an Efficient System of Staff Support
in Different Locations with Different Cultures

In dealing with traumatic stress, UNHCR needed to learn about working on different continents and with people of different origins. In some cultures, for example, dreams or nightmares are seen as coming from spirits and containing certain messages. In such a context, dreams are taboo. In other cultures, talking about negative experiences weakens the strength: one should forget and move on. Understanding, or at least respecting, local cultures is a key factor.

Ensuring the Balance Between Staff Support and
Organizational Needs

In the process of providing various services, it is necessary to ensure that staff support reaches its objectives without hampering and delaying operational goals. UNHCR is in the process of strengthening the Staff Welfare Unit at its headquarters and in the field so that services to staff can be provided in a timely manner.

Building a Knowledge Base on Current Experiences

Dealing with traumatic stress in an international humanitarian organization is professionally enriching and it enables the collection of valuable data for further development of a stress management strategy. A research component needs to be developed in order to document the work done, monitor trends and guide further development of stress and human resources management strategy.

3. STAFF SUPPORT TODAY

UNHCR uses an interdisciplinary approach involving different professionals to provide staff support. Although addressing trauma is predominantly a psychosocial issue, the involvement of staff development and learning, staff security and health care is extremely important.

Mission Readiness

According to UNHCR rules, all staff going on mission must obtain prior security and medical clearances. Staff going on mission or reassignment from Headquarters receive from the JMS a medical kit appropriate for the regional conditions. JMS staff also provide information about the physical environment and living conditions, as well as giving the necessary vaccinations. Pre-mission briefings are presently done:

- For new recruits during a five-day induction course in Geneva. Most of the participants in this briefing are young professionals often completely new to UNHCR and humanitarian work. Technical sessions include one on security (4 hrs) and another on stress (1.5 hrs). Each participant has an individual appointment with the JMS.
- Training for Emergency Response Teams, an eight-day Workshop on Emergency Management, is provided to staff members who would normally constitute the first-line emergency team. Apart from operational issues, emphasis is put on security, health, and welfare, with approximately three hours devoted to stress management.
- During major emergency operations, staff departing from Geneva can undergo psychological briefings with one of the Staff Welfare Officers. This, however, is not being done consistently.

The organization of pre-mission briefings is sometimes rendered difficult by the need for a high degree of mobility of UNHCR personnel and by other resource constraints.

Staff Support Following Critical Incidents

In the case of critical incidents or traumatic events, regardless of the level of impact, the field staff safety officers usually inform the Staff Welfare Unit and the JMS. Upon receiving such information, the Staff Welfare Officers establish contact with the staff and assess the situation in terms of what action needs to be taken. If possible, the situation is managed locally through:

- the "Peer Support Personnel Network";
- field staff safety advisors who are often the first contact for the survivors following an incident; and
- the UN staff counselors' network.

If none of the above is possible, the Staff Welfare Unit will organize a mission to the location of the incident or the place where the staff are relocated. When the incident is particularly grave (such as in West Timor or in Guinea in September 2000), the Staff Welfare Unit will also invite other professionals to join the team to provide psychosocial support.

The protocol of critical incident stress management used in UNHCR consists of the following elements:

- General introduction and meeting of debriefers with all staff (setting the roles, expectations, and responsibilities).
- Group and/or individual debriefings as necessary and appropriate.
- Meeting with management in order to define the necessary managerial/ organizational support.
- Individual meetings with staff and, if need be, referrals to the JMS.
- Referrals of individuals to external resources for longer term therapy.
- If possible, organizing a follow-up debriefing to set the conditions for self-help.
- Briefing with the management on follow-up action.

In some cases it is necessary to reassign staff members to less stressful duty stations. On the basis of observations, recommendations are made to the Human Resources Section.

UNHCR is constantly working on improving its approaches and strategies. As mentioned earlier, the UN Counselors' Network has been of great value. UNHCR is also committed to the continuation of the Peer Support Personnel Network. This year, 40 staff members will be trained to deal with different types of stress.

Staff Support in Long-Term Hazardous Situations

An increasing number of UNHCR staff members work in continuously hazardous environments and are exposed to high levels of cumulative stress, the effects of which are often delayed. UNHCR staff working in Sarajevo in the early nineties became used to constant shelling and danger but many of them experienced the consequences of this exposure much later.

The following are some of the measures already being implemented in some field offices to counter possible delayed effects of cumulative stress:

- The availability of recreational facilities, as well as access to the current news of the world, are important for the staff. These contribute to the diversity of their activities. Taking short-term breaks is important for self-care and stress management. Currently most remote offices are provided with basic sports facilities, audio-visual equipment, and satellite TV.

- To ensure better dietary habits, major emergencies usually employ catering services but smaller offices cannot always afford the same luxury.
- Better preparation of managers to lead teams in hazardous environments. Teams that are well cared for operate and support each other better, create time for self-care and, in the long run, suffer less from long-lasting effects of stress.
- Preparation of peers to support their colleagues.
- Organizing occasional visits by the Staff Welfare Officers so that actual levels of stress and living and working conditions can be assessed.
- The introduction of a "mental health travel scheme" allows the staff to leave their duty station on a mandatory or voluntary basis (depending on the gravity of the conditions) for approximately one week every two months. During the Kosovo crisis in 1999, the medical team closely followed the staff deployed in the operation. The team observed extreme fatigue and exhaustion due to poor living conditions and an extremely demanding workload. It was concluded that the interval between travel was too long, given the conditions. As a result, today upon the assessment by the Medical Officer or the Staff Welfare Officer, travel can be approved in shorter intervals such as every four or six weeks. This policy has proven successful.
- Undertaking Stress Management Training for staff in the most seriously affected offices. On some occasions, Staff Welfare Officers facilitate mini-workshops during their mission. The training is usually focused on identifying one's own sources of stress, stress reactions, and coping mechanisms. There are also discussions on coping mechanisms at the team level.

Cases of staff who, due to overwhelming levels of stress, are not able to continue working in the operation or in the given duty station, are dealt with by the JMS and the Staff Welfare Unit. On the recommendation of either service, the staff member will be given a special leave to allow time to deal with his or her problem while not having to worry about job security.

Post-Mission Debriefing

Post-mission psychological debriefings are important but difficult to organize, again due to the high mobility of staff and other resource constraints. While there are post-mission discussions in less formal settings, usually between old colleagues or with good friends, often such informal sharing does not facilitate the expression of the most troubling details.

4. OTHER SOURCES OF STRESS

UNHCR recognizes that stress is present in non-emergency situations. Some of the most important sources of stress are job insecurity, rotation, interpersonal relationships, abuse of power, poor performance management, lack of clarity of tasks, and long working hours.

Interestingly, traumatic stress seems to be more accepted by individual staff members and the organization since it can be blamed on abnormal factors such as civil strife and war. The aforementioned job-related stress is more connected to internal factors and also to staff members' choices regarding deployment and careers.

CONCLUSION

Raising awareness about the impact of stress and normalizing it within the work context seems to have contributed a great deal toward laying the foundation for the development of a stress management strategy. Having the in-house capacities to deal with stress management, first through the JMS and then through the Staff Welfare Unit, was crucial in that process. In an effort to improve staff support strategies, UNHCR is currently exploring various possibilities of cooperating with external partners such as universities and professional volunteers.

On the whole, more consideration is being given in UNHCR to the prevention of cumulative and traumatic stress, and burnout. Strategies and protocols contain the elements UNHCR needs in order to deal with traumatic situations. Making them work requires a continued commitment, as well as adequate financial resources.

Voices

SERVICE INCURRED
Martin Barber

In 1978 and 1979 the numbers of "boat people" leaving Vietnam soared. Many of them arrived on the shores of Malaysia and Southern Thailand, where they were taken to camps set up with the assistance of the UN High Commissioner for Refugees (UNHCR). UNHCR scrambled to recruit field officers to serve in the seaside towns where these camps were established. Most were young European or North American graduates, with limited experience in humanitarian work.

The field officers were involved alongside the local officials in Malaysia and Thailand in every aspect of the work to assist these refugees. They monitored the construction of camps, the arrival of food and other supplies, helped the refugees with their applications for resettlement in the West, and tried to deal with the consequences of the piracy which many boat loads of refugees had suffered.

For reasons which were incomprehensible to me, gangs of pirates preyed on the refugee boats with extraordinary savagery. Not only were refugees stripped of all their valuables, but many women and girls were brutally raped, people of all ages were butchered and thrown into the sea, and others were left to drift in boats without supplies or abandoned on uninhabited islands off the coast.

We were a close-knit band of young UNHCR field officers. While I was posted in Northeast Thailand, working with refugees crossing the border from Laos, one of my colleagues was working in the south. He decided that he had to do something about the atrocities. He persuaded the local police to take him out in their boats to the islands where the refugees were being dumped. In situations of great personal danger, and without formal clearance from his superiors, he rescued many families, and on more than one occasion effectively interrupted and prevented acts of piracy while they were happening.

After several months this experience affected his mind. He became unable to work normally. It was clear that he would have to go home and seek treatment.

For staff in the service of the United Nations, who need to leave their posts for medical reasons, the compensation is dramatically improved if the illness is deemed to have been "service incurred." It was painfully obvious to his colleagues that in this case the only reason for our friend's condition was the horrendous experience which he had been living, while trying to save Vietnamese boat people from piracy and death. But the officials dealing with his claim were skeptical. It took us many months of correspondence, in which several of us separately attested to the events which he had been part of, before he was granted "service incurred" compensation. In those days we were unaware of the condition called "Post Traumatic Stress Disorder," but we certainly observed it in our colleague.

These events had a profound effect on me. I asked myself if I would have dared to do what he did. Almost certainly not. I wondered at the impact which taking part in these events could have on the mind of an apparently stable and mature young man. It reminded me of the stories my father had told me of refugees who came to England after the Second World War. Some of them had only started to relive the traumatic events of the war when they retired from full-time employment, and became belated victims of post-traumatic stress.

Since my first-hand experience of trying to help a colleague in distress over 20 years ago, I have tried to encourage the humanitarian agencies I have worked for to consider the psychosocial impact of traumatic stress on their staff. Agencies are rightly putting increased emphasis on ensuring the physical safety of their staff. They need to remember the psychological side too.

TRANSFORMED BY THE FRONT LINE

Yasmine Sherif

For seven years, I lived among those whose lives had been torn in pieces by rockets, mines, executions, rape, torture, and an unspeakable climate of fear that could shatter the sanity of any human mind. As I worked in the wars and post-war situations in Afghanistan, the Balkans, Cambodia, and the Democratic Republic of Congo, I found myself in environments for which no human being is prepared. These are extreme situations that invoke our survival instincts, expecting us to tap into our ultimate capacities of strength and courage.

As a UN civil servant, I was not prepared for the inhumanity of man. My education at the university had taught me the legal provisions of human rights and humanitarian law, and my subsequent work at UN headquarters guided me to an intellectual comprehension of humanitarian disasters. Neither taught me the dynamics of war. Those lessons can only be experienced the moment we face the gruesome reality of cruelty and desolation.

As a humanitarian worker I could only understand the dark forces of war as I lived through the fate of those I had come to help. Eventually, civilians caught in armed conflict became my teachers. A major lesson that they and their hellish environment taught me was that unless, I, as a humanitarian worker, conquered my personal fears, I could not be of service to those who were the direct targets in this painful reality.

In truth, it is impossible to suppress fully one's fears in the midst of daily rocket attacks and abuses by distorted minds of murderous militia and armies, whose presence can eliminate your own in a second. But, it is possible to hide those fears for the sake of the work. When you see the immense suffering of those you are attempting to help, you are morally and emotionally compelled to put aside your own fears. Temporarily. You function under pressure in the present by postponing your relief to the future. That kind of pressured living and working builds tensions within that will have to be released at some point, when you leave the frontlines.

When you finally return to a more peaceful society, often after several years and several different operations, your experiences resurface. You encounter anew the pictures of human suffering; the smell of death and poverty; the pressure of persecution; and the sadness of leaving behind all those who have nowhere to return.

What do you do with these experiences? There is not much follow-up at the UN. And if there were, what kind of follow-up should it be? Judging from my own experience, you need to find ways and means of mirroring and channeling your accumulated experiences into something constructive that will serve not only yourself, but all those people whom you have encountered on the frontlines.

My own inward search has been my relief. I could not have grown as a person without the experiences I encountered in the field. By witnessing the inhumanity of man, I have cultivated a desire to understand it so that I can defy it.

UN personnel on their return from the field should be encouraged to remember, not to forget, their experiences. We should be guided to unfold them in a profound and transformative way. We should be inspired to see our darkest experiences as tools that can shed light on our path toward a greater understanding of our ideals, our cause, and our duties as UN officials. Only then can we challenge our feelings of helplessness and grow beyond the bureaucratic and programmed attitudes that sometimes prevails among those who have not had these experiences.

Such transformative support goes beyond simplistic means of dealing with trauma and band-aid approaches. It aims at inspiring an internal search and change that will generate a genuine expansion of our consciousness. It asks us to transcend ourselves for the sake of others, to turn our own memories of war and humanitarian disasters into living testimonies that will motivate us to continue to alleviate suffering in this world.

We cannot afford to forget our experiences at the frontlines. We must learn not to indulge in, and continuously move beyond, our insulated existence away from the frontlines. Only then can our experiences become meaningful to us, to those who will never be able to "return" from hell, and to those who should never enter it.

4

Protecting the Protectors

Catherine A. Bertini

Humanitarian workers in the fields of war and natural disasters live by an immutable rule: risk goes with the job. Delivering food, shelter, or medical aid to refugees, displaced people, or the victims of floods, earthquakes, or drought requires sacrifices, large and small, of one's personal comfort and safety.

For a long time, the humanitarian community accepted this hard fact and, occasionally, its tragic consequences—a violent death or a fatal accident in a faraway place, the news received by shocked colleagues, heart-broken families and friends. These were like bolts out of the blue in a kinder world in which the flags of the United Nations or the Red Cross constituted an unassailable shield for their personnel.

Not any more. In lands without the rule of law, the humanitarian flag can become a target, and humanitarian aid booty for armed bands. Cold-blooded terrorism against aid workers is becoming, alarmingly, all too commonplace. In Somalia, Sudan, and Afghanistan, UN relief convoys are hijacked, our drivers beaten or killed. In Angola, UN planes have been shot down. In Sierra Leone, the Great Lakes, the Balkans, and the Caucasus, our staff have been taken hostage. Every day, our workers, and the employees of numerous other aid agencies, are risking their own lives in their efforts to save the lives of others.

The number of casualties in humanitarian missions has risen to shocking and unacceptable levels. Between 1992 and 2000, the United Nations lost 198 civilian employees to violence, terrorism, and aircraft accidents. In 1998, more civilian relief workers died than armed and trained UN military peacekeepers. Since 1994, there have been 59 incidents of kidnapping and hostage taking affecting 228 of our colleagues. In 1999 alone, there were 292 violent incidents including robberies, assaults, rapes, and vehicle hijackings.

The World Food Programme (WFP) has the tragic distinction of having one of the highest death tolls among UN agencies. Since 1988, 56 WFP employees have died or been murdered in the line of duty. In the lobby of the WFP headquarters in Rome, a plaque on the wall commemorates the employees who died in the line of duty. But names engraved in brass cannot possibly convey the fullness of their lives, the depth of their contributions, and the utter waste of their deaths. As one example, Saskia van Meijenfeldt, a Dutch logistics officer, who was only 34 years old when she died on a rebel's whim, along with Luis Zuniga, a senior official of UNICEF. The two were shot in the head, point blank, in a moment of madness and confusion in a displaced persons camp in Burundi. The other four members of what should have been a routine assessment mission scattered and ran for their lives—literally. The killers have never been brought to justice, despite repeated interventions by the United Nations to the authorities of Burundi. Saskia's story is one of the more brutal, but all of the deaths are equally tragic.

Death can also come wearing a more banal face: a car accident, perhaps, or an infection that proves to be fatal. In the regions where humanitarian agencies are needed, the roads are all too often bad, drivers negligent, mosquitoes infectious, and water contaminated. Crime can be chillingly violent: in some countries, you risk a carjacking or armed assault every time you drive to the office. In all these guises, mortality haunts the front lines, claiming its victims at random.

Far more often, however, the risk of the front lines is not death but damage. The hazards of the job are such that they may not kill, but they can leave people crippled, weakened, or with broken marriages. That all-inclusive human condition we call stress can eat away at you silently and insidiously, undermining your mental and physical stability.

Out of concern for its staff members, the vast majority of whom are stationed in the field, WFP developed three innovative programs to help them minimize the dangers and potential harm.

In 1998—a year in which 12 staff members died, seven of them by murder—WFP created a security task force to examine ways to better protect our people. One of the results was the Security Awareness Training (SAT) Program, the first training initiative of this magnitude in WFP's history. Designed for *all* WFP employees, even headquarters staff who may never be sent to the field, it has "graduated" nearly 6,000 staff members worldwide.

This mandatory course covers all aspects of security, from the home to the office to the vehicle. Over the course of two days at headquarters or three days in the field, staff members learn the chain of command for security in the UN system, and engage in role-playing to arrive at the right reactions in a high-risk situation. Between March 1999 and June 2000, approximately 5,650 staff and 200 managers in almost all the countries in which WFP operates received this vital security training. The manuals and other teaching materials were produced in English, French, Spanish, Arabic, Russian, and Portuguese; additionally, training was also carried out in local languages in East Africa, Afghanistan, and Bangladesh. Leading this massive exercise was a team of 58 Security Awareness Trainers, selected from the WFP staff and deployed to the field for an average of three months each.

As the SAT instructors went from country office to country office on their security mission, what they heard from the staff members convinced them that there was an equally great need for counseling and psychological support for employees. Relief workers see the worst that life on this planet can inflict—slaughters, the brutal exploitation of other human beings, random and destructive natural disasters, famines, and hopeless, grinding poverty. Relief workers are thrown into crowded and chaotic settings with poor communications systems and constantly changing circumstances. Consequently, they can suffer from a broad range of ailments: chronic fatigue, headaches, sleep disorders, risk-prone behavior, depression, a sense of hopelessness: in a single word, burnout.

It was for them that the Peer Support Program was created. Under this program, staff members, selected from country offices around the world for their inherent empathy and extensive field experience, were trained in communication and stress management techniques. Called "Peer Support Volunteers," they constitute an informal source of comfort—a solid shoulder to cry on—for colleagues struggling with stress and work-related problems. The volunteers also give effective emotional support for handling the burnout symptoms. The program, launched in 2000 with 77 trainees, has proven to be a success; WFP intends to continue this training in order to have a minimum of 100 volunteers worldwide, particularly in high-intensity operations.

Meanwhile, since the mid-1990s, WFP has maintained professionally trained staff counselors who travel extensively to the country offices, supervising the Peer Support Volunteers and discussing personal and/or work-related issues with staff members. (As of 2001, there were seven such counselors.) In the event of a traumatic incident, a counselor is dispatched to the country in question within 72 hours to debrief the staff member(s) involved. This procedure was made mandatory in 2000.

Thirdly, WFP developed Emergency Response Training (ERT), an intensive 10-day course held in a field setting. Staff members are instructed in such practical subjects as first aid, survival in the wild, hostage negotiations, off-road driving, and deep field communication. They also participate in seminars in more theoretical subjects like humanitarian law, civil-military cooperation, and inter-agency cooperation. The ERT course, which was introduced in November 2000, will be mandatory for WFP employees sent to emergencies. The enthusiasm staff members have shown for this highly specialized training indicates that it is not just needed but highly valued by the people for whom it was designed.

WFP will continue to listen to staff members who are literally and metaphorically under fire, and will continue to respond to their needs and problems. WFP's training and support programs may well evolve over the years to fit the changing circumstances of the operations, especially as emergencies continue to overtake development operations. Every humanitarian agency concerned about the welfare of its staff must listen to its employees and learn from them how the front lines are affecting their life.

But there are other remedies that can be taken by the international community as a whole. The UN family can act in concert with humanitarian organizations, governments, and non-governmental organizations to forge a kind of global customary law recognizing and protecting aid workers. Host governments must be obliged to provide protection, if necessary, for humanitarian agents working in their jurisdictions and to cooperate fully in the prosecution of those responsible for violence against UN staff and all humanitarian workers.

Those who commit crimes against humanitarian workers must be brought to account. They cannot go unpunished. And the countries that fail to take action against them should be made to understand that all available pressures can be brought to bear. When aid workers are killed, kidnapped, robbed, or abused, when food convoys are attacked or vehicles hijacked, the international community should be entitled to apply serious measures. We do not currently hold governments responsible for investigating murders and prosecuting the guilty. It is profoundly shameful that only four people have ever been tried for and convicted of their crimes against UN staff members.

To achieve this will require a concerted effort by all of us in the United Nations—government, agencies, and secretariat—and by the entire international community. Together, we must forge an inviolable recognition that the safety and well-being of humanitarian workers in the field are to be respected at all times. This principle must carry the same force as other portions of the Geneva Convention; it must be scrupulously observed and forcefully defended for the sake of the men and women around the globe who are dedicated to helping victims.

And within the international community, there needs to be a common recognition that the job of "humanitarian worker" is now, more often than not, a dangerous one. Soldiers, who may spend only a small part of their time in life-threatening situations, are instilled with an awareness of security and equipped with the hardware to protect themselves. Humanitarian aid workers, on the other hand, who may spend most of their time in equally high-risk environments, are not always taught to be aware of risks. It is time they were.

This means that we need to increase the awareness of security in the UN culture and, more importantly, to embrace security management as an integral part of all UN humanitarian operations. We need to confront the simple fact that the United Nations sends unarmed aid workers into environments where member governments sometimes will not send their own armed troops.

Humanitarian agencies are being forced to grapple with some difficult questions. The most difficult of all is: When is the security risk for our staff so great that we cannot reach the victims of war, who then die for lack of food, shelter, water, and medicine? Where do you draw the line? This is the question that we in the UN family must answer. Because, while we cannot forfeit our mandate to help people in need, neither can we endanger the lives of people responding to the need. To paraphrase the poet John Donne, "Any death diminishes us, because we are involved in humankind."

RECOMMENDATIONS

1. The humanitarian principles of impartiality must be maintained in all crises. And they should be taken into account even when the Security Council takes its decisions on conflict situations. The humanitarian principles of impartiality must be accepted and the terms of engagement must allow aid workers to reach innocent civilians wherever they are on either side of a conflict. It must be reaffirmed, for instance, that no innocent child or adult should starve because of a war or conflict.

2. The Security Council should examine its authorization of peacekeepers in crisis situations. The Council regularly spells out peacekeepers' role in protecting civilians but does not clarify their role in protecting aid workers. The Council must explicitly define how future peacekeeping operations would protect humanitarian workers as well.

3. The international community must be mobilized to punish those responsible for crimes against humanitarian workers. A strong message must be sent to governments and groups under whose jurisdiction murders, kidnappings, and harassment take place that they will be held accountable if they fail to respect aid workers' lives. In the case of countries that do not take serious action to prevent or investigate and prosecute crimes against humanitarian workers, the Council must call for a system to monitor such violations, leading to penalties. Too often, in cases of attacks on UN relief convoys, murder, or hostage taking, responsible governments or groups enjoy total impunity. All too often we hear, "It wasn't our troops who were responsible, it was the rebels," or the other way around. This practice is not acceptable and must change.

4. Security training must be conducted for all UN staff members who work in insecure environments. This should be a pre-condition for staff to participate in high-risk operations. UN managers and officials must be fully trained in security management and be responsible for integrating security into their operations. Each agency should review its facilities, equipment, and technology to ensure it is providing the best support possible to staff.

5. The United Nations Security Coordinator's (UNSECOORD) role of coordination and clearinghouse for security information must be enhanced through increases in its staff and funding. I welcome the Secretary-General's decision to appoint a full-time security coordinator. The UN budget should be revised to accommodate a larger staff. Once expanded, UNSECOORD could have the capacity to address many other management issues, including deploying security officers to all major UN humanitarian projects in crisis areas. Please note that currently there are only 13 staff members in UNSECOORD. And nine of those staff are paid for by agency budgets. Minus malicious acts insurance, UNSECOORD's own budget for 2000 was $537,000—that is for coordinating security for tens of thousands of United Nations staff worldwide.

Voices

FROM WYOMING TO SOMALIA
Dale Skoric, 28, Logistics Officer

When I went to Somalia for WFP, I was young and energetic and ready to take on whatever any war zone threw at me. It was the spring of 1993 and anarchy still reigned in this leaderless country despite the efforts of Operation Restore Hope. After 18 months of a stressful, non-stop operation under extremely dangerous conditions to help get WFP emergency food aid to the Somali population, I went home to Cody, Wyoming (in the United States) for annual leave.

One night while I was there, I turned on the television news and saw that gunmen had shot and killed a UN colleague I had worked with closely in Somalia. It came as a complete shock that someone with whom I had talked regularly I would never see again—all for the sake of trying to help the most vulnerable under chaotic conditions. The sad news was to change my view of life and work completely.

I still work in these types of operations but I realize just what the risks are. You can't have false heroics because the goal is to help the people who might starve without us. These places are a long way from Cody, where I grew up, and the journey has opened my eyes to a lot of hard facts about life and death for people who are poor and hungry and deprived of opportunities to improve their circumstances.

THE WORST IS THE LONELINESS
Hiro Matsumura, 51, WFP Country Director

In the 18 years I have spent working in Africa for WFP, I found the conditions in Bissau to be the worst I have ever experienced. Every day was a nightmare. No electricity, no water. Once, our office telephone didn't work for over two weeks. Almost all the electrical appliances in my house were destroyed by electricity breakdowns. Even the voltage regulators burned out.

The worst is the loneliness. I was without my wife for the first time in 22 years because Bissau is a non-family duty station. I even lost my dog Indy, my pet for six years, who disappeared in the evacuation. He was down to skin and bones when I found him again a month later. He had contracted a virus that made him slowly bleed to death, and nothing I did could stop it. Every night in Bissau, I came home at 9 or 10 P.M., knowing that no one waited for me in the darkness, not even Indy.

On my next home leave, my wife and I went one day to the Shinjuku train station in Tokyo. It is the busiest station in Japan with more than 1 million passengers a day. I became completely disoriented by the crowds and when we got on the train, I fainted. The next day, I went to a doctor who diagnosed a stress reaction to Japan after the mental stress I had in Bissau.

THE ENGULFING SOUND AND THE SILENCE
Rhian Gastineau, 25, Food Aid Monitor

I was standing at an airdrop zone near a village called Malual Bai in southern Sudan watching a Hercules C-130 make a "dry run." The noise was deafening, and the ground shook as the huge aircraft passed overhead. When the pilot radioed he was starting the "live run"—during which he would drop the sacks of food—we noticed that he was coming in just to the right of the drop zone. This normally wouldn't have mattered, but at the one-minute mark, when we gave him the "clear for drop" signal, the wind instantly picked up.

When the first wooden pallet with the bags on it left the back of the aircraft I knew we were in trouble. The wind took the 50-kilogram bags and blew them right over to where we were standing. My heart stopped. I tried to figure out which way to run. I turned and started to run away from the drop zone. The bags were falling fast. Then I heard the horrifying sound of the bags falling behind me. It was like standing in front of a firing squad but not knowing where they were positioned. The bags were falling behind me, in front of me, beside me. I could feel, as well as hear, the bags dropping like lead weights. I finally realized that I could not outrun the bags and so I stopped and just waited for all 162 bags to fall. Everything seemed to happen in slow motion. I could hear the Sudanese screaming as they fled the falling bags. The aircraft had passed overhead by now but the noise was still deafening.

What still stands out for me today is the engulfing sound of the bags hitting the ground around me. This continued for no more than 15 to 20 seconds. Then there was an absolute silence like I have never heard in all of the years I have lived in Africa. There were no birds singing, no crickets making their chirps, and no people yelling. I wondered if I was actually alive.

WE CANNOT ALLOW EMOTIONAL INVOLVEMENT
Erika MacLean, 47, Food Aid Monitor

The day we were bombed in Sudan, I was on the radio trying to get approval for the aircraft to drop enough food to give each woman a bag of grain. Suddenly I heard a loud thud. I looked to my right and saw clouds of sand smoke. It's amazing how in these situations you're somewhere between consciousness and automatic pilot. I heard myself saying over the radio, "We've been bombed." The radio operator said, "When, yesterday?" I replied, "No, now!" As soon as I'd said the words, the first waves of panic started to take over.

The next thing I remember was the radio operator saying, "I suggest you take cover." I ran out of the compound, which was deserted except for the WFP Sudanese field officer screaming and waving his arms at the exit for me to follow him. We ran to a water hole, dry at that time of year, where I found 10 women crouched with their knees up to their chins. I was not going to throw my body on top of theirs so I took cover by a tree. Scared stiff, I watched as the Antonov came round again and again. In total, it dropped 24 bombs.

During those first few minutes of the bomb attack, the radio operator's voice was a lifeline—kind, steady, and reassuring. He asked if I wanted to be pulled out. No, I said, I wanted to finish the food distribution. We were in Akak, where the people had not been fed for two months. Despite the danger, I wanted to stay and finish what I had come to do.

But I knew that if I were to sleep that night, I would have to find the crying baby who had kept me awake the night before. Just outside the compound, there was a family sleeping on food bags. It was their baby that was crying because it was hungry and the mother was sick and couldn't care for it. I made some instant porridge and fed the child, gave the mother an aspirin, and went to bed.

We do what we have to do, although we are surrounded by the horrors of families trying to survive in the most desperate of conditions. We cannot allow emotional involvement; otherwise we would not be able to do the work. It may sound hard to some, but for those of us who work in the field it is a necessity.

LUNCH IN AFGHANISTAN

Georges Dubin, 41, Logistics Officer

I was the leader of a WFP convoy traveling from Bamiyan in central Afghanistan to deliver food in a valley controlled by the Taliban. We reached a village where we were summoned to the quarters of the local commander. He and his entourage were waiting for us in the garden. The meeting started courteously enough but I could see from the faces of our local escorts that trouble was brewing. The commander informed us that he was going to take one truckload of food for his village. I put forward the usual reasons why he couldn't and the discussion grew very heated.

I knew we had to get out of there, but the commander insisted we stay for lunch. The meal took ages to get through. The commander then made it clear that the only way for us to reach the Taliban side of the valley was through his village. The atmosphere was extremely tense. When we went back to the vehicles, our escorts suddenly began cocking their guns. I knew that if they started shooting in this narrow road we would end up in a massacre. Fortunately, the escorts were brought under control and we went back to our base camp five kilometers away.

But the escort chief was still angry and offended and I was told he wanted to go back and kill the commander. Using my satellite phone, I briefed my boss in Islamabad. He advised me to bypass the commander and negotiate with the village elders for safe passage to deliver the food. We proceeded, but we had to cross the front line with the commander's death threats hanging over our heads. We accomplished the mission but I knew my nerves were shot when I was back home in Islamabad and opened a can of soda and found myself jumping out of the chair at the sound of the lid popping off.

5

Risk and Protection for UNICEF Field Staff

Nils Arne Kastberg

There was already a high level of violence when the new Programme Coordinator for UNICEF arrived at her posting in the summer of 1999. She was familiar with violence. Five years earlier she had been traveling with a UNICEF team when her vehicle was ambushed, she had been shot, and a colleague mortally wounded. Now, a few months after assuming her post, the UNICEF Country Representative and another colleague from WFP were shot and killed.

Following the deaths, she became Officer-in-Charge of the country mission during a state of increasing tension. She was surrounded by war. She often visited areas where violence was commonplace, where the UNICEF team witnessed atrocities inflicted on children and where large numbers of civilians had been killed. She worked incessantly to fill a deep void and immersed herself in her work. She even dismissed reports of threats on her own life. She writes:

> I hadn't realized the danger at first because in the middle of hectic and high-speed work, the adrenaline is so high and things are happening so fast that you don't notice when you are at risk. With the ethnic tension, every decision was (seen) from an ethnic perspective and consequently as an ethnic preference. This resulted in harassment and threats that I dismissed as part of the job. I went out for a few days for R&R and then received orders from security not to return. I had to leave friends, so many good people, my whole life . . . It was so hard never being able to come to closure or at least to say goodbye.
>
> After the ambush incident in Egypt, where a colleague and four police officers were killed and I was shot, the group of us who survived hardly talked about it. Stress counseling and debriefings were not yet popular. I suppose they would have been even considered a sign of weakness. We all just thought that time would make a difference and we'd get over it. After six months, the situation didn't improve as we all suffered from one symptom or another. Headquarters sent us a specialist in stress counseling and we went through rapid-eye movement desensitization and debriefing sessions where we all recounted our part of the incident and put the picture together again: what we felt, heard, saw, and thought. The whole picture of what really happened was suddenly clear and the gaps were filled. It is only when you recollect all the missing points and talk about them over

and over again that you come to grips with your fearful memories and get them out of your system. It is like waking from a bad dream and seeing, my God, there is sunshine again.

This new traumatic experience was much more complex because it involved the loss of friends, colleagues, evacuation of very much needed staff, the war, the insistent rumors of the atrocities being committed, the scenes of children getting hurt, the threats, and my own evacuation in the end. I was tormented for months after my evacuation with the memories of the children crying, with the memories of the stories of the raped young girls, and with a terrible guilt that I have let them down by leaving. Building on my previous round of stress counseling, I knew that I had to share these experiences and deal with the intense emotions. Generally, you can't discuss these very complicated emotions only with friends and family. You need professionals to guide you on how to deal with them, and you also need to share them with people with common experiences. I attended a critical incidents management course in the United States. It is extremely interesting how people from different backgrounds, culture, and experiences react to stress and trauma in the same ways.

As humanitarians, we are generally not trained to handle this extreme stress. We think, "It's my fault that I can't cope." There is sometimes the sense that you are not doing enough, and there is the guilt as well, especially when people around you die. When you have a professional debriefing, you have a chance to discuss your experiences with people who understand because they have gone through similar things. It is wonderful when you also suddenly realize that you are not alone and that your feelings and reactions are normal reactions to abnormal situations [1].

THE PLAGUE OF COMPLEX EMERGENCIES

This is a new era for international organizations that step into the breach of political conflict to provide for civilians caught in the crossfire of intrastate hostilities. Until the 1990s, emergencies had typically been natural disasters and acute ones; complex emergencies are political and chronic. They are more tenacious than natural ones; they persist and their numbers accumulate year by year. The number of countries where the United Nations has recognized "formal complex emergencies" increased from six in 1989, to nine in 1991, to 11 in 1993, and then to 13 in 1995 [2]. They have risen on average by one per year over 11 years. In 1991, UNICEF emergency funds were dispersed to 25 countries [3]. Four years later, a subsequent UNICEF report counted "25 existing complex emergencies, and at least ten more where the potential for violent political disorder was a strong possibility" [4]. In January 2000, the UNICEF Executive Director's annual report to the Economic and Social Council Executive Board noted that there are "now more than 50 countries (where UNICEF has programs) experiencing some form of crisis and requiring humanitarian disaster relief assistance" [5]. Nine of the eleven formal complex emergencies recognized in 1993 continue to appear on the list of complex emergency countries in 2000, spreading and compounding in a way that resembles a plague. Political emergencies in one country spread easily into others, in the way that the

Rwanda emergency became a crisis encompassing the Great Lakes Region and as the Liberian emergency in the early 1990s has subsequently aggravated political disorder in Sierra Leone and Guinea.

But this new era of response to complex emergencies is different in another way. Complex emergencies expose the staff of an intervening organization to the same risks as those victims whom they are to assist. It is only too common to find humanitarian workers side by side in the bowels of an overcrowded basement crouched beside the victims they serve, as explosions from the fighting above shake the walls. Fear mingles with confusion. Instead of being the outside providers reducing the crisis, they are as likely to become part of the crisis itself, even abetting hostilities in some instances, and just as likely to be targets of local aggression as anyone else in the struggles for plunder and political domination.

UNICEF's EMBRACE OF HUMAN RIGHTS

Children may be the most evocative of victims, but up to now, this has not given those who represent them any special standing. The reverse is more common. A UNICEF senior official in Rwanda observed with chagrin that "children per se will not usually get us to the table for the key political discussions in any country. Children do not (yet at least) represent a viable, unified, or vocal constituency. I asked myself repeatedly in Rwanda why UNHCR was so visible and why they had such frequent contact with the top levels of government . . . It appeared to me that the real reason they had clout was that they represented the donors to the refugees ($1.0 million per day) and the wishes of those governments that the refugees return" [6]. Even though children may evoke the most heartfelt response, their defense does not always carry the equivalent level of political currency.

UNICEF resolved, in the last decade, to increase the political currency of children, namely to advocate publicly for states to protect children as a matter of priority. UNICEF sought a principled approach to the needs of children to set a standard for treatment in conflict, in poverty, and in all forms of neglect. The decade witnessed a shift in UNICEF orientation. The Convention on the Rights of the Child, adopted by the General Assembly in November 1989, became part of UNICEF's mission statement in 1996. The United Nations Committee on the Rights of the Child recommended that the General Assembly mandate a study on the protection of children affected by armed conflict. Graca Machel headed the study and in 1996, the study made a ten point call for urgent action including the explicit implementation of international standards, monitoring/reporting violations of child rights, promoting physical and psychological recovery for children, demobilization of child soldiers, increasing commitment to assist refugee and internally displaced children, and ending the scourge of landmines. Many of these ten points have figured significantly in guiding UNICEF's shift toward integrating a human rights perspective into its policy and programming initiatives.

The primacy of rights in UNICEF policy has led the organization to take an ethnical stand against the violations which repressive regimes and warring factions perpetrate against civilians. This has been a bold initiative with far-reaching implications, since UNICEF's support of these ethical values implicitly challenges the right of states to exercise a sovereign prerogative in the way they treat their citizens. This UNICEF position has subsequently been embraced and articulated by the Secretary-General as the right of international organizations to accord greater priority to the rights of individuals than to the rights of states [7]. One of the implications of UNICEF's rights-based initiatives has been to question the principle of neutrality in the delivery of international assistance and to search for a principle which replaces neutrality and yet carries its respectability. In order to ensure the security of its staff and to implement programs in conformity with its ethical values, UNICEF has experimented with ways of doing this, i.e.,with consent frameworks, ground rules, modalities of conditionality, and formulas for compliance—sometimes negotiated with warring factions, sometimes with repressive regimes, and sometimes with non-state entities—to establish the basis for humanitarian intervention. UNICEF's humanitarian interventions are increasingly hedged with some kind of accord on how their clients must treat women and children.

There are benefits from these experiments. A rights-based program provides a language and a corporate imperative—even if specific guidelines are still evolving in UNICEF—for bridging the gap between responding to complex emergencies and meeting children's needs more generally. There are also costs. The more political exposure, the greater the likelihood of reprisals. UNICEF's active advocacy of protecting children and women increases its political exposure and inevitably, the risks to the organization. Risk increases for those who intervene in political emergencies, and it increases especially for those who are on the front line of advocacy. Many staff members have experienced trauma, witnessing death, assaults, robberies, rapes—human and in particular—child suffering. UNICEF has suffered the deaths of 29 staff members over the past nine years.

PLANNING FOR EMERGENCIES

Rwanda in 1994 was a debacle for all organizations. Up to then staff losses came in twos and threes, in Rwanda they came in dozens. Eleven UNICEF national staff members were killed during a three-month long convulsion of violence, seven national staff were arrested, and there were numerous medical evacuations for trauma exposure to these disturbing events. In the aftermath of Rwanda, preparedness within UNICEF and the need for greater coordination with collaborating organizations took on a higher priority. Between 1994 and 1998, UNICEF made a commitment to increase its capacity to respond to complex emergencies, and took a number of initiatives. Only two of these are mentioned here.

First, UNICEF has improved communications between headquarters and the field, and among field missions, to help missions make sound security decisions based on reliable intelligence and supportive contact. In 1998, OPSCEN, UNICEF's communication center, began operating around the clock, gathering and relaying information as it was needed, maintaining close contact with missions in crisis.

Testimonies of appreciation confirm OPSCEN as a flagship feature of UNICEF's increasing resolve to protect staff under siege with current intelligence, options, advice, and comfort. One of UNICEF's senior country officers wrote about OPSCEN following her recent experience in the midst of a civil war when young rebel fighters flooded the streets.

> I was trapped in the UNICEF offices for five days with 300 people—staff, their families, and other sheltering (nationals), while young rebel fighters armed with AK47s, rocket launchers, grenades, etc. systematically looted every building on the street. The staff at OPSCEN in New York were knowledgeable and ready to provide support—in fact, this proved to be life saving in the end . . . OPSCEN has to be not just a UNICEF best practice but a world first in excellence. Their support to me personally over the phone every hour—advice, moral support, humor, love, and concern—was incredible. I think I would have cracked under the strain if I hadn't had them talk to me all the time. They also passed messages to my family, which was very reassuring. We were always the first to get information, and our colleagues in the other agencies automatically looked to UNICEF for briefing [8].

Second, UNICEF has recognized the dangers of staff exposure to trauma and stress and resolved to make stress management facilities more available. The approach to stress management that an organization like UNICEF adopts depends on how exposure to violence, and especially violence inflicted on children, is understood. There is a temptation to discount the value of stress management expertise since stress and trauma are experienced so differently by different individuals; and if each individual's experience is different, so must the therapy differ from case to case. What then is the value of building in stress management expertise if the coverage and success rate may be low, if treatments are as diverse as each person's experience?

Yet, there is another point of view. While the experience of stress may differ, the reactions and symptoms are generally predictable, so much so in fact that almost everyone, from police to humanitarians to soldiers and even those who have suffered abuse as children, show the same symptoms and can be treated in roughly similar ways [9]. And there is the further point, that those who care for children in crisis, like UNICEF, are likely to find the experience of violence inflicted on children so disturbing that they may deny the experiences and their effects altogether. Caretakers themselves need special care [10].

This chapter opened with testimonies of one staff member's experience with death and how she subsequently coped with the trauma. Her account concludes:

> . . . UNICEF has to take more steps to address the issue of stress and trauma management for staff who have served in extreme situations. We can't just hope that a good person will notice and step in to offer support; we need to institutionalize the concepts of counseling and debriefing. While some of us at UNICEF still tend to be shy or sarcastic about the issue of counseling, at other organizations it is obligatory [1].

RECOMMENDATION:
BUILDING CONSENSUS ON BUILDING PEACE

For all the priority UNICEF has given the matter of security preparedness, UNICEF's own efforts—ranging from better communications to more experienced staff to stress management support that recognizes the special nature of exposure to violence toward children—cannot stand on their own. All humanitarian workers, and especially all civilian employees of the United Nations, share the same vulnerability. The actions of one organization affect the others just as the protection services for one readily benefit the others.

ACKNOWLEDGMENT

Special acknowledgment is made of the contribution of Jim Freedman and others who have made this chapter possible.

REFERENCES

1. Managing Stress in the Midst of War, *UNICEF Staff News*, March 2001.
2. United Nations Department of Public Information, 1999.
3. J. Richardson, *Assessment of UNICEF Emergency Response*, Office of Emergency Programmes, 1995.
4. J. Richardson, *Emergency Response Based on Staff Perspectives*, UNICEF Office of Emergency Programmes, 1995.
5. UNICEF Executive Director, *Annual Report to the ECOSOC Executive Board, Progress Report 31*, January 2000.
6. UNICEF, *Internal Report*, February 1997.
7. K. A. Annan, Two Concepts of Sovereignty, *The Question of Intervention, Statements by the Secretary General*, United Nations Department of Public Information, New York, 1999.
8. A Phone Line to the Outside World, *UNICEF Staff News*, March 2001.
9. J. L. Herman, *Trauma and Recovery, the Aftermath of Violence from Domestic Abuse to Political Terror*, Basic Books, New York, pp. 33-50, 1992.
10. Y. Danieli, Who Takes Care of the Caretakers? The Emotional Consequences of Working with Children Traumatized by War and Communal Violence, in *Minefields in Their Hearts: The Mental Health of Children in War and Communal Violence*, R. J. Apfel and B. Simon (eds.), Yale University, New Haven, pp. 313-343, 1996.

6

Health Workers on the Front Line

Xavier Leus and Hilary Bower

Health workers are, by profession, in harm's way. Ill health, traumatic circumstances, and human frailty are par for the course, and even in stable societies, many work in situations of high tension and significant risk. But when it comes to humanitarian health activities, such "normal" working conditions are compounded by unfamiliar environments far from home, by insecurity and uncertainty, by lack of creature comforts and, in the worst scenarios, by the threat of physical and psychological violence.

One of the cornerstones of humanitarian action is the quick deployment of capable staff to the crisis site. But unlike military organizations that routinely have large numbers of staff at the ready, UN agencies and NGOs face great challenges in planning for and maintaining contingents of well prepared staff able to go into the field at short notice, and in supporting their physical and mental security when there.

International health workers go to countries and cultures that are not their own, often with little advance information or training about the situation they are about to go into. National health workers in countries suffering natural or man-made crisis often continue to work despite situations of grave danger and uncertainty for themselves and for their families. Both groups are charged with being where normal health services cannot or do not function, and they accomplish many things.

In the southern states of Sudan, for example, local and international health workers have, for years, braved the threat of aerial bombing in towns and villages as well as attacks by militias of shifting loyalties to run health centers and makeshift hospitals in areas where all state health provision has disintegrated.

In Somalia, local health workers, supported by UN agencies and non-governmental organizations, have managed to maintain and supply rudimentary health clinics throughout years of complete breakdown of the state, the continuous presence of armed militia and the constant threat, and frequent occurrence, of kidnap.

In the Palestinian Self Rule Areas and Occupied Territories, humanitarian health workers are confronting checkpoints and traveling through areas torn by violence to ensure supplies get through to villages and towns isolated by security measures.

In terms of global public health, diseases like smallpox and polio could not be eradicated without the bravery of health workers who are willing to go into the A to Z of conflict zones, to trust cease-fires negotiated with notoriously unreliable parties, and to face volatile and disturbed populations.

But these accomplishments are sometimes exacted at a heavy price. Every year humanitarian health workers die or suffer injury as a result of their activities. Still more burn out from the pressure of working in such difficult and desperate environments.

Like the populations in conflict they serve, many humanitarian health workers are exposed to the threats to life and limb embodied in armed attack, bombardment, and mines. They often have to cross checkpoints manned by volatile and unpredictable elements, cope with shifting and uncertain frontlines, and sometimes have to accept "protection" from far-from-reassuring "security" elements just to move through their communities.

While international health workers can draw unwanted attention as a potential source of income, goods, or public relations, national staff can be at even greater risk due to suspicions regarding their relationship to particular factions of the conflict, and have often been specifically targeted by warring parties.

An Angolan doctor working as national staff for WHO in his own country describes traveling into a National Union for the Total Independence of Angola (UNITA) area to investigate an outbreak of anthrax as "disturbing," even though his mission had been requested by UNITA and permitted by the government. "They knew who I was and why I was there, but some soldiers at a faraway check post could still think I was a spy. We were stopped and questioned numerous times. I just tried to keep calm." The same trip saw the team returning in the dark in torrential rain along a road lined with landmines.

Kidnap is a constant worry in many situations of complex emergency. One international WHO representative was kidnapped and held hostage twice in Somalia, despite apparently high level security arrangements. "My big mistake was to let my staff, who were small in number and had been working hard all week, go instead of asking them to drive me to the airport. Instead I caught a lift with another UN agency, whose staff were very new, and we walked into the situation blind. My staff were nationals, old hands, they knew who to trust and how to deal with situations, but when it came down to it, we didn't have enough staff capacity on the ground to mean that they could always be available."

Local health workers are at no less risk. In Guinea, for example, Sierra Leonean refugee health workers have been sought out and held by rebels because their services are needed. In Sierra Leone, health workers have been kept hostage behind RUF lines for the same reason.

But threats to physical safety come not only from combatants. Like those delivering other forms of aid, health workers are at risk because they move in situations where humans are desperate, where the care they can offer is often limited, and the rationale they work by because of this can be misunderstood. Trying to apply good public health principles can put health workers in danger.

"One of our NGO partner staff was killed in Merka (Somalia) because a clan decided we were being partisan in our treatment of patients suspected of having tuberculosis. In fact, given the scarce resources, we were choosing people who were least likely to default on treatment and therefore most likely to be cured. Could we have seen this coming? Could we have prevented it? I don't know, but what we could have done is trained our people better so that they could anticipate some of the dangers in certain strategies, and we could have had security people whose job it is to keep track of local response to our work," says one WHO coordinator.

Attacks on humanitarian staff have become disturbingly more common in recent years. A study by researchers from the Center for Refugee and Disaster Studies at Johns Hopkins School of Hygiene and Public Health published in the *British Medical Journal* [1] found 382 deaths among relief workers from 32 organizations between 1985 and 1998. Though these peaked in 1994 (almost 90 deaths), the 20 deaths that occurred in 1998 were almost 10 times more than those recorded in 1985. The majority of these deaths (253 people or 68 percent) resulted from intentional violence. Among health workers 57 percent of deaths were caused by intentional violence.

"In complex situations where there are one or more clans, tribes, or armies fighting, much of the insecurity for humanitarian workers is related to one side perceiving that another is getting more assistance—so they bombard those providing the assistance, or kidnap you, or try anything to even things up," says another WHO officer with long experience in complex emergencies.

Describing a case where a doctor was killed because the relative of a dead patient thought he had been negligent in his treatment, he adds that one of the major failings of the current system of recruitment to humanitarian work is that new people are simply not well enough prepared on how to work in dangerous settings.

"In places where everyone carries a gun, disagreement can be fatal. We don't prepare our colleagues enough. I have seen people engage in arguments over money or treatment which is simply not worth putting yourself at risk for. Putting someone really green into an emergency is dangerous, but often it is these people who are the most motivated to go. There has to be a real orientation and training so that we can tap the enthusiasm and dedication of these people while still keeping them as safe as possible in the circumstances."

Quite aside from the actual threat of warfare, the pressure to work quickly and long hours, to drive off road or in difficult conditions, and to live and work in unsound buildings place humanitarian workers at increased risk of accidents, while in many countries there is also increased risk of illness from disease. Yet, a study by WHO and the UN Joint Medical Services in 1998 of over 200 relief workers found that less than half had received any medical briefing before departure [2]. A similar percentage had been given no information about food safety or what measures to take in case of problems, and less than 40 percent had had any specific briefing about AIDS/HIV despite respondents being stationed in countries of high HIV prevalence.

But it is not just physical perils that threaten the well-being of health workers in humanitarian settings. The impact of psychological stress is equally evident. An experienced pediatrician who spent a year in a hospital for unaccompanied children in Rwanda at the height of the crisis in 1994 tells of not being able to work for over a year after returning from his mission.

"There were so many children and I could only help some of them. Everyday we lost children. We had so little to do anything with, and militia were constantly at the gates, threatening. I do believe that it was important for me to have been there, that I did save some lives, even if I couldn't save them all. But for a long time afterwards I was in depression. Even now I feel my whole approach to life has changed. Before I was an optimist, I thought humans were essentially good. Now I know there is evil in the world."

Another speaks of trying to come to terms with the "ruthless triage" she had to carry out again in those terrible days in Rwanda when millions of people were stranded on a desiccated plateau. "You are like the finger of God. You know that the ones you leave behind will be dead when you come back. Every day we went back, we stepped over the bodies of people we couldn't help the day before. When I came home, I couldn't stop seeing the faces and the bodies."

Another health worker described feeling distraught as he struggled to make sense of his patients and their behavior. "One of the most disturbing things I experienced—quite aside from the shock of the physical violence—was the change in mentality of the people I was dealing with. People become so ruthless. All pretence of caring, of the strong looking after the weak, goes. It's everyone for themselves. It really knocked me because I found myself feeling less and less sympathy for the people I was trying to help."

Like many humanitarian workers, these health workers felt little support during or after the mission, and all took at least several months to recover their confidence and ability to work. They were anxious months since as "short-term professionals," like so many recruited to humanitarian causes, they had no financial or medical support after their contract ended. Indeed, many short-term humanitarian workers point to lack of job security and benefits to their families, such as insurance and pensions, as major stress factors in emergency settings.

Short-term employment is a double-edged sword: it can prevent people from voicing their anxieties—or their security needs—for fear of being seen to be weak or unsuitable for field work, while the premature "exit" which can come about when people have no help to integrate their experiences reduces the store of experience that an organization can draw on.

The mental health and well-being of people working in complex emergency settings can also be compromised by such apparently simple factors as lack of visible backup, perceived lack of organizational interest in individual security (experienced, for example, through the high hassle quota when trying to get essentials for security such as radios), inability to communicate with central offices, or bureaucratic procedures.

"On a number of occasions, I have been in danger because of administrative problems and delays in making payments which I have no control over. We often throw people into the field without adequate support or means to honor obligations and this can be very dangerous in some countries," says a WHO officer.

Even how organizations react to the death of employees has a profound impact on how well supported those who remain in the field feel. Strangely, in many United Nations organizations where multiculturalism is a Holy Grail, the prevailing culture for dealing with death is solidly litigation-oriented, according to several senior WHO officials who have been faced with reacting to a colleague's untimely demise.

"In the Arab world, the amount of respect you show a person in his or her death is soothing balm to his family and his colleagues. But very often the first concern of our organizations is for the type of contract a person is on, which then governs the response. This can be very demoralizing for people who have to carry on after a tragic event, and it undermines their confidence in the organization's ability to take care of them, which in turn damages their effectiveness."

Opinions differ on how to address these many different aspects of "security" for health workers, but two aspects that most agree on are the need for sensitive and detailed preparation before a mission and clear tangible support during and afterwards.

A WHO occupational health physician puts it this way: "Health workers going into complex emergencies face almost the same risk as army personnel, but we don't prepare ourselves like armies. What I would like to see is a proper systematic approach that includes medical clearance with briefing, precise information about insurance, evacuation and repatriation as well as potential health problems, a field staff training program in the basics in terms of first aid, security and protection that will give staff more confidence, and debriefing with the ability to refer for specialist counseling if necessary. This should be part of the operating costs of any field operation. It shouldn't be seen as a luxury, but as a necessity."

Others suggest some "reality" training is also required before people venture out. "People need to have some idea what it is like to face a gun, to be surrounded by gunfire, to face a soldier at a check point," said one WHO field worker. "They need to experience their own reactions, to practice their reactions. It doesn't matter that you are supposed to be a health worker in a hospital—in complex emergencies, nowhere is risk free."

Another long-term emergency health officer stresses that promoting the development of interpersonal skills can be a vital support and protection for staff in the field. Taking the crises of Sierra Leone as an example, he says: "So much of how you cope depends on the quality and intensity of your relationship with the people around you. Developing relationships within and outside of our own mission is a good investment of time and effort in complex emergencies and should be seen as a crucial part of programming. For myself, if I hadn't felt supported, defended, and protected by the relationships we built, I would not have been able to take the difficult decisions that we had to take."

However, very few UN agencies or NGOs currently systematically prepare their staff in this way, or use specific methods to recruit those most able to cope—and WHO is no exception. And, though medical kits and advice are available on request, there is not always obligation for a medical release or debriefing on return.

"Often we don't even know that people are traveling. Some come for their medical kit or for vaccines, but there is no obligation. And people can slip through the gaps," says a WHO occupational health physician.

Debriefing of staff regarding their health and welfare, their personal experiences and their needs is not only important for mental and physical well-being, but morale too. For staff moving from one field situation to another, the lack of debriefing is often taken as indicative of the lack of interest in their welfare. But, she notes, debriefing has to be more than a collection of signatures and it is crucial that staff have access to specialist counseling if necessary.

"In some cases, simply talking through experiences with supervisors or peers is enough, but often if staff have been through very difficult conditions, when they come back to their home base, it can be difficult communicating their experience to colleagues. It is important to be able to refer to counseling, and particularly to social workers or psychologists who are trained particularly in this kind of support."

And it is not only staff members who may need this support. "When we first went to Somalia, there was an outbreak of hostilities. A lot of people were killed in front of our home and a grenade was thrown into the compound," recalls a WHO officer. "My wife and five children saw some pretty terrible things but were offered no counseling or R and R (rest and recuperation), though other UN agency staff were. Personally I didn't feel I needed it but it would have been nice to know the organization cared."

For the most part, however, agencies and NGOs rely on their employees' strength of character, resources, and enthusiasm to get them through. Part of this is due to the difficulty of attracting funds that can be used for such preparation. WHO's emergency and humanitarian work around the world is funded almost entirely from donor contributions. The "regular" budget of WHO country offices—allocated from the pot of member states' annual contributions and designed to last two years—can be swallowed in just a few days of emergency, leaving health services critically under-resourced when people are at their most vulnerable. Yet it could be argued that in terms of health of a population in crisis, the first and most critical thing to achieve is security, mobility, and presence of health workers since without them no health care can be done.

In the face of increasingly urgent need to achieve this, WHO has put a proposal to the Inter-Agency Standing Committee [3] to set up a reference group on the occupational health of humanitarian workers in its broadest sense, from behavior and environmental-related risks to risks related to conflict and violence.

The aim of the reference group would be to develop inter-agency standards and guidelines which define:

- occupational risks for humanitarian workers and roles and responsibilities for managing risks,
- pre-departure and in-field preventative activities,
- minimum operational "safety net" in the field (such as first-aid kits, minimum communication support, minimum transport support, medical evacuation procedures and so on), and
- methods of assessment, monitoring, and reporting on health security measures and incidents.

It is also proposed that the group establish coordination mechanisms and mobilize crucial resources required to ensure that security of health workers becomes an inseparable part of humanitarian programs.

If these things can be achieved, humanitarian organizations will be one step closer to protecting and defending those who often risk their lives to help others.

REFERENCES

1. M. Sheik, M. I. Guttierrez, P. Spiegel, M. Thieren, and G. Burnham, Deaths among Humanitarian Workers, *British Medical Journal, 321,* pp. 166-168, July 15, 2000.
2. Division of Emergency and Humanitarian Action WHO, UN Joint Medical Services, International Centre for Migration and Health, *Occupational Health of Field Personnel in Complex Emergencies: Report of a Pilot Study,* July 1998.
3. The Inter-Agency Standing Committee (IASC), chaired by the Emergency Relief Coordinator (ERC), ensures inter-agency decision-making in response to complex emergencies. The IASC is formed by the executive heads of sixteen leading agencies and NGO consortia, providing a good representation of today's composite humanitarian world.

7

Women on the Front Lines: UNIFEM's Work to Promote Women, Peace, and Security

Noeleen Heyzer

A decade ago, UNIFEM launched its innovative African Women in Crisis (AFWIC) program to respond to the special concerns of women in countries in or after conflict. This has provided important first-hand knowledge about the situation of women living in war-affected countries; it also created unique challenges for our frontline staff members.

The AFWIC experience led us to examine critically the need for an expanded and intensified program on issues of women, peace, and security. We learned that a quick-response mechanism is essential, yet at the same time, there is a need for a long-term strategy for working with women in crisis and post-crisis situations. There was also a clear and urgent need to take the lessons we were learning on the ground, both working with women and as UN staff working in crisis situations, to influence and shape policies at the formulation stage.

In 2000, with these lessons from AFWIC helping to shape a global initiative, UNIFEM developed a "Women, Peace and Security Framework." It is intended to guide UNIFEM's work as well as to identify areas of knowledge that will benefit diverse agencies assisting those in conflict situations. The five-point framework includes:

1. UNDERSTANDING THE IMPACT OF ARMED CONFLICT ON WOMEN AND GIRLS

UNIFEM supports assessments of the impact of conflict on women to help ensure that policies and programs of assistance address the gender dimensions of conflict. Key aspects of this work include collecting and disseminating information, disaggregating data, assessing lessons learned, and fostering cross-regional and inter-agency collaboration and learning.

An example of a very simple but compelling lesson is that the location and lighting of toilets in refugee camps can help reduce the risk of violence against women. Understanding risks to women's security can help ensure women's safe resettlement and return. This is true for both women refugees in the camps, and women who are working there as either international or national staff.

The consequences of insensitivity in dealing with the impact of conflict on women and girls can be severe. This was the case in Kosovo last year, in an attempt to respond to the massive numbers of women who survived rape during the genocide. Thousands of displaced men, women, and children had gathered together in a stadium. A man with a megaphone called for all women who had been raped to report to a particular area. Needless to say, not a single woman risked identifying herself, the stigma, the accusation or the potential repercussions, even though it meant losing the opportunity to hold her aggressors accountable or to receive life-saving support.

The kind of insensitivity and lack of sophistication in approach demonstrated in this example obviously affects working with women nationals on issues around rape and other forms of sexual violence, reproductive rights, and HIV/AIDS, who are struggling with the same lack of awareness, information and data, and therefore lack sufficient support for their efforts. This awareness is critical in order to properly identify the issues and bring appropriate and necessary assistance to women in conflict and post-conflict situations, as well as to those working on their behalf.

2. IMPROVING PROTECTION AND ASSISTANCE FOR WOMEN

The specific interests of women and girls are often neglected in the delivery of protection and assistance in post-conflict reconstruction. UNIFEM helps mobilize protection, as well as humanitarian, psychosocial, and economic assistance for women, and focuses particularly on preventing gender-based violence and sexual exploitation, including the verification of gender-based violations, improved monitoring and reporting, and special protection measures.

On a visit to Colombia, UNIFEM staff witnessed with poignant clarity the significant gaps that exist in the protection of women and girls in armed conflict. We learned of the huge majority of women among the internally displaced. The area was called the Valley of Widows. Edendale Valley in South Africa has the same name. Cambodia is called the Land of Widows. Most of the women were left to fend for themselves with little, if any, support. On a limited basis UNIFEM, UNFPA, UNHCR, and others provide reproductive health care, and psychosocial and economic support for these women and girls. However, absolutely clear is the disproportionate way in which women and girls are affected and displaced by conflict, and the glaring inadequacy of humanitarian assistance to meet their special needs.

The implications are enormous for staff working on these issues. Currently, the support systems for female staff working in unstable conditions are inadequate. Time and time again we hear from staff who have been poorly prepared and left without support to deal with the kind of trauma women experience in conflict. These staff require full briefings on the impact of armed conflict on women and girls, the dimensions of what can happen to them in conflict zones, the kinds of stories they will hear, the kind of help they will be asked to provide, and the personal nature of many requests for assistance and support. These interveners will be on the frontlines, often the first or only person that women will have to turn to for help. Even when staff members are prepared, the effects on staff can be devastating. We need to provide constant support and counseling, and experienced gender experts for them to turn to for networking and consultation.

We have found, as well, that staff receives little or no training on documentation of violations, which is a critical gap. If they witness violations of women's human rights, they need special skills to document, report, and monitor them. They need to know to whom to submit such reports. Where violations of women's rights have occurred, by nationals in a country and/or by UN staff, how should they be codified so that an intervener-witness can correctly identify, document, and report them? How does an intervener working with women cope with the stress and distress of such violations if they are not even recognized adequately to have clear procedural directives attached to them? These questions need urgent attention.

3. SUPPORTING WOMEN'S PARTICIPATION IN PEACE PROCESSES

Women often assume activist roles while holding together their families and communities. From the grass roots level to the negotiating table, UNIFEM supports women's participation in peace-building, and helps to leverage the political, financial, and technical support needed for endeavors to have positive impact both nationally and regionally.

While the credibility of peace processes that exclude participants on the basis of caste, ethnicity, religion, or political affiliation are often called into question, the systematic exclusion of more than 50 percent of the population on the basis of gender is rarely challenged, despite the assertion that, ". . . women's representation at the negotiating table is the sine qua non of gender equality and inclusion" [1].

4. BRINGING A GENDER PERSPECTIVE TO INTER-GOVERNMENTAL PEACE AND SECURITY INITIATIVES

UNIFEM fosters strategic partnerships with regional and multilateral bodies and provides policy support, information and gender analysis of the political, humanitarian, and human rights aspects of conflicts and seeks to mainstream gender.

UNIFEM concurs wholeheartedly with the conclusion that:

The mandates of preventive peace missions, peacekeeping operations and peace-building need to include provisions for women's protection and address gender issues. All peace support operations should include appropriately staffed and integrated gender units and gender advisers, and give priority to the verification of gender-based violations and the protection of women's human rights. Field operations should protect and support the delivery of humanitarian assistance for affected women and girls, and in particular for refugee and displaced women [1].

5. GENDER JUSTICE IN POST-CONFLICT PEACE BUILDING

During the transition to peace, a unique window of opportunity exists to put in place a gender responsive framework for a country's reconstruction. As a central element of peace building, UNIFEM seeks to strengthen a gender focus in electoral, constitutional, and judicial reform.

UNIFEM's EXPERIENCE ASSISTING THE NEGOTIATION OF PEACE IN BURUNDI

Until the summer of 2000, the situation of Burundian women and girls had been completely ignored by the senior international officials negotiating peace. But in July, UNIFEM had an opportunity to brief the heads of Burundi's 19 negotiating parties on gender issues relating to the negotiations. This led to the first All Party Burundi Women's Peace Conference that month in Arusha.

Negotiating peace is not a simple, straightforward matter. Peace must encompass all members of a society, women as well as men, children and youth. Yet all too often it is the men alone who come to the peace table. Women now are championing their rightful place at that table.

When women's recommendations were incorporated into the Arusha Accord it was the first time that the contribution of Burundi women to the peace effort for their war-torn land had been officially recognized. Together with the men, they could develop a common vision for Burundi's future, in which peace and reconstruction were the most pressing and immediate concerns. This was also the first time there was a breakthrough on gender exclusion. One outcome of this conference was that men began to think differently about women's contribution to the peace process.

UNIFEM and the Mwalimu Nyerere Foundation (MNF), together with all those who worked for the inclusion of women and gender issues in the Burundi peace negotiations, garnered many lessons during the process of successfully convening this gathering.

The conference was the culmination of a long struggle to have gender issues reflected in the Arusha Peace and Reconciliation Agreement for Burundi. More than 50 Burundi women delegates and observers participated. The women's conference was convened by UNIFEM and MNF, and each of the 19 Burundi parties represented at the peace negotiations (begun in 1998) sent two women delegates to the conference, as requested. Nelson Mandela presented the women's proposals to the draft peace accord, that included provisions to guarantee girls access to education; to punish war crimes against women and girls; to ensure women's rights to inheritance, property and custody, and to include constitutional provisions guaranteeing children's and women's rights and equality.

With the exception of one recommendation—a proposal for 30 percent representation of women in all decision-making during and after the transition period—all the women's recommendations were accepted by the 19 parties and incorporated in the Arusha Peace Accord that was signed on August 28, 2000.

What were the issues in working with and on behalf of these women to assist in making these gains? The first was understanding the context in which the women were working, and the burdens, challenges, and hopes that they brought to the process. Below are some of their voices, a critical prelude and centerpiece to our understanding of how to support them to achieve their goals, and the starting point for understanding the issues UNIFEM would face as part of this process.

> No one wins in this kind of contest, says Alice Ntwarante, observer (administrative and finance director of the Direction Generale de l'Hydraulique et Energies Rurales). It was frustrating not to be allowed to negotiate alongside the men at Arusha . . . We did achieve something: . . . we were united in purpose, despite our ethnic split—three Hutus, three Tutsis. The various political parties to which we belonged tried to split us up, but we resisted them. . . . After each round of negotiations, we took the action into the rural areas of Burundi, inviting country people to attend meetings to inform them, in Kirundi, of what had taken place and to explain our position as women regarding the peace process. These rural women provided valuable feedback.

Women are never a homogeneous group. They differ in race, ethnicity, religion, political affiliation, ideology, geographic location, age, and attitude. Well aware of these differences, the conference did not strive for total harmony or accord. Women from different factions strongly disagreed with each other on political grounds. Nevertheless, the participants, and the UN staff facilitating the process, recognized that, regardless of the differences, all women, from all groups, saw being involved in the peace negotiations and the ultimate agreement as their right. It was critical that the facilitating group was also mixed both in terms of regions and disciplines, with a common understanding and briefing on the issues and the challenges. The goals were to find common ground, to ensure that the solutions and debates were inclusive, and that the achievements were owned by the women themselves.

Further, the realization that women from rural areas, who were often not literate, or spoke only Kirundi, needed to be involved, meant that the UN staff had to support efforts to reach out in a way that would validate the indigenous process, and not favor one group over another. The women who participated were taking personal risks to attend the meeting, given the nature of the Burundi conflict, and the size of the gathering, which involved public and political personalities.

> Because of the travel restrictions for Burundians going out of the country, just to get there (Arusha) was a tremendous achievement—by any means available: bus, plane, and private cars, says Imelda Nzirorrera, observer (acting director of the Center for Promoting Human Rights and Genocide Prevention). . . . we tried to find a way to join in the negotiations. Even after we got there we noticed the men were not happy with our presence. "We don't see any reason for you women to be here," they said. "You should return home. These issues on peace are exclusively men's business!" We must continue the struggle to assert women's place at the peace table.

Burundi was a particularly exhilarating and successful intervention on the part of the women. However, an important part of the work for UN staff in such an instance is to be aware that with enhanced visibility there are sometimes dangers, which necessitate intensified support and security to ensure and enable ongoing efforts. In UNIFEM's experience, there are instances in which funding or assisting women to participate in the political processes and have their voices heard—a necessary part of reconstruction and post-conflict response—can be threatening to women and interveners. Enhanced protection and security strategies are critical in these situations.

PREVENTIVE PROTECTION FOR WOMEN

As mentioned above, violence and the other risks associated with supporting women in conflict and post-conflict societies require much more serious attention by those currently involved in such work.

• Adequate training, preparation, and protection are essential for interveners considering the heightened risk to themselves and the women they are working with when supporting and promoting critical issues in post-conflict contexts such as: women's right to own land; identifying, combating and addressing sexual violence in all its forms; and women's reproductive rights and political rights. These issues are often inflammatory and unpopular, and need to be pursued with women in a way that does not make them and the interveners targets for violence or censure from other citizens, including State actors. UNIFEM's experience has shown that even research and the production of materials on violence against women, and documentation of women's experiences in conflict, can be contentious, and adequate understanding of how to address the risks and the provision of appropriate support are critical.

• Many UNIFEM staff and partners have stressed that this is particularly true for national staff, who are especially vulnerable in the context of working publicly on such issues. Much greater support and protection need to be provided for national staff who work with women and women's issues.

• Security is currently inadequate and an emergency in and of itself. There are several dimensions to this: much of the work with women is rooted in the grassroots, often in remote areas, where there may be no UN presence and provisions for women interveners are lacking.

• Ensuring that they have adequate equipment such as phones and two-way radios in cars is basic and essential. Violence, rape, abductions and the presence of arms in refugee camps create a dangerous environment for both female refugees and interveners, but gender aware responses to these dangers has been sorely lacking.

• Women interveners working in conflict or post-conflict contexts are often most likely to be approached by women who have been sexually assaulted (nationals, refugees, and even UN staff). This can put the female intervener in the dangerous position of being perceived as the "whistle blower," and she may become the target of violence and/or aggression for retribution from both colleagues and male (and sometimes female) nationals. Greater recognition of this reality must permeate training, protection measures, security, and support systems. Additionally, other staff who have not been properly sensitized to issues of sexual violence may act as potential psychological and systemic obstacles to an intervener in this situation: they not only create an unreceptive or poisoned environment for her to operate in, but impede her ability to service and respond adequately to the women she works with.

• It has been noted that protection for those who have been violated comes *after* the violation. Serious priority and commitment must be devoted to understanding and exploring preventive measures and preventive protection; innovative measures must be employed to discover what will really be effective. In order to minimize violations and work toward their eradication, much more gender awareness and sensitivity, and exploration of what works in situations in which women and girls are vulnerable, need to be ensured. These may include improved communication systems, sanctions against staff who do not respond immediately and effectively, stronger security, better lighting, tighter controls on arms in refugee camps, and self-defense training.

• Working with women, interveners find that there are complex, interrelated issues, tying social, cultural, political, civil, and economic conditions inextricably together, not to mention issues around rape, torture, HIV, and AIDS. As mentioned earlier, counseling is essential for the intervener, as is sophisticated training in how to understand and address the integrated nature of challenges women face.

• In working with women who are at risk in conflict situations, we also have to be clear about what constitutes a risk for the intervener. For instance, staff must have better methods to assess the gender specific challenges and demands they will face, and what support they will need and have. Not being adequately prepared or supported has led to ineffective interventions, and may be damaging to staff members.

• The pandemics of HIV and AIDS must be addressed for interveners working with women, both in terms of the issues they will be dealing with and the need to understand the gender and human rights dimensions of the pandemics, but also in terms of the support and services that must be made available to staff. Awareness training is simply not enough. Staff are vulnerable to sexual assault and other forms of assault which hugely increase their vulnerability to the disease, and protection, treatment, counseling, and other services must be immediately available to them.

We know that women play a critical role in peace-building and reconstruction of societies. Women at all levels in a war-torn society, and women who enter complex and dangerous situations working with women are an essential and integral part of all systems, solutions, processes, negotiations, and resolutions that take place.

This is no longer the wisdom solely of women activists, organizations, or experts; it is now accepted universal common sense. Knowing this, we must make it possible for women to participate in every capacity to promote gender-sensitive and gender-inclusive responses to conflict, peace-building and violations without the threat, fear, or reality of further violence and egregious attacks. Until everyone engaged in this work is doing his or her part to ensure that the training, protection, support systems, safe spaces, and responses are gender sensitive in a meaningful and serious way, we will continue to put women at further and unnecessary risk.

REFERENCE

1. The Machel Review 1996-2000: A Critical Analysis of Progress Made and Obstacles Encountered in Increasing Protection for War-Affected Children. UNIFEM, the Government of Norway, UNICEF and the Canadian Department of Foreign Affairs and International Trade.

Voice

SEX, VIOLENCE, LOVE, LOSS, HOPE:
MEN AND WOMEN IN THE CAMPS SPEAK TO US

Janet Albrecht

In a crisis situation, people have essential needs for survival: food, water, clothing, shelter. But even when these basics are provided, high rates of morbidity and mortality persist, particularly among women and infants, if reproductive health services are not also provided. Emergency reproductive health services are crucial to save lives and prevent illness. Women need trained assistance during labor and delivery, or if they must deliver their own babies, they need clean delivery kits to avoid deadly infections; skilled care to manage pregnancy complications such as haemorrhage, eclampsia, obstructed labor, and retained placenta; and, appropriate treatment for miscarriages and the consequences of unsafe abortions. Men, women, and youth all need family planning information and services to prevent unwanted pregnancies, and to prevent and manage reproductive tract infections and sexually transmitted diseases (STDs), including HIV/AIDS. They are often more vulnerable to rape, sexual exploitation and violence and need access to psychosocial and medical care, including emergency contraception.

Recognition of the importance of reproductive health in emergency situations as vital to humanitarian aid is relatively new. The United Nations Population Fund (UNFPA) went into camps for internally displaced persons (IDPs) in Angola to learn about their reproductive health. We collected quantitative data indicating extremely high rates of infant and maternal mortality, low life expectancy, low rates of assisted deliveries, high birth rates, low use of family planning, very high rates of adolescent pregnancy, poor knowledge of and access to treatment for STDs, and widespread violence. We also collected qualitative data to give more life and meaning to the numbers. The IDPs spoke openly to us about their lives: the incredible losses, uncertainty, changing social roles, violence, family life, love, dreams for the future, and hopes for their children. They told us their thoughts on contraception, sexuality, STDs, and gender roles. In their own words:

> Since we arrived here, the hardships have been many: no clothing, food, money.
> If I complain to my husband, he hits me. He goes out and returns drunk. If I say I
> don't want sex, he insists and we wind up doing it. I said the children we have are
> enough because we don't have the means to take care of more children. I don't
> want more children. My husband beats me if I refuse to have sex with him. But I
> don't want to have more children.

I don't have a husband. Since we got here we started getting pregnant. At first the men said they wanted to stay with us, but it's a lie. They leave you and the baby. After giving birth, the problems start because you're alone without knowing what to do because the men don't assume their responsibilities.

The men feel powerless, living on the land of others, dependent upon charity: ". . . as a father and husband my role has changed in the sense that my worries have increased and my means of subsistence have diminished . . . now, in this position, I'm desperate."

Going into the camps gave us the opportunity to study the realities of life there, and to experience it for ourselves. We were exposed to contagious diseases and sickened by parasites and malaria, just as the IDPs are. One team was physically and verbally harassed by an intoxicated army major who threatened to carry one of the women off into the bush, as has happened to countless women and girls. Another group of interviewers was stoned by IDPs who mistrusted our questions and intentions. Others feared that we were sent by the military to seek out young men for conscription. The difference between the IDPs and us was that we had a lifetime of good nutrition to fortify us, access to medical treatment, protection of the international community, and the ability and means to leave the camps and return to the safety and comfort of our homes. Any hardships we encountered were diminished by the hunger, illness, and desperation we saw.

As researchers, we went into the camps to collect data. We listened to the IDPs, felt their emotions, saw how they lived, and carefully documented our findings. It is hard to remain truly objective in the face of such overwhelming need. You want to help, but you realize how powerless you are to do so. It's something you never forget.

8

Supporting Staff During Crisis and on the Path to Development

Omar Bakhet and Marie Dimond

UNDP's ROLE IN CRISIS AND POST-CONFLICT SITUATIONS

Chances are that the United Nations Development Programme (UNDP) is not among the first organizations to come to mind when thinking of the multiplicity of actors working in crisis situations. Especially for people less familiar with the many UN bodies, the name alone, it seems, would imply that this is the international agency mandated to address longer-term development in countries where conditions are sufficiently stable to do so. However, while UNDP has generally focused on more traditional development assistance with an emphasis on capacity-building and poverty eradication, a growing awareness of its key role in crisis and post-conflict situations, especially over the course of the 1990s, led to a gradual strengthening of its work in these areas. The UN Secretary-General, Kofi Annan, recently reiterated that ". . . war is the worst enemy of development, and broad-based development is the best form of long-term conflict prevention." In fact, owing to the unique, multi-track nature of its work, UNDP is better characterized as the organization that is present not only "before, during, and after" the outbreak of crisis but at the front line as well as in the back hills.

One reason for this is UNDP's central coordination mandate. Based on a series of General Assembly (GA) resolutions, UNDP was given leadership of the Resident Coordinator (RC)[1] system which applies to the nearly 130 program countries, including the approximately 30 that are considered crisis and post-conflict environments. This means that the Resident Representative (RR) of UNDP is normally designated as the RC and hence also usually coordinates the humanitarian assistance of the UN

---

[1] The concept of a single official for the coordination of operational activities for development within the UN System stems from the restructuring of the economic and social sectors of the System initiated by GA resolution 32/197 (1977) in which it was decided to entrust overall responsibility for, and the coordination of, operational activities for development carried out at the country level to a single official who should exercise team leadership and ensure a multidisciplinary dimension in sectoral development programs.

system. Managed and funded by UNDP, the RC system provides the overall framework for the coordination of operational activities, a critical factor in advancing the success of any multi-dimensional intervention. The merger of the Resident and Humanitarian Coordinator (HC) positions not only ensures a more unified and coherent UN approach; it also facilitates the early integration of a more longer-term, development-oriented perspective essential to a smooth transition out of the emergency phase.

The growing recognition that preventive and curative development must be addressed simultaneously in the midst of crises has led to an awareness of the critical link between relief and development. As a result, the RC was additionally mandated by the GA to "facilitate the preparedness of the UN system and assist in a speedy transition from relief to development." Finally, it is important to point out that UNDP's role in crisis situations is not confined to those considered complex political emergencies but extends to natural disasters as well. The responsibility assigned UNDP for operational activities for natural disaster mitigation, prevention and preparedness, as well as for capacity-building for the effective response to the problem of land mines and its socioeconomic aspects only serves to consolidate further its key role in this area.

THE ROLE OF UNDP's EMERGENCY RESPONSE DIVISION

Within UNDP, the Emergency Response Division (ERD) has been tasked to address the transition between the relief and recovery phases. Since a strong recovery program is essential if recurrence of conflict is to be minimized, ERD has recently established the Transitional Recovery Team concept as a means through which UNDP seeks to facilitate this overlap. The teams will provide crucial support to the RC/HC in the preparation and implementation of a transitional strategy. UNDP thus seeks to build on its traditional multi-sectoral programming, its long-term engagement in countries, and its role in developmental and humanitarian coordination to provide an effective bridge that spans the relief-to-development gaps that so often have hindered recovery efforts. A recovery approach focuses on how best to restore the capacity of the government and communities to rebuild and recover from crisis and to prevent relapses. In so doing, recovery seeks not only to catalyze sustainable development activities but also to build upon earlier humanitarian programs to ensure that their inputs become assets for development. ERD will support the teams by continuing to provide specific technical support in key related areas such as small arms, demobilization, reintegration, governance, rule of law, and mine action.

UNDP believes, for instance, that mitigating the causes that lead people to revert to small arms for their survival, safety, and livelihood, and stemming the flow of illicit arms is a major part of the solution in halting armed conflict. It therefore seeks to confront root causes of strife and create an environment where people again feel secure enough to live without guns. In the Republic of Congo, for instance, UNDP is working to collect and destroy firearms while integrating this activity with the transition to civilian life for ex-combatants. UNDP thus welcomes the emphasis placed in the Brahimi Report [1] on integrating the development aspects of peace-building, such as the active engagement of local parties, effective civilian governance and the disarmament, demobilization, and reintegration of former combatants.

In the coming years, UNDP intends to strengthen significantly its operations in crisis and post-conflict situations. It will continue to work in close collaboration with program country Governments and local communities to help enhance national capacities to prevent conflicts, to minimize the damage caused by natural and man-made disasters, and to manage recovery and peace-building processes effectively. It will strengthen its role as a key partner within the United Nations system and beyond, and as a mobilizer and coordinator of international assistance in crisis and post-conflict situations.

STAFF SUPPORT IN CRISIS AND POST-CONFLICT SITUATIONS

As a result of UNDP's broad mandate outlined above through which it is invariably present before, after, and during crisis, its staff work in most countries is affected by natural and man-made disaster. UNDP staff, particularly those specializing in transitional activities, are just as exposed to the particular hardships and challenges faced by the average relief worker. It could even be argued that, in some ways, UNDP staff may face a unique burden: as an emergency wanes and fades from the international limelight and as the flurry of relief workers phase out their operations and depart, UNDP staff are the ones who remain behind to devote themselves to the much more long-term task of rebuilding a shattered country. In some ways, this adds an additional pressure, particularly in face of the immense responsibility of ensuring that optimum advantage is taken of the window of opportunity that has presented itself and that a relapse into conflict is avoided.

Indeed, a recovery environment brings with it challenges all of its own. The focus of interventions is no longer restricted to, for instance, the identification of beneficiaries and the distribution of food, water, blankets, sheeting, and jerry cans but is based on a more complex, multi-dimensional and integrated approach with a view toward rebuilding the socioeconomic fabric of a fragmented society. At times these postings can prove all the more difficult, particularly if a relapse occurs after initial progress has been made. While relief workers may be fortunate enough to experience, over time and as a result of their interventions, alleviation of the suffering caused by drought, flooding, or displacement, staff working in a recovery environment risk witnessing a deterioration and the loss of hard-won development gains. Thus, UNDP staff, who are not necessarily viewed as part of the traditional community of relief workers, and who remain after the emergency has passed, tend to receive less recognition for and understanding of the particular challenges they face.

UNDP plays an especially important role in-country as the RC/HC most often is also the Designated Official and, as such, the person ultimately responsible for UN security matters. S/he coordinates actions at the country level aimed at ensuring the safety and well-being of all staff of the UN system in the designated area of responsibility; convenes and leads the work of the inter-agency security management team for effective and joint action on all security-related aspects; and ensures proper planning, implementation, and reporting. In carrying out these responsibilities, s/he receives instructions and guidance directly from the Office of the UN Security Coordinator (UNSECOORD) while drawing on the UNDP Country Office for administrative support.

UN field personnel have not always received adequate support in terms of security. This has led some staff to rely more on their embassies that, in some cases, have demonstrated more care, concern, and commitment toward the safety of their nationals than the UN did toward its staff. This must change. More often than not, staff has been dispatched with little or no preparation in terms of what to expect from a security and hardship point of view once they arrive on the ground. No systematic briefing, support, and debriefing structure is yet in place. Instead, it has mainly been in the interest of the individual to glean information haphazardly from colleagues who have been to the particular country or area or know others who have. Needless to say, this can provide for the sharing of very slanted and subjective views based on individual experience and character and is far from the more professional type of briefing required.

As within other UN organizations active in crisis and post-conflict situations, there is growing acknowledgment that far more needs to be done to support staff who are being deployed to some of the most challenging working environments in the world. Not only do these staff have to deal with the "usual" hardships such as cultural and language barriers, physical hardship, risk of disease, reduced access to quality health services, being away from family and friends and the accompanying sense of isolation and deprivation. UNDP staff also face the same stressors as their more relief-oriented colleagues, including the risk of being caught in ambushes and cross fire, kidnappings, land mines, threats and intimidation, curfews, checkpoints, and the need for armed guards and escorts. UNDP staff also share the same sorrow, anger, and sometimes guilt when they leave local colleagues and friends behind to an unknown fate while they are evacuated or relocated to safety when worse comes to worse. In this regard, UNDP has made provisions to have local staff and their eligible family members included in evacuation plans.

During missions, those who essentially provide the most support are colleagues, often on no less a ground than simply being "all in the same boat." Clearly, bonds develop much more quickly and more deeply than they would in more normal situations. UNDP recognizes that their staff should not be reduced to resorting to receiving emotional support only from fellow staff members, especially following particularly traumatic events such as the violent death of a colleague. While considerable focus has been, and continues to be, placed on ensuring physical safety, far more attention needs to be paid to the psychological well-being of staff. It is common knowledge that this is in the best interest of the organization as healthy, happy, and well-balanced staff are also more productive and more committed to their work as compared to those who are disillusioned, depressed, and burned out.

The type of UNDP support offered to date has usually consisted of the system-wide adoption of the policy entitling staff serving in difficult duty stations to Rest and Recuperation (R&R) which normally entails five days off every two months. However, owing to a variety of reasons often related to the nature of an organization's mandate, not all UN agencies have the same policies, whether pertaining to R&R or other entitlements. UNDP recognizes that significant discrepancies in pay and benefits among UN staff working in crisis situations can lead to poor morale and are not conducive toward fostering a strong sense of community so essential to good coordination, especially during and in the aftermath of emergencies. UNDP therefore supports the system-wide effort to harmonize salary and benefit scales among staff from different agencies. Over the course of the last few years, field-oriented UN agencies have made a concerted effort to better coordinate special entitlements and benefits. While there is room for further harmonization, significant progress has been made.

UNDP also recognizes that more attention needs to be paid to the special needs of staff returning from prolonged and/or particularly difficult assignments in the field. In New York, UNDP/UNFPA staff can avail themselves of the confidential services of the Program for Staff Assistance (PSA), a counseling center designed to assist staff and their families in dealing with concerns of a personal nature, free of charge. The center offers information, assessment, short-term counseling, emergency intervention and referral services depending on the particular need of the staff member, including those related to reassignment and adaptation to the New York area. The extension of PSA services to the field offices may be considered. UN staff can also seek psychological counseling services on their own which, in principle, are covered by UN health insurance plans.

In conclusion, UNDP notes that increased awareness of and appreciation for the hazards and hardships staff face needs to be established, particularly in the upper echelons of what can at times appear as a removed bureaucracy disconnected from the realities of the field. Indeed, while UNDP prides itself in providing assistance to program countries before, during and after crisis, it should not overlook that its staff is deserving and in need of adequate support as well, especially before, during, and after their missions to crisis countries.

POLICY AND PROGRAM RECOMMENDATIONS

UNDP:

- must recognize the toll that work in crisis and post-conflict situations can take on its staff.
- is committed to work within the UN system to further the safety and security of staff and supports the Secretary-General's proposal stipulating that staff security should increasingly be funded from the UN regular budget rather than depending on voluntary funds.
- will continue to contribute funds to assist UNSECOORD in carrying out its responsibility of providing common security services to the UN system.

- is in support of the Minimum Operating Security Standards (MOSS) recently established by UNSECOORD in response to the Secretary-General's wish for a critical review of UN security procedures in the field. This initiative is linked to the undertaking of common threat assessments and the identification of criteria for suspension of operations in cases of non-compliance.
- is also strengthening its own capacity to assist the RR/RC in his/her role as DO, and to address the UNDP specific security needs affecting the delivery of programs in the field including staff awareness training. ERD will strengthen its security focal point role within UNDP through establishment of a security unit tasked with providing improved backstopping and policy support to country offices.
- urges that, along with provisions for international staff, appropriate attention be given to security management of national staff and their eligible family members.
- urges that the harmonization of remuneration and entitlements among UN agencies be expedited.
- will consider recruiting counselors to provide psychological services to staff working in crisis and post-conflict situations. Ideally, the medical facility available at country level exclusively to UN staff and their dependents should have someone with counseling experience or who is able to refer the person to another source.

REFERENCE

1. United Nations, *Report of the Panel on United Nations Peace Operations,* A/55/305-S/2000/809, August 21, 2000.

Voices

HEALING IS AN INDIVIDUAL PROCESS
Kathleen Cravero

In the aftermath of tragedy, many things go wrong. Organizations—and people—become confused and chaotic. They overreact, they underreact, they take action too quickly, or they fail to act at all. The response to the ambush in Burundi was no exception.

First, there were those who sought to blame the victims. Why were you there? Why didn't you have a larger military escort? Why wasn't Rutana's request for help put in writing? In other words, why couldn't you predict the unpredictable? Why didn't you control the uncontrollable? There must be a way to "explain" this unthinkable, tragic event.

The truth is that tragedies happen in places like Burundi not because mistakes are made or unnecessary risks are taken. They happen because the UN is operating in increasingly dangerous environments in which we are seen as belligerents by one side or the other. Neither our neutrality nor our moral authority is accepted by those wielding the guns. Most of them simply don't care if we or the people we serve live or die.

Second, there were those who sought to solve the crimes. They insisted on explanations, sought evidence for their theories, pointed fingers at the "guilty." Rage was vented at the government, at rebel groups, at the international community.

The reality is that we will never know who pulled the trigger in Rutana—or even who planned the attack. Those of us who delivered assistance on a daily basis knew that the levels of deceit, of fear, and of hatred in Burundi were far too deep for truth to penetrate. This is one of the reasons the violence never ends.

Third, there were those who sought to comfort. They encouraged us to talk, to remember, to relive the events in order to get past them. These people were well-meaning but not always helpful. Some of us were not immediately ready to "talk through" the most traumatic experience of our lives. We sought to bury the memories until we had the time and space to mourn properly.

The fact is that healing is an individual process. It varies among cultures and within peoples and cannot be forced or hurried along. For some people, counseling is a welcome release. For others it increases levels of distress.

Finally, there were those who asked what they could do to help us most and those who, without asking, did things that saved us time and worry. These included many members of the UN community in Burundi like the person who translated letters and documents into Spanish so Luis Zuniga's family could read them; the people who arranged a memorial service for our murdered colleagues; and the person who obtained clearances for flying the bodies to Nairobi. They also included colleagues at the international level: Sergio de Mello, who visited Burundi the day after the murders and provided much-needed leadership and reassurance; Mark Powe, the UNICEF Security Coordinator, who came to Burundi and investigated the incident with sensitivity and compassion; and Kevin Kennedy, who refused to allow a "blame the victims" mentality to take hold in New York.

They also included a number of UNDP colleagues. UNDP provided, in fact, a model of constructive institutional response. Both the Administrator and Deputy Administrator remained in close contact but were not overbearing. The Africa Bureau provided guidance without interfering in decisions made in-country. The office of Human Resources, under the leadership of Deborah Landey, offered sensitive, rapid, and effective support both to me and to the UNDP staff member wounded in the attack. These colleagues, and the many wonderful friends who called or sent messages (saying simply "we're thinking of you") were sources of light during very dark days.

I know now, through painful personal experience, how to respond to people in trouble. I let them know that I'm available. I offer practical support. And I remind them that bad things happen to good people, but good people survive.

WHAT AID WORKERS AND FROGS HAVE IN COMMON
Marie Dimond

We all have different views on what constitutes acceptable working conditions. This applies particularly to the area of aid work where a certain amount of exposure to physical and emotional hardship is to be expected. But the degree of personal risk a person should be prepared to take while carrying out his/her job raises far more questions.

Is it, for instance, acceptable to expect staff to operate in environments in which they can only move outside the confines of their compound donned with helmets and flak jackets, accompanied by armed guards and an escort vehicle? Or to expect them to sleep with their clothes and sneakers on and have their "quick-run-kit" handy at all times in order to have a head start when they come under attack and be able to fend for themselves in the bush for a few days before they are (hopefully) rescued? Is it acceptable to routinely avoid potholes while commuting between home and the office to minimize the risk of running over a concealed anti-tank mine?

While very few, these examples illustrate the varying ways in which the United Nations has adapted to environments that, from the perspective of most of the outside world, seem, at the very least, unacceptable. Very early on into my field service, I was introduced to the concept of taking "a calculated risk," based on a somewhat nebulous computation in which differing degrees of danger and their potential consequences were weighed in the context of the gravity of the humanitarian situation, the moral imperative to intervene, and an almighty factor called luck or timing or being in the wrong place at the wrong time.

Not all relief workers decide to work at the front lines for entirely altruistic reasons. There are a number, albeit in the minority, who seek more adventure in their lives and enjoy the sense of thrill that can accompany the adrenalin rush brought on by high-risk situations. Over time this can lead to a culture of toughness, in which some staff who have "been around the block" may become hardened to the madness of war and the suffering it brings with it. War stories are exchanged with no little sense of bravado under the theme "the closer the call, the better." A week after taking up my first posting in Mogadishu, when intense militia fighting in the neighborhood became a little too close for comfort, we went through the first of what were to become a number of hairy evacuations. Upon arrival in Nairobi, I was greeted, oddly, with "Congratulations. Now you're a veteran," as if I had graduated into a higher class of aid work.

In the years that followed, I was confronted with many situations in which, to any "reasonable" outsider, the abnormal had become normal. After some time, I could not help but be reminded of an experiment in which a frog is first dropped into boiling, or near boiling, water. Not surprisingly, it immediately jumps out. Then, however, it is put in cold water with a slow flame. The frog, liking the warmth, gets comfortable and sleepy and eventually gets cooked.

How many stories have we heard about people being lulled into complacency? Where they slowly but surely adjust to ever more hazardous environments, becoming careless and neglecting to draw the line, often to their own detriment. Much has been said about having to know when to "get out." Most often this point comes once a security incident finally ends up hitting too close to home, once the people injured or killed are no longer simply statistics but someone you personally knew. Not everyone, however, is able to admit when "enough is enough." In this respect, the UN and others need to do far more to support staff who are nearing, or who have passed, the boiling point.

Ironically, the UN, despite its noble mandate, is probably one of the organizations that is the least humanitarian toward its own staff. Generally, they work in an environment where they are expected to be strong and know what they were getting themselves into. More often than not, in the midst or aftermath of traumatic events, relief and development workers alike find themselves confronted with the underlying assumption that hardship and risk, including to one's own life, come with the territory.

Aid workers may be reluctant to show signs of buckling under pressure or admit to emotional difficulties for fear of seeming weak or in the wrong job. The lack of empathy and support may be even greater for those transitioning back to "the real world" after a prolonged stint in hardship postings. This can often be made even more difficult owing to the UN's harrowing administrative services that result in having to spend inordinate amounts of time and energy chasing down issues related to contracts, shipments, and outstanding payments.

No one is tough enough to go through near surreal experiences without eventually having to deal with effects of one form or another. While awareness for the counseling needs of victims who have lived through the most unspeakable horrors is gaining ground, support for those who have come to provide assistance to them should also not be overlooked.

9

Managing Projects on the Ground

Reinhart Helmke

United Nations Office for Project Services (UNOPS) is in the unique position of being a service provider to other entities of the United Nations system without a substantive or sector mandate of its own. While this avoids conflicts of interest in the course of implementing project work on the ground, UNOPS relies more than other UN entities upon the entire UN system framework for all substantive matters.

This is why UNOPS has not developed a unique policy on issues such as security, or political and humanitarian affairs. These are dealt with by dedicated and specialized offices within the UN system, which may or may not themselves be users of UNOPS services. The UN Resident Coordinator has such a function, aiming at effective coordination of operational activities for development. This is often undertaken in crisis situations, whether attributable to natural disaster or civil strife. Another entity dealing with such issues is the Department of Political Affairs which monitors, analyzes, and assesses political developments throughout the world. Furthermore, the Office of the United Nations Security Coordinator (UNSECOORD), is the fundamental provider of services relevant to the protection of UN staff.

Through years of experience with helping to carry out the mandates of its UN clients, UNOPS has developed a unique hands-on expertise in project implementation. UNOPS weighs with great care any feedback relevant to crisis situations which is received from its personnel in the field. When and where appropriate, UNOPS will also draw the attention of its clients to lessons learned in the field, for their consideration when designing a future project or considering a change in policy. This exchange is an important added value that UNOPS owes and delivers to its clients.

UNOPS can have an ongoing presence throughout different phases of peace-keeping, peace building, and development, whereas other mandate-specific UN missions may have a presence of more limited duration. This has helped to bridge the continuum ranging from conflict or crisis situations to long-term development.

It is therefore quite natural that UNOPS demonstrates particular interest in the well-being of field personnel in crisis situations. UNOPS makes every effort to avail its field personnel of the best possible lodgings, communication equipment, and means of transportation, in compliance with generally applicable UN requirements as well as specific instructions issued by responsible UN entities such as UNSECOORD.

Based on the prevailing situation in each area where UNOPS has been charged with carrying out project activities, UNOPS field personnel often formulate requests for support and propose practical solutions.

Special attention has to be given to the recruitment and management of national staff, to promote fairness and take due account of all local cultural, economic, educational, and other social factors. This is in the best interests of both the communities and the program. In the foregoing connection, UNOPS should:

- Conduct in-depth briefings of staff on the dynamics and political, ethnic, or other causes of any local conflict, as well as the prospects for resolution thereof;
- Adequately train staff who will recruit national staff on the various cultural and other issues which need to be taken into account when doing so;
- Raise awareness among international staff about the social, economic, and other challenges that national staff may be facing.

UNOPS takes due note of such requests from its field personnel. Many of them are aimed at better preparation to deal with crisis situations. UNOPS also invests in improving relevant training provided to its personnel, notably as regards the political environment in which they will operate.

An increasing number of United Nations staff works in conditions that require special attention. The following real life scenarios, contributed by UNOPS project staff, may illustrate this better than statistical data, however impressive.

Voices

HUMANE HUMAN RESOURCES MANAGEMENT
Alicia Noeli Escursell

I was assigned from 1997 through 1999 to work for a demining program as the Senior Finance Officer. The main goal was to assist, train, and build the capacity of the local demining authority to destroy landmines, which had been laid during the recent war. It was a large program with a total of 38 staff members: 8 local support staff, 6 UNOPS international staff, and 24 international supervisors (landmine specialists) provided by various donor governments. Regretfully, the cease-fire agreement reached earlier by the warring parties was not being fully observed; attacks continued and landmines were laid again.

I had to travel for one week each month to all of the provinces where we had demining units in order to pay the monthly allowance to international supervisors and deminers, a total of over 600 people. This task required travel from the capital to the countryside on World Food Program (WFP) planes, carrying large amounts of cash and without any accompanying security guards. At the beginning, I traveled alone. My risk was fairly high, since everybody knew that I was arriving with money to pay them. But after the first of the two incidents described below, some of my international colleagues accompanied me for (primary moral) support.

One day, when I was ready to start paying in a particular province, three deminers who, because of unjustified absences, were not to receive the full salary, came toward me and threatened me with traditional knives, with the intention of taking the cash. Thanks to the quick intervention of international supervisors and some of the other local deminers, I am alive today and telling this story. When I reached the car carrying with me the money, walking slowly and surrounded by my colleagues, I drove away safely and was able to reflect on the gravity of the danger with which I had been confronted.

The second incident had a dramatic effect on me. Just one month after my arrival in the country, I was requested to arrange the transportation of a landmine victim to a hospital, from which he would be transferred by a WFP plane to the military base in the capital. I assisted without any briefing; I was confronted with a 22-year-old man who had lost his limbs and whose face was severely burned. He had essentially been dumped on the tarmac by the paramedics. One might understand that an unconscious survival/self-defense technique which people adopt in such çircum-stances is indifference to others' suffering. But this is hard to accept. The paramedics' and the ambulance driver's slow reaction to saving the victim's life was unnerving to me. I had to assert myself, just to ensure that the victim was placed in the ambulance and driven to the hospital. There I again had to intervene to see that he received prompt medical attention.

On a lighter note, I would like also to share a valuable strategy for managing staff in crisis situations. The environment in which we were working was indeed stressful, and frequently our communications with New York and/or our home countries were cut. At such times we did not receive any support, professional or emotional, from our colleagues/relatives abroad. Thus, I started inviting the office staff (both national and international) for a coffee at the beginning of the day. It was an opportunity to exchange ideas or news, but served primarily to boost our morale through the identification and sharing of humorous aspects interspersed with the seriousness of our daily tasks.

We had a strong need to feel that we were not on our own, that we were struggling together, side-by-side, and that we would collectively be able to succeed in our tasks. The morning coffees made us more aware and sensitive to the dangers that each of us was exposed to; the levity helped us to recognize and cement our mutual dependence. I consider it to be extremely important that we develop local means for providing assistance/support to staff working in hardship environments.

PERSEVERANCE DESPITE ADVERSITY
Basil Comnas

From early 1993 to mid-1995, I was UNOPS Area Manager for a UNDP-funded rehabilitation program executed by UNOPS in a war-torn country. My job was to manage a team of three internationals and approximately 25 national professionals, engineers, doctors, agronomists, water engineers, gender experts, and support staff.

From early 1993 when we first arrived, we experienced numerous security incidents and threats. Being assaulted and threatened at checkpoints that were set up by militia or bandits became a common occurrence. On several occasions, my colleague and I were held for short periods at checkpoints with automatic rifles put against out heads. This was especially terrifying when the person holding the gun was a virtual child. Racing through one's mind is the thought: "How can a 12 year old know the value of life and will this person understand the consequences if he pulls the trigger?"

One night in October 1993, a female UNOPS colleague and I were injured following an attack as she was returning by vehicle to the UNDP/UNOPS compound. Trying to offer some feeble assistance, and avoiding small arms fire at close range, I fell in the darkness into a culvert and broke my knee and several ribs and dislocated my shoulder. With the bandits not knowing my fate and still firing shots into the darkness, I crawled with my one good arm, not knowing what to fear more, the bullets or the snakes.

My colleague was abducted, dragged kicking and fighting into a waiting armed vehicle and driven out of town. When the bandits stopped the vehicle in the desert, she managed to escape in the near-total darkness. She hid from and eluded her abductors. Later she found the road and made her way back, arriving by 4 A.M. There she found me lying in bed with a broom and rope tied to my damaged leg, as there was no possibility of medical attention until morning. That night we felt ourselves quite lucky to be alive and to have escaped this close encounter with death. We employed humor and laughter to vanquish the feelings of affront that the assault had made on our pride.

The following morning my medical evacuation took place by air. I was then taken to the hospital for surgery. Three weeks later, on crutches, I returned to continue the project work. After some weeks, when UNOPS had demonstrated that we would not let these events halt this important program, I was brought to New York for debriefing. I had several sessions with a UN psychologist at the Secretariat, who sent me to Johns Hopkins University where I was evaluated for post-critical incident stress. After passing all examinations, and after a course of physiotherapy for the leg, in March 1994 I returned to work.

THE MANAGER'S PERSPECTIVE

Voices:

REASON FOR HOPE

Shashi Tharoor

The experience of working, as a young man, as head of the Office of the United Nations High Commissioner for Refugees in Singapore at the height of the "boat people" crisis was utterly extraordinary. It was my job, with a tiny staff, to handle the refugees rescued at sea and brought into the bustling port of Singapore; to negotiate their disembarkation with the Government's Immigration Department, the shipping company, the company's agents, and sometimes its embassy; to persuade the Government's Home Ministry and Foreign Ministry to cooperate with us despite an official policy aimed at discouraging the arrival of refugees in Singapore; to work with the embassies of third countries to establish resettlement possibilities for the refugees and to obtain the guarantees without which their disembarkation was not permitted; to persuade immigration officers to accept a particular family even if they didn't quite qualify for admission to their country under the official rules; and, as if all this wasn't enough, to manage and run the refugee camp (which, unlike every other country in the region, the Government wanted the United Nations to run). Each day brought with it its own challenges and rewards, demanding patience, creativity, problem-solving abilities, and negotiating skills, as well as a basic commitment to the cause of helping people who had lost everything.

The work was emotionally charged, but I discovered that I was able to put my head to the pillow at night each night knowing that things I had done had made a difference to people's lives—real people, whom I met and spoke to and shared meals and songs with at the camp. I will never forget one family which had left Vietnam in a little boat, powered by a weak engine cannibalized from a tractor. The engine broke down, and the boat drifted helplessly in the South China Sea. The family ran out of their meager supplies of food and water; the two parents slit their fingers and asked their infants to suck the blood to stay alive. For days they subsisted on rainwater and hope. When they were finally rescued by an American ship, they were too weak to stand. We got them off the ship on stretchers and rushed them straight to intensive care in a Singapore hospital. To see them a few months later, healthy, well dressed, and ready for a new life in the United States, was to see the power of dedicated UN work to transform suffering into hope.

Some ask if this could not have been done by ordinary volunteers or church groups. Indeed, I worked closely with non-governmental organizations who were my "operational partners" in the camp, and I appealed to kind souls in Singapore and in the diplomatic community (usually wives of diplomats) to volunteer their time to teach foreign languages, offer cooking classes, and so on. But I also knew that volunteers and NGOs could not have persuaded a Government to offer asylum, or other Governments to find resettlement places. The effectiveness of the United Nations lay as much in the fact that it was an intergovernmental organization whose Member States felt some legal and political obligation to accede to its demands. It was through this experience that I developed my faith in the indispensability of the United Nations system as a force to do good in a world where too many problems, like refugees themselves, cross frontiers and can only be resolved by means that themselves transcend frontiers.

THESE DECISIONS HAUNT ME STILL
Kathleen Cravero

When I accepted the job as UN Resident Coordinator in Burundi, I knew the country's troubled history. The airport had been bombed just one month before I arrived and the fighting between Government and "rebel" groups had almost reached the capital. And so I expected to hear the sound of gunfire far into the night. I was not surprised to meet roadblocks everywhere I went. I knew that half a million Burundians were refugees within their own country. These were all sources of stress, but they were obvious—and shared by all UN staff.

The most overwhelming, gut-wrenching challenge for me was more insidious: each day became a relentless series of life-and-death decisions. Decisions, for example, on where food and supplies could be delivered, which in turn determined who would eat, who would freeze, who would get shelter from the wind and the rain. Decisions on which staff could be involved in these missions, and what level of security was sufficient. Decisions on how to interpret the onslaught of daily information, filled with conflicting facts from questionable sources, diverging views on the same situation, polar opposite explanations of the same events. Decisions on when the UN would cooperate (however reluctantly) with Government edicts and when we would draw a line in the sand; decisions on when principles would prevail over collaboration, over expediency, over "getting the job done." What to believe, when to be firm, when to give in, when to take risks, when to hold back—every waking moment was spent either making one of these choices or preparing for the next one.

Of course, Resident Coordinators are not alone in these decisions. There are program committees, security teams, humanitarian coordination groups—some more effective than others but all designed to help determine "risk thresholds," the term that experts used to describe this horrifying daily reality. But at the end of the day, it is one person who accepts responsibility for what happens; one person who is accountable for the collective judgment of the UN country team.

I am convinced that there is no way to prepare oneself for this level of responsibility. From the day I arrived in Burundi until the day I left, these decisions bore down on me—and never got easier. They haunt me still.

COMPLICITY WITH TORTURE:
MANAGING HUMANITARIAN ASSISTANCE UNDER ECONOMIC SANCTIONS, HAITI 1992-1994

Elizabeth D. Gibbons

People privileged enough to work for the United Nations or one of its agencies feel proud and honored to serve the mandate laid out in the UN Charter:

> To maintain peace and security . . . to achieve international cooperation in solving international problems of an economic, social, cultural, or humanitarian character, and in promoting and encouraging respect for human rights and for fundamental freedoms for all without distinction as to race, sex, language, or religion" (Articles 1.1, 1.3).

Advancing that mandate is ample compensation for the tremendous sacrifices made by UN staff, whose voices are heard throughout this volume. But those of us serving the mandate in countries such as Haiti or Iraq, against which the UN Security Council has imposed comprehensive economic sanctions, find that instead of encouraging respect for human rights, by virtue of being UN staff and hence bound to support Security Council decisions, we are compelled to participate in sanctions-provoked violations of social and economic rights, and of the fundamental right to life for the most vulnerable populations: children and the poor. It is but small compensation that the UN attempts to offset the very same damage resulting from its own sanctions by a robust humanitarian assistance program, administered by the UN agencies such as UNICEF. This is the "voice" of the UNICEF Representative in Haiti from 1992-1996, and attempts to articulate the personal struggle of living through such a contradictory experience, which one UN colleague has likened to that of being a doctor forced to be present at a torture session in order to administer just enough care to ensure that the wounds inflicted do not kill the victim [1].

THE HAITIAN CONTEXT 1991-1994

In response to the September 1991 military coup d'etat against the democratically elected President Jean-Bertrand Aristide, the United Nations and the Organisation of American States (OAS) imposed a sanctions regime against Haiti as a means to punish the coup leaders and force a return to application of the national Constitution and full respect for human rights. By the end of the three years which Haitians suffered under sanctions, unemployment increased from 50 percent to 75 percent, agricultural output declined 20 percent, prices of basic foodstuffs increased 100 percent while per-capita income declined 30 percent to a mere $250. Child malnutrition doubled and thousands of children perished in a measles epidemic; maternal mortality increased 29 percent and under five mortality increased by almost 10 percent; school enrolments dropped by one third and the number of street children doubled [2]. UN sanctions were responsible for much of the violations of economic and social rights which this precipitous decline represented for Haiti's poor and vulnerable.

The irony was, of course, that the UN, which should be supporting indivisible human rights was, through the instrument of sanctions, violating one set of human rights (economic and social) for the sake of advancing another (civil and political). Despite the mounting evidence that sanctions were harming the very people which the nascent democracy aimed to benefit, they were vociferously supported by the pro-democracy forces within Haiti, led by the exiled President, who in all international fora called for a "real, complete and total embargo" as a means of forcing the military to step aside. The irony of using an international policy which violated rights as an instrument to advance their respect was never acknowledged; throughout the sanctions period, "human rights" only meant civil and political rights. Not a single one of the UN, OAS, or Non-governmental Organization (NGO) human rights reports written during the 1991-1994 made any observations pertaining to the violations of economic and social rights, and only a handful commented on the economic hardships of sanctions. In the highly politicized context of the time, this meant that humanitarian assistance to offset the impact of sanctions on the poor was viewed by some who championed the defence of human rights as a Trojan Horse which gave solace to the military and weakened the embargo. Those of us in UN agencies such as UNICEF, charged with administering humanitarian programs in Haiti, found ourselves attacked by the pro-coup elements and the pro-democracy forces. The former pronounced UNICEF to be an organization that supported sanctions by virtue both of being a UN agency and of maintaining silence on their corrosive effect, and whose staff had joined "the cowards who stab a child in the back without batting an eyelid" [3]. The latter accused us of siding with the military by providing aid which undermined the impact of the sanctions, and most particularly, by publishing a report, commissioned from the Harvard University School of Public Health by UNICEF and the UN Fund for Population Activities, which provided evidence that sanctions were among a complex set of factors contributing to a rise in child mortality. This report, in fact, caused an international uproar, due to a sensationalist headline in the *New York Times* which read "Study says sanctions kill up to 1,000 children a month" [4]. The White House immediately issued a statement attacking the report's credibility on the basis of a "questionable methodology," while those who considered themselves to be part of the international pro-democracy forces discredited UNICEF by suggesting the organization had allowed itself to be manipulated by the Haitian military.

THE PERSONAL TRAUMA OF MANAGING THE
HUMANITARIAN ANTIDOTE TO SANCTIONS' POISON

As head of UNICEF-Haiti (which constantly monitored the situation of children as part of its mandated daily work), and as a witness to sanctions' devastating effect on the vulnerable population, the strenuous denial of any such effect by the political and human rights actors gave me the feeling of living under a repressive dictatorship in which truth is suppressed and distorted by Orwellian double-speak. Giving interviews to the international media was obviously especially stressful under these circumstances. How far I felt from noble participation in "solving international problems of an economic, social, cultural or humanitarian character, and in promoting and encouraging respect for human rights!" Not only was I, a United Nations employee, witnessing horrendous violations of social and economic rights brought about by UN-supported sanctions, but was also unable to exercise my own right to freedom of expression.

Presenting a public face of denial was just one of many trade-offs we had to make between respecting UNICEF's mandate to protect children's rights, and respecting the political imperatives imposed by sanctions. Every programmatic decision, which in any other circumstance would be so routine that the head of office would not even need to know about it, let alone be involved, required that I evaluate the potential trade-off. Emblematic of these decisions was that which we in UNICEF Port-au-Prince took in reaction to the measles epidemic that rocked Haiti from 1991 to 1993. With the malnutrition and breakdown in vaccination programs resulting from sanctions, the fatality from measles was known to be high (up to 14 percent of cases in some health institutions), although we could not be certain how high. But we were certain that measles, an easily preventable disease, was debilitating or killing thousands of Haitian children. Although the humanitarian agencies had the funds available to launch a massive campaign to combat the epidemic, the majority decision of the agencies was to take no action out of respect for President Aristide's constitutional government, which was concerned that by preventing children's death from measles, the *de facto* military government would gain the support of poor parents; hence the outcome of the campaign would be a lessening in the population's support for a return to democracy. UNICEF opposed the majority decision, but nonetheless had to comply. We found ourselves in an impossible political and moral situation, not wanting to undermine democracy by risking the perception that UNICEF supported the military, but neither wanting to compromise a child's fundamental right to life. Ultimately, we found a middle ground which once again, brought the organization attacks from the pro-coup and the pro-democracy forces.

These attacks from both sides were a constant during the sanctions period, and served to undermine my spirit further. Since my actions derived largely from my own moral compass, supported by my dedicated Haiti team and the wider UNICEF mandate, I had no objective measure to judge the rightness of our chosen path. I was always acutely aware that any programmatic decision risked my personal reputation and, more importantly, that of UNICEF. While Headquarters invariably supported my commitment to our mandate, and was particularly instrumental in allowing the Harvard Study to be carried out and publicly released, the highly politicized national and international environment in which I operated meant that HQ was reluctant to give me written instructions. Even when I requested them, HQ answered most of my queries with "use your best judgement."

Although UNICEF-Haiti successfully managed an ever-increasing humanitarian program which, furthermore, complied with the political requirement that it be implemented entirely outside the sanctioned state structure, I felt personally party to the collective punishment of the innocent population, and complicity in its torture. This sense of personal responsibility for the malnutrition or death of thousands of Haitian children, which derived from my status as a United Nations staff member, together with the attacks against UNICEF for sticking to our mandate, the lack of guidance and the repressive silence I had to observe, brought me to the brink of resignation from the organization. The advice of a senior UNICEF colleague saved me from that fateful decision; he pointed out that while resigning and breaking my silence about sanctions' impact would doubtless assuage my own personal pain, it would do nothing to help the children of Haiti. First of all, the military regime would use my statement to justify their own propaganda against the embargo and UNICEF would lose all credibility with the democratic forces; secondly, UNICEF-Haiti's principal donors would flee the organization, drastically reducing the funding available to do even the little we were able to do; and, finally, my action might have wider political consequences for UNICEF, harming children elsewhere in the world. I found great comfort in this advice, and while it did not reduce the day-to-day pain of administering the humanitarian antidote to sanctions' poison, it did strengthen my sense of purpose and confidence in the path we, as an office, had chosen. Indeed, once sanctions had been lifted and democracy restored, a wide-ranging evaluation of UNICEF's program during the embargo period, which interviewed some 40 Haitian and international actors, indicated that in the view of these erstwhile critics:

> in the end, UNICEF's loyalty to its mandate . . . (represented) one of its greatest achievements during the 1992-1994 period. This allowed the organization an identity above partisan interests and enabled it to continue working through highly politicised times without being unnecessarily compromised [5].

EPILOGUE: PROCESSING THE TRAUMA

Although over time I was able to recognize that during 1992-1994 UNICEF's staff had implemented a humanitarian program which responded about as well as the contradictory political context would allow, I still could not process the guilty sense that I had been complicit in the violations of human rights which resulted from sanctions, particularly of the rights of Haiti's children. I felt an added sense of guilt from my inability to protect my own staff from the consequences of carrying out the UNICEF mandate in the highly politicized context of sanctions. Too often, although we seek a leadership rather than a protector role, the head of office is looked to as an omnipotent parent, responsible for making sure things work out. This was something I could not do, neither for the Haitian staff, who saw their country and their personal circumstances deteriorate around them, nor for the international staff, who were subject to the trauma of a sudden office of the UN Security Coordinator (UNSECOORD)-ordered evacuation of all dependents and "non-essential" staff of humanitarian agencies. The security menace which provoked the order to evacuate, whereby UN families were separated for a full year, and remaining UN staff in Haiti were confined to a hotel for four months, was never adequately explained to any of the heads of UN agencies operating in Haiti. Faced with a persistent refusal by the chief of the UN political mission, and by UNSECOORD, to specify the nature of the threat against UN staff, we were left to speculate that the real purpose of the evacuation had been to "send a message" to the military (who at that point, October 1993, were being particularly uncooperative in the negotiations), that something dramatic was about to happen so they had better agree to the terms being offered. If this indeed were the case, it would not have been the first time the mission of the humanitarian agencies was subjugated to the political imperative. On the occasion of the release of the UN/OAS Humanitarian Plan in March of the same year, we were advised to be "continuously sensitized as to the political implications of the humanitarian aid program on the negotiating process" [6].

The pain and humiliation of that evacuation, that left the UN the laughing stock of Port-au-Prince, the way in which we agency heads were treated as children who had do as we were told, no questions asked, and the sense of responsibility for dividing staff from their families, all created in me an anger, a bitterness, and a lamentable disrespect for security measures from which it took several years to recover. This unprocessed anger, together with my guilt and the overall sadness which being a witness to sanctions had created, meant that as late as 1996, I could not speak of sanctions without a catch in my throat, or tears welling in my eyes. I knew then that I could not take another UNICEF assignment until I had somehow come to terms with what had happened to me, and to Haiti, during the 1992-1994 period. I felt that documenting the experience would serve as the needed therapy. UNICEF granted me the sabbatical I asked for in 1997. I was also offered short-term psychological counseling, which pinpointed my grief as coming from the death of my idealistic belief in the nobility of serving the UN Charter. UN work, like any work, is a series of moral compromises.

Writing *Sanctions in Haiti* [2] greatly helped me process the trauma, and even more so when the manuscript was found to be of publishable quality. The official denial of my views' validity throughout the sanctions period had led me to think no one would believe or be interested in what I had to say. That the book ultimately had a modest influence on international sanctions policy further contributed to my recovery. Although I was often depressed for several years after leaving Haiti, I concluded my sanctions experience convinced that those of us who suffer personally as a consequence of our UN roles can greatly benefit by believing in ourselves, and by writing down our experience both to help our own recovery, and to help others to understand.

REFERENCES

1. Dr. Xavier Leus, PAHO/WHO Representative in Haiti 1988-1993, quoted in Tardif, Francine, *Regard sur l'Humanitaire: une analyse de l'experience haitienne dans le secteur sante entre 1991 et 1994,* Preface, Harmattan, Montreal, 1997.
2. For complete analysis of sanctions humanitarian and political impact inside Haiti, as well as additional information on issues treated in this essay, see Elizabeth D. Gibbons, *Sanctions in Haiti: Human Rights and Democracy under Assault,* Praeger Publishers with The Center for Strategic & International Studies, Westport, 1999.
3. Francois Latour, Editorial, *La Nouvelliste,* June 8, 1994 (Children's Day).
4. Howard French, Study Says Sanctions Kill 1000 Children a Month, *New York Times,* Section A1, November 9, 1993.
5. Kate Alley, John Richardson, and Jacques Berard, *UNICEF-Haiti Country Programme Evaluation, 1992-mid 1996: Programme Choices in Political Crisis and Transition,* UNICEF Evaluation Office, New York, 1996.
6. Ambassador Christopher Thomas, assistant secretary general, OAS, in *Aide Memoire* of March 4, 1993.

WATCHING FOR THE SIGNALS

Paul E. Arès

Something changed in me after the hostage taking. It was as if my nervous system had been shaken. It ranged from stomach disorders, numbness in my arms and legs to a strange internal vibration all over my chest like waves moving up and down, to a squeezing tightness in my head.

I kept looking for a cause . . . a physical cause because I didn't want to admit that it might be psychological. Every conceivable test came out negative. I finally saw a neurologist who diagnosed it as Post Traumatic Stress Disorder. Then I wondered how one was supposed to deal with that.

I had often felt that I was pushing myself to the limit both physically and emotionally. I may have done it once too often. I used to think that I could cope with absolutely anything and that working in areas of high risk would not affect me. You don't realize that stress is actually affecting you physically until much later. I kept thinking that my mind is sound so it has to be some kind of stomach disorder, or allergy. My body was clearly sending signals.

LOUD VOICES AND SHOOTING IN THE NIGHT

We were taken hostage in the northern part of Liberia in April 1999. I wasn't sure we were going to get out of this one alive (this was my second).

Around four o'clock in the morning we were awakened by gunfire somewhere in the distance. Then the shooting stopped and I laid awake listening. We had been assured by all levels that the area was safe. At five o'clock it started up again, but this time it was right outside the World Food Programme (WFP) compound. Within minutes we heard loud voices and the sound of an automatic weapon just outside the door. Armed men and boys barged in, herded us into the front room of our guesthouse, and demanded keys for all our vehicles. We were told to get into the cars and go with them.

There were eight of us and they kept us throughout the fighting, even as they retreated under fire from the advancing Liberian forces. We didn't know what they planned to do with us: did they want to use us as human shields? Did they want to take us with them into the bush and hold us longer? I remember going over in my mind the points I had read in a security document on what to do if you are a victim of a hostage taking so that I could guide myself, and the others with me. One of the rebels pointed an AK 47 at my face and said that he would "fire" me. What was most unnerving was the look in his eyes; they were glazed and he appeared to be on drugs. As the situation worsened I even thought about what it would be like to take a bullet in the chest, and I was preparing myself mentally for it.

After this second hostage taking, I really felt that it had to be the last. The emotions that you feel weeks and months after the experience can be quite draining. It certainly has a lasting impression. At the time, I was surprised at how cool and calm I was as I guided the team out of the worst part of it. I was also impressed by how calm everyone else remained and how we were able to agree on what course of action to take. There were times where we just had to flow with it; others when we had to take a decision and make a move. I kept looking for an opening, for an opportunity to get us out.

I watched the others in the group to see how they were coping and talked to them to see how they would respond. Some spoke readily, others withdrew. We all felt fear and knew that we had to stay together and handle it as a group. When the firing got heavy, we would all hunker down in some corner away from the windows and wait until it stopped. You think of many things as you are down on the floor: What am I doing here? How did we get caught up in this mess? I hope nobody gets hurt. How painful it would be for our families if we get killed.

A few times I had to make difficult calls and I simply did. People look to you for direction, especially in a crisis. If you are Head of Mission, you are the leader. You put your innermost fears and feelings aside and concentrate on helping your team through. It is hard on you, but you have to do it. You can't let events overtake you, you must make decisions and take risks.

There were very emotional moments. I can still hear a little girl crying in the darkness of a room where we had taken refuge during the fighting (our captors had herded us into a hospital where we joined some Liberians). The child's mother was trying to comfort her. I listened, then there was silence, and then it was the mother who started weeping. It was such a deep, sorrowful sound. I knew why it was so painful a cry. Liberia had recently come out of seven years of war and these people had just come back home to Voinjama full of hope. And now the fighting was starting up again. If she got out alive she would have to leave, one more time, with everything on her back, to seek asylum in Guinea.

Then I heard a loud explosion. The walls trembled, dust and plaster fell as a bomb exploded right next to the hospital. There was real panic as there was nowhere to go. One could only hope that the next shell would not come through the roof. Now, whenever I hear unusually loud voices or a bang, every nerve in my body goes on alert.

We did manage to wrest ourselves away from our captors during one of the battles, but it was only the next day, as the fighting continued, that we were evacuated.

CHILD SOLDIERS

We had been taken hostage by a group that included child soldiers, similar to the ones I had been meeting since January 1996. I got to know some of these child soldiers and youth combatants and have taken their pictures on a few occasions. The ones on the border between Liberia and Guinea used to refer to me as Mr. Paul. They would recognize me because I was one of the rare white persons who passed through.

These child soldiers are nevertheless dangerous and become vicious in combat. They are unpaid, undisciplined, completely unpredictable, and merciless when in battle or when pillaging. They are kids, teenagers, and yet they can use an automatic weapon like an experienced fighter. One moment they are in a tee shirt playing soccer in the street, the next they are aiming an AK 47 at you. Because they engage in non-conventional warfare, they are feared even by adult soldiers.

They are, in fact, "well-trained" and "brain-washed" by the older ones. In many instances, they are forcibly recruited and then subjected to a series of transforming initiations. There are "older brothers" responsible for the younger ones, all part of a command structure. For child combatants in the Revolutionary United Front (RUF) in Sierra Leone, the initiation involves breaking the bonds with the child's village or family. Some of the children have reported that they, or their "brothers," were brought back to the village and forced to kill or maim a member of their immediate family. This brings the child to a point of no return. Tough and inhuman persuasive measures are used, including drugs, to send child combatants into battle and commit atrocities. They are not mature enough to cope, resist, or to make any judgments on their own.

IT JUST CREEPS UP ON YOU

I used to think that I was kind of hardened to suffering and misery. As time passed, however, the opposite happened. You really deny yourself the right to feel their pain and grief. You learn to deal with it and hold it at bay while you are working. It's when you're alone that it creeps up on you.

There were many times in Liberia and later in Sierra Leone when I would look out the window of the plane or helicopter and wonder if this would be, as one field security officer put it, "our unlucky day." Will some rebel or militia shoot us down? Even though you know that the mission has been cleared and that it should be safe, it's a real concern. You learn to live with these feelings and to put them aside. On several occasions I have had to sign a document that absolves the UN of all responsibility. There is a lingering sense that the risk level is still quite high.

SIGNALS OF STRESS

Humanitarian workers living in countries in crisis and conflict are subjected to a great deal of stress. They deny themselves the right to feel tired and exhausted, and at times they are at the limits of their capabilities without realizing it. The stress manifests itself in different ways: some develop a drinking problem, others become aggressive or withdrawn. Some simply can't handle it, while others adjust. As managers we must be prepared to deal with the problems as they happen, or preferably even before they occur. We have to watch for the signals, watch for the symptoms such as those that crept up on me. Staff should not be sent to one hardship duty station after another. There should be a break so that their minds and bodies can recuperate. You need a normal family life for a while, to be closer to your children and not have to worry about their safety. National staff are in an even worse situation and so little, to date, has been done about it.

I could deal with taking calculated risks in order to do my work, but I found it far more difficult when the safety of my wife and children were at risk eight months later during the coup d'etat in Abidjan. For three days and nights there was constant shooting on both sides of our house. It wasn't right to put my family through this. I was part of the UN Security Management Team making decisions that would affect UN staff and their families. We were working on an evacuation plan knowing full well that it would be very difficult to implement. The threat to my family was harder on me than anything I had been exposed to. I'm sure it's the same for colleagues.

HOW DO I FEEL AS A MANAGER?

I traveled constantly throughout West Africa's coastal region to get a handle on the difficult situations and the problems that the countries and the UN faced. As a Regional Manager, it was very important to have first-hand knowledge of the whole region. I worried about the security of the WFP staff traveling and working up-country in some very difficult places in Liberia and Sierra Leone during and after the wars, which is why I have been to all of these places myself. I firmly believe that I cannot send staff to places where I would not dare to go myself. I should be able to identify with the situation of those out in the field and they should feel that I understand their work and share in the burden. I found that just being there for a day or two seemed to reassure them. They need to talk to someone who feels it the same way, someone who can relate. It certainly enabled me to make better decisions later on.

When I traveled to Freetown, Monrovia, and into the back hills, I always slept with one ear open as situations can change so quickly. Sensing the stress, we made sure that staff took their R&R and at times we had to rotate them out of a high-stress duty station. We also hired a stress counselor for the region to help people cope.

To share some of the responsibility, I always participated with the Country Director in taking decisions on difficult missions, where people could get hurt if things went wrong. There is always an element of risk in the work we do; we just have to gauge it properly and keep the risk to a minimum. As managers, we have to take our role very seriously because our staff place their security in our hands.

I DO THIS WORK BECAUSE I BELIEVE IN IT

Walking through a refugee or displaced persons camp is very moving for me. This is where I feel the importance of the work we do. Without the help of the UN, and many NGOs, these people would suffer even more and many would die. There are no words to describe what you feel when you come upon a family that has just crossed over from Sierra Leone, their children so severely malnourished that they are literally dying before your eyes. Some have spent weeks in the bush trying to get here. They come carrying those who have been raped or have had limbs cut off. And many have died along the way. What else can you feel other than a tremendous desire to help and bring immediate relief? For that moment you deny your right to feel so that you can get on with the job. But inside you feel torn apart: we have so much and they have so little. There are mixed feelings of guilt, despair, and empathy as they cling to you. The children out of sheer joy and awe because you are like a savior to them; the adults who are full of gratitude while trying to maintain some sense of dignity as they ask for more help.

I ask my staff to take their sunglasses off when they meet these people. They need to see your eyes, to recognize another human being and to be able to communicate, at least visually. We are all at the same level. You could just as well have been born here and have to face the same miserable fate. Count your blessings and share some of them.

I do this type of work because I believe in what we are trying to achieve and experience a tremendous sense of satisfaction in actually making a difference in someone's life. You see severely malnourished children on one trip and, when you return a month later they are running around, smiling. It's good to be able to see people—poverty stricken refugees, displaced, and school children—eat and stay healthy because you and your team have been able to provide them with food. It gives you a greater sense of purpose, certainly a meaningful way of earning a living.

I have always felt safe when traveling up-country as the people knew that WFP brought them food. I rarely felt threatened. But that is changing. In Sierra Leone, the RUF no longer sees the UN as neutral, but rather on the side of the government, their enemy. Under these circumstances, the security of staff is even more critical than before. This change in attitude toward the UN impacts our decision-making. On two occasions we decided to opt out of convoys when we were not convinced that the situation on the ground was safe enough. Both times the soldiers in the convoys were taken hostage.

It's on the front line that you can really see the people and organizations such as Médecins Sans Frontières (MSF), the International Committee of the Red Cross (ICRC), and the many NGOs who are prepared to take great risks to help those most in need. I have a lot of respect for these people and the organizations they work for. They labor under very difficult conditions, and their health and lives are often at risk. They meet the worst cases: the massively traumatized, the dying, the maimed and the starving. They are also the ones who will be taken hostage, get caught in a crossfire, attacked, killed, raped or aggressed, get malaria and other diseases, or suffer from stress and trauma. There are no comforts of home in these duty stations; just barely enough to get by. In crisis, there is no distinction between the work week and the weekend; it just never ends.

Some of the humanitarian UN agencies are also there sharing the front line and the back hills. We all work together and face the same problems. There is a price to pay for taking risks and for taking on some of the pain and trauma of the people we wish to help. It is hard on our bodies and on our minds.

NOTHING PREPARED ME

Linda Champoux-Arès

Nothing prepared me for that phone call. Nothing! I listened in disbelief as I was told that my husband had been taken hostage in northern Liberia. They didn't know who had taken him or why. It must have been difficult for Mohammed to make that call. He spoke calmly, slowly; he gave me time to collect myself. One of Paul's colleagues had also been taken hostage and we discussed briefly how best to inform his wife, Nancy.

Within seconds of hanging up, Nancy called. She had heard about the hostage taking. News travels fast in the field! I did what Mohammed had done for me. I went over each detail as he had told me. I assured her that the office was trying to reach her as we spoke and I suggested that we spend the day together. Then I hung up and cried. It was overwhelming. I felt completely alone and I didn't know how I was supposed to handle this. I realized that I might never see Paul again.

I had been informed that this incident would not be reported to the media since it was possible that the captors wanted a platform for their cause. Because of this I decided to wait before telling our children and his parents. Our youngest son had spent a year with us in Abidjan. There had been a few uncomfortable experiences with groups of older boys and more and more car hijackings and house break-ins. Then one day he came home and told us about a friend's father who had been killed outside his house. After that he reminded us to lock the doors each time we got into the car and he no longer wanted to walk the streets on his own. The following year we sent him to school in Canada and I was so relieved that he would not have to live through this.

I decided to carry on my day as planned with one of my good friends. Nancy joined us and we kept our cell phones out waiting for news. The Regional Manager for GTZ (Gesellschaft für Technische Zusammenarbeit) was a personal friend of Nancy's and since someone from their organization happened to be in Voinjama at the time, he was able to give her additional updates. At the end of each call, he set the time for the next one.

I knew Paul's office was doing everything they could to get them out safely and to keep us informed. I also knew that they didn't need a worried wife calling every hour, but I might have had we not had the GTZ contact. He was getting information directly by satellite telephone. We were so appreciative. I don't know how to express how helpless and vulnerable we felt. Afterwards I asked some of the women how they had coped, what they had done. One of them, for whom this was a second experience, had immediately arranged for someone to care for her young children. She knew that she would be too preoccupied. Life does "stop" for the families.

Late in the afternoon, we received the news that the hostages had broken away from their captors and were safe inside the HCR (UN High Commissioner for Refugees) compound. That evening, however, my relief changed to fear when Paul called. I could hear shooting in the background and I could tell from his voice that they were not out of danger. The Liberian government would not give clearance for the UN helicopter to go into Voinjama for fear that it would be shot down. I did not sleep that night. I had no piece of mind until I got the call that he was finally safe in Monrovia.

What would I have done if the news had not been good? Who would I have turned to? In the field, we don't have that network of family and old friends that one needs in difficult times. I thought of the other spouses who one day would have to live through this. In crisis situations, WFP's attention is focused on getting their people out safely. They set up a crisis center in Rome to coordinate their work. There should be someone in that room dedicated to the family since we are also part of the crisis.

On a human level we can't forget the families of those caught in dangerous situations. We cannot assume that they are coping. We have to take that extra step because some will need to be cared for and comforted. I was lucky; Paul came back unharmed. As the situation becomes more and more dangerous for humanitarian workers, I think that we have to do something to prepare families for that phone call.

10

Stress and Mine Action

Martin Barber

In 1992 two young British officers, who had left the Army to help organize mine clearance work near Kabul in Afghanistan, were using a Russian tank to push a large roller across suspected mined areas. They were taking turns in joining their Afghan colleague in the tank. The one in the tank saw something up ahead. He called to his colleague to look. It looked like a mine. They decided to test the roller. Three of them were now in the tank. They moved slowly ahead. The roller exploded the mine as planned, but, unknown to them, the mine had been linked to a large demolition charge placed directly under where the tank was expected to be. The charge exploded, penetrating the gear box inspection belly plate and setting the tank on fire. The three men escaped from the tank with horrible burns. The two British men were evacuated by air to London. The Afghan man was cared for in a Kabul hospital. All three died of their injuries within two weeks.

This is the most dramatic mine accident which took place during my six-year association with the mine action program in Afghanistan. But it was by no means the only one. There are now about 3,000 men involved in mine clearance in Afghanistan. Every year since 1990 an average of five people have lost their lives and more than 20 have been injured in accidents while they worked.

Every accident is a traumatic event for the surviving deminer, for his family, for the colleagues in his team who witnessed the incident, for the paramedics who have to intervene immediately, and even for deminers in other teams, who are reminded once again of the risks they take every day while they are at work. So how do the individuals and the organizations involved in demining cope with these traumatic events, and with the stress of the daily work environment?

A rapid poll of major mine clearance organizations currently employing deminers produced a wide range of responses.[1]

The organizations most involved in mine clearance and minefield survey work come from two quite distinct traditions and disciplines: the military and the humanitarian.

---

[1] I define a "deminer" as somebody whose job brings them regularly into close proximity of live mines. The individual may be prodding for mines, using a mine detector, handling a dog looking for mines, or working on the disposal of unexploded ordnance.

THE MILITARY TRADITION

The organizations with a more military background tend to see mine clearance work as basically similar to other military work. The deminer is exposed to risks and stresses which are similar to those facing all military personnel. Indeed some organizations clearly try to market their mine clearance work as routine, and not inherently more dangerous than many other activities.

One agency responded to our enquiry as follows:

> Demining may be seen as being "stressful," but it should not actually be stressful. It is more agricultural or horticultural. Staff are very carefully and continuously monitored (every 10 minutes or so) on their attention spans and drills. They also have 10-minute breaks every 30 minutes. They are all part of teams, camaraderie, and so on. Most are aged 23–33, most come from a military/militia background and are demobilized soldiers. Most will never see a fellow/team casualty, though all will have extensive and repeated first aid training. All have the latest equipment for detecting mines and all have seen a demonstration of just how good the personal protective clothing is. Most, if not all, will have discussed mine clearance (perceived to be dangerous), with their families before deciding to join a training course. In the event of a team casualty, the agency immediately conducts an accident investigation and then everyone gets back to work—led onto the actual minefield and into lanes by our international and senior staff. During desk officer/director visits, we also clear mines on our hands and knees. The greatest stress is probably financial pressure from extended families—as deminers are often the only breadwinners. Delays in funding contracts mean that deminers always work with the threat of redundancy or pay cuts looming over them.

Another agency took basically the same line:

> Our approach to demining is to put the deminer into a very controlled and structured environment and ensure high levels of discipline and quality management. We benefit from the fact that the majority of our organization is made up of ex-soldiers (not engineers), many with combat experience. Within this environment we have reduced the role of a deminer to "just another job." There are, of course, many occupations which have varying levels of risk associated with them and, as with demining, subject to training, operating procedures and quality management this risk is reduced to a very low level.

THE HUMANITARIAN VIEW

Humanitarian organizations with a long tradition of humanitarian work, and that have recently become involved in managing mine clearance operations, have a different perspective from their military counterparts. Although I sense that there is no unanimity, even among the staff of individual organizations, some do recognize that demining can be highly stressful, and believe that they have a duty to provide advice and counseling which will prepare their personnel for the experience, and assist them in coping with the traumatic stress that may follow their involvement in an incident. The following extract is from the response provided by one mine clearance organization with a humanitarian background;

We have no institutionalized procedure for providing counseling to personnel before they take up their assignments. (That is if you mean by counseling a systematic procedure that addresses [deep] emotional aspects of the hazards of the work the deminers will do.) However, all international personnel are briefed on general aspects of working in stressful environments; but the emphasis is on the practicalities rather than the emotional and personal aspects.

We have provided counseling for injured deminers, and for deminers who have been exposed to extremely stressful tasks. International deminers, as well as locally recruited deminers from one of our national programs assisted international forensic experts in Bosnia excavating mass graves. These teams were provided with professional support by a psychologist during and after the work. It is not clear how effective this was. Some of the deminers later stated that they felt that the counseling was inadequate. One explanation for this may be that this experience broke new ground, both for the psychologist and for our organization. Equally, the concept of counseling appears to have been unfamiliar to male professional deminers with a military background. We have now contracted a team of counselors, with competence in post-traumatic stress work, who are on standby for deployment when needed.

Injured deminers are offered counseling as part of their rehabilitation. Injured deminers may also be included in our organization's post-war psychosocial rehabilitation program for civilians.

Families of deminers who have died in the service of our organization have not systematically been offered counseling, but they are provided with general practical support.

We know that some of our deminers have experienced post-traumatic stress, either from particular experiences or from working under dangerous conditions in general. We have an ongoing debate within the organization over whether we need to introduce better procedures to monitor our staff, so that we can intervene appropriately if required. For us one of the most important issues is: how do we ensure that deminers who may have been working at the job for some years maintain the mental alertness they need to avoid accidents? Should we institutionalize rotation between the stressful work of actual clearance and other less stressful support tasks?

This communication illustrates how seriously some organizations are now taking this issue, but also how uncertain they are about how to respond to the evident needs of their personnel. The last paragraph raises an issue that has troubled the managers of all demining teams since such work began. The Director of one of the major mine clearance agencies in Afghanistan, who has employed over 1,000 deminers for several years, came up with some interesting observations. He believes that deminers become more prone to lapses of concentration and risky behavior, if they are under stress for reasons unconnected with their work environment. He believes that a highly disciplined, predictable, and well-organized environment helps deminers to maintain their concentration. Recently, funding for the program ran out altogether. Until new money became available, some teams were obliged to work without salaries. He noted a rise in the normal number of accidents during this period, which he ascribes to worries about the well-being of families when the bread winner is unable to send the usual monthly remittance. This finding echoes the view of one of the "military" organizations that the greatest stress for deminers can be uncertainty about their job prospects! He also believes that illiterate men from the countryside have better concentration, and are less prone to accidents than educated men from the cities. He ascribes this to their tough physical upbringing and their belief that they are unusually fortunate to have obtained a relatively well paid and regular job. It would be interesting to test this informal observation by systematic study.

Managers regularly take the painful decision that the "nerve" of an individual deminer has "gone," and that he is now a danger to himself and others. The deminers themselves sometimes reach the same conclusion. But they may feel pressure from their families to continue in the work because of the lack of other opportunities. Is there any scientific basis for this kind of decision? Can the "symptoms" of "lost nerve" be described, learned by managers and applied by them to their teams? Should managers receive formal training in this task, or should their teams be submitted to regular review by a qualified counselor/psychologist? Should there be an agreed maximum period for people to do this kind of work on a daily basis? Or should demining be considered as just another regular job, which the employer should make as routine as possible?

These issues are ones which I believe organizations involved in mine action should consider, with the help of experts from the field of traumatic stress. Some agencies may understandably be reluctant to take this on, fearing that such a debate would open a "Pandora's box," and even prompt suggestions that they might have a legal obligation to provide psychosocial care for their personnel if international standards were to be developed in this field. Some of these agencies pointed out in their responses that most of their deminers had participated in one way or another in the wars which saw the mines being laid, and that they had surely witnessed more traumatic events during the course of those wars than during their work as deminers. This may well be true, but I believe it would be in everybody's interest, and most of all in the interest of those who do this work, if we discovered whatever we can about the psychological processes which influence the behavior of deminers, both during their usual work and in response to the traumatic experience of an accident.

Voice

AN EYE WITNESS IN CAMBODIA

Becky Jordan, Handicap International, Cambodia, 1996

There are certain stories that should not be permitted to collect dust and be forgotten with their details fading even into dreams or nightmares.

What happened today has become a sinister ritual. Yet another mine victim. Flesh and bones. First aid . . . [But] for me, this was no ritual. . . . In fact, there was nothing for me to do other than violently throw up, before all and sundry, outside the house where the young bonze had been injured. It is possible that the sight of a foreign, white volunteer throwing up her lunch will provide more matter for gossip in the villages than the accident itself. . . .

Russ, a friend of mine, provided first aid and afterwards reproached himself with having made mistakes. But he was alone and he got on with it. We just looked on like a load of idiots, totally sick and paralyzed.

About 5 inches of white bone projected from the wound. Above it a mass of dark red, burned, mangled flesh. It had been exposed to the fresh air for only 5 minutes, yet it was already horrible. The young bonze was barely 16 years old, swathed in his saffron robe and with his head shaven like his colleagues. . . . How young he looked. He was probably not committed for life, and just as well because now it was no longer possible for him, because a bonze has to be intact, or so I have been told. Now, thus depleted, "Baï Lao! Ont mien huiy! Finito!"

I think I shall go and see him tomorrow after he has come out of surgery that will give him some chance of walking again. (He will live) but I can already imagine him dragging around with that block of distorted flesh where his knee ought to be.

My job will be to do the paperwork and ensure that he is fitted with a proper prosthesis in one of our workshops, but I shall never forget that sight. And I know from my own physical and moral suffering that the most important thing to do today in Cambodia is to work to rid these people of antipersonnel landmines!

I wanted to be strong and to help but, above all, I felt the burden of my own uselessness. And I am left with the horrible feeling that I was capable of nothing better than vomiting and, what is more, of feeling better for it!

My God, why do You permit us to see any need to create, produce, distribute, sell for profit, and disseminate millions of these revolting weapons? Why? Is mine disposal possible? Will we be able to combine the quality of our minds and our intelligence, our money, our hands and arms for this humanly essential task? Please.

126

At least let no civilian ever again see his foot evaporate into thin air like that, reduced to nought but 5 inches of white bone and a mass of mangled, gory flesh where a knee ought to be.

There is no way of ending this story on a dignified note. This is the end yet it will never stop. We really must rid the planet of these mines.

11

Handle With Care:
A View from the Staff Counsellor's Office

Jean-Guy Morisset

THE SPIRIT OF SWISSAIR 111

As the UN Staff Counsellor on emergency assignment to Halifax, I witnessed a long, painful week unfolding for the families. This is where I first encountered "the spirit of Swissair 111," a spirit akin to the highest ideals of the United Nations. It seemed to envelop the members of our "UN family," the families of the victims, and the families of Halifax. They worked together as a team: the press and the police, the hotel clerk and the owner of the photo service, the social workers and the mothers, and the children and the fishermen. This community had lost many of its own at sea and had cared for the victims of the Titanic. A few generations ago the town of Halifax had been flattened when a munitions ship exploded in its friendly harbor. Everyone seemed to understand the pain of grief and no one was afraid to care. They all stood by to help.

Three years later, the same caring feeling suddenly emerged at a United Nations memorial honoring victims of the helicopter crash in Mongolia. For a brief moment, everyone focused on the spirit of those who believed in making it a better world, who did not run away from human pain, who were concerned enough to make a difference day by day. For a brief moment, propelled by grief, we rose above the budget lines, the national boundaries, the bureaucratic pettiness. For a brief moment, we remembered who we really are, we the peoples. For a brief moment, we dared to care and the pain was almost palpable.

HONOR THE DEAD: CARE FOR THE LIVING

And why, I thought, is it so difficult to get our administrative machines to act consistently in a caring way? Why do we turn our backs on the psychological challenges of peacekeeping missions and complex humanitarian emergencies? Why are we so reluctant to find funds and provide real support to those who are taking on these challenges in the field or in the bureaucratic jungles of headquarters offices? Why are we so sadly lacking when it comes to supporting and encouraging and counseling our own people? Why must our staff so often feel that no one cares?

How often will we grieve before we learn, as an organization, that those who live and work with us must be handled with care?

BEFORE, DURING, AFTER

Back in 1990, staff counselors were already concerned about the stress and trauma that came with the United Nations' new efforts in peacekeeping missions. It was immediately apparent that civilians were being thrown into high-risk environments that had normally been left to trained soldiers. Based on the lessons learned by the military, however, a number of preventive measures had already been identified. These new high-risk assignments required some serious pre-departure training and expert psycho-social support in the field combined with post-mission debriefings and follow-up. Prepare, support, and debrief: a simple, proven model that is still not applied after ten years of hard knocks and errors dearly paid for.

THE HIGH COST OF DENIAL

Maybe we just don't have the organizational fortitude to face certain facts. Maybe this is just a massive case of denial, the same kind that is operating in the AIDS pandemic. Maybe it's still too difficult to keep focusing on the loneliness, the terror of being targeted from both sides, the abuse, the horror of the refugee camps, the family breakups, the alcohol and drug problems, the fatal accidents, the mines, the orphaned children, the abandoned spouses, the wasted lives. There is a price to pay, the diplomats will say, for attempting the impossible in outrageous circumstances. Partly true, but somewhat facile and irresponsible. In fact, the huge burden of personal hardship, with its concomitant financial waste, could be considerably reduced if it were managed rather than denied.

BURUNDI ON MY MIND

As a 21-year-old volunteer teacher heading out to Burundi with Canadian University Services Overseas (SUCO), I felt that I was taking a fair amount of risk. In 1965, many countries were testing their newly-acquired independence and I witnessed three coups d'état during my two-year assignment. Many of my students lost their parents and I remember how I feared, standing by the closed gates at night, that a spear might come whistling out of the dark. The fact is, I was never threatened, targeted, or insulted. There was plenty to deal with, emotionally and physically, but I felt respected and supported. And to this day, I reap new lessons from this unique experience.

As I reflect on the selection process I had gone through, the pre-departure training sessions, the support systems on site and the return process, I realize that I was surrounded by a lot of caring people. Whatever the personal costs and the problems, I did not feel that I was wasting my time or that my life was at risk because no one cared. Today, from the vantage point of my fifth floor United Nations office, it makes me sick at heart to see how people can be thrown into harm's way with virtually no preparation, no psychosocial support on site, little understanding of security procedures, and no assistance in coming back to a "normal" world that can never be the same for them.

Take a look at my office. After more than ten years of discussions, committees, reports, personal letters, proposals, recommendations, draft policies, and job descriptions I have accumulated about twenty feet of files on the topic. After four years of ardent pleading and explaining I actually succeeded in obtaining one "P-3" post for a "Staff Counsellor Peacekeeping." Two years later, this post was abolished in four minutes, with no discussion, no explanations, and no regrets, in the midst of a bureaucratic shuffle that did not concern my office. We had fully developed a Mission-Readiness Program and passed it on to the training service. This program was simply dropped, again with no discussion and not a trace of care. My personal definition of "organizational denial" was taking shape.

ERRORS IN RWANDA

You may recall the Rwanda debacle, when hundreds of terrified staff were haphazardly extracted from an instant war zone, the same war zone that led to a Canadian General's well-publicized brush with Post Traumatic Stress Disorder. Three months before, we were heading for Nairobi to contact expert resources and develop some professional readiness to handle possible critical incidents in the region. Bear in mind that we had already experienced a number of murderous car-jackings and abductions. This had profoundly affected a number of our staff. Records show that the project was not only overruled but it was ridiculed. When all hell broke loose soon after, a Staff Counsellor was rushed to Nairobi with two experts graciously offered by the Canadian armed forces. They faced painful improvisation as they tried to help staff, families, and children. My definition of "organizational denial" was reinforced.

EASIER TO DENY

The organizations who put staff in these situations, whether they are national, non-governmental, or international, must eventually come to terms with the long-term welfare of their staff. They must manage trauma suffered in the line of duty, psychological hardship as well as broken legs, in addition to less newsworthy pain and suffering such as depression, alcohol and substance abuse, grief, nightmares, and the loss of appetite. The present organizational denial is costing us a fortune in sick leave, disability pensions, accelerated turnover rates, administrative errors, accidents, and dysfunctional work units. This is a well-known secret. Quite incredibly, this significant financial loss is never accounted for in budget exercises, for the simple reason that it does not fit into any of our antiquated budget lines.

Such is the legacy of untreated trauma, big and small, from those who suffered World War I and World War II. We may see the legacy passing on from generation to generation in the refugee camps. However, we may not have noticed as it moved from generation to generation of managers in international organizations. Struggling with denial, they can only give sporadic and disorganized attention to a number of painful issues, such as the trauma of helicopter accidents and abductions, the abuse of managerial authority, sexual harassment or, of more recent notoriety, workplace violence. The attention peaks when hearts are wrenched open by another tragic accident or the senseless murder of a dedicated colleague. Photographs haunt us, the Secretary-General walks from the memorial holding the hand of a courageous young girl and we briefly take note that we are dealing with real people here, and real lives. For a moment we agree that we should be as careful as we possibly can in managing our human resources.

REINVENTING THE WHEEL, AGAIN

Unfortunately, in our panic, we rush into action and have no time to review all the pieces that were put in place by others, in and out of the organization. As a consequence, meager resources are dilapidated in the process of reinventing the proverbial wheel. For example, after ten years of starts and stops, you will still find well-meaning people with impossible deadlines writing yet again a paper on mission readiness, creating booklets that already exist, and reinventing job descriptions rather than consolidating existing services and providing new resources to match increasing needs.

WHEN WILL THEY EVER LEARN?

In line with the simple design of helping staff throughout the full cycle of a mission assignment, how much progress have I seen in the past ten years? First of all, precious little mission readiness gets done, and it usually rests on the extraordinary efforts of a few dedicated individuals who eventually move on. Most of our civilian peacekeepers and humanitarian workers, staff or volunteer, novice or experienced, are not getting a single day of formal preparation. Quite ironically, military personnel, who make a career of facing high risk situations, get more preparation than the civilians who go to the same area. As a matter of fact, many aid workers operate in areas where member states refuse to send their troops. This rather casual approach to readiness has not improved significantly, despite the fact that civilian loss of life has overtaken military loss of life in many United Nations operations.

Psychosocial support in the field is still not an established practice. In the past two years, the United Nations has placed staff counselors in three missions, but the vast majority of the missions have no such support. The United Nations High Commissioner for Refugees (UNHCR) will soon have regional counselors in the field and has trained peer counselors. The World Food Programme (WFP), in the wake of the airplane crash that took 23 lives, now has 6 part-time counselors in the field and is also taking rapid strides in the area of peer counseling. Stress counselors accompany safety teams in the field to provide an initiation to stress management. Overall, we are beginning to recognize the validity of psychosocial support for our staff but resources are sparse, compared to other functions which have a guaranteed place in every mission budget, such as financial, personnel, procurement, or legal support.

The debriefing phase is still getting the least attention. I haven't heard of any systematic debriefing since the pilot sessions organized by the Staff Counsellor's Office in 1995. The word "debriefing," in this context, takes on a broad meaning. It includes a process wherein staff are asked to share their experience and contribute to lessons learned. It also includes a review of health-related issues and should provide an opportunity to consider the impact of positive experiences and professional growth as well as the impact of stress and critical incidents and exposure to physical disease. In addition, this process should provide for guidance and support for appropriate reinsertion or reassignment within the Organization. Unfortunately, staff are largely left to their own devices at this stage.

WHO NEEDS DEBRIEFING?

In fact, the most common complaint I have heard from mission appointees is that they had no one to talk to, even in extremely stressful circumstances or after a critical incident. The following is a small sample of situations which were reported to the Staff Counsellor's Office in New York. In all these cases, a sound debriefing process would have eased the hardship of the staff and probably reduced administrative costs in the final analysis. There was, for example, the case of the young lady whose friend was shot dead in front of her and who was herself shot at and left for dead. There were staff who survived a wild car-jacking or an armed ambush and had to nurse bullet wounds for years. Others survived helicopter crashes where close friends perished and got no help in dealing with the psychological trauma. There were also cases of colleagues who were not able to get back home in time to talk to a dying spouse or parent.

Some came to our office because of sudden episodes of sadness and crying and others could not forget a lonely airport arrival and an empty home. Those who happened to visit the office after a mission have told numerous stories of abusive supervisory practices, alcohol abuse, Kalishnikovs pressed to people's heads, and daily shellings.

Some of the staff members in the above situations were questioned within the framework of investigative procedures, but they all returned from mission without the benefit of a systematic debriefing process or routine counseling support. They had no one to talk to.

PUSHING FORWARD

Immediately following the tragic Swissair incident three years ago, the office of Human Resources Management created a working group to help develop a more caring approach to tragedies that involved our staff. Even though the issues were not easy to face, many people were eager to give their time and efforts and a very special spirit of dedication emerged. This inter-organizational group has produced a "Handbook for Actions in Cases of Death in Service" and introduced the practice of assigning one contact person from the organization to provide focused assistance for the family of deceased staff. This has worked very well and the handbook has proven to be of genuine help to many staff trying to achieve some measure of poise and dignity in dealing with the loss of colleagues. Recommendations of the group led to a more compassionate stance in the administration of the education grant benefit, to give one example. Memorial ceremonies were designed to reflect the character of the United Nations family and pay tribute to the ideals and accomplishments of our staff.

DRIVEN BY DENIAL OR GOVERNED BY CARE?

In addressing the day-to-day needs of staff, Staff Counsellors are typically struggling with very meager resources to serve large client groups. They are learning to use the Internet to share their knowledge and experience and often collaborate across organizational boundaries. They often form effective and caring teams with managers to resolve complex issues involving performance improvement, mental health, or alcohol abuse.

The sad truth remains that, in terms of resource allocation, we are still facing an obstinate refusal to address the mental health and security of staff in a fiscally responsible and efficient fashion. Legal exposure is created by the failure to provide adequate preparation and support and it is highly doubtful that this would be tolerated in the private sector. At this point in my career, short of writing it off as malevolence and ignorance, I have concluded that, in a very human fashion, our managers are simply overwhelmed and frightened by these issues. As mentioned above, many of them have inherited a culture that denied their own trauma and pain. Nevertheless, it is not too soon to acknowledge the wealth of research provided by the World Health Organization (WHO) and the International Labour Organization (ILO) concerning mental health and the workplace. We have learned enough. We should now know better.

Many of us have been touched deeply by "the spirit of Swissair 111," by colleagues' capacity to recognize the suffering of others and by their resolve to show up and deal with it. Therein lie the deepest values of the United Nations and these values should not be reserved for memorials. They need to be freed up to celebrate the lives and the daily work of every member of the United Nations family. Every person deserves to be handled with care. As WHO so ably phrases it, let us "DARE TO CARE."

Voices

SEPARATION FROM FAMILIES
Kim Robinson

In July 1999, the Victorian Foundation for Survivors of Torture (Australia) was contracted by AusAID to provide supportive counseling and debriefing for the UN Assistance Mission in East Timor (UNAMET) staff. These debriefings revealed a high level of distress, anxiety, and fear. Many reported feeling re-traumatized as a result of having been on previous UN missions, which were dangerous and exposed them to violence and war.

UNAMET staff reported that there had not been adequate support or debriefing available in previous missions. Staff reported a hostile attitude by some senior UN staff toward debriefing, and a lack of information or offers of support for re-entry to their country of origin. Many perceived the UN as unable or unwilling to prioritize their emotional needs.

One man described having lost four close colleagues in helicopter crashes in Africa, and his resulting terror at having to travel by helicopter in East Timor. Many reported marital breakdown and feelings of loss due to separation from children and family.

> Family? How do we keep in touch?! You work long enough for the UN and you don't have a family. Problem solved. (UNV)

> My son drew a picture of the family at school. He left me out. I feel so terrible about that. (UN International staff)

> My daughter spoke to me on the phone and said "Mum you have to come to school tomorrow to look at my school books with the teacher." I replied that I couldn't, that I was working far away, and she asked me "Are you my real mother," and I said "Of course I am, but your Auntie Rose can go with you to school." She said OK. I got off the phone and cried. (UN International staff; widow with four children)

Many staff actively took up the opportunity for one to one counseling, and reported finding relief in being able to talk to someone about their stress and any critical incidents. A number of people were experiencing the effects of cumulative trauma as a result of work on previous missions. For some, a critical incident in East Timor trigger memories and fears they had experienced in Angola, Bosnia, Rwanda, and other places.

Group workshops and open forums often provided an opportunity to describe what people were experiencing in the mission, including feelings about issues such as security, coping with fatigue, frustrations with the administration, and difficulties keeping in contact with home. The Staff Support Team played a role in permitting people to articulate and cope better with their fears. It is thus recommended that clinicians equipped with counseling and debriefing skills be available for staff on future mission.

THE STORY OF SOMEBODY WHO WENT OUT
TO LEARN ABOUT FEAR . . .*

Petra Miczaika

Angola. Outside the office, not very far away, there is a massive explosion. Nobody in the room moves and I continue with the discussion on stress management and the effects of trauma. Even my heart did not miss a beat, at one with the behavior of our staff. The eyes around the table show different levels of traumatization. There are open eyes and eyes so hurt that they will not let me in at all.

This is my working day in Kuito, a destroyed city in central Angola. Early in the morning we have left Luanda on an old B727, sitting in the dark hull of the aircraft. There is no light except for a lonely bulb dangling from the ceiling. We are a small group of people and, for once, I am not traveling alone. One of our peer support volunteers is helping me and translates for staff who do not speak English.

The sad face of a man on the plane attracts my attention. After our bumpy arrival in Kuito—the airstrip had holes so big that the airplane rocked and groaned—I understand. In the luggage compartment lies the dead body of a little girl, his daughter, who had been sent to Germany for medical treatment—unsuccessfully.

After this long day in Kuito, both my travel companion and I are emotionally distraught and physically exhausted to a point that I refuse to go out the next day at dawn to yet another location. I need a break and a day of normal office work to be able to confront more despair and trauma in yet another Angolan city.

Democratic People's Republic of Korea (DPRK). When the ancient Russian plane touches down in Pyongyang I am surprised to see a man hosing down the tires of the plane with water. There is a hissing sound which explains the action and leaves me worried. The plane, whenever it leaves Beijing, is packed with mountains of goods and food. Inside, beautiful female voices chant socialist songs to distract from the dilapidated interior and paralyze the anxious brain. Perfect service gives us an introduction to the strangest country on earth.

As a German national, I had traveled to East European countries before the fall of the Berlin wall and made friends there. DPRK made me face my limits. How could I be a Staff Counselor to national staff if staff were not allowed to communicate with me except on the work level? It took two trips to realize that meaningful contact

*Das Maerchen von einem, der auszog das Fuerchten zu lernen (Gebr. Grimm).

can be made on the nonverbal level. Into the team building exercise I smuggled socialist slogans which harmonized with my objectives and had staff participating enthusiastically. International staff listened patiently to my explanations of the dangers faced by national staff and changed their feelings of being rejected and judged.

Loneliness and isolation challenge even the hardiest introverted staff member in our sub offices. After a first winter in hotels without heating and electricity, with temperatures below zero in their rooms, staff spoke up and caused a change in their work and life environments. Work for me in DPRK is winter work, when staff feel more isolated and desperate. The WFP pub animates the lonely soul and increases team spirit, and the regular visit of the Staff Counselor brings stimulation and the opportunity for sharing and expression.

Kosovo. The Serbian driver who takes me from Belgrade to the Kosovo border scrutinizes his waiting Albanian WFP colleague cautiously and, looking aside, even shakes hands. Embarrassed silence. Then some instructions and off we go across the parking lot to the waiting car, waving good-bye a last time. The atmosphere is grim and grey, and the dirty snow and the cold deepen the gloom of the military controls.

Diversity on several levels is the big issue in the Balkans. Privately, staff share with me that they have friends among the enemies, because before they used to be neighbors and business partners. All sides feel treated badly and are not yet ready for change and forgiveness. In communication exercises I have them face their judgmental attitudes and find denial and resistance so high that it leaves me speechless. As in the other countries I visit, the country as a nation is traumatized. Unlike some other countries I visit, the expression of anger and aggression is literally simmering at the surface.

The individual stories of our staff are similar on all sides. They talk about the pain of life as a refugee, of the loneliness away from their homes and families, of the lost dreams of an education and of the loss of loved ones.

Wherever I travel for WFP I meet wonderful staff, dedicated to the point of stubbornness in their attitudes and determination. National staff express their gratitude for my visits and the hope that they seem to instill. How often do I wish I had a magic wand, because my visits are short and rare.

12

United Nations Human Rights Field Officers

Ben Majekodunmi*

UNANSWERED QUESTIONS

How do you react when month after month, you return to the same prison and see, with no improvement, thousands of men and women detained in rooms so small that they cannot even sit on the floor at the same time? What do you feel as you count the scattered bodies of hundreds of massacred human beings? Do you ask "is my presence not a little late?" What is your reaction at the end of the day when you finish your report and go home? Does showing no emotion mean that you don't care that much? How can you begin to claim that you work for human rights when this silence is all the reaction you have when confronted by the intense pain of so many?

A man comes to your office with information of human rights violations committed against people in the community. Later that day, the man is himself arrested, beaten and thrown into detention as punishment for contacting UN Human Rights Officers (HROs). Your efforts on his behalf show no results and, as you walk away, his cell door clangs shut. What happened to the "do no harm" principle of human rights work? Your bottom line "don't make things worse," is now flapping loose in the wind. Would it not be better to just pack up your things and leave, to stop giving people false hopes and expectations?

Ending months of work, your office has prepared a thorough report, detailing serious violations across the country—summary executions, forced disappearances, rape, the recruitment of underage children. Your Operation's Chief presents the report to the host country's Head of State and to the Ministers of Justice and Defense. You await a response from the Government indicating a determination to end impunity and seek respect for human rights. It never comes. The State authorities have other priorities. What the operation requires is the concerted support of other UN bodies, a loud reaction from headquarters, and

---

*Ben Majekodunmi participates in this book in his personal capacity. The views expressed do not necessarily reflect those of the UN.

action from UN Member States. Some of these actors show willingness to respond, but coordination is awkward, the consent of other organizations' headquarters and capital cities is needed. As time passes, other events take front stage, the report slips out of date and the momentum is lost. As you realize that no major change will occur, your mind goes back to the many persons interviewed; to the man who cried as he gave testimony of the killing of his wife and children; to the seven-year-old child found alone in his home with no food, waiting for parents who you knew would never return.

Driving with a colleague, deep in the empty countryside, you meet a barrier of branches across your path. Before there is time to reverse, a gun is poking into you through the open window of the jeep. Forced violently out of the vehicle, you are convinced by the agitation of your attackers that you will be killed and thrown to the side of the road. Minutes pass; it becomes clear, as your captors relax, that they only want money and will probably let you go. It is only once back in the jeep, the scene a few hundred meters behind, that your hands begin to tremble; when you have time to think of that one person who, more than anyone else in the world, you love and want to see again. You imagine being quietly killed out here and never again seeing that face, holding those hands. You think of the children you want to have and of the family you want to build. You ask yourself "What am I doing? Does my presence here make such a difference that I can take these risks?" "How much longer should I stay?"

INTRODUCTION

Some of the difficulties UN human rights fieldworkers confront are the same as those faced by colleagues with other UN or non-governmental organizations (NGOs): problems such as access to vulnerable populations, security and communications. There are other challenges, however, that are particular to UN human rights field activities. They find their source, above all, in the essence of human rights work and in the presence, or lack of, support provided to UN human rights field activities by the UN and Member States. Other factors such as slow recruitment procedures, limited training, and short contracts can aggravate conditions.

There are several different types of UN human rights fieldwork, and a broad distinction can be made between short and long-term activities. Senior members of the UN Secretariat, UN Special Rapporteurs, and the members of special Commissions, for example, conduct short-term visits to a few specific locations in a country lasting from a few hours to a few weeks at most. Longer-term missions to a country usually involve a human rights "field presence" or larger "operation" and will continue from a minimum of several months to several years. These different interventions, nevertheless, share the aim of promoting and protecting human rights. The focus here is on HROs working in field operations below the level of senior management, drawing from my own, and other UN human rights colleagues' experiences.

1) THE COMPLEX ROLE OF UN HUMAN RIGHTS OFFICERS—"CATCH 22"?

The Essence of Human Rights Work— Pressures, Conflicting Motivations

While the range of actors considered to bear responsibility for respecting human rights is expanding, international human rights obligations are traditionally owed by a State to persons within the State's jurisdiction; and human rights violations are acts or omissions attributable to State authorities and officials. At the basis of UN human rights work lie 3 closely linked types of action:

1. efforts to *assist* States in their implementation of international human rights standards, for example, through human rights training, assistance in the establishment of independent national human rights institutions and other *technical cooperation* activities;
2. efforts to *monitor* States' progress in meeting their *responsibility* for the respect of human rights standards, for example, through investigations and publication of reports; and
3. efforts to ensure *accountability* for violations, for example through monitoring a State's prosecution of officials for acts of torture.

Every UN human rights field operation is conducted according to a mandate negotiated between the UN and national authorities, with mandates generally including one or more of the above areas. Past operations have focused largely on civil and political rights, however, very positively, increasing attention is being given to economic, social, and cultural rights. Other organizations arrive with food, medicine, big budgets, loans, and programs to improve infrastructure. In contrast, UN human rights operations arrive with technical assistance and a sometimes less welcome focus on responsibility and accountability for violations of international law. States agree to UN human rights activities within their territory for a variety of complex human rights, political, financial, and other reasons. Important to note is that the objectives of a UN human rights operation and those of the State are not necessarily the same. Areas of disagreement, on key human rights issues, are often grave, carrying major political implications within the country.

Protecting the most vulnerable: UN HROs are called upon to represent, among others, convicted prisoners, excluded indigenous populations, women marginalized by gender discrimination, trafficked children, a silenced media. We are needed precisely by people who are unable to benefit from the full protection of their own State, at times because the State lacks sufficient resources, at others because elements of the State itself may threaten their rights. Perpetually called upon to represent vulnerable groups—these least represented persons—we are fundamentally focused on stimulating change in a State's behavior; a role that inevitably complicates our work. The essence of UN human rights work and some conflicts between UN and State motivations can create a very difficult working environment.

(Mis)Perceptions of Human Rights Officers at a Local Level

Contradictory motivations may lead to some uncertainty in capitals, but it is primarily at a local provincial level that they can lead to difficulties in the work of individual HROs. Provincial level officials are frequently not even aware of a UN mandate's existence and some may feel more vulnerable, than national authorities, to the UN's monitoring and investigating work. Responsibility for violations can be directly linked to them, and may affect their careers. Where HROs are nationals of wealthy nations, their presence in a much poorer country can be perceived as a new form of colonialism, paternalistic at best. Where HROs are from a country with a very poor human rights record, local officials sometimes question on what moral basis these HROs give human rights "lessons." "Go and preach human rights at home," they tell us.

Pressures Created by an Unbalanced Mandate

Some UN human rights field activities focus exclusively on monitoring, investigating, and accountability. These limited mandates can create great difficulties for staff in the field. Some local officials refused outright to allow HROs to interview refugees during investigations into alleged human rights violations. They regarded us with suspicion, unsure of our motives or how we would use the information we gathered. In such situations, we would invest time in implementing the assistance aspects of our mandate: human rights training for officials, making local radio human rights broadcasts. Only after developing a relationship of mutual trust with local authorities could we implement our monitoring and investigating roles. Without the assistance aspect of our mandate—important in and of itself—we would never have succeeded in seeking accountability for violations.

Impunity—Getting Tangled in History

Most human rights mandates define a particular time frame, often focusing on current human rights violations, sometimes stretching back a year or two. But what do HROs do when confronted by a furious local population who demand attention to injustices they had suffered for years before the UN seeks to resolve a current situation. The mandate—drafted in New York, signed in the capital city—makes no mention of these decades old acts. Yet, you are facing a situation infinitely more human and real than the text of a distant agreement. Grappling with sensitive history that, for those who survived it, represents the lost lives of loved ones is a vast task in itself, one that brings untold complications to the relationship between HROs and the communities within which they work.

The Obstacle of Priorities

While impunity looms as a big problem today, efforts to seek justice for these past violations can be presented tomorrow as an obstacle to peace and reconciliation. Human rights standards (justice and an end to impunity) may be sacrificed by an accord through which the international community encourages State authorities to offer amnesties to individuals in exchange for their agreement to lay down their weapons. Immediate peace, at all costs, is presented as a priority. With the scrawl of a pen, HROs find that human rights standards we proffer so forcefully, as the basis for our every action and spoken word, are no longer. The framework gradually constructed for implementation of our mandate at a local level is turned upside down placing doubt on the credibility of staff and our work.

The factors detailed above reveal a potentially awkward basis for a working environment, and are the source of many of the difficulties confronting HROs.

2) PHYSICAL SECURITY

A complex work environment is exacerbated by delicate security situations. UN HROs, because of their human rights work, have been the victims of deliberate killings, beatings, illegal arrest, and detention. Some have been victims of more indiscriminate attacks, including mine explosions and stray bullets. Most escape direct violence, but almost all experience periods—an hour, a week, or months on end—of tension. HROs have guns pointed at them in mock shootings. They are verbally abused, receive threatening calls and letters and are held for hours at check points. They are followed as they conduct their daily work and find that people with whom they have contact are subsequently attacked or threatened.

Investigating the Persons Responsible for Your Protection

National security forces, generally police and army, usually bear primary responsibility for the physical security of HROs. Where UN peacekeepers are present they provide valuable additional security, although usually secondary to the role of local forces. National sovereignty and simple logistics make it difficult for security arrangements to be any different. Nevertheless, for HROs, these arrangements can lead to circumstances in which we are investigating reports of alleged human rights violations by the same civilian, police, and military officials upon whom we must depend for our security in a particular region; a bizarre situation, to say the least.

Moral Dilemmas

UN security guidelines are used to limit the movement and presence of UN field staff in regions where security is poor. However, where security risks for UN staff are high the risks of human rights violations for the local population are often also high. Thus, HROs may be most urgently needed in precisely the places and times that security guidelines forbid us from attending. Indeed, in several recent instances, State soldiers or armed opposition groups deliberately killed UN or NGO staff specifically to prompt the complete evacuation of all personnel. Emptied of potential witnesses, subsequent massive human rights violations have gone unreported in the region.

Serious ethical questions are raised when the UN evacuates all its personnel, including HROs, leaving behind local populations who had gathered in a particular area precisely because they had expected to be protected by the UN. To evacuate a

UN presence in response to killings committed with the very objective of ensuring that no witnesses of human rights abuses will be present implies that some UN strategies are seriously flawed. As HROs on the ground we are of course concerned for our own personal security and aware that our effectiveness in addressing violations will be increasingly limited as security conditions deteriorate. However, we often question evacuating HROs in terms of the UN's moral and, arguably, legal responsibility.

3) HUMAN RIGHTS WORK AT A PERSONAL LEVEL

A Privilege and Responsibility

As HROs we find ourselves in distant countries, our days regulated by curfews, our every minute attended by the crackle of a walkie-talkie. We have to be humble, yet firm; patient, yet determined; sensitive to a local reality, yet consistent with an international standard. We must be black and white, yet also color blind, embracing differences to the extent that they are no longer such. Although the working environment is often difficult, serving as a human rights officer for the UN in a field situation is a tremendous privilege. HROs have the opportunity to assist in the birth of new States, the realization of the dreams of entire populations. We are plunged into the heart of a country and entrusted with caring enough about its people to help them deal with difficulties at fundamental junctions in their history. And, despite the aforementioned difficulties, we are generally welcomed by local people with wide-open arms, invited to join their festivities and share their sorrows. We believe in our work as a means to achieve essential progress in promoting and protecting rights. Even where all else fails, the joy at being able to genuinely assist just one person is a great reward. Indeed privileged, we carry also a proportional responsibility toward the UN, toward the State to which we are deployed and toward its people.

Relationships

One of the great pleasures and essential supports of fieldwork is the friendships we are able to make. HROs tend to develop very strong relationships with colleagues from human rights operations and partner organizations, some becoming lifelong. Making friends in the local community is an equal pleasure; however, languages, cultural barriers, and the role and status of HROs can prove to be obstacles. The need for neutrality requires that we keep some distance from our main working partners, local State officials. Friendships with members of local NGOs, church leaders, and others can sometimes place these persons at risk. HROs remain far from their families, and miss their partners and children.

Witnessing Human Rights Violations

Returning from a difficult human rights situation, many people ask "What is it like to see the victims of human rights violations?" "How do you cope with that?" Perhaps the most severe form of this sort of pressure lies in the failure of an HRO to make a difference, particularly when this means a lost life, severe pain, or permanent injury to the victim.

Coping

We all live these pressures in different ways. A small number suffers psychological trauma from witnessing violations, while most HROs seek to keep a minimum emotional distance from events. One of my tactics is to shake hands with the persons who seem to pose the most immediate threat, assuming that it will be that little bit harder for them to deliberately harm my colleagues or myself in the next few minutes. The instinct to take a proffered hand is so strong that aggressors can be surprised and find themselves reaching out, before realizing that this is not what they want to do. Once a hand has been accepted the act creates, temporarily, a bond that precludes violence; a strategy leading to bizarre situations.

I recall sitting at the wheel of a jeep, with my colleague standing next to the vehicle, as a soldier came running up, charged his gun and screamed "*je vais vous tuer*" (I am going to kill you). Little room for doubt in that statement but, in the stress of this moment, I found myself wondering if the soldier's use of "vous" was the plural form of "you" indicating that he intended to kill both of us. Or was it, instead, the singular polite form of "you" suggesting that he was planning to kill only my colleague, at whom the gun was pointed? The second or two needed to consider these questions and conclude it was unlikely the soldier would be polite in this particular context and the threat was thus to us both, kept me calm and helped me deal better with the other decisions I had to make on the spur of the moment. My tactics are perhaps poor, but they illustrate the very personal manner in which HROs experience different pressures.

The Importance of Making a Difference

The coping mechanism perhaps most common to all of us is being sure that we are improving a human rights situation. When we no longer see the positive effect of our presence, a delicate balance—between choosing to remain with an operation or to depart—is rapidly upset. Individual HROs can positively influence local and specific situations; however, we cannot hope to influence an overall countrywide human rights context unless our operation itself functions well and is supported at the international level. As HROs, frustrated at our inability to make a difference, we find ourselves asking, rhetorically, how it is possible that soldiers and armed groups continue to kill civilians with impunity an entire year after our reports were published? We ask how our operation can find its mandate utterly ignored by some State authorities and how UN and NGO workers can become the deliberate targets of violence? It is not enough for the UN and Member States to send HROs to a country and cast them adrift once there, paying only lip service to UN human rights resolutions. Human rights operations can do little without continued political and material support from across the UN system and Member States. It is the presence or absence of such support that can make the biggest difference to an operation's success. I believe that the same support also makes a fundamental difference to how well HROs are received in a country, the respect given their mandate, their physical protection, and their personal well-being and sense of accomplishment.

In April 2000, the UN Commission on Human Rights adopted a resolution (E/CN.4/RES/2000/61) emphasizing the important role of human rights defenders in the promotion and protection of human rights, and noting with concern the threats, harassment, insecurity, arbitrary detention, and extrajudicial executions to which these persons are subjected. The resolution requested the Secretary-General to appoint a special representative to report on the situation of human rights defenders and on means to enhance their protection. The resolution and subsequent appointment of Ms. Hina Jilani as Special Representative mark important and very welcome efforts by the UN and States.

On the ground, international politics is of little immediate relevance when you spend your days witnessing suffering from human rights abuse. Were we, as HROs, to be invited to express our views at an international level, for example at the Commission on Human Rights, we would ask decision-makers to base their decisions not on politics but solely on the human impact of violations. We would ask them to respond "as though this were your wife, husband, child suffering the violations described in our report."

4) THE EXCEPTIONAL RISKS FACED BY NATIONAL STAFF

As international HROs in the field we like to think of ourselves as being on the "front-line" of human rights work. However, we are rarely as much on the front line as staff who are nationals of the countries in which we work. For reasons of neutrality and safety, national staff are rarely employed as "human rights officers" but fulfil, nevertheless, essential roles providing expertise, and working as interpreters, translators, drivers, and administrative assistants. Nationals of a country almost invariably face greater risks than internationals and are often also responsible for their families. Unlike internationals, they do not have the easy option of simply leaving the country if a situation worsens, unless as refugees or asylum seekers. The arbitrary imprisonment, beating, torture, and killing of national staff are not given the same media or political attention as that of international workers, a fact not in keeping with the notion of equality at the heart of the human rights message we seek to share.

5) RECRUITMENT, CONTRACTS, TRAINING, AND INSURANCE

Reference needs also to be made to some regularly overlooked, practical factors. Recruitment procedures are often slow, with long delays. Applicants are kept waiting for months on end, told each week that a final decision is imminent. Contracts are sometimes very short and few applicants—with school fees and house rental to pay for in their home country—are prepared to quit secure jobs, leave their families, and travel to a country in the midst of armed conflict with an assurance of only three months of work and salary. Training of HROs is organized only on an ad hoc basis, depending on the uncertain availability of funding and the initiative of operation chiefs. "Malicious act" insurance—covering, for example, the deliberate killing of staff in the course of their work—is of particular importance for human rights personnel, and yet is not systematically accorded to national staff. In addition, Malicious Act Insurance expires with the end of a staff member's contract; national staff remaining in their country after UN employment may be attacked months later in retaliation for having assisted the UN, and will no longer be covered.

6) LEAVING AN OPERATION— RETURNING "HOME" AND MOVING ON

Leaving a human rights operation can come as a relief, release of tension, and escape from the continuous pressure of working long, seven day weeks. After a few years of fieldwork, HROs often feel that they have more in common with colleagues in the international environment than with friends and family left at home, leading to a sense that "home" no longer truly exists. Leaving a field operation, for most, involves choosing not to renew contracts and thus also means "unemployment." While a break from work is usually needed, the pressures common to any person in between jobs need to be addressed. Hence it is particularly important that the post-mission period involve follow-up contact with headquarters, debriefing, information on employment possibilities, and access to counseling for any trauma. It has proved difficult for the UN to obtain resources for post-mission follow-up. None of these forms of assistance are systematically available, and HROs are left largely on their own to do everything from searching for jobs to identifying a need for counseling and seeking, and paying for, such support.

7) RECOMMENDATIONS

a) International Support

The field work and reports of UN human rights mechanisms—human rights operations, Special Rapporteurs, and others—should be given much greater consideration and acted upon by relevant UN agencies, headquarters, and Member States. The well-being of HROs depends above all upon substantial international commitment to human rights.

b) A Balanced Mandate

The mandates of human rights operations should be broad, including, if possible, a focus on assistance, responsibility, and accountability. Careful drafting of a mandate is fundamental to an operation's success and to the safety of HROs.

c) Guidance/Training

All human rights staff should have access to guidance/training. UN headquarters should develop the capacity to provide such support. Greater consideration should be given to sharing training capacities among different UN bodies.

d) Recruitment and Contracts

Staff recruited as HROs must be extremely competent, with attention given to human rights commitment as well as academic qualifications. Contracts should be of a reasonable length.

e) Security

Parties to a conflict must be made responsible and held politically and judicially accountable for every action that threatens the security of UN and NGO staff in the field. This fact should be made clear in all high-level contacts with such entities. UN security rules should take into account UN human rights mandates.

f) Insurance

All national staff with human rights operations should be given "malicious act" insurance and coverage should continue for some time after the end of employment.

g) Post-Mission

Staff, their partners and family should have access to psychological counseling during and following their work with an operation. Upon leaving, staff members should be debriefed, with a record kept of the work conducted. Staff should be systematically supported in developing a career and obtaining future positions.

CONCLUSION

This chapter necessarily focuses on the difficult aspects of human rights field work. There is another side in which, as HROs, our cooperation with States is extremely positive and in which we are inspired by the efforts of local officials who seek to strengthen respect for human rights in their country. UN human rights interventions at a field level contribute, in many different ways, to the promotion and protection of human rights, and are an invaluable resource for individuals, for States and for the UN. This resource needs to be given much greater support.

Voice

"YOU AND YOUR PEOPLE WILL NEVER LIVE HERE AGAIN"

Bosnian Serb Municipal Councilors to Bosniak (Muslim) Returnees in Kozarac

Milburn Line

"WHERE WERE YOU IN 1992? . . ."
IDP/Refugees Question to Members of the International Community

How could the world have allowed the atrocities of the ethnic cleansing to have occurred? How could we have watched on television as millions of people were expelled from their homes? The world knew about the concentration camps in Prijedor in 1992. The UN system of "safe-areas" became an international farce as 7,000 Bosniaks were murdered in the worst single act of genocide in Europe since World War II. In 1997, the international community hotly debated whether to attempt to implement fully the Dayton peace accords guaranteeing right of return for minorities expelled during the conflict or just to leave them separated. In fact, the whole scenario of several million displaced and refugees often appeared to be a battle lost before begun. By not acting to prevent the atrocities, the world had allowed the cycle of violence based on ethnicity to become institutionalized.

In the face of such injustice and given the demonstrated impotence of the world's response, how could I address these people, who had been expelled from their homes, as a representative of the international community in the name of human rights? Their faces betrayed their anger and lack of faith in a system that had failed them. I could not look into their faces and deny them the right to return to their homes and expect them ever to respect the rights of others. As I struggled personally and professionally with not wanting to disappoint the displaced persons I knew, but also not wanting them to be exposed to further ethno-nationalist violence, I came to believe that the only responsible answer was not to compromise standards of the rule of law. But maybe we were unrealistic about the possibilities of respect for law in a country where it had never prevailed.

After three and a half years struggling with refugee return issues, I made one last visit to the field areas where we supported returns. I was most struck by the normalcy of it all. In Kozarac, where we were told that people would never be allowed to return, kids were playing and laundry was drying among the 1,000 reconstructed homes of returning Bosniaks. Three newly reconstructed minarets stood under the shadow of the Kozara mountains. On the other side of the ethnic divide in Sanski Most I saw Bosnian Serb returnees walking down the main street. Some 5,000 Bosnian Serbs had returned to their native Drvar despite the tenuous security situation that the international community seemed unable or unwilling to resolve.

Driving away, I worried about whether any of what we had worked for would last. Again, the international mission was selling small steps as big victories and unwilling to take the larger, more risky, steps to improve the chances that things might work over the long term. Since some people had returned, it would be easier to declare the process, though far from complete, a victory and not address the tougher questions of sustainable integration of returnees. But we still accomplished what we never expected to be able to do: getting thousands of people home without getting them killed in the process.

Many of us field officers spent long hours debating, and sleepless nights wondering, if we would become lost in the process jousting against the windmills of evil despite the reality of unhealed scars left by the war. We knew we had over-estimated our capability to transform a shattered society by the power of idealistic principles. But at least we didn't sell out the right of people to return to their homes because they weren't the right ethnicity, even though many in the international community found it tempting to do so. Perhaps I had been drawn in and become lost in the process, but I couldn't help but think that it was worth it if only one Bosnian realized that a few of the internationals, who had disappointed them over and over again, finally got it right.

What else could we have done when faced with the determination and dignity of so many IDPs and returnees in so many places who, perhaps as deluded and idealistic as we in the international community, were thinking we could guide a process of reintegration and reconciliation only a few years after a brutal war? Despite having been failed by the international community both during the conflict and after, they would not give up on returning to what was theirs: their homes, their jobs, their lives. The Bosnian challenge will continue for generations: to ensure that conditions of tolerance and respect for human rights exist so people can get their lives back. It was now time for me to get mine back as well.

PART III. VOLUNTEERS

13

Eternal Vigilance

Sharon Capeling-Alakija

For the United Nations Volunteers program (UNV), which began in 1971, the security of its now around 5,000 volunteers annually is a bottom-line issue and one of serious concern.

In the 1990s, the United Nations Volunteers (UNVs) came to play, individually and collectively, a significant part in the efforts of the UN to make and keep the peace and to promote democracy and respect for human rights. In its work, UNV is faced with the same reality as the rest of the UN system: the working environment is now different, less secure. People bent on ethnic cleansing, genocide, persecution, torture, trafficking, or destruction do not pause to make the distinction between volunteers and others among the servants of the international community who seek to curb their activities.

While the number of major security incidents involving UNVs has been limited, the program's experience unfortunately reflects the general trend where UN personnel are not only not exempt from aggression, but indeed are at times specifically targeted.

A Japanese UNV, Atsuhito Nakata, was murdered in the course of—indeed, quite possibly because of—his duties for the United Nations in Cambodia in 1993. A Cambodian UNV, Chim Chan Sastra, was one of several local and international staff murdered in an ambush while serving with the UN Human Rights Field Operation in Rwanda in 1997. Two UNVs, an Australian named Lisa Malone and Omar Aguirre, from Bolivia, were among the five UN personnel killed in a 1998 helicopter accident in Guatemala.

Impelled by these and other tragedies, the UNV program aims to do all it can to ensure that the risks to the volunteers are minimized. However, this is not an area where one can readily be satisfied that all has been done. There is more which the program itself, the UN system, and the international community can and must do. As with liberty, so with security: the price is eternal vigilance.

The United Nations Volunteers program is the volunteer arm of the United Nations system. Today, UNV has some 5,000 volunteers every year. They come from nearly 150 countries. They are academically well qualified, many with master's or doctoral degrees. To be considered, they must also have several years of professional experience. Their average age is 39. According to the organization, "most importantly, they bring an intangible but crucial asset, that of idealism and motivation."

Thirty-six percent are women and around two thirds come from developing and economic transition countries. In the 1970s and 1980s, they were mostly involved in technical cooperation for social and economic development under the general auspices of the United Nations Development Programme (UNDP). In the last decade, the UNVs have come to play an increasingly important role in peacekeeping, elections, and in interventions of other international bodies such as the European Union and the Organization for Security and Cooperation in Europe.

The assignments of the UNVs have been exclusively civilian. There are roles that UNV does not consider appropriate to its volunteers; for example, in 1991 UNV declined to furnish UN security officers in northern Iraq because of their requirement that they carry side-arms. Civilian policing is also not a job for UNVs. The physical operation of de-mining is also seen as best left to specialist organizations.

The UNVs who participate in UN missions are integrated into the staffing of the particular mission and the chain of command. The UNV program is not a separate operational agency: it contracts with entities such as the Department of Peacekeeping Operations and the Office of the Coordinator for Humanitarian Affairs to identify candidates, select them in collaboration with officials of the operation in question, field them with the minimum of delay and repatriate them on completion of their assignment.

With regards to numbers, the trend is clearly upward as the UNV program has been called to provide volunteers in support of the mandates of the UN. In the past two years alone, there has been a tremendous increase in the number of UNVs serving in countries and territories with inherent security risks. In 1999, about 45 percent of that year's total of 4,383 UNVs served in such situations: 1,972 volunteers. The figure rose in the year 2000 to almost 50 percent of 5,181 assignments, or 2,590.

The element of risk is demonstrated by the fact that in August of 1999, 500 UNVs serving in East Timor were evacuated under difficult circumstances to Darwin in Australia, amid the carnage which followed the Popular Consultations. As soon as the situation allowed, some 60 went back in and were the human face of the UN. In other cases between May and October 2000, UNVs were evacuated from Eritrea, Guinea, the Palestinian Territories, Sierra Leone, and West Timor.

Besides numerical strength, the UNV contributions to these operations are noteworthy for the diversity of nationalities, professions, and roles in support of a very wide range of the overall UN involvement.

In Cambodia in 1992-93, a total of 674 UN Volunteers from 65 countries served in the UN Transitional Authority in Cambodia (UNTAC). The majority of them were district electoral supervisors but also as doctors and nurses, lawyers, camp managers, builders, mechanics, electricians and computer and video technicians, air traffic control, agriculture, and small business management. In UNTAC, the UNVs comprised 10 percent of the total civilian component.

In June 2000, 693 UN Volunteers were at work in Former Yugoslavia representing 83 different nationalities. Forty percent of the civilians within the UN Mission in Kosovo (UNMIK) were volunteers and 83 percent of those involved in civil registration were volunteers.

In East Timor as of 31 December 2000, 552 volunteers from 86 countries served in about 150 different functional capacities.

Other examples:

- 200 helped monitor the historic elections which brought apartheid to an end in South Africa;
- 280 helped maintain peace in demobilization camps in Mozambique between 1993 and 1995, and another 110 helped UNDP prepare the multi-party elections there;
- nearly 100 fulfilled human rights observer and other functions in support of the UN Mission in Guatemala.

It is clear that, if only for numerical reasons, UN Volunteers should be factored in when provisions are made for the security of UN personnel in potentially hazardous operations. However, should those provisions make any distinction between the volunteers and the UN *staff* deployed in the same operations? The answer will normally be "no" and as an answer it will usually suffice. However, it can be open to challenge if and when things go badly wrong from the standpoint of security.

Ultimately, there *is* a distinction to be made between people who have volunteered their services to an undertaking, and others for whom the involvement is part of their tenured, or temporary, salaried job. UN Volunteers bring an intangible but crucial asset to their tasks, a strong sense of motivation and solidarity. In their giving, there is also reciprocity, for when the UN Volunteers give, they receive just as much. That is what volunteerism is all about.

Of course, with 5,000 individuals from 150 countries motivation is bound to vary, from social or religious conviction about helping one's disadvantaged neighbor, through the desire for encounter and adventure, to welcoming the monthly living allowance as a steady, if modest, income and enhancing personal and technical skills that can open up new career opportunities.

The net result with regards to the UN Volunteers is a remarkable degree of esprit de corps in serving the United Nations on a volunteer basis. This came into play when Atsuhito Nakata was murdered in Cambodia. The UN's and the national security forces had failed to prevent this outrage and there were substantial misgivings among the UNV District Electoral Supervisors as to whether the political situation might not deteriorate further and their exposure be even worse.

In those particularly difficult circumstances, the choice was offered to all the UNVs individually between continuing with their tasks of civic education and preparation of the elections or withdrawing fully, honorably, and with all benefits maintained and references provided. While a few withdrew, the overwhelming majority decided to remain and, with their UN staff colleagues, brought the elections to a successful conclusion. It seems clear that best practice in preparing for and carrying out the more sensitive UN operations should build recognition of this choice into contingency planning.

The particular contribution that volunteers can make and wish to make, underlines well the wisdom of entitling this book "Sharing the Front Line and the Back Hills." For it is the back hills to which most UNVs are drawn and assigned in every such operation and where they play their best roles. Volunteers believe that to succeed their work must be grounded in the lived reality and the needs and aspirations of the great majority of the population who live in the villages of the countryside and the urban slums.

"It is not to exaggerate," said Secretary-General Kofi Annan on a visit to UNV headquarters in Bonn, "to see UNVs as the grassroots ambassadors of the UN. If you didn't do what you do, the UN would remain very distant."

It was precisely because UNVs in Cambodia went out two by two into every distant community to register electors and encourage voting that they were more exposed to the interplay of local animosities. It was precisely because the oppressed indigenous peoples of Guatemala have taken refuge in the most distant mountain and forest villages that UNVs had to take out to them the message of The Mission for the Verification of Human Rights in Guatemala (MINUGUA) of new hopes for respect for human rights (and in the process check out allegations of torture and mass murder), and were thus more exposed to the mischance of the helicopter accident.

Some UNVs will indeed partner UN staff colleagues in the back hills, but most, by far, will not be in on the strategy sessions in the capital city but out in the frontlines, making the crucial link, people-to-people, with the human beings whom the operation is designed to benefit. Without such linkage there is little prospect of real or sustainable success. The UN system must take this into account when establishing its security arrangements, but, more importantly, the international community must recognize the inexorable implications for the resourcing of the operations in terms of security, transport, communications, and the like.

In practice, UN Volunteers in the field and local staff working for UNV Support Offices are integrated into the UN security coordination structure, a management team headed by the Designated Official (usually the UNDP Resident Representative) or delegated nominee, with membership from the agencies participating in the operation. Generally, UNVs are subject to the direction and guidance of the Designated Official with respect to security matters and are incorporated in all applicable security plans. In the event of evacuation, they are taken out with other UN international staff to a safe haven or other destination approved by the Secretary-General. As part of their contractual arrangements, UNVs also benefit from life and medical insurance coverage.

Review and enhancement of security provisions is a standing agenda item for UNV and it must rely on the UN Security Coordinator (UNSECOORD) and on the arrangements of UN agencies using the volunteers. The program must therefore seek a balance between its role as a service provider to the UN system and its responsibilities to the volunteers whom it has recruited. This, of course, begins with the initial policy decision as to whether or not to make UNVs available in the specific situation, which entails deciding what are and are not acceptable risks.

In these circumstances, the first priority is to raise the awareness of the security dimensions of the operation as they may impact on volunteers. To the fullest extent feasible, therefore, UNV participates in UNSECOORD's—or undertakes its own—pre-assignment security assessment missions. In these missions, the physical situation at the proposed duty station/s is reviewed and the existence of security plans, the nature of security installations and communications equipment and the level of identification available to UN personnel are determined.

Once the decision is made to proceed, the quality of selection is crucial. UNV is fortunate to have built up a register of people who have had prior experience of assignment as UNV refugee camp administrators, electoral supervisors, or human rights defenders, to name but three categories. The ability to turn to the register, to academic and training institutions in the relevant discipline and to UNV's cooperating organizations readily permits rapid recruitment of suitable candidates, even in the significant numbers cited. Increased emphasis is being placed on systematic briefing prior to departure, and to training of UNVs upon arrival at the duty station. UNV staff also makes special security monitoring visits while the volunteers are in place: a recent example was a visit to Sierra Leone, where 75 UNVs were serving with the UN Assistance Mission.

The program also has, at its Bonn headquarters, in-house security focal points in charge of monitoring and coordinating security arrangements and responding to situations as they occur. An acknowledged weaker point is debriefing. The logistic difficulties in debriefing volunteers who return to their many different home countries are part of the reason for the lack of comprehensive debriefing of volunteers returning from the field.

The Government of Japan has been particularly generous to UNV in helping it enhance its security provisions. It has financed a Trust Fund specifically to address these concerns, totalling $1,855,000 between 1994 and 2000. This funding has enabled UNV both to mount a series of regional security workshops and to adopt several special measures.

Regional security workshops were held in 1998 for the African continent, the Arab States and the Commonwealth of Independent States, Asia and the Pacific, and Latin America. They were attended by some 50 UNV program officers, those entrusted with the first-line responsibility for their UNV peers on the ground. The intention was to create a multiplier effect by providing them with the knowledge and means to conduct similar training sessions for all serving UN Volunteers in their respective countries of assignment. The result was improved safety and security awareness among about 1,500 UNVs in all.

The first of the workshops was held for the Africa region. It brought together program managers/officers with responsibility for 700 UNVs in eleven countries. Joining them were colleagues and resource persons from UNSECOORD, the UN High Commissioner for Refugees (UNHCR), UNDP, and the International Committee of the Red Cross. Each participant presented a plan for follow-up workshops to be discussed with her/his Designated Official, Security Management Team and Field Security Officers back at base. The plans were referred to UNV headquarters for review and funding. Specific issues that emerged included the need to build the topic of stress management into pre-assignment briefings and into the training of program officers; a recommendation that the UNV program officer be a member of the Security Management Team in each country; and shortcomings such as delays in pouch services in crisis situations, speed of recruitment, slow response times and insufficient communications between headquarters and the field.

A second round has now begun with a regional workshop in Dhaka in 2000 for 11 countries of the Asia and Pacific region. This time, UNV Country Operations Assistants (the national staff of the UNV Support Units) were included.

The Dhaka agenda headings convey some impression of the extensive ground covered in these sessions:

- The Security Management System
- The Security Plan
- Crowds, demonstrations, targeted attacks, and personal security awareness
- Convoy planning, travel and vehicle security, anti-hijacking, checkpoint procedure
- Communication procedures and practical exercise on use of equipment
- Malicious acts insurance, residential and office security
- Natural disaster security consideration
- Stress management and trauma counseling
- Sexual harassment awareness
- Explosives and mine awareness
- AIDS in the workplace
- First Aid procedures
- Hostage incident management
- Post-workshop: country level tentative proposals/plans
- UNV conditions of service and clarifications on country-specific adminis- trative issues
- Course evaluation and feed-back for future workshops

The first of two new workshops for the African continent was held in Nairobi during 2001. At the 1998 African workshop, a handbook was distributed for the first time. It was a supplementary field manual for UNVs that emphasized security and safety issues, produced with Japanese support. UNV is currently finalizing a CD-ROM, in partnership with UNSECOORD and UNHCR, aimed at increasing awareness of security in general and in the situation specific to the proposed country of assignment to be distributed prior to fielding. UNV has also produced a 20-minute video entitled "Notes from the Field" that provided an overview of potential security risks and scenarios which UNVs may encounter. It was made available to 60 serving UNV program officers, selected UNDP country offices and cooperating organizations.

Other special measures enabled by the Japanese Trust Fund have been:

- the exceptional provision of additional radios to UNVs serving in Cambodia, Rwanda, and Georgia, in areas where only a limited number of hand-held radios and mobile communications was available;
- the provision of on-site UNV Stress Management specialists in Rwanda following the security incidents of February 1997, as well as in Somalia, Kosovo, and East Timor.

Safety and security enhancement workshops have also been conducted *within* special operations. In October 2000, with the help of resource persons from

UNSECOORD, two UNVs were trained from each of the thirteen districts in East Timor where volunteers are assigned to the UN Transitional Administration. They are expected to organize follow-up workshops for their peers. Similar workshops were planned in Kosovo and Sierra Leone.

Despite all these measures, there are outstanding issues. For example, the Hazardous Duty Station Supplement is made available to UNVs, when approved by UNSECOORD for a specific location, albeit as volunteers at a lower rate than to international staff. Similarly, since they are not considered to be UN staff proper, UNVs are not entitled to carry the UN Laissez-Passer. UNV's concerns have been expressed in several cases where the absence of a Laissez-Passer may have security implications, especially when frequent crossing of borders in war zones is part of the duties. UNHCR has also pointed out that this poses a problem in its use of UNVs.

Yet, UNV itself must also seek to preserve that delicate balance that will not overly institutionalize its volunteers, will permit them to bring their special contribution to UN operations, and, in extremis, voluntarily to withdraw from them. Fine judgment is required, perhaps more flexibly on a case-by-case basis.

To sum up: a greater degree of risk was perhaps inevitable as international, cross-border warfare has given way to intra-national civil conflict. In these new contexts, UN personnel are at best caught in the crossfire of local power plays, at worst seen by one side as biased in favor of its opponents. The international community must seek to educate men and women worldwide to have respect for those who seek to bring objectivity and impartiality to bear for the benefit of all, and it should introduce deterrent penalties for contravening that principle. Meantime, the UN itself can do more, and more efficiently, to protect all involved.

For its part, UNV should continue to garner all there is to learn from its experience, assignment by assignment, and compare notes with others equally or more familiar with the issues. UNV clearly has a degree of responsibility and a great deal to contribute to this end.

Voices

SHOWING "PRESENCE"

Benny Ben Otim (Uganda)
UNV Protection Officer, UNHCR, Banja Luka,
Bosnia-Herzegovina, 1992/3

Protection work in the former Yugoslavia was often done by the seat of the pants, determined as it was by the fluctuating daily circumstances confronting minorities. The range of protection activities to moderate the wanton killings of minorities included mediation with the "central" government, local municipalities, militia, and often individual soldiers at the roadblocks, who were law unto themselves. UN Volunteer specialists were involved in all of this work.

We also monitored and reported human rights violations, provided protection to "extremely vulnerable individuals," i.e., the elderly, sick, unaccompanied minors, and those under direct threat of violence, and provided the UN presence in threatening situations. Sometimes when we received advance notice of planned attacks on particular families or villages, the UNHCR and UNV staff would position themselves between the attackers and the minorities, often intermingling physically with those threatened until the threat passed or until the people concerned could leave the area safely. This approach was consistent with the concept of showing "presence" and was not discouraged by UNHCR. To my knowledge, no UN Volunteers were injured in these activities.

HONORED TO BE ABLE TO DEFEND

Manuel Amat (Peru)
National UNV, Ombudsman's Office,
Arequipa Department, Peru, 1998

Ayacucho, 23 December. Police officers arrive at my house at 4 A.M. We have a glass of juice before leaving for the jail, where I will make sure the police respect prisoners' rights in their monthly search for drugs, alcohol, or weapons. I can't watch in every part of the jail, but I always choose the "C" area, where the most dangerous prisoners are held and the most problems likely to arise.

When we get there we find that eight of the prisoners have been sent to a high security cell. They were planning to kidnap the police officers—and me, too!—and use us as human shields. They had assembled diverse "home-made" but dangerous weapons. In spite of this frightening experience, I remain committed to this work—thousands of prisoners in Peruvian jails need our constant presence to guarantee their rights.

By early afternoon I'm at the Ombudsman's Office to handle the other part of my job: answering citizens' questions, following up on cases, and looking for ways to resolve complaints and demands. A woman comes to see us after trying to get the police to do something about her situation of domestic violence. They had told her "Family problems should be solved at home." I go to the police station and explain to the officer in charge that the situation legally requires investigation. By the end of the day, the officer who had rejected the woman's complaint receives a reprimand. I talk to the police about another man as well, who had been detained without a lawyer and was tied up in his cell.

I leave for home after 7 in the evening, tired but satisfied with the work done. I feel honored to be able to defend other citizens' rights in our society, which includes educating them so they can defend themselves.

14

The Peace Corps Volunteer
Safety Support System

Michael D. O'Neill and Elizabeth Kramer

Since 1961, the Peace Corps, an independent agency of the United States government, has worked in developing countries under its mission to promote international peace and friendship through the service abroad of American volunteers. In nearly 40 years more than 163,000 volunteers have served in 135 countries. In addition to the technical assistance the volunteers provide, they have fostered people-to-people relationships that help establish a foundation for peace. Upon their return to the United States they help expand Americans' knowledge of the world by bringing their personal understanding of the cultures, customs, languages, and traditions of other people.

Safety and security of the volunteer is the agency's highest priority. The Peace Corps often operates programs in some of the least developed countries and in some of the most remote areas in the world where health, safety, and security risks are an unavoidable part of volunteer service. While it is not reasonable to expect that the agency can ensure the safety of its volunteers, as there exist many variables beyond Peace Corps' control that impact volunteer welfare, Peace Corps does strive to provide the volunteers with the information, training, resources, and support they need to navigate successfully the risks they will encounter.

In matters of safety and security, Peace Corps makes the following key assumptions: Serving as a volunteer overseas entails certain safety and security risks; each volunteer is expected to adopt a culturally appropriate lifestyle that promotes his/her safety; and, each Peace Corps post will establish and maintain a volunteer safety support system as prescribed by Peace Corps policy. The Peace Corps approach to safety and security is characterized by obtaining and maintaining the acceptance and consent of host country authorities and the population at large for its presence and the work volunteers have been recruited to perform. The operative assumption has been: the better integrated the volunteer becomes with the local culture and people, the more productive and safer the volunteer will be. Within the scope of its mission, the Peace Corps takes a systematic approach to increase volunteers' capacity to keep themselves safe and to minimize risks through information sharing, training, site development, incident reporting and response, and crisis management planning.

VOLUNTEER SELECTION

All applicants to the Peace Corps are required to have a personal interview to assess the motivation, life skills, and special abilities they bring to volunteer service. The interview also offers applicants the opportunity to discuss any questions or concerns they may have about Peace Corps. The personal attributes by which applicants are assessed are: motivation and commitment, productive competence, social sensitivity and cultural awareness, emotional maturity and adaptability. Prior to departure, all applicants must pass rigorous medical and legal screening.

Applicants are provided with information packets that describe the nature and conditions of Peace Corps service, the many challenges volunteers face, the impact serving in another culture will have on individual lifestyle, comfort, and safety (for example, living with host families, conservative dress, restrictions on movement, and night travel) and the support volunteers will receive in their respective countries of service. These challenges often include unwanted attention, harassment, health and personal safety risks, and cultural behaviors that a volunteer might find offensive or uncomfortable. Based on this information, applicants make an informed decision whether or not the Peace Corps assignment is suitable for them. The invitation materials reinforce the expectation that volunteers are responsible for behaving in an appropriate manner, adapting to their environment, and developing relationships within their new communities. Throughout their service, volunteers are kept informed by the Peace Corps administration in country of emerging security issues and given guidance for maintaining their safety and well-being as appropriate.

PREPARATION FOR SAFE LIVING

Before reporting to their assigned sites, volunteers participate in a 10–12 week intensive training in the country of service, often living with host families. Peace Corps uses a competency-based, adult learning approach to training that includes group discussions, role playing, and experiential exercises, rather than straight classroom instruction. Training is complemented by practice teaching, participation in community programs, and demonstration activities. Its design emphasizes the integration of personal health and safety, technical, cross-cultural and language training components which, taken together, provide a comprehensive approach to prepare volunteers for their assignments and to equip them with the skills they need to negotiate safely in their country of service. From this early experience forward, volunteers begin to build a network of friends and contacts in the host country that will support their efforts for a safe, healthy, productive service. Continuous training is offered throughout the 27-month tour of duty and is designed to raise awareness of their new environment, build their capacity to cope effectively with the many challenges they will face, and provide them with the tools they need to maintain a safe and appropriate lifestyle.

SITE DEVELOPMENT AND PLACEMENT

During training, volunteers are assessed in order to match the environment of a site with their personal characteristics and preferences. Such characteristics include: age, gender, physical capability, language proficiency, marital status, demonstrated coping skills, and any past experience they bring. The relative merits of privacy vs. security and proximity to neighbors are discussed openly with volunteers prior to placement. Volunteer sites are assessed and approved by Peace Corps and/or host government officials before volunteers arrive to ensure the placement is appropriate and reasonably safe. Site selection is based on established safety and security criteria that reflect consideration of history, access to medical, banking, postal, and other essential services; access to communication, transportation, and markets; availability of different housing options and living arrangements; and, obtaining and maintaining the acceptance and consent of the host community. During the course of service volunteers are visited by Peace Corps program supervisors and medical staff members.

VOLUNTEER SUPPORT

Peace Corps expects that host communities and local agencies will provide the first level of support to volunteers. To this end, host communities and families are oriented to the expectations and challenges of supporting a volunteer, and offered the opportunity to express their own concerns and questions. Pre-service training is designed to enable the volunteer to integrate with the host community and establish a support system. Many posts have formal and informal peer support networks among volunteers. These peer advocates are often trained in listening skills, supportive feedback, crisis intervention, and specific in-country policies. Trained counselors from the Peace Corps Office of Special Services (OSS) provide this training, and often the Peace Corps Medical Officer (PCMO) is a member of the staff advisory panel.

Volunteers are expected to report safety concerns or incidents to the PCMO. The PCMO and other staff members are prepared to provide appropriate medical, emotional, and administrative support as each case warrants. The Peace Corps maintains a collaborative relationship with the U.S. Embassy and host government in order to respond to volunteers' safety and security concerns as they arise.

RETURNED PEACE CORPS VOLUNTEERS

As the time approaches for the volunteers to complete service, they are brought together for several days to reflect on their service, celebrate their accomplishments, give feedback to the program, and prepare for the upcoming transition. Sessions are provided on the psychological/emotional impact of re-entry to the United States reflecting a sudden change in lifestyles, work, and cultural expectations. Volunteers are assisted in capturing their experience in a personal résumé and developing future educational and/or career strategies.

Extraordinary re-adjustment assistance is provided by OSS for volunteers and staff who have been evacuated from a country. These transitional conferences include critical incident stress debriefing and individual counseling to help volunteers and staff come to terms with sudden loss, trauma, and the need to adjust under duress. Peace Corps has arranged with a medical insurance provider to allow returned volunteers access to continued health insurance coverage at a preferred premium rate. The Peace Corps Office of Medical Services provides direct benefits to returned volunteers for post-service medical evaluation, and assists returned volunteers in filing claims for worker's compensation.

The Peace Corps Office of Returned Volunteer Services provides career, educational and re-entry related assistance and information to returned volunteers who often maintain contact with fellow returnees through country of service groups, or regional returned volunteer associations. The National Peace Corps Association, a private alumni organization of returned volunteers, Peace Corps staff, and friends, coordinates many of the activities and communication among these returned volunteer groups.

15

Precious Lives Honored To Serve

*Kris Hurlburt**

The International Federation of Red Cross and Red Crescent Societies is comprised of 176 member National Societies around the world, making it the largest humanitarian organization with 97 million volunteers and 296,000 employees as at the end of 1999. The International Federation works to improve the lives of vulnerable people by mobilizing the power of humanity. It provides relief and development support to its membership and to National Societies in formation. Each year several hundred expatriates (delegates) and thousands of national staff are hired to fulfill this mandate. Because of its unique network which reaches local communities, members of the Federation are often first on the spot to respond to emergencies.

HOME AWAY FROM HOME AWAY FROM HOME

The opportunity to join the operations of the International Federation is an honor *and* a life altering experience. As a delegate remarked recently, "I knew my life would be changed forever, that I would never be the same or even entirely fit into my own culture again. This I met with some sadness, grieving over what I would lose while at the same time eager and excited about the new opportunities I faced. Giving up part of my life to gain another required a very deep-felt decision. I am so much richer for my experiences serving with the Red Cross."

Aid workers, who have lived as expatriates for several years, are often silent for a few seconds when asked where they are from. They see vibrant images of past missions mingled with childhood memories and visions of their families. Some recall previous deployments or even where they last made their bed. All are reflections of just where home might be.

Home could be a tent next to a refugee camp in Tanzania or a hotel room under continuous surveillance by the authorities through one-way mirrors. It could be a compound surrounded by stone walls and unarmed security guards in Afghanistan or an unheated apartment in the steppes of Mongolia or even a patch of ground in

---

*Kris Hurlburt contributed to this book in her personal capacity. The views expressed do not necessarily represent those of the International Federation of Red Cross and Red Crescent Societies.

earthquake ravaged Gujarat, India. Usually it is less dramatic: sharing a house with other expatriates or alone in a small apartment in the city. Sometimes it is a place of exceptional beauty: overlooking the Adriatic Sea, or next to a garden full of exotic fruit trees in Sri Lanka. All places have their memories, often intense and dominant in such profound situations. One delegate who, like most others, loved to tell a good story, described waking up to find a six-foot-long python slithering through his tent.

Some feel a little sadness, confusion, discomfort, and even embarrassment explaining where they are from. It is insufficient to simply say Calgary, Seoul, or Helsinki when you just spent an intense year or two in a conflict zone or disaster setting where your little plot becomes your refuge, your safety, your home, and your history. Strangers quickly become family sharing incredible experiences, sometimes wrought with dramatic events and the enticing element of fear.

PSYCHOLOGICAL SUPPORT: AN ONGOING EVOLUTION IN THE INTERNATIONAL FEDERATION

In some respects the emphasis on psychological well-being took the International Federation back to the birth of the Red Cross and Red Crescent Movement when its founder, Henry Dunant, saw a need to provide aid *and* comfort to soldiers on the battlefields of Solferino, Italy in 1859. He mobilized local villagers to assist without regard for the side they had been fighting on [1]. Shortly after, The International Committee of the Red Cross was formed and in 1919 the League of Red Cross Societies (known today as the International Federation of Red Cross and Red Crescent Societies) was founded. Several decades and numerous disasters later, the International Federation began exploring a new path of providing psychological support to disaster victims. There was another role in addition to supplying food, water, medical care, and shelter: mental health was deemed an important need in a world filled with so much ugliness.

The Federation convened its first working group on psychological support in 1991. Representatives of the American, Belgium, British, Danish, and German Red Cross Societies were designated to develop the first set of guidelines addressing this need. The International Federation Psychological Support Program (PSP) was launched in May 1991. In 1993, the Federation adopted Decision No. 25 "Psychological support to victims of disasters and stressful life events" and opened its Reference Center for Psychological Support, based at Danish Red Cross Headquarters in Copenhagen. Since then, psychological support programs have developed within other National Societies and continue to evolve with each major catastrophe.

The horrifying events in Somalia, the former Yugoslavia, and Rwanda reinforced the need to prioritize psychological support to delegates, not just disaster victims. Film footage of bodies being dragged through angry crowds, hundreds of thousands fleeing war-torn Bosnia and the horrific scenes from Rwanda filled television screens with images of tremendous psychological pain, terror, and hardship brought on by the savage conflicts and devastating disasters. While many watched in the comfort of their homes, Red Cross and Red Crescent delegates, national staff, and volunteers were providing humanitarian aid, risking their own physical and mental health. Sometimes they too became victims, forced to flee to safe refuge, endured air raids and artillery fire, or suffered the loss of a colleague killed in action, coming face to face with their own mortality. More than one delegation huddled together in fear as the confrontation line passed over their compound.

They witnessed the physical consequences of landmines, machetes, nuclear disasters, and disease on the people they were there to serve. They shared the psychological pain of children who saw their parents killed, of mothers who forcibly watched while their offspring were sexually assaulted. They heard detailed and intimate horror stories over and over again. In disaster settings they heard the cries of victims trapped in the rubble resulting from earthquakes or found stiff bodies wrapped around tree limbs after the cyclone subsided. They smelled the odor of death, felt the rumbles of aftershocks, and heard the sounds of dying. They looked into thousands of eyes harboring the aftermath of the most unimaginable acts committed by other human beings. All the while they kept handing out food, setting up shelters, providing first aid, and sharing knowledge, sometimes working days without sleep. Delegates returned from their missions exhausted with minds filled with visions and memories they couldn't erase. Severe stress symptoms including flashbacks, night terrors, extreme anxiety, and depression were noted. Several delegates were diagnosed with post-traumatic stress disorder and referred for treatment.

Decision makers were learning how humanitarian missions impacted on their staff and gained an understanding of the help that could be provided. In response, the International Federation contracted a psychotherapist in 1993 to brief and debrief delegates at its Secretariat through which each delegate passed pre- and post-mission, as well in delegations when conditions warranted extra support. Following a rapid progression of critical incidents affecting several delegations in Africa, a psychologist was hired locally to provide psychological support to the delegates in specific operations. In 1994, another Geneva-based psychotherapist was contracted.

While this was a step in the right direction it was not enough. In 1996 a short chapter on the workplace stress was included in the *Handbook for Delegates* [2]. A one-hour session on managing stress in the work place was given to staff and later added to the induction course attended by all first time delegates. In 1997, the Danish Red Cross published *Psychological First Aid and Human Support* [3] which was later translated into numerous languages.

Concurrently some National Societies began to offer their own psychological support services in the delegate's country of origin. One Icelandic delegate said she was more comfortable talking about her experiences and concerns in her mother tongue. Others expressed their appreciation for the services based in Geneva. Slowly the defenses of the non-believers and mission-hardened delegates began to erode and the awareness was born that anyone can be affected by serving on the front lines. The support in Geneva was especially important for delegates coming from regions where such services were non-existent, highly stigmatized, or otherwise unavailable.

Concerns about international humanitarian aid workers and peacekeepers grow with each kidnapping, murder, and threat. A composite of improved services reduces the risk. Adequate and appropriate equipment allows important needed communications. What is it like for the majority of aid workers who never face these critical events or work on the periphery of them? The stressful situations experienced by delegates and local staff are less likely to be sudden and traumatic than cumulative. Some issues are obvious: cultural differences, foreign languages, separation from family and friends, loneliness, and fear. But others linger in the background waiting to be addressed.

SECURITY AND PREVENTION SAVES LIVES

A sound security system is the best prevention in terms of both physical and psychological safety. Red Cross and Red Crescent staff, by the nature of their work, often find themselves in unstable political and social environments requiring special measures. Security translates into prevention and can mean the difference between life and death. Those managers who place appropriate emphasis on safety also contribute to the psychological well-being of staff, reducing the risk of exposure to traumatic incidents and the subsequent ramifications. With staff safety in mind, another important initiative was undertaken in 1996 when the International Federation created the position of Security Officer, responsible for global staff and operations security. A security briefing became a part of delegate preparation, providing them with survival tools for a variety of settings: during shelling, mob violence, and hostage situations, among others. Security, always an important concern of the International Federation, was prioritized in delegations and today each is required to have an updated security plan that includes evacuation procedures. Knowing the context one works in, being sensitive to cultural norms, adhering to the security regulations, and anticipating events that might occur help keep a delegate safe.

The biggest risk remains motor vehicle accidents [4] that result in more death and injury than any other threat. Causes include chaotic traffic patterns, lack of familiarity with local driving customs, compromised infrastructure (eroded roadbeds, broken traffic lights and illegible street signs), inexperience driving large 4-wheel-drive vehicles, driving under the influence of alcohol, and not using local drivers. The onus is on delegates to follow the security regulations and to take responsibility for their own, and others', security.

Travel by air, essential to most operations, presents anxiety for some individuals. The International Federation has guidelines prohibiting travel on airlines with questionable repair and maintenance schedules. In times of emergency however, the temptation to get access quickly can be overwhelming. Several humanitarian workers have lost their lives in air disasters. This concern was underscored in November 1999 when a United Nations plane filled with aid workers crashed into a Kosovo mountainside killing all on board. Rescue operations were hampered by landmines at the crash site. Events like this cause every delegate to pause and consider his or her own vulnerability.

TELECOMMUNICATIONS

The emphasis on doing everything possible to ensure the safety of the delegations and their assets included equipping offices and residences with adequate communications equipment. Long before the Internet and e-mail were born, delegations in high risk settings communicated electronically, first orally over HF and VHF radio networks and then through written radio messaging (PACTOR). While initially installed for security measures, the development of communication technology has provided the single, most effective support for expatriates worldwide. Even in countries where telephones don't work or postal systems are unreliable, electronic messages can be beamed into space through satellite systems. The ability to connect with family and friends almost immediately fills many gaps previously experienced during deployment and greatly reduces the sense of isolation. It helps maintain cultural ties: accessing local newspapers, keeping tallies on sporting competitions, exchanging the latest jokes. Personal business can be conducted: banking, shopping, real estate, insurance claims. Technical information can be gleaned and photographs readily shared. Even advanced education can be completed. For organizations it is an investment in the well-being and longevity of the employee. As one experienced delegate recalled, "a happy delegate is a good delegate."

PREPARING FOR MISSION

As missions seemed to gain more complexity and risk, and awareness grew regarding the psychological impact on delegates, more emphasis was put on determining fitness for work and matching qualifications and experience with positions. All prospective delegates attend a Basic Training Course organized by National Societies throughout the world. Upon selection, a week-long induction course for new delegates helped prepare them better for their mission by teaching International Federation standards and answering the many questions first timers have. Included were sessions on mission stress and security. All these initiatives contributed to the mental preparation of each delegate and increased their confidence that systems were in place for their well-being. In addition to the knowledge gained, the workshop provided elements of stress inoculation about what they might face in the field.

Most delegates are contracted from one mission to the next. Job insecurity results in some taking on new assignments before they are adequately rested. After several years in the field, delegates start losing their place in the job market since, while interesting, a resume filled with humanitarian missions does not easily translate into local skills. People give up careers to join and when the time comes to return home they may find themselves unemployable in the domestic market or face starting again at the entry level. Health insurance coverage often ceases at the end of the mission while symptoms may manifest much later.

GOING BUSH IN THE BACK HILLS

Aid worker jargon includes "going bush," and while rare, this phenomenon occurs when a worker sheds his or her own identity and assumes that of the local culture. It may be the manifestation of extreme cases of burnout combined with predisposing factors and a lack of adequate coping skills. It is most possibly the same noted in history when, years after the conflict has ended, a soldier deemed missing in action resurfaces from the jungle having assimilated the local culture. Anecdotal evidence suggests certain indicators of going bush that tend to intensify over time: adopting local dress, customs, language and religion, withdrawal and rejection of compatriots, and a decrease in family contacts that sometimes cease entirely. Other indicators are an increase in risk taking behavior, circumventing security rules, and placing themselves and others in danger. Often some of the actions may take on an air of mystery and intrigue which may serve as an enticement.

The standard intervention used to be mandatory time off out of the country, reassignment to another mission area or termination of the mission, possibly effective when done early. In extreme cases, the worker chooses to leave the mission, often staying in the country attempting to find positions with other organizations or disappearing to the hills, leaving behind confusion and tragedy for all involved. For those who succumb there is a large network of family, friends, and colleagues affected yet little is done to address their well-being. It is suggested that a number of different approaches be taken including raising awareness among managers about indicators and creating an environment to address the issues. More important is to empower and place responsibility on the shoulders of the aid worker for his or her own self-care. At the same time they need a working environment that encourages dialogue, peer support and honors requests for time off. The selection process and screening of potential workers is vital to ensure they have both the technical skills and coping mechanisms to work in difficult circumstances in foreign lands. Better screening and the increasing emphasis on psychological support should help address this phenomenon by identifying early warning signs and providing supportive interventions, including longer term psychotherapy when appropriate.

AGING PARENTS AND SICK RELATIVES

Older aid workers are often better prepared for international assignments. They have more life experience and developed technical skills that bring added value to an operation. But they also bring with them worries for elderly parents or sick loved ones. It is an additional and chronic stress factor that intermingles with guilt about choosing an assignment far from home. Recently a group of 40–50-year-old women working in the humanitarian field shared their thoughts and feelings about their parents, learning they weren't alone with frightening thoughts of "what if." They confronted the conflicting emotions resulting from their career choice vs. providing care for those who raised them. During various missions someone in the group had received that dreaded telephone call informing them of the death of a father by a massive heart attack, a mother's emergency cardiac bypass surgery, a loved one whose breast cancer had metastasized, a caretaker who had broken her hip, the need to decide whether to stop life support. All shared feelings of trepidation for the long trip home frightened, worried, anxious, and alone.

One expatriate told how she was denied access by a much younger colleague to a telephone call to comfort her elderly parents by informing them of her safe arrival. "It was like being slapped in the face with the reality of just how difficult it was to contact loved ones. What if they needed me?" One mother of three adult children, all of whom have been deployed abroad at some time, stated, "I think it's the daughters who feel most responsible. As they get older and roles start to reverse, they become the caretakers. My sons just don't react the same way."

The eight women represented five different nationalities. Not one was confident that their employer could handle a family crisis thoroughly or quickly or how their elderly parents would be informed if they were hurt, abducted, or killed in action. Simple mistakes by human resource personnel reinforced that concern. One example was when there was a miscalculation of time zones. A 75-year-old parent woke to a phone call at 5:45 in the morning. Her initial fear was exacerbated when the caller identified herself as being from the organization her daughter was working for. The parent's first thought was that something horrible had happened to her daughter when actually all that was needed was the answer to a simple question about a banking transaction.

The compassionate leave benefit usually provides several days off plus travel time. This is inadequate when one has to pass multiple time zones: an exhausted delegate arrives to help a parent heal from major surgery or plan a funeral. No time or energy remains to move beyond shock and start the grieving process. What results is an expatriate emotionally torn between two realities returning to the field. Leave without pay for emergency situations should be readily granted. However, many delegates are not aware of this possibility.

How do they cope? The most important step was to discuss different scenarios with their parents and other family members before the mission. They established a network of friends and relatives who agreed to notify them quickly and to keep them updated about parental needs. Trust that these people would follow through was essential. Everyone had a plan if an emergency occurred up to and including resignation from their job if the situation was extreme. Most had established e-mail exchanges with their elderly parent(s) and their support network. Not one had a way to rid themselves completely of feelings of guilt.

TIME OFF

International Federation delegates are available for duty 24 hours a day 7 days a week and typically work in demanding environments. Adequate time off is essential but for some it can be exhausting and stressful. Most delegates either have rented out their homes or given up their leases so they do not have a place to settle into easily. Many spend their holidays living out of a suitcase. They have nowhere privately to entertain guests and end up on a progressive tour of visiting friends and family. They are often the guests of honor amid many who want to hear all about their experiences. Others are afraid to ask but, at the same time, have many unanswered questions creating an uncomfortable void. Parents, spouses, children, and best friends all want private time. They want to show their hero off proudly to their friends, the storekeeper, the librarian, and the neighbors. Hence, a trip home can be a whirlwind experience filled with conflicting emotions that has left more than one delegate who had been pulled in so many directions glad to return to their mission to rest.

There are ways for delegates to manage "going home stress." The most important is to identify one's own priorities, set limits with friends and family about events and activities, and to take time for dialogue with those closest about one's emotional needs and the impact on oneself of moving from a mission to home so they know how to give the needed support. Organizing a "vacation within a vacation" and taking personal time can be very helpful.

A number of career delegates have created an oasis for themselves where they can maintain a sense of control, groundedness, and normalcy for the period they have off. A few long timers have farms or ranches that allow them to live a very different lifestyle during down time. Some have small cottages in beautiful surroundings. Others return to the same hotel year after year. A comment frequently heard is that "I just want to get rid of the suitcase, sleep in a good bed, wake up when I want, use my own language, and be around things that are mine for a while." But for most delegates who work from one contract to the next, it is a luxury to be able to maintain one's own home.

After a few years out going home can feel like being a guest in your own country. The landscape changes, old friends have developed new friends, parents have aged, and people have died. Politicians have come and gone. New fads and fashions are evident. The last known television success has been reduced to reruns. Old jokes have been replaced by new ones. Neighbors have changed. Even the slang is different. An International Federation delegate from Kenya said recently, "Each time I go home I find that my social circle has changed and become smaller. Friends have moved, married, had children, and established new friends. The points that connected us are weakened, and then I leave again."

Mission friendships are often mission specific encompassing expatriates from other organizations and the local community. No one really says goodbye for more often than not paths cross again and new stories are shared. Delegates experience incredible situations together and depend upon each other for socializing and support. Not all situations are dramatic and difficult. They are privileged to have experiences most would never dream of and travel to areas of the world tourists would never see, getting an insider's view. They experience the everyday kindness of total strangers who share their culture freely. They meet high government officials, appear on television, and are auspicious guests of local authorities. Most missions involve many expatriates and friendships also develop with those in other organizations. Delegates belong to a special breed, changing their lives to help others. Sharing the front lines and the back hills.

DEVELOPING SUPPORT

Since 1997 the International Federation Health Officer and the two psychotherapists comprised the psychological support program (PSP) team, seeing all delegates pre- and post-mission. The former acquired additional duties as the liaison between the Secretariat, National Society, delegates, and the psychotherapists. The briefing by the psychotherapists focused on stress inoculation, educating outgoing delegates about typical reactions, stress, and traumatic stress, while the Health

Officer advised on physical health and self-care. All became available to delegates by telephone and e-mail in addition to in-person confidential consultations.

Based upon an external evaluation of the PSP conducted in 1998, a set of recommendations to improve the system was instituted:

- continue the present briefing and debriefing program with minor modifications
- develop an integral and required PS component for Heads of Delegation training
- develop a training workshop on PS for desk officers and department heads in Geneva
- assign a PS delegate to regional delegations (covering several delegations each)

Selva Sinnadurai, a long time International Federation delegate who has worked in Croatia, Bosnia, Afghanistan, and Papua New Guinea recently said, "Since I first started I've seen the International Federation place increasing emphasis on psychological support. I think we are ahead of other humanitarian organizations but sometimes wonder if we are viewed as pampered children by the mission hardened? I do not think so. I was not referred to the psychotherapist straight after my evacuation. I was treated like a mature adult and not forced into a session. I think this was a fair way of addressing the issue for we all know *now* such services are available."

THE FUTURE OF PSYCHOLOGICAL SUPPORT

The International Federation is taking many new steps at the dawn of the new millennium. Senior managers participate in comprehensive workshops on mission stress. Mental health specialists are contracted locally when the situation demands. Psychological support programming was extended to delegation hired staff. Additional initiatives were underway for supporting family members. Special consideration was given to the Secretariat and National Society headquarters staff, many of whom are veterans of past missions. A handbook, *Managing Stress in the Field* [5], was distributed. And most importantly, both accumulated and traumatic stress started to be openly discussed. The taboo's power began to weaken.

REFERENCES

1. H. Dunant, *A Memory of Solferino*, H. Dunant, Geneva, 1862.
2. Danish Red Cross, *Psychological First Aid and Human Support*, Copenhagen, Denmark, 1997.
3. International Federation of Red Cross and Red Crescent Societies, *Handbook for Delegates*, Geneva, Switzerland, 1996.
4. International Federation of Red Cross and Red Crescent Societies, *World Disasters Report*, Geneva, Switzerland, 1998.
5. International Federation of Red Cross and Red Crescent Societies, *Managing Stress in the Field*, Geneva, Switzerland, 2001.

Voice

RED CRAYON

Janet Shriberg

In this picture you are mocking us. Why not mock us? We came so abruptly in your life and forced our awkward laughter on your small ears. You're right to sit alone while other kids show me how to chase a hog away from the tortillas sizzling over the fire. You are right to lift your left shoulder to hide your wet eyes. And, you are right to shrug off my questions because perhaps you know I have no answers.

Why should I know more about the terrible shakes that bring down homes and trap babies in dirt and stone. I want to reach out and ask you for forgiveness. Without a word you sit quietly outside the circle and watch the other children listen to my directions. "Draw the earthquake, what did it look like?"

They draw with fury. Their small hands grasp the broken crayons I gave them. Blue, yellow, orange, each color transforming a child's last nightmare. Each child has only one color. Certainly there are not enough colors for everyone. And kids don't share when they are drawing earthquakes that kill people.

There was no red crayon to match your red shirt. I am sorry about that. I think of this each time I stare at the photograph of you on my wall. There should have been a red crayon, maybe then you would've joined us. Or, maybe you would have stayed outside, watching us. You did let me take this picture, and you smiled but you didn't draw with us. There should have been a red crayon for you to draw with later, after we left.

16

The Dangers of Aid Work

Barbara Smith

The International Rescue Committee (IRC) was founded in 1933 to assist and resettle refugees in World War II. IRC currently operates resettlement offices in 17 U.S. cities and overseas offices in 28 countries. It is a beneficiary-driven organization in that we only define our mandate assisting refugees worldwide, thus fielding programs based on the needs and capacities of the refugees and not on pre-selected sectors (such as health or shelter) or time frames (such as emergencies or post-conflict). IRC currently has programs in seven different sectors and has country programs that are 22 to 1 year old, averaging 8 years per country. From programs to security, IRC relies on acceptance by the community and disciplined communications as the cornerstone of overseas work. Currently half of its staff works in active war zones and three-fourths in areas where there are terrorist threats.

IRC's security policy is structured on the United Nations model of five phases of security risk: our movements and work are guided by whether no unusual risk exists (phase 1), through evacuation (phase 5). We participate in the warden system with other NGOs. IRC conducts annual training of trainers in security precautions, covering topics from personal behavior to radio use. The trainers are then responsible for holding classes for all staff in their country of assignment. Each country is required to maintain and update a security plan with precautions and contingency plans. The focal person for security, who designs and monitors security readiness at IRC headquarters in New York, reviews all security plans. RedR is IRC's prime consultant for training and policies. Like other NGOs, IRC has experienced hostage situations, mine accidents, and violent armed robberies. However, its only fatalities have been from car accidents: one international and, in the last five years, three local staff have been killed in vehicle accidents.

Adequately protecting the bodies and minds of aid workers in refugee situations is perhaps now an oxymoron. Wars operate without rules, target civilians, are aimed at inflicting suffering, even without a political motive. Aid workers are presented with unremitting chaos, moral issues for which nothing, even in their imagination, could prepare them, and inadequate responses from their supervisors; and, they receive marginally relevant stress management paradigms from mental health and security professionals. The increasing numbers of deaths, many hideous, among their ranks and problems returning fully to their prior lives after humanitarian service are the tragic toll.

Novice aid workers often believe that, with malice toward none, they have come to "do something" more than just be a bystander to the suffering, and that they truly have no part in the war around them. The Red Cross has subtly instilled a doctrine of neutrality and impartiality in many aid workers. Caretakers in hospitals and shelters in every country should be respected, afforded a modicum of both protection and dignity, and not share the illness and conflicts of the people they serve. Experienced aid workers know that their presence and activity become part of the conflict.

Relief workers, almost by design, move from country to country and situation to situation almost like they are on a golf course. Often one renews acquaintances, several years later, with a person casually met in another war, on another continent. It is not unusual to find aid workers who have been in Ethiopia, Goma, and Bosnia, but rare to find one who has stayed in the same place over a period of years. Novice or experienced, aid workers are generally strangers without access to the more hidden and powerful societal forces at play around them. It is not unusual for aid workers, in the midst of open warfare, to "suspend the laws of physics." Americans who wouldn't walk alone at night in Central Park venture near and into lines of fire in Bosnia, live and work with gangs of murderers in West Timor, refuse to give hungry, drunken armed men at checkpoints supplies that they would immediately give up if accosted on the streets of their hometowns. In Sarajevo, aid workers walked on streets open to sniper fire just to get a pizza at night (and get shot at). In Guinea, staff go for a run passing checkpoints manned by armed drunken soldiers (and get accosted); people go for walks alone while armed technicals with stolen food in trucks pass by (and point guns at them). Every aid agency has stories like these from IRC.

One aid worker, seeking relief from the Somali sun under the wing of a loud C-130 engine required to be kept running at all times for fast takeoff, pulls out a cigarette and a lighter. With fumes of jet fuel visible overhead, he lights the cigarette and nonchalantly begins to smoke. He would have never thought of smoking in restricted European airport zones, but in Somalia it didn't matter. He was living where the world was upside down; so the threat of a spark near jet fuel did not matter. He even refused a request to move away until he was made to by the pilot. Under the doctrine of "force protection," aid workers, in civilian clothes, frequently take more risks and sustain more injuries than do the military.

Whereas aid workers' governments can issue travel restrictions that workers can ignore, military proscriptions against exposing staff to danger are airtight. Not only did U.S. soldiers stay behind barbed wire near the lake in an airport in Goma in 1994, but the rare ones sent beyond the perimeter were not allowed to get out of their Humvees. I personally asked two such soldiers for water stored in canisters in their Humvees and they declined, amidst people dying of thirst, saying they weren't allowed to.

UNPROFOR, for protection, built a barbed wire fence that jutted far into the sidewalk of a Sarajevo street where sniper attacks were common. Civilians and aid workers hugged the wall to avoid being shot but were forced, when they came to the armed headquarters, to walk into the street, thus becoming open targets. Shootings occurred often. In many places, notably Somalia and Bosnia, the UN peacekeepers were not tasked with protecting civilians but only relief supplies. Trucks were protected with guns, but not the civilians working on or relying upon supplies brought by them. With the emphasis on forced protection, in a mandate absent any commitment to protect aid workers and other civilians, the level of risk rises dramatically.

Local armed groups clearly use the presence and security risks of aid workers as a tool as well. Stories of killings and kidnappings abound, and are on the increase. The International Committee of the Red Cross (ICRC), historically the group most protected by international law, has sustained the most casualties. One of the most shocking incidents of all was in Chechnya where, under a large Red Cross symbol covering the roof of a tent and every other sign possible to identify a hospital as a Red Cross facility, doctors and nurses were killed in their beds. The usual conventions and rules of war offer less and less protection in recent years. It is literally true that many people engaged in and leading the shooting have neither heard of nor can they read the Geneva conventions. It is unclear what they even know of the Red Cross movement. Some of these people are children, some have themselves been reared without education in war zones. Others know full well what they are doing but know they operate with near impunity.

Many aid workers have noticed that different sides to a conflict are more concerned and more attentive to how they are being perceived in the media than they are about protection of civilians and upholding international law. It may be that the news media are the best vehicle to inform and hold some armed groups accountable to the rule of law. Others are absolutely not susceptible to outside pressure and operate at will. Peacekeeping forces will not protect aid workers, local authorities will not protect aid workers and, in some respect, the behavior of aid workers compromises their own protection. There is no security for them. They can only seek to understand the risks they are taking and ways to minimize the danger to themselves.

One of the first and most pronounced effects of the stress that aid workers undergo can truly jeopardize their security; over time, people get overwhelmed by the suffering, become fatigued and undernourished, and totally immerse themselves in work and tragedy. The result is loss of judgment and concentration, which can lead to poor choices about security. After prolonged exposure to danger, it is common for people to accept it as part of everyday living. Aid workers can also decide that since the local population must live with this danger and are suffering so much more than they are, it is almost unconscionable for them to protect themselves overtly in ways the local people cannot. This is often manifest in the differences and disagreements between the headquarters of aid agencies and the staff on the ground.

Headquarters staff try to insist on stricter security measures than field staff are willing to accept. They think that field staff have impaired judgment about the risks and believe that headquarters understands the situation and what must be done if any useful work is to happen. As the death toll of workers has risen over the last several years, aid agencies have adopted stricter security measures, but it is not infrequent for field staff to take unnecessary risks in the course of their job.

In addition to desensitization to danger, another problem of people who cannot manage the level of stress to which they are exposed is that their personal relationships deteriorate. People form unwise relationships and get into protracted problems with colleagues. Staff conflict disrupts programs and can compromise security. In most dangerous situations, the staff must rely on each other to insure that everyone is safe. When staff will not speak to each other or mistrust each others' motivations, the unity required to keep people watching out for each other, sharing information, and covering for each other's mistakes is lost. This most certainly compromises security.

The problem is not that aid workers are doomed to lose their sense of reality, nor that they suffer dysfunctional stress reactions or live as targets minute by minute. But these situations are common and do impinge on the functioning of whole teams when they happen.

AID WORKERS PROTECTING THEMSELVES

Aid workers have most definitely taken steps to analyze the problems that they face and outline concepts and concrete steps that can be taken to protect themselves. One widely utilized framework for minimizing risk for aid workers is the security triangle, developed originally by Konraad Van Brabant [1]. The triangle is comprised of three security elements: acceptance, protection, and deterrence. According to this framework, staff safety is only as strong as their acceptance in the area in which they live. Local people have knowledge of the situation, and a better understanding of the dangers and how to assess the risks and minimize the threat. Indeed, in many situations, including East and West Timor in 2000, local people literally hid aid workers in their houses as the militia were killing civilians. Aid workers are more likely to be accepted not on the appropriate and transparent behavior of individuals, but based on the local populations' acceptance of the values, mandate, and mission of the agency.

The second cornerstone is deterrence. People and teams must have skills in managing crises, be they outbreaks of shooting or mob violence. Standard operating procedures, staff training, and marking of all vehicles contribute to deterrence. Closely related is the third leg of the triangle, protection. Equipment such as road worthy cars, communications gear, and sometimes flak jackets provide needed safety.

Most agencies rely heavily on acceptance to provide protection (it often feels like luck). Some workers understand the issues so poorly that they cannot articulate why they can function so easily in unusual and dangerous areas. Since aid workers have access to more resources than local people, and pay relatively little for them, personal services like cooking and laundry have been conferred on them because they are well fed, highly educated expatriates largely from developed countries. Aid workers have an out; they can leave. Local people may somehow seem "smaller" because they must react and cannot escape the issues and violence surrounding the conflict.

It is the rare aid worker who thinks or expresses how separate, sheltered, and relatively pampered he or she is, and attaches a feeling of superiority. There are very few aid workers who are not decently motivated and mean to be helpful. Most arrive because of a common humanity. But insidiously, aid workers who are protected above other people, who have personal services most couldn't expect at home, who are not wracked by the effect of the conflict, and who are by and large well treated by the local population, do not recognize how much this protection comes from local people.

A study of deaths among aid workers showed that most occur within the first three months of arrival in a country, rather than after they have spent time and made enough mistakes to make some enemies on one side of a conflict or another or have angered some black marketers or local authorities [2]. Indeed, it is the people who have been in the country for a brief time who do not know how to protect themselves and who, more importantly than having no enemies, have yet to make friends in and be accepted by the community, who are the ones most likely to be killed.

On a day-by-day, even minute-by-minute, basis, aid workers survive in significant measure because the local community protects them. In the recent deaths of UNHCR workers in Kupang, West Timor, the UN staff who had gone to local houses survived. The three remaining in the office without local protection were brutally murdered. Local people also hint and behave as if aid workers are in a special category. Kindness and hospitality are evident for reasons ranging from genuine appreciation for their assistance and presence, to hope for employment, to pure curiosity, to trying to find a way to pilfer goods and services. In societies where local women are not invited to make decisions, share meals, or have any interaction with or equality to men, female aid workers are invited to do all of these things with local men. Where local females cannot hope to find respect, female aid workers experience respect, even deference.

In current wars and conflicts, it is well known that civilians have become common targets, children are increasingly the soldiers, and terror is used as a weapon. In Bosnia early in the war, an estimated 90 percent of casualties were civilians. In Congo, three million civilians have died of the effects of war in two years. Aid workers are increasingly at risk, and will continue to be killed if they are present where there is war. Though efforts are made to protect aid workers, and there is increasing pressure to stop targeting them, there is no denying the fact that not all aid workers who enter conflict zones can or will be protected.

Difficult as it has been for staff overseas to develop and maintain protocols to minimize security risks, it has proven even more so to institutionalize mental health principles into the management of programs. While it is no longer unusual to speak about the emotional status of staff, its effects on staff functioning, and the need for psychological care, still very few are willing to admit that they themselves cannot cope. In addition, perhaps therefore, the development of programs to safeguard staff mental health is in its infancy.

Many NGOs rely on the combination of time away from work and critical stress debriefing following an incident. Staff are given relatively long leave time both to rest during an assignment at routine intervals, and time enough to go home. This can attenuate the process of becoming overwhelmed but, just as frequently the time away allows the staff members to regain their equilibrium, but on return, they feel like they had never left. After a particularly stressful and dangerous event, such as a car jacking or hostage taking, many NGOs provide debriefing for the affected staff, based on the belief that retelling the stories and sharing the various perspectives of their experience, will minimize any lasting effect and trauma. Critical Incident Debriefing, while not presented as a mental health exercise, usually also does not make follow-up available.

There are precious few techniques available for people who must live in extremely stressful, dangerous situations, work, socialize and depend for their own physical safety on the same people 24 hours a day, seven days a week. They are told that a dead, ill, or burned out aid worker cannot help anyone, in order to illicit the most deeply held belief of aid workers: "to help someone else." Teams who are working in dangerous situations often develop splits among themselves. Arguably, inability to manage personal relationships as one once did is a hallmark of stress reactions. Generic stress management techniques of taking time away, developing a hobby or eating fresh food are many times impossible. These techniques may be taught both by the human resource department staff at headquarters, where most have little formal training and even less international experience, as well intentioned as they may be.

The seeming increase of stress reactions attests to the desirability of other ideas, techniques and practitioners than those trained and working in the developed world, which separates between work and leisure. Many NGOs recognize the inadequacy of their policies, but have few resources and less staff depth to make needed changes.

But, most staff members can complete a tour of duty with few lasting problems to their functioning. We at IRC see that the experienced, creative, and brave aid workers, the kind that is crucial to good humanitarian programs, experience so many types of stress, danger and injury, in close living quarters, that over a period of years they inexorably lose too much of the resilience that made them so effective in the first place. This is a tragedy. Long-term staff and their mental health deserve much attention and research.

REFERENCES

1. K. Van Brabant, *Operational Security Management in Violent Environments: A Field Manual for Aid Agencies,* Overseas Development Institute, London, 2000.
2. M. Sheik, I. Gutierrez, P. Bolton, P. Speigel, M. Thieren, and G. Burnham, Death among Humanitarian Workers, *British Medical Journal, 321*:1, pp. 166-168, July 15, 2000.

Voice

AN UNSPOKEN AGREEMENT

Gerald Martone

Some have referred to our time as among the most violent in human history. Relentless open warfare, ethnic violence, and political oppression rampages over thirty countries around the world. Fighting armies and rebel groups have used forced movements and violent deportations of people as a deliberate military strategy on countless occasions. Being displaced and uprooted used to be a side effect of war. Now it has become a deliberate objective of ruthless demagogues and their fighters.

Over the last ten years I have seen refugees flee on foot, by car and tractor, and on buses. Just two years ago, I witnessed Kosovars forcefully deported out of their country on trains. But last summer I was even more disturbed as I watched East Timorese civilians forcefully purged from their homeland on commercial airliners. I stood helplessly by on the blistering tarmac of the airport in Atambua, West Timor as barefoot women and children, with bundles on their heads, were marched at gunpoint off jumbo jets.

Yet even amid these atrocities and unspeakable horrors, refugees display extraordinary courage, compassion, and dignity. People outside this profession often ask, "How can you stand all that suffering?" I have wondered just the opposite: how can anyone stand *not* having the chance to see the nobility and fortitude of the human spirit in the face of tragedy?

For me, the hardest part of our work is trying to reconcile the contradictions, the inconsistencies, the utter defiance of these horrific situations to conform to any familiar explanation of reality. Each crisis only seems to bring more contradiction and moral confusion. These dilemmas flout rational understanding. There is hardly a place to turn to find the solace of a ready explanation or even acknowledgement of this irreconcilable and unconscionable reality. What possible explanation can reconcile an understanding of the intense fear and paranoia that drives a people to ethnicide? How am I to understand why some of the most severe and extreme hatreds and attempted annihilations are between groups of people who are most similar to each other?

At times we portray a façade of competence and effectiveness while facing insurmountable situations of tragic suffering. It is as if we have an unspoken agreement that we won't acknowledge the futility of what we are attempting to do. I find myself denying any expression of hopelessness or impotence to alter the course of staggering human misery.

There is even a dichotomy of reactions to the very beneficiaries we serve. While we romanticize refugees as helpless, violated objects worthy of our charity and sympathy, we are sometimes confused about who these people really are. They might be innocent victims or culpable, conspiring perpetrators. Each refugee population seems to have wolves among the sheep, confusing my generalized compassion. Are they refugees or fugitives, hostages or captors, victims or villains?

Some outsiders revere humanitarian workers as possessing an extraordinary measure of compassion. I am viscerally embarrassed at the implication of my own saintliness. In fact, the attraction to this field in my case is far less noble. It is a ghoulish fascination with the frightening moment of violent anarchy. It is a repetition compulsion that draws me toward what I fear, rather than run from it. Perhaps I am seduced by the sense of invincibility from escaping death's grip so near at hand.

There is also an inherent contradiction in our magnanimous humanitarian exertion against the backdrop of world apathy, indifference, and anti-international-ism. When I was in the Peace Corps I was warned not to expect more than fifteen minutes of sustained interest in my precious two-year odyssey from my family and friends back home.

As we watch the metastasizing populations recoil from frightening traumatic experiences and grotesque human rights violations, we do little to provide an alter-native or temporary reprieve from a bleak and dreary life in exile. We make little available to distract these victims from the haunting recollections of their plight. While the large-scale, broad sector approaches to emergency relief provide a narrow emphasis on material and physical needs, a critical niche is unmet as the emotional suffering of people is overlooked.

"We will die with full stomachs" was the refrain of Bosnians, still suffering emotional turmoil and legitimate fears of further persecution long after their material needs had been met. In the refugee camps in Goma, Zaire in 1994 we used to hypothesize about the existence of a "failure to thrive" syndrome; people surrender-ing the will to live despite the extraordinary efforts to reverse the effects of severe dehydration.

Finally, we face the inconsistency and contradiction of our own organizational mandates. Most of these simple covenants are imbued with the rhetorical atonement of a commitment to the dignity of those we serve. But we only seem to recognize dignity when we are mortified to learn that it has been a neglected aspect of our craftsmanship.

Last winter in Ingushetia I met an old Chechen man. We were in an aban-doned pig farm that had been converted into an Internally Displaced Persons camp. Thoughtlessly, we neglected to consider the religious taboo against pork as we converted the farm into a camp. Sitting in a pig stall, the old man announced to me, with mixed emotions, the birth of his new granddaughter. He smiled and then he sighed: "We are Muslims you know."

17

Psychosocial Care for Humanitarian Aid Workers: The Médecins Sans Frontières Holland Experience

Piet van Gelder and Reinoud van den Berkhof

Médecins Sans Frontières Holland (MSF Holland) is one of five operational sections of the MSF organization. The other four are Médecins Sans Frontières France, Belgium, Switzerland, and Spain. MSF Holland works independently in 30 countries worldwide, but in several countries together with other operational MSF sections. MSF Holland is a strictly impartial operating emergency humanitarian aid organization. After the initial emergency aid is provided, projects are handed over to longer term international as well as national humanitarian aid organizations.

MSF Holland has a variety of humanitarian aid programs, such as mental health (Sierra Leone), HIV/AIDS (Ethiopia), drought (Mongolia), refugee aid, Kala-azar, Sleeping Sickness, nutrition, drug distribution, vaccination campaigns (measles, cholera), and aid to natural disasters (El Salvador, India, and Turkey).

PSYCHOSOCIAL CARE AND SUPPORT

Psychosocial care is used to support emergency workers who have been exposed to cumulative and critical incident stress while working in the field during both short- and long-term missions. The work involves ongoing and cumulative stress, often compounded by critical incident stress. Ideally, therefore, psychosocial care should be integrated into a humanitarian aid organization as a standard service for employees who work in the field. There are strong arguments for the integration of such services. The goal of psychosocial care is to protect and support aid workers, and to minimize the development of abnormal stress response syndromes that may cause lost time and a drop in effectiveness of work. The goal of MSF Holland, as an organization, is to keep aid workers sustained during their missions.

Aid workers themselves do not always acknowledge the stress involved in humanitarian aid work. They are generally professionals who are confident about their ability to maintain their "edge" or invulnerability [1, 2]. Many tend to downplay or ignore stress; others may be simply unaware that they may be affected. Moreover, aid workers will not be convinced of the benefits of psychosocial care and support if the management does not acknowledge the need for these services. The organization may assume that selection procedures will single out individuals who are sufficiently resilient to handle stressful conditions in the field and for whom training will provide sufficient protection [1, 2].

Dyregrov [3] argues that it is easier to respond to the worker's needs in the event of a critical incident if psychosocial care or debriefing has become part of the normal organizational response to certain kinds of events.

When psychosocial care and support are a standard in a humanitarian aid organization, these services have organizational validity. MSF Holland has provided these services for their aid workers, international as well as national, in the field since 1993 through the Psychosocial Care Unit. Psychosocial care and support for the people working in the field have become important components of the organizational philosophy of the Dutch operational section of MSF.

THE PSYCHO SOCIAL CARE UNIT (PSCU) OF MSF HOLLAND

The PSCU at MSF Holland is a team of 16 volunteer-professionals who are familiar with on-site conditions and can be deployed within 24 hours in the event of critical incidents. These professionals also provide stress management support on the site. Managers in the field may be advised how to ensure that continued attention is devoted to stress management, how to promote group cohesion in the wake of a critical incident, how to monitor the aid workers' psychological welfare and refer for psychotherapy if necessary, and how to set up a "defusing" session [2, 4] in the event of renewed unrest or danger.

Because of the legitimacy and credibility achieved in the MSF Holland organization by the PSCU through 8 years of hard work, interventions on site by the PSCU now are effective and its rapport with the workers is established prior to missions. The PSCU is a permanent multidisciplinary team of psychologists, psychiatrists, social workers, and psychotherapists, associated with the organization so the services it provides can be accessed easily and speedily.

Psychosocial care and support, a "circle of full support," is an integral part of the whole mission: preparation, the mission itself, coming home and aftercare.

PREPARATION

All fieldworkers should be prepared for their missions.

Preparation for the job to be done in the field takes place at various in-company training and courses for different levels of responsibility:

• Preparation Primary Departure Course for first mission aid workers;
• Basic Management Course for field coordinators;
• Advanced Management Course for country managers.

Preparation Primary Departure Course

In this course, first mission people are familiarized with the MSF Holland basics, such as the organization, human resource management in the field, safety and security, working and living in teams, introduction to emergencies, data gathering in emergencies, health programs and policy, cross cultural communication, water and sanitation, pharmacy stock management, mass vaccination campaigns, introduction to finances, nutrition, and "Coping with Stress" offered by a team of the PSCU.

In this "Coping with Stress" module, the PSCU pays attention to the following basic issues on stress and stress management:

- Individual and (international and national staff) team stress
- Coping with individual and team stress
- Stressors in the field: day-to-day work stress, cumulative
- Stress and critical incident stress
- Awareness of stressors experienced by others and how to support one another
- Individual and team stress management
- The role of support of the PSCU for people in the field

The Basic Management Course

In this course future field coordinators are trained in basic management skills, such as the MSF mission, advocacy, role of the (Project/Logistic/Medical) Coordinator, project planning (project cycle, initial assessment, problem analysis, logistical framework, monitoring, and evaluation), budgeting, security, human resource management, and "Stress Management."

A team of the PSCU offers the "Stress Management" module. Important issues are:

- Recognizing, identifying and analyzing different forms of day to day, cumulative and critical incident work-related stress in the field: organizational stressors, work relationships, working conditions, cultural differences, robbing, and shooting incidents
- Recognizing the emotional and physical reactions of people to the various stressors
- Critical incident stress and Post Traumatic Stress Disorders symptoms
- Basic skills to manage the after-effects of critical incidents
- Basic skills to manage stress: prevention, management of team stress, and of organizational stressors
- Basic cognitive techniques to cope with personal stress

Advanced Management Course

This has the same content as that of the Basic Management Course, but is related to the highest level of responsibility in the field, that of the Country Manager. In this course, the PSCU offers the module on "Advanced Stress Management Skills for Country Managers."

Important issues in this module are:

- Thorough understanding of stress prevention and stress management from the perspective of the Country Manager
- Identifying and analyzing the different stressors in the field and designing a stress management plan based on stressor analysis
- Providing basic psychological support for individuals and teams in the field following critical incidents and cumulative stress
- Techniques of a defusing or decompression debriefing
- Mastering cognitive techniques to cope with personal stressors
- Post Traumatic Stress Disorder symptoms and the need for referral
- Appointments in the field with the PSCU if necessary

Part of the preparation is that before coordinators and country managers go for a mission, they have to be briefed by the PSCU, in particular when they leave for high security risk countries.

Psychosocial Care and Support in the Field

The services of the PSCU in the field are the following:

- Offering cumulative and critical incident stress (management) interventions
- Providing specific psychosocial care in the field for those who have been traumatized and helping the international as well as the national teams to deal with the aftermath of their experiences
- Providing workshops in the field to elaborate further (basic and advanced) stress management skills for those already trained in the various courses mentioned above

COMING HOME AND AFTERCARE

The PSCU provides specific psychosocial care and support to people returning from the field, such as debriefings following high security risk projects, short-term psychotherapy, to a maximum of 16 sessions, when needed or requested (recommended), referring non-Dutch people to colleagues from the PSCU network in different countries. People are referred to professional helpers when long-term psychotherapy is needed.

PEER SUPPORT NETWORKS

As far as we know, only MSF Belgium has a unit somewhat similar to the MSF Holland PSCU. But there is a major difference: their "422 unit" consists of staff who perform their normal, daily tasks at Brussels headquarters. They are expatriates (expats) who do their "office turn" after their "field turn." In the event of a critical incident, a team of two of these workers goes to the field to debrief the affected staff. They have had only a short, practical training in debriefing techniques. Mostly non-professionals, they are volunteers with field experience who want to provide support in case of critical incidents. This kind of support is comparable to the military tradition of "comrades helping comrades." Their professional training and experience are not sufficient to enable them to determine whether a person needs specific psychosocial care or to be referred for professional helpers.

As part of the office hierarchy and organization, there may be links between these debriefers, the organization, and the people who need the debriefing, which could affect the latter's future careers within MSF Belgium. Indeed, some of them felt safer being debriefed by us than by their own people, who do not have the full impartiality and independence of the PSCU in MSF Holland.

MSF France, MSF Spain, and MSF Switzerland do not have a Psycho Social Care Unit or a Peer Support Network.

Because of the proven value of the MSF Holland psychosocial care and peer support systems we have been approached by partner sections to assist them in establishing a peer support network as well as a back-up professional psychosocial care system. The PSCU of MSF Holland supports the development of the MSF Peer Support Networks in The Netherlands, United Kingdom, United States/New York, Canada, Germany, and Norway. This consists of providing workshops on work and traumatic stress, vicarious traumatization and family support and assisting the Peer Support Networks in identifying, organizing, and establishing a network of psychologists to whom to refer returnees suffering from their field-related traumatic stress.

The Peer Support Network system was established in the Netherlands in 1991 as a voluntary organization of former MSF expats, to support the reintegration process into society of MSF colleagues returning from the field. Although MSF Holland finances most of the costs of the Peer Support Network Holland organization, PSN Holland is independent of the MSF Holland organization. Peer support may play an important role in the work and private life of an expat. It has been shown to be an effective form of emotional support because peers recognize and immediately understand most of the positive and negative aspects of being an expat, having been expats themselves. Peers understand and can support the expat during a period in which he or she feels sad or depressed for missing the specific MSF work and life atmosphere, something one can never explain to people who are not familiar with "MSF life." Peers understand why and when one needs psychosocial therapeutic care. They know this may be necessary after a complicated, long, intense, and stressful period in the field.

We feel that other MSF organizations are slowly becoming aware of the importance of psychosocial care and support for humanitarian aid workers. It is tragic that severe critical incidents are necessary to activate this awareness, such as that of the six ICRC team members who, in April 2001, were killed and chopped to pieces near Bunya, Congo.

LESSONS LEARNED AND FUTURE DIRECTIONS

The first lesson we learned over the past years was the importance of a well organized HRM department, one able to recruit and match the prospective candidates to the post. This process takes at least a fortnight with the group of candidates together to be trained and educated. This is done with great care in order to achieve the desired results. There is a high rate of intersubjective reliability when a decision to select a candidate is taken.

Even after such preparation, it is still difficult to predict the behavior of people in field conditions. We keep on working to improve our methods. Meanwhile, a lot of work is done to increase coaching and education in the field for both the international and the national staff. Good and fair working contracts that demonstrate how coworkers should be treated and managed are important as well. These are preconditions for the work of the PSCU to take place effectively.

The second lesson we learned was that no matter the state of scientific discussion about early interventions, including debriefing and its positive or negative results in traumatic situations in the field, when critical incidents happen, being present and meeting the victims as soon as possible (within 24 hours) is essential. We thus use any method available to prevent our people, including national staff, from being traumatized. We are not wedded to one method. We will persevere in this direction of multi-methodology and well-reflected eclecticism, which is very different from the non-professional idea that "anything goes."

We frequently noticed that expats suffered sooner from burnout symptoms when they were working with a traumatized national staff. We thus considered it necessary to make psychological maintenance visits to educate the national staff and help them cope with trauma within their own settings and cultures. We were able to establish self-help groups that have worked out very satisfactorily in Sierra Leone, Angola, Guinea, and Uzbekistan. We are monitoring this new initiative closely.

Another lesson learned was how important it is to establish peer support groups in as many home countries as possible. Why? An MSF mission always leads, to a greater or lesser extent, to a certain estrangement from friends and family: sometimes they will listen one time to the expat's story but that's it. So missions frequently include a personal feeling of isolation and loneliness. The only persons who really understand what happens to you in the field are fellow expats. MSF Holland has taken the lead in establishing these groups (peer support and PSCU) in the partner sections. We also select therapists or advanced social workers to do the more therapeutic treatments. We train these groups and, when requested, we do the maintenance work as well. However, most of them have become self-supporting and create their own national and cultural style to deal with these issues.

We have lively international contact on matters of caring and support and we will continue to do so. We will internationalize further the idea of the complete circle of support and care and implement it whenever it is possible. Of course, this set of ideas is not limited to MSF Holland alone.

In this ever changing world we have already done just a little bit of what is needed for "les populations en dangers" and for our own expats and national staff. That is why we must continue our activities with the knowledge that we are not only builders of humanitarian ideas but also, sadly enough, must seek to be rebuilders of humanitarian dignity wherever and whenever it is trampled underfoot.

SUMMARY AND RECOMMENDATIONS

Psychosocial care and support of humanitarian aid workers is an essential part of human aid for the people who provide human aid to others. The added value of psychosocial care to these aid workers is recognized and legitimated more and more by the management of international humanitarian aid organizations. This book is realistic proof of that awareness. MSF Holland is one of the first international humanitarian aid organizations to pay attention to and care for their own humanitarian aid workers by setting up a specific psychosocial care and support unit. That was necessary in order to address increasingly stressful situations in the field, such as robberies, shooting incidents, kidnapping, and abduction. Constructive and positive feedback from people in the field who have been emotionally supported after cumulative stress situations and critical stress incidents encourages psychologists to continue with their work on behalf of their colleagues working in the field in stressful situations.

It is seriously recommended that every international humanitarian aid organization develop this kind of essential support for the hardworking people in the field. The benefits of psychosocial care and support to the aid workers in the field are immeasurable.

It is also recommended that psychologists in this specific area of their profession try to work together to develop it on every level. This book should stimulate and enhance the implementation of this recommendation.

REFERENCES

1. C. Dunning, Mental Health Response to Mass Emergencies, in *Interventions Strategies for Emergency Workers*, M. Lystad (ed.). Brunner-Mazel, New York, 1988.
2. N. Cohen de Lara-Kroon, R. van den Berkhof, and M. Lis-Turlejska, Debriefing Procedures for Humanitarian Aid Workers, *Nowiny Psychologiczn*, 2001.
3. A. Dyregrov, The Process in Psychological Debriefings, *Journal of Traumatic Stress, 4*, 1989.
4. J. T. Mitchell and G. S. Everly, *Critical Incident Stress Debriefing: An Operations Manual for the Prevention of Traumatic Stress among Emergency Services and Disaster Workers*, Chevron Publishing Company, Ellicot City, Maryland, 1993.

Voice

LIKE A SQUEEZED LEMON
Marc Vachon

It is difficult to talk about Goma because it was a huge nightmare from beginning to end.

In June 1994 I was living in Maputo, Mozambique, working on short-term emergency missions for MSF France as a logistics officer. I came back from a two-month mission to the southern part of Sudan, and was asked to go to Goma, Zaire (now Republic of Congo) to put in place a 740-bed field hospital. This hospital remains today the largest ever built by MSF.

When I arrived in Goma the only word I could find to describe it was: Hell. You saw it on TV: a lot of dead bodies everywhere; 500,000 refugees from Rwanda; cholera, dysentery, shigellosis. I began work immediately; four days later we opened the hospital, and within ten days it was 100 percent operational. I spent another ten days starting the construction of a therapeutic feeding center. Then I became ill. On my last day, en route home, I was stopped by the military and threatened by a 9-mm. gun when a soldier argued that I was a terrorist working for the Tutsi invaders. That was enough. But the day after I left the field hospital had 560 patients and the feeding center was almost ready to welcome 450 children.

I spent only four days in Paris. I went to MSF Headquarters for what proved to be a very short—three hours—and cold debriefing. It seemed to me that nobody there knew what was happening in Zaire.

> Thanks for everything, Marc. You look a bit tired . . . You should rest. Thanks again for everything.

I went back to Maputo for three weeks. From the beginning I had bad nightmares. They were always the same. I was sitting in a car, driving slowly, looking at the bodies lying side by side along the road. I started to drink, to drink a lot—whisky for breakfast, a bottle a day, and pills to sleep. Every night I got into fights in bars. At the end of the three weeks, my fiancee did not want to talk with me anymore. Finally, I dropped everything and flew back to France without looking back.

I don't know why people were so cold at MSF Headquarters. I think that everybody was looking at me as a piece of shit or as a mad man. Sure, I have a few friends who were OK, but appeared embarrassed. When I went to talk to someone he is busy, she is not there. When I asked for another appointment in the field I was told: "No, there is nothing now, nothing in the pipeline."

In Paris I not only got drunk but very badly drunk. Six weeks of whisky and pills. Go back to MSF each week. "Nothing for you now." What had I done wrong? Finally I met a friend who told me that he was on his way to Afghanistan. This was the short-term appointment that had been offered to me before I went to Goma, and which I was told would be held for me until I returned. From that moment, I knew that I had been blacklisted by MSF.

WHY?

This lasted three months. I looked like a zombie . . . lost 10 kilograms . . . my eyes always red . . . I was a total mess.

To be sure, someone would tell me that I should talk to this particular person, but this person was not available until a week from now. And, anyway, what was I to talk about? When you cut yourself and are bleeding it is obvious that something has happened and people are looking at you. But when something happens inside your head, how do you know what to do? I thought I was OK; it was the people around me who were not. I only wanted to go back to work and put something else in my head, to change what is in my mind.

Finally, I was told by the office of human resources at MSF that I had been blacklisted for "non-humanitarian conduct" while in Zaire.

Non-humanitarian conduct?

In Goma?

What does this mean?

I don't know, but that is what they said, that was the reason they gave me.

Demoralized is not a strong enough word. I was really depressed and sad. Everything was black. I was sad for MSF, for me, for Rwandans, for the whole damn world.

Luckily, at the end of October a friend offered me a position with a small NGO in Kirgistan, a former part of the Soviet Union. I went there and started to work. I began to have other people and things on my mind: daily problems of snow, cold, and organizing convoys. Slowly I stopped having nightmares every night. I drank less alcohol and slowly started to smile again.

It is difficult for me to put these things on paper and to make sense of them. It was not until three years ago that I could speak of Goma without sweating.

What is hardest for me to take? Goma, or the way MSF treated me?

When you go into the field, you believe that the people back at Headquarters are professionals who will take care of you if something happens to you. In reality, you feel like a lemon, squeezed and thrown away when they do not need you anymore.

18

GOAL—A Champion of the Poor

Andrew Spearman

Founded in Dublin in 1977 by John O'Shea and four friends, GOAL is an international relief and development NGO dedicated to the alleviation of suffering among the poorest of the poor in the developing world and to assisting those coping with the aftermath of war and disaster. It is non-denominational, non-political and its guiding ethos is the belief that every human being has a right to the fundamentals of life, i.e., food, water, shelter, literacy, and medical attention.

GOAL has responded to almost every major natural and man-made disaster and catastrophe in the past 24 years and is currently implementing programs in 14 countries. It also provides financial support to a whole range of indigenous groups and missionaries with similar philosophies.

Since its inception GOAL has sent in excess of 800 volunteer workers to work on its many programs around the developing world. These would typically be people with such skills as nursing, medicine, dentistry, engineering, accountancy, or logistics and would normally volunteer their services for a minimum of a year. Many give up well-paid and secure jobs at home to travel abroad, often to very remote regions of the world, to be of service to their fellow men and women.

Some of these people have had prior experience in relief or development work but many are new to such activity and are therefore obliged to undergo orientation training to prepare themselves for living and working overseas. They attend a course that gives them information about the country they are to visit, the history, political situation, and the social and religious habits of the people among whom they will be working.

Because applicants are being recruited for some of the world's remoter areas and sometimes in regions that are politically unstable or volatile, GOAL takes very seriously its responsibility to appoint only people with the necessary strength of character. From the very first contact with a potential volunteer, experienced head-quarters staff are on the lookout for signs that the candidate might not, for a variety of reasons, be psychologically suitable for such a posting.

Assuming that a candidate has the required professional qualifications, she or he undergoes a series of informal briefing sessions with the various departments and desk officers at the organization's headquarters. This not only informs the candidates about conditions in the area they are to be working in and the problems that they can anticipate but it also gives GOAL a chance to assess their suitability for the posting.

In practice it is very seldom that a person who is patently not suited to working in such a totally different milieu puts him or herself forward. Usually people have thought long and hard about volunteering and it is something that they have wanted to do for years. Many have taken special educational courses with a view to equipping themselves better for humanitarian work. The few people who apply for the wrong reasons are usually easy to pick out.

Staff at headquarters keep contact with field workers (GOALies) to ensure that they are settling in well. All returning GOALies are asked to attend a final debriefing and have a medical check-up. If anything arises from the medical check, and if further screening is required, GOAL pays for referrals.

GOAL keeps a list of psychologists and trauma specialists to whom volunteers can be referred because it realizes that issues can arise from experiences overseas. It is part of the Field Directors' brief to ensure that the basic health and security needs of their fellow workers are looked after. Field Directors generally have a minimum five years experience of working overseas.

There is a definite awareness of the possibility of people being stressed, traumatized, and shocked, and in emergency situations, where life and death judgments might be called for, mental exhaustion can be a hazard. Aid workers can sometimes be struck by an overwhelming despair brought on by the feeling that a few individuals just can't do enough to satisfy such a huge need.

Physical security is, of course, of paramount importance. All Field Directors are well-versed in emergency procedures; it is GOAL's policy to evacuate personnel as soon as life threatening situations arise. All missions have a well thought out emergency evacuation procedure that can be initiated either from Dublin headquarters or the field office. Personnel have been evacuated on several occasions in recent years from such places as Somalia and Sudan. GOALies are always ready to evacuate at a moment's notice.

The evacuation plan would typically take less than 24 hours from its initiation to successful completion even, as happened recently, from one of the remotest areas of south Sudan. As soon as the word is given to implement an emergency evacuation, staff are ordered back to base where they remain until their rescue flight arrives. Communication lines are kept open at all times. GOAL contacts families if there is danger where their loved ones are based to reassure them that we are keeping an eye on the situation.

Only one person has ever been killed while working for GOAL. In November 1999 Andrea Curry, a young engineer from Armagh in Northern Ireland, paid the ultimate price in her efforts to bring aid to the people of Kosova. She died when the World Food Programme plane in which she was traveling crashed in fog as it approached Pristina Airport.

Andrea had not been with GOAL long: in fact, she was flying in to take up her first assignment, one that she was looking forward to and had been working toward for some time. Her untimely death left an indelible mark on the lives of everyone in GOAL and, just as the news of the death of any aid worker anywhere is greeted with shock, it also somehow served to strengthen people's resolve to continue on with the work.

Volunteers have often seen up close the dangers faced by aid workers. Several years ago GOAL personnel in Ethiopia witnessed the murder of two Danish aid workers from another organization.

GOAL is immensely proud of its volunteers and their work with people affected by some of the worst humanitarian disasters and crises in the past 24 years. Naturally, our attention is focused on the victims of these tragedies, but the volunteer doctors, nurses, logisticians, engineers who quietly get on with the work of helping as many of these victims as possible are deserving of immense respect. The type of people who volunteer for humanitarian work are typically unlikely to seek praise or thanks for what they do. If they were to be asked it is certain that aid workers would fairly unanimously prefer to be given the wherewithal to do their work rather than awards or medals.

The tragedy of Somalia in 1992 where several million innocent victims perished due to war and starvation, will be forever etched in our collective memory. In response to overwhelming needs, GOAL mounted a huge humanitarian operation, doing its best to provide as many people as possible with regular food supplies and medical care. GOAL volunteer doctors and nurses worked tirelessly to provide relief to the hungry and infirm, but they reckoned that up to 25 percent of Somali children under the age of five died from severe malnutrition.

In January 1992, GOAL donated drugs and medical equipment to one of the main hospitals in the capital city, Mogadishu. Serious consideration was given to sending personnel to Somalia but the extremely volatile security situation ruled out this option at that time. However, as the nutritional and health situation deteriorated and the security situation stabilized somewhat, GOAL sent volunteers into Somalia in August. GOAL then expanded its operation, and at any one time had 28 GOAL staff involved in life-saving work in Mogadishu, Baidoa, and surrounding villages and in refugee camps.

One of GOAL's greatest supporters at the time was Irish President Mary Robinson who is now the UN High Commissioner for Human Rights. GOAL is also immensely proud that our former President has shown by her actions and her courage that she cares for those in the greatest need. Her inspiration gave hope to many in the dark days of the Somalian crisis and she continues to give hope to the oppressed and the poor throughout the developing world.

In southern Sudan in 1993 there was human suffering and misery on a scale akin to that seen in Somalia, and again GOAL had to cease operations due to heightened insecurity. GOAL has since returned to Sudan and is doing some very valuable work both in government and rebel held areas.

On April 7th 1994, an orgy of genocide exploded in the tiny African state of Rwanda which over the next six weeks was to leave at least 800,000 people dead, many killed in a brutal and grotesque fashion. GOAL mounted an immediate response to the unfolding nightmare, sending medical and logistical experts to Rwanda.

By July, at the height of the crisis, GOAL had 70 expatriates working alongside over 1,100 local staff at the Goma refugee camp in neighboring Zaire. The level of suffering being heaped upon the Rwandan people was appalling and much of the work that the GOALies were called on to perform in Goma was of a particularly distressing nature.

Volunteers came from all walks of life, predominantly medical, but firemen, journalists, hotel managers, teachers, army officers, and others all gave their time and energies toward easing the suffering in the hellish camps. Field hospitals were established, feeding centers set up, people were clothed, fed, nursed, and, inevitably, many were buried in mass graves, miles from the beloved country from which they had fled.

Mary Robinson visited the mass graveyard in Goma and afterwards, in unequivocal terms, she castigated the international community for its failure to halt the flow of death in Rwanda and in the refugee camps. She also called on the world's governments to show political will to address the shocking imbalance which exists between the haves and have-nots.

Her tears and outrage brought home to the Irish public and viewers around the world the sense of despair and helplessness aid workers felt in the difficult task of stemming the overwhelming tide of misery and suffering. These brave individuals, many of them volunteers, witnessed suffering on a terrifying scale. Their strength and resolve kept them going in the darkest hours. They could not avert their eyes, break down or run away. They had to keep going. Nobody that was there, will ever forget Rwanda.

Everyone who worked in Rwanda and Zaire has their own personal, painful memories of those days and nights of dark despair, working around the clock to defeat death, to save lives, to afford a modicum of dignity to the corpses that had to be buried. Writing in 1995, former GOAL volunteer Fr. Gerry O'Connor, recalled his experiences in Rwanda.

> I had worked in the war-torn countries of Sudan and Angola. I was confident I could cope with anything I was going to witness.
>
> That first morning in Goma numbed me. Every muscle in my body froze as I watched in disbelief. My eyes stayed open though I wanted to close them. I kept shaking my head. My heart beat in anguish, my mind wrestled with ideas about how to help these people. In that first morning we witnessed thousands of corpses, covering every inch of the margin of the road. We stopped at roundabouts and viewed people slipping rapidly into death.
>
> That first day in Goma was sickening. I remained composed for most of the day, until toward evening time, when I came across a center full of unaccompanied children. There were thousands of children, and their faces were paralyzed with despair. Not even a hug or a kiss or playfulness could provoke a smile. I broke down and cried and cried. Goma became a reservoir of tears, as Rwandans, aid workers, and Zairians all found hell on earth too much to take.
>
> GOAL commenced operations by hiring some buses that had carried people to Zaire in the exodus from Rwanda. We transformed these buses into mobile clinics and stuffed them with medical personnel who quite simply traveled all the roads in and out of Goma, lifting people out of the gutter, rehydrating them, treating them for cholera and bringing them to the health clinics that GOAL and other agencies had established in the refugee camps.

A journalist with us described these bus journeys in an Irish Sunday newspaper as a "bus journey to hell." The scenes on those buses were harrowing. GOAL workers saw so many people die every day in their hands. People traveled with their cholera-ridden loved ones, daughters, sons, mothers, and fathers. When they died on the bus, family members departed, having neither the will nor the means to bury or cover their loved ones.

Families destroyed by the war, evil, and cholera abandoned the corpses in the bus, in a strange land, knowing that they would never even know where the deceased were to be buried. GOAL aid workers buried them.

The corpses in Goma and surrounding areas mounted everywhere with disastrous consequences. First, they posed a serious sanitation risk. Second, even in death these humans were deprived of dignity. Third, these corpses had a profoundly negative impact on the morale of both the living refugees and aid workers.

The Zairian authorities refused to bury the dead. Rwandans were not going to bury their own dead and international agencies argued it wasn't their task. GOAL declared that this was an intolerable situation, and began the process of putting trucks on the roads to remove the corpses and to bury them. The images of mass graves which were flashed on television screens of the world will be an eternal memory of what happened in Goma.

Coping in Goma was difficult. Within the GOAL team we were blessed to have dynamic, resourceful and committed men and women. On behalf of the Irish people, GOALies made a truly remarkable contribution to the relief effort. . . . I am sure all GOAL volunteers have memories that will never fade and will continually resurface. Many of us are scarred for life. Things will never be the same again.

I myself cannot stop thinking about those who died in my arms; about the girl I hit and injured as I drove through the camp, about driving over and smashing the corpse of a healthy-looking 20 year old and then trying to put the body back in place again, about the 70-year-old granny who walked for four days to reach Goma and injured herself and died of gangrene on our doorstep.

A GLOBAL POLICY RECOMMENDATION

Another important aspect of GOAL's work is to be a voice for the poorest of the poor. It seeks redress where there is injustice or suffering. It campaigns on behalf of the poor of the world and is tireless in its defense of the rights of humans to the basics of life.

One issue that GOAL has stressed for some time is that of corruption which is rife throughout the developing world. Director John O'Shea has been forthright in his condemnation of politicians and officials who seek to make themselves wealthy at the expense of their people, often among the poorest in the world.

"In my 24 years experience of GOAL bringing aid to the needy I would say that the greatest problem, the biggest barrier that we have had to overcome, is that of official corruption," he has said.

"This is why I have been trying to get Western governments to rethink their policies on aid to the developing world. Bilateral, or government to government aid is the easy option for the donating government. Basically, all they need to do is to write the check and hand it over to the recipient government. Rather like handing money to a beggar in the street, what they do with it is largely up to them. In practice this money seldom trickles down to the people who need it the most, the poorest of the poor, in sufficient amounts.

The safest way of getting assistance to people who need it is by providing the operational NGOs and the missionary organizations the wherewithal to do the work that needs to be done. The big difference is that, unlike governments, especially dictatorships, these organizations have a genuine interest in helping people. They want to get to work in the slums and villages and start solving problems along with the local community.

The NGOs and missionaries are like an army of caring people with a sense of justice and a great desire to help others. It is one of the great failures of the international community that they are by and large not given sufficient assistance in doing so. Instead, they must spend much energy and time in appealing to the public and the donor community, convincing people to part with their money so they can go to work.

19

Supporting and Equipping National and International Humanitarian Non-Governmental Organizations and Their Workers

Alastair Ager, Erik Flapper, Tineke van Pietersom, and Winnifred Simon

CASE STUDY

The Antares Foundation began its psychosocial support program for local NGOs in Zugdidi, Georgia, in May 2000. Beset by ethnic and civil strife since independence from the Soviet Union in December 1991, Georgia began to stabilize in 1994. However, political settlement of separatist conflicts in South Ossetia and Abkhazia remains elusive. The Zugdidi region hosts some 60,000 IDPs from Abkhazia, in a context where social services, health care, and education for the indigenous population continue to suffer due to the economic situation. Zugdidi region was the focus of considerable international humanitarian aid in the early 1990s, but the interest of most international NGOs has—with continuing political instability—subsequently waned and they frequently handed over activities to national NGOs. These local NGOs are staffed with motivated but frequently young and inexperienced workers, and are typically reliant upon short-term and insecure funding arrangements.

The Antares Foundation program has sought to strengthen the human resource management and psychosocial skills of a number of these organizations. With such poor coverage of governmental social services, much of the population is dependent on alternative support given through these NGOs. Adequate financial and operational support are key issues for such organizations, but staff support and management are also crucial if they are to constitute a sustainable source of assistance to the area.

Accordingly, the Antares Foundation program has been involved in providing a range of training inputs on stress management and organizational development, combined with the installation of a staff psychosocial support system suitable for the local environment. In Zugdidi, since no (mental) health or social systems are available, nor are referrals a feasible means of support, an "intercollegial" consultancy system has been established for the participating NGOs. This enabled them to share ideas and knowledge, and mobilize effectively appropriate assistance.

OVERVIEW OF APPROACH

The above case example illustrates a common context for many of Antares' programs with NGOs working in the field of humanitarian assistance in unstable and demanding conditions with significant physical and financial insecurity. Recurrent themes in framing support to such agencies are the initial lack of awareness, at times denial of the psychosocial needs of workers, the resulting lack of skills to address such needs, and the limited organizational capacity to cope with such challenges.

The four key levels at which Antares works are: provision of field consultations to individuals; staff training and support; organizational support and development; and inter-agency networking and support ("intervision"). The approach assumes the direct linkage of these various levels to create an integrated approach to psychosocial support. While direct work with field staff (for example through debriefing or counseling) may establish credentials and credibility with staff, the thrust of Antares' work is to establish awareness and skills at an organizational level regarding the prevention of stress and anguish among fieldworkers.

PROVISION OF FIELD CONSULTATIONS TO INDIVIDUALS

The Antares Foundation has identified a particular need for individual, field consultation for managers of national NGOs. While their position may be perceived by staff of international agencies as unambiguously that of "manager," in relation to local, national staff colleagues, they may be viewed more informally as a "coordinator," and also as friend, relative, neighbor, and compatriot. Such additional roles bring with them many obligations and responsibilities but often no formal power.

In the face of this ambiguity, many managers feel vulnerable and lonely. Their history in their organization, the challenges of formalizing relationships, tasks and responsibilities and the direct pressures that they often experience (themselves being part of a population in danger in a context that is still unstable) all contribute to a frequent sense of isolation, uncertainty, and hypervigilence.

International staff frequently perceives national staff as demanding and difficult to deal with. Much of this may be attributed to the disparity between expectations regarding the separation of formal work roles from wider personal needs and circumstances. National staff has needs beyond their immediate work situation regarding money, family, career, and personal adjustment, which international staff are impotent to address and are thus essentially encouraged to deny [1]. However, national NGO managers are less able to distinguish between the job and the wider needs of their staff. Working relationships with expatriates and their organizations also rank high on the list of stressors of national staff.

Because of their isolated position in relation to both international staff and their national staff, managers frequently express the desire to be able to share their stress-related problems and thoughts, both those at work and at home, and the interrelationship between the two. Talking with someone "neutral," who is not part of the local context, is particularly valued. The discussion frequently provides an opportunity for an open assessment of the work of members of the national "team." The security and openness can help establish an overview and a sense of connectedness and control.

The following convey managers' perceptions of the value of these consultations: "I felt completely stuck and demotivated. This consultation gives [new] options"; "Somehow I felt responsible for everything, guilty and isolated from my team. It has been good to share and to get back some realistic ideas and ways to handle my crisis"; "I never cry, I don't, I can't. I do not want to. It is good that you focus on my strengths and on how to improve things that I am not good at"; "At home it is cold and sad. At work I feel happier. I am with friends and I am doing something useful. But work never ends and I am tired. I cannot concentrate or make proper decisions anymore. I felt like a failure. Now I understand more about how my life at home influences the work and not just in my case."

STAFF TRAINING AND SUPPORT

It is essential to be clear and transparent with all training, debriefings, and support of field staff. Objectives, activities, and codes of conduct need to be agreed upon by all parties and, preferably, formally stated in advance in Terms of Reference (TOR). Specific goals described in the TOR could involve:

1. To debrief and provide psychoeducation to national staff of NGOs to equip them to deal with the actual and potential effects of acute and ongoing extreme stressful situations;
2. To give support, education, and coaching to (national) coordinators, managers and directors in the management of national staff suffering from ongoing and traumatic stress;
3. To assess and define the need for follow-up for future activities.

Our integrated approach links project management (with a special focus on safety and security analysis) with stress management at the team level, since a significant proportion of team stress is traceable to poor project and team management. Any assumption that (external) trainers, coaches or therapists will be welcomed with open arms by field managers and their teams is frequently erroneous. Very often we meet, and need to work through, a lot of initial resistance, depending on the history of the project, the prevailing management style, past incidents, and overall team dynamics. We view this as normal reactions from teams working under abnormal circumstances. We try to begin with an individual debriefing and assessment of the work performance and psychosocial status of the team members prior to group work and training. Subsequent support (practical and psychological) from the team leader for group debriefings and individual consultations is vital in a field context. As consultants, we are significantly dependent on this attitude toward stress management and team support. The individual consultations enable us to create a safe personal support structure for the team members and gain useful insight into the team's psychosocial status and its dynamics.

Although in the training we work with handouts on stress management as a guideline, a lot of material is adapted for the specific context, taking into account cross-cultural and gender issues, and relevant local safety and security topics.

Providing the opportunity for team members to discuss and reflect upon their personal stressors and coping strategies is always the "core" of such field interventions. Training is built around: (a) psycho-education on basic stress theory and symptoms of acute chronic stress; (b) interactive group work on recognizing and developing coping tools; (c) "first aid" tools for use after critical incidents: how to help yourself and others; and (d) defining a mechanism for staff to receive supportive counseling regarding work and organization-related stressors, with appropriate feedback to management.

ORGANIZATIONAL SUPPORT AND DEVELOPMENT

Work at the levels of individual support and of training teams often indicates systemic organizational issues that need to be addressed by NGOs if they are to function effectively and sustainably. There are four recurrent organizational challenges Antares faces in the work with national NGOs.

1. Low priority for self-care: NGOs working in the humanitarian field appropriately have their first priorities and resources aimed at their beneficiaries, the ones who need protection and care. Staff generally have an altruistic attitude; they feel a need to assist those who are worse off than themselves. Working conditions thus have a low priority in these organizations, a belief generally shared by both employees and employers. The culture of the humanitarian work is no payment for extra work; being present and available 24 hours, 7 days a week, especially in emergencies.

2. From feeling responsible to being responsible: Studies and interviews have repeatedly made clear that being listened to and respected for what they do is the one thing needed to keep people going in humanitarian jobs. Management bears a clear responsibility. People in the field, working in very bad circumstances and not always knowing what to expect and how to react, have a right to good information, guidance, and care. However, when severe emergencies strike, there is little time for preparation, guidance, or care. The whole organization is occupied with operations, logistics, fundraising, and coordination. Staff care thus needs to be addressed at an earlier stage; policies have to be formulated and agreed upon throughout the organization.

3. Need for training management and staff: Before starting training, an assessment of needs and suitable support for the managers and the fieldworkers has to be made. This can be done through interviews with managers (not excluding the managers as "users") and a sample of fieldworkers. Only then can a strategy be designed for addressing needs of all levels of the organization. As well, there is a need for training in stress management and psychosocial support for managers. They have to know how to prepare themselves and their staff, to make decisions for withdrawal or evacuation, or they must anticipate possible difficult and dangerous situations for their staff and have understanding of the psychosocial consequences of stress. They

must set the example and give the subject legitimacy for discussion, encouraging people to speak out and ask for help. Only then will psychosocial care for staff be accepted by the staff themselves.

4. Allocating resources, human and financial: Training and support are frequently the first activities to be cut when there is a shortage of funds. This means systems have to be built when finances are available. Donors rightly demand that staff be deployed effectively and efficiently. Organizations need to request more explicitly funding for this. Much can be done with fairly minimal funding: people can help each other as soon as they know how. The intervision method, the network consultation system, described next, is a relatively low cost means for national NGOs to strengthen effectiveness and moral.

INTERVISION: NETWORKING AND COLLEGIAL CONSULTATION

Intervision is a strategy which, in an environment where care and aid systems have partly or completely ceased to function, seeks through consultation among equals to reach solutions to work-related problems. It typically involves a group of colleagues utilizing their training, common sense, and practical experience to advise one another.

Managers embarking on the use of intervision will typically need to go through:

Phase 1: where they will require training and counseling to become acquainted with the different methods and techniques;

Phase 2: where they go through a period of applying the method with selected colleagues within the humanitarian world;

Phase 3: where they are offered the opportunity to discuss possible bottlenecks with supervision by coaches/trainers and, if necessary, to adjust methods and techniques;

Phase 4: where they will then be able to set up, carry out, expand, and evaluate mutual professional consultation among managers.

Key prerequisites are equality, cooperation, transparency, and respect. Cultural adaptation, effort, and commitment are additional ingredients for which the parties involved are responsible. In this way, at low cost, organizations can identify needed and available resources, and thus become both less vulnerable and more independent.

Examples of problems that have been discussed using this method include: "Stress is 'sky high' in my organization"; 'How can I help my team to cope with stress?"; "I am very grateful that he supported me in very difficult crisis situations. Now I fear that he does not function well anymore in the team and I don't know what to do"; "I feel a lack of commitment to the job in my team members. They are just there for the money. What can I do to change this?"; "Because I am a woman, men do not really accept my decisions, they undermine them through negative remarks and other behaviors. Is it just me? How do I manage?"; "My team has a critical approach toward cooperation with international staff. Since we have to cooperate: what can I do?"

An example of the "intervision" working method is the Incident Method [2]: This method is suitable for groups of 5–20 persons, takes minimal 75 minutes and needs one chairman to direct and monitor structure and time. Through a sequence of nine defined phases an ongoing work challenge or incident will be tackled. The participants are putting themselves in someone's else's place and formulate different advices. This method promotes expertise, cooperation and team spirit.

SUPPORT OF INTERNATIONAL NGOs

The issues described above are with some notable and significant exceptions, such as the availability of referral facilities in the home country, faced by the staff of international as well as national NGOs. However, staff working within international NGOs enjoy some significant advantages over their local counterparts. In general, international NGOs offer better working conditions for their staff and have more resources for psychosocial support. Human resource management departments will also be in place to take care of primary and, often, also secondary working conditions.

On the other hand, the institutional complexity of established international NGOs [3] can create barriers to effective deployment. Further, even within the best-resourced international agencies we have frequently seen how lack of time and knowledge of psychosocial support can foster a denial of staff problems. The first priority of support to management in this area is thus to create awareness of, and potentially challenge, organizational culture and attitudes. The goal is creation of positive professional behavior regarding stress and traumatic experience among staff. Secondly, training and support of management is, alongside support of more general cultural change, vital.

Those organizations that are frequently working particularly in high-risk countries need to prepare their staff more rigorously. Though people working in those areas are usually quite experienced, they are vulnerable and at risk as well, and the strain of operating in such environments over an extended period can accumulate. In such settings there is a clear need to have a "second level" support system in place for major incidents and problems. If the basic system is in place, it is generally easy to extend it. If there is no system available, however, outside professional assistance will be required to establish appropriate back-up and support.

What activities might be offered by such "second level" support? If a team is involved in an evacuation, armed attack, hostage taking, death or any other life-threatening situation, we would recommend the following basic steps:

1. Direct support through field managers: support "on the spot" through the most skilled person, the manager or someone else with relevant knowledge of the local program.
2. Field support from headquarters (HQ): counseling/debriefing of personnel in the field by qualified professionals. If no specialists are available locally, HQ should provide them within 48 hours. A team of specialists should always be ready to leave at short notice.

3. Debriefing/counseling at HQ after return: have suitable support in place, including a referral system.
4. Follow up: evaluation of the support is always necessary after every incident and procedures are to be adapted if necessary.

Though such a system might appear complex to develop, it can be built with the help of one appropriately qualified professional. The goal is the prevention or minimization of PTSD, burnout syndrome, or mental disorders among affected staff. Provision of such support is not just an ethical issue; it is necessary for operational effectiveness and efficiency of NGOs [4]. A better functioning humanitarian worker is the aim of all involved: fieldworkers, their organizations, and their beneficiaries.

CONCLUSION

NGOs working in the field of humanitarian assistance need to support and protect the well-being of their staff—often working in very demanding situations—if they are to be effective in their assistance to beneficiaries. Such support and protection needs to be an integrated function of the organization (impacting its procedures and culture) rather than something mobilized only in crisis contexts [4]. Local NGOs, given their limited institutional capacity, are likely to find addressing such needs most difficult, although their staff may be particularly vulnerable. Inter-organizational collaboration, through such mechanisms as "intervision" is, in these circumstances, likely to prove of significant benefit.

REFERENCES

1. M. Walkup, Policy Dysfunction in Humanitarian Organizations: The Role of Coping Strategies, Institutions and Organizational Culture, *Journal of Refugee Studies, 10*:1, pp. 37-60, 1997.
2. J. Hendriksen, *Intervisie bij werkproblemen, procesmatig taakgericht probleem oplossen,* Nelissen, 9de druk, 1986.
3. C. Fyvie and A. Ager, NGOs and Innovation: Organizational Characteristics and Constraints in Development Assistance Work in The Gambia, *World Development, 27*:8, pp. 1383-1396, 1999.
4. A. Ager, Psychology and Humanitarian Assistance, in *The Applied Psychologist* (2nd Edition), J. Hartley and A. Branthwaite (eds.), OUP, Milton Keynes, pp. 226-243, 1999.

Voice

BEING KNOWLEDGEABLE CAN HELP ENORMOUSLY

Maria Blacque-Belair

When I was in the field, I knew nothing about self-care, secondary traumatization, or burnout. After four years in besieged Sarajevo, all I knew was that I wanted a long break. Looking back, I think it is unfortunate that both the French and U.S. NGOs I worked for did not educate us more about such things.

Instead, I wondered why I was so irritable and tired all the time, and dreaded hearing one more tragic story. To keep my sanity, I focused on pleasant things: looking at the small rabbits that my neighbors raised, hearing the chickens in the morning, and watching the roses growing in the garden. Instinctively, I felt that in order to last until the end of my assignment, that is what I had to do. Most of the time I kept my feelings of exhaustion to myself. Because I wasn't educated on the effects of secondary traumatization, I thought that it was my own problem. I should not allow myself to be weak, I kept saying to myself, yet realizing full well that when I got angry for no reason there was something wrong. I shared these feelings with a few other relief workers who had become good friends and I could trust. At the time, we felt that we could not speak openly. In fact, we had to keep these feelings hidden, especially from the program managers at headquarters. Too many times, we had heard that so and so was removed from his or her post because "s/he was too burned out," but we did not know exactly what it meant.

The worst was when new relief workers arrived; they had so much enthusiasm, so much patience, that we felt even more guilty about being so tired. Personally, I knew that each time I took a break—and we were allowed a lot of R&R—I would come back full of enthusiasm and promise myself not to lose perspective . . . but two months later the exhaustion came back. And with it came the feeling of being inadequate and assaulted by the problems.

When I came back home to New York, I decided to educate myself on these things and the first book I read was *International Responses to Traumatic Stress* [1]. It was a big relief because a lot of the symptoms I had felt were described as normal reactions to extreme stress. I saw too many of my fellow relief workers get totally burned out. I am certain that if they had been more reassured that their reactions were mostly normal, they would have known how to cope rather than internalize their reactions, leading to depression. Being more knowledgeable can help enormously.

There are no ready-made formulae to deal with secondary stress. The danger— and it seems it seems to be the current trend—is to overemphasize self-care. Relief workers, like firemen, emergency doctors, and war reporters, have chosen this type of work. They have deliberately followed a path that involves self-sacrifice; over-emphasizing self-care compromises those values. Taking risks and being exhausted come with the territory, but the rewards of this kind of work are priceless. It is crucial, however, to provide information and support to relief workers so that they can be aware of stress symptoms and how to manage them better.

Relief workers often find that it is not that simple to resettle at home. After the initial euphoria of being back in their old environment, many experience a rift with their loved ones. They find it hard to explain what they went through. Further, their friends and families are willing to hear their "heroic stories" but only for five minutes or so and then they move on to more mundane issues. As a result, some relief workers prefer not to talk about their experiences. They find it painful that their intense experiences become so trivialized. This may lead some to isolate themselves. Others become very nostalgic about their relief life and tend to aggrandize what they did.

In addition to the social and emotional rift of fitting in, many relief workers also face difficulties in reinserting themselves professionally. Since there are a limited number of management positions at headquarters, the vast majority of relief workers have to face the job market. Relief experience often is not understood and, until recently, was not even considered a profession. For some relief workers, especially those who had significant responsibilities, it is difficult emotionally to have to start from scratch again. Some will find administrative work boring and pale in comparison with the responsibilities and direct involvement they had in the field.

It is during this transition period that relief workers are very vulnerable and risk emotional decompensation and, sometimes, depression. Others will grab at more field work because trying to fit in at home turns out to be too difficult.

At this crucial moment, relief organizations should play a supportive role. Unfortunately, it is often at this time that many organizations relieve themselves of any responsibilities, aside from an occasional "debriefing session." Organizations who pride themselves on how their workers risk their lives to fulfill their missions must support them in building their lives after relief work. It should be seen as a moral obligation.

Here are a few suggestions of what can be done:

Offer support groups *before, during,* and *after* assignments. These should not be seen as "debriefing sessions with a psychologist"; instead, these groups should be led by experienced relief workers. A mental health professional could come occasionally to provide information on stress-related symptoms and also be available for individual or group therapy upon request.

The advantage of having support groups run by experienced relief workers is that they would not focus only on psychological topics such as burnout and secondary traumatization. The values of relief workers, the political context in the country, the actions of the international community and cultural differences need to be addressed as well.

For example, a relief worker who sees the job as a stepping stone for his or her career may react very differently than another who is there because of political commitment. The situation in each country will affect the relief workers differently: in Kurdistan, relief workers were welcomed with open arms after the Gulf War, but in Bosnia they were resented for being an alibi for the international community not to intervene.

Every relief agency should have an in-house support group or at least refer to one. They could function as alumni groups do in universities. The groups could provide emotional peer support, exchange tips on job opportunities, and refer to relevant professional expertise. Staff and funds must be allocated to these activities, including funds for professional counseling when needed; none of these should be done only on a volunteer basis.

A Web site should be developed that would give updates on former relief workers as well as their contact addresses. Job opportunities outside the humanitarian field could be posted. In addition, most large relief agencies have powerful board members with good connections in the job market. They could counsel relief workers, especially those who had many hardship missions, on ways to find new jobs.

REFERENCE

1. Y. Danieli, N. S. Rodley, and L. Weisaeth (ed.), *International Responses to Traumatic Stress,* Baywood, Amityville, New York, 1996.

20

Sustaining the Humanitarian Work Force: Increasing Violence, Increasing Vulnerability

Sheila M. Platt, Milagros Bacareza,
and Sonia Margallo

The work is not easy. All my assignments have been in security risk areas and some in isolated non-family posts. With other workers, I was evacuated from Cambodia, and later from West Timor, when three UNHCR colleagues were killed and our own colleague stabbed. Often I went alone to a new service site to set up a ground base. Homesickness was constant and the adjustment process took time. Yet I remain with the agency through all these years.

Sonia, Psychologist

This is an account of how one Asia-based NGO has worked to devise ways of supporting a workforce carrying heavy responsibilities for a variety of vulnerable populations in difficult conditions. It describes the development of an approach toward staff support that grew from concern as well as a need to preserve the most valuable asset of any humanitarian organization: the workers who get the work done.

Community and Family Services International (CFSI) is a non-profit social development organization formed in 1981 at the Bataan Philippine Refugee Processing Center with a mission to address the psychosocial needs of people uprooted by persecution, armed conflict, disasters, poverty, and other destabilizing conditions. The creation of the organization was a direct response to the needs of Vietnamese, Cambodian, and Lao refugees as well as local Filipinos with two major goals: the first to empower and equip such people to address and prevent social and mental health problems; and the second to avoid uprooting and displacement by promoting peace, respect for human rights, and the equitable distribution of resources. Subsequently the internally displaced, disaster survivors, and others in exceptionally difficult circumstances have also been served, with children, women, men, and minorities as priority groups.

From headquarters in Manila, CFSI has worked closely with the international community as well as national and local authorities responsible for uprooted persons in the Philippines, Hong Kong, Indonesia, Malaysia, Thailand, Vietnam, Cambodia, and Myanmar. An important aim has been to build the capacity of national social welfare organizations and local NGOs to meet the needs of this vulnerable population.

204

None of the work, past or present, would have been possible without the devotion of a group of individuals dedicated to the goals and mission of the organization. The project-oriented nature of the work led to a pattern of light staffing at headquarters, augmented by the formation of teams to carry out the projects at hand. These teams often include colleagues who started with the organization in Bataan and choose to return over the years for various assignments. The Filipino and international alumnae group of staff, spread all over the world, includes social workers, community development workers, psychiatrists, psychologists, public health specialists, and engineers.

In addition, the agency trains uprooted persons, as employees or volunteers, for service to and with others, using culturally specific programs to teach casework as well as community education and outreach skills. These past and present workers form a network, have remained attached to the organization, and can be counted upon when needed. Some reflect a perception of the agency as a "*Holding Environment*" providing nurturing and support bound together by shared experience [1].

The psychosocial needs of humanitarian assistance personnel were a concern of CFSI from its inception. The organization was established by social service professionals who had a good understanding of common human needs and capacities. They truly respected the dignity of every human being and made the welfare of their colleagues their abiding concern. The aim was better-adjusted workers with an increased capacity for coping with the stressful demands inherent in refugee service, leading to longer terms of service and decreased expenses related to new worker training. Also, CFSI was a product of the environment. Virtually the entire humanitarian assistance workforce at Bataan lived in the isolated Philippine Refugee Processing Center sharing the same facilities with the refugees. They were on duty, on call, or living within a "fishbowl" every single hour of every single day. Everyone felt the pressure and the stress.

Early efforts included stress management training, education campaigns on depression, and a "Mental Health Awareness Week." Response to the availability of counseling services was positive. In fact, more than 10 percent of all persons seen for counseling in camps during the first 14 months of operation were humanitarian personnel who voluntarily sought this service. Internally, CFSI devoted significant attention to preparing and supporting its personnel by providing newly recruited workers with detailed briefings about worksite challenges and conditions. A thorough on-site orientation program helped establish equilibrium. "Mental Health Day" outings for the entire staff were designed to reduce the impact of stress and promote worker resilience.

In 1989 asylum seekers in Southeast Asia violently protested implementation of the Comprehensive Plan of Action (CPA).[1] The organization realized the need for

---

[1] The CPA was an agreement between countries of first asylum in Southeast Asia and UNHCR requiring every asylum seeker to present their case to a pair of UN lawyers. If the interview and the lone appeal failed to support refugee status, the alternatives were either voluntary or involuntary repatriation to the country of origin. Asylum seekers reacted strongly with demonstrations and widespread violence aimed at host governments and camp staff.

immediate specific support to manage the resulting stress and security problems. As the camps became turbulent, staff suddenly found themselves living in a changed work environment. They were being perceived as the cause rather than the solution to the asylum seeker's problems, and were consequently the target of threats. Feeling disoriented by the loss of what had been seen as a helper role, they were anxious about outbreaks of violence, fearing for their own security.

> As repatriation loomed, problems worsened, with frequent critical events such as suicide threats and attempts, drug overdose, poisoning, self-immolation and stabbing. During hunger strikes and protracted mass demonstration, our Vietnamese paraprofessionals got harassed by the mob and pressured not to report for work. There were threats to life and of kidnapping.
>
> *Dr. Mila, Psychiatrist*

The agency responded with one day Crisis Management Workshops for staff that were educational in content, and highly interactive in nature. In order to foster trust and respect for one another's privacy and to allow sharing of personal information, participants agreed to a rule of confidentiality about any personal experience. Morning and afternoon snacks were served, along with lunch to emphasize an atmosphere of care for staff by the organization. Those attending were administratively cleared from work responsibilities for the day. Beyond the core service providers, participants eventually included the whole staff of the organization: senior management, line workers, as well as administrative and logistic support personnel.

The goal of the workshops was to provide a framework and vocabulary enabling staff to understand their current reactions as related to stress arising from their work, identify all the major and minor sources of the stress currently impacting them, and become proactive in managing the situation. Participants worked on three objectives. Together they developed personal and work-group strategies for managing the stress of their current situation, agency security policies and plans for current emergencies, and guidelines to manage critical events anticipated. The day was organized to lead participants through a process of learning to recognize and then begin to manage both the cumulative and traumatic stress now inherent in their work in three steps.

I. RECOGNIZING SIGNS AND SOURCES OF STRESS

Workshops opened with a brief discussion of the nature and physiology of stress. A section on physical, emotional, cognitive, spiritual/philosophical, and behavioral reactions to both cumulative and traumatic stress invited participants to identify their personal pattern of reactions in relation to a realistic scenario. Grief and vicarious traumatization were discussed. Emphasis was placed on how communication is negatively affected by stress. This was seen as especially true in multi-cultural, multi-functional, and multi-lingual or dialect work groups and situations that depend on interpreters to link service providers with beneficiaries. As participants identified and discussed all the sources of the stress then affecting them the link between stress and security became clear. The result was a comprehensive picture of the situation in the camps highlighting how alarmed people were about what might happen next.

II. STRESS MANAGEMENT FOR HUMANITARIAN WORKERS

Basic elements of stress management were presented. These included starting with one's own body, using the notion that while cumulative stress disrupts healthy routines gradually, traumatic events disrupt them suddenly and dramatically. Responding to the idea that stress management starts with one's self, participants worked in small groups to present recommendations to their colleagues for exercise, rest and sleep, stress-decreasing nutrition, relaxation and communication. A final exercise was the choosing by each participant of a "buddy" for mutual support in making and carrying out a personal stress management plan.

III. MANAGING CRITICAL EVENTS

Basic crisis theory, the stages of crisis, and a model of crisis intervention introduced the final section of the workshop. Using their experience, participants made an exhaustive list of factors causing stress for crisis teams, such as lack of accurate information, time pressure, and intense media coverage. They collected anticipated critical events and formed small groups to discuss handling hostage taking of a staff member, hunger strike, riot, and other situations. These discussions later evolved into agency crisis management and security plans.

Participants were enthusiastic about the workshops. They began to rely on their buddies, held work group discussions about how to address sources of stress within their power to modify, and reported feeling more empowered to cope with both the existing situation and future emergencies. Because some stress was coming from the agency itself, patterns of communication within the organization and in the camp settings were examined and new ones created to assure both horizontal and vertical improvement in accessing information and communicating with management.

Staff strongly recommended that participation be expanded to include partner NGOs as well as the security forces in the various refugee camps. The resulting series of workshops brought together organizations and personnel to work on improving operational security and contingency plans. People unfamiliar with each other's functions and work styles found common ground in jointly responding to stress, and welcomed the opportunity to cross language and cultural differences in order to plan for crisis.

In 1989, UNHCR asked the agency to set up mental health and community development services in the troubled camps in the then Crown Colony of Hong Kong. Reasons for the chronically high stress included intense crowding in urban sites and remote island locations. Hong Kong citizens were hostile toward the asylum seekers at a time when their own relatives in China were not allowed to enter the colony. Constant media scrutiny of relief work and the violence associated with implementation of voluntary and forced repatriations as required by the CPA was an added factor.

At UNHCR's request, Crisis Management workshops were provided for UN, NGO, and host government security authority staff in Hong Kong and a number of camps in Southeast Asia. The resulting Critical Event Guidelines, together with other workshop material, became the basis for UNHCR's widely distributed pilot guide *Coping With Stress in Crisis Situations* [2].

In more recent years, as "humanitarian space" continued to shrink, organizations frequently found themselves working to provide aid to refugees and internally displaced people in complex humanitarian emergencies within war zones. Attacks on aid workers increased yearly and fatalities mounted. The AIDS pandemic entered the picture with its harrowing loss of life and creation of orphaned children. Wars seemed to multiply, some of them fought by child soldiers. In these conditions of ever increasing stress on the work force, CFSI responded to frequent requests from UN agencies, national and international NGOs and government departments to provide both consultation and training in staff support and protection before, during and after critical events. Often the impetus for such training came from the field.

Recognizing that each organization is different and there are many ways of addressing employee needs, what follows are the interlocking elements organizations may wish to consider in developing a comprehensive human resource management process designed to support staff operating in hazardous environments. An initial step involves review by an organization of strategic development plans and ongoing operations regarding protection and support mechanisms necessary to ensure employee safety, capacity for service, and general well-being. Prevention, preparation, and alleviation are all part of a comprehensive approach designed to promote resilience in physically and psychologically hazardous work environments.

Prevention encompasses measures taken before the start of service to minimize vulnerability of individual workers to general and specific hazards of a given assignment:

> *Vacancy announcements* that make reference to the possibility of difficult work environments both alert applicants to challenges and provide opportunity for self de-selection.
>
> *Applications for employment* that ask applicants to describe previous difficult life experiences with a particular emphasis on coping strategies utilized in these situations provide a useful focus for interviews.
>
> *Interviews* that include discussion of possible challenges to safety and well-being on assignment, as well as institutional response capacities, provide applicants the opportunity to make choices about their own suitability for a given assignment. When perceived coping capacity and stress management skills are considered in offering employment to qualified individuals, a more resilient work group may result. Conducting such interviews requires frankness, as well as sensitivity to the applicant's situation given that factors such as recent significant loss or involvement in a current life crisis may create vulnerability in highly stressful assignments.

Preparation involves organizational, work group, and individual arrangements designed to equip workers for service in unstable environments where crises are likely to occur.

Orientation including a thorough introduction to the structure of the organization, its mission, history, and key players, benefits new employees with a feeling of being grounded as well as identified with the organization.

Briefings that are up to date and discuss elements of the cultural, political, and security environment pertaining to the mission equip new workers to engage sooner in productive work. Such briefings are most effectively delivered by colleagues who have recently worked in or visited the project site. Information about institutional response and support capacities, as well as protocols for emergency situations and other difficulties, allay the anxiety of new workers. When personnel policies are discussed with specific reference to provisions and procedures regarding emergency leaves, sick leaves, "mental health days" and worker well-being resources, employees tend to start the work feeling supported and cared for by the organization.

Staff Development and Routine Support may include development of employee capacity by providing supervision, in-service training, participation in external conferences, and career as well as personal counseling services.

Pre-assignment Stress Briefing is a staff support option delivered to the work group either before departure or at the work site. This is an educational session with brief written materials reviewing reactions to both cumulative and critical event stress. The briefing group has opportunities to identify possible sources of stress in the new assignment, pick a stress buddy and begin together to map out individual and work group stress management plans for use on the assignment.

The group may also receive an introduction to critical event debriefing to familiarize them with what to expect. When presented at this stage, workers are prepared to anticipate and receive such service themselves, should the need arise. Explanation of debriefing includes a brief description of its purpose, how it is organized and contingency plans. Opportunity for questions and comments concludes the session.

Alleviation involves the provision of post critical event and post assignment support and care. When a work group, an individual worker, or an entire workforce is exposed to traumatic occurrences, the special support needed may take many forms depending on the circumstances and resources available. For example, when three UNHCR workers were murdered in September 2000 in Atambua, West Timor, measures to support both the UN and NGO international and national work forces at the site included evacuation to safe locations. There administrative and financial arrangements for leave periods, stress debriefings and psychological support were all provided. With UNHCR, CFSI assembled a team of mental health professionals to deliver group debriefings, individual sessions, consultation and support to whomever requested or required it, and long-term follow up as needed.

Exit Debriefing is a follow-up measure provided to workers completing assignments in difficult environments. This can be useful in several respects. The worker is given a chance to reflect on the positives and negatives of the experience in ways that may be helpful in achieving closure. Discussion prepares them for the challenges of adjusting to environments outside humanitarian emergencies where there is often little comprehension or actual interest by others in one's experience. In addition the interviewer, on behalf of the agency, can both express appreciation for the service given and make sure the organization benefits from lessons learned by and from individual workers.

CFSI's long experience in supporting its own work force and working with others suggests the following core concepts in respect to care and support of humanitarian workers by their organizations:

1. *Care and concern for the physical and mental health of workers should be a significant component of organizational policies and operational priorities.* The quality of services rendered to vulnerable clientele groups of humanitarian organizations is directly related to the well-being of their workers. No one can continue effectively to provide support and assistance to other people in distress if he or she is in a worse psychological state.

2. *Communication lines between the humanitarian worker and the employing organization, as well as with family, are a major concern. Organizations have the responsibility to see that these remain open to the extent possible.* Generally, work sites are isolated, lacking in recreational facilities and basic life amenities. The nature of the work involves exposure to daily pressures and stresses, life-threatening situations, and horrific experiences. At certain points in time there is an urgent need to connect with someone trusted. It could be to consult about a pending critical decision, to ventilate frustration, anger, pain or share joy, to be updated on home developments, or just to have someone to talk to. This is tremendously helpful and every effort should be made by the organization to meet this legitimate staff concern.

3. *Contingency plans provide a sense of security and assure the frontline worker that personal safety and well-being are serious concerns to the employing organization.* Before a humanitarian worker accepts an assignment, he or she needs to know the risks to be taken and to be amply briefed on what to expect in the prospective work site. Further, it is the responsibility of the employer to make sure that the risks are minimized and that the worker is provided with a relatively reliable protection and safety net while performing humanitarian tasks.

> My wish for everyone in this new millennium is that we continue to care for each other and recharge each other with uplifting and comforting words, especially when the going gets more rough. I think that this is our legacy to the people we worked with. Let us continue to practice our caring attitude.
>
> *Ines, Social Worker*

REFERENCES

1. B. Smith, I. Agger, Y. Danieli, and L. Weisaeth, Health Activities Across Traumatized Populations: Emotional Responses of International Humanitarian Aid Workers, in *International Responses to Traumatic Stress*, Y. Danieli, N. Rodley, and L. Weisaeth (eds.), Baywood, Amityville, New York, pp. 416-417, 1996.
2. *Coping With Stress in Crisis Situations*, UNHCR, Geneva, 1992.

21

Limiting the Risks and the Vulnerability of Humanitarian Aid Workers

Clémentine Olivier

INTRODUCING HANDICAP INTERNATIONAL

Handicap International is a non-governmental organization created in 1982 and working in the field of international aid and cooperation. Its objective is to help all those in a vulnerable situation for whatever reason, such as underdevelopment, poverty, exclusion, exploitation, violence and armed conflict, grave violations or negations of human rights, failures of social services, and ecological disasters. The Association works in particular with people with disabilities, regardless of the origins of their impairment, which may be congenital or antenatal, malnutrition, illness, accident, violence or trauma, physical, sensory, or mental.

Vivre Debout (Live Upright), the Association's motto, reflects a philosophy of action based on promoting and defending human dignity. It relies on values of *solidarity,* interlinked with notions of mutual aid and fraternity, and of *equity,* associated with notions of justice, of equality, and impartiality. The notion of equal opportunities is founded on these values.

Handicap International is currently running rehabilitation programs in 40 countries. Since the creation of the Mines Coordination Unit in 1994, the Association has developed acknowledged skills in anti-mine action: mine-clearance, mine-risk education, studies on the presence of mines and their socioeconomic impact, technical, and technological research.

HANDICAP INTERNATIONAL AND SECURITY

Working in the field of humanitarian action very often means working in difficult and unstable political, economic, and social circumstances. Therefore, not having the calling to pursue our humanitarian aid programs regardless of any danger, thereby justifying a higher degree of risk-taking, security is an extremely serious concern for the management of Handicap International. We are continually faced with decisions of whether a team should remain in the field, which is why the analysis of security problems is an important part of the work and responsibility of those managing missions in the field.

It is rare that the 1949 Geneva Convention and its Additional Protocols of 1977 apply fully. And the increase in the different type of attacker that may include war

211

barons, terrorists, and bandits, has brought with it a consequent lack of respect for "the rules of war," notably, the principle of not attacking non-combatants, which applies to humanitarian aid workers. What is more, teams in the field can be undesirable witnesses of violations of human rights. Faced with this kind of environment, new means must be developed to ensure the security of aid workers in the field.

The security regulations in the field and the accompanying methods for managing security issues are intended for both expatriate and national team members equally. Inasmuch as security is likely to affect all aspects of the Association's work, it concerns all members of Handicap International's teams. This being said, certain measures need to be adapted to the specific nature of expatriate status, particularly regarding evacuation, as elaborated below.

For Handicap International, insuring the security of teams in the field means adapting behavior to the particular environment and the context. The security rules and behavior to be adopted by teams should not be frozen, but must be defined and adapted according to objective contextual information. Indeed, an apparently stable situation can become dangerous if team and individuals do not take into consideration or do not respect the specific cultural, religious, political, and historical customs of the country. It is also possible to achieve an acceptable degree of security in a war situation when the rules of behavior, logistics, telecommunications, and coordination with other humanitarian aid teams are satisfactory.

Situations where the insecurity is ill-defined can be as wearing and dangerous as those of open conflict. A situation generating stress of medium intensity on a permanent and lasting basis can inflict real psychological damage on the individual, leaving after-effects that, though less visible, are as serious as physical injury. Furthermore, one becomes accustomed to danger, and is less vigilant when the danger is less perceptible, which can be catastrophic.

Expatriates may also come to absorb some of the psychological sufferings of the victims they are helping, and this transfer of suffering can be very wearing and unnerving.

Finally, the violence teams in the field face is not limited to situations of tension, armed conflicts or banditry. Working in humanitarian aid can lead an expatriate to loose some of his or her bearings. The social and cultural codes of their own country may not be valid in the country where they are working. They must identify and respect new socio-cultural codes, a process that can be extremely difficult, even violent. This violence, if not controlled, can have serious psychological after-effects for certain expatriates.

INSURE A PRESENCE IN THE FIELD: AT WHAT PRICE?

The basic rule is never to send a team to an area where we are not able to guarantee a satisfactory level of security.[1] Furthermore, as soon as the Head Office

---

[1] The decision to open a program in the field depends on a number of variables, such as the existence of identified needs to which the Association is in a position to respond. The security status and knowledge of the geopolitical context form a part of these variables.

considers that individuals are no longer secure, whether it be because the environment has become too unstable for the mission to continue, or because someone's psychological distress is such that he or she is in danger, we evacuate them.

Security regulations apply to all Handicap International team members, and the risk management tools for use in humanitarian action in an unstable context are the same for expatriate and national staff. However, when people's lives are directly threatened, we evacuate our teams, and measures will be adapted according to whether the staff member is an expatriate or national.

THE FUNDAMENTAL PRINCIPLES OF HANDICAP INTERNATIONAL

Anticipating the Risks

This principle—the keystone of security management—requires adequate staff, equipment, and logistics. A team where the roles and responsibilities are clear, where the vehicles are well maintained, the means of communication adequate, where detailed security and evacuation plans are familiar to everyone and regularly updated, are all signs of a satisfactory approach to risk management. In certain situations, body protection (bulletproof vests and armored vehicles) may be considered. Security regulations for traveling will be adapted according to the confirmed or suspected presence of mines. Finally, Handicap International is careful always to inform national authorities, embassies, and consulates of the presence of expatriates on missions in the field.

The aim of security regulations is not to punish in cases of transgression, but to avoid risks and to anticipate dangerous situations. In order to help teams in the field define a satisfactory security code, Handicap International produced a "Security Guide."[2] The Guide must be adapted by teams to the local situation and takes into account recommendations made by other NGOs (in particular Médecins Sans Frontières) or international organizations such as the United Nations High Commissioner for Refugees.

Handicap International contracts a private specialized repatriation company that evacuates teams at any moment from any location.

Finally, the effectiveness of risk management tools depends greatly on the way in which they are used, and the good sense of the teams in the field; the human factor is vital. We also try to remain alert to incidents which could be the first symptoms of a team being in difficulty, no longer able to protect itself or even putting itself in danger. For instance, while an increase in the number of road accidents could be due to inadequate security regulations, it could also be a sign indicating that the team is troubled, that manifests itself, unconsciously, by endangering the expatriates in the field.

---

[2] "Security Guide" in the Administrative Reference Manual (Handicap International internal document).

Designation of a Security Officer

At the Handicap International Head Office one person is responsible for the security of programs, including all missions. This person validates the security arrangements for each mission, and can be consulted at any moment by the manager of a program. The Head Office maintains a 24-hour-a-day emergency service, in addition to the services of the repatriation company. One person is responsible for the security of the mission in the field, usually the Country Director.

Respect of Local Laws and Customs

Whatever the level of instability surrounding the humanitarian mission, adopting a code of conduct respecting local traditions is essential to limiting risks. Failing to do so could easily be experienced as provocation.

Individual conduct can influence and compromise not only other members of the mission, but all the humanitarian aid workers in the area. Each expatriate is therefore a representative of Handicap International, even outside working hours.

Individual Conduct

Security is above all a question of conduct. It is therefore important to be on the lookout for signs indicating that an individual does not have the stability and calmness necessary for good "risk management." The "symptoms" can be apparent in all areas in the administrative management of the mission or in questions of strategic positioning of the programs. In the same way, we are watchful when a team member has trouble sleeping or has a tendency toward problems with drug or alcohol abuse.

Collective Conduct

First, and important in all humanitarian aid missions, good communication between all the different parties involved in humanitarian aid (national and international) in the field is a minimum requirement, not only for risk management, but also for the successful management of aid programs. As far as NGOs are concerned, it is even more important to re-emphasize the presence and the identity of non-governmental activity, and to avoid being lumped together with other parties present in the field. NGOs should not only remain non-governmental, independent, and impartial, but should also be seen to be so. The protection of non-governmental organizations can be strengthened by drawing up of a "code of conduct," that all NGOs would agree to respect while on missions in the field.[3]

Regulations Prohibiting the Carrying of Firearms

In order to avoid confusion as to the intentions of humanitarian aid workers, they should never carry arms, without any exception to this rule. In very exceptional

---

[3] This was the case in Sierra Leone: "Code of conduct for Humanitarian Agencies in Sierra Leone— 21 November 1998."

circumstances, and within the limits of local legislation, armed guards[4] may protect buildings that house provisions of aids. However, providing aid should never be the object of armed protection. Access to the buildings or the Association's vehicles is prohibited to anyone carrying arms.[5] In practice, however, it can be dangerous to refuse access to armed men, and in case of threat we advise teams to comply.

VISIBILITY AND IDENTITY

The visible identity of humanitarian aid workers—particularly when they are non-governmental—can also be a means of limiting risk in an unstable environment when immunity for humanitarian aid workers is realized in the country in question. Signs identifying NGOs will be attached to vehicles and buildings. When traveling in a convoy, it may be decided to inform local authorities or even belligerents of the route to be taken to allow them to recognize us as being independent, neutral, and unarmed. The choice of color of the vehicles will depend on local symbolic interpretation and on the desire not to be confused with other organizations, especially military ones, white often denoting neutrality and the non-aggressive nature of the convoy. However, in countries with a high rate of crime, we would favor keeping the association's visibility low, so as not to attract the wrong kind of attention.

HUMAN MANAGEMENT OF RESOURCES

The Itinerary of an Expatriate

The itinerary of an expatriate at Handicap International is divided into 5 phases: recruitment (1 day), preparation for departure (14 to 20 days), the decision on a posting, individualized support during the mission, and upon return from mission.[6]

One of the objectives of the recruitment and training processes is to make certain, as far as possible, that the candidate's professional competence and psychological profile are adequate. A psychologist is always present during the recruitment process. This being said, as we have already stressed: "la séléction des candidats est sans doute relativement efficace pour les autres difficultés psychiques, le caractère effractif du traumatisme nous laisse peu de chances pour une anticipation."[7]

---

[4] In this situation, the Association could contract an external security firm that would employ the guards.

[5] "No weapons" stickers are systematically stuck to the Association's buildings and vehicles.

[6] Handicap International expatriates can have two kinds of statute, volunteer or salaried, depending on whether their assignment is short- or long-term period. Expatriates receive the same social security coverage and are paid, regardless of their legal statute: the volunteer staff are given allowances, the salaried staff, salary.

[7] A. Devaux, L'expatriation et l'humanitaire: 'Pendant, après,' *La Revue Française de Psychiatrie et de Psychologie Médicale, 29,* June 1999, pp. 17-23, at p. 18. Whereas the selection process can be relied upon to reveal other psychological difficulties inherent in the personality of the candidate, the nature of expatriation in itself can trigger previously apparently non-existent psychological difficulties, which are almost impossible to anticipate.

When the posting is made, the expatriate is informed by the Desk Officer and the Head Office security officer of the possible security risks, including presence of landmines,[8] and behavior to adopt when traveling, curfews, and historical and geopolitical contexts, among others.

When determining a posting, we take account, as far as possible, of the wishes and skills of the candidate on the one hand, and the constraints in the field and the needs of the Association on the other. Unfortunately, a perfect fit cannot be guaranteed due to the shortage of human resources. In addition, an experienced expatriate, capable of running a mission in a country where security is unstable, may not or does not want, or, if s/he is taking a family, for example, to be posted again to a potentially unstable zone.

There is Head Office supervision for the full duration of the mission, covering technical, human, security, and financial aspects of the project. In addition, there are regular visits to the project by Head Office staff, including the Desk Officer, technical coordinators, and financial controllers. This provides regular opportunities to evaluate changes in the security situation in the country. Having to cope with tension on a daily basis can prevent teams in the field from making a realistic assessment of the situation. For this reason, a permanent watch is maintained by the Head Office.

Finally, returning from mission is a pivotal transition. There is always a debriefing addressing not only the technical aspects of the program, but also the security and human aspects. Handicap International has produced a "Return from mission guide,"[9] as a complement to the "Departure Guide,"[10] to help expatriates adjust to a return that is often experienced as another separation.

SOME RECURRENT PROBLEMS

Managing people is not an exact science. When we form a team we try to send only people with an apparently stable psychological profile. However, zero risk does not exist. Expatriation can have a triggering effect that may activate a latent psychological problem or create a new one.

Furthermore, the fact that a person already has long experience as an expatriate is no guarantee of being able to adapt successfully to a new environment. In fact, a "career" as an expatriate requires more and more professionalism, involving difficult mental gymnastics as each new situation demands identification and adaptation to new socio-cultural norms.

A recurrent problem is a lack of human resources immediately available for duty in the field. The effectiveness of a humanitarian aid activity in case of catastrophe— natural or man-made—is measured by the capacity of the organization to send rapidly

---

[8] All expatriates receive specific information on the management of risks related to landmines.

[9] "The guide for expatriates returning from mission and planning to resettle definitively in France," Handicap International, updated in March 2000, 47 pages (internal document).

[10] "Departure guide for future expatriates," Handicap International, updated in January 2001, 14 pages (internal document).

an experienced team qualified to carry out a mission in a country where the security situation is unstable. However, it is not always possible to put together quickly a team of individuals who are complementary both in human and professional terms.

In order to manage human resources as well as possible and to protect expatriates against serious psychological problems, administrative procedures are adapted to each mission. In certain countries, for example, an expatriate's mission may be limited to a maximum of 12 months.

It may also be decided that holidays should be taken regularly, perhaps every two or three months, with an obligation to leave the territory in order to obtain maximum benefit from the rest period. Satisfactory management of the rest periods helps to limit the risks of trauma. In general, the quality of working conditions has a direct impact on the team's individual and collective psychological well-being.

THE QUESTION OF WHETHER TO EVACUATE EXPATRIATES

Whether to evacuate an individual or a team is always a difficult decision. The risk of error cannot be excluded, since the appreciation of a security situation is never certain. The consequences of evacuation should also be taken into account, as far as possible. The withdrawal of a team from the field always affects the links between the Association and its local partners and workers, and therefore has an impact on both the immediate and future effectiveness of aid programs in the area.

Two situations—rare in practice—are relatively simple to deal with: an evacuation imposed by the national or international authorities, or a voluntary evacuation decided upon by the Handicap International Head Office after receiving reliable and validated information from its network of contacts making the withdrawal of teams unavoidable.

However, the situation is rarely so clear cut. For example, it is possible that the expatriate team suggests maintaining a presence in the field when the other humanitarian aid teams have decided to evacuate. It is also possible that within the same expatriate team, there is disagreement on the need to evacuate. While any expatriate who feels in danger is always authorized to leave, the decision for total evacuation cannot be taken without weighing various elements. Limiting the risk of error in the appreciation of the situation depends on several factors: the experience and personality of the expatriate responsible for security; his or her ability to collect and analyze all information available in the field by setting up an "intelligence" network with all other local and international parties; the ability to separate rumor from fact and take an objective view of the situation in a tense and unstable environment; the ability to establish a relationship of mutual confidence with the Head Office and a reliable and regular system of communication and situation analysis. While the final decision to evacuate is made by the Head Office, this decision is largely based on analyses which only the team in the field can provide. The Desk Officer at the Head Office should stay alert to the risks of error resulting from the fairly frequent contrasting attitudes, consisting of refusing to recognize danger or giving way to panic.

When an evacuation is necessary for security reasons, the evacuated team often feels that it has abandoned its colleagues, local partners, and the beneficiaries of the mission. While evacuation safeguards the team members physically, the psychological suffering caused by a sudden departure and the feeling of having abandoned their fellow team members can have serious consequences, even though they may be less visible and, for this reason, often neglected. This sense of guilt should be heeded and attended to. It may also prevent expatriates from being able to appreciate objectively the danger of staying. Therefore, Handicap International may be forced to impose an unwelcome evacuation if it determines that the risks the team would be running in attempting to continue its activities are too high. Such a decision taken by the Head Office is, to a certain extent, a way of protecting the teams from the painful dilemma of having to choose between their need and desire to protect themselves, and their fear of "abandoning" their local partners.

Indeed, when an evacuation is decided upon, in theory only expatriates and their families are repatriated. The security of nationals is the responsibility of the national authorities or the United Nations High Commissioner for Refugees for those seeking asylum. The fact that a person is an employee of Handicap International does not alter the responsibility of the public authorities. However, if somebody is in danger *because* of their links with Handicap International, specific measures are taken. For example, we have in the past been obliged to destroy our personnel files to prevent anyone from being identified as a member of the Association. We have also been able to establish contact between national staff members who consider themselves to be in danger, and the authorities able to insure their protection (UN High Commissioner for Refugees or local authorities).

Additional measures are taken to help our national staff face the situation. A "security envelope" is given to each employee, containing a Handicap International membership card and a salary advance of several months. Procedures are put in place to enable our national staff who remain behind to communicate, if need be, with the team members evacuated to neighboring countries (radio, telephone, e-mail).

As a potential source of distress, the impossibility of evacuating nationals is always clearly explained to the whole team, and forms part of the internal regulations of every mission in the field. In any case, national staff generally do not wish to be evacuated, preferring to remain with their families. Handicap International could not handle the evacuation of all the national staff (often several dozen individuals, together with their families). And how would one decide who should be evacuated and who should remain behind? What is more, the responsibility of the Association does not end with the decision to evacuate, and the evacuation process does not end once the border has been crossed. An evacuated team has to be cared for physically, psychologically, and administratively upon its return. These would be impossible to ensure for national staff in a host country due to lack of means, of visas and administrative authorization at immigration, not to mention the moral responsibility of separating a person from his or her country and familiar environment with no way of guaranteeing eventual return.

Bearing Witness

For an expatriate to witness violations of human rights is of course in itself a violent and traumatic experience. Beyond that, the failure of the international community to condemn these violations can provoke disillusionment and bitterness in the teams in the field. This constitutes another form of violence not only for the direct victims, but also for those who have witnessed these violations.

In order to help expatriates cope with the difficulties they may experience in being such a witness, Handicap International's management assumes a monitoring role toward expatriates, discusses with them what they may experience, and has also instituted a formalized framework within which expatriates can give evidence of what they have experienced in the field.[11]

The Role of Mental Health Professionals in Handicap International

Since the beginning of the 1990s the role of mental health professionals (psychologists, psychiatrists, psychiatric nurses, psychometricians) has continued to develop in the Association. Psychological support programs for vulnerable populations led to the creation of a technical service by the same name. One element of this service is the availability of psychologists and psychiatrist to assist distressed expatriates.

In order to encourage maximum freedom of speech for expatriates in need of psychological support, and the professionals' neutrality, the professionals are not part of Handicap International's management or organization structure, but are external to the organization and bound by professional confidentiality.

While there is always a debriefing with the Human Resources Department, the Technical Coordination Unit and the program's management upon return from mission, a meeting with a psychologist is at the expatriate's own initiative. Each expatriate is provided with a list of addresses and telephone numbers of mental health workers inside and outside the Association.

The Human Resources Department and the program coordination structure at the Head Office are responsible for alerting the management of the Association when an expatriate or a team begins to show signs of psychological distress. In the past, for example, weekly telephone calls between a psychiatrist at Handicap International and expatriates in the field were initiated. A visit from a mental health professional or a mediator may be suggested to teams in the field to help solve problems and conflicts, or deal with distress. In the same way, for certain humanitarian missions considered

[11] See for example, "Handicap International and the witness question," Monitoring and Positioning Unit, Handicap International, April 2001 (internal document).

to be "sensitive" (for example, following the evacuation of a team or an individual, or when the mission has experienced painful events), medical and/or psychological follow-up is suggested to the members of the team concerned.

Finally, it is strongly advised that expatriates returning from a mission have a medical check up, which becomes mandatory if there is to be a further posting. This can be an opportunity to discuss certain problems—physical or psychological—that the expatriate has had to handle during the mission.

The incorporation of psychological support for teams is thus a characteristic of Handicap International. Unfortunately, as expatriation can be a destabilizing experience in itself, it is not possible to avoid all the risks involved since each case is, by definition, unique.

Voices

A PRISON WITHOUT BARS

C. O.
Expatriate in Croatia (1994) and Bosnia (1996)

The first time I dared put my foot on anything other than tarmac after spending several months in the Former Yugoslavia in mine-infested areas, I was overcome by panic and vertigo. It was impossible to move. Knots in my stomach, cold sweats, I was sure I was going to die. And yet, I had always managed to stay calm in the field!

It had become an obsession to study the ground where I walked: never on bare earth, never on grass, always on tarmac and always on roads that had been identified as mine-free. It had become a survival reflex, as vital as eating, drinking, and sleeping. For several months, the presence of mines had dominated my whole behavior in the field. I was in a prison without bars, my liberty of movement limited to the journeys necessary for the mission.

Upon returning to France, I regained my physical freedom of movement. Emotionally, I could not detach myself from these acquired reflexes. I continued to notice the slightest irregularity in the soil, an old tin can, a patch of tall grass as a potential threat!

It was several weeks before I was able to raise my head and stop studying the ground under my feet. But what of those who are condemned to live forever in that "prison without bars"? How do they cope?

YET ANOTHER EVACUATION

P. C.
Psychologist in Guinea,
from July 2000 to January 2001

Early December 2000: The attacks on Guinean villages by armed groups are getting closer to Kissidougou, where all the NGOs are based. The town of Guéckédou has been taken and the road linking us with most of the refugee camps is now cut off. In a wave of panic the civilian population, Guineans and refugees alike, are fleeing from the region *en masse;* the lucky ones with some money are cramming into bush taxis or the decrepit local buses, while the others are leaving on foot through the bush with their belongings in bundles on their heads.

The NGOs are organizing themselves to meet the situation as best they can; permanent radio contact with the heads of mission based in the capital allows us to follow the advance of the fightings and assess the risks. We are ready to leave town at any moment, having already experienced a similar situation barely two months ago, which ended in the evacuation of Guéckédou.

I have lost contact with most of my Sierra Leone colleagues who worked with me for eighteen months in the camps. Only those in the camp at Massacoundou, 15 minutes from our base, will get a farewell visit. Joy at seeing them again quickly gives way to trepidation. I have to tell them that we could be leaving at any moment. The prospect of our departure only increases their anxiety as they feel that as long as the whites are still here the danger cannot be so great. The distress of the refugees is overwhelming. Chased out again by the violence from the place where they had found refuge, they do not know where to go, they have no hope and seek from me answers and solutions that I am at a loss to give them. What are we going to do? Where should we go? What are the United Nations and the NGOs doing to protect us?

Deal first with the most urgent problems—explain the situation to my colleagues and give them a two months advance salary to help them face the crisis. I could not even visit the children to whom I have been providing therapy for over a year. With the passing months, they had begun to recover psychologically, regaining the ability to laugh and play together, to tell of tragic past experiences without being overwhelmed by emotion, to be able to look to the future again. I have to leave the camp not knowing whether I shall ever see them again, with feelings of impotence and guilt which will remain with me for a long time. When it is time to leave, my colleagues manage, in spite of everything, to smile and wish me well. They don't forget the old customs, sending greetings to my family, wishing me a good journey and hoping to see me again soon, God willing.

AN EVACUATION FROM SIERRA LEONE
I. A. R.
Psychologist in Sierra Leone

Friday the 5th May 2000: The decision has been made to evacuate Freetown. It is a shock. Of course, we were more or less expecting it. For a week events have been following on rapidly, one after the other: attacks on the demobilization camps, 500 UN troops taken hostage in the country, and advances by rebels toward the capital. We are not surprised, and yet, do we really realize what is happening? Perhaps, but it is not certain. Time is running out, we must organize meetings with our Sierra Leone colleagues, try to think of everything so that work can continue during our absence, try to anticipate, share responsibilities, inform the teams still in the camp at Murraytown. Try to stay calm, don't panic or collapse. Recover the generator and store it in a safe place, pack our bags, announce our departure to the watchmen and the domestic staff and tell them what is provided for them. A difficult moment. They tell us that we are right to leave. Because of our white skin we could be in danger, that the rebels will not take Freetown, that we will soon be back.

And then we wait. The evacuation will not take place until tomorrow morning. We are in a bar with other expatriates, one of whom has already lived through the evacuation of December 1998. Only then do we realize that it is really an evacuation and not just a stay at Conakry until things quiet down, and that we shall not be back soon, as we had thought. When we were leaving, we had even said ". . . see you Tuesday or Wednesday" to the psychology program assistant. What an illusion! Between what we know and what we realize afterward when the action is over and all we can do is wait for the next day, we have plenty of time to imagine what could happen if the rebels take Freetown, and to think about those who were left behind. The children in the therapy groups are already suffering greatly; how will they survive another trauma? Will people be able to protect themselves? What chance do the girls in the team have of avoiding being raped if the rebels break into their houses? We are afraid for them. Our worries are fed by memories of the accounts told by patients already in our care. We have a whole sleepless night to imagine the worst, which is certainly going to happen.

And then the feeling of guilt at the moment of leaving, goodbye to the ideals of humanitarian aid. We are leaving because things could turn nasty. Of course we know that nothing would be gained by staying behind and that it could even put the whole Sierra Leone team in danger; that it is not our country. We are happy to climb into the helicopter, sure, but the anguish and feelings of guilt are still there. In the future, there will always be a "before" and an "after" the evacuation, when we speak of our mission in Sierra Leone.

22

Preventing Broken Hearts, Healing Broken Minds

John Fawcett

World Vision International (WVI) is one of the largest faith-based humanitarian aid and emergency relief organizations in the world with an annual budget close to one billion U.S. dollars and 11,000 staff. WVI is a multicultural international agency with a complex management structure, program offices in nearly 100 countries and staff from over 40 different nationalities. Growth in the last decade has been phenomenal. In the early 1990s, country programs of five million dollars were large. Today, emergency relief responses top ten million dollars in the first month. Many chapters in this book describe staff support programs in different stages of development. This chapter discusses staff support through the experience of World Vision. While answers to some issues are clear, consistent quality staff support will only come through interagency collaboration and the strengthening of the relationships between research institutions and field-based organizations.

In 2001, in a country (unnamed for security reasons) in Africa, an international NGO was coming to the end of its grant funding. Local staff needed to be laid off. Aware of the issues and concerns of the local community and how important salaries were to family survival, the Field Director worked closely with local elders and senior local staff to ensure as smooth a transition as possible. However, when layoffs commenced, one local manager grew angry and physically attacked the international Field Director. Disgruntled staff, some armed with AK47 assault rifles, were outside the building demanding money. Other senior local staff intervened and managed to calm the situation. Within a few hours, however, it deteriorated. Staff and family members surrounded the building and shouted verbal threats. All the international staff were in the building at the time and could not leave.

Overnight the scene quieted but there was no resolution. At 4 A.M., under cover of a noisy generator and the first daily prayer of the local Muslim community, the international staff slipped out of the compound and began a swift retreat. An hour later the escape was revealed and angered locals began to attack the compound with guns and other weapons. Local armed guards fired back and for a period of 15 minutes a gun battle ensued. Fortunately, no one was killed in the incident, but the NGO temporarily halted operations.

This is the face of humanitarian work at the commencement of the new millennium. A work birthed in compassion and care, sheltered for decades by an aura of neutrality and impartiality, is now increasingly viewed as partisan, wealthy, subjective and, in some instances, potentially destructive to the communities being assisted. Instead of being observers of wars, NGO staff have become participants, victims and sometimes, politically biased. The distance between participant and perpetrator is much narrower today than ever before. The stakes are higher. The dollar amounts are enormous. The political influence and potential power of NGOs are recognized by individuals and governments all over the world. How, in the face of this increasing complexity, is it possible to provide appropriate and sufficient organizational support for both local and international staff?

KEY ISSUES IN DEVELOPING A FRAMEWORK OF SUPPORT

Characteristics of the present staffing environment include:

- Chronically stressed and burned out staff
- Increased security risks
- Huge increases in job vacancies
- New entrants without required skills and expertise
- Existing staff whose skills are no longer relevant
- Organizations unable to provide culturally appropriate support
- Organizational structures collapsing under the pressures of rapid growth
- Senior leaders with little ability to manage multinational corporate entities.

PAIN AND SUFFERING

In Rwanda in 1994, humanitarian workers and UN peacekeepers were faced with a situation not previously encountered in such depth or magnitude. For what was the first time, at such an extreme level, humanitarian workers lived and worked in the midst of ongoing genocide and were apparently unable to stop the killing.

A colleague, who arrived in Rwanda as the international humanitarian effort commenced, still talks of the almost surrealistic experiences of working there. She and her team toiled desperately to provide basic health services to injured and traumatized refugees. At the end of the day, unable to stay in the camp because of the heightened dangers at night, they returned to their vehicle to drive back to their tents. Before driving away, however, they had to clear away the bodies of those who had crawled into the shade afforded by the vehicle during the heat of the day and had subsequently succumbed to injury, thirst, disease, or trauma. The next day they would return to the camp to find that some of those treated the previous day had been murdered in the nighttime ritual of revenge and ongoing genocide. This pattern of daily life repeated itself for a period of weeks. This colleague still has nightmares of the experience.

Clearly there is a psychological impact on staff exposed to extreme circumstances. Psychological expertise has indeed influenced the direction of staff support services in recent years. Mobile trauma support teams and internal organizational services are positive outcomes of this expertise. Potential negative consequences include the tendencies to seek unidimensional explanations for such complex phenomena [1], and to apply the diagnosis almost indiscriminately to both victim [2] and communities [3].

World Vision International developed a psychological debriefing intervention service, adapted loosely on the Mitchell and Everly model [4]. Anecdotal reports from staff provided with debriefing indicated that the level of organizational response was of more importance than the actual debriefing itself. World Vision staff reported the presence or absence of senior managers as being important factors in how they coped with trauma immediately after a critical event. The presence of the most senior manager during and following a major event was interpreted as a demonstration of organizational support and care. Practical aspects such as the provision of money, the replacement of personal items, care of children, options for future employment and the ability to continue, even at a distance, the work for which they had been originally employed were reportedly more important than psychological debriefing. The subject of psychological debriefing is elaborated on in chapter 32 in this volume.

SECURITY MANAGEMENT

Humanitarian work is extraordinarily difficult, challenging, and often painful and very dangerous. Security of staff has also become a major issue for NGOs and the UN and has influenced considerations of staff support. Between 1989 and 1998, 32 staff members of the World Food Program were murdered and in 1996 the International Committee of the Red Cross had six staff killed as a result of targeted assassination in Chechnya [5]. In 1998 UNHCR reported the deaths of 17 civilian aid workers compared with eight military peacekeepers during the same period [6]. Many NGOs now have their own internal security training program and others, such as RedR, offer security training for NGO and UN staff around the world [7]. However, most NGO resources go into programs, and very little is allocated for security. WVI, which views the security of its 12,000 personnel serving in over 100 countries as vital and has invested resources in, among other measures, creating the post of director of corporate security. WVI believes that "prevention is the remedy": the way to enhance staff safety and security. The organization has therefore invested many resources into security awareness and prevention training, and distributes security manuals [8] to its staff worldwide. It conducts security training at several levels: for decision-makers at the management level, and for all staff at the personal safety level. It has also set up regional security management teams, with officers to oversee security in countries and regions (Africa, for example, is divided into three regions). Ample resources go into communications equipment for staff, as WVI believes that, in the field, "if you can't talk to each other, you don't have security."

RETENTION OF STAFF

Experienced humanitarian workers are extremely valuable assets to any NGO and international agency. The good-hearted volunteer, while still important, is a minority today. International humanitarian work is a career requiring very high levels of expertise, knowledge, and experience. In recognition of this, salary levels continue to rise and NGOs compete with each other for the very best staff. Field workers now plan their careers around successive assignments and move readily between organizations. Retention of skilled staff is a serious challenge to all organizations.

The principles and practices of human resource management must evolve to meet effectively needs of staff both internationally and locally. It may not be possible in the future for multinational NGOs to have significantly different employment policies for expatriates and nationals. Local staff may have considerable training, education and expertise and, being well aware of first world employment practices, requires full employment contracts, with comparable benefit, if not salary, packages to international staff. NGOs need to face the cost implications of equity to avoid employment discrimination.

Rapid increases in job vacancies have contributed to high worker mobility. This mobility has obscured the "darker" side of doing humanitarian work, the psychological impairments that trauma professionals have quite appropriately focused on in the recent years. Incidences of severe traumatic disability among humanitarian workers may be significantly less of a concern than previously believed. Nevertheless, Acute Stress Reactions (ASR) or Post Traumatic Stress Disorder (PTSD) are extremely disabling for the individual and expensive for the employer. Extreme trauma may result in the end of a career. While some reject outright psychological trauma in relief workers [9], it would be irresponsible to dismiss it totally in determining appropriate support structures for field staff. The author's own experiences resonate with those who have described similar profoundly disturbing psychological experiences during and following dangerous field assignments.

Advances in Employee Assistance Programs (EAP) in business environments have been slow to transfer to NGOs. However most NGOs and government agencies today acknowledge the need for proper psychological support alongside other medical services. There is an increase in the availability of counseling in major cities close to field operations, as well as mobile rapid response psychological units.

Issues relating to the cross-cultural applicability of both trauma diagnosis and psychological interventions are of major importance as well. Individual focused talk therapy does not, it turns out, translate well across cultures. Therapy, for example, is not justice, and therapy alone may not enhance healing [10].

Community psychological trauma work may be based on a series of untested assumptions [11]. Some organizations, such as The Transcultural Psychosocial Organisation, have focused their trauma recovery programs on community based approaches where the primary intervention is with families and groups within the local cultural context [12]. It should be a relatively simple matter for agencies with strong human resource management to incorporate mental health services and support alongside existing health services.

CROSSCULTURAL AND MULTICULTURAL STAFFING

Humanitarian personnel no longer come primarily from first world countries. For example, World Vision International employs approximately 500 staff internationally of which nearly 55 percent are hired from Africa, and only 22 percent come from North America. International staff within World Vision work in over 90 different countries, but the traditional North–South relocation routes are a thing of the past. Nigerians work in Kosovo, Brazilians work in Mozambique, Ghanaians work in Cambodia. Issues of cross cultural relocation and transition have become intricately more complex than they were in the 1950s when international work was dominated by largely European first world expatriates traveling the world delivering charity.

A faith-based Christian organization, WVI has expanded since its inception fifty years ago; while the founding group, North American conservative evangelicals, is now very small but still very influential, today WVI employs Christians from Eastern Orthodox to Protestant evangelists, Liberal Catholics to Southern Baptists, as well as Muslims and Buddhists (the latter only in field programs). This has created a major issue of identity for the organization. Founder-generation staff often revert to simplistic solutions to issues of faith through statements that sacred texts or ritual behaviors will either heal or protect staff. While openness is increasing to discussing these issues in WVI there is still a substantial way to go before a real, effective communication becomes an integral part of the organization's lifestyle. Organizations that have more distance from this issue may be in a more objective position to evaluate the role of faith in providing support to staff.

RECOMMENDATIONS

World Vision has identified the following factors as being critical in developing consistent and effective staff support. More has been achieved in some areas than others. Some of the recommendations may appear idealistic or even unattainable; however, without appropriate standards of quality it is unlikely that sufficient progress will be made.

EMPLOYMENT POLICIES

- International humanitarian organizations must adopt human resource practices that are professional, effective and consistent across local and international staff. Guidelines such as the People In Aid Code [13] should be integrated into organizational policies.

RECRUITMENT PROCESSES

- People recruited for humanitarian work must have the competencies to be able to perform to levels of organizational expectations. In determining program objectives and outcomes, recognized standards of performance such as the Sphere Standards [14] should form the basis of designs and job descriptions. The practice of "finding a warm body" to fill the job is more commonplace than is generally realized. Pressures from donors on NGOs to commence a project can lead to inappropriate recruitment and subsequent project failure. In the Balkans during 2000, the author spent time with the manager of a large housing reconstruction project who later confessed to being totally out of his professional depth. His previous experience in housing construction had been as an account manager at a first world mortgage agency, and he was finding the task of providing skilled leadership in rebuilding bombed houses something of a personal and organizational challenge. The NGO had been under considerable pressure from the donor to commence work and rather than lose the grant had opted for the relatively high-risk solution of placing an accountant in charge of building hundreds of houses.
- Staff hired locally must be employed according to both international and local employment law and with account to the complexity of multi-national employment realities. Every job must have a clear and accurate job description. Every staff person must have a clear, accurate, and written legal employment contract.
- Selection of staff, especially those recruited for the most challenging disaster environments, should include a full psychiatric history, including that of the immediate family.[1] Indications of any psychotic episodes, including eating disorders and recent depressive or anxiety related disorders, should be referred for psychiatric evaluation. Past mental health problems almost certainly contribute to the decrease of resilience of individuals [15]. Any previous history of ASR or PTSD should automatically exclude the applicant from significantly stressful field placements.
- At interview, applicants should be assessed for evidence of resilience. The shattering of worldviews and the development of negative self-images may lead to psychological disability [16]. Workers who have rigidly held beliefs are particularly vulnerable to experiencing a fundamental shattering of their belief structures after a traumatic experience and then going on to experience a loss of self-esteem [17]. Resilience is a function of a person's strength of "faith" in self, the goodness of people, the goodness of God, and the future and in a sustaining religion [18]. While resilience still affords much opportunity for further study it is recommended that new applicants for international humanitarian work be assessed for evidence of coping skills as well as

---

[1] Most psychological tools are based on Western modems of mental health and should be used in other cultures only with appropriate guidance and advice. Some tools have been validated with specific cultural groups but care is recommended in use of management processes birthed and developed mono-culturally.

examining their belief structures. The flexibility with which a belief structure is held is more relevant for these purposes than the content of the belief.
- The ability to secure and retain a good social network should be assessed. Military literature identifies social support as being significant in reducing the incidence of negative psychological conditions [19]. Social factors therefore play a key role in determining stress reaction vulnerability to traumatic events.[2]
- Prior life events, especially during the past 12 months, should be audited using a standardized tool. Evidence of ability to handle life transitions should be provided by applicants. Patterns of failing to manage transitions should be considered as partial grounds for excluding candidates.
- Previous career posts should be reviewed. Early data analysis of field research hints that field staff with as few as five front line assignments in a career show significantly increased levels of clinical psychological conditions. While data do not permit drawing strong conclusions, recruiting agencies would be wise to review the number and type of previous field experiences when considering career humanitarian workers.
- Leadership applicants must be assessed in ability to provide a consultative leadership style, especially for management of emergency relief projects. In particular, they should be assessed on their competency relative to their team rather than on an absolute level of competency. Team leaders must be perceived by members as being more competent than the members in times of high stress. Competency is an essential factor in credibility [20]. Team cohesion and trust in leadership (competent leadership) are factors most likely to lead to the mitigation of ASR. Recovery from ASR appears to relate to previous life events and personality variables. The health, effectiveness and productivity of a team is a direct function of stress related behavior.

TRAINING AND CAPACITY BUILDING

- Organizations must provide appropriate and effective training. Security management training is essential. Training in the use of equipment such as communication systems, vehicles, and specialized tools is necessary. Knowledge of first aid is essential.
- Individual and team (corporate) stress management training should be provided. Such training should include focus on the importance of team cohesion, morale, and its components and leadership issues.
- Military literature identifies two critical aspects of social support; team cohesion and consultative leadership style. When teams are created, team-building exercises should be undertaken. Team cohesion is a powerful protective factor for ASR and PTSD. A major factor enabling a person to keep

[2] The same study demonstrated that combat exposure accounted for less than 20 percent of the variance, suggesting that critical events themselves may be less traumatizing than social support factors.

going in the face of danger is the near presence or presumed presence of a comrade [21].

- It is essential that team leaders, not just team members, participate fully in team building exercises [22].
- Leaders need to have a solid training in organizational stress management methods and techniques. In addition to understanding individual stress management, leaders need to assess environmental and organizational stress causes and symptoms, and how to reduce them.

SUPPORT SYSTEMS

- Management structures and organizational hierarchy must be clear and defined, with accountability and responsibility requirements understood by all.
- Individuals and teams must be provided with sufficient equipment, supplies, and funds. Failure adequately to prepare funding and program proposals is a significant. cause of stress and decreased morale. Organizations should not require staff to continue attempting to meet program objectives with insufficient resources.
- Local staff support services must be designed in the context of the prevailing culture. The knowledge of cultural anthropologists, ethnographers, sociologists, and local experts should be relied upon.
- The present tendency to utilize Western psychological frameworks to determine causes and impacts of stress and design interventions must be resisted until full cultural and ethnographic assessment has been undertaken.
- Adequate provisions must be made for time away from work, and for leisure activities. Annual vacation time must be provided and staff must actually take leave and not enter into covert agreements with management to forgo leave in order to either conserve organizational resources or meet deadlines or other organizational objectives.
- Staff must be able to access external social support networks such as family, friends, and professional groups. Organizations need to ensure that policies relating to such matters as telecommunications and e-mail are flexible and open enough to ensure the maintenance of social networks. Policies that restrict phone personal phone calls to 15 minutes per week should be abandoned in favor of ones that encourage field staff to continue with external relationships. Program proposals need to factor these costs into financial estimates. These supports should not be sacrificed if funding is an issue. Social support is one of the strongest prophylactic factors for stress management.
- Staff must be provided access to full and comprehensive health services, including mental health services [23]. Particular attention must be paid to environments of extreme hardship, emergency disaster relief, war and especially mass killings or genocide. Health services must be designed on the basis of local and cultural appropriateness and must be readily available.

Networking with other agencies and health providers is strongly recommended. The nature of ASR in humanitarian work must be more fully researched.

• Organizations must have local, regional, and international crisis response strategies. In the event of major incidents such as employee murder, full field evacuations or significantly traumatic incidents, competent, trained, and senior staff must be available on or as near as possible to those impacted. The presence of senior managers, even if they are not trained in emergency procedures, is a powerful factor in assisting recovery and maintaining morale.

• Organizations need to attempt to maintain stable and long-term teams, as team cohesion is a highly protective factor in avoiding ASR and PTSD. Despite the high mobility of staff, organizations need to address such issues actively, especially for those involved in front line emergency situations.

• Organizations need to develop career path mechanisms that reduce exposure to the highest risk environments. Exposure does not increase resilience; in fact, it appears that exposure may increase the possibility of ASR and PTSD. Rotation over a lifetime career may involve periods of direct fieldwork followed by headquarters type assignments interspersed with study or skill enhancement opportunities. Organizations need to avoid the temptation to have staff members permanently assigned to major relief programs.

REFERENCES

1. Y. Danieli (ed.), *International Handbook of Multigenerational Legacies of Trauma*, Plenum Press, New York, 1998.
2. D. Summerfield, The Invention of Post-Traumatic Stress Disorder and the Social Usefulness of a Psychiatric Category, *British Medical Journal, 322,* pp. 95-98, 2001.
3. I. Agger, S. Vuk, and J. Mimica, *Theory and Practice of Psychosocial Projects Under War Conditions in Bosnia-Herzegovina and Croatia*, ECHO/ECTF, Zagreb, 1995.
4. J. T. Mitchell and G. S. Everly, *Critical Incident Stress Debriefing: An Operations Manual for the Prevention of Traumatic Stress Among Emergency Services and Disaster Workers*, Chevron, Ellicott City, Maryland, 1996.
5. K. Van Brabant, *Operational Security Management in Violent Environments*, Overseas Development Institute, London, p. 330, 2000.
6. *The Los Angeles Times*, p. A8, August 2, 1998.
7. For details contact RedR Training Dept. RedR, 1 Great George Street, London, SW1P 3AA, UK.
8. C. Rogers and B. Sytsma, *World Vision Security Manual*, World Vision International, Geneva, 2000.
9. D. Summerfield, Book Review, *British Medical Journal,* 2000; available at, <http://www.bmj.com/cgi/content/full/320/7243/1216>
10. P. J. Bracken and C. Petty, *Rethinking the Trauma of War*, Free Association Books Ltd., London, p. 191, 1998.
11. D. Summerfield, *The Impact of War and Atrocity on Civilian Populations: Basic Principles for NGO Interventions and a Critique of Psychosocial Trauma Projects*, Overseas Development Institute/RRN, *Network Paper 14,* London, 1996.

12. D. Somasudaram, *Community Mental Health in Cambodia*, TPO, Phnom Penh, Cambodia, 1997.
13. *People In Aid Code of Best Practices in the Management and Support of Aid Personnel*, available at <www.peopleinaid.org/codemain.htm>
14. *Humanitarian Charter and Minimum Standards in Disaster Response*, Oxfam, Sphere Project, Oxford, United Kingdom, 2000.
15. G. Fawcett, *Ad-Mission; The Briefing and Debriefing of Teams of Missionaries and Aid Workers*, Harpendon, United Kingdom, 1999.
16. J. Bulmam, in *Compassion Fatigue: Coping with Secondary Traumatic Stress Disorder in Those Who Treat the Traumatized*, C. Figley (ed.), Brunner/Mazel, New York, 1995.
17. D. M. Lovell, *Psychological Adjustment Amongst Returned Overseas Aid Workers*, unpublished D. Clin. Psy. thesis, University of Wales, Bangor, Wales, 1997.
18. G. Higgins, *Resilient Adults, Overcoming a Cruel Past*, Jossey-Bass, San Francisco, 1994.
19. T. W. Barrett and J. S. Mizes, Combat Level and Social Support in the Development of PTSD in Vietnam Veterans, *Behavior Modification, 12,* pp. 100-115, 1998.
20. S. Noy, Stress and Personality as Factors in the Causation and Prognosis of Combat Reaction, in *Handbook of Military Psychology*, R. Gal and A. Mangelsdorff (eds.), John Wiley, Chichester, United Kingdom, 1991.
21. S. Noy, Combat Stress Reaction, in *Handbook of Military Psychology*, R. Gal and A. Mangelsdorff (eds.), John Wiley, Chichester, United Kingdom, 1991.
22. From an unpublished literature review prepared by G. Fawcett, YWAM, Highfield Oval, Harpenden, Herts AL5 4BX, UK, for World Vision International, 2000.
23. J. Fawcett, Managing Staff Stress and Trauma, in *Complex Humanitarian Emergencies: Lessons from Practitioners*, M. Janz and J. Slead (eds.), World Vision, Monrovia, California, pp. 92-125, 2000.

Voice

IN GOD'S LAP

M. R.

One of my earliest memories is of trauma transformed by the care of an emergency room physician. I was four years old and, in the era before safety restraints, was riding in the back of our station wagon along with the spare tire. So when my dad stopped too suddenly, I flew forward gashing my forehead at the eyebrow and spewing blood everywhere. Conveniently, we were on our way to the hospital to pick up my mom and new baby sister. My dad was mad at me for getting hurt and I was terrified. What I remember most is that the doctor's voice was soft and kind, his hands were gentle and confident, and he had me "play possum" while he stitched up my head. I left calm, comforted, and even happy. This experience, only a few months after our arrival in Japan as missionaries, sustained me in the lonely years to come. This warm human connection was an island of peace in a dark sea of chaos.

My mother had health complications after the baby was born. She spent several more weeks in the hospital over the next few months while my dad and the newly arrived Japanese maid attended as best they could to the newborn and the rest of us three kids. Even once my mom was well, the pervasive chaos of those early months persisted.

So, it was a relief to me when I could go to kindergarten with my six-year-old brother. Although riding the Tokyo train by ourselves every day was sometimes quite scary, it was better than staying at home. I had my older brother for security and my mother prayed for our safe return each day. Prayer was the main coping skill in our family. "The Lord will provide. The Lord will take care of us." We only needed to keep praying. This in spite of the fact that we were in Japan less than a decade after the end of the war, and had already had both stones and curses thrown at us.

Toward the end of this first year when I was almost five, my sister broke her leg by falling down the stairs. Our almost three-year-old brother had opened the gate and, of course, not bothered to close it. My mother was furious with me and verbally accosted me as was her way, "Why didn't you keep a better watch over them? How could you have let this happen? Your sister might be crippled for life now and it's all your fault! You should be ashamed of yourself!" I was terribly frightened and confused and deeply ashamed. I began to resent my younger brother and sister for somehow getting me into trouble. The animosity, especially toward my sister, deepened as my mother repeatedly compared me unfavorably to her. "Why can't you be more like your sister? She's always so good to go to bed when she's told (or whatever behavior was desired from me), she never whines and fusses like you." My sister and I found out years later that my mom said similar things about me to her. It's no wonder we were always fighting. Both of us were sure that the other had cornered the market on our mother's affection that each of us so desperately craved.

My experience with the ER doctor along with my own sense of abandonment and aching loneliness spurred me to try to take care of others like he had taken care of me. I began to collect stray kittens and puppies in various stages of starvation. There was no shortage of them in Japan at that time. Their religions forbid killing and so litters of young animals would just be left by the side of the road. My young heart went out to them . . . so little and soft and helpless . . . and I would carry them home translating their hungry, plaintive mews into equally plaintive pleas of "Can't she stay? Can't I just feed her a little bit? We have lots of scraps. She can have some of my food." The puppies never stayed around long, but at one point I had collected over 40 cats and kittens. My parents finally said they had to go. I could keep only one. And of course since our Japanese pastor had recently given us a kitten, that was the one we had to keep. But it was a mean cat and eventually my father had to kill it—after it attacked my mother as she was taking some meat out of the refrigerator. The cat we really loved we kept secretly for as long as we could. We made a cozy nest for her out of doll blankets in the gutter outside our house. But when the rains came she was washed away—one more of many beloved pets to be carried away by the tides.

About that time my father took me to visit "the bomb center" in Hiroshima. Here it was not kittens and puppies left to die, but children and grandmas, mommies and daddies. I was horrified, terrified by the bleak, dark emptiness of that hollow, rusting dome and the pictures and all the sad, too sad people. But from that scary, dark place I plunged even deeper into what seemed like a bottomless pit when my father tried to explain things to me. He told me that the only tragedy here was that these people had not had an opportunity to hear the Word of God, that they had died without being saved as Christians from the eternal damnation of hell. I felt like I was drowning with nothing to hold on to. The birds were all that saved me—the bright-colored origami cranes hanging singly and in chains all around the memorial caught my attention. They were a lifeline for me back to hope and healing and human connection. Our Japanese maid taught me to fold these colorful, lively birds and many other things besides. She taught me Japanese as she told me Japanese fairytales, played Japanese games with me, and even took me to visit at her parents' farm, all of which nurtured my human connection back to life. Her care sustained me.

Having learned some Japanese, I easily made friends with the local Japanese girls. I had one friend in particular and we would visit back and forth at each other's homes, both of us quite fascinated by the other's life. My dad also began to take an interest in my friend and I was quite delighted with having gained his ever-elusive attention. He talked to her about Jesus and invited her and her family to church. One day quite abruptly she was no longer allowed to play with me or even to talk to me. I was devastated and confused and couldn't understand. My father consoled me by saying that having no friends at all was much better than having friends who weren't Christian. I just missed my friend terribly.

I began to have nightmares about being lost, abandoned, and in danger, chased by an unimaginably terrifying, all-powerful malevolent pursuer. I would courageously brave the abyss to my parent's room. But, after being spanked repeatedly and finally, dunked in a bathtub of cold water, I preferred the terrors of my own bed to the terrors of my father's wrath. And when the pain was too unbearable, I would imagine that Buddha was there and I could crawl into his lap and he would hold me and love me and comfort me. I didn't think Jesus would mind, it was hard to get much consolation from Him hanging on the cross. I sort of thought that since Jesus was God he must have sent Buddha to Japan, since he couldn't be there himself. But I knew my father would be enraged, so I kept this secret to myself. I knew about Buddha, of course, since his statues were everywhere. I knew that the Japanese thought he was God, just like we thought Jesus was God. From the upper story of our house in Tokyo, I could look out and see into the gardens of a Buddhist monastery or temple. It looked so calm and peaceful and orderly. People would walk there, slowly, and they seemed so deep and quiet. It was another "island of peace, in the dark sea of chaos." I thought of the Buddha like that, as a place of deep profound rest and peace and comfort. And so I sought the sanctuary of his lap when it seemed like I just couldn't go on anymore.

The last year we were in Japan was especially lonely because my older brother went off to boarding school. He was in the fourth grade; I was in third. I just read more comic books. At Christmas, he and I exchanged comic books. I felt connected to him and to the homeland as I read and reread those American comic book stories. Things "American" took on a special charm for us in Japan. We eagerly looked forward to packages from the States and the goodies enclosed—Kool-Aid, chocolate chips, peanut butter and jelly, Jell-O, and other American treats. The 4th of July was also a highlight with fireworks in the middle of Lake Nojiri and hymns reverberating out over the water accompanied by my father on his portable pump organ.

After five years in Japan, we moved back to the Midwest. This was as much of a culture shock as going to Japan. We had not had much money in Japan, but had lived a life-style of the wealthy in some ways. We had our Japanese maid. We spent summers in our cabin at the lake. Now we were just poor. My schoolmates were farmers' children, who had never been out of the state, let alone out of the country. Their ideas of the world and expectations of their futures seemed similarly restricted. Things "American" no longer seemed so special. I was adrift on the lonely seas of cultural homelessness. Only it would be years before I would connect with this term that named my experience. Only years later would I finally meet others who had had similarly painful and alienating cross-cultural experiences as children.

It has taken me years . . . decades . . . of painful investigation to unravel the reality of my actual experience from the myth of "what a wonderful opportunity it was." I have certainly gained from my time in Japan, but the costs for me (and for the whole family) were huge, especially as they are still so largely unacknowledged. Writing this story has continued the healing process for me. It has prompted first conversations with some family members, corroborating the painful chaos of our life in Japan yet initiating a new closeness. I am grateful for the opportunity to revisit this territory.

23

Local Community Capacity: The Source of Renewal

Ian D. Campbell and Alison Rader

It matters greatly that our response to and understanding of suffering is shaped by the degree of our proximity to it. How we touch it determines our relevance, integrity, and effectiveness as organizations. In short, the choice is to observe and provide or to feel and participate. The perspectives within us, at least, are starkly different. On the one hand, we act and evaluate our capacity; on the other, we experience, reflect, act, and rely on the capacity of those who seem weak and vulnerable because they suffer. This has been a key foundation for learning and sustained response by a small team of international consultants who together have comprised The Salvation Army's International Headquarters program facilitation team with a focus on HIV/AIDS, health, and development.

HIV/AIDS signifies voices that are speaking and are yet to be heard. The global experience and response to HIV/AIDS is a paradox, characterized by valuing of expertise or of known relational experience, of belief in the strength of intervening organizations, or in communities that can respond; of providing for people in contrast to participating with them; of a focus on populations or on persons, and on individuals or persons who are in relationships that greatly influence quality and progress in life. The capacity of local communities to respond is the vision shared by the facilitation team. The way of approaching the work of supporting implementers in more than 40 countries has been by strengthening capacity of these implementing teams to encourage local communities to respond to their situations rather than just "receive." Where there has been belief expressed in local implementers, there has inevitably been an expression of strength and hope by these people. This is seen strongly in local community response also, and this in fact is a major source of strength, hope, and renewal for implementing teams.

Many voices clamor. Which ones have reached me and the team with which I work? How have we sustained our hope over 15 years of intense involvement?

In 1987, an HIV positive young man, living in a village in Southern Zambia, was depressed. He burned himself alive while alone in his hut.

His father, a headman, felt shame and loss. The HIV/AIDS team, exploring an innovative team approach to home care, had encountered other voices: the desire for care by the presence of persons and families with HIV/AIDS; a sense of yearning by neighbors for community belonging somehow obstructed by not knowing how to acknowledge this new disease; and the voices of those who could see that the process of change requires hard work at reconciliation in families and neighborhoods, yet find it almost impossible to speak alone from within these neighborhood and communities.

The headman made a decision that saved years of community indecision for the catchment population of 80,000 people; he called a meeting of leaders and asked the team to help the conversation happen. He may have asked for information, but he really wanted to know how to respond as a father and a leader to other leaders and ordinary community members. He wanted to correct a wrong: his son should not have died, especially alone. And he sensed the need to build community resilience for the future. So he asked for acknowledgment and opened up the first community counseling process that over the next two years spread throughout the area. Communities began to make change happen. Hope replaced denial and paralyzing fear. For these communities, acknowledgment of present and future loss was necessary to the discovery of hope.

The passage for these people has not been smooth in the last 12 years. At times their voices have seemed muted. Then questions raised again about the truth of HIV and, always, among the voices of long-term concern and responsibility, there were those pushing for quick cures; interventions driven by ready money from donors who think they know, in contrast with nurturing community capacity for care, belonging, change, leadership, and hope.

This capacity is a source of our hope and can be the source for implementers who engage daily in the living environment of people with HIV/AIDS. This is our "front line."

The voices of village people in Southern Zambia were heard by a team of people of different nationalities who worked with them, and who learned of the immense strength of human relationship that is the foundation for expansion of community capacity. We learned that organizational and team development can be dynamically renewing if it is based in learning from and with people who are living with the impact of HIV/AIDS.

A team from the outside cannot intrude into community intimacy. It needs to be invited; and there is no better entry point than a mutual recognition of authentic participatory caring, of love for one another. Love is a hard word in the world of development organizations. From Long Chuan, a border county of the Yunnan Province in China, the county chief participated during 1999 in an "exposure" visit to India where she saw home care and community counseling. She was inspired by its genuineness and, upon return, she started a similar process in her county. Within three months, neighborhood destigmatization had happened. "Love in action" was the phrase used to describe this and it was the context also for an invitation to our team to return to continue to support and learn.

Another learning encountered is that long-term change in attitudes and behaviors, in all cultures in which our international facilitation team has worked in the last decade, depends on a capacity for shared safe intimacy within a group that can become a shared confidentiality, in contrast to shared secrets or knowledge.

Woven around this capacity is the approach by the team doing the work and of the larger organization that supports the implementing team. That is what our international team does: a community process that works within is needed in the approach by those from without. In practice this means that the "technical support team" (which in 1994 we more accurately called a "program facilitation team") bases its conscience in local community life; design, evaluation, and process analysis are deliberately shaped by actual visits to homes and neighborhoods. Questions are explored about concerns rather than immediate needs; about hopes and vision rather than immediate objectives; and about ways of thinking and approaching a conflict often hidden within family or neighborhood.

On our part, there has been an expansion of the capacity of "front line" teams to keep going in the face of many constraints. This seems to happen in proportion to the belief in the local community capacity.

The working culture of our organization has been shaped by voices from local neighborhoods. There is an ongoing shift from a welfare paradigm to participation in development; from expert individual to team, validated by local experience; from intervention to facilitation; and, above all, from self-assurance to belief in the capacity of communities to cope and change and hope.

The practical expression of this has been the opening of HIV-related programs set in a context of health-related community development in 40 countries; of intercountry (regional) facilitation teams in Africa, India, and Asia Pacific that exist as a counterpoint to a continuing, yet changing, culture of hierarchy and supervision. These regional teams are grown through inclusion of field people as co-facilitators and community members with passion for their future, rather than relying on increasing numbers of international experts with advanced academic qualifications, yet with shallow personal experience of the community capacity development approach.

Vitality keeps returning to the facilitation team members and me as long as we immerse ourselves in the ordinary life struggle and joys of local neighborhoods. We learn in China, Bolivia, Bangladesh, Tonga, Russia, and Canada, to name but a few countries, that a local community capacity development approach is vital in contrast to a dominant reliance on the strength of organizations. Technical capacity in organizations is another question and is generally tangential to the living community reality, unless its development is based in experiential learning.

Does involvement destroy our objectivity? No. It refreshes, given that partnership with implementing teams and with local communities is based in mutual listening and receiving. Good facilitation requires effective participation.

In a recent Pacific consultation of facilitators, the Tonga team members shared an experience of facilitating reconciliation. A young woman living in one of the island groups was known to be HIV positive. As a result of participatory conversation, the local implementing team developed a deep trust. Counseling with the young woman and her immediate family became possible. Her parents responded by increasingly caring. They even went beyond their own circle by "coming out" on the radio as a family with HIV. This experience has solidly motivated the Tonga team many months after the interaction.

Within and between organizations that care, there can be a radiation of the voices of fathers, mothers, friends, and neighborhood people. These voices are central to our own health, to our shared vision and to clarity for learning about ways of participating, of embracing experience that can hurt yet can also release our courage and hope for long-term community progress. This means we can sustain our work. Energy is not so much recycled as renewed.

Our voices and those of people of other international organizations dedicated to doing good in the world are only potent as they are informed by people within the suffering. Energy is found for local action, for facilitation of expansion and going to scale, for organizational learning and for interorganizational sharing.

We are authentic because we feel yet another paradox: the burden lifts as it is shared. We can be truthful about our personal and organizational weakness. Strangely, we seem to be growing because we are freshly alive to the mystery that living in hope requires acknowledgment of loss, and the discipline of justice and grace.

Voice

A FAMILY BLOOD FEUD IN KOSOVA

Stevan Weine

In the year following its supposed liberation, I was traveling to Kosova with a group of Americans as part of a collaborative project that brings together American and Kosovar professionals concerned with families. On one of our visits to Pristina, we were present when two persons were shot in a blood feud.

Directly in front of the Grand Hotel, men from two Kosovar Albanian families faced off in an explosion of bullets and terror in the early afternoon. Our Kosovar and American collaborative group was in a meeting room a few paces away. When the shots were fired I was looking out my hotel window and saw the attack that in a frightening moment left blood and a body on the pavement where we walked.

One gunman escaped into the hotel and men in the uniforms of many different forces surrounded it. A huge crowd gathered. As the hotel was searched, I fidgeted in my hotel room. Were the others OK? What are we doing here? How could I ever consider bringing my children to this place? The telephone was broken. I packed my bags, figuring that for sure we had to go.

After several hours, we were allowed in the lobby and I was reunited with our group. The first thing I did was to call home and spoke with Ivan Pavkovic, my partner and mentor. He told me, "If you are able to finish your work, then it would be better to stay."

When we sat in a big circle and shared our thoughts and feelings about the incident, the Kosovars explained that what happened was a version of a blood feud. They regretted that shootings happen in Kosova, but reminded us that they happen all the time in Chicago and New York. The Americans wanted the work to continue, but were concerned at how unprepared we were to respond to such incidents. If there was a shooting or a hostage situation, we should know how to react and how not to react. The group moved to return to the tasks at hand.

I thought I knew myself and what we were doing here. Our aim was to help Kosovar professionals learn to navigate through the new realities. Suddenly it seemed as if I had not sensed the danger in Kosova. It was only an idea and it had no teeth. If I did not know that, then what could I claim to know that would be of use in Kosova?

As professionals, our work was committed to advancing a family-oriented approach to mental health. But the shooting that day was from families and their code of honor. Had we been engaging in a romance of the Kosovar families?

Before the shooting, I felt a growing sensation of being at home in Kosova. There was engaging work, good friends, cafes to sit, places to walk, and connectedness with the hopes and struggles of a people. Then comes the shooting, my unexpected reaction, and the place is not what it was for me.

Redescribing Kosova and myself allowed me to stay. Our job was to engage collaboratively with Kosovar professionals in mental health reform and family-focused training. We wanted to help them find ways to have hope, where hope is based upon their legitimate professional work within the Kosovar framework, and not only the short-term promise of money from abroad. We still shared the commitment to Kosovar families.

Instead of chasing me away, the events of that afternoon, and the process of reflection it evoked, added to and deepened the slow accumulation of obligations that comes with each conversation with professionals and families in Kosova.

24

Mental Health of Humanitarian Aid Workers in Complex Emergencies

Barbara Lopes Cardozo and Peter Salama

Since the end of the Cold War in 1989-1990, most violent conflicts in the world could be characterized as complex emergencies, that is, "relatively acute situations affecting large civilian populations, usually involving a combination of war and civil strife, food shortages, and population displacement, resulting in significant excess mortality" [1]. The nature of humanitarian aid work in such emergencies has fundamentally changed since the end of the Cold War and differs from humanitarian missions associated with natural disasters. Wars between nation states, upon which most international legal conventions have focused, are now the exception. Today humanitarian assistance is implemented amid the anarchy of weakened or collapsed states and the chaos of internal conflicts, and civil wars. These changes in the environment in which humanitarian action takes place have contributed to the increased violence directed toward aid workers. Since the early 1990s, intentional violence has become the leading cause of death among aid workers in complex emergencies, with death from motor vehicle accidents a distant second [2, 3].

In this chapter, we will outline the major types of stressors faced by aid workers in complex emergencies, as well as the associated mental health problems and the risk factors and protective factors for such outcomes. To illustrate these points, we will describe the results of a mental health survey conducted in Kosovo among aid workers.

CDC MENTAL HEALTH SURVEY IN KOSOVO

A major complex emergency occurred in the province of Kosovo in 1999 [4]. The wide-scale human rights abuses suffered by the Kosovar Albanian population have been reported elsewhere [5]. A household survey of Kosovar Albanians in 1999 demonstrated the frequency of major traumatic events experienced by the ethnic majority in Kosovo; 62 percent reported being close to death; 49 percent had been tortured or abused; and 4 percent raped [6]. These experiences were associated with high prevalence rates of mental health problems among the Kosovar Albanian population; 17 percent of the population was reported to be suffering from symptoms of Post Traumatic Stress Disorder (PTSD), and more than 43 percent felt anger and revenge toward Serbs. Indeed, reprisal attacks against the Serbian minority, largely confined to living in enclaves in Kosovo, began almost immediately after the refugees had returned. The mental health effects of this physical danger and isolation among Serbs, compounded by feelings of being victimized by the international community, have also been documented [7] and rates of mental health problems were similar to those of the highly traumatized Kosovar Albanian population. Enormous tension existed between the Kosovar Albanian and Serbian communities, and aid workers, who often worked with both traumatized populations, found themselves in a mediating role. In the initial months, international aid organizations provided one of the few forums for interaction between the two communities. Furthermore, the widespread euphoria with which Kosovar Albanians had greeted aid workers initially soon turned to suspicion and, at times, hostility.

In June 2000, international aid organizations in Kosovo concerned about the mental health of their staff contacted the International Emergency and Refugee Health Branch of the Centers for Disease Control and Prevention (CDC). As a result, we conducted a survey of humanitarian aid workers employed by 22 prominent international aid organizations in Kosovo. The objectives of the survey were to gather information about the demographics of humanitarian aid workers, assess the prevalence of mental health problems among expatriate and Kosovar Albanian aid workers, and determine the demographic and specific occupational risk factors associated with negative mental health outcomes. We also sought to improve our understanding of the syndrome known as "burnout" which is frequently mentioned by aid workers and human resources staff of international aid organizations but has no exact clinical correlate. Finally, we sought to make practical recommendations for preventing and alleviating mental health problems in aid workers.

The demographic results of the survey are shown in Table 1. Expatriate aid workers came from 55 countries; approximately 50 percent were from English-speaking countries in North America, the United Kingdom, Ireland or Australia, and 30 percent were from Western Europe including Scandinavia. The mean age of 36 years for the expatriate group was higher than expected; 25 percent, however, were less than 30 years of age. In general, expatriates were well educated and 54 percent held managerial positions within their organizations. Their significant others generally did not accompany them on mission. A higher proportion of Kosovar Albanian aid workers than expatriate aid workers were male, and their mean age of 32 years was lower. In addition, as a group, Kosovar Albanian aid workers were less educated and in positions of less responsibility within their organizations.

STRESSORS IN COMPLEX EMERGENCIES

The increased risk for violent physical assault and death [2] is one example of the psychologically traumatic events confronting humanitarian aid workers today. The recent murders of aid workers in Timor, central Africa, and Chechnya illustrate the dangers of violent assault, such as shooting, sniper fire, shelling, robbery, and rape, in complex emergencies. However, humanitarian aid workers in complex emergencies are exposed to a number of other stressors and traumatic events that may

Table 1. Demographic Characteristics of Expatriate and Kosovar
Albanian Aid Workers, CDC Mental Health Survey, Kosovo, June 2000

Demographic characteristics	Expatriate staff Percent (N = 285)	Kosovar Albanian staff Percent (N = 325)	Total Percent (N = 610)
Sex			
Male	49.1	70.5	60.4
Female	50.9	29.5	39.6
Marital status			
Single	44.1	32.8	38.1
Married	24.6	51.1	38.7
Separated	1.1	0.9	1.0
Divorced	8.5	0	4.0
Widowed	1.1	0.9	1.0
In a relationship	19.9	12.4	15.9
Other	0.7	1.9	1.3
Presence of significant other in Kosovo			
Yes	23.3	83.3	52.7
No	76.7	16.7	47.3
Children			
Yes	27.0	48.6	38.5
No	73.0	51.4	61.5
Highest educational level			
Primary school	0	1.9	1.0
High school	14.1	41.0	28.4
University degree	38.2	55.0	47.1
Post-graduate degree	40.3	1.9	19.8
Doctorate/Doctor	7.4	0.3	3.6
Previous psychiatric history			
Any major illness	9.4	6.9	7.9
Major depression	3.2	3.1	3.1
Acute stress disorder	1.1	0	0.5
PTSD	2.5	1.2	1.8
Panic/anxiety disorder	3.2	3.1	3.1
Bipolar affective disorder	0	0.3	0.2
Schizophrenia	0.3	0	0.2

result in stress-related illness, which in turn may be a major cause of morbidity [8]. Aid workers may suffer primary traumatization by being exposed directly to severe traumatic events, such as sniper fire. In addition, they may suffer secondary traumatization when colleagues or friends are targeted; families of aid workers who suffer from primary traumatization can also suffer from secondary traumatization. Finally, aid workers may be subject to tertiary traumatization through work-related exposure to trauma, such as listening to first-hand accounts of people traumatized by war [9].

Event-Related and Organizational Stressors

The stressors affecting humanitarian aid workers may be divided into event-related stress and organizational stress [10]. In Kosovo, event-related stressors were common experiences among both expatriate and Kosovar Albanian aid workers and included a situation that was very frightening (57 percent for expatriate and 67 percent for national staff), hostility of the local population (38 percent and 21 percent respectively), attack on vehicles or convoy (15 percent and 11 percent respectively), armed attack or robbery (20 percent and 17 percent respectively), verbal or physical threats to life (36 percent and 37 percent respectively), handling dead bodies (26 percent and 23 percent respectively), murder of a co-worker (7 percent and 7 percent respectively), and being taken hostage (6 percent and 6 percent respectively) (CDC, unpublished data).

Aid workers also suffer more mundane stressors related to the difficult situations in the field [11]. Living conditions may be poor, with lack of privacy, lack of separation between work and living space, and intermittent or non-existent running water and electricity. The job may require traveling on hazardous roads and in unreliable airplanes. Access to medical care is often limited, and evacuation in case of illness or injury may be difficult. In addition to these difficult working conditions, expatriate aid workers are not surrounded by their usual social network and family. Separation from family and friends for extended periods of time may be a stressor in itself. Furthermore, communication with the outside world may be limited due to a lack of access to phone lines, e-mail, and international newspapers or television.

Organizational stressors may include the lack of well-structured management plans for field operations, unclear organizational decision-making processes, and tension between the expectations and needs of headquarters and field offices. Interpersonal conflicts among a heterogeneous group of expatriates suddenly expected to function as a team under difficult and sometimes dangerous conditions are not uncommon. Poor remuneration, inadequate rest and recreation, and obscure career pathways are also frequent sources of stress. Many of these problems may be exacerbated by factors particular to the humanitarian profession itself. First, unlike military personnel, aid workers do not usually benefit from being in a well-trained, tightly knit unit with a clear command structure [12]. Second, training and briefing, particularly in the management of psychological stress, are generally inadequate [11]. Such training is particularly important for organizations that deploy a high proportion of first assignment "volunteers" to emergency situations. Third, aid workers are often called upon to perform duties that are outside their realm of professional competency and experience; indeed, job descriptions may be fluid, vague, irrelevant, or non-existent. Even if their work is confined to their usual profession, the type of work that they are required to perform, the level of resources at their disposal, and their degree of responsibility may all represent new challenges. Fourth, aid workers generally feel pressure at some stage from their own management, when the drive to ensure the visibility of their organization may override questions of the appropriateness or quality of interventions.

Personal Ethics and Organizational Mandate

Two other issues deserve mention because they are relatively modern sources of stress in the humanitarian sector. First, aid workers may discover that their personal ethics and preferred approach may not match the mandate of a particular organization. Some humanitarian agencies have a specific mandate to intervene in acute relief settings, whereas others may emphasize longer-term projects; some are religiously motivated or use a charity model; others pride themselves on a rigorous and secular professionalism; some rely heavily on expatriates; others work predominantly through local organizations. Increasingly relevant is an organization's attitude toward advocacy and human rights; some may regard any involvement in human rights work as a violation of neutrality and fear that it may jeopardize the organization's field presence and operations; others believe that their presence obliges them morally to bear witness to these human rights abuses and sometimes to denounce them publicly.

Second, the culture of humanitarian work is changing. Organizations are more self-critical than in the past and are increasingly allocating resources to the external evaluation of their own activities. Inevitably, external criticism, even if constructive, leads to a reassessment of an individual's perception of his or her own effectiveness. This reassessment may be especially difficult if the individual's original expectations of what could be achieved under the circumstances were unrealistic. The perception that one has not been effective professionally, or worse, that one has contributed to an intervention that has resulted in negative consequences, may cause significant stress.

REACTIONS TO TRAUMATIC STRESS AND ASSESSMENT OF DISORDERS

Stress is a normal response to demands of the human system to prepare for "fight or flight" and is not harmful in itself. The physiologic response to stress enables a person to mobilize energy, to act quickly in an acute situation, and to focus attention by blocking out other thoughts. Afterwards both physical and emotional fatigue are to be expected [8]. Stress becomes problematic only when it occurs too often, lasts too long, or is too severe. Humanitarian aid workers are exposed to single, severe traumatic events as well as to cumulative stress with relatively minor stressors over a long period of time.

PTSD and ASD

Debilitating psychological reactions to severe stress were first documented among soldiers at war. The symptoms recognized in U.S. Civil War soldiers as "soldier's heart" came to be known as "shell shock" in World War I and "battle fatigue" in World War II. Since the classification of these symptoms as a diagnostic category in the Diagnostic and Statistical Manual (DSM III) in 1980, this disorder has become widely known as Post Traumatic Stress Disorder (PTSD) [13]. The symptom profile of PTSD includes symptoms of arousal, such as feeling jumpy or easily startled, symptoms of excessive recall of the trauma events, such as recurrent nightmares, and symptoms of avoidance, such as an inability to remember certain aspects of the traumatic event. Similar reactions to traumatic experiences have now been recognized among victims of many types of severe trauma (e.g., physical and sexual abuse, torture, accidents, and disasters). The symptoms of Acute Stress Disorder (ASD) are similar to those of PTSD but, by definition, last fewer than four weeks and often resolve spontaneously over time. The symptoms associated with PTSD last longer and are more severe, and recovery often requires the help of mental health professionals. ASD and PTSD are both classified as anxiety disorders in the DSM IV.

Other Stress-Related Illness

Other reactions to stress that occur in people working under difficult conditions, such as in complex emergencies, include adjustment disorder, major depression, pathological grief reactions, and substance abuse. These disorders have a complex interaction with PTSD and may occur together or independently; some authors have even suggested that there may be a progression from PTSD to depression [14].

Another syndrome associated with job-related stress is "burnout" [15-18]. This syndrome, although not as stringently defined as the psychiatric diagnoses listed above, is reported to be common among aid workers. It seems to represent a process of exposure to emotionally demanding situations that leads to physical, mental, and emotional exhaustion. Burnout begins gradually and progressively worsens. The risk factors for burnout are: excessive demands from self, others, and the situation; lack of resources, personnel, and time to complete the job; lack of control over the situation and unrealistic expectations; and lack of acceptance, acknowledgment, and recognition.

In their attempt to reconcile their experiences, aid workers may also respond to unresolved stress with subtler behavioral changes. One such reaction, termed "enmeshment," is akin to survivor guilt, with an over-identification with the beneficiary population [19]. This reaction may be more common in younger, more idealistic aid workers. By contrast, avoidance reactions of distancing, withdrawal, and denial may be more common among experienced personnel. Finally, aid workers may exhibit self-destructive behaviors such as working to the point of exhaustion, consuming excessive amounts of alcohol, or engaging in unprotected sex. The individual feels dissociated—distant from his or her previous self and the environment in which he or she may have acted more cautiously.

Screening Tools

The mental health problems described above can be assessed on a population level using standard self-reported questionnaires. Standardized screening tools such as the General Health Questionnaire-28 (GHQ-28) are available to assess non-specific psychiatric morbidity [20]. In this questionnaire, each question is scored from 1 to 4; the higher the total score, the higher the morbidity. It has been validated in many international settings and has frequently been used by the World Health Organization to gather information on psychiatric morbidity at a population level [21]. The Harvard Trauma Questionnaire (HTQ) is one tool used to screen for PTSD [22]. The HTQ was developed by the Harvard refugee group initially for screening for PTSD among refugees from Indo-China who had been granted asylum in the United States. These refugees had suffered from trauma events, as these stressful incidents were termed, prior to and during their flight from Indo-China. The HTQ has also been used extensively among refugees from Bosnia. The HTQ comprises two parts, a description of trauma events and a list of PTSD symptoms. Another questionnaire, the Hopkins Symptom Checklist (HSCL-25) [23], is often used as a screening tool for anxiety and depression; scores higher than 1.75 have been correlated with clinical diagnosis.

In our survey in Kosovo, using trauma events derived from our previous work in Kosovo, from the literature on domestic rescue workers [24], and from our own experience, we adapted the trauma events from the HTQ in order to increase their relevance to the experience of aid workers. Our questionnaire also included an extensive demographic and occupational history designed to gather basic information, as well as more specific occupational data such as length of service and type of employment. Factors potentially associated with a higher risk for mental health problems, such as psychiatric history, were also included, as were factors that might alleviate mental health problems, such as the type of organizational assistance available to the employee.

The reactions to traumatic stress that we found among aid workers in Kosovo included many of the mental health problems described above. However, given the nature and frequency of traumatic exposures reported, we expected a higher prevalence of PTSD in both groups; fewer than 2 percent of expatriates were suffering from symptoms of PTSD, which is similar to the lower range of the prevalence in the general population [25]. Furthermore, fewer than 7 percent of Kosovar Albanian aid workers suffered symptoms of PTSD, which is much lower than rates in the general population in Kosovo [6]. These low prevalence rates may be explained by the fact that the population was self-selected, that is by definition, participants were well enough to be currently working for international aid organizations. Those suffering PTSD or other major mental health problems may have dropped out of relief work early or after their first mission.

Although rates of PTSD were low, rates of other mental health problems were high. More than 20 percent of expatriates and more than 10 percent of Kosovar Albanians had GHQ-28 scores greater than 9, indicating symptoms of psychiatric morbidity. Approximately 15 percent of aid workers in both groups had symptoms of depression. Approximately 10 percent of expatriates and 15 percent of Kosovar Albanians had anxiety symptoms. Figure 1 shows the relationship between the number of trauma events reported and anxiety symptoms of clinical importance. A similar relationship was observed for depression. Furthermore, more than 15 percent of expatriates drank alcohol at a hazardous level, defined as the daily consumption of three or more standard alcoholic drinks per day. As would be expected in a Muslim society, few Kosovar Albanians drank alcohol heavily.

RISK AND MITIGATING FACTORS IN COMPLEX EMERGENCIES

Individual Factors

The ability to cope with stressful situations depends on an individual's psychological strengths and on external factors that can be viewed in terms of personal and external resources. Personal resources include the characteristics that constitute "resiliency" including resourcefulness, flexibility in emotional experience, intellectual mastery, need and ability to help others, and a vision of moral order [26]. Others include self-esteem, hardiness, and a strong physical and psychological constitution. Studies among war veterans [27] and domestic disaster workers [28] have attempted to identify personality risk factors for stress-related illness such as introversion, neuroticism, adverse life events prior to the trauma, and previous psychiatric illness. Of concern was that 9 percent of expatriates and 7 percent of Kosovar Albanians in our study had a prior history of major psychiatric disorder. The most common prior diagnoses were major depression, anxiety disorder, and PTSD (Table 2). Previous studies suggest that this group is likely to have a higher risk of developing subsequent mental health problems.

However, in studies among veterans, personality characteristics alone could not account for their high prevalence of mental illness [29]. Several studies have found a correlation between the prevalence of PTSD and the cumulative number of traumatic events [6]. A relationship between trauma events and depression has also been observed. In addition, personality risk factors appear to play a less important role as the intensity of the traumatic experience increases. As shown in Figure 1, aid workers are frequently exposed to intense trauma. Clearly, external environment plays a major role in the etiology of stress-related illness among this group.

External Factors

Organizational support becomes critical in highly demanding occupations. In the military setting, intensive training and tight-knit groups may be protective factors for soldiers, allowing them to be better prepared mentally to function amid violent conflicts. To what extent this military experience can be extrapolated to the civilian domain is unclear. Studies in various settings have suggested that untrained, poorly briefed staff suffer most from stress-related illness [30]. In our survey, as expected, a greater proportion of Kosovar Albanians aid workers, who had generally been recruited in-country as aid organizations began operations in 1999, were on their first mission and had worked for their organization for less than six months. Those with no previous experience in the humanitarian sector, however, made up an important proportion of both groups. In addition, there was an important group of more experienced workers; although only 12 percent of expatriates had worked in five or more humanitarian emergencies, 38 percent had worked in the humanitarian sector for three or more years.

Support strategies for aid workers include family and social networks, preventive measures of self-care, and organizational support structures, such as briefing before departure, psychological support while working in the field, and debriefing after completing the assignment. Social support networks and family can be particularly important in offsetting stressors encountered by aid workers. International staff are often temporarily separated from families and friends. This is usually not the case for national staff. On the other hand, national staff may be faced with additional stressors; they are often selected from the population that the humanitarian agency serves and may have suffered traumatic events directly related to the events that precipitated the humanitarian intervention. In contrast to international staff, national staff cannot generally go home to a safe and stable environment after the assignment is over.

In our survey, the proportion of aid workers offered important support services by their organization was low (Table 2); stress management training, psychological support during assignments, and post-mission psychological debriefing are still not common practice among international aid organizations. Preliminary analysis of data from this survey indicates that there is a relationship between organizational support

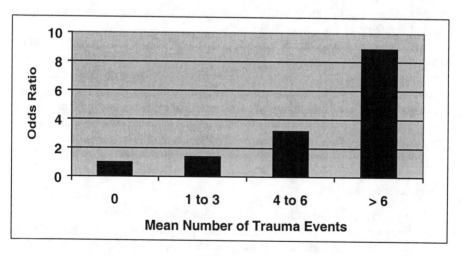

Figure 1. Odds of suffering anxiety symptoms of clinical significance by mean number of trauma events experienced, expatriate and Kosovar Albanian aid workers, CDC Mental Health Survey, Kosovo, June 2000 (controlling for all major demographic variables) ($N = 610$).

Table 2. Occupational Characteristics of Expatriate and Kosovar Albanian Aid Workers Participating in CDC Mental Health Survey, Kosovo, June 2000

Occupational characteristics	Expatriate staff Percent (N = 285)	Kosovar Albanian staff Percent (N = 325)	Total Percent (N = 610)
Job Function			
Director/coordinator/project manager	54.4	9.6	30.6
Technical—health/nutrition/food	12.3	7.8	9.9
Technical—water/sanitation	2.5	0	1.2
Technical—shelter	2.1	2.2	2.2
Logistics	6.4	9.3	7.9
Administrative	8.1	6.2	7.1
Translator	0	6.5	3.5
Program assistant	4.6	13.1	9.1
Driver	0	13.4	7.1
Other	9.5	31.8	21.4
Prior Number of Humanitarian Emergencies			
0 emergencies	38.6	74.9	57.9
1 emergency	21.8	16.3	18.9
2-4 emergencies	27.5	7.5	16.9
5-9 emergencies	10.0	0.6	5.0
≥10 emergencies	2.1	0.6	1.3
Provision of Services by NGO			
Medical insurance	91.2	26.8	57.5
Medical evacuation for serious illness	86.3	21.7	52.5
Adequate time for rest	63.9	49.2	56.2
Stress management training prior to mission	9.5	11.5	10.5
Psychological debriefing after mission	22.5	2.6	12.0
Psychological support/counseling on mission	25.6	9.3	17.1
Condition of Living Environment			
Excellent	21.9	20.6	21.2
Good	57.6	35.3	45.7
Average	19.4	40.3	30.6
Poor	1.1	3.8	2.5
Adequate Running Water/Electricity			
Yes	59.9	54.3	56.9
No	40.1	45.7	43.1

Table 2. (Cont'd.)

Occupational characteristics	Expatriate staff Percent (N = 285)	Kosovar Albanian staff Percent (N = 325)	Total Percent (N = 610)
Ability to Communicate with Family Back Home Adequately			
Yes	54.0	70.2	62.5
No	46.0	29.8	37.5
Level of Job Satisfaction			
Very satisfied	29.9	55.2	43.3
Satisfied	64.1	42.6	52.7
Dissatisfied	5.7	1.6	3.5
Very dissatisfied	0.4	0.6	0.5
Plans to Renew Contract			
Yes	84.0	82.0	83.0
No	16.0	18.0	17.0

policies and mental health outcomes among humanitarian aid workers. Social factors such as access to communication with family and friends appear particularly important (CDC, unpublished data). Our cross-sectional study did not clarify whether interventions such as stress management training have a direct affect on mental health outcomes or simply represent a marker for a more caring organization. Longitudinal intervention studies of aid workers will be required to answer these questions definitively.

RECOMMENDATIONS AND FUTURE DIRECTIONS

Current Issues

In the past, the typical humanitarian aid worker could be characterized as a young "volunteer" devoting a short period of his or her life to a charitable cause. Nowadays, aid workers are becoming more professional and viewing their work as a distinct career choice. Our survey confirms that there are two important subgroups of expatriate aid workers that will probably demand separate organizational approaches: new recruits (many of whom are volunteers) and career aid workers. Special attention should be given to staff on their first mission to ensure that their training needs are met and their skills match those required for the job. Our study also indicates, however, that mental health problems may be correlated with the number of trauma events experienced, which are, in turn, related to number of missions and amount of time spent in the field. This indicates that experienced aid workers may also be at risk for negative mental health outcomes. These results raise certain questions about the syndrome of "burnout." This syndrome may in fact represent a combination of symptoms of anxiety and depression related to trauma events and the more mundane stressors associated with relief work, not studied here, such as job security, career development opportunities, salaries, and conditions.

Although many humanitarian organizations, including the United Nations and non-governmental organizations, employ far more national than expatriate staff, organizational policies for national staff, including selection and recruitment, remuneration, insurance and psychological support are rarely fully developed. Policies such as staff evacuation procedures in times of serious security situations may differ considerably depending on nationality and are not always articulated in advance. This may lead not only to threats to the lives of these workers but also to intense feelings of guilt for expatriate co-workers who are evacuated to safer places while their national colleagues are left behind. The regular event-related and organizational stressors are compounded for national staff who are members of the emergency-affected population that the humanitarian organizations seek to serve.

One of the key questions for the modern humanitarian aid organizations is how best to select, prepare, train, and support aid workers so as to maximize their efficiency, minimize both physical and mental illness, and retain staff. The personnel policies of humanitarian organizations have not always kept up with the demands of volunteers and career aid workers and the new reality of providing assistance in increasingly volatile situations where the Geneva conventions may no longer protect aid workers [31].

A careful match should be made between the assignment and the level of experience so that inexperienced personnel are not deployed to the most stressful situations. For more experienced aid workers, guaranteed access to occupational benefits, such as adequate life and medical insurance, disability and retirement benefits, may help in retaining staff for a longer period of time [11]. Transparent evaluation of performance and clear career promotion pathways also become important for this group.

Formal organizational policies on the prevention of stress are important for all aid workers. At present these policies are non-existent or incomplete and vary significantly from one organization to the next [12]. Within the framework of institutional policies, mechanisms to support aid workers in the field need elaboration. A formal mentoring system for new personnel or the designation of a particular worker chosen by his or her peers in the field to act as the support person for that particular area are two examples of current practice. Ad hoc peer support networks of regional managers often exist but should be formalized by headquarters.

It is imperative that all organizations have formal policies on stress prevention [11]. Policies on the use of critical incident stress debriefing (CISD) also need to be put in place [32-35]. A full discussion about psychological debriefing can be found in chapter 32. Managers of international aid organizations should implement simple, common sense measures to help prevent stress-related illness in their staff. These include educating staff members about the health effects of heavy alcohol consumption, improving staff access to communications, such as satellite phones and e-mail, facilitating families and spouses accompanying aid workers or at least visiting them in the field, encouraging and even enforcing regular rest and recreation, and offering a package of care that includes stress management, psychological support while in field in difficult environments and psychological debriefing in some situations. A thorough assessment of the cross-cultural appropriateness of offering such services to national staff should be made. Finally, human resources systems should be upgraded so that information regarding staff turnover rates can be tracked within each organization to facilitate access to peer support for aid workers integrating back into their own society.

REFERENCES

1. B. Burkholder and M. J. Toole, Evolution of Complex Disasters, *Lancet, 346,* pp. 1012-1015, 1995.
2. M. Sheik, M. I. Gutierrez, P. Bolton, P. Spiegel, M. Thieren, and G. Burnham, Deaths among Humanitarian Aid Workers, *British Medical Journal, 231,* pp. 166-168, 2000.
3. B. Seet and G. M. Burnham, Fatality Trends in United Nations Peacekeeping Operations, 1948-1998, *Journal of the American Medical Association, 284,* pp. 598-603, 2000.
4. United States Agency for International Development (USAID), Kosovo Crisis Fact Sheet. Available at <http://www.usaid.gov/ofda/kosofs144.html>. Accessed January 5, 2001.
5. P. B. Spiegel and P. Salama, War and Mortality in Kosovo, 1998-1999: An Epidemiological Testimony, *Lancet, 335,* pp. 2204-2209, 2000.
6. B. Lopes Cardozo, A. Vergara, F. Agani, and C. A. Gotway, Mental Health, Social Functioning and Attitudes of Kosovar Albanians Following the War in Kosovo, *Journal of the American Medical Association, 284,* pp. 569-577, 2000.
7. P. Salama, P. Spiegel, M. Van Dyke, L. Phelps, and C. Wilkinson, Mental Health and Nutritional Status among the Adult Serbian Minority in Kosovo, *Journal of the American Medical Association, 284,* pp. 578-584, 2000.
8. Y. Danieli, N. S. Rodley, and L. Weisaeth (eds.), *International Responses to Traumatic Stress,* Baywood, Amityville, New York, 1996.
9. S. B. Jensen, *Taking Care of the Care-Takers Under War Conditions, Who Cares?* European University Centre for Mental Health and Human Rights, 1999.
10. J. Wilson and J. Lindy, *Counter Transference in the Treatment of PTSD,* Guilford Press, New York, 1994.
11. M. McCall and P. Salama, Selection, Training and Support of Relief Workers: An Occupational Health Issue, *British Medical Journal, 318,* pp. 113-116, 1999.
12. L. T. C. Jacob, M. Romo, R. May, and J. Schreider, Disaster, Psychiatric Casualties and Implications for Future War, *Journal of the Royal Army Medical Corps, 128,* pp. 93-99, 1982.
13. American Psychiatric Association, *Diagnostic and Statistical Manual of Mental Disorders,* Fourth Edition, American Psychiatric Association, Washington, D.C., 1994.
14. T. Mellman, C. Randolph, O. Brawman-Minzter, L. Flores, and F. Milanes, Phenomenology and Course of Psychiatric Disorders Associated with Combat-Related Posttraumatic Stress Disorder, *American Journal of Psychiatry, 149,* pp. 1568-1574, 1992.
15. H. J. Freudenberger, Staff Burnout, *Journal of Social Sciences, 30,* pp. 159-165, 1974.
16. C. Maslach, *The Burnout: A Cost of Caring,* Prentice-Hall, Englewood Cliffs, New Jersey, 1982.

17. A. M. Pines and E. Aronson, *Career Burnout, 1988: Causes and Cures,* Free Press, New York, 1988.
18. S. Kahill, Interventions for Burnout in the Helping Professions: A Review of the Empirical Evidence, *Canadian Journal of Counseling Review, 22,* pp. 310-342, 1988.
19. B. Smith, I. Agger, Y. Danieli, and L. Weisaeth, Health Activities across Populations: Emotional Response of International Humanitarian Aid Workers, in *International Responses to Traumatic Stress,* Y. Danieli, N. Rodley, and L. L. Weisaeth (eds.), Baywood, Amityville, New York, 1996.
20. D. P. Goldberg and V. F. Hillier, A Scaled Version of the General Health Questionnaire, *Psychological Medicine, 9,* pp. 139-145, 1979.
21. D. P. Goldberg et al., The Validity of Two Versions of the GHQ in the WHO Study of Mental Illness in General Health Care, *Psychological Medicine, 27,* pp. 191-197, 1997.
22. R. F. Mollica, Y. Caspi-Yavin, P. Bollini, T. Truong, S. Tor, and J. Lavelle, The Harvard Trauma Questionnaire. Validating a Cross-Cultural Instrument for Measuring Torture, Trauma, and Posttraumatic Stress Disorder in Indochinese Refugees, *Journal of Nervous and Mental Disease, 180,* pp. 111-116, 1992.
23. R. F. Mollica, G. Wyshak, D. de Marneffe, F. Khuon, and J. Lavelle, Indochinese Versions of the Hopkins Symptom Checklist-25: A Screening Instrument for the Psychiatric Care of Refugees, *American Journal of Psychiatry, 144,* pp. 497-500, 1987.
24. C. S. Fullerton, J. E. McCarroll, R. J. Ursano, and K. M. Wright, Psychological Respects of Rescue Workers: Fire Fighters and Trauma, *American Journal of Orthopsychiatry, 62,* pp. 371-378, 1992.
25. S. Melty-Brody, R. Hidalgo, K. Connor, and J. Davidson, PTSD: Prevalence, Health Care Use and Costs and Pharmacological Considerations, *Psychiatric Annals, 30,* pp. 722-730, 2000.
26. R. J. Apfel and B. Simon, Psychological Interventions for Children of War: The Value of a Model of Resiliency, *Medical Global Survival, 3,* p. A2, 1996.
27. N. Milgram (ed.), *Stress and Coping in Time of War: Generalizations from the Israeli Experience,* Brunner/Mazel, New York, 1986.
28. A. C. McFarlane, The Longitudinal Course of Posttraumatic Morbidity: The Range of Outcomes and Their Predictors, *Journal of Nervous and Mental Disease, 176,* pp. 30-39, 1988.
29. D. W. King, L. A. King, D. M. Gudanowski, and D. L. Vreven, Alternative Representations of War Zone Stressors: Relationships to Posttraumatic Stress Disorder in Male and Female Vietnam Veterans, *Journal of Abnormal Psychology, 104,* pp. 184-195, 1995.
30. R. J. Ursano, B. G. McCaughey, and C. Fullerton (eds.), *The Structure of Human Chaos: Individual and Community Response to Trauma and Disaster,* Cambridge University Press, Cambridge, 1994.
31. Division of Emergency and Humanitarian Action, WHO, UN Joint Medical Services, International Center for Migration and Health, *Occupational Health of Field Personnel in Complex Emergencies: Report of a Pilot Study,* Division of Emergency and Humanitarian Action, World Health Organization, Geneva, 1998.
32. J. M. Curtis, Elements of Critical Incident Debriefing, *Psychology Report, 77,* pp. 91-96, 1995.
33. G. Yamey, Psychologists Question "Debriefing" for Traumatized Employees, *British Medical Journal, 320,* p. 140, 2000.
34. P. Salama, The Psychological Health of Relief Workers: Some Practical Suggestions, *Relief and Rehabilitation Newsletter 15,* 1999.
35. B. Raphael and J. P. Wilson (eds.), *Psychological Debriefing: Series Practice and Evidence,* Cambridge, Cambridge University Press, 2000.

25

Surviving with the Dead:
Forensic Investigations in the Service
of Human Rights

William D. Haglund and Susannah M. Sirkin

> . . . the communication of the dead is tongued with fire beyond the language of the living.
>
> T. S. Eliot [1]

Convoys of humanitarian workers have come to the aid of the living and those desperately clinging to life in the wake of brutal atrocities during the past two decades. A separate army of volunteers and professionals has also entered country after country to respond to the dead: victims of war crimes, crimes against humanity, and genocide.

This second "army" consists of forensic scientists from dozens of countries. They investigate reports of victims who are missing, dead, or buried in mass graves. They give voice to the stories of those who can no longer speak. These are stories of blindfolds and bound wrists, beatings, and bullets to the back of the head. Unraveling the stories of these victims is painstaking scientific work, often conducted in settings devoid of security, technical supplies, or appropriate facilities. And, for those trained in the science of death investigation, who are used to the meticulous collection of evidence for one specific death at a time, the horror of uncovering and detailing the final moments of victims of mass killings is profound. This chapter will illustrate the experience of many of these investigators, particularly in the context of the excavation and examination of a mass grave in Kibuye, Rwanda.

BACKGROUND

The horrors of Nazi atrocities and the resulting Nuremburg trials set the stage for the development of human rights and humanitarian law. Lamentably, the promise of a human rights regime that would bring perpetrators to justice lay dormant for almost four decades until the clarion call of Argentina's disappeared awakened their relatives after the "dirty war" of the 1970s. In response to Argentina's 1984 request for scientific assistance under the newly elected President Alfonsín, the American Association for the Advancement of Science's Committee on Scientific Freedom and Responsibility deployed a team of forensic scientists.

A forensic pathologist who participated in the Argentina investigations, concluded his summary of the value of this precedent-setting work, stating, "[The] lesson of Argentina was the recognition that forensic documentation of human rights abuses provides an irrefutable documentation of the historic record, preventing revisionists from later claiming that the abuses never occurred, were not as extreme as stated, or were only a measured response to a national emergency."[1]

In addition to providing a record that was resistant to historical revisionists, scientists demonstrated that they were able to collect narrative and physical evidence that could be presented in court and information that assisted in the identification of victims so they might be returned to their families. Throughout the process, abuses of the "dirty war" were exposed to world public opinion. These outcomes continue to be bedrock ideals of international forensic efforts. A further significant impetus for such investigations is the affirmation of the dignity of victims and, for survivors, the hope that such investigations serve as a deterrent to repetitions of such atrocities in the future.

In a dramatic expansion of the scope of forensic human rights work, the UN International Criminal Tribunals for the former Yugoslavia Physicians for Human Rights (ICTY) and Rwanda (ICTR) recruited dozens of forensic scientists in the late 1990s, initially from PHR, to conduct exhumations of mass graves to collect crucial evidence of genocide and war crimes.

PHR has also filled a gaping void by providing humanitarian assistance for the establishment of databases, training, and technical aids for the identification of human remains resulting from armed conflicts past and current, such as in Cyprus, Bosnia and Herzegovina, and Kosovo. Hundreds of forensic experts have been fielded in such missions over the past decade and a half. As a result, the application of forensics to the investigation of human rights abuses has become an expectation on every continent.

MISSION TRENDS

Mandates for early investigative missions in the 1980s came largely from governments or local human rights groups. Administrative and logistical support needs were minimal. For the most part, the teams were relatively small. A few volunteer experts including pathologists, archaeologists, and anthropologists fit these trips into busy work schedules. Extra laborers were employed locally. The experts could carry their own equipment such as cameras, trowels, calipers, and laptops. For examination facilities, they utilized existing local morgues or hospitals. If extra

---

[1] Robert Kirschner, M.D., former director of the International Forensic Program, Physicians for Human Rights, personal communication.

expertise or laboratory services were needed, they were donated by university-based scientists [2].

These early expeditions usually lasted a few days to several weeks. Relatively little planning was involved. The requirements for documentation, storage, and physical evidence were fairly simple. Budgetary needs were also modest, limited to travel, communication, living expenses, and report writing. Hence, conventional funding raised by the principal non-profit organizations provided sufficient support.

Today, the international demand for scientific death investigation is immense and the landscape has changed dramatically with the emergence of national and international criminal tribunals. No longer is the purpose of this work primarily to expose atrocities and ensure that the truth be recorded forever. It is also a critical component of international criminal investigation and prosecution, with all of the evidence collection standards entailed. In addition, many investigations are carried out in the context of recent conflict or uneasy peace with high security concerns. Intervening governments or institutions frequently require immediate response.

In the 1990s scientists were called in to exhume the bodies and identify remains of thousands of victims of genocide in Rwanda and Bosnia [3-5]. As they quickly realized, extraordinary levels of funding, planning, and preparedness are necessary for such interventions. A majority of experts are no longer volunteers and are now paid. They may remain in the field for weeks, or even months. Complete examination facilities need to be set up and equipped. The scope of the work now frequently requires UN or government funding, including for NGOs that do not normally accept such funds.

The professional and technical challenges for the scientists in these settings have been unprecedented. Victims are often fleshed rather than skeletal, necessitating adequate morgue facilities, storage, equipment, and pathologists on site for extended periods of time. In addition, the work often takes place in countries with little or no infrastructure, which limits conventional identification of victims, thus requiring recourse to DNA technology. Vast logistical and administrative support is critical, but in recent forensic investigations, scientists have been unusually creative in adapting to less than adequate facilities and conditions. Any organization expecting to undertake large investigations needs to be proactively involved in planning, resourcing, and staffing.

THE EXPERTS AND THE EXPERTISE

Literally, the term "forensics" applies to any discourse in the legal setting. In the mind of the public, mention of forensic experts in the context of international investigations conjures up the disciplines of forensic archaeology, anthropology, and pathology. However, the forensic investigations under discussion typically require a much wider array of medical and scientific specialties as well as considerable support staff.

In addition to the disciplines noted above, particular investigations may call for a range of interdisciplinary expertise: specialists in ballistics, entomology, botany, statistics, toxicology, and epidemiology. Large projects require local laborers, clothes washers, electricians, drivers, backhoe operators, de-mining teams, and security personnel. For smaller investigations, a particular expert may fill several roles simultaneously, for example, an anthropologist may assist the pathologist in the autopsy, collect the evidence, and take photographs.

The experts represent the international forensic community. Many come from Latin America, where they have applied their skills in exposing atrocities in their homelands: Argentina, Chile, Guatemala, Honduras, and Peru. Others come from the United States, Canada, the United Kingdom, Australia, France, and the Netherlands. Among other nationalities represented in recent PHR projects are Costa Rica, Cyprus, Denmark, Germany, Greece, Italy, Korea, Somaliland, Spain, Sri Lanka, and Turkey. Many of these individuals have demanding employment in their home countries, but take their vacations and leaves of absence in order to respond to the international need. For most, their expertise entails years of schooling and experience, as well as graduate degrees in medicine and the sciences.

EMOTIONAL AND PSYCHOLOGICAL PREPAREDNESS

Many of the scientific experts recruited for these projects have spent their professional lives studying and documenting death. Forensic pathologists have usually conducted dozens or hundreds of autopsies on individuals who died violent deaths, including victims of gunshot wounds, domestic violence, or car accidents. The work of pathologists and death investigators has involved contact with death notifications and working with grieving families. Others, particularly anthropologists and archaeologists, have spent years studying ancient burial grounds, documenting long lost cultures. Because these professionals deal with bodies and bones, gravesites and morgues, there is a perception that they are immune to the emotional and psychological consequences of the grim nature of this work. Some allege that they are morbidly drawn to death investigation in choosing such professions. There are those who are proud of the fact that nothing shocks them and they, therefore, approach going into rugged or dangerous terrain with some bravado. However, most see themselves as scientists using their training and skill to piece together a challenging puzzle that forwards justice.

Few of the experts involved in PHR's work in Rwanda and the former Yugoslavia had ever participated in an effort to investigate a large-scale atrocity, let alone a scientific project in such a difficult physical environment. The majority was experienced in working with the dead in their homelands, but the magnitude and horrific context were unparalleled. The threat of mines, sinister checkpoints and the ever-present weaponry and military were also new and difficult experiences.

Nothing could have prepared tribunal teams for the spectacle of mass graves containing hundreds of bodies, slaughtered and dumped like garbage. Anticipating the difficult emotional responses of PHR investigators, the organization provided briefing materials on secondary trauma to team members. PHR had previously conducted the first training on secondary trauma for ICTY investigators and prosecutors in the Hague who were preparing to go into the region in 1994. The materials included information about the normal responses that exposure to such horrors might trigger, including sleep difficulties, sudden onset of crying, feelings of helplessness, inadequacy, or guilt. They also suggested crucial coping mechanisms such as regular nourishment, time off, conversations with colleagues, exposure to the beauty of nature or art, and physical exercise. PHR also offered referrals to professional support services for returning experts, upon request. Very few have availed themselves of these services.

Perhaps due to the culture of toughness within the forensic science field, most PHR participants reported initially that they had no need for psychological support, and that the environment had not overwhelmed them emotionally. However, quite a few participants have reported traumatic responses many months later. One forensic pathologist wrote: "I cried for the first time two years after my first tour, while watching a film which depicted a massacre, the bodies from which I autopsied in 1996. Where were my tears during those weeks when I stood surrounded by 200 body bags on a daily basis? Where were those tears while I was analyzing hundreds, probably thousands, of gunshot wounds and preparing a report documenting these atrocities?"[2] This scientist concluded that the intense concentration and pressure of the scientific work at hand had resulted in a form of "dissociation" necessary to "get the job done." This account indicates a need for follow-up months and even years after a project is completed and "interveners" return to their home countries. It also demonstrates the necessary defensive mechanisms that many interveners need to rely on in order to accomplish their assigned tasks.

PHR has also initiated a practice of sending psychosocial workers into the field along with its forensic experts, largely to deal with the needs of survivors and relatives of the "missing," but also to advise the staff when needed.

THE FORENSIC INVESTIGATIONS

Two major environmental considerations are paramount for any project: security and weather conditions. One tries to avoid snow, cold, and rainy seasons, and it is essential that sites of work are cleared of mines and unexploded ordnance. Of course, even the best-laid plans are always subject to frustration. The organizers experience much anxiety that fragile security and logistic arrangements may not hold.

Before launching the actual forensic investigations in Rwanda, Bosnia, and Croatia, PHR experts conducted assessments in 1995. These were followed in 1996 by forensic investigations that would provide physical evidence to be used in court by Tribunal prosecutors. Over a period of 11 months that year, more than a hundred international experts representing over a dozen countries participated in the work. At that time, co-author Haglund, acting as Senior Forensic Advisor for both tribunals, was responsible for the fieldwork. The following overview uses the investigations at the Home Saint Jean and Kibuye Roman Catholic Church, Kibuye, Rwanda, as well as those in Bosnia, to illustrate experiences of the forensic experts.

---

[2]Yvonne Milewsky, M.D., personal communication.

WILLIAM HAGLUND'S ACCOUNT

I arrived at the Tribunal office in Kigali, Rwanda in September of 1995, a year and a half after the genocide of 1994. I was struck with the military presence, the show of automatic weapons and the general destruction of the airport as well as the pervasive presence of the dead. The four-story building that then housed the Investigators and Deputy Prosecutor was just getting up and running. The tribunal was underfunded. Supplies and resources were at a minimum. I wondered at all the missing office doors, until I realized they had been removed to be used as desks. This appeared to be an ominous beginning for an International Tribunal.

Of the hundreds of sites and graves to investigate, our choice was guided by the tribunal indictment connected with Clemont Kiashima, the former Prefect of Kibuye Prefecture. The first choice of sites fell on the Kibuye Roman Catholic Church and Home St. Jean, occupying a peninsula that jutted into Lake Kivu in the lush central western border of the country. Our goal was to exhume and examine surface skeletons and the victims of a large mass grave at the rear of the church. In all 493 individuals, mostly women and children, would be recovered.

Kibuye was a parish a little over a hundred kilometers, three to four hours drive from Kigali. In a common scenario in Rwanda in the spring of 1994, Tutsi villagers fleeing the slaughter found sanctuary in churches and stadiums. Estimates vary widely regarding the number of persons who gathered on the peninsula.[3] In all, four gravesites were located and only the largest would be fully excavated. In addition to bodies in graves, skeletons were strewn about the slopes and it is likely that many victims disappeared in the lake. According to the indictment, the killings in the church began on the 17th of April and continued on the next day. A period of several days passed before a resident returned to the town. When his young daughter asked him, "Daddy, why are all the people sleeping?" he said he knew he had to do something about the dead. With the aid of a Chinese bulldozer from a road building project, and assisted by prisoners from the local prison, he had a grave dug behind the church and they pitched bodies into it for three days straight.

First among the experts to arrive in Kibuye were three archaeologists in mid-December of 1995. They topographically mapped the landscape, the buildings, the rooms, photographed the bloody walls, and the locations of skeletal remains and graves. UN sources had assured us that the war in Rwanda has been "low tech" and that we would not encounter mines and sophisticated ordnance. A rude awakening occurred during the initial days when, in the area being mapped, a mother and her child were walking through and the child picked up what he thought was a bottle. It turned out to be what UN military ordnance experts said was an unexploded rocket launched grenade. It blew off the child's hands and part of his face. The mother had lost her other two children to the genocide. From then on, it became a hard and fast rule that areas would be checked for potential explosive devices before sites were processed. Security issues would cause frustrating delays later in Bosnia, when

---

[3] Estimates of the dead by the French Military and locals at the Home St. Jean range from 2,000 to 4,000.

through oversight, ordnance assessment of the scene was not properly arranged in advance of the forensic team's arrival.

The anthropologists arrived in the first part of January and began documenting and collecting skeletons that lay scattered over the terraced slopes between the church and Lake Kivu. Soon convoys of equipment were arriving to set up our field examination area. Essential equipment included blow-up modular tents in which to perform autopsies, a backhoe, an x-ray machine and processor, and a range of supplies necessary to excavate and perform autopsies.

One of the first nights after the initial team members had arrived I gave a slide show of graves I had visited the previous September. We discussed the condition of the bodies and what that might mean for our exhumations. The presentation ended with five large pits containing bodies and crania that had been collected by government authorities near Magunza. I estimated that a minimum of 6,000 persons had been placed in these open pits for public viewing. Our experience of such monstrous collections of dead was limited to photos from War II. The horrific magnitude of the numbers of dead were unprecedented in their experience.

Each day there were problems to be solved, only to be supplanted by more the next. We needed to truck water to the site. This water was essential for the processing of x-ray film and to supply what became the most eagerly anticipated event of the day, a hot shower. In order to develop x-rays, the water had to be passed through a filtration system. Each day the team was beset by a host of logistical challenges: the lack of electrical cord, plumbing pipe, the non-arrival of the x-ray darkroom, and what to do about dogs and foxes that haunted the grave at night. Nevertheless, through ingenuity, we solved those problems only to be met by more on the next day.

I recall asking one of the archeologists what part of the grave she was about to work in on a particular day. "One of the nurseries," she quietly said. The grave contained nearly one hundred and forty children and infants and often they would be grouped in parts of the grave euphemistically referred to as "nurseries." Especially for the young anthropologists, accustomed to dealing with "clean" bones, the decomposed, fleshed remains were an abrasive assault to their sensibilities. Sometimes a mother would be recovered only to find out that in the folds of her dress was an infant. Seeing these tiny bodies of babies swaddled at their mother's backs, seeing faces and hands and feet, proved extraordinarily difficult.

Each day spent removing bodies from the grave, one was immersed in a smell that one could not leave behind, even after luxuriously hot showers. The smell lingered in our clothing, in our hair and on our skin. It slept with us.

The pathologists and autopsy assistants were the last group of experts to arrive. The exhumations and examinations continued simultaneously with archaeologists and anthropologists switching from the grave to the examination area to provide assistance for the autopsies. The pathologists were the most accustomed to recent death, but even they became overwhelmed at times.

The fifteen to twenty laborers who worked with us became great friends and one day we decided to have a party. Beforehand, they had protested that the curfew would prevent them from attending. I told them there was no need to worry and that we would drive them home. After the festivities, we piled our passengers into in a Land

Rover and they began to guide me to their residences. First to be let off were the ones from town, then it was six kilometers outside of town, until the last passenger was let off 19 kilometers from the gravesite. We realized how much distance they traveled on foot as they walked to and from the grave every day, some needing as much as three hours each way. I took to driving the roads early in the morning in order to give them rides. Whenever I return to Rwanda, they somehow find out I am in the country and at least one or two make the trip to Kigali to see me. They never talk about the genocide.

The team lived and ate together. In one break that was taken away from the site many went to see the mountain gorillas. Each morning and especially at night we talked a lot. We talked about the work, its problems, and strategies to make it go more easily. We reminisced about home, our families, and our pets. We fantasized about food much of the time, and wondered what the next arriving expert might bring by way of treats. And we found ourselves wondering whether our work would ever see the light of the courtroom and what that might mean for the future. We drank a lot of beer. In the mornings, some would swim in Lake Kivu. Two people fell in love, while the rest anticipated their weekly phone call home. The landscape could be serene.

I would often go to the graveside in the early dawn. Aside from the smell of the grave, it seemed so inconceivable that such horrors had occurred in this tranquil landscape. As the sun rose, voices from the town wafted with the smoke, the first stirrings of morning life. Brightly colored birds flitted through the banana grove at the edge of the grave.

One aspect of our work that gives us resolution and an extreme sense of satisfaction is interacting with families and identifying and repatriating the dead. We had hoped to be able to identify scientifically some of the dead in Rwanda, although this was not a primary goal of our mandate from the Tribunal. Of the nearly five hundred victims examined, only six had identity cards associated with their remains. In an effort to elicit more leads to identities, the most idiosyncratic clothing and artifacts recovered from the remains were displayed for the local population to view. Among these were t-shirts with logos, a priest's vestments, and an artificial leg. Eleven more potential names came from this effort. So, of nearly five hundred people, we had the potential to identify 17 and, because of the lack of conventional scientific documentation of dental and medical care, the only recourse would be to resort to DNA technology. In order to achieve an identification in this way, one needed blood samples from families and of these members of only two families could be located. This was a severe disappointment for many investigators, and left them feeling unresolved in their expectation of what they had come to do.

Many members of this team would be joined by scores of more experts throughout the rest of the year in the former Yugoslavia. Security became tighter and logistics nightmarish. The technical and personal challenges persisted. Some of the original experts were at my side for eight months. The work was grim. The hours were long and arduous with added stresses associated with living conditions, exhaustion, security, and deadlines, always deadlines. The rainy season arrived, then the cold weather, yet we had not completed the work. The mud was so deep in the floors of later Bosnian graves that a step would plunge ones wellies into the mud and, when trying to extract oneself for the next step, the wellie would remain stuck as one stepped out of it. Many were drained physically and psychologically.

THE AFTERMATH

Many experts felt unease at being able to return to the safety and comfort of their homeland with so much left undone. Some carried with them a sense of guilt for being able to return to lives that were easy and predictable and leaving behind whole populations in desperation. Many of the experts returned to countries where the amount of money spent on a single homicide investigation and prosecution would have supported hundreds of investigations that they had left. For many of us there was frustration and a sense of helplessness, even anger, at having to leave behind so much undone. Hundreds of graves and thousands of victims remained unexamined. The vast majority of survivors would never know the fate of those most dear to them. They were deprived of giving them a decent burial and grieving their loss. Numerous participants in the first Tribunal investigations have returned in subsequent years, and some continue to participate in other international projects in countries such as Sri Lanka, East Timor, and Cyprus. In part, these anxieties underscore limitations and inadequacies of the context in which responses to international forensic missions are presently carried out.

Although forensic experts have been involved in international investigations for over a decade and a half, the ability of the international community to respond to past and ongoing forensic needs is still primitive. Recent international experience has framed at least six issues that need attention: 1) rapid response capacity; 2) addressing the humanitarian vacuum in which survivors find themselves in the wake of current, large-scale forensic investigations;[4] 3) identification and repatriation of the dead; 4) creation and empowerment of local forensic capacity; 5) provision for forensic investigations in the International Criminal Court; and, 6) appropriate psychological preparation and support for investigative teams before, during and after missions.

CONCLUSIONS

Our experience has taught us that secondary casualties may result among experts we send on investigations. In recognition of the physical and emotional toll exacted by this work, PHR attempts to screen for those deemed most able to stand up to the strains and stresses of such interventions. We seek persons experienced with travel and accustomed to minimal living comforts and those whose personal security

---

[4] To survivors, primary among these expectations are the identification and return of their dead. Tragically, positive, personal identifications are usually impossible in poor nations and areas suffering from recent conflicts, where the infrastructure has been severely compromised or non-existent. Rwanda is but one example. In Bosnia and Herzegovina there are currently 4,420 body bags being warehoused in Tuzla. Of these, 1,895 contain complete bodies, 1,799 bags contain body parts of single persons, 694 bags enclose the body parts of two or more persons, and 32 have yet to be examined. Only 81 have been positively identified! DNA technology to identify these individuals will cost millions of dollars [6].

thresholds are not so restrained that they are incapacitated by military presence and post-war environments of heightened security. We try to prepare our experts both physically and emotionally for what they will encounter, professionally and personally. A large part of the disappointment experienced by experts is their inability to utilize their professional skills to the fullest extent possible.

It is critical that experts receive a comprehensive overview of the context of their investigative project: how it will differ from their usual work; the limitations they need to adjust to; and the protocols to be followed in such a team effort. They may have to contend with the potentially hostile reactions of the community which may not be ready to accept the brutal truth about the fate of their "missing." Worst, they leave these countries with a job undone, and continue to bear this knowledge for the rest of their lives.

REFERENCES

1. T. S. Eliot, Little Gidding, in *Four Quartets*, Harcourt and Brace, New York, 1991.
2. M. Harvey and M. C. King, The Use of DNA in the Identification of Postmortem Remains, in *Advances in Forensic Taphonomy*, W. Haglund and M. Sorg (eds.), CPR Press, New York, 2001.
3. E. Stover and G. Peress, *The Graves: Srebrenica and Vukovar*, Scalo, New York, 1998.
4. E. Stover and M. Ryan, Breaking Bread with the Dead, *Journal of Historical Archeology*, 35:1, pp. 7-25, 2001.
5. W. D. Haglund, M. Connor, and D. D. Scott, The Archeology of Contemporary Mass Graves, *Journal of Historical Archeology 35*:1, pp. 57-69, 2001.
6. G. Knight and D. Rhodes, Warehouse of the Dead, *New York Times Magazine*, pp. 46-47, March 11, 2001.

Voices

A VOICE FOR VICTIMS

M. Cherif Bassiouni

If one asks why we should intervene, there are no more eloquent words than those of John Donne: "No man is an island, entire of itself; every man is a piece of the continent, a part of the main . . . Any man's death diminishes me because I am involved in mankind, and therefore never send to know for whom the bell tolls; it tolls for thee. . . ." This is why I shall always be engaged in whatever way I can and try to do what is right.

What makes a person intervene in a distress situation? I assume that the motivation is the result of inner moral conviction which is so overpowering that it overcomes fear and disregards the temptations of any rewards for looking the other way. In my case, it was something that I learned as a child, though I am not really sure how, but which has guided me throughout life. It is what led me in 1943 at the age of seven to run out of my house in Cairo with a toy gun during a night raid to try to shoot down a German plane that I thought Hitler piloted. Later, it was what led me to oppose government practices that violated human rights in my country of origin, resulting in my being placed under house arrest for seven months.

We intervene to lend assistance to others because of a sense of human and social solidarity, without which a civilized society could not exist. In small and big ways, we must all intervene, not only because we can save or help others, but because in so doing we reaffirm our own humanity. I strongly believe in what the Old Testament and the Qu'ran hold: that he who saves a life is as if he saved all of humanity.

It was my firm conviction as a gatherer of the evidence of terrible crimes that I had a moral responsibility to bear witness and to bring the facts to the attention of the international community. There were many disincentives for me to pursue the course of conduct that I did, and many incentives for me not to do it. That is why, when I was nominated by the Secretary-General to be the first prosecutor of the ad hoc International Criminal Tribunal for the former Yugoslavia, certain major powers in the Security Council blocked it. But I did what I believed was right, irrespective of the rewards that would have come my way had I not done my duty. I overcame the hurdles that were put in my way to prevent what I believed was necessary to fulfill the mandate. Above all, it was the fulfillment of a moral obligation.

The Commission of Experts to investigate crimes in the former Yugoslavia was established with the support of some members of the Security Council, especially by the United States and Non-Aligned States. It was grudgingly accepted by others who could not publicly oppose it because of its legal and moral symbolism.

The task of the Commission was enormous. A war was ongoing, there was no precedent to guide the Commission, and no resources available; but worst was the lack of political will to have the Commission accomplish its mandate. At the time, certain major powers had political concerns about what the Commission could uncover. Thus, financial and bureaucratic hurdles were placed in its way to prevent it from carrying out its mandate. I had the option of accepting this political reality or trying to overcome it. Undaunted, I established a database at DePaul University, Chicago, staffing it with a few paid, but mostly volunteer, lawyers and law students, supported by private grants. In two years, over 160 persons worked on the database project, to which evidence and information flowed from governments, NGOs, investigators, and individuals, including victims. The operation worked around the clock seven days a week and collected, correlated and analyzed over 65,000 documents, 300 hours of videotapes, and hundreds of pictures. Concurrently, the Commission conducted 35 field investigations. The database and investigations uncovered: 151 mass graves with reportedly between 5 and 3,000 bodies; and over 800 places of detention, through which passed 500,000 persons, an estimated 50,000 of whom were tortured. The Commission also undertook the world's first and largest investigation of rapes. It accumulated 575 affidavits of rape victims, interviewed in the field 223 victims and witnesses, identified 1453 other potential victims and gathered information about another potential 4500 victims. Another major investigation involved the siege and shelling of Sarajevo which included documentation on more than 12,000 civilian victims, on the destruction of civilian and cultural property, and on attacks on hospitals. The day-by-day analysis of the shelling and sniping over three years produced statistical data that clearly showed a pattern of intentional attacks on prohibited targets, in violation of international humanitarian law. All of this, and more, provided the basis for the Security Council to establish the Tribunal, for initial prosecutions, and for the Prosecutor's Office to conduct further investigations leading to evidence sufficient to indict certain individuals.

As Prophet Muhammad said: "If you see a wrong right it; With your hand if you can, or With your words, or With your stare, or In your heart, and that is the weakest of faith."

MY INTRODUCTION TO GENOCIDE

Ben Kiernan

What first brought home to me the concept of genocide was talking with my maternal grandfather, Abraham Gershon Silk. I remember one conversation in 1969, the year before he died. I was sixteen. His parents, Moses Zeidan and Frances Shudmak, had married in 1873 in Krakow (then in Austria-Hungary, now Poland). They set off by land and sea for London, and eventually sailed for Australia, where they arrived in 1885. They soon anglicized their names. Abe Silk was born in Melbourne in 1893. At the age of 76, he told me of relatives in Krakow he had never met. They had written to him in the 1930s. But once war broke out, he did not hear from them again. "They are probably all dead," he said, with regret at not having done anything for them from Australia. Across the table, my grandmother, Grace O'Sullivan, listened. Her family had left County Kerry after the 1840's famine in Ireland. Grace had married Abe in 1924 in a Melbourne hotel. It was a neutral venue: each family objected to the other's sanctuaries, perhaps national as well as religious. Grace's mother, Kate Kiniry, who had been the first pupil to attend Mrs. Howard's Catholic Ladies College in West Melbourne, had founded the Victorian branch of the republican Young Ireland Society, which in 1917 had given her a clock from Connecticut "as a token of esteem." Two years later Grace's father James appeared on the steps of Melbourne's St. Patrick's Cathedral, in the front row in a photo of a gathering for Irish independence. At the other end of the row is my paternal grandfather, Esmond Kiernan, who grew up on the Victorian goldfields. His father, John Joseph, had also left Ireland during the Famine. He had gone first to the United States, and then, on disembarking in Melbourne in 1854, gave his nationality as "American," rather than "British subject."

During the 1930s, as Hitler's shadow loomed over Europe, James O'Sullivan taught my mother, Joan Silk, and her brother, Kevin, to say their prayers in Irish. Kevin also picked up a smattering of Yiddish jokes from his other grandfather, Morris Silk. Sixty years later my father, Peter Kiernan, would organize Melbourne's sesquicentennial memorial to the victims of the Irish Famine. But in 1969 I had little knowledge of any of these issues. The headlines were dominated by issues like the struggle for Aboriginal rights, and the Vietnam War, about to engulf neighboring Cambodia. I had no idea that within a few years, I would begin a quarter century of work documenting the Cambodian genocide that was to follow that war [1]. Nor that I would end up in Connecticut, where Gilbert Brothers of Winsted had set that clock ticking. But I need not have been surprised in 1998 to find myself at a conference on Ethnopolitical Warfare in Derry, Northern Ireland, with my parents and two children, Mia-lia and Derry. At 73, on her first visit to Ireland, my mother sat down in a Sligo pub and suddenly began to pray aloud in Irish. I'm not sure what Abe Silk would have made of it, but it all seemed to make sense to me.

REFERENCE

1. B. Kiernan, Bringing the Khmer Rouge to Justice, *Human Rights Review, 1*:3, pp. 92-108, April-June 2000.

WE MUST DO MORE

B. M.

UN Human Rights Officer in Rwanda 1994

I was investigating a massacre site in a countryside school complex where several thousand Tutsis and moderate Hutus had been trapped and gradually killed as their attackers set fire to room after room forcing them out. Almost all of the bodies had been buried in two mass graves. I clearly recall entering a room in which the ceiling had fallen in following the fire. At the end of the room, about 3 meters from the doorway, there stood, 1 meter high, a white plaster statue of the virgin Mary, half burnt, and with her hands outstretched and a peaceful smile on her face. Just to the right of the statue, and slightly closer to the doorway, there was a hand-print on the white wall. The print was from the hand of a small child, and it was in blood. I have thought many times of that child walking through the middle of a massacre with blood on her hands and a burning virgin Mary standing, as tall as herself, smiling on. The world seen through that child's eyes could surely not have appeared more terrible.

Returning from an investigation into another massacre site in the countryside of southeast Rwanda, I remember in particular an elderly man who stopped us as we were driving down a track. He asked our interpreter if we were investigating the genocide in this area and, when we confirmed this, he led us to a house in the brush about a kilometer away. Inside were the bodies of about 14 people, adults and children, squashed into a small room and half submerged in rain water which had gathered on the floor. The man showed us burn marks where the roof had been set afire, and bullet casings on the ground. To the rear of the house a woman's body lay covered in a cloth. The man started crying as he explained that this was his family lying dead and that he had managed to escape by running through the ring of attackers and hiding in the brush. I felt that telling us what had happened had done him some good but, much more, I felt that he would be waiting and waiting for some sign that justice had been done, and that the statement he had made against the killers of his family would be used. I feared he would wait for years and would see nothing! I was bitter and angry; angry as much with myself as with the world for not providing him with the justice he wanted and needed in order to continue his life.

It was at times like these that the enormity of what had happened in Rwanda overcame me and led me to question my continuing presence there. I felt angry that my colleagues and I had arrived after the events rather than before, in time to prevent them; I felt frustrated with my own powerlessness, with my knowledge that human rights violations continued, and with the insufficient attention and care of the rest of the world for events in Rwanda. I sometimes felt great doubt as to whether I was making any genuine difference whatsoever, at least as a symbolic balance to the UN's failure to act earlier and to the serious personal security concerns.

I found the bottom line of my own motivation in the need to create a record of events. I tried to imagine the situation if the work was not done, if the years went by until the graves were overgrown, the bodies decayed and the witnesses dispersed, and I felt that this would be the worst that could happen. In contrast, if the Rwandan

Government could one day publish a document detailing the precise events of the genocide, the names of those thought to have died and a confirmation of the principal people involved in the killing, then I felt that the record would at least be there and that it might somehow help to prevent future violations.

Human rights work and the pressures faced by UN Human Rights Officers find their source in the very nature of our work. The fundamental answers to those pressures must start with strengthening the UN's commitment and action to address human rights violations. We must do more.

PROSECUTING WAR CRIMES

Minna Schrag
Former Senior Trial Attorney,
International Criminal Tribunal for the Former Yugoslavia

I was in my law firm office one day in November 1993, talking over an approach to a particularly complex and intriguing corporate settlement negotiation, when Conrad Harper, then Legal Adviser at the State Department, called to ask if I would be willing to have the United States nominate me to a senior position at the Yugoslav War Crimes Tribunal then being organized in The Hague. That call changed my life.

At the time, I was dimly aware of the new tribunal, and I knew about as much about international human rights law as I suppose most supporters of Lawyers Committee for Human Rights and Human Rights Watch do, that is, very little. I had only recently had my first professional encounter with international law, having represented investors in a lawsuit against Lloyd's of London in which I contended with the significant differences in approach between British and American law regarding investor protection and litigation procedures. But I was a former federal prosecutor in New York, and I was general counsel of the NOW Legal Defense and Education Fund, the premier women's advocacy organization in the country, and I suppose the State Department thought that experience would prepare me for the position.

Before I left for The Hague, I read as much as I could about Yugoslavia. I reread Telford Taylor's book about the Nuremburg trials, and got in touch with him (he had taught me constitutional law at Columbia Law School) and received his good wishes. That was the sum total of my orientation.

My work at the Tribunal was the most challenging, and frustrating, of my life. Working with prosecutors and investigators from diverse legal traditions who carried with them equally diverse assumptions about just about everything a prosecutor does, we tried to create, with no precedent or guidance, a truly international prosecutor's office. We argued a lot. That we succeeded, however imperfectly, is a tribute to the dedication and good sense of many people who were my colleagues as the Tribunal began, and who were willing, at least sometimes, to suspend their professional perspectives derived from their own national training and consider different points of view.

Most of my work was on that cerebral level. But as we prepared cases for indictment, I read countless witness statements prepared by investigators, and I interviewed some witnesses myself, all of them victims of particularly egregious trauma. None of us at ICTY received any serious training about engaging with trauma victims, let alone about the effect on ourselves of working so closely with people who had suffered greatly. I suppose most of us, if we thought about it at all, thought that our professional experience would serve as a kind of armor to shield us from our own reactions to the unthinkable terror of the events in Bosnia. As we talked about what we were doing, I think we provided a sort of communal safety net for one another. But I have no doubt that we would have done much better, and been much more effective, if we had at least some empathetic support from people who knew a lot more about trauma than we did.

But the Tribunal began its operations with an insufficient budget (since then, greatly increased), and the Office of the Prosecutor was structured along the lines of an ordinary domestic law enforcement office. That original structure and budget failed to reflect our extraordinary mission, and needs. And so, while there was a unit set up outside the Office of the Prosecutor to attend to needs of victims and witnesses (with insufficient mandate, funds, and staff) there was no provision for helping the professional staff with the emotional toll of our work.

As for the work in The Hague changing my life, it gave me haunting dreams, and memories of people and their stories that will always be with me. I like to think it made me more open to new ideas. And it made me unequivocally committed to the search for effective ways to address wide scale human rights violations.

IMPARTIAL OBSERVER DRAWN INTO SLEEPLESS MORAL CONFLICT

Mariana Goetz
Written in Enaboishu (Masaai for "togetherness"),
a village outside Arusha, on the foot of Mt. Meru, Tanzania

I woke up with a strange sense of intense unease. Perhaps it is fear. I'm not quite sure. It has been raining hard, drumming on the corrugated metal roof. Now it has stopped and the crickets and bush babies are in full symphony all around me, life teeming through the open windows.

There were a few branch cracking noises which made me jump, or more accurately, made me freeze in my bed, missing a heart beat before being able to move and perk up my ears. I am listening hard, but I don't think that there is anybody out there. All I can hear is a group of dogs fighting in the distance. One of the dogs had been hurt and is making a desperate yelping noise. Now all is calm again. Just the dense lush jungle around me. The dogs are at it again. Something really eerie about all that yelping in the distance.

I woke up from this dream. I was an inmate in a strange prison in the mountains. I was detained for crimes I had not committed. There had been some long-standing mistake, along the lines that I had been a warden, or at the prison for such a long time that I became an inmate. There had been a fight or battle and some American servicemen's bodies were still lying around the back of the prison decaying. Nobody had bothered to bury them.

One day some visitors came to the prison. Another inmate and I were supposed to entertain them by organizing a light display in the lush green valley in front of the prison, while the visitors had dinner. I remember vividly that after the display we walked back up to the prison building and were invited by the visitors to sit with them at the dinner table. I had been running around the countryside barefoot and my feet were dirty. I felt a little disconcerted and would have preferred to have a wash first. One of the visitors sensed my shyness and pulled up a chair for me and my fellow inmate and made us feel comfortable. He looked at me and said that it must feel great to run around barefoot in the countryside. It did.

We looked at the view which was a mixture of the Jura mountains in France where I grew up and the jungle around Mt. Meru in Arusha. The view was spectacular as the moon was out and it had been raining a lot and everything looked so fresh. I was trying to explain that I grew up near here and pointed in the direction. The man seemed to be absorbed by his own thoughts, and at times I felt like he was deliberately ignoring what I was saying. The conversation that we managed to have was, on the whole, agreeable. However, I could not help feeling that even though he was not here to help, at some level he acknowledged my existence, listened and perhaps for a split second tried to understand. He said a few nice things and he thought: "I was a funny one." I answered: "just very cynical."

It is 5 A.M. I can hear the call of prayer in the distance, it's the middle of Ramadan here.

In my dream, there was a flashback to when I was a prison warden. The prison had glass walls, and had a strange feeling of being like a modern shopping center. There was an issue about getting people out of the building in the evenings so that we could lock up. There was a little commotion at lock-up time, getting the inmates back where they were supposed to be. This happened in good humor, and us wardens used to joke with the inmates that since the lights were always on "there is no sleeping here, we are just as much prisoners as you."

It was clear that the visitors were human rights observers, and I had some hope that they would help to get me out of there. I had a dull feeling of disappointment dawning upon me. For some reason, but not malicious, and probably only because they did not know really what was going on, or what to say, they simply did not get it. They knew I was a prisoner, but did not ask any questions really. The hints I was dropping passed them by completely.

Then I had my 1-week-a-year parole, where I was let out and allowed to go home. I went to London to my brother's flat. My brother was not there. His flat was not entirely empty, but it was obvious that he was not really living there. At this point I was just trying to stay sane. I was telling myself out loud: "He probably has a girlfriend and is staying with her for a while." Everything I could have needed was there. Only he wasn't. I thought of calling, but I didn't know who or where to call. I was not even sure that the phone was connected. Then I thought that perhaps he had not forgotten that it was my week out. I thought that maybe he was embarrassed or, like the others, he did not know how to deal with me and my situation. So, I decided to get a grip. I would not impose. I would enjoy being in London, and I would try to make the most of my time out to get myself together. Then I woke up.

I imagined that working for justice, witnessing a genocide, would be passive. Like a neutral observer detached from the problem and able to stand back. But it's not like that, it touches your conscience. You get sucked in and you become part of the problem.

SURVIVORS AND OBSERVERS

Priscilla B. Hayner
Author, Unspeakable Truths: Confronting State
Terror and Atrocity[1]

I'm not infrequently asked how I feel after having spoken with so many victims and survivors of indescribable human rights atrocities. Behind the question is sometimes a hint in the voice that any normal person might feel a bit traumatized if they did my kind of work.

It's true, I've seen pits of thousands of decomposing bodies in Rwanda, which smelled so bad it was difficult to breathe. I've interviewed groups of amputees from the mad violence in Sierra Leone. I've spoken with women whose husbands "disappeared" in Chile, and kids whose parents "disappeared" in Argentina. I received a tour of unmarked graves—it had been too dangerous to honor the dead—on a hilltop in Guatemala, with a detailed description of the massacres that were witnessed by my guide. I drove through towns that had been all but flattened by ravaging gangs in East Timor and Sierra Leone.

Working as an independent researcher and writer, and then as an independent consultant, I've traveled in recent years to over two dozen countries emerging from a period of unspeakable crimes. In each place, I spoke with those who had suffered some of the worst. So I'm asked: how is it, this kind of research? The answer is three-fold. Working alone, it is logistically very difficult. Working in so many different countries, always comparing them, it is intellectually difficult, but extremely engaging. And emotionally, peering into these survivors' lives, it is

[1] Published by Routledge (New York and London), 2001. *Unspeakable Truths* is a comparative study of over 20 truth commissions around the world.

always a humbling experience, each time pointing again to how very lucky we are, those of us who have not had to confront such pain, nor grow up in a society that has torn itself apart.

As an observer, interested in understanding how survivors cope, I have had one consistent reaction. I am amazed and impressed with the ability of persons who have witnessed or directly experienced these atrocities to go on with their daily lives, often with an incredible strength of spirit. In the end, I don't feel traumatized. Mostly, I feel impressed and honored to speak with those who have survived.

26

We Have a Long Way to Go

Chris Cramer

By and large—despite their apparent intelligence—members of the media believe they are immune from that which they cover. They sally forth in their thousands each year to cover hostilities and disturbances the world over, safe in the belief that they cannot be touched—mentally or physically—by the mayhem around them. Then they return to the safety of their homes and their families and pick up where they left off. For many of them, as Anthony Lloyd describes it in his book *My War Gone By, I Miss It So* [1], it can be like jumping off a speeding train: surreal, frightening, and frequently resulting in acute depression.

Much of the media industry is in denial that post-traumatic stress disorder affects reporters, photographers, and others in the news business. Only recently have many news organizations even accepted the most basic thinking when it comes to preparedness for what many of them do on a regular basis.

Let us first of all turn to physical safety training.

Until very recently—perhaps only 10 years ago—the media at large believed that journalists simply did what they had to do: get into a war zone or hostile environment, cover whatever story was unfolding, report the story, and get out again. To do so unscathed was mostly a matter of luck rather than judgment. Tell the story, get back home, do your expenses, and relax until the next time.

There was no training before you arrived. You learned on the job, kept your feelings and experiences to yourself and, if you were lucky, got assigned again when the next story went pear-shaped.

Recently things have started to change.

At the BBC, change coincided with some particularly onerous legislation in the early 1990s which made it clear—in my view quite properly—that employers were liable for where they sent their staff, what they asked them to do, and how they asked them to do it.

The wake-up call for me came when BBC newsmen covered the siege of Dubrovnik in October 1991. The team I had assigned there decided the situation was too dangerous to stay: the city was under constant bombardment and their lives were at risk. They told me they were leaving.

I was furious, knowing that our media competitors were going to stay and, as it turned out, produce remarkable coverage which won several broadcast awards.

How could my staff do this to me? How could they leave a story of such magnitude when the world needed to know what it looked like and how it felt to the people who lived there.

Then—my epiphany. How could I react this way? This was not only the wrong emotion; it was and is fundamentally bad management. Since I had deployed staff to a war zone or hostile environment, then I was legally—and for that matter, morally—responsible for their safety. Everything else was secondary.

Nonetheless, I was personally still troubled. Media men and women, I thought, did what they did—they always had. Our profession was inherently dangerous.

For years journalists had set out to cover the world at large with nothing but a pen and paper, occasionally a tape recorder or still camera and, more recently, a video camera. There were occasions where they would don a steel helmet, sometimes a flak jacket, but for the most part they had only their vocation, and precious little else, to protect them.

A Safety Officer for BBC's News department, Peter Hunter, convinced other managers and me that appropriate safety training and safety awareness was a prerequisite for a responsible media company. "Do you think for a moment that fire officers and members of the armed forces go and do what they do without safety awareness and first aid training?" he argued. "Why should members of the media be any different?" He was right. And the media industry worldwide owes him a huge debt for raising the issue and giving it the recognition it deserved.

For years, journalists from all parts of the business had adopted the principle that you never refused an assignment, no matter how dangerous it might turn out to be; that doing so would run you the risk of losing some professional esteem. For men and for women, it was all a matter of "balls." And there was the added hazard many of us felt, that if you displayed a lack of courage to your bosses there was a real risk of losing the assignment.

But Peter Hunter's campaigning led to BBC managers like myself wanting to change the system. We wanted to send out a very strident signal that it was perfectly OK to talk about safety and safety training. That it wasn't in any way "wimpish."

And change it we did, though it was an uphill and frequently depressing experience.

In 1991 and 1992 the BBC's Deputy Head of Newsgathering, Ray Gowdridge, and I drew up a mantra for reporters, producers, and technicians. And then we communicated it to all other staff and freelancers working for the BBC:

> No story is worth a life. No picture sequence is worth an injury. No piece of audio is worth endangering our staff.

And we went much further. We committed ourselves to spend all it took to provide the best equipment, the best training, the best vehicles, and the best insurance for our staff, including freelancers, in harm's way. We eventually got support from BBC's Boards of Management and Governors.

We also declared that no staff member would be deployed to a war zone without training in battlefield first aid and battlefield knowledge. That policy was painful and meant that some reporters did not go. But we were rigid: only the most experienced of correspondents and crews were allowed to bypass this policy, and then only if they went on refresher courses.

We put these courses out for tender. Companies sought the business and we adapted their programs to suit our needs. Senior management took the training programs, introduced some of the sessions, and endorsed the courses back at head-quarters. Veteran correspondents went, listened—and appreciated what they learned.

However, some of our staff, still in denial, were appalled. They accused us of using this safety policy as an insurance scam to avoid our responsibilities. They refused to wear their flak jackets, and ridiculed us as managers. But we persevered.

I've heard all the excuses as to why correspondents and support staff don't wear flak jackets: "they are too heavy," "they get stolen," "they become targets," and "they distinguish us from the local population and render us incapable of doing our job." What they were really saying to me was: "Let me do my job. Let me get killed in the course of my work. Let me be a martyr to my cause."

Another excuse we frequently heard from bosses and employers was: "Print is different from Broadcasting." Their theory was that print journalists travel much more safely by themselves, are more experienced, and don't need safety awareness training.

Nonsense. This was and still is the worst form of arrogance from employers. My view has always been that print journalists, more likely to operate away from the media "pack," are probably in more danger than their broadcast colleagues. They tend to be less well equipped, less able to afford armored or properly protected vehicles, and more likely to be targeted.

And there were other excuses from some media bosses: "we don't send staff, we send freelancers"; "we couldn't possibly afford to insure them." I find this really dangerous and irresponsible talk from employers. My experience has always been that some newspaper bosses are more irresponsible than those in broadcast when it comes to deploying their staff without regard to their safety.

News organizations in the United States, for all their sophistication , are the most reluctant to confront the issues I have been talking about. With notable exceptions—including my own company, CNN, NBC, and the *New York Times*—few American news organizations have any formal safety training schemes for journalists traveling into harm's way.

Who is taking the lead? Where are the guidelines? Where are the best practices?

In Britain, courtesy of the BBC, CNN, and some other organizations such as Independent Television News, Reuters, and APTN, a new set of safety guidelines has recently been endorsed and agreed to at the Newsworld Conference in Barcelona in November 2000. They are as follows:

1. The preservation of human life and safety is paramount. Staff and free-lancers should be made aware that unwarranted risks in pursuit of a story are unacceptable and must be strongly discouraged. Assignments to war zones or hostile environments must be voluntary, and should only involve experienced newsgathering practitioners.

2. All staff and freelancers asked to work in hostile environments must have access to appropriate safety training and retraining. Employers are encouraged to make this mandatory.

3. Employers must provide efficient safety equipment to all staff and freelancers assigned to hazardous locations, including personal issue kevlar vest/jackets, protective headgear, and properly protected vehicles, if necessary.

4. All staff and freelancers should be afforded personal insurance while working in hostile areas, including cover against death and personal injury.

5. Employers are to provide and encourage the use of voluntary and confidential counseling for staff and freelancers returning from hostile areas or after the coverage of distressing events. (This is likely to require some training of media managers in the recognition of the symptoms of Post Traumatic Stress Disorder.)

6. Media companies and their representatives are neutral observers. No member of the media would carry a firearm in the course of his or her work.

7. Media companies should work together to establish a data bank of safety information, including the exchange of up-to-date safety assessments of hostile and dangerous areas.

These guidelines, I believe, are just the beginning, and there is already evidence that many media organizations are prepared to sign on to them. But what they do not address is the large number of indigenous journalists around the world who need to report on the hostilities inside their own countries *without* the benefit of proper training or safety equipment. They are likely to be the most at risk.

Greater safety awareness by the media won't stop the profession being targeted or being killed or injured by accident. But it is a start, one which needs to spread across the world, together with the strident message that the intimidation of journalists by governments or organizations will not be tolerated by the international community.

POST TRAUMATIC STRESS DISORDER

Let me now turn to another, more controversial area of concern: what I have described as "Safety Training for the Mind." That is Post Traumatic Stress Disorder: PTSD. And here, the media industry has only recently started to wake up to the need for another kind of recognition: protection for the mind as well as for the body.

I speak from bitter experience or, in common parlance, I have a victim's eye view.

In May 1980, I briefly became a hostage in the Iranian embassy in London. I was there to take delivery of a visa to visit Teheran for the BBC, where a large number of other hostages had been seized by Iranian revolutionaries inside the United States embassy. For me, it was a masterpiece of bad timing as, within minutes of arriving inside the building in Princes Gate in Kensington, it was stormed by six Iraqi-backed terrorists from a disputed border region in Iran. Before the siege was broken six days later by Britain's Special Air Services, the gunmen had killed one hostage and were threatening to murder another each hour before blowing the building up and all of us with it.

On the second day, after personal intimidation and a pistol-whipping, I faked a heart attack to get out.

Back at the BBC my bosses offered me counseling. Another suggested that I go out that night and get drunk and come back to work the following day. I took the latter's advice, mainly because I then belonged to the school of journalism that believed that real men (and women) simply returned to work and shrugged off their memories and anxieties. So I refused any form of psychiatric counseling, and refused two additional offers over the next few years or so.

I know now that I could not have been more wrong. I personally went through many years of hell, for the most part concealing this from all those around me. I couldn't travel in planes, in elevators, on escalators, couldn't go to restaurants, cinemas, or theaters. I drank too much, went from one unsatisfactory relationship to another and only avoided drugs because I figured I might enjoy them too much! For years I was, in my mind, persecuted. I looked under my car for bombs each day for a while and, of course, didn't find any.

My problem was typical. I was afraid to admit I had lost my nerve.

These days I am much wiser and better understand that journalists cannot be immune from the stories they cover or are involved in. That the flak jackets they wear and the armored vehicles they may travel in are not effective protection against mental and emotional stress.

At the BBC in the early 90s we introduced confidential counseling for staff and training for managers to spot the effects of PTSD. It was, and still is, very, very controversial.

As in the case of safety training, we managers were told that real men or women didn't need it. They were journalists, not victims. They got over their pain in more conventional ways—like drinking or drugs or smacking their partners.

It has taken the media industry far too long to realize that it is perfectly natural for journalists, like other folk, to feel the effects of trauma. There is nothing particular about the work they do that keeps them immune from what they experience; to deny it and think otherwise is unnatural at best and dangerous at worst.

These days I have my own personal profile of a media person who is probably suffering from PTSD. He or she would start conversations with, "This is my thirtieth war, you know"; "When I get home I go out and get drunk, or laid, or whatever, and then I am fine."

I personally find it most curious that in the United States of all places, where, they invented the notion of grief counselors, most people in the media haven't until fairly recently given it a moment's thought. There is virtually no acknowledgment at all within the industry, apart from some exceptions such as CNN, that PTSD even exists among their ranks.

The first study on the prevalence of symptoms of PTSD and depression in members of the media was conducted by Dr. Anthony Feinstein during 2000 (see chapter 27, this volume) and aided by BBC, CNN, and the European office of the

Freedom Forum. When his results were first discussed by the industry during the Newsworld Conference mentioned above, they made startling reading. This study is an important milestone in what I believe is the maturing of the media industry. But much still needs to be done.

The media, in particular in the United States, must wake up to the need for safety training as an issue as worthy of debate as say, editorial integrity, the invasion of privacy, or corporatization. Worldwide there need to be formal training programs for all journalists and those who work with them, for freelancers, and for indigenous media. There needs to be proper insurance for media staff and freelancers. The industry must accept that members of the profession are more than likely to be affected by the stories and conflicts they cover. And their bosses need to recognize that and take steps to provide voluntary, and confidential, counseling.

We still have a long way to go.

REFERENCE

1. A. Lloyd, *My War Gone By, I Miss It So,* Atlantic Monthly Press, New York, 1999.

Voices

COURAGE ISN'T ENOUGH: LEARNING FROM OTHER PEOPLE'S MISTAKES

John Owen

It all came back to me that day in March 1984 when someone handed me a wire story from El Salvador reporting that the American photographer John Hoagland had been killed in a cross fire. It was Hoagland, on assignment for Newsweek, who had upbraided me (when I met him earlier that year) outside of the Camino Real Hotel, one of those hotels forever linked in journalists' minds as the Salvador war hotel. I was then a senior journalist and field producer for a CBC TV news team that had been in San Salvador long enough to get press credentials, a translator, and a van that we'd loaded with our gear. We were ready to roll out and find some "bang-bang." I introduced myself to Hoagland and asked him a few questions about where the fighting was taking place. But what I got in return were expletives: "You fucking TV guys. You come in here and think that you can just head out somewhere without first doing your homework," or something to that effect.

"Do you have any idea where you are going? You are heading right into a contested area that is dangerous!" He shook his head and abruptly walked away. I was shaken, and jolted back to reality. In my eagerness to demonstrate my gutsiness to our correspondent who'd never been to Salvador and our TV crew, I was about to put us all at risk. We spent our time cruising the outskirts of San Salvador instead.

The irony wasn't lost on me when I thought about Hoagland's death. He knew what he was doing—he didn't take foolish chances—and still he lost his life because he'd got himself caught in a cross fire trying, like most remarkable still photographers, to get as close to the action as possible. Our Freedom Forum Journalists Memorial that honors journalists who've been killed on assignment carries this note about Hoagland: "The last two pictures in his camera show the ground swirling up to meet the falling photographer, who kept his finger on the shutter until he died."

If ego got in the way of the safety of me and my crew in El Salvador, then it was stupidity that nearly did me in at the conclusion in 1983 of the bloody Shouf war in the mountains above Beirut. Again on assignment after working as an executive producer, I wanted to test myself back in the field. I volunteered to relieve the CBC's exhausted field producer who had done a long and dangerous stint in Beirut. Several weeks after arriving there, a cease-fire was negotiated, and the fighting among the warring factions in the Shouf Mountains, once home to popular ski resorts, was finally called to a bloody halt. We decided that the story could best be told by driving to the mountain village of Kfar Matta, where some of the most ferocious fighting had taken place and where the Canadian correspondent Clark Todd, who worked for a rival TV network, had been killed—perhaps murdered—earlier in the war. If peace was restored there, we thought, there was indeed some hope that it might last.

But to get to the village and back in time to edit and feed our piece by satellite that evening, we had to leave early, shoot quickly, and race back. While driving into the mountains we spotted what appeared to be a convoy of open trucks, filled with refugees and their belongings, headed for their home villages. It would make an excellent opening establishing shot, and our cameraman and soundman jumped out to record it. Suddenly the convoy came to a halt. Across the road from where I had remained by our van, I could see that our cameraman and soundman were now being held by someone, not a fighter, who appeared to be waving a pistol at them. He gestured quite wildly and seemed to demand our camera. While it didn't appear that any of us was in danger, this disruption was eating into our scarce time to get to the village. While our cameraman and soundman tried to reason with the man, I noted that our camera was unattended and that I might just be able to retrieve it. But as I made my move, the man wielding the pistol moved rapidly in my direction and pointed the pistol at me. He fired, I dropped—as I understand is a natural reflex—to a fetal position. I assumed that I'd been killed or was about to be. But the man had fired off to one side.

Alive and in shock, the next thing I knew we were all surrounded by members of one of the warring Shouf factions, a jeep full of armed Druze militia. They had watched this drama unfold and swept in once they saw what was about to happen. The man, a thieving carpet merchant who didn't want pictures of his booty or him recorded, was disarmed and taken away. Hours later we got our camera back, slightly damaged and inoperative, and we were released from custody. There was now no prospect of traveling on to Kfar Matta.

I am uncomfortable telling these stories. They undermine the pride I felt at the time, thinking that I enjoyed a reputation of sorts for being willing to put myself at risk in these dangerous war zones, and they highlight the clumsiness and inexperience that marked my forays into hostile environments. As I reflect on these ventures, I think that what propelled me was a mixture of motives, ranging from a personal need to come to terms with never having served in Vietnam, owing to a medical deferment, to a professional sense of curiosity about what was really happening in the trouble spots of the world. Both of these impulses sent me toward zones of danger, but neither would have given me the slightest sort of survival skills once there.

I was also aware that it wouldn't hurt my news career to be on these high-profile assignments. I had already figured out that those who'd been in the field enjoyed more status than those who'd never put themselves on the line covering conflicts.

As I moved up the CBC executive ladder, I tended to appoint to senior positions those journalists who were aware of the risks and dangers that they were asking others to take in the field. Like other managers, I believed that I also shared a view common for those times that someone's refusal of any assignment to a potentially dangerous area smacked of cowardice, especially if that person willingly accepted pleasant assignments to exotic locales.

Now, I realize that the willingness to go into dangerous places was not enough to guarantee my safety, the safety of anyone who worked with me, or our ability to capture an important story and bring it home to our viewers. We needed the kind of training for "hostile environments" that is now readily available in Britain for both staff journalists and freelancers. In fact, following the devastating deaths of Kurt Schork of Reuters and Miguel Moreno Gil of Associated Press Television News in Sierra Leone in May of 2000, the journalistic community in uncharacteristic fashion pledged to provide this type of training and support counseling to their fellow journalists upon their return from emotionally difficult assignments.

Unfortunately, those who head news organizations today are more likely to come from marketing, news media, corporate law, or the news-lite magazine programs that dominate (certainly in the United States) prime time airwaves. Meanwhile, front line journalists continue to risk their lives covering conflicts that their bosses care about only because they want pictures and stories if something dramatic happens. No news boss should rest easily at night until every staff or freelance journalist under his or her command knows the difference between *true* courage and foolish courage.

DON'T GO IF YOU CAN'T DEAL WITH THE CONSEQUENCES
Gary Knight

EXPERIENCE

Modern air travel made it possible for me to be in Sarajevo taking photographs in a front line trench and city morgue in the morning and by evening be back in London drinking a glass of wine with friends. That is a long way for the mind to travel.

I am a photographer and have worked in areas of conflict for the last 14 years, including the Former Yugoslavia, Burma, Afghanistan, Liberia, Zaire (Congo) Israel, and many others.

My work in war zones has been positive, although traumatic. I can't emphasize enough the huge degree to which the things I have seen, and the people I have photographed and formed relationships with, have shaped my life. They have affected every aspect of my existence. There have been times of great joy and times of incalculable desperation; but both have been vital to me.

Each time I leave my home I accumulate more traumatic experiences. I am not trying to contend with one or two experiences in the context of a relatively normal life. I have nothing in common with those who are unexpectedly visited by trauma during the course of their ordinary working lives. I cannot see one of these experiences as being any different from another; there is no "worst experience." In a sense I seek out emotional trauma; I court it. I seek no emotional support from the people I work for nor do I hold them responsible for my state of mind or my actions.

I don't think the editors I work for really understand what I experience, but why should I expect them to? Who could? Do I really understand it myself? They are supportive in the best way they know how. They will take care of me if I am hurt and they make provision for me to have the equipment and training I need if I ask for it.

That I "suffer" from emotional trauma is indisputable but it does not really concern me to any great degree, I try to live with it and accommodate it. There is room in my life for trauma; it is an essential part of the creative process.

METHOD

To work in areas of conflict, in any capacity, one must expect to bear the pain. Ultimately one must expect that it will cost you or your colleagues your lives. Unfortunately, working in conflict zones has become something of a highly collectable macho badge of honor for many journalists, aid workers, and UN staff. This has led to many people working in these areas who are unable to live with the emotional stress that comes with the job. It may sound insensitive, but I am of the belief that if you can't deal with being in a war zone then find something else to do. Anyone entering a situation that is likely to result in a traumatic experience should walk in with his or her eyes open.

Coping with emotional trauma often takes a long time, is very complex, very costly, and often unsuccessful. I advocate an approach that tries to minimize its impact at the beginning.

When I work in areas of conflict I tend to isolate myself from the organizations I am working for and I build my own support mechanisms in the field. I try to be as emotionally self-sufficient on the ground as possible. This process usually involves:

1. Traveling with one of a small number of very intimate colleagues with whom I can talk about the events I witness. Combat photographers have a very tight knit community, which for many is essential in dealing with trauma. Photographers generally take the greatest risks and receive the least logistical and emotional support from their clients. Without each other they are isolated. Without my colleagues, I would probably have debilitating emotional difficulties.
2. A firm belief that my work is morally important.
3. Creating a very stable life at home, particularly the supportive relationship with my wife.

TO CONSIDER

Don't go if you can't deal with the consequences.
Keep staff in the field to a minimum.
Avoid working in isolation.
If you are prepared as much as possible for what you will see, you will be better placed to deal with it. Unfortunately, many media organizations and individuals

labor under the somewhat arrogant belief that attending one of the multitudes of "hazardous environment" courses available is somehow unmanly and inappropriate. I have attended one and I am convinced that they are of enormous value, even to those who consider themselves experienced.

HOW I LEARNED TO LIVE WITH TRAUMA

Josh Friedman

Did you know that some Native Americans who emigrated from Iowa to Chicago were so overwhelmed by urban stimuli that they suffered paralyzing indecision, breakdowns, and even death?

I didn't know this when I finished Peace Corps service in a tiny Costa Rican mountain village and arrived in the middle of the frigid winter of 1966 to study history at the University of Chicago—the first time I had ever lived in a big city. After several weeks of loneliness, despair, and terrible longing for my Costa Rican friends in the little village, the traumatized Indians were just one of several discoveries I made as I searched the library for an answer to my condition.

I read books about returning World War II GIs. I mooned around the International House chatting with foreign students. I went to a shrink at the University health service. I did everything but study. Looking back, it took me more than a year to really begin to recover from the culture shock I was experiencing.

In the years since then, after covering war and humanitarian disasters as a *Newsday* reporter, I have experienced that same feeling I had that winter in Chicago. I now consider it sort of like having a chronic bad back. If I see violence or people dying, I know I'll pay for it—but I never know when. It was only many months after I covered the 1984-85 Ethiopian famine, for instance, that the results began to show up. I was watching a lighthearted movie in New York when I started crying for no particular reason. Then I began snapping at people. I had no patience.

I've seen this phenomenon—call it culture shock or post-traumatic shock or whatever—affect other people. My unscientific observation is that self-knowledge and the duration of the shock or trauma controls how long it takes to recover.

The Americans who were held hostage in Beirut for many years during the 1980s—I have met most of them—seem permanently shaken, with the exception of Terry Anderson, whose U.S. Army training and service in Vietnam helped him survive the awful treatment he received. The most striking victim of trauma I know was a very cocky, very powerful New York City political boss convicted for corruption and sent for eight years to a maximum security prison where he feared constantly for his life. Shortly after his release he agreed to speak to my students at Columbia University. I was shocked when he begged me to help him prepare for his lecture because he felt so insecure about standing up in public in front of a few students. I don't think he has ever regained his former pluckiness completely.

In my own experiences as a reporter, I think the danger of repeated bouts of trauma and recovery is the development of a protective carapace, the uniform of the legendary, battle-hardened, hard-drinking journalist. Underneath that tough exterior, unfortunately, often lurks self-protective insensitivity and self-medication. I have feared this in myself for years. I try to fight against it but it keeps creeping up as I get older. Covering thousands of Albanians fleeing Kosovo recently, I had to force myself to push aside that hardened exterior and feel the refugees' misery and fear.

All this self-knowledge does have its benefits. Soon after I covered Kosovo, I discovered I had an aggressive form of often-fatal bladder cancer. Eager to go on vacation, the surgeon dropped this information on me by phone and left town. For several minutes I felt as if I had stuck my finger in an electric socket.

But soon, the old familiar feeling returned, only this time instead of bullets and bombs, the "incoming" consisted of mutant cancer cells. The cancer turned into just another assignment and two years of surgery and chemo later, I'm still feeling pretty unfazed by it. I guess the danger will be when I'm finally told, as I hope to be, that I'm better. This may turn out to be the mother of all PTSDs.

A PIECE OF OUR SOUL
Elizabeth Neuffer

I left Bosnia as a reporter three years ago. What I didn't realize then is that Bosnia—and the experience of covering the war there from 1994 onward—will never leave me.

Loud, sudden noises still make me duck for cover as if there were shellfire nearby. I still dream, from time to time, about a foot clad in a tennis shoe that I saw poking from mass grave. I now always sleep lightly, one ear cocked for danger.

But most of all what stays with me is my guilt.

Why, for example, didn't I realize that massacres would result—and warn the world accordingly—when I heard of how the Bosnian Serb army had separated the men from the women of the UN safe area of Srebrenica in July 1995?

Why, that day in Sarajevo when a sniper hit the elderly woman on the street just behind me, did I never even write a story?

And why did I once risk my translator's life, insisting that we track down and confront men we knew to be mass executioners?

There are many answers: stupidity, exhaustion, hubris. But the real answer is that ours is a profession in which success is measured by getting the best story out on time, not by the compassion we show for those around us. It is the clash between those two conflicting demands, I think, that proved most difficult for me during the Bosnian war. The resulting heartbreak is one that our editors need to come to understand.

Today's wars are not like reporting on World War II, Vietnam, or even the Gulf War which I also covered. Bosnia's war was an intimate, messy conflict, in which civilians were deliberately targeted as part of a policy of "ethnic cleansing." There were no no-man's zones, not really. There were no armies to hide behind. There was no distance between the reporter and the conflict; in Sarajevo, the shell of the Holiday Inn where most journalists stayed was right on the front lines. Everyone who reported from Bosnia made friends, took lovers, adopted families from among the Bosnians, no matter their ethnic stripe.

But how to show compassion for their plight and yet get the job done, much less keep a professional distance? I did what I thought best: I let people cry on my shoulder as I took notes with one hand. I brought food to families whom I was interviewing. I carried letters in and out for families I befriended who turned up in stories, over and over again. But as the weeks turned into months that turned into years—as Bosnia's war turned into Kosovo's—there came a day when I realized I could no longer report a story and still have the strength to be compassionate, as well.

"You're the one whose mother was just shot," I snapped once to a young, distraught man on the street following a killing in Kosovo. "So, tell me the details." It was only as he sobbed out the story that I realized I had forgotten to tell him how sorry I was. It was then I realized it was time for me to put down my pen and let someone else cover the conflict.

During the war, as I returned each year to the newsroom of the *Boston Globe* in Massachusetts on an annual visit, I found myself unable to talk about just how heart-wrenching my assignment was proving. My editors were always concerned for my safety, and never wished me to take unnecessary risks to get a story, and for that they deserve great credit. Not all editors were so wise.

But we never talked about Bosnia's legacy, about how I walked out of that newsroom to go to Bosnia as one woman and returned to it as someone else. We never spoke about how guilty I felt for not having done more, about how responsible I still feel for the people I know there, for how much I wished I had more power to change events than just that of my pen. We never talked about the fact that Bosnia will always haunt me—in both positive and negative ways.

Our profession needs to acknowledge that the work we ask reporters to do is hazardous in more ways than one. There is a physical risk to being a war reporter, but there is an emotional burden, too. Editors cannot look on wars simply as another assignment. In today's wars, you are asking reporters not just to write stories, but also to give up a piece of their soul in the process, as well.

A DINNER BY CANDLELIGHT

Bill Berkeley

It was nearly midnight before we finally sat down to dinner. My wife, Mary Jane, and I had been reporting since dawn. It was June 1994. Rwanda's genocide was still unfolding in the south of the country. Hutu death squads known as the

Interahamwe—"those who attack together"—were still stabbing, hacking, and clubbing to death their ethnic Tutsi brethren in a state-orchestrated slaughter that would claim the lives of more than 500,000 in 100 days. Several thousand dazed survivors of the massacres, some of them wrapped in gauze that barely concealed their hideous machete wounds, had taken up residence in the national soccer stadium nearby.

We had begun our day at a makeshift hospital in a churchyard in Byumba, high in the heartbreakingly beautiful hills of northern Rwanda—the Switzerland of Africa, they used to call it. Amid the stench of fresh machete wounds and the vacant stares of children with stumps for limbs, we had met a 30-year-old woman named Odette, who carried a baby on her back named Dominique, aged two. The baby wasn't hers. The Presidential Guard had killed Dominique's parents, neighbors of Odette's. On that same day they had broken into Odette's home at five o'clock in the morning. They had grabbed her husband and bayoneted him to death, then rounded up her three brothers and four children—ages thirteen, eleven, eight, and four—and shot them one by one. Odette said she had fainted behind the sofa and was left for dead. She wept quietly as she told us her story. "I find it unbelievable that somebody can have the cruelty of killing even a baby," she had said.

From there we had visited a hastily assembled refugee camp on a steep mountain slope to the south, where we met a wide-eyed 11-year-old girl named Umulisa, dressed in a threadbare blue and red sweater, with smudged cheeks and a luminous smile. Umulisa had laughed at us hysterically, irrepressibly, rather than tell us in her own words about the day two weeks earlier when she had fled from her home as the militia arrived, then returned an hour later to discover her mother and father, brothers and sisters, aunts and uncles in a heap of severed heads and arms and legs on the floor of her living room.

From there we had headed further south, and visited a plain brick church by a dirt road south of Kigali, the Rwandan capital. The church was filled waist-high with about 200 putrid, maggot-riddled, freshly slaughtered corpses. Returning home through a rubble-strewn, rebel-held town called Kabuga, on the outskirts of Kigali, we met a middle-aged man named Francois, 40 years old and balding, with thin wrists and thickly-callused fingers. Francois had recently been taken into custody by rebel troops. By his own account, he had joined up with the *Interahamwe* and killed, among others, his own brother-in-law. "Everyone had to join," Francois told us. "It was the thing to do."

We were spending the night now in an abandoned monastery on the edge of Kigali that had itself been the scene of a massacre just weeks before. The smell from the pockmarked room where thirteen priests and two visiting nuns had been rounded up and shot wafted over the premises. Upon our arrival that evening, our Tutsi rebel escorts had arranged for us to interview about a dozen more survivors of the massacres who were now living in the nearby stadium. We had gathered in a sweltering, airless study of the monastery. Mary Jane, a photojournalist and human rights activist, was also serving as my French interpreter. A soldier translated from Kinyarwandan, the local dialect, into French. Mary Jane translated from French into English, then back around again from my questions in English.

One by one, for hour after hour, we had listened to their stories—unspeakable, unbelievable, inexplicable. There was a weird, surreal, science-fiction quality to this catastrophe that defied easy emotions. "I was very much surprised," said a middle-aged man named Isadore. He had survived with his wife and children but lost 20 immediate relatives. Isadore had stared at us with quizzical eyes. "Looking at my neighbors, I thought they were friends. I was very much surprised that they were among the people who came to kill us."

By then we were numb and exhausted. Mary Jane could scarcely keep up her interpreting. She stumbled and paused. I grew agitated and snapped at her, and she snapped back. Here were these traumatized survivors of genocide, painstakingly baring their souls, describing the most appalling horrors, and the two of us could barely stay awake.

Now, finally, we repaired to the bare-walled room occupied by our bodyguard, a Tutsi rebel fighter named Tom Ndahiro. He propped his Kalashnikov against the wall and promptly fell asleep on the bed. We lay out our sleeping bags on the cement floor and took our seats at the desk beneath a crucifix. We neatly set the table: two white paper towels, our bottles of water and pocket knives, and a single candle. It's important at such times to "maintain standards," we believed. There were, of course, no lights or electricity in Rwanda then, for the country was finished. And there was no food to be had. Dinner for us was a fresh avocado, stuffed with canned tuna, obtained a week earlier in neighboring Uganda.

And there was silence. Pure silence. Not a word passed between us as we ate. It was as intimate a moment as we had ever shared, or ever will.

PHOTOGRAPHER OR PHOTOJOURNALIST?

John Isaac

In 1994, I documented the situation of Rwandan refugees in Goma, Zaire for the UN. Later, I went to Rwanda to document the returning refugees. I saw the unaccompanied children in Goma, who had either lost their parents or been separated from them.

When I got back from that trip I had a nervous breakdown and, on the UN medical service's recommendation, was treated for several months, including medications for my depression and trauma. My final recovery was very interesting. One Saturday morning I was outside my Queens, New York apartment and saw a beautiful butterfly sit on a sunflower in my neighbor's yard. I do not know what happened to me. I ran inside the house and took my camera that I had packed and not touched for almost three months, loaded a roll of film and photographed the butterfly and the sunflower.

During my therapy, the doctor had tried to bring out all that I had bottled up inside me for the past several years, being a witness to genocide, wars, and the plight of refugees. Photography was not a job for me. In many ways, it was a way of life since I got into photojournalism after being in love with photography. I felt that the best way to express my creative photography was by telling a story about other human beings. To photograph a situation was very important to me, but I was a human being first and then only a photographer. Many times I chose to help some one rather than take a photograph. I was criticized by many, as "not a true photo-journalist." I accepted that, and learned to live with it, even though it is a contradiction when you have chosen to be a photojournalist and make decisions as to whether to take a photo or not.

In 1984, I was in Ethiopia covering the famine in Korem, in the north, with UN Secretary-General Perez de Cuellar. Many journalists were trying to get the best photographs and everyone was pushing each other. I was shocked to see some who stepped over dying kids to get the best shot they could. Peter Magubane (a well known South African photographer) and I tried to make some of the photographers aware of what they were doing. But in the frenzy we were also being pushed aside.

Ten years later, when I arrived in Goma, the scene was similar. The whole town was flooded with journalists and TV crews. It was amazing. I overheard a cameraman shouting to the director that it was fantastic and beautiful and to come and have a look in the viewfinder. I ran to look at the sight. It was a line of bodies in a row. He had set the camera on a tripod in a low angle and was describing the view in his viewfinder with such exclamations. It really did not make any sense to me. Later, seeing the unaccompanied children and a pile of dead bodies that were shoveled into a truck, this little boy named "Innocent" who had lost both his parents told me that I reminded him of his father. When I was about to leave the scene he asked if I ever came back to this place, would I please look him up.

With all of this in my head, I returned to New York. One day, some three weeks later when I went to work, I could not stop crying and my hands were shaking and I just could not function at all.

FULL CIRCLE

Ron Haviv

Several of my colleagues and I were on the outskirts of the Bihac pocket, an area supposedly under protection as a UN declared safe haven which was continually under attack by Serb forces. In winter of 1994 it was in danger of falling. I wanted to try to photograph the attack as well as see if it was possible to cross into the Bosnian territory. Serb forces in the Kraijina, a part of Croatia held by Serbs, were attacking in concert with the Bosnian Serbs. The Kraijina Serbs were letting journalists into their "republic." It was difficult to work and nearly impossible to cross over. I would drive around the front trying to document the attack. I went to photograph artillery positions with a colleague. As we drove around, we were chased and stopped by a red jeep filled with heavily armed and very angry Serb forces. We were immediately arrested and taken to a local police station. It was nothing new; I was arrested almost on a daily basis. On top of it, we had done nothing wrong and had all the proper papers. After waiting around all day we were to be deported. We were unconcerned and looked forward to leaving as it was impossible to work. I was escorted to my hotel, watched as I packed, and taken to reception. As I paid I left a note for a friend saying what had happened. I walked outside and waited for the escort. Instead, a Serb general, a stern grandfatherly type, came up to us and without saying a word handcuffed us together and we were thrown in the back of a jeep. We drove off in complete silence into the night.

We were taken to a farm and were promptly put into a tool shed. We had no idea what was happening and things felt like they had taken a turn for the worse. A few minutes later the door burst open and two soldiers laughing hysterically doused us with cold water. The door then shut. Some hours went by and the door opened again and we were brought into the command center. We explained who we were and what we did. The commander smiled and said we were liars and spies and were under arrest.

Back in the shed, we sat shivering and cold. We were then separated. I heard a gunshot and I was taken into the command center again. They told me they had just killed my friend, yet I was told if I would confess to being a spy all would be fine. I was back in the shed alone. Several more hours passed. The door burst open once again and they came in and put a hood over my head and dragged me into a room. All I could hear was breathing. Then the questions began: "Are you a spy for the Muslims?" I would answer, "No I am a journalist." A punch to the face. Question. Answer. Beating. The program continued until I lost track of time and was back in the shed again. I wasn't sure if my colleague was dead or not. A few minutes after returning they removed the hood from my head. Time passed, and as morning arrived I was dragged out again and put face up against a wall. A soldier came up from behind and doused me with cold water. I screamed in shock. Later I heard the splash of water and a scream. I knew he was alive. Meanwhile, both the United States and the Russian governments were negotiating with the Serbs for our release. By the third day we were handed over to a Russian working for the UN and finally deported.

Several months later I found myself in the same region again. This time the Serbs were under attack and were fleeing. As I walked among the refugees and their tractors and belongings, a Serb in uniform came up to me and smiled. He said: "Do you remember me? You were my prisoner. Let's have a drink." This is life in the Balkans. Everything comes full circle.

292 / Sharing the Front Line and the Back Hills

THE CHANCE TO CRY

Frank Smyth

The Oscar-winning film, "Life is Beautiful," compels its audience to identify with a man who confronts the evil of a Nazi concentration camp and replaces it with the hope of a fantasy world. He is an Italian Jew played by the film's director, Roberto Benigni, who loves his wife and son. While the couple are separated and detained to be used as slave labor, the man manages to save his son from harm by hiding him in his own bunk bed from the prison guards.

Like many people, I loved the film and said so to my date as we left a Washington, D.C. theater. But soon in a nearby bar I began to sweat. Before I finished my first beer the beads were pouring down so much I wondered if any other patrons besides my date noticed as they began to drip from first my forehead onto our table and then from my chin onto the cement floor when I leaned back in my chair. I was taking short breaths but could still not seem to get enough air. The toes of my right foot were curling and soon my entire right leg began to pump. Blood turned my cheeks red. I told my date I hated the film. Wouldn't the guards have found the boy? Although a tune from a live jazz band filled the basement café, in my head I heard the high-pitched cries of an Iraqi boy named Jaffer.

Exposure to trauma affects all first responders including police, fire, and ambulance employees. What separates them from journalists? Their respective professions recognize the predictable impact that repeated interaction with tragedies may have on their staff, while journalism as a profession by and large does not. Entities from the U.S. Secret Service to the Geneva-based International Committee of the Red Cross now provide routine counseling services to their people. How many newsrooms do? At least one does now, although its learning curve was slow.

The Daily Oklahoman offered counseling to reporters after the 1995 Oklahoma City bombing, but not many reporters went. "What I really needed was time with fellow journalists who went through the trauma with me to talk about all the things that happened—you know, the stuff you can't put in the paper because it is too gruesome or too out there or whatever," said feature writer Penny Owen. "(But) by the time we slowed down, everyone was so tired of the bombing that we never really got (to) have that big hashing out session." Four years later, however, after the Oklahoma City area was hit by a tornado, managing editor Joe Hight ordered "(e)veryone involved in the actual coverage" to attend at least one debriefing session with a trained counselor.

Reporters are no different from cops or emergency crews in that most are more comfortable opening up before peers than a stranger. A coffee shop or a bar may provide colleagues with an invaluable venue in which to talk and perhaps debrief each other about the emotions of their work. Honest debriefings, however, require no showmanship, something that the anthropologist, Mark Pedelty, says is ingrained in journalists' "machista" culture [1]. What is required to compel anyone to open up is an environment that makes one feel safe enough to reveal among other things what Pedelty calls "the nagging doubts, fears, and lies of press work."

The "lies" are perhaps better described as contradictions. For unlike other emergency responders who rush to tragedies to help, we run in to record. The ethics of our profession mandate that we not intervene, although I admit I once used my four-by-four with TV written in masking tape on its windows to evacuate civilians from a parish under fire. Rarely do journalists experience immediate gratification; rather we interact with evolving tragedies more like vultures who pick at the scene.

Recognizing the need for debriefing or the opportunity to articulate emotions in the aftermath, for example, of a school-yard massacre is not a sign of weakness, as too many journalists and others still seem to think. Instead, when done success-fully, debriefing fosters strength. The act of articulation—writing, drawing, painting, talking, or crying—seems to change the way a traumatic memory is stored in the brain, as if it somehow moves the memory from one part of the hard drive to another. Child survivors, for example, from Guatemala to Bosnia have begun to heal by drawing or coloring out images of attacks. Especially when the act is coupled with the opportunity to grieve, articulation often provides a release of the emotions associated with the event that leaves its author able to recall the memory in the future with less or no pain.

If not, the emotions may remain bottled up in a way that can spill over. Sounds and smells, especially, can pop the cork. I was imprisoned with Jaffer and others in 1991 after the Gulf War in Iraq, where another young Western stringer, Alain Buu, and I were detained for over two weeks. Although Jaffer's cries remain etched in my mind, I did not hear anything that sounded like the outburst he repeatedly made in an Iraq prison back in 1991 until nine years later back home on a warm winter day. I was in a D.C. park talking on my cell phone and not watching my golden retriever, Marty, when she cried out after she was bitten through the nose by a Rottweiler.

The Iraqi boy named Jaffer was at most 16. In the first cellblock of a large Iraqi prison, I only glimpsed him once or twice during daylight, although I saw and heard him a lot at night. It was spring in the Tigris-Euphrates valley and in the wake of Desert Storm millions of ethnic Shia and Kurdish Iraqis had risen up in an "intifada" or an attempted "shaking off" of Saddam's regime. Alain Buu and I had been traveling with Kurdish rebels in northern Iraq when we were captured and we soon found ourselves alone among dozens of cells in a two-story block made of cement with a large open floor.

Nearly every prisoner in the block was accused of sedition for having played a role in the just-crushed intifada, including us as well as Jaffer. He was the only boy in the block and he was singled out like many war victims for his ethnicity. A non-political prisoner told me that Jaffer was from the south and he was a Shia. From the second-floor cell that Alain and I were sharing, we could see almost the entire floor. There was a ping-pong table as well as some smaller tables with chairs where guards played dominoes. Every night, for several nights in a row, the guards chased Jaffer around the cellblock floor in a pack as they beat him with rubber hoses.

One night shift of guards always tortured victims every night for hours while they laughed. Trauma is often associated with memory loss. The Ursuline nun, Dianna Ortiz, from New Mexico was burned by Guatemalan guards only to be saved by a man she said spoke American English. She lost the memory of her own personal past including her dearest friends and family, as if her brain shut down that part of her mind to protect her from the pain of hot cigarettes. Neither Alain Buu nor I were ever physically harmed while in Iraqi custody. But we stood accused of being spies and Iraq was holding us incognito and we were missing.

I began to recall the faces, but not the names, of dear friends, as if parts of my mind, in anticipation of possible torture, were shutting down like large steel garage doors slamming down on rollers hard enough to crack cement. Alain and I both once heard a man audibly undergoing a severe form of sustained pain coming from deeper within the prison. Our block was a holding tank, and most Iraqi prisoners in it were later released. I do not remember dreaming at all while I was detained, although I had vivid nightmares thereafter.

Looking at Jaffer's gaunt face with his large eyes open wide like his mouth, while listening to his repeated cries, I was glad not to be the one being tortured. A moment later, I felt guilty for not volunteering to change places with him or any other tortured prisoner. The emotions clashed in my mind as I listened to Iraqis being tortured for hours including Jaffer who cried out like Marty at every stroke.

Not all my prison memories are bad. Nearly every reporter who has covered a blood-and-guts beat knows that trauma can also bring out the best in people. I do not know the name of my hero and I am not even sure what he looked like. But like Jaffer's, I will never forget his voice. This man was quietly taken out of our cellblock some days before Jaffer arrived, but he was there the first day Alain and I were brought to the prison.

That night, after the last domino fell, the guards began what for one night shift would become a daily routine. They were still discussing the domino match as they rose to walk about and (in most cases) randomly choose a victim to bring to a large open area by the stairwell of the second floor at the Eastern end of the block. Only with the first light of dawn did I see that the man who was the victim was standing with his arms over his head as if his wrists were tied to the ceiling. From before midnight to almost dawn, the guards beat him to encourage him to properly imitate a barnyard animal. I thought they were trying to make him bleat like a sheep, as he seemed to be going, "Ba-ha-ha, ba-ha-ha."

One guard at a time stood behind the man, and, at the encouragement of other guards, swung at him with a long flat board to hit what sounded like his bare buttocks. The guards took turns and each one swung whenever he or one of his peers judged one of the man's animal noises to be somehow inadequate. Some guards were more merciless than others. I was wrong about the noise and I realized it around dawn when a rooster crowed in a field somewhere outside the prison. It took a moment before the guards collectively broke into laughter. I heard several guffaws.

It was hours before, during the same torture game, that my hero suddenly began to sing. He was across the atrium and a few cells nearer to the victim than we were. By then I was wondering whether the guards would end up killing the victim. The singer had waited for hours until he was no longer crowing loudly and clearly enough to avoid receiving endless swings. Once the singer began it soon became apparent that he was vocalizing in solidarity with the victim. He sang in solidarity with every nightly torture victim the four or five days he was there, and he seemed to get away with it because he may have been a Shia cleric and his songs were filled with references to Allah.

The first night Alain and I were there the singer prayed on for hours as the guards went on as well with the crowing game. One guard began to beat the victim more fiercely once the singer started, but two other guards walked away from the group to go downstairs and play ping-pong. The sounds of pain, prayer, and the bouncing ball echoed in the dark throughout the damp block.

Smells can be even more intense, and the olfactory gland itself is hard-wired to the emotional part of the brain. One smell I inhaled in Iraq was so powerful that I forgot about it for seven-and-a-half years. Alain and I had been traveling with two other young men, Gad Gross, a Newsweek photographer, and Bakhtiar Abdel al-Rahman, an economics student at the University of Baghdad, who was now an armed Kurdish rebel and our guide. We last saw the two of them in the afternoon on March 28, 1991 just north of Kirkuk in northern Iraq as together they ran under fire toward a cluster of small cinder block houses, as Alain and I were diving into a ditch. An Iraqi tank later parked on the other side of a long dirt mound between us and a road.

The next morning at around eight we heard a commotion coming from the nearby houses, as if the soldiers had captured two people. Minutes later we heard a burst from an automatic rifle. Maybe another minute passed before we heard a loud, sustained scream that was cut short by another burst. Looking over the ditch's edge, Alain and I minutes later both saw a soldier walking away with Gad's camera bag in his hand. I suppressed my desire to grieve, as Alain and I were still hiding from the same soldiers. We were spotted while hiding in the ditch an hour later and soldiers were about to kill us too when an intelligence officer, who seemed to be newly arrived at the scene, argued that we be saved for interrogation. Alain and I were released eighteen days later on Saddam's order.

I forgot one thing about the ditch, although it sometimes manifested itself anyway. About five years after being imprisoned in Iraq I began working on a novel, one of those unpublished manuscripts that more than a few journalists have lying around. In one scene, prison guards torture a young captured Salvadoran guerrilla in the cell next to an imprisoned journalist, and they do so whenever the journalist's needs are met. For example, after the journalist is allowed to relieve himself in a bucket, the guards bring the bucket to the boy and force in his head. At one point, the guards take the boy around the corner of the cellblock out of sight of the journalist, who then hears a gunshot. (He never sees the boy again.) Several moments later, he inhales burnt gunpowder.

I thought I had made up the smell after a few shooting sessions at an indoor pistol range in Hoboken, New Jersey.

About two more years later I was working on a non-fiction version of the Iraqi event and I wrote for days, day and night, trying to recall the details, however painful some were. I brushed in more color and layered on more texture on the part where Alain and I heard the capture of Gad and Bakhtiar. I always remembered having an emotional reaction not long after hearing the gunshots, and shrinking in my mind like a little boy who was too big for his britches and who had really messed up. But I forgot what had triggered this sensation.

There was a slight breeze that day, and it took a few minutes for the smell of burnt gunpowder to travel over the ground to our ditch. It was sweet and I remembered inhaling it for the first time. I thought about the memory before I tapped the words into my keyboard. I made a few changes to the paragraph that included my feeling like a little boy in need of a savior. I walked to my bed, collapsed into a fetal position, and began to moan, shake and tear and did so nearly loud enough for the neighbors to hear for what seemed like an hour. A friend held me as I wailed for Gad and Bakhtiar seven years after Alain and I heard them die.

Journalists are people who, like almost everyone else who is exposed to pain, feel it whether it is their's or not. Keeping it bottled up may lead to drinking, smoking, philandering, working, or doing something else in a compulsive way that provides a distraction, but not release. The need to articulate feelings after exposure to trauma is obvious, and it is more likely to happen sooner than later if a counselor who is paid to listen is on hand. Once I finally faced up to it, I paid for a counselor out of my pocket. I took the chance to cry.

REFERENCE

1. M. Pedelty, *War Stories: The Culture of Foreign Correspondents,* Routledge Press, New York, 1995.

ALL FOR THE STORY?

Paddi Clay

Last night, after years of searching, I finally listened to a recording of the burst of gunfire that killed my father somewhere on the road to Stanleyville in the Congo 37 years ago.

I've been trying to locate that recording for most of my adult life, ever since I became a journalist and his old buddies mentioned that it existed.

No sooner had I heard it than I ran into one of my father's former colleagues, Peter Hawthorne, who had come into the radio station to talk about Africa and Africa correspondents. It was a coincidence that heightened every emotion I was feeling.

Perhaps the final catharsis will be when I go to Washington—with my son— to see my father's name on the Freedom Forum Memorial. Like the families of the Vietnam fallen I would like to trace my fingers along his name and make up for the fact that I only found out about the memorial by accident and through the Internet three years ago.

I'm slightly embarrassed by the fact that I've taken so long to piece together the patchwork quilt of my father's history—embarrassed because I've also been a hack in Africa and somehow I should have made the time to put together this story, which is so close to me.

For years I've been bumping into his remaining buddies by chance and hearing the odd anecdote, or picking up snippets when people who knew him in South Africa meet me for the first time. I've also been discovering references to him in other people's books about Africa, correspondents and South Africa's sixties political history. But I had never really tackled the project—or my search for the recording—head-on.

I was given the recording by an old friend of my late mother. She had given him a disc recording for safekeeping. She didn't want me to know about it when I was young, and then genuinely forgot where it was when we lost contact with the friend.

Now I have most of the facts and the recording. And it's time to access the buried feelings for a father whose funeral I didn't attend.

I wrote a poem about my memories during my teenage years, about faded photographs in suitcases, in cupboards. Those pictures linger in my memory. Me, rowdy in the hotel pool and my father with his fellow journalists at the pool bar, trading hack talk, and consuming whisky. Me, with a label on my lapel, clinging to my suitcase and the hand of an annoyed air hostess in the empty hall of Nairobi airport. We're waiting for my father who is late in fetching me because he's covering a story.

The postscript to that memory is that when he arrived he charmed the air hostess and placated her with a drink in the bar while I kicked my heels with a pile of comics at his side. My father charmed many people and especially me.

I cried when I heard the gunfire that killed him.

My mother's note in my diary on the morning after his death told me he died doing what he loved. That didn't help me much as a nine year old or a teenager, but I was always proud of him and I now understand why he chose to do the job he did.

I've also experienced the thrill of covering the best story of my career in Africa for foreign networks. I've also toted recording equipment into dusty villages and weaved my way round gun toting maniacs.

But understanding what motivated him to "get the story out" at all costs doesn't really counteract the anger and the regret. I gave up dangerous jobs when I was pregnant and I won't go back to that way of life now that I am a parent. My father went on doing his work even though I existed.

I share his genes. But not his obsession with the story. Maybe I'm also more aware of the dangers facing journalists. His death was a wake-up call for his generation of journalists in Africa. Until then they hadn't really grasped that war and war coverage was changing, that there was a strong chance they could also become victims.

Today I can listen to the shots that killed my father and wonder at the circumstances (or inherited genes) that led me into a similar career. I can think of that gunfire as the most powerful soundbite of my life, and go on with my life. But I will always regret that I never got to sit over drinks with my father, journalist to journalist, arguing about journalism and Africa.

Perhaps our biggest argument would have been about journalistic commitment. Is it something we can control? Or are some of us born with more of it than others?

DYING TO TELL THE STORY

Kathy Eldon, author and filmmaker living in Los Angeles

My son Dan, a Reuters photographer, was killed by an angry mob in Mogadishu on July 12th, 1993. Three other journalists, Hos Maina and Anthony Macharia of Reuters, and Hansi Krauss, of the Associated Press, also died that day, killed by the very people they were trying to help. The situation was tragic: believing that the hated warlord General Aideed was there, United Nations forces had bombed a house, killing or wounding over 50 men, women, and children. Survivors raced to the journalists' hotel, and begged the photographers to return with them to photograph what had happened. Assured of protection, Dan and his colleagues drove to the site of the bombing. When they arrived, and began shooting the carnage, the enraged crowd blamed the "foreigners" (two of those killed were Kenyan) and set upon them with sticks and stones, killing four and seriously wounding Mohamed Shaffi, a Reuters cameraman.

Dan was 22 when he died. Though young, his photographs had appeared on the front pages of newspapers around the world. I was proud of what he was doing in Somalia. As a former journalist, I had always encouraged Dan to stand up for the truth, to tell stories that mattered, and speak out when he saw injustice. When I heard that he had been killed, I blamed myself. If I had not encouraged him to follow his heart, he would not have died. Minutes after I heard the news, I got a call from Mark Wood, the Editor-in-Chief of Reuters. My heart cracked open, I begged him to do something to commemorate the work of the journalists who had died. "We must transform this tragedy into something positive." I cried. "I will do everything in my power to help." Mark promised.

In a strange way, I was lucky, for Dan's and the other deaths were widely publicized as one of the biggest tragedies in journalistic history. Three months later, the Associated Press and Reuters produced together a book and an exhibition of the work of the three dead journalists, entitled *Images of Conflict,* which was shown in many countries. Dan's death gave me a voice, and I used it to speak out about the role of journalists, campaigning for insurance for freelancers, and public awareness of the importance of the news. I was able to do something positive with my grief.

Reuters and the Associated Press have been supportive throughout, funding seminars and the traveling exhibition, and offering free footage when my daughter Amy and I produced a TBS special, *Dying to Tell the Story,* profiling journalists who risk their lives to do their jobs. (In the past three years, we have lost two of those featured in the film: Carlos Mavroleon, who died while on assignment in Afghanistan for 60 Minutes, and our friend, Mohamned Shaffi, who died recently while on assignment in Jerusalem.)

I was fortunate. Other mothers aren't so "lucky." Their loved ones don't die in high profile tragedies and most aren't former journalists who can transform their pain into media projects. Losing a child is the worst that can happen to a mother. You never get over it. If you're lucky, you might get through it. It means a lot if something can be done to commemorate the person who has died. It helps me to know that Dan is included in a book that commemorates Reuters' journalists who have died while working. The book is in the main reception area of Reuters' head office in London. It's big and beautiful, printed on hand-made paper, and I cry every time I see it.

Organizations can help mothers, siblings, spouses, and other relatives get through by being attentive to their feelings. We need to believe that our loved ones died for something, and that they are remembered. When someone dies, don't be shy about expressing your feelings directly to the survivor. Many of us feel uncomfortable around death. I know I did. But all we survivors really need is to have a chance to hear good things about our loved ones and to talk about them. Be a good listener. Don't escape from those who have deep pain in their hearts. Just be there.

In a world sadly lacking in heroes, peace keepers, humanitarian aid workers, human rights defenders, cameramen and women, journalists and photographers, are heroes. Their lives may have been cut short but, for the most part, they knew the risks they were taking and chose to continue. They died trying to make the world a better place. No matter what, we must not forget them.

WORKING IN THE THIRD WORLD

Beryl Goldberg, freelance photographer and writer, NYC

The pain for me of working in the third world is to be confronted with the contrast in the lives between us and them. People have so little and make do with so little. We have so much and want always more. When I visit villages in Africa or Latin America I see often projects in which a small expenditure would make a huge difference in people's lives. In a recent visit to a village in Burkina Faso the women were involved in a project that would be income earning for them. The main things that were lacking were merely little carts to carry their supplies and basins to carry water, very inexpensive items. There, one realized that every drop of water is precious. Water may be used for cooking and what's left over used to feed the animals or water plants. In the village there is no such thing as a freely flowing tap. Water often arrives in a basin on someone's head after having been carried a significant distance.

When I return home from one of these visits I face a closet overflowing with clothing; a refrigerator stuffed with food. I go to a restaurant and am served enough food for at least two. I wash my face and the dishes by turning on the tap and running the water. We have so much. I know I can't send water to Burkina Faso. I don't think we in the West must change our lives totally. We don't have to starve, we don't have to empty our closets. But can't we be more generous?

Foreign aid and relief agencies can make a big difference. I have seen small programs where people's lives do change through microcredit programs and health programs. When I try to explain this to people here, a few care but others can't be bothered. I fear a cynical mood has overtaken many. The third world, especially Africa, is presented as a cesspool of war, disease, and corruption. Not to say that this does not exist. It does, but there are committed people doing good work. There are families with children and grandchildren who study and work and raise families. These stories are hard to find in the Western media but we should get them out there so there is a truer picture of this world. If there is hope and positive news, I believe it will be much more difficult to dismiss these countries.

WHO CARES FOR THOSE WHO CARE?

Barbara Bertoncin

I'd say my job sends me more to the back hills than to the front line. I follow mostly the Balkans, but I have always arrived there when the real (and dangerous) things had already happened. Yet I still become troubled.

"Bosnia is not interesting any more" Irfanka Pasagic[1] reminds me every time I am surprised when another international organization leaves her country. During the winter I had traveled around a Kosovo full of all kinds of organizations and UN white cars.

In Tuzla immediately after the war, in just this small and unlucky town, there were dozens of organizations. Today all of them have left, and you have just to visit Mihatovici, a big center housing 2000 refugees, 600 of whom are children, to see if it were really time to leave.

How long will Kosovo last?

I fear that the "Bosnia lesson" has not been learned.

I think most of the mistakes come from a lack of preparation, both in terms of knowledge and in the ability and willingness to listen to the local people and learn their needs. And the biggest mistake remains the short terms of the projects.

So, speaking in paradoxes, I would prefer more interveners and decision makers to become troubled. But then again, will there be anybody to care about them: the best, the most involved, the ones who will really suffer during and after?

Two years ago, in the same month, I spent ten days in Bosnia, participating in a very psychologically intense and tiring workshop in Republika Srpska, then went to Serbia at a critical time. When I returned, I needed months to recover from all the pain I had heard and seen.

Because this kind of empathy, of proximity, makes you discover victims and persecutors in the same family, sometimes in the same person, soon you lose any kind of Manichean vision. You'd just like to stop speaking, writing, also thinking, but you have to report and, when you enter that dimension, you have to report more than ever. That is what I mean by "troubled."

---

[1] A psychiatrist from Srebrenica, now working in Tuzla with traumatized women and children.

And still I am lucky, because I work in a warm and comfortable environment, my colleagues listen to me, and my reports convinced the magazine to pay more attention to trauma as a key factor, not only in the Balkans.

I am pleased to see that there is a will to recognize even the interveners' feelings, because the risk is that the brave ones, those who are willing to share the suffering and the frustrations of the people they work with, will just increase the number of traumatized people.

PERSONAL ARMOR
Christine Spolar

I've never forgotten that day. A young man squeezed next to me in the armored truck, which was our safe passage through war torn Sarajevo, and we peered through the bulletproof window at the wreckage of his neighborhood. "I'm leaving my life behind," he whispered, tears falling down his cheeks as we passed a row of buildings that had been reduced to bare steel girders by shells and grenades. "My mother, my brother, I'm leaving everything I know."

I closed my eyes and, out of compassion or exhaustion, let my own tears fall. I tried to hold onto my composure and to focus on anything but what I had seen that week in February 1993. As the truck careered down the road known as sniper's alley, so did my thoughts.

As a staff writer for the Washington Post, I ventured into Bosnia during the early and worst days of fighting. My job was to relieve co-workers who were assigned full-time to cover the war. I returned, from 1995 through 1998, as the Post's bureau chief for Eastern Europe and spent much of my time in the Balkans. I had been a reporter for nearly a dozen years when I met Sarajevo. Nothing could prepare me, really, for its deadly game of chance.

In those first months, the Post editors made sure I had the requisite flak jacket and helmet, the kind of armor that would allow me to board UN flights into the war zone. An armored car, deemed necessary by the wire services, the BBC and the New York Times, came later. I had no special war training, no seminars, no extra pay, no special insurance. But I went into Bosnia as one of the most fortunate reporters there.

My paper had deep financial pockets and a journalistic commitment to the story. If I had serious physical ailments—my arms, in fact, gave out to a debilitating case of carpal tunnel syndrome after two years of hoisting computers, satellite phones, and backpacks in and out of the region—the paper could quickly address the problem. I also knew whatever made it into the Post's pages could influence policy makers and people who could help resolve the worst conflict in Europe since World War II.

Yet . . . no one ever spoke much about the personal armor needed to weather a war. Months into my work, I wondered if no one wanted to acknowledge the emotional risks involved in writing about war, or the editors were just too far removed from the war zone to understand. I came to realize that the paper, perhaps rightly so, focused solely on the story, whatever it took to produce. Talk was brief in a land where phone connections broke off within seconds. "Great story today, very sad, what will you have tomorrow?" There was no time or place to tell the private battles waged to capture the trauma on paper.

There were good times, when I could relate the uncommon bravery of the people in their daily lives. How they ignored the random rat-tat-tat of machine guns to gather wood or when they shrugged off danger to draw fresh water from an outdoor pump or, on a particularly good day, how Sarajevans ventured down the street to find friends in nearby apartments to share pieces of "war cake," a sodden sweet concocted from the sugar, oil, and flour found in UN aid packages.

The bad times came in a blur of sound, fury, and silence that, to my critical eye, never translated well enough on paper. The searing whine of an incoming shell. The pause between artillery rounds. A crack of a mortar strike and then the hushed, hushed, hushed seconds before awful screams. I saw a young girl—no more than 12—my first week in 1993. Half her face appeared gone, raked over by shrapnel from a noontime attack. This was a war where I would see much worse, but that night, as now, I couldn't forget her bloody, broken face. Would she date? Would she marry? In a mountain town where pretty girls had families early, what was her future? That small moment was worth not more than a line in a story then. It still glints, sharp and tough, in my mind.

I grew close to my interpreters, one Serb, one Muslim, who traveled miles with me in search of stories. We had days that were too exhausting, too complicated, or just too plain frightening to relate to editors miles away. Does it sound like an explanation or an excuse when you tell them that you have no story that day because the car slipped off a muddy mountain road onto the edge of a field studded with mines? Better to recount the accident with a sense of bravado, a couple of quips and not the nasty shards of truth: Zoran, my interpreter from Belgrade, and I had been deeply frightened, tiptoeing around the car until we rocked it out of the mud. Teary-eyed from the mental and physical exhaustion, we didn't talk for hours.

How do you prepare for war? I'm not sure you can. How do you endure the war? With help from fellow travelers who need to talk as much as you do. How do you recover from war? It is a most personal reckoning.

I don't talk much about those times. Gatherings where people swap old war stories hold no allure. I don't want to relive the moments as much as I want to hold them dear. They give me strength.

WAR CHILDREN: THE HIGHLY PERSONAL "SPIN"

Sherry Ricchiardi

Tuga Tarle took a deep breath and sat silently for a few moments, weighing the consequences of the offer she was about to make to me. "The children will talk to you, but it will be heartbreaking," the aid worker warned. "They are the walking wounded, the little ones with ruined lives."

Tarle offered a pile of gray file folders as proof. Each one contained material macabre enough for a horror film featuring Bosnian and Croatian children as witnesses to unspeakable crimes. At times, the details brought tears to my eyes, yet, as a reporter, I knew these little survivors were invaluable sources of information. I agonized over whether they should be sought out and interviewed. The files contained accounts of youngsters who saw their mothers and sisters raped, fathers and brothers executed, villages ransacked and burned. Many reported seeing bodies blown apart by mortars and limbs severed by razor-sharp shrapnel.

One child described seeing a pregnant neighbor thrown to the ground, screaming wildly as her stomach was slashed open and the fetus torn out. Another told of helping to drag nine corpses—all boys from her village who had been rounded up and shot—into a backyard for burial in a shallow grave.

To aid workers like Tarle, these children were "the true innocents and precious survivors who must be protected from further harm." To journalists, these children represented a treasure trove of information on how genocide and mass destruction were carried out in the back hills and towns of Bosnia and Herzegovina. They could also provide insight into how the youngest survivors were coping in the aftermath of the bloodiest European war since Hitler's armies roamed these regions.

But how do journalists go about documenting these stories without risking further damage to fragile young minds? Where do we draw the line in pushing for details from children who have witnessed horror? When does the pursuit of information become exploitation? Is it ever justifiable to ask a child to relive hellish experiences for the sake of a richer or more relevant news story? Does the end—raising consciousness about horrendous events, such as genocide in the Balkans—ever justify the means? Under what circumstances should reporters protect the identity of minors? These were some of the questions I anguished over as I moved through refugee centers packed with the war's most vulnerable victims. The issue of using children as primary sources, especially when they have experienced traumatic events, is a thorny one.

Just as therapists seek new and better public health models to help children work through trauma, journalists also need to explore better information-gathering models to help them edge closer to the truth of how cataclysmic events affect one of society's most defenseless populations. Sometimes, it means seeking alternatives: some therapists, with the proper permission from parents or guardians, will allow journalists to be unseen observers while they interview children about their experiences; another viable source can be found in the creative products: the art, poetry and letters children produce as part of the healing process.

Sometimes the decision boils down to pure common sense. During a visit to a refugee camp in the Bosnian town of Siroki Brijeg, a Red Cross worker told of a 14-year-old Muslim child who was about to give birth after being released from what he described as a "rape center." The Red Cross worker, eager to have the girl tell of her captivity and rape at the hands of the Serbs, offered to request an interview.

Girls impregnated and held until it was too late for them to abort had become a common scenario amid the charges of systematic rape in Bosnia. In this case, the child had been reunited with relatives who feared she was dead. The pain already inflicted was so great, there was no hesitation in settling instead for information from those who had talked with the girl and knew the intimate details of her story. It was a lost opportunity for an exclusive story on the child's experience with extreme sexual terror. But interviewing a 14-year-old impregnated rape victim seemed too gross a violation.

No doubt the story lost the power of the girl's own account of how it felt to go from being a carefree schoolgirl with loving parents to a terrified Muslim child horribly abused at the hands of her captors. It lost the richness of the highly personal "spin," but the information was powerful enough coming from her family members.

Did the compromise reflect a sound journalistic decision or an emotional response to a child's suffering? One thing I am certain of: I am better able to sleep at night because I did not ask that tormented child to relive her horror.

27

Journalists, War, and Post Traumatic Stress Disorder*

Anthony Feinstein and John Owen

As we enter the new millennium it is unusual to come across a topic in the behavioral sciences that has not been studied, at least from a clinical perspective. The researcher starting out on a new project begins by doing a literature search to see who has been there before him or her and what the nature of that work was. Invariably the computer search engines come up with a number of citations, certain areas of interest proving more crowded than others. And crowded would best describe the field of psychological trauma, particularly over the past two decades.

There is now a large literature devoted to how individuals respond to overwhelming trauma, which may be visited upon them in many different ways. How veterans react to combat [1, 2] or civilians to man-made [3, 4] or natural disasters [5, 6] have all been thoroughly studied. On an individual basis, how victims of rape [7], assault [8], domestic violence [9], and motor vehicle accidents [10], to mention but a few, respond psychologically has been carefully documented. However, within this burgeoning field of trauma studies the psychological health of war reporters has not been addressed. When it comes to this topic, the computer search draws a blank. This omission is surprising given the dangerous nature of war journalism. Personal anecdote attests to this fact and published memoirs of war journalists rank among the classic accounts of war. Robert Capa and the second world war [11], Michael Herr and Vietnam [12], and Anthony Loyd and the Balkans [13] are three examples of a genre that spells out the considerable risks journalists go to in order to capture news, or as they prefer to call it, history in the making.

In addition to the eloquent voices preceding this chapter, consider the following. In a series of interviews with war journalists that were conducted by the authors recently, the group reported such typical experiences as: getting shot (one photographer had been shot on four separate occasions), being shot at, subject to mock execution, assault, having a bounty placed on their heads, having colleagues killed alongside them as they worked on an assignment, having close colleagues commit suicide, having their plane shot down and surviving the crash that killed both pilots

*This study was funded by the Freedom Forum.

only to have personal possessions looted by renegade militia who stormed the wreckage, and surviving a mortar that came through a hotel wall and lodged in a cupboard that stood at the head of a bed as the journalist lay resting.

How these experiences and countless others affect war journalists can be surmised, but empirical data are needed to record the psychological consequences of traumatic stressors that often rank in intensity alongside those of combat veterans. We have addressed this question in a study that investigated the prevalence of symptoms of Post Traumatic Stress Disorder in a representative sample of 140 war journalists.

However, before discussing the methodology and results of this study, a few words on the psychiatric sequelae of trauma are called for.

PSYCHOLOGICAL CONSEQUENCES OF TRAUMATIC EVENTS

Post Traumatic Stress Disorder (PTSD): For individuals to develop symptoms of PTSD they need to have been exposed to a traumatic event in which two factors by definition, are present. First, they must have experienced, witnessed, or confronted an event that involved actual or threatened death or serious injury to self or others, and second, the person's response involved intense fear, hopelessness, or horror [14]. To sustain a diagnosis of PTSD following an overwhelming stressor, the person must display a set of symptoms that fall into three categories, namely re-experiencing the trauma, a persistent avoidance of stimuli associated with the trauma coupled with an emotional numbing of responsiveness and, finally, persistent symptoms of physiological arousal.

PSYCHIATRIC CONDITIONS CO-MORBID WITH PTSD

While PTSD, which is classified as an anxiety disorder, may stand alone as a diagnosis, it frequently occurs with other psychiatric conditions such as major depression, substance abuse, and other anxiety disorders.

THE STUDY

The *aim* of this study was to explore the frequency of PTSD symptoms in journalists who report on war. The present report is part of a larger study that is currently also investigating depression and personality factors in war journalists.

The *method of study* first involved discussing the project with the world's leading news organizations to elicit their cooperation in providing a list of names of journalists to survey. To that end, CNN, BBC, Reuters, The Canadian Broadcasting Corporation, Associated Press Television News, and an organization representing freelance cameramen and women (Rory Peck Trust) were approached and the purpose of the study explained. All agreed to participate and provide a list of names, addresses, and e-mail addresses of their journalists who covered war zones. One hundred and seventy names were provided. Only those journalists fluent in English and currently working in war zones were included.

A study of this kind presented a particular set of logistical difficulties. War journalists lead an itinerant life and it soon became apparent that trying to reach them via regular mail was ineffectual. Furthermore, mail services in areas of conflict are either erratic or non-existent. Faxing questions and replies back and forth also was impractical given the volume of paperwork involved. Taking these facts into consideration, an interactive Web site was developed and each journalist was assigned an individual case identification number. Strict confidentiality was maintained, not only between journalists but also with their employers. Indeed it was a prerequisite of ethical approval that the journalists replies were kept confidential from their bosses.

The journalists were asked to complete a number of questionnaires. In addition to detailed demographic data (age, marital status, years worked as a war journalist, etc.) information was collected on drinking habits (number of average size bottles of beer, glasses of wine, shots of spirits consumed per week) and other drugs used (cannabis, amphetamines, cocaine, LSD, barbiturates, opiates). Journalists were also asked to complete a series of self-report questionnaires, of which data from two are presented here.

1. The revised Impact of Event Scale [15] contains questions that closely follow the diagnostic criteria for PTSD as defined by the American Psychiatric Association in their Fourth Edition of the Diagnostic and Statistical Manual of Mental Disorders (DSM-1V) [14]. Thus, 8 questions are devoted to re-experiencing phenomena, 8 to avoidance (*numbing*) phenomena, and 6 to the hyperarousal criteria. Subjects are asked to respond to the frequency with which symptoms have occurred in the past 7 days and are offered a choice of 5 responses per question, i.e., "not at all"; "a little bit"; "moderately"; "quite a bit"; and "extremely." While the scale cannot by itself make a diagnosis of PTSD, a particular constellation of symptoms endorsed can give the researcher a good idea of whether the person is suffering from PTSD or not. Using DSM-1V criteria, if a journalist endorsed at least one re-experiencing symptom, at least three avoidance symptoms and at least two hyperarousal symptoms at an intensity of "moderately," "quite a bit," or "extremely," they were deemed to have probable PTSD. The scale can therefore provide an index of *current,* but not lifetime, PTSD.

2. The 28-item General Health Questionnaire [16] contains four subscales of 7 questions each, namely somatic complaints, anxiety, social dysfunction, and depression. A choice of 4 responses are provided for each question and scored 0-0-1-1. Each subscale provides a score, which then is summed to provide a total score as a global index of psychological distress, which by convention is taken as GHQ ≥ 5.

ETHICAL APPROVAL

Ethical approval for the study (both paper and Internet versions) was obtained from the Ethics Committee at Sunnybrook and Women's College Health Science Centre, which is affiliated to the University of Toronto.

RESULTS

The hazardous nature of war journalism was demonstrated tragically during the course of the study. One of the most experienced war journalists was killed on assignment while the questionnaires were en route to him. Of the remaining 169 journalists, 140 (82.2 percent) gave their consent and completed the study. The war group had spent on average 15 years reporting war and covered every major conflagration during this period, including Bosnia, Rwanda, Chechnya, the Gulf War, Middle East, Congo, Sierra Leone, Indonesia, Somalia, and Ethiopia. A breakdown of the most frequently covered conflicts is shown in Figure 1. Of note was the fact that the war group were on average 39 years old and yet only 46.4 percent were married. A breakdown of basic demographic characteristics appears in Table 1.

Alcohol and Drug Use

Male journalists drink on average 15.0 (sd = 9.4) units of alcohol (as defined in the methods section) per week. Females drink 11.0 (sd = 9.4) units per week. The upper limit of what constitutes acceptable drinking has been set at 14 units and 9 units per week for males and females respectively [17]. Based on these guidelines, 41.2 percent of male war journalists were rated as drinking excessively. The figure for females was 51.7 percent.

Forty-seven (33.8 percent) journalists smoke cigarettes and 24.3 percent use cannabis. Hard drugs, i.e., cocaine, amphetamines, etc. are used by 6.4 percent.

Symptoms of Post Traumatic Stress Disorder

A breakdown of the individual PTSD symptoms and how frequently they were endorsed appears in Tables 2, 3, and 4. The percentage figures refer to three levels of intensity from the Impact of Event Scale, namely "moderately," "quite a bit," and "extremely." A cumulative total is supplied for these three rating responses. Data are not given for the remaining two Impact of Event Scale categories, i.e., "not at all," and "a little bit."

The total subscale scores for intrusion were 9.2 (sd = 7.1), avoidance 6.7 (6.2), and hyperarousal 4.7 (4.9). The total impact of event scale score was 20.2 (16.0).

Applying DSM-1V criteria for a diagnosis of PTSD, described in the methods section, 19.7 percent of the sample had sufficient symptomatology to receive a diagnosis of "probable" PTSD.

Psychological Distress

The mean subscale scores for the GHQ were: somatic complaints 1.0 (sd = 1.5); anxiety 1.2 (sd = 1.8); social dysfunction 1.0 (sd = 1.6); and depression 0.5 (sd = 1.1). The mean total score was 3.6 (sd = 4.6). Based on a cut-off point of 5, 33.3 percent of the sample were classified as "psychologically" distressed.

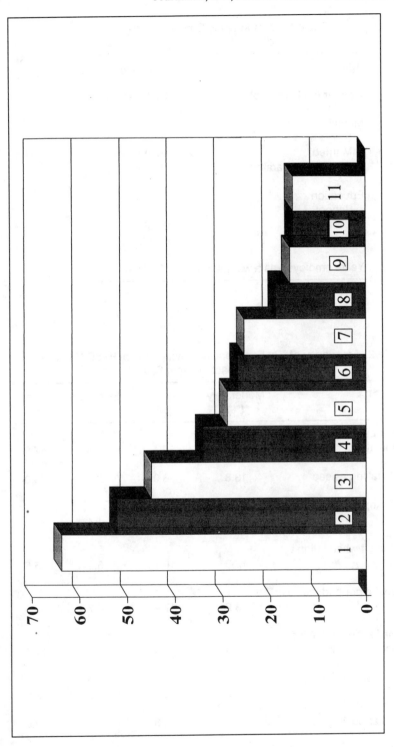

Figure 1. Percentage of war correspondents covering various locations.

Legend: 1 = Yugoslavia (Bosnia/Croatia/Serbia), 2 = Kosovo, 3 = Gulf War/Iran/Iraq, 4 = Rwanda/Burundi, 5 = Congo/Zaire, 6 = Chechnya, 7 = Somalia, 8 = Israel/Gaza, 9 = Lebanon, 10 = Sierra Leone, 11 = Afghanistan.

Table 1. Demographic Characteristics
of War Journalists

Age	39.2 (6.4)
Gender (male:female)	78.8%:21.2%
Marital	
Single	42.8%
Married	46.4%
Divorced/separated	10.9%
Education	
School	14.7%
College	20.6%
University	64.7%
Years employed as a war journalist	15.6 (6.8)

Table 2. Frequency of "Re-Experiencing" Symptoms of PTSD Rated
According to the Impact of Event Scale-R

Symptom	Moderately (%)	Quite a bit (%)	Extremely (%)	Total (%)
Any reminder brought back feelings about it	24.6	16.7	6.5	47.8
I had trouble falling asleep	13.8	8.0	2.2	24.0
Other things kept making me think about it	14.5	15.9	1.4	31.8
I thought about it when I didn't mean to	12.3	16.7	6.5	35.5
Pictures about it popped into my mind	23.2	17.4	8.7	49.3
I found myself acting or feeling like I was back at that time	6.5	4.4	0.7	11.7
I had waves of strong feelings about it	17.3	18.7	6.5	42.5
I had dreams about it	15.3	8.8	4.4	28.5

Table 3. Frequency of "Avoidance" Symptoms of PTSD Rated
According to the Impact of Event Scale-R

Symptom	Moderately (%)	Quite a bit (%)	Extremely (%)	Total (%)
I avoided letting myself get upset when I thought about it or was reminded of it	26.3	9.5	1.5	37.3
I felt as if it hadn't happened or wasn't real	8.7	8.0	4.3	21.0
I stayed away from reminders of it	8.0	6.5	1.4	15.9
I tried not to think about it	10.1	10.1	2.2	22.4
I was aware that I still had a lot of feelings about it, but didn't deal with it	15.3	12.4	8.8	36.5
My feelings about it were kind of numb	13.1	9.5	4.4	27.0
I tried to remove it from memory	5.1	8.7	0	13.8
I tried not to talk about it	13.9	5.8	4.4	24.1

Table 4. Frequency of "Hyperarousal" Symptoms of PTSD Rated
According to the Impact of Event Scale-R

Symptom	Moderately (%)	Quite a bit (%)	Extremely (%)	Total (%)
I felt irritable and angry	13.1	13.1	5.1	31.3
I was jumpy and easily startled	8.1	9.6	6.6	24.3
I had trouble falling asleep	10.3	9.6	1.5	21.4
I had trouble concentrating	6.5	7.2	5.1	18.8
Reminders caused me to have physical reactions, such as sweating, trouble breathing, nausea, or a pounding heart	4.3	4.3	1.4	10.0
I felt watchful and on guard	11.6	11.6	5.1	28.3

The Relationship between PTSD and Psychological Distress (GHQ)

Correlations were sought between scores on the Impact of Event Scale as an index of PTSD and a rating of general psychological distress, namely the General Health Questionnaire. A modest but statistically significant correlation was found between the IES and GHQ scores ® = .3, p = .003).

DISCUSSION

In this study of how war journalists deal with the stresses and physical dangers of their work, we found that approximately one in five journalists had "probable" PTSD while one in three showed evidence of psychological distress. Before discussing these results in greater detail, some comment on the sample composition is called for.

In completing this study, we were fortunate in having the cooperation of many of the world's large news organizations. War journalists as a group are few in number and given our access to them by the news organizations we feel confident that the sample collected is representative of the group as a whole. The fact that the journalists had been working in this area for an average of 15 years attests to their experience and also validates our impression that the sample represents "bona fide" war journalists as opposed to journalists who may cover a conflict or two before moving on to other aspects of journalism. Finally, by confining our selection process to names from reputable news organizations we avoided the potential pitfall of including adventurers who style themselves as war journalists and who are invariably to be found in areas of conflict.

With respect to the demographic data, a number of points stand out. First, war journalists are predominantly male, females accounting for only 20 percent of the sample. Second, journalists are frequently single, which is noteworthy given their average age of 40 years. Within the general population, the comparative data show that 80 percent of males and 90 percent of females are married [18]. The itinerant lifestyle, being called on to travel at short notice, prolonged periods away from home, the unpredictability of organizing a social life within the confines of home: all these factors are likely to affect the ability of journalists to form and sustain long-term relationships and could account for the relatively high numbers of single men and women in the sample. Finally, the average age of 40 years with a standard deviation of 6 years indicates that the majority of war journalists are either young or in early middle age. Only 9 journalists were over the age of 50 years, suggesting that the rigors of a job that combines frequent exposure to danger and intermittent physical hardship make it difficult to sustain this type of work throughout a career until retirement.

Concerning symptoms of PTSD, it was notable that scores were highest on the re-experiencing subscale. Every item was endorsed and almost 50 percent of the group were still experiencing symptoms such as flashbacks and intrusive, emotion laden reminders. Avoidance symptomatology was less in evidence which may, in part, be related to the fundamental nature of what journalists, in particular writers and producers, do. Journalists have to tell a story. They have to revisit what has just occurred, check the facts, interview survivors, recreate the event, and rely on recall in the process, all these actions the very antithesis of avoidance, denial, and a numbing of responsiveness. Journalists who have themselves been traumatized by war therefore find themselves in an unique situation, the very mechanism by which they practice their profession at odds with their psyche's attempt at dealing with overwhelming trauma. The tension set up between what the profession dictates and what their mind may unconsciously demand is likely to generate further intrapsychic tension and may account for the fact that one third of the group fell into the psychologically distressed category as defined by the GHQ. Drinking to excess may aggravate this process.

While it needs to be emphasized that a self-report questionnaire cannot by itself generate a psychiatric diagnosis, the correlation between the Impact of Event Scale and a valid diagnosis of PTSD is robust [19]. Thus, the figure of almost one in five war journalists having a diagnosis of PTSD is likely to be close to the mark. A point prevalence of approximately 20 percent for PTSD is well above the rate in the general population [20] and higher than that for traumatized police officers [21]. Comparison with the latter is, however, misleading. Police spend years in training, learning how to confront and deal with dangerous situations. Journalists do not. The "typical" war journalist is someone who is sent early in his or her career into a war zone without any preparation for the multitude of hazards that lie in wait.

Complicating the clinical picture is excessive alcohol intake in almost half the sample. War journalists often tend to use alcohol to relax and as an aid to sleep. A thriving black market ensures that liquor is always readily available during war. Hunkered down in a war zone, with nothing to do at night other than wait for morning, alcohol frequently becomes an antidote to boredom and tension. Cannabis has a similar function. However, the overwhelming majority of journalists made it clear they did not drink or smoke cannabis while working as such behavior was recognized as dangerous and likely to compromise not only their physical safety and that of others, but also the quality of what they were doing.

A final observation pertains to treatment. Some of the large news organizations have belatedly woken up to the fact that war journalists are at risk for disorders such as PTSD. While confidential psychiatric help is now offered to war journalists within these organizations, the same does not apply to freelance journalists. The latter also lack the logistical back-up provided by the large organizations to their journalists in the field. Thus, the freelancer is potentially at greater risk for developing more frequent and enduring psychological difficulties. PTSD is potentially a chronic disorder [22]. It also impacts adversely on quality of life [23] and is known to effect the lives of family members too [24]. For all these reasons, it behoves the news organizations to provide speedy access to therapy for their staff and any freelance journalists whom they may employ on a contract basis. It is equally important that no stigma be attached to those journalists requiring therapy. There is much machismo surrounding war, but this should not color the perceptions of the news bosses, general public, and indeed the war journalists themselves that those who voluntarily chose the battlefield as their workplace are immune from the disabling psychological consequences of violence.

REFERENCES

1. K. A. Lee, G. E. Vaillant, W. C. Torrey, and G. H. Elder, A 50 Year Prospective Study of the Psychological Sequelae of World War II Combat, *American Journal of Psychiatry, 152,* pp. 516-522, 1995.
2. J. Wolfe, D. J. Erickson, E. J. Sharkansky, D. W. King, and L. A. King, Course and Predictors of Posttraumatic Stress Disorder among Gulf War Veterans: A Prospective Analysis, *Journal of Consulting Clinical Psychology, 67,* pp. 520-528, 1999.
3. W. H. Sack, J. R. Seeley, and G. N. Clarke, Does PTSD Transcend Cultural Barriers? A Study from the Khmer Adolescent Refugee Project, *Journal of the American Academy of Child and Adolescent Psychiatry, 36,* pp. 49-54, 1997.
4. D. Michultka, E. B. Blanchard, and T. Kalous, Responses to Civilian War Experiences: Predictors of Psychological Functioning and Coping, *Journal of Trauma Stress, 11,* pp. 571-577, 1998.
5. X. Wang, L. Gao, N. Shinfuku, H. Zhang, C. Zhao, and Y. Shen, Longitudinal Study of Earthquake Related PTSD in a Randomly Selected Community Sample in North China, *American Journal of Psychiatry, 157,* pp. 1260-1266, 2000.
6. L. M. Najarian, A. K. Goenjian, D. Pelcovitz, F. Mandel, and B. Najarian, Relocation After a Disaster: Posttraumatic Stress Disorder in Armenia After the Earthquake, *Journal of the American Academy of Child and Adolescent Psychiatry, 35,* pp. 374-383, 1996.
7. J. R. Davidson, L. A. Tupler, and W. H. Wilson, A Study of Chronic Post-Traumatic Stress Disorder following Rape Trauma, *Journal of Psychiatric Research, 32,* pp. 301-309, 1998.
8. N. Breslau, H. D. Chilcoat, R. C. Kessler et al. Vulnerability to Assaultive Violence: Further Specification of the Sex Difference in Posttraumatic Stress Disorder, *Psychological Medicine, 29,* pp. 813-821, 1999.
9. S. Roth, W. Newman, D. Pelcovitz et al. Complex PTSD in Victims Exposed to Sexual and Physical Abuse: Results from the DSM-1V Field Trial for Posttraumatic Stress Disorder, *Journal of Traumatic Stress, 10,* pp. 539-555, 1997.
10. A. Feinstein, S. Hershkop, D. Ouchterlony et al., *Journal of Neuropsychiatry and Clinical Neurosciences,* 2001 (in press).
11. R. Capa, *Slightly Out of Focus,* Modern Library Edition, 1999.
12. M. Herr, *Despatches,* Vintage Books, New York, 1991.
13. A. Loyd, *My War Gone By, I Miss It So,* Atlantic Monthly Press, New York, 1999.
14. American Psychiatric Association, *The Diagnostic and Statistical Manual of Mental Disorders* (Fourth Edition), APA, Washington, 1994.
15. D. Weiss and C. R. Marmar, The Impact of Event Scale-Revised, in *Assessing Psychological Trauma and PTSD: A Practitioner's Handbook,* J. P. Wilson and T. M. Keane (eds.), Guilford Press, New York, pp. 399-428, 2000.
16. D. P. Goldberg and V. F. Hillier, A Scaled Version of the General Health Questionnaire, *Psychological Medicine, 9,* pp. 139-145, 1979.
17. S. Bondy, M. J. Ashley, J. T. Rehm, and G. Walsh, Low Risk Drinking Guidelines: The Scientific Evidence, *The Canadian Journal of Public Health, 90,* pp. 272-276, 1999.
18. Statistics Canada, 1996.
19. A. Feinstein and R. Dolan, Predictors of Psychiatric Morbidity following Physical Trauma, *Psychological Medicine, 21,* pp. 85-91, 1991.
20. R. C. Kessler, K. A. McGonagle, S. Zhao, C. B. Nelson, M. Hughes, S. Eshleman et al., Lifetime and 12 Month Prevalence of DSM-111-R Psychiatric Disorders in the United States, *Archives of General Psychiatry, 51,* pp. 8-19, 1994.

21. I. V. Carlier, R. D. Lamberts, and B. P. Gersons, Risk Factors for Posttraumatic Stress Symptomatology in Police Officers: A Prospective Analysis, *Journal of Nervous and Mental Disease, 185,* pp. 498-506, 1997.
22. D. F. Zatzick, C. R. Marmar, D. S. Weiss, W. S. Browner, T. J. Metzler, J. M. Golding et al., Posttraumatic Stress Disorder and Functioning and Quality of Life Outcomes in a Nationally Representative Sample of Male Vietnam Veterans, *American Journal of Psychiatry, 154,* pp. 1690-1695, 1997.
23. R. Hierhollzer, J. Munson, C. Peabody, and J. Rosenberg, Clinical Presentation of PTSD in World War II Combat Veterans, *Hospital Community Psychiatry, 43,* pp. 816-820, 1992.
24. R. A. Kulka, W. E. Shlenger, J. A. Fairbank et al., *Trauma and the War Generation. Report of Findings from the National Vietnam Veterans Readjustment Study,* Chapter X, Brunner-Mazel, New York, pp. 236-257, 1990.

28

The Bridge between Sorrow and Knowledge: Journalists and Traumatic Stress

Elana Newman

Journalists occupy a special role in society as a conduit between the afflicted and the public. They are responsible for informing the public about injustices and social problems, while upholding standards of impartiality and truth. This may place them in complex overlapping roles. Newsgatherers simultaneously may be rescuers, bystanders, witnesses, advocates, victims, and even, at times, victimizers of the people whose situations they depict. Although journalists *are* first responders, their mission is to mediate public awareness and response to humanitarian crises and natural disasters, not to intervene directly. Thus, newsgatherers confront unique moral, psychological, and ethical dilemmas, which are compounded when organizational support or training is lacking. This chapter reviews challenges and successes they face and suggests training, research and policy agendas to support media personnel covering human rights violations.

FACING ADVERSITY

Journalists are exposed to a wide range of human suffering. Studies of American journalists *not* in war zones suggest that most—86, 96, and 98 percent—journalists and/or photojournalists reported covering at least one story in which someone was killed or hurt, with most covering more than one such event [1-3]. Although such research has focused on exposure to death, journalists encounter other types of emotionally wrenching experiences [4]. One [3] left police reporting, "not because it was stressful, but because [he started] not to care very much" and exposure to death was minor compared to "remaining human" and not "breaking down yourself" when interviewing shocked and grief stricken individuals. These challenges may be magnified in cultures where human rights violations abound, such as when interviewing family members whose loved ones have disappeared or individuals in refugee camps. Like mental health workers, journalists may have difficulty sustaining focus without being challenged and changed by interacting with bereaved suffering individuals [5, 6]. Reporters may feel overwhelmed by this pain and/or detached from it through numbing all feelings, likely amplified among foreign correspondents covering war and atrocities [7].

Newsgatherers may also face grave personal risks [8]. In war-torn countries, or countries that limit freedom of the press, journalists often are in jeopardy. For example, in 2000, the Committee to Protect Journalists (CPJ) documented 24 journalists killed and 81 journalists imprisoned for practicing their profession [9]. Reporters Without Borders' (RWB) indicated that 85 journalists were imprisoned since the beginning of 2001. Further, 446 newsgatherers were arrested and 653 were attacked or threatened in 2000 [10]. These figures likely underestimate a significant problem for the profession. In addition, women journalists face sexual harassment [11]. Such violence is counter to Article 79 of the 1977 Protocol I to the Geneva Convention, which stipulates that journalists in areas of armed conflict shall be considered civilians and not be attacked.

COPING WITH ADVERSITY

Increasingly, journalists and photojournalists acknowledge the potential adverse effects of their work on physical, emotional, and family life [12-16]. Particularly harrowing assignments may cause long-standing symptoms of fear, numbing, guilt, nightmares, substance abuse, difficulty sleeping, intrusive recollections, irritability, mistrust of others, isolation, avoidance of trauma-related reminders, hypervigilance, and exaggerated startle responses [7, 17, 18]. Many of these symptoms are associated with post-traumatic adaptations, including Post Traumatic Stress Disorder (PTSD). They are observed in other first responders [19-22]. Understanding the extent of such post-traumatic symptomatology among journalists is critical. Thus far, five studies examined journalists' responses to traumatic events, including Feinstein's in this volume (chapter 27). In one study, 15 journalists who witnessed an execution demonstrated short-term, trauma-related anxiety responses including symptoms of dissociation [23]. More recently, 131 respondents from seven U.S. newspapers endorsed high rates of exposure and moderate levels of intrusive and avoidance symptomatology [1]. In two studies, one of photojournalists and one of journalists, trauma exposure was common in both groups, and rates of PTSD were approximately 6 percent and 4 percent respectively [2, 3]. This is roughly equivalent to the estimated lifetime prevalence of PTSD among American adult males (5 percent) as reported by the National Comorbidity Survey and just slightly lower than the average lifetime prevalence (7.8 percent) for American women [24].

Substance abuse and depression also may be reactions to newsgathering. Loyd depicts the depression and outlook changes from covering a war zone [25]. Future research needs to address other mental health reactions, and risks for such reactions, so that empirically-based policy can be determined.

ORGANIZATIONAL ISSUES

The organizational policies and culture of the news industry create conditions that can affect the mental health of journalists and their subjects. In an effort to document the truth, many news agencies have policies about the minimum number of non-anonymous sources necessary for a story to be published or aired. Often journalists must wait for brave informants, who risk their lives and those of their family, to supply both information and names. Journalists, thus, must conduct difficult cost-benefit analyses to balance the public's right to know with their duty to protect the vulnerable [26, 27]. These ethical and moral dilemmas can create distress, and memories can haunt newsgatherers long after stories are published.

Furthermore, a correspondent's appraisal of a situation and/or promises made to participants can be overturned by editors or changed when other agencies use the material. One American photojournalist discovered that in a video he created, although he had "masked" a gruesome image of a child's desecrated body, another network unmasked it, featuring not only the "new" image but taped the family's anguished response to it. He remains haunted by the knowledge that his video caused this family additional pain [2]. Certainly these circumstances are more likely to occur when human rights violations abound and cross-cultural issues are not understood, and require further documentation.

Freelancers, in particular, may feel extremely isolated and vulnerable. John Rodstead, reflecting on his experiences as a photojournalist in war zones, reports that freelancers, without organizational support (personal communication, 2000):

> face the increased pressure of the competitive environment set up for them by the market agencies (the best photo on the day gets the sale) . . . creating an attitude of one-upmanship. It also gets many photographers killed. . . . Some drink, some do drugs, and some you never see again due to burnout (and) breakdown.

Little is known about the range of policies designed to assist newsgatherers and their families when correspondents are hurt, killed, or imprisoned. For example, it is unknown how many news companies have kidnapping and evacuation insurance for newsgatherers in dangerous areas. While kidnapping insurance is controversial and may promote kidnapping, the advantages and disadvantages of these policies should be carefully assessed. Second, many news agencies require critical incident debriefing for correspondents who cover mass destruction or return from dangerous areas. Although the costs and benefits of formal debriefing are hotly debated (see chapter 32), those who participate voluntarily indicate high satisfaction [28]. Furthermore, most clinicians and journalists agree that fostering peer support and accessing professional help as needed is helpful to many [18, 29]. While this may not be available in war zones or impoverished countries, newsgatherers may find support in other ways (i.e., through e-mail). Many reported that they would feel much better if an editor simply took them aside to thank them for their dedicated, hard work.

The presence of international reporters can help local journalists, particularly in repressive or war-torn countries. Local journalists with foreign credentials have greater mobility and security than those working for local media outlets. Repressive governments reduce the presence of international media by expulsion or complicated permit laws.

TRAINING

Finding the angle to depict traumatic events may be difficult, especially in ways that are simultaneously truthful, sensitive to victims, and capable of mobilizing aid [15]. One journalist remarked, "The greater stressor for reporters, . . . is the desire to tell a story fully and truthfully . . . in the shrinking amount of space" [3]. Telling concise sensitive stories about trauma survivors can be fostered through training.

Through training programs, journalists can familiarize themselves with the needs and issues of victims, and the rapidly expanding scientific understanding of traumatic stress. Cote and Simpson provide specific information for journalists regarding trauma, journalists' responses, framing stories, and interviewing victims in a sensitive but effective manner. They suggest that journalists should introduce themselves, check to see if interviewing the victim will cause harm, and clarify what will be written or photographed before collecting information [30]. Also, journalists can provide victims a sense of control by allowing them to view the story before publishing and correct inaccuracies [31]. Many journalism programs currently prepare students to cover traumatic events, and initial evaluations suggest that students' knowledge is increased [32], although longitudinal studies need to determine if such training affects behavior in the field.

A study of American journalists revealed that few were warned that covering news could be deleterious to their mental health [2]. This is a tragic oversight, as they can be taught how to cope with vicarious traumatization, the transformation of beliefs and emotions from empathic listening to survivors [5, 6, 33]. Changing the workplace to support and foster resiliency is needed.

CONCLUSION

Journalists may potentially play a pivotal role in reconciliation and healing from trauma and human rights violations. As the UN Special Rapporteur on the Promotion and Protection of the Right to Freedom of Opinion and Expression, Organization for Security and Cooperation in Europe Representative on Freedom of the Media, and Organization of American States Special Rapporteur on Freedom of Expression stated:

> States are under an obligation to take adequate measures to end the climate of impunity and such measures should include devoting sufficient resources and attention to preventing attacks on journalists and others exercising their right to freedom of expression, investigating such attacks when they do occur, bringing those responsible to justice and compensating victims [34].

Conditions must be created to promote journalists' mental health, safety, and professional performance. Support for their work fosters favorable conditions for citizens and a sustainable democratic process in general. Table 1 lists relevant recommendations. Many initiatives related to them are already underway, but we must continue to ensure that those who enlighten us about human suffering do not themselves become victims.

Table 1. Recommendations

---

1. Document risks to journalists

2. Reduce risks to journalists
   a. Provide security measures for journalists working in dangerous areas
   b. Promote international policy to reduce risk
   c. Evaluate the efficacy of these interventions
   d. Monitor and protest the expulsion of foreign correspondents
   e. Advocate for journalists who are in danger

3. Prepare journalists for covering trauma
   a. Provide technical training on covering such events
   b. Provide trauma-specific skills
   c. Provide emotional training
   d. Evaluate the efficacy of these interventions

4. Change newspaper policies and/or governmental policies to help journalists do their work
   a. Examine insurance policies
   b. Examine evacuation policies
   c. Provide ongoing training to help newsgatherers decide difficult decisions
   d. Provide support to correspondents after difficult stories
   e. Foster collaboration between mental health professionals and news professionals regarding ways to help correspondents
   f. Evaluate the efficacy of these interventions
   g. Provide freelancers with peer support networks

5. Examine the physical and mental health effects upon journalists and conditions that reduce and increase risk

---

REFERENCES

1. R. A. Simpson and J. G. Boggs, An Exploratory Study of Traumatic Stress among Newspaper Journalists, *Journalism and Communication Monographs, 1,* pp. 1-26, 1999.
2. E. Newman, R. A. Simpson, and D. Handschuch, *Trauma Exposure and Post-Traumatic Stress Disorder among Photojournalists,* manuscript submitted for publication, 2001.
3. C. M. Pyevich, *The Relationship among Cognitive Schemata, Job-Related Traumatic Exposure, and PTSD in Journalists,* unpublished doctoral dissertation draft, University of Tulsa, Oklahoma, 2001.
4. E. Caldwell, Be a Person First When Covering Stories Involving Grief, *Editor and Publisher, 126,* pp. 50, 56-57, 1993.
5. Y. Danieli, Countertransference, Trauma, and Training, in *Countertransference in the Treatment of PTSD,* J. P. Wilson and J. D. Lindy (eds.), Guilford Press, New York, pp. 368-388, 1994.
6. Y. Danieli, Who Takes Care of the Caretakers?: The Emotional Consequences of Working with Children Traumatized by War and Communal Violence, in *Minefields in Their*

Hearts: The Mental Health of Children in War and Communal Violence, R. J. Apfel and B. Simon (eds.), Yale University Press, New Haven, pp. 189-205, 1996.

7. B. Gassaway, Making Sense of War: An Autobiographical Account of a Vietnam War Correspondent, *The Journal of Applied Behavioral Science, 25,* pp. 327-349, 1989.

8. S. Ricchiardi, A Ticket to Hell, *American Journalism Review, 21,* p. 32, 1999.

9. The Committee to Protect Journalists, *Attacks On The Press In 2000: A Worldwide Survey by the Committee to Protect Journalists,* Committee to Protect Journalists, New York, 2001.

10. Reporters without Borders (May 19, 2001). [On-line]. Available: http://www.rsf.fr/uk/home.html.

11. Women on the Frontlines: Do They Have a Different Agenda? *Media Report to Women, 25,* pp. 4-6, 1997.

12. C. Aiken, Reporters are Victims Too, *Neiman Reports, 50,* pp. 3, 30-32, 1996.

13. M. Fitzgerald, Stress and Burnout, *Editor and Publisher,* pp. 11, 38, 1989.

14. S. Ricchiardi, Confronting the Horror, *American Journalism Review, 24,* p. 34, 1999.

15. F. Ochberg, A Primer on Covering Victims, *Neiman Reports, 50,* pp. 21-26, 1996.

16. M. I. Pinsky, Covering the Crimes: What a Steady Diet of Death and Depravity Can Do to a Reporter, *Columbia Journalism Review, 31,* pp. 5, 28, 1993.

17. C. Harvey, The High-Stress Police Beat, *American Journalism Review, 17*:6, pp. 28-33, 1995.

18. Dealing with the Trauma of Covering War, *Neiman Reports, 53*:2, p. 24, 1999.

19. T. Harvey-Lintz and R. Tidwell, Effects of the 1992 Los Angeles Civil Unrest: Post-traumatic Stress Disorder Symptomatology among Law Enforcement Officers, *Social Science Journal, 34,* pp. 171-183, 1997.

20. W. Corneil, R. Beaton, S. Murphy, C. Johnson, and K. Pike, Exposure to Traumatic Incidents and Prevalence of Posttraumatic Stress Symptomatology in Urban Firefighters in Two Countries, *Journal of Occupational Health Psychology, 4,* pp. 131-141, 1999.

21. B. Smith, I. Agger, Y. Danieli, and L. Weisaeth, Health Activities across Traumatized Populations: Emotional Responses of International Humanitarian Aid Workers: The Contribution of Non-Governmental Organizations, in *International Responses to Traumatic Stress: Humanitarian, Human Rights, Justice, Peace and Development Contributions, Collaborative Actions and Future Initiatives,* Y. Danieli, N. S. Rodley, and L. Weisaeth (eds.), Baywood, Amityville, New York, pp. 397-442, 1996.

22. B. T. Litz, L. A. King, D. W. King, S. M. Orsillo, and M. J. Friedman, Warriors as Peacekeepers: Features of the Somalia Experience and PTSD, *Journal of Consulting and Clinical Psychology, 65,* pp. 1001-1010, 1997.

23. A. Freinkel, C. Koopman, and D. Spiegel, Dissociative Symptoms in Media Eyewitnesses of an Execution, *American Journal of Psychiatry, 151,* pp. 1335-1339, 1994.

24. R. C. Kessler, A. Sonnega, E. Bromet, M. Hughes, and C. B. Nelson, Posttraumatic Stress Disorder in the National Comorbidity Survey, *Archives of General Psychiatry, 52,* pp. 1048-1060, 1995.

25. A. Loyd, *My War Gone By, I Miss It So,* Atlantic Monthly Press, New York, 1999.

26. J. E. Brown, News Photographs and the Pornography of Grief, *Journal of Mass Media Ethics, 2,* pp. 75-81, 1987.

27. R. P. Clark, Covering Crime: Journalists Face Difficult Choices, *RTNDA Communicator,* pp. 14-15, December 1987.

28. J. I. Bisson, A. C. McFarlane, and S. Rose, Psychological Debriefing, in *Effective Treatments for PTSD: Practice Guidelines from the International Society for Traumatic Stress Studies,* E. B. Foa, T. M. Keane, and M. J. Friedman (eds.), Guilford Press, New York, pp. 317-319, 2000.

29. J. Zibluk, Remembering Jonesboro: "Critical" to Treat Stress, Trauma, *News Photographer, 54,* p. 35, 1999.
30. W. Cote and R. Simpson, *Covering Violence: A Guide to Ethical Reporting about Victims and Trauma,* Columbia University Press, New York, 2000.
31. L. Zalin, *Columns, 21,* pp. 22-25, 2001.
32. L. J. Mills, R. Simpson, E. Newman, P. Reynolds-Ablacas, M. Scherer, J. Maxson, and J. Boggs, *Examining the Effectiveness of a Trauma Training Program for Journalists,* paper presented to Annual Convention of the International Society for Traumatic Stress Studies, Miami, Florida, 1999.
33. L. A. Pearlman and K. W. Saakvitne, *Trauma and the Therapist: Countertransference and Vicarious Traumatization in Psychotherapy with Incest Survivors,* Norton, New York, 1995.
34. A. Hussain, F. Duve, and S. Canton (December 1, 2000), United Nations Press Release: *International Mechanisms for Promoting Freedom of Expression Condemn Use of Various Threats to Silence Journalists* [On-line]. Available: http://www.unhchr.ch/huricane/huricane.nsf/newsroom.

29

Centurion: Shielding Journalists and Aid Workers

Bo Mills, Paul Rees, and Gordon J. Turnbull

PREPARING FOR THE FRONT LINE

Centurion recently received the following message:

> My name is Yannis Behrakis and I'm a Reuters photographer based in Athens. I did the first course of Reuters journalists a few years ago with my friend Kurt Schork. . . . Kurt was killed in an ambush in the jungle of Sierra Leone on May 24, 2000 along with APTN cameraman Miguel Gil Moreno. It was me, Kurt, Miguel, and Reuters TV cameraman Mark Chisholm, and 8 Sierra Leone soldiers traveling in two civilian vehicles in no-man's land some 100-km northeast of Freetown when we were ambushed by RUF rebels . . . Kurt, Miguel, and the 8 soldiers died in the 30 or more minutes of gun battle. Only me and Mark (injured) survived. I hid for more than three hours in the jungle using all my survival skills, but one of the things I remembered well when I started crawling away from the ambush was a day in a forest in England. When walking through a path, one of us triggered a booby trap. I also remembered the small anti-personnel mines (in the demonstration). Then I decided to move through the most difficult path to avoid possible traps, thinking that if there were traps they would be placed on a path used by humans . . . it was a good day on the course and a horrific day in the jungle. Thanks for that day. Cheers Yannis

What had started out as a "normal" day for four newsgatherers ended in a terrible tragedy. Kurt Schork, an experienced reporter, and Miguel Gil Moreno, an award-winning cameraman, were ambushed and murdered in a hail of gunfire by rebel soldiers in the jungle of Sierra Leone, a country in the midst of a vicious civil war where no one was quite sure where the front line began. The news of Kurt and Miguel's deaths sent shock waves through news corridors everywhere, and questions about whether the tragedy could have been avoided. In reality, military people would agree that no one is supposed to survive such an ambush, but when both Yannis and Mark credited their survival to training they had received at the instigation of their agencies in the days leading up to their assignment, there was renewed interest in Hostile Environments Training, and in preparing people, both physically and mentally, for dangerous work.

WHAT IS A HOSTILE ENVIRONMENT?

A hostile environment can be anywhere where there is a threat to personal safety or security, not just war zones or countries like Sierra Leone in the midst of civil strife. Less obvious examples are natural disasters where the dangers are not from weapons and hostile forces but lack of clean water and the increased risk of contracting diseases. Hot and cold climates are also hostile environments. Lack of attention and planning given to proper clothing and equipment for filming in cold climates carries with it the risk of avoidable injury, for example from frostbite or exposure. Likewise, in hot climates, dehydration or heat exhaustion may quickly turn a healthy camera-man into a casualty, at the same time a burden to the rest of the crew. In some countries, just looking different invites danger. The course teaches important personal security measures, including dressing down for assignments in countries where poverty and crime go hand in hand. The training also addresses difficulties faced when working in countries with unfriendly regimes or religious fanaticism. In such countries a simple gesture can be misinterpreted as a lack of respect for local customs and result in illegal detention or worse. In many cases, camera crews and other observers are not welcome at all.

Throughout the week, the course includes the practicalities of working on the ground in volatile areas. Filming demonstrations has often resulted in some of the worst injuries to camera crews. When a crowd becomes angry it often doesn't want its activities to be recorded, for fear of prosecution. The camera crew often becomes the target of its hatred. The training teaches how to identify mob danger signs, and shows the tactics employed by both rioters and the security forces. For a camera crew it's important not to get caught in the middle, or misinterpreted by one side as being on the other side.

Throughout the course the emphasis is on heightening **awareness** (to see the hidden dangers), and **risk assessment** (using awareness to make sound judgments to minimize risks to safety). Subjects covered in the Hostile Environments course are: *risk assessment; detection of dangerous items; awareness trail; emergency clothing and equipment; hostage abduction and enduring captivity; personal security and personal protective equipment; emergency shelters; mines and booby traps; Post Traumatic Stress Disorder; urban awareness and building security; weapons and ballistics awareness; observation; cold weather injuries; vehicle security; emergency navigation; hot climates and diseases; emergency field first aid; emergency stretchers and carries; civil disturbances; working with helicopters/light aircraft; vehicle checkpoints/border crossings, and outdoor practicals.*

THE RACE TO GET THE NEWS AND ETHICAL REPORTING

Ironically, many of the problems faced by journalists in the field may be a result of the unquestionable influence the media have in shaping public opinion. Camera teams are no longer seen as impartial observers of a country's troubles. Today, opposing sides of a conflict, no matter how unworldly, understand all too well the benefit of media attention for their chosen cause as well as its potentially negative effects. While one faction may want to show the world atrocities committed against its people, the opposing side will not want the same footage shown if they are the accused perpetrators.

The speed at which news is gathered also generates problems. The advantage of this immediacy is that journalistic teams bring to the world's attention events as they are unfolding. The disadvantage is that journalists no longer have time to "acclimatize" to the area, and the changing dangers they face. They have no time to find out which roads are safe, or where the shifting front line begins and ends *that day*. There is scant time to build relationships or to gather local intelligence. While the news has become faster and slicker, the risks faced by those who gather it gain momentum at the same pace. In the last two years 149 journalists were killed in the course of their job.

On the psychological side there is another danger. Since the American Civil War correspondents have been able to reach the epicenters of modern conflicts, sending back actual images of conflict from the front line. Today, they can transmit these images in real time into the homes of the general public who find themselves transported to the raw edge of conflict, viewing the images of mass global suffering. The immediacy and accessibility of news highlights the plight of millions of people every day. But these images of suffering can also traumatize a wider audience. Often the only people to have contact with the victims of their reports are the newsgatherers themselves. This puts them in a unique position: they must tell the story but at the same time remain wary of creating further trauma for either the victims or the viewers through imprudent and sensationalized reporting. By learning the effects of trauma on the mind they can help limit the impact of trauma on themselves and others [1].

The aim of Hostile Environments Training is to counter the problem of journalists hitting the ground running, and minimize the risks they face by giving them a better understanding of the dangers *before* they leave home. The Centurion course covers not only the everyday practicalities of *physical* survival in hostile environments, but also *psychological* survival, not only for journalists and aid workers themselves, but anyone else they encounter in the course of their work [1].

SHIELDING THE JOURNALISTS AND AID WORKERS

Journalism and aid work are solitary professions. In journalism, small teams are deployed to one news event one week, and then often straight on to the next the following week without returning to base. In the past, little consideration has been given to the psychological effects involved in covering traumatic news stories. An important part of the week's training is the subject of *traumatic stress reactions,* including Post Traumatic Stress Disorder (PTSD), depression, and other anxiety states. A wide range of personally-threatening situations are discussed, from surviving a hostage-taking to coping at the scene of large scale disasters. The mental health professionals taking part in the hostile environments training emphasize practical, commonsense, and *"here and now"* coping with the impact of trauma rather than psychoanalytic interpretations. The audiences tend to be robust and rugged characters, many of whom have been exposed to trauma repetitively. The subjects covered are therefore geared to topics such as stress management, impact of trauma on partners and families, and surviving hostage situations.

PTSD THROUGH HISTORY

Observers of history have always referred to PTSD [2, 3]. Arguably, the First World War represented the first major, global conflict to provide psychiatrists with convincing evidence of the damaging effects of warfare on the mind. *"Shell shock"* was also observed first hand by an unprecedented number of war correspondents. Even though they could see what was happening, lessons learned about combat stress reactions were quickly buried, only to be rediscovered during the Second World War. The observations of military psychiatrists [4] made in the early 1920s had to wait until WWII to be published. War correspondents contributed to keeping the pressure for the world to acknowledge the existence of psychological trauma throughout the Korean and Vietnam conflicts, until PTSD was finally recognized in the third edition of the psychiatric classification manual, DSM III [5].

STRESS

Stress should be seen as potentially adaptive. It encourages survival, inventiveness, and vigilance. However, extreme stress causes a substantial imbalance between the demands of the emergency and the personal resources required to cope with them. Short-term imbalance can be tolerated but longer-term disequilibrium leads to stress reactions and the evolution of the symptoms of strain. The course covers the broad range of principles in the primary **prevention** of stress, early **recognition** of stress symptoms (cognitive, behavioral, physical, or emotional), and **alleviation** of stress reactions. They include: trying to rest more and make contact with friends; maintaining a normal schedule and a reasonable level of activity; eating well-balanced meals even if not hungry; expressing feelings with immediacy and talking to others; finding a confidante if feelings are intense and prolonged; not becoming addicted to destructive ways of seeking endorphins such as alcohol, nicotine, caffeine or chocolate, and trying to keep a sense of humor if at all possible.

STOICISM

Calm and phlegmatic behavior in the face of adversity is appealing and has been an integral component of the "psychological armor" for people working in the field. Pat Barker writes eloquently about stoicism in her book "Regeneration" [6]:

> "I'm glad you're not going back." Without warning, Prior again saw the shovel, the sack, the scattered lime. The eyeball lay in the palm of his hand. "Yes," he said. She would never know, because he would never tell her. Somehow if she'd known the worst parts, she couldn't have gone on being a haven for him. He was groping for an idea that he couldn't grasp. Men said they didn't tell their women about France because they didn't want to worry them. But it was more than that.

He needed her ignorance to hide in. Yet, at the same time, he wanted to know and be known as deeply as possible. And the two desires were irreconcilable.

THE KEY ROLE OF NEWSGATHERERS IN CHANGING THE "DENIAL CULTURE"

In order to be able to survive, psychological defenses that involve denial are more frequently found in newsgatherers and aid workers and certain other sections of the community such as emergency service workers, police officers, the military, and doctors and nurses, where exposure to victims of trauma is inevitable as part of the job. The sight of devastation, suffering, or destruction is a stark reminder of the reality of their own vulnerability, which needs to be denied consistently to permit completion of the task. There is a profound difference between "healthy" and "unhealthy" denial. *Healthy* denial is helpful and adaptive when used appropriately. For example, the cameraman can look at an image of devastation through his lens without being affected at the time. The lens acts as a barrier and a vehicle that facilitates denial. *Unhealthy* denial eventually causes distortions of thinking, such as viewing victims as responsible for their own misfortune or viewing suffering as an expression of underlying weakness. Alcohol and illicit drugs are known to increase the capacity to deny.

CRITICAL INCIDENTS

Newsgatherers, emergency, rescue, relief and medical workers may become **secondary** victims of disasters [7]. They are affected by the sheer magnitude of the incident, their connection with survivors and the dead, and translation of the meaning of the disaster into personal thoughts of vulnerability, mortality, and loss of control. Critical incidents that challenge newsgatherers include: life threat; colleague injured/ killed "in the line of duty"; colleague committing suicide; mass disasters; children injured or killed; use of firearms; situations of extreme strain/long duration/high intensity; extreme sensory impressions; symbolic meaning of objects (such as children's toys in air crashes), and any other event that has an unusually powerful impact on participants. Psychological support provided by **outside** helpers is not always useful in the immediate aftermath. Natural human healing factors, such as coming to terms with exposure to trauma through discussion with friendly colleagues, or using the coded language of *gallows* humor are helpful and may be disrupted by intrusions from the outside.

ACUTE STRESS REACTIONS

Acute Stress Reactions (ASR) [8] following exposure to trauma are normal, common, usually self-limiting, and affect more than 50 percent of those exposed to trauma. They are adaptive psychobiological processes that are implicated in the assimilation of new information with an intense survival emphasis. ASRs contain elements of post-traumatic stress, depression, grief, anger, and dissociation. They follow exposure to intense threats to life and limb. Newsgatherers and aid workers are characteristically resilient to adversity. However, some events will overwhelm even the most robust of psychological defenses. Adrenal gland-modulated "*fight or flight*" responses create a state of "*high alert*" designed to optimize the chances of survival. It works well because less than half of ASRs progress to PTSD. An understanding of ASR not only helps journalists themselves, but also enables them to understand the mental conditioning of traumatized people whom they will inevitably meet in the course of their work.

CRITICAL INCIDENT STRESS MANAGEMENT

Survivors often need support to carry them through their exposure to traumatic situations. Critical Incident Stress Management (CISM) includes pre-exposure stress inoculation training, immediate and informal post-exposure supports, and longer-term organizational resources, creating a complete safety net [9, 10]. Its key elements are:

Pre-incident education: giving accurate information to help carry out tasks, desensitizing to the sight of dead bodies, educating about stress reactions, and practical steps needed to manage them. Hostile Environment Training is a good first step in this process;

On-scene support: assisting distressed primary victims or secondary victims such as rescuers and newsgatherers at the scene of critical incidents;

Defusing: brief group meetings led by peer debriefers shortly after the trauma;

Demobilization: in the case of large scale, mass casualty incidents between shifts;

Debriefing: by mental health professionals and trained peers, allowing trauma victims to feel accepted, be given a chance to articulate what happened, "normalize" their reactions; hear different perspectives, and feel that they are being cared for [10].

POST TRAUMATIC STRESS SYNDROMES

Failure to process ASRs leads to PTSD, depression, anxiety states, and substance abuse. Chronic reactions tend to occur in individuals who have been helpless to respond to the trauma. Newsgatherers, aid workers, and peacekeepers are often unable to respond to traumatic situations instinctually and feel paralyzed and powerless. PTSD is a long-term reaction to the impact of unresolved traumatic exposure. (See chapters 24 and 27 for a detailed description of reactions to traumatic stress.) PTSD can merge months or years after traumatic exposure, known as "*delayed-onset PTSD*." Chronic PTSD affects personal relationships, causing *loss of intimacy; breakdown in communications; decreased or increased sexual activity; detachment; increased anger and irritability; fears of abandonment, and loss of interest in shared activities* [11].

HOSTAGES

The Hostile Environments Course highlights fear as being fundamentally important for survival. At one point delegates are kidnapped and taken hostage. This is increasingly important as newsgatherers and aid workers become targeted, particularly in third world countries. Handling of hostages involves physical restraint, sensory deprivation, interrogation, brainwashing, verbal abuse and humiliation, threats of injury and death, and physical abuse or torture. Training demonstrates how bodies and minds involuntarily react to captivity and how best to cope with these reactions. Delegates discover how quickly freedom can be snatched away from them, and how touch, smell and hearing are heightened when vision is denied. On a practical level, the exercise also teaches valuable lessons on how to differentiate between "amateur" and "professional" captors to measure the degree of threat to life, and how best to react to captivity to survive. The stages of psychological adaptation to captivity are:

Panic: (in the first few minutes); because hostage situations are not anticipated and are perceived as life-threatening, the abrupt transition makes it impossible to assimilate the new situation instantly;

Disbelief: (first few hours); "We'll be rescued shortly, this can't be happening;"

Hypervigilance: (first few days); becoming wary and alert to smallest details;

Resistance/Compliance: (after the first few weeks); hostage behavior very variable;

Depression: (after the first few months); loss of freedom, isolation, cruel treatment, and lack of contact with the outside world cause depression and passivity in the hardiest;

Gradual acceptance: (after months or years); final stages of adaptation are reached.

The course also discusses ways to retain some degree of control over life in captivity and use the time constructively including: *maintaining composure and controlling initial shock as soon as possible; keeping a low-key and unprovocative profile; gaining recognition as a dignified human being rather than an object; maintaining some degree of control over the environment, however small and insignificant it might seem; eating and exercising as much as possible to reduce stress and maintain health; keeping an active mind; looking positively into the future, and being determined to survive.* The *Stockholm Syndrome* is a relationship that may develop between captor and hostage. Hostages see captors as protectors and government, police and family as jeopardizing their safety. "*Stockholming*" involves regression to a childlike state of dependency and is an adaptive response to helplessness in conditions of great danger, designed to enhance survival. Journalists need to allow enough time and space for adequate "*re-entry*" following the release of hostages before attempting in-depth interviews [12]. The results will be much more objective and authentic.

CONCLUSIONS

The Hostile Environments Training prepares journalists and aid workers both physically and mentally for dangerous work. There is no easy way to measure its success. One way to evaluate the training is to discover how useful it has been in coping with subsequent exposure to trauma. Positive feedback about its effectiveness in saving lives is gratifying but the irony is that to find out that it works usually means someone, somewhere has had a horrendous experience. Preparing newsgatherers and aid workers in advance for what they may encounter in volatile regions leads to a greater awareness of the dangers they face, and greater confidence when attempting to cope when practical difficulties and life-threatening events arise. Preparing people emotionally as well can lead to enhanced emotional literacy that improves the quality of balanced reporting. The Hostile Environments course is seen by many organizations as an investment in healthier people and safer reporting that reflects back to the public the way the world really is, which is the essence of quality journalism.

REFERENCES

1. W. Cote and R. Simpson, *Covering Violence: A Guide to Ethical Reporting About Victims and Trauma*, Columbia University Press, New York, 2000.
2. J. Shay, *Achilles in Viet Nam: Combat Trauma and the Undoing of Character*, Atheneum, New York, 1994.
3. W. Shakespeare, *The First Part of King Henry the Fourth*, Act 2, Scene 3, lines 42-69, 1598.
4. A. Kardiner, *The Traumatic Neuroses of War*, P. B. Hoeber, New York, 1941.
5. American Psychiatric Association, *Diagnostic and Statistical Manual of Mental Disorders* (3rd Edition), APA, Washington, D.C., 1980.
6. P. Barker, *Regeneration* Penguin, London, 1992.
7. C. R. Figley, *Trauma and Its Wake*, Brunner/Mazel, New York, 1985.
8. World Health Organisation, *The International Classification of Mental and Behavioural Disorders, International Classification of Diseases* (10th Edition) (ICD-10), WHO, Geneva, 1992.
9. J. T. Mitchell, When Disaster Strikes: The Critical Incident Stress Debriefing, *Journal of Emergency Medical Services, 8*, pp. 36-39, 1983.
10. A. Dyregrov, *Proceedings of the Fifth World Congress on Stress, Trauma and Coping in the Emergency Services Professions*, Baltimore, April 1999.
11. Y. Danieli, The Treatment and Prevention of Long-Term Effects and Intergenerational Transmission of Victimization: A Lesson from Holocaust Survivors and Their Children, in *Trauma and Its Wake*, C. R. Figley (ed.), Brunner/Mazel, New York, pp. 295-313, 1985.
12. G. J. Turnbull, Debriefing of Released British Hostages from Lebanon, *Clinical Quarterly of the National Center for PTSD, 1*:4, pp. 21-22, 1994.

30

The Forgotten Tribe

Newscoverage Unlimited:
How an International Tragedy Spurred
an Initiative to Help Newspeople
Who Must Cover Grisly Stories

Robert M. Frank

During the first week of September 1998, the telephone rang while I was working on my computer in my basement, catching up on some very overdue and tedious bookkeeping.

The call was from Captain Mike Short, who works for the operational headquarters of Canada's Air Force. I had served as an Air Force Reserve public affairs officer for many years. Swissair 111 had crashed, September 2, into the ocean while attempting an emergency landing in Halifax, Nova Scotia. Newspeople from around the world were converging on the scene and my help was needed. Fast.

Like many others, I had seen the initial news reports of the crash and had reacted with sadness and compassion, but also with the detachment of an observer who is not in a position to do anything about it. Now I was involved, learning every known fact and rumor about the crash. I flew to Halifax to work at the Canadian Forces desk at the media operations center.

The crash of a flight which originated in New York City and was bound for Switzerland had drawn hundreds of newspeople from all over the United States, Canada, and Europe. Just telling who was who was a challenge amid the chaos. My arrival coincided with the news conference that revealed the trajectory of the doomed aircraft.

The cavernous news conference room in the Halifax Convention Centre overflowed. I headed to the adjacent media operations center where, on a video monitor, I watched the news conference unfold. As experts for the first time traced the final flight path, a local disaster worker standing beside me exclaimed: "Ohmigod. It went right over my house!"

The media operations center was an equally cavernous chamber the size of a large ballroom. It served as a joint operations center that let spokespeople for the

various responding agencies, including the military, police, transportation authorities, and relief organizations, quickly compare notes.

A very intense period ensued, with few opportunities to pause, think, and feel.
The frenzy of media activity simply leaves little time to consider the human cost. One
gets caught up in the pace. Indeed, after a few days I had to stop and remind myself
that this was a terrible tragedy. I believed that it was essential to stay centered and not
lose sight of why we were there. The only occasions when I had enough time to reflect
were on the drive to and from my room at the Air Force base at Shearwater, where I
would catch a couple of hours of sleep each night. It was across the flight line from the
hangers where Sea King helicopters continually shuttled whatever the cruel sea had
yielded to Navy divers.

At the end of the first week of the recovery operation, the Canadian military,
for the first time, held a news conference during a major operation to acknowledge
publicly the effects of traumatic stress. The director of the Atlantic Region military
operational mental health center outlined the comprehensive measures that had been
implemented to sound out every participant in the recovery operation and to provide
help to any who needed it.

During the news conference, a sergeant from the province of Newfoundland
spoke up: "You folks in the news media . . ." he began forcefully, prompting the
public affairs staff in the audience needlessly to brace themselves for whatever
comments might ensue, ". . . are the forgotten tribe."

He went on to observe, accurately, that an extensive system had been implemented to ensure that every supervisor offered assistance to every person exposed to
the grisly disaster response: military, civilian, police, volunteers. Everyone, that is,
except for members of the news media—and some newspeople had indeed seen too
much. Too ugly. Too fast.

Soon afterward, a toll-free telephone help line was made available to newsgatherers. We posted a terse news release:

FOR IMMEDIATE RELEASE September 10, 1998

Toll free line available for personal assistance

HALIFAX, N.S.—Any media who have been involved in any aspect of the
Swissair Flight 111 tragedy can call toll free 1-877-xxx-xxxx starting Friday,
September 11 at 8 A.M. if they require personal assistance in dealing with this
tragedy.

I don't know how many people availed themselves of this service; that wasn't
my preoccupation at the time. It was a half-measure hastily cobbled together for
the noblest of reasons.

Although the media operations center was off limits to newspeople, we frequently granted individual interviews in one of the smaller rooms on the opposite side
of the corridor. Occasionally, during rare lulls in the action, the dénouement of a
one-on-one interview with a reporter would turn into a private conversation between
two people.

During some of those conversations, I recognized what seemed to be symptoms of traumatic stress. Occasionally I mentioned this. Afterward I wrote:

> The debriefing is unfortunately the exception rather than the rule. Most media (remember the photogs and crew are there too, not just the reporters) are internalizing, maintaining a semblance of normalcy and suppressing emotions that still lurk, just below the surface. Some are not conscious or semi-conscious of this until I point it out. It is fascinating to see the change in demeanor on their faces as their stories pour out. Human beings are not machines. We have emotions, and they are important to us.

Some recounted tales of horror going as far back as the Vietnam War. I had the impression that some of those tales had never before been spoken aloud.

Then back to the action. There was simply too much to do other than note it—and press on.

What I observed, though, was that a group of reporters from the Canadian Broadcasting Corporation (CBC) seemed to fare best. Every night they would get together for about an hour and let off steam over a beer. They said that they were amazed to discover that they were experiencing the same reactions as everyone else, but it was not affecting their ability to cover the story well. And the next morning they were able to go out again to do their work.

Still, these were isolated conversations. I did not know at the time that the CBC reporters' spontaneous self-help and mutual support would become a model for me. Rather, I put the entire subject out of my mind. I only pieced the various bits together on the plane home, when I was able to sift through my recollections and conclude that trauma had been the common thread, and that no one was there to help the newspeople afterward.

What is more, stoic cultures like the newsroom add to their isolation, as does the fear of career consequences. Many newspeople believe, often with good reason, that they will lose their job or that their editor will pull them off important projects if they admit that covering a story has affected them. So they mask the effect that their news coverage has had on them. Most try to return to a semblance of normalcy as quickly as they are able, but the after-effects can persist or reappear long afterward out of the blue. Others cope, but risk suffering burnout later.

Peering out the aircraft window as Halifax and the Atlantic Ocean receded from view, I realized that unless something were done, newspeople would continue to suffer in silence. I envisioned an organization that would promote this self-help and involve clinical experts where mutual support is not enough.

However, I remained skeptical. Perhaps I had simply imagined that newspeople in Halifax were experiencing some degree of traumatic stress. So, in 1999, I visited Denver in the aftermath of the Columbine shooting tragedy. I left convinced that covering grisly stories did indeed affect newsgatherers; that the ensuing anger, blame, or numbing that accompany trauma can undermine the quality of reporting. In other cases, newspeople simply leave the craft, depriving the public of their well-honed skills. Worst, it sours many to the view that reporting serves the public interest.

Newspeople themselves need to be reminded that their work is both good and essential, even when they must deliver bad news that we would rather not hear.

Searching further, through much networking, I found that I was not alone. As a result, a number of pioneers in the United States, Canada, the United Kingdom, and Australia have helped to found *Newscoverage Unlimited* (www.newscoverage.org). Its mission is to help newspeople who experience trauma during the course of their work.

The initiative is founded on the self-help and mutual support inspired by those CBC reporters in Halifax. This will involve recruiting a volunteer team of current and former newspeople who would like to help their colleagues. Many probably already do so spontaneously: the person in the newsroom to whom one naturally turns. Newscoverage Unlimited will simply organize them; train them how to help someone who has seen too much, too fast or too ugly, and how to refer those who need expert help to appropriate professionals.

Some large news organizations already have implemented excellent programs to help their staff. Newscoverage Unlimited will complement those efforts, particularly in terms of helping those who are reluctant to express their own vulnerabilities to their employer. It will also help the majority of newspeople who don't have these programs at their disposal, as well as the growing proportion of freelancers who have no employer to turn to for support.

The aim is to pool expertise on newsgathering and trauma, share that knowledge and help those who need it.

The timing could not be more appropriate. Chapters 27 by Anthony Feinstein and 28 by Elana Newman report findings of studies on how trauma affects newspeople. Feinstein has discovered that more than a third of war correspondents suffer from Post Traumatic Stress Disorder. In terms of sheer numbers, an even greater need lurks for those who cover daily fare at home: In November 2000, Elana Newman reported at the annual conference of the International Society for Traumatic Stress Studies that data from a survey of hundreds of American news photographers showed that the most frequently reported trauma-producing incident is the automobile crash. For as long as most people can remember, newspeople were simply expected to tough it out. No one expresses that better than Chris Cramer (chapter 26).

In a few newsrooms, well-meaning help is imposed. Sometimes this is welcomed. Other times it is resented.

Ultimately, I hope, newspeople themselves will drive demand, uninhibited about asking for help when they need it, from their employer or from a third party.

Trauma will shed its stigma in the newsroom once newspeople recognize that it is a normal reaction to horrific events that does not reflect flawed or weak character, poor judgment or foolishness.

After the Swissair 111 recovery operation, we concluded that it was impossible to term our efforts "a success." How could anything associated with such a tragedy be considered a success? Instead "we did good"—as much good as anyone can muster in such terrible circumstances.

If newspeople themselves decide that Newscoverage Unlimited will truly help colleagues who experience trauma during the course of their work, it too cannot help but do good.

Newspeople need to hear, from each other and from their readers, listeners and viewers: " We know that it is not easy to witness evil or misfortune, and we are sorry if this reporting has become painful for you. Thanks for illuminating an otherwise dark world for us. We hope that you find the courage to go on and report another day."

31

Issues of Security in the United Nations System

Diana Russler and Shirley N. Brownell

However you look at staff security—whether at UN duty stations, in peace-keeping missions, or in the operations of non-governmental humanitarian agencies—everything boils down to resources; in any language, money. You need money to hire staff; to strengthen the security apparatus at headquarters and in the field; to train staff as to their personal responsibility for security; to provide stress management counseling; and to purchase proper equipment, including vehicles and communications gear. Without the money for each of these elements, you cannot have an effective security management system to protect those who put their lives on the line to help others.

There is absolutely no reason why a UN staff member should die in the field doing the Organization's work. Staff in the field must, after all, be taken care of, not taken advantage of. And, yet, the UN has not fared very well as a system in preventing the tragic deaths of 196 of its staff in the field. One explanation given is that, with so many priorities confronting the UN, security has, until very recently, been considered a luxury. Because it was not seen as part of the price of doing business, funding for staff security was never included in budgets. As proof, currently the UN system's annual spending rate on security is $21 per staff member.

In statement after statement by senior United Nations officials, the request for increased or expanded resources to address escalating security problems is a constant. Secretary-General Kofi Annan wrote, in a recent report to the General Assembly on the safety and security of United Nations personnel (A/55/494):

> There can be no question that good security requires adequate and predictable funding. There should be nothing discretionary about the financing of staff security: it is neither a luxury nor a perk. It is something we owe those who are willing to serve humanity under the most challenging of circumstances.

The report outlined measures aimed at improving staff security, because the Secretary-General said that UN personnel could no longer be required to carry out functions in dangerous environments, at great personal risk, without the minimum level of training, stress counseling, and equipment being provided to them. He called for resources to strengthen the Office of the United Nations Security Coordinator

(UNSECOORD), including the appointment of a full-time Security Coordinator; for more field security officers; for security training and stress-management counseling for staff, and for urgent communications and other critical equipment.

THE UN SECURITY MANAGEMENT SYSTEM

The UN security management system dates back to 1980 when the Administrative Committee on Coordination (ACC), consisting of all executive heads of agencies, programs, and funds, and chaired by the Secretary-General, decided that there should be an integrated approach to managing the security of UN system staff. At that time, staff were evacuated at the slightest hint of trouble in a country, and the ACC wanted to make sure that organizations would not refuse to evacuate their staff by claiming that they lacked the funds. The system, it was agreed, would be managed from a neutral office whose only interest was staff safety and security.

The purpose of UNSECOORD is to ensure that staff working in the field can carry out their assignments safely, without undue risks for their lives. Its role is to make sure that security policies are in place; that there is adherence to, and compliance with, those policies; and that there is training and counseling for staff. The additional staff now being recruited will allow UNSECOORD to start a program of compliance inspections at UN duty stations located in 150 countries, for which the Office has direct security responsibility. As such, it will no longer have to take at face value what the security management team at a duty station reports about its security plan.

UNSECOORD has been pushing, for years, but with few supporters, for the inclusion of security provisions, arguing that, just as provisions are made for home leave and for education grants for staff, there should also be provisions for security whenever a project is set up or a post created. In other words, the cost of keeping that staff member alive should be factored into the planning. UNSECOORD believes that with 75,000 UN system staff members worldwide, plus all those with Special Services Agreement (SSA) contracts, it is possible to put a certain percentage of money—not a huge sum when calculated in this way—into a special account to fund security. Unfortunately, others have not been persuaded to adopt this approach.

Other reasons cited for the low priority given staff security include institutional inertia: there is no single constituency pushing the issue; and, even though the UN has had fatalities, it has been very lucky in that it has not suffered major catastrophes.

Managing Security

The most effective approach in the way the UN deals with security in the field has been the naming of a designated official in a country, usually the Resident Coordinator, who has overall responsibility for the security and protection of UN system personnel, and the appointment of a security management team, consisting of all the heads of agencies at a duty station. Through training, raising their consciousness and making sure they remain engaged, it is possible to improve the way security is managed.

Training is an important component of any security management. By putting all staff through a security awareness program, they can learn what to do and how to react in various situations. Simple things can save lives, such as how to behave when carjacked or taken hostage. UNSECOORD is working with the Department of Peacekeeping Operations (DPKO) to re-establish, at Headquarters, the program of mission readiness workshops, which had been discontinued.

In the absence of training resources, the next best thing is disseminating information about training. A UN booklet, *Security in the Field,* contains practical, common sense measures staff members can take to minimize the risks they may face in duty stations. It tells what to do if taken hostage, to protect your children, when walking on the street or driving, how to secure your house, and more. UNSECOORD has printed and distributed over 100,000 copies of the booklet in the UN's six official languages, and is now on the third printing of the next 300,000 copies. It sent the booklet to all staff, local and international, in the field.

The resources for training must come from UN Member States. To date, only 10 countries have contributed to the trust fund for the security of UN system staff, the most generous being Japan, with a donation of $2 million. With that money, UNSECOORD has trained over 6,500 staff at 20 duty stations, and another 19 duty stations will complete training by the end of 2001, so that some 15,000 staff in high-risk areas will have been trained. During 2002-03, training will take place in 40 more countries. However, this is a one-time exercise, and resources are needed for sustained training. A much greater commitment to training is required, for it makes no sense to send unarmed and untrained civilian staff into areas where the military, with extensive training and weapons, will not venture. In addition, many Governments have 10–15 mobile teams to train their embassy staff, while the entire UN system has a single, three-person team that is on the road constantly.

Managing Stress

In addition to security training, staff must have access to stress management counseling to aid them in coping with day-to-day stress as well as critical incident stress. The drive to get the resources to recruit a full-time stress counselor at UN Headquarters began in 1992. Yet, it was not until October 2000 that one was hired. A second stress counselor is expected in 2001.

UNSECOORD became involved with stress counseling in the early 1990s when the number of staff fatalities began increasing, and its own Headquarters staff needed help in dealing with the fatalities and with the families of the victims. Realizing that the situation for colleagues on the ground who had suffered a traumatic incident must be far worse, the Office began assembling, with the help of experts, a mechanism for providing psychosocial help to UN system staff. The final section of the field security booklet, "Coping with Stress," reflects this concern. It soon became evident that the UN needed to have full-time stress counselors because, when faced with a crisis, there would be a scramble to find somebody who was not committed to their own private practice, and who could spend weeks in the crisis area.

The Organization's first attempt at stress counseling in a consistent manner occurred following the 1994 genocide in Rwanda, where many UN personnel and their children were traumatized by the atrocities they had witnessed. The counseling, held in Nairobi, made a remarkable difference to everyone, including those who were reluctant to participate, viewing such an activity as a Western invention. The greatest impact, however, was on the children, who went from drawing pictures of people being decapitated, of tanks and of guns, to those of cars and flowers and rainbows by the end of the week-long counseling session. Very slowly, stress counseling has become accepted, and is today the first request to UNSECOORD. With additional resources, that Office would hire more stress counselors at Headquarters and regionally, and at peacekeeping missions. They could not only respond to critical incidents, but also do preventive work and handle harassment issues, alcoholism, drug abuse, and other problems.

Funding Security

The resources to overhaul the UN security management system have to come from Member States, and recently they have been more willing to help. General Assembly resolution 55/238, adopted on December 23, 2000, was in response to the aforementioned Secretary-General's report. For 2001, as an interim measure, the Assembly approved eight more professional posts at Headquarters, eight in the field plus 16 local-level staff. However, the resolution included a proviso, namely, that all security expenditures be cost-shared by all the agencies and programs of the UN system. Over the past few months, there has been much discussion on resolving this issue. There is reason to believe that this matter will be resolved before the start of the fall 2001 General Assembly.

The Secretary-General proposed, in the report cited, regular budget funding for staff security, declaring the present cost-sharing system, which relies on "unpredictable and piecemeal funding and outdated, cumbersome and complex procedures" as not suited for the difficult and dangerous situations in which UN personnel are obliged to work. His proposal would establish one formula under which all field security officers would be funded from Headquarters and the costs distributed throughout the system. For the 2002-03 biennium, he called for a post of a full-time Security Coordinator, at the Assistant-Secretary-General level; for $60 million to strengthen the capacity of field security officers by establishing another 40 positions to supplement the existing 60 posts, and for personnel to conduct security training in the field. These proposals are also tied to an agreement being reached on cost-sharing arrangements.

The Security Council Weighs In on Staff Security

May 2001 witnessed the first meeting ever of the Security Council with United Nations staff. Following the murder of three UNHCR staff members in Atambua, West Timor, in September 2000, more than 14,000 staff from duty stations all over the world signed a petition calling for a special meeting of the Council to address staff safety. That initiative resulted in a closed meeting of the Security Council at which the Federation of International Civil Servants Associations (FICSA), which represents staff from 27 organizations and regional offices belonging to the UN family, made statements.

FICSA presented a document entitled "Elements for a Strengthened Security System for United Nations Staff and Associated Personnel." It urged the Council to address staff security regularly to ensure that words were translated into effective action, including regular briefings by the Secretary-General and agencies' heads on the progress made, and the difficulties encountered, in developing and coordinating security arrangements; meetings with staff representatives and rank-and-file staff members, especially those in difficult environments; field visits to assess the situation on the ground; and reports every time a major security incident occurs to ensure that lessons were learned. In the short term, FICSA said there was a need for a strong message of support for the measures already proposed by the Secretary-General in his report on staff security; called on the Secretary-General to develop his proposals further, based on an assessment of needs rather than of what was politically and financially achievable; called for inter-agency cooperation and coordination; and for adequate funding.

Council members, in turn, stressed their strong commitment to staff security and protection, and agreed that more needed to be done to mainstream security issues; establish an integrated approach to staff security, under UNSECOORD; improve security from UN system chiefs and implement cost-sharing arrangements among agencies and programs. They also saw the need for more resources for security; better training of staff about conditions they would face in the field; greater security from host Governments and more follow-up in apprehending and bringing to justice those who perpetrated violence against UN staff; and for promoting universal ratification of the relevant Convention, among other measures.

SECURITY IN PEACEKEEPING MISSIONS

UNSECOORD is responsible for the security of the personnel of the United Nations agencies, funds, and programs. Responsibility for the security of military, civilian police, and civilian personnel serving in peacekeeping operations rests with the head of the peacekeeping mission, reporting to the Under-Secretary-General for Peacekeeping Operations. A May 2001 report of the Secretary-General on the implementation of the recommendations of the Special Committee on Peacekeeping Operations and the Panel of United Nations Peace Operations (A/55/977) provides a comprehensive review of security requirements in peacekeeping missions. The study assessed security management in peacekeeping and identified existing weaknesses, along with practical ways of rectifying them. It raised concern over the need to clarify current arrangements for security management. In particular, it noted the need to codify security policy, procedures, and standards for peacekeeping, as well as command and reporting arrangements, and to clarify their relation to those established for the UN agencies, programs, and funds, as laid out in the Field Security Handbook.

The study proposed that, in devising the initial security infrastructure, special attention be given to the necessary material resources needed to support it. In order better to protect staff in the most vulnerable areas, it is imperative that missions allocate equipment according to security needs, ensure the full integration of regional sites into security planning, and improve information exchange among all locations and components. The study warned that the deployment of personnel without adequate security equipment constituted a serious breach of the Organization's Duty of Care. Managers with responsibilities for the safety of staff should have them clearly recorded in their terms of reference, and all staff should receive security awareness training consistent with their role and responsibilities, the study urged.

DPKO is responsible for day-to-day executive direction, management, and logistical support for UN peacekeeping operations worldwide. However, no office within that Department is specifically responsible for establishing and enforcing mission security and safety standards. UNSECOORD has the lead for mission security planning, but DPKO should strengthen its involvement to ensure that staff security is adequately planned, resourced, and regularly exercised. The two should work in partnership to clarify responsibilities and improve mission security programs.

ADHERENCE TO INTERNATIONAL INSTRUMENTS

It doesn't take resources to sign and/or ratify international instruments, however, and two are frequently mentioned in connection with staff safety and security: the 1994 Convention on the Safety of United Nations and Associated Personnel, which entered into force in 1999 (chapter 35); and the Statute of the International Criminal Court, adopted in 1998. Member States are called upon with great regularity to become parties to these documents. But ratification alone would not enhance the security of staff in the field. The purpose of the Convention is to prosecute the people who have killed you after you're dead. It merely facilitates the arrest of the perpetrators. The ICC Statute, for its part, would set up a venue where the accused could be brought for prosecution. Once it is functioning, the Court could be helpful in arresting, prosecuting and convicting people who have killed UN staff. The record of Governments in bringing such people to justice is abysmal—only six arrests for the 196 UN personnel killed in the field. Security Council members, at their historic meeting with UN staff in May, expressed shock, and protested at the light sentences handed out by Indonesia's courts to the murderers of UN staff in West Timor. Governments were urged to bring to justice the perpetrators of atrocities against United Nations staff and associated personnel.

CONCLUSION

The challenges faced by the UN system and humanitarian personnel working in dangerous places make security, and its management, an imperative. People may be willing to do humanitarian work, and to take certain risks, but no one is willing to die in the process. And unless they can be assured of their safety—through greater support and caring, quality training, top-level security officers, protective and communications equipment and vehicles—few persons will come forward for such assignments, if doing so means that they might pay the ultimate price: their lives. Which brings us back to the premise of this chapter: it takes money, and plenty of it, if you want quality security.

32

Psychological Debriefing

Beverley Raphael and Robert J. Ursano

Debriefing is a word now popularized in the English language. It is also an intervention that is widely used in response to a range of traumatic and stressful experiences. Debriefing infers a capacity to relinquish or unload what has happened or is known. It is customary now to consider it as applicable as an acute intervention in situations ranging from stresses and incidents in the workplace to the violence of war, ethnic conflict, and the devastation of natural disasters. Ursano states that "debriefing is a systematic process of education, emotional expression, cognitive reorganization through provision of information, fostering meaningful integration and group support" [1]. Debriefing as an intervention is applied typically in the immediate post trauma period. While there have been many different formats, some focusing more on a continuum of care with building coping skills, and others on education, the most widely used model is that of Critical Incident Stress Debriefing (CISD), developed and more recently evolved by Mitchell and Everly [2].

This form of debriefing was originally developed for emergency personnel but has been applied to populations as diverse as: those affected by disaster; the newly bereaved; those affected by work related incidents; emergency service workers; combat soldiers; peace-keepers; and numerous other individuals and groups. There is a growing body of evidence that its utility across such diverse populations is limited, and that it is inappropriate for a great many [3]. Although debriefing is frequently perceived as helpful, there is no correlation between such perceived helpfulness and better outcomes [4]. Indeed, it may be perceived as most helpful by those who by all indications appear to need it least [5].

McFarlane notes that debriefing is not a therapy as the person is not ill [6]. The motives of those providing debriefing and their aims are often less clear, but some of these may also be complex. For instance, there is the wish to take away pain and suffering; to prevent problems such as PTSD; to undo what has happened; to gain mastery over horror and terror or to experience these vicariously and to make money or satisfy role expectations.

The complexity of trauma experiences, the diversity of reactions, and the strengths of human adaptation and resilience, even in overwhelming circumstances, complicate the determination of what should be provided, by whom, and for what purposes at these early times. Debriefing has been taken up as a simple and almost

343

magical solution in the face of these complexities, and has become a powerful social movement. Research development for debriefing and early intervention must be alongside and supportive of the humanitarian response that is central.

THE BACKGROUND TO TRAUMA, LOSS, AND CATASTROPHIC EXPERIENCE

Population studies show a high frequency of traumatic experiences in the general population, frequently for those in adverse social circumstances. This is particularly so for those populations affected by war, violence, repeated disasters, other conflicts, famine, mutilating, and multiple deaths. It is also so for those who share their experience as UN, NGO, or other helpers. This background of trauma may contribute to individual vulnerability or adaptational strengths.

Those working with traumatized populations have been shown to benefit from training, experience, preparation, and briefing for what they are to face personally [3]. These factors may be more important than any subsequent intervention in mitigating negative impacts and facilitating better outcomes. In addition, there needs to be respect for and recognition of those adaptations that have been made [7].

THE STRESSORS THAT MAY BE EXPERIENCED

Stressors range from personal life threat, violence, exposure to the deaths of others, threats or loss of loved ones and primary attachment figures, losses of multiple kinds, devastation of home, community environment, war and combat, to malevolent physical and psychological environments. Exposure to intended and meaningless human malevolence and destructiveness adds a particular level of stress. Each of these stressor components may involve different reactive processes and these may interact to add to the complexity and severity of the experience. Stressors may be acute, unexpected or ongoing, profound and chronic. Any simple brief intervention such as debriefing cannot encompass this level and may be superficial as a response where any ongoing experiences are the source of the most profound negative consequences.

All the available evidence suggests that the majority of individuals adapt to such experiences: they grieve, resolve psychological trauma and find meaning and mastery of the experience. Nevertheless, there is a correlation between the intensity and severity of the exposure, the individual's coping style, past experience, such as childhood abuse; successful management of other adverse experiences; training and preparation; social support and the recovery environment. All these factors should be taken into account when targeting interventions to those at higher risk and modifying relevant factors to facilitate optimal adaptation. The event cannot be "taken away," nor can the experience of it, but there are interventions of demonstrated effectiveness to facilitate recovery. To date, there is not adequate evidence that debriefing contributes to recovery in such contexts.

ADAPTATIONS OF INDIVIDUALS, POPULATIONS, AND CULTURES

The literature on coping has contributed only partially to understanding the reactions of those directly traumatized and those who work with them. Cultural influences are significant, both in rituals involved [8], and in whether narrative is appropriate or when [9, 10], or indeed, if psychological trauma and debriefing are even cultural concepts [7].

DEBRIEFING AND NEGATIVE OUTCOMES

A number of studies have shown either no benefit of debriefing as it has been applied, or potentially negative outcomes. For instance Watts [4] showed no benefit, even though debriefing was perceived as helpful for populations after bus crashes. Similar findings exist for those affected by other motor vehicle accidents [11]. After a major earthquake [12], debriefing was not shown to facilitate recovery and even, for some, was correlated with less improvement in symptoms over time to a potentially negative outcome [12]. Lundin investigated debriefing as applied in different settings; the Armenian earthquake; the Estonian ferry disaster; and Swedish NATO soldiers in Bosnia [13]. He found that traumatic stress symptoms tended to decrease over time but this did not relate to debriefing. Rather, it related to degrees of preparation, training, previous experience and "professional" as compared to "non-professional" roles.

A follow-up of a well established CISD program for emergency workers in the United Kingdom found that perceived helpfulness was inversely related to outcomes [5, 14]. Bisson and colleagues found burn victims who were debriefed were worse at follow-up compared to those who were not [15]. The Cochrane review of debriefing concluded "there is not current evidence that psychological debriefing is useful for prevention of Post Traumatic Stress Disorder" [16]. Solomon and colleagues also reviewed debriefing and its relevance in the military context and found limited evidence of benefits [17].

ELEMENTS RELATED TO DEBRIEFING MODALITIES AND APPLICATIONS THAT MAY BE OF BENEFIT

Shalev draws on the model of Historical Group Debriefing and suggests that reducing arousal, shortly after exposure, may be the most important aspect [18]. He reports the non-structured non-interventionist type of debriefing involving "simple reconstruction of group narrative" was effective in reducing anxiety in soldiers recently exposed to combat.

Weisaeth also looks at group stress debriefing (GSD) with a focus on different types of groups [8]. Debriefing should be for those who have been briefed. He believes that trained leaders of professional teams may best provide debriefing through normal operational review and stand down.

These findings are also supported by the more integrated approach described by Alexander [19] and his work with police officers involved in body recovery after an oil rig disaster, where debriefing was integrated into management and utilized informally with other supportive structures [19].

Debriefing models have been explored in general health services settings [20] and in obstetrics for mothers after miscarriage and "traumatic" childbirth [21]. In these instances, findings support aspects of good practice rather than a new type of intervention.

Debriefing as a formal procedure in the CISD modality has been taken up by emergency services. While it is perceived as helpful, it has not been shown to prevent development of Post Traumatic Stress Disorder. However, as reported, it may lessen absences from work for sick leave, job turnover, and perhaps other stress effects or staff assault in a stress management framework [2]. It is also suggested as potentially helpful in a systematic program to lessen the negative effects of assaults on staff in mental health facilities [22]. This does not really cover severe, profound and highly traumatic stressor exposures.

ELEMENTS THAT NEED TO BE ADDRESSED IN EARLY INTERVENTION

Sharing and Making Meaning of Experience

This has been part of the reaction to trauma and loss since time immemorial [8]. Weisaeth notes that in historical times men openly expressed their grief, but less so their fears or reactions to life threatening experiences, so often glorified instead by heroic tales, and "war stories" [8]. Debriefing has provided a new socially sanctioned ritual for men to talk of these experiences.

Ursano et al. have further investigated the potential beneficial effects of "talking" in "natural debriefing" after a disaster [1]. When they followed up these people several months after the disaster, there was no evidence that this talking had mitigated or prevented levels of PTSD symptoms or depressive symptoms. These continued and were related still to the high levels of exposure as assessed earlier.

What is clear from many reports is that there is a popular belief, held both by the public and those who offer help, that it will be helpful to talk about what has happened, to make meaning and share the experience. The extensive testimony provided in books and other research by those who have survived horror and terror also attest to this.

Trauma and Loss

Another issue of "talking" about what has happened, about reviewing it, making meaning, and sharing feelings is its *timing* and this may be a critical issue when considering debriefing interventions. Reports from those offered debriefing suggest that they would have liked to talk about what had happened, but not at that time, rather at a time when they were ready, later. This may relate to ongoing tasks on which they are focused; or a fear of being overwhelmed; or a need to talk to specific others; or a need to come to some internal and personal adaptation before it was shared externally.

The model of debriefing so widely followed has focused on immediacy effect at 24–48–72 hours, although this is a little more flexible in recent times [2]. There is evidence that this timing is inappropriate for those acutely traumatically bereaved, and that effective interventions can be provided for those at high risk of adverse outcomes in the weeks and months, rather than the immediate days after the loss [23]. This does not obviate the need for a compassionate contact, ensuring safety and supporting attachment: leading into more specialized and targeted counseling when needed [24, 25]. For both trauma and loss stressors, there is good evidence of beneficial intervention offered to individuals at a later and more psychologically appropriate time for them.

Two debriefing studies report benefit of this modality when offered at a much later time. Stallard found it helpful for adolescents offered it at three months after a disaster [26]. Chemtob [27] applied the debriefing model to disaster affected populations in Hawaii six months or more after the disaster.

Learning

As suggested by most models of debriefing, there are processes of education and learning involved. The operational debriefing or formal review is aimed at learning what was done well, what could have been done differently, and what procedures may need to be changed. This operational review and associated active learning process is likely to be helpful not only for the acknowledgment of what has been achieved, but also what can be contributed constructively to future responses. It is likely that this process is also psychologically helpful. The types of debriefing suggested by Shalev [18] and Weisaeth [8] may also facilitate active learning among those involved.

Much more needs to be known about memory and learning as they occur in post-trauma phenomenology and as they may be influenced by acute and early interventions, including debriefing. It can be concluded, however, that it is likely that learning will occur in this time of high arousal; that modern educational theory supports the benefits of active, problem solving learning approaches; that what is learned should ideally not only assist with adaptation to this experience but be able to be generalized to other circumstances of adversity; and that learning may also build on earlier experience including training and preparation and briefing, as well as what has been learned in past circumstances of trauma.

POLICY AND PRACTICE OF DEBRIEFING AND EARLY INTERVENTION

Arising from the themes addressed above, it is possible to make a number of recommendations that should govern policy and practice in this field.

1. Preparation, Education, and Structural Support

Wherever possible, workers should be prepared not only for the practical tasks their work will entail, but also for the emotional tasks. This should involve a review of potentially traumatic experiences, preferably with those who have themselves mastered them, and an exploration of adaptations. Practical exercises are also helpful. Recognizing their own style of response and adaptation and what helpful self-care steps they can take should be a part of the process. Safety, attachment, mutual support, and the use of cognitive strategies of problem solving can be mobilized and enhanced. Preparation should cover normal reactions and adaptation and what can be done to facilitate these for the self and others. Timing of reactions and expectations of change over time should be dealt with. Briefing should be used to prepare specifically when likely threats and outcomes are known, such as dealing with bodies after mass deaths. Specific attention should be given to the stresses and frustrations of being unable to act or help as with peacekeepers, or the failure of actions to achieve desired outcomes. Structural processes include tours of duty, limitations on exposure, environments of support, privacy, and relief. Protection from over-involvement or the disengagement of burnout can be facilitated by recognition of achievement, maintaining personal hopefulness and ensuring that attachments are maintained.

2. First Ensure Safety

Protecting and making safe those who have been affected is the first prerequisite. This must focus on physical survival in the first instance, and then psychological. Psychological safety may be enhanced by *compassionate* and *protective* responses and interventions to mitigate: high levels of arousal; behaviors that may be harmful to the person or others, cognitive impairment related to shock, and dissociation or organic factors. These interventions can be seen as *psychological first aid* alongside physical first aid. Both are provided in emergency and both have rubrics of A, B, C—for psychological first aid this is: Arousal; Behavior; Cognition. The person or persons are assessed in the emergency and if necessary transferred to mental health or other care.

3. Do No Harm

A compassionate *outreach,* expression of concern, offer to help can do no harm. Debriefing universally applied in this early setting as a formal technique *can* do harm. It should never be provided as a compulsory intervention and, if offered at all, should be offered in a supportive context for naturally occurring groups or as part of an operational debrief. For workers, rotation and limiting of exposure, and limitation of tours of duty may also be helpful in lessening harm.

4. Support and Attachment

The need for human contact and for ensuring the safety of family and loved ones is primary. Interventions should aim to provide information on the whereabouts of significant others; family; loved ones; teammates and co-workers. Reunion should be sought if safety can be guaranteed, or communication at the least. If there is separation, loss, or unknown outcomes, it should be recognized that this will be an ongoing source of distress that may drive behaviors. Workers who have been engaged with populations and individuals who are threatened or killed may also experience intense distress for these attachments. Support of team members and other workers may be vital and groups may come together for this mutual support. Peer support as well as attachment can be one of the benefits of such groups.

5. Making Meaning, Dealing with the Experience

Information may be central to making meaning of traumatic experiences and can have psychological value in its own right. Sharing meaning in a group of supportive others may also facilitate some attempts to make meaning. But the evidence suggests this is best as part of a supportive review by the team leader with groups that naturally work together; that the narrative of this discussion may take considerable time and should not be intruded upon or interpreted; that the timing in the early phase is inappropriate for some, if not many; that some believe that it would be better for them in an individual, rather than a group, setting; that it may further traumatize some; and that for some it is seen as better not to review or discuss. It might be recommended here that:

- *Informal group processes* be supported and not intruded upon, allowing discussion of the experience as mentioned above.
- *Supportive debriefing* be provided for those groups that are trained and work together either as part of an operational review led by their team leader or through processes such as group stress debriefing, or historical group debriefing [8, 18].
- *Integrated debriefing* [19] may be a useful strategy if known mental health support can be built into responses.
- Any such interventions should be sensitive to *individual, group,* and *cultural* needs and to timing. These interventions may or may not facilitate emotional release: this should not be demanded. The potential cognitive and affective strategies that are relevant for different individuals should be taken into account also.
- *Adaptation* should be *facilitated.* It should be recognized that most will adapt in their own ways and these should be respected. It is unethical to disrupt such adaptations without evidence that they will be harmful or that intervention will be beneficial.
- *Outreach and contact* can provide information and offer help. They may also, as may the above processes, identify those at high risk and in need of follow-up and more specific interventions.
- *Justice and meaning* are particularly relevant when human rights are violated in trauma and disaster. Justice will be a powerful demand even if it cannot be achieved, and its psychological meaning needs also to be recognized.

6. Counseling

Although there is a widespread belief in Western societies of the benefits of trauma counseling, this is often a nebulous concept offered from the earliest period after loss. While practical support, compassionate assistance and the offer to help and listen can be of general value, the need for specialized trauma and other counseling is more clearly defined. Specialized counseling should be separate from such generalized support.

- *Trauma counseling* focuses on psychological trauma and should be offered to those at high risk two or more weeks after the event. It may follow supportive outreach and relevant screening [24].
- *Bereavement counseling* focuses on loss and grief and provides a framework to facilitate the working through of the separation, protest, and recovery [23].
- *Traumatic bereavements* are frequent in such settings and may require complex psychological interventions [28, 29].

Other aspects of experience may require further targeted interventions over time: the more severe exposure, the more interventions may need carefully to "dose" the affect and to facilitate those resolutions that can be achieved.

CONCLUSIONS

There is some evidence to support the policy and practice recommendations outlined above. They must be carried forward in a climate of humane and humanitarian response. Nevertheless, this climate must also be one that recognizes the complexity of trauma, of being a helper and of individual experience and reaction. It must be better informed by science in order to build a strong knowledge base to inform the future.

REFERENCES

1. R. J. Ursano, C. S. Fullerton, K. Vance, and L. Wang, Debriefing: Its Role in the Spectrum of Prevention and Acute Management of Psychological Trauma, in *Psychological Debriefing: Theory, Practice and Evidence*, B. Raphael and J. P. Wilson (eds.), Cambridge University Press, London, pp. 32-42, 2000.
2. J. T. Mitchell and G. S. Everly, Critical Incident Stress Management and Critical Incident Stress Debriefings: Evolutions, Effects and Outcomes, in *Psychological Debriefing: Theory, Practice and Evidence*, B. Raphael and J. P. Wilson (eds.), Cambridge University Press, London, pp. 71-90, 2000.
3. B. Raphael and J. P. Wilson, Introduction and Overview: Key Issues in the Conceptualization of Debriefing, in *Psychological Debriefing: Theory, Practice and Evidence*, B. Raphael and J. P. Wilson (eds.), Cambridge University Press, London, pp. 241-253, 2000.
4. R. Watts, Debriefing After Massive Road Trauma: Perceptions and Outcomes, in *Psychological Debriefing: Theory, Practice and Evidence*, B. Raphael and J. P. Wilson (eds.), Cambridge University Press, London, pp. 131-144, 2000.

5. A. Avery and R. Orner, First Report of Psychological Debriefing Abandoned. The End of an Era? Traumatic Stress Points, *International Society for Traumatic Stress Studies, 12*:3, Summer 1998.

6. A. McFarlane, Can Debriefing Work? Critical Appraisal of Theories of Interventions and Outcomes, with Directions for Future Research, in *Psychological Debriefing: Theory, Practice and Evidence,* B. Raphael and J. P. Wilson (eds.), Cambridge University Press, London, pp. 327-336, 2000.

7. D. Silove, A Conceptual Framework for Mass Trauma: Implications for Adaptation, Intervention and Debriefing, in *Psychological Debriefing: Theory, Practice and Evidence,* B. Raphael and J. P. Wilson (eds.), Cambridge University Press, London, pp. 337-350, 2000.

8. L. Weisaeth, Briefing and Debriefing: Group Psychological Interventions in Acute Stressor Situations, in *Psychological Debriefing: Theory, Practice and Evidence,* B. Raphael and J. P. Wilson (eds.), Cambridge University Press, London, pp. 43-57, 2000.

9. C. Ober, L. Peeters, R. Archer, and K. Kelly, Debriefing in Different Cultural Frameworks: Responding to Acute Trauma in Australian Aboriginal Contexts, in *Psychological Debriefing: Theory, Practice and Evidence,* B. Raphael and J. P. Wilson (eds.), Cambridge University Press, London, pp. 241-253, 2000.

10. J. P. Wilson and M. R. Sigman, Theoretical Perspectives of Traumatic Stress and Debriefings, in *Psychological Debriefing: Theory, Practice and Evidence,* B. Raphael and J. P. Wilson (eds.), Cambridge University Press, London, pp. 58-68, 2000.

11. M. Hobbs and R. Mayon, Debriefing and Motor Vehicle Accidents: Interventions and Outcomes, in *Psychological Debriefing: Theory, Practice and Evidence,* B. Raphael and J. P. Wilson (eds.), Cambridge University Press, London, pp. 145-160, 2000.

12. J. A. Kenardy and V. J. Carr, Debriefing Post Disaster; Follow-Up After a Major Earthquake, in *Psychological Debriefing: Theory, Practice and Evidence,* B. Raphael and J. P. Wilson (eds.), Cambridge University Press, London, pp. 174-181, 2000.

13. T. Lundin, Debriefing After Disaster, in *Psychological Debriefing: Theory, Practice and Evidence,* B. Raphael and J. P. Wilson (eds.), Cambridge University Press, London, pp. 182-194, 2000.

14. A. Avery and R. Orner, More on Debriefing: Report of Psychological Debriefing Abandoned. The End of an Era? *Australian Traumatic Stress Points, Newsletter of the Australian Society for Traumatic Stress Studies,* July 4-6, 1998.

15. J. I. Bisson, J. A. Jenkins, and C. Bannister, Randomised Controlled Trial of Psychological Debriefing for Victims of Acute Burn Trauma, *British Journal of Psychiatry, 171,* pp. 78-81, 1997.

16. S. Wesely, S. Rose, and J. Bisson, Brief Psychological Interventions ('Debriefing') for Immediate Trauma Related Symptoms and the Prevention of Post Traumatic Stress Disorder (Cochrane Review), *The Cochrane Library, 4,* Update Software, Oxford, 1999.

17. A. Solomon, Y. Neria, and E. Witztum, Debriefing with Service Personnel in War and Peace Roles; Experience and Outcomes, in *Psychological Debriefing: Theory, Practice and Evidence,* B. Raphael and J. P. Wilson (eds.), Cambridge University Press, London, pp. 161-173, 2000.

18. A. Y. Shalev, Stress Management and Debriefing: Historical Concepts and Present Patterns, in *Psychological Debriefing: Theory, Practice and Evidence,* B. Raphael and J. P. Wilson (eds.), Cambridge University Press, London, pp. 17-31, 2000.

19. D. Alexander, Debriefing and Body Recovery: Police in a Civilian Disaster, in *Psychological Debriefing: Theory, Practice and Evidence,* B. Raphael and J. P. Wilson (eds.), Cambridge University Press, London, pp. 118-130, 2000.

20. J. Turner and B. Kelly, The Concept of Debriefing and Its Applications to Staff Dealing with Life-Threatening Illnesses such as Cancer, AIDS and Other Conditions, in *Psychological Debriefing: Theory, Practice and Evidence*, B. Raphael and J. P. Wilson (eds.), Cambridge University Press, London, pp. 254-271, 2000.

21. P. Boyce and J. Condon, Traumatic Childbirth and the Role of Debriefing, in *Psychological Debriefing: Theory, Practice and Evidence*, B. Raphael and J. P. Wilson (eds.), Cambridge University Press, London, pp. 272-280, 2000.

22. R. B. Flannery, Jr., Debriefing Health Care Staff After Assaults by Patients, in *Psychological Debriefing: Theory, Practice and Evidence*, B. Raphael and J. P. Wilson (eds.), Cambridge University Press, London, pp. 281-289, 2000.

23. B. Raphael, C. Minkov, and M. Dobson, Psychotherapeutic and Pharmacological Intervention for Bereaved Persons, in *Handbook of Bereavement Research: Consequences, Coping, and Care*, M. S. Stroebe, R. O. Hansson, W. Stroebe, and H. Schut (eds.), American Psychological Association, Washington, D.C., pp. 1-14, 2001.

24. R. A. Bryant, A. G. Harvey, S. T. Dang, and T. Sackville, Treatment of Acute Stress Disorder: A Comparison of Cognitive-Behavioural Therapy and Supportive Counselling, *Journal of Consulting and Clinical Psychology, 66,* pp. 862-866, 1998.

25. S. D. Solomon, Interventions for Acute Trauma Response, *Current Opinion in Psychiatry, 12,* pp. 175-180, 1999.

26. P. Stallard, Debriefing Adolescents after Critical Life Events, in *Psychological Debriefing: Theory, Practice and Evidence*, B. Raphael and J. P. Wilson (eds.), Cambridge University Press, London, pp. 213-224, 2000.

27. C. M. Chemtob, Delayed Debriefing: After a Disaster, in *Psychological Debriefing: Theory, Practice and Evidence*, B. Raphael and J. P. Wilson (eds.), Cambridge University Press, London, pp. 227-240, 2000.

28. B. Raphael and N. Martinek, Assessing Traumatic Bereavements and PTSD, in *Assessing Psychological Trauma and PTSD*, J. P. Wilson and T. M. Keane (eds.), Guilford Press, New York, pp. 373-395, 1997.

29. E. K. Rynearson, *Retelling Violent Death*, Brunner-Routledge, Philadelphia (in press).

33

Humanitarianism at Risk:
From Threatened Aid Workers to
Self-Deceiving Organizations

Mark Walkup*

The complex emergencies facing the humanitarian community today require aid workers to possess nothing less than "superhuman" characteristics [1]. They must not only be technically competent in economics, agronomy, medicine, and engineering, they must be fearless "moral philosophers" who engage in the essential crafts of political analysis and conflict management with deep understanding of history and culture [2]. Unfortunately, aid workers are *not* humanitarian superhumans. They are real people. They have limits. Yet the performance of the humanitarian regime and the quality of international benevolence ultimately rest on their shoulders.

The weight of this massive burden placed, perhaps unfairly, on these aid workers by the international community is compounded by very tangible demands of their needy beneficiaries in the field and the tasks of negotiating the conflicting ideals of neutrality, justice, and solidarity. These personnel must encounter the troubling ethical dilemmas of relief work, face the limits of their helping capacity, and realize that their goals may sometimes conflict with those of the people they are supposedly assisting. Aid workers try to remain accountable to multiple groups of unsatisfied clients in this environment of incessant appeals, widespread criticism, and intractable conflicts. As a result, they endure degrees of psychological distress—involving elements of cognitive dissonance, angst, and guilt—in order to persist in their mission.

This chapter argues that psychological distress is one of the main causes of operational dysfunction in humanitarian organizations (HOs). The coping strategies used by aid workers to manage this distress become institutionalized into organizational behavior and culture. These cultural institutions inhibit organizational performance by fostering insensitivity to clients, defensiveness toward evaluation and learning, and resistance to change. Unless HOs find ways of reducing the effects

---

*The author works for the U.S. Department of State's Bureau of Population, Refugees, and Migration. The views expressed are his own and do not necessarily reflect those of the U.S. Department of State.

of psychological distress, they will be constrained in their capacity to improve the delivery of assistance and protection to vulnerable populations in need.

THE CAUSTIC CONTEXT OF HUMANITARIANISM

Aid workers operate on the front lines where the generosity of donors directly confronts the demands, politics, and social structures of the beneficiaries. The milieu and behavior of these aid workers is not unlike those of "field-level bureaucrats" in other social organizations, who have constant interaction with nonvoluntary clients, considerable independence and wide discretionary power in decision making and policy application, and extensive potential impact on the livelihood of clients [3]. Their work environment includes inadequate resources for the assigned tasks, physical and/or psychological threats against them, and ambiguous and/or contradictory expectations about job performance, which is also difficult to measure. Field-level bureaucrats in HOs not only influence organizational performance; they have considerable impact on clients' lives. They socialize clients to the expectations and rules of the HO services. They control client eligibility and access to the benefits of the humanitarian regime. In short, their capacities and actions determine the relationship between the organization and the clients, and between humanitarian policy objectives and actual impact.

But the capacities and actions of aid workers are constrained by many factors. The logistical impediments are well known. The increasing violence and threats to aid workers' physical security are already well documented by others in this volume. What is less evident is the insidious nature of the typical environment of humanitarianism, where conflicting ideals, competing interests, and hidden evils assail the psychological health of aid workers.

Unfulfilled Expectations

Many aid workers suffer when their naiveté, lack of preparation, and unreasonable expectations meet head-on with the demanding work requirements in humanitarian operations. Though many humanitarians seek uplifting experiences "helping people help themselves" and "building peace," too many of them bitterly report that what they find are greedy, conniving, ungrateful people who lie, cheat, and steal in order to survive. Hoping to receive appreciation, self-fulfillment, and bonding experiences, they instead are faced with caustic realities that erode their self-esteem and worldview.

Ethical Dilemmas

Aid workers encounter debilitating ethical dilemmas when they must make life-affecting decisions despite the contradictions and dissonance involved in their actions. For example, the distribution of insufficient resources sometimes forces relief workers to decide who eats and who does not, and in many cases, who lives and who dies. HO staff must decide whether to cut programs that may support aggressors in armed conflicts, while knowing that doing so will place thousands of innocent people at risk.

Demands of Beneficiaries

Although the voices of beneficiaries are not as loud as those of donors, beneficiaries, too, persistently complain about the inadequacies of resources and services. They are keenly aware of the organizational dysfunctions; they pay the price for them every day. Whereas HO workers can often disguise policy failures from donors, they find it very difficult to hide mistakes from the affected populations. For aid workers in the field who directly interact with affected populations, these voices are the hardest for the conscience to ignore.

Fear

For clear reasons, aid workers endure fears about personal security when working in conflict zones among warring groups. Horrifying evidence shows that aid workers are increasingly targeted themselves for the role they play in conflicts. Fear of violence from rebel groups is hard enough; but when humanitarians begin to fear the very people they are making personal sacrifices to serve, the threat to the aid workers' psyche and spirit is especially severe.

Market-Based Survival

HOs, as all organizations, must generate and sustain resources in order to survive. Fundraising strategies depend on skills such as the marketing of suffering, enhancing image, buying donor fashions, competing for credit and visibility, and selectively avoiding coordination mechanisms. These "necessary evils" of humanitarian work ensure organizational survival, but ironically reduce the appropriateness and efficiency of assistance delivered to affected populations. Knowing that they must be more accountable to donors than to affected populations, aid workers struggle to justify the problems that result from organizational survival-based policy decisions.

Operational Inconsistencies

Confusion is also caused when aid workers learn that beneficiaries are to be simultaneously helped and feared; both empowered and controlled. As Hyndman observes of refugees: "One moment they are asked to become leaders and decision makers in the camp; the next they are herded behind barricades at gunpoint in order to be counted for a UNHCR census" [4]. Refugees are encouraged to be self-reliant, but not so much as to delay their repatriation. Aid workers are torn by the inherent conflicts between humanitarian ideology and operational practice.

THE PSYCHOLOGICAL EFFECTS

The resulting psychological distress from living in this environment is a combination of cognitive dissonance, angst, and guilt. First, *cognitive dissonance* is produced when there are inconsistencies among one's "cognitions," defined as "any knowledge, opinion, or belief about the environment, about oneself, or about one's behavior" [5]. Making these cognitions consistent is a basic human drive, but one that cannot be easily satisfied when managing the contradictions in the humanitarian industry. Second, aid workers experience a set of emotional conditions that collectively can be called *angst*, including anxiety (a state of tiresome suspense in which a person waits for unknown stimuli or information to clarify his or her situation of persistent discord or perceived threat); and frustration (a state of discord resulting from the perception of continued inability of a person's action to change environmental factors). Third, despite knowing they are not responsible for their clients' suffering, many aid workers experience various degrees and forms of *guilt* because of their inability to fulfill the humanitarian job that is expected of them. In some aid workers, this guilt is compounded because of their perceived "original sin" of being rich or white or European, thus being indirectly associated with exploitation and fueling conflicts in the developing world. Guilt can also be "a convenient substitute for action where action is impossible" [6].

Wrestling with this psychological distress, aid workers have several options: they can *exit* the organization (contributing to the extremely high personnel turnover rate in HOs), they can *voice* their concerns (risking their jobs or essential social support of peers), or they can remain *loyal* (to the organization, the cause, or the financial security) [7]. Those who remain must somehow cope with the distress that threatens their psyche, and most aid workers display behaviors that can be categorized into at least four identifiable stages of conscious and subconscious coping mechanisms: overwork, detachment, projection, and delusion. First, personnel *overwork* to alleviate guilt, to reduce boredom, or to attract desired recognition. Overworking leads to work hoarding, reduced participation by others, and ultimately results in "burnout," a clinically-documented psycho-physiological condition. Second, personnel *detach* themselves from the source of their distress by withdrawing to paperwork in the compounds, avoiding direct interaction with needy clients, and retreating behind rules and procedures that effectively limit client demands and reduce essential communication. Third, aid workers deal with policy failures by *projecting* the blame onto others—other competing HOs, unresponsive donors, or restrictive host governments—and they often blame the affected populations themselves for their problems. Last, when faced with criticism and obvious shortcomings, personnel often create *delusions* of success by reconceptualizing the suffering or deservedness of their clients, creating a false supply-demand equilibrium, or promoting and celebrating a heroic self-image. This self-deception enables them to sustain self-esteem despite their powerlessness to alleviate their organizational problems or the miserable conditions of their clients.

FROM INDIVIDUAL COPING TO ORGANIZATIONAL SELF-DECEPTION

As these individual behaviors associated with the coping mechanisms are shared and become expected and legitimized by the close-knit aid worker community, they form "institutions" that shape organizational behavior. Institutions are the rules, rituals, patterns of interaction, codes of conduct, standard operating procedures, values, and unspoken understandings among a group. Institutions serve many purposes for an organization: they reduce uncertainty, regulate and give meaning to life and activities, foster identity, structure rites of passage, establish expectations about ethics and performance, and foster cohesion [8, 9]. These institutions form the basis of a collective "organizational culture," the assumptions, values, and beliefs that are learned responses to a group's dual needs for survival in its external environment and for internal cohesion [10].

Using a psychoanalytic approach to organizational analysis, Kets de Vries and Miller classify dysfunctional organizational culture types by uncovering an organization's predominant "motivating fantasy," that is, the underlying perceptions shared by individual personnel about their relationship with their environment [11]. From the motivating fantasy emerges a specific kind of policy structure. For example, a fantasy of "persecution" produces a structure of "paranoia," and a fantasy of "control" leads to a "compulsive" structure. HOs, however, encounter a significantly different milieu of institutional dynamics and related behavior patterns than the organizations examined by Kets de Vries and Miller. The harsh HO environment of criticism and inadequacy produces a fantasy of "guilt" shared by HO personnel. The organizational efforts to respond to the fantasy of guilt require a policy structure based on "defensiveness." But a defensive policy structure does not fit with the survival-based need to promote a positive image to donors and the media. So, in order for the image-conscious HOs to maintain these defensive policies in the climate of public scrutiny and personal introspection, HOs must shroud them in carefully fabricated facades. For HO personnel to save face and sustain morale, they, too, must begin to believe their own misrepresentations.

HOs develop shared "mediatory myths" that allow personnel to mediate the dissonance between what *should* be done and what *can* be done [12, 13]. These myths become encoded into organizational culture through language and jargon, written and oral histories, and ritual ceremonies. For HOs, one predominant myth is unrealistic organizational proficiency and policy success, designed to reduce the distress caused by the obvious inadequacy of their humanitarian efforts. This myth is more than a public relations strategy to promote a favorable image through the media. The function of the myth goes much deeper because it is constructed by HO personnel to justify their actions not just to the public, but also to themselves. This ceremonial process of social and psychological re-visualization creates patterns of cultural institutions that perpetuate an alternative socially-constructed reality. Hence, the culture that upholds these facades to assuage the collective guilt becomes *self-deceiving*.

While these myths enable individuals to "get on with their work," the resulting institutions diminish the capacity of individuals and organizations to process information effectively, learn from experience, and constructively modify behavior accordingly. Thus, needed changes are resisted, whether initiated by headquarters leaders, field personnel, or independent evaluators. Although HOs are overcoming their historical aversion to evaluations, there still is little evidence that they are actually learning and changing behaviors in spite of the increased numbers of evaluations. Dysfunctions persist because they are tied to institutionalized myths that support the collective self-deception and protect against perceived threats from their external environment. While protective of organizational coherence and survival, the myths undermine the organization's ability to deal sensitively with affected populations, to learn and change from evaluation, and to coordinate with other HOs. These failures, in turn, contribute to more dissonance and hence more distress for HO personnel. So, the vicious cycle continues.

RECOMMENDATIONS

At the individual level, subtle resistance by aid workers to formal organizational objectives, or "everyday forms of policy dysfunction," is not simply "shirking" of responsibilities. Rather, it should be viewed as individual coping behavior that is instrumental for psychological stability. Likewise, at the organizational level, subtle collective resistance to formal policy objectives is not irrational behavior; it is an informal strategy to sustain internal coherence and market survival. At both levels, the survival motive does not excuse the behavior, which is often detrimental to policy success and client interests. But it indicates that many dysfunctional behaviors cannot be treated simply as a failure to follow policy. In fact, this analysis demonstrates that such behaviors are functional, and in some cases essential, for survival. Those working for reform in HOs should understand the purposes of these strategies and institutional forms. Then they can learn to redirect them, gradually replacing them with other institutions that are more consistent with policy objectives and client interests, while still sustaining the capacities of individuals to cope and organizations to survive.

Toward this aim, research can help answer some key questions. For example, what is the relationship between degree of psychological distress and the amount of training or psychological support offered by HOs? What variables affect aid workers' speed and nature of progression from one coping mechanism to another? Why do some HOs appear to have "healthier" cultures? Do these "healthier" HO cultures actually promote better performance? Improving HO health and performance requires an increased openness by HO leadership to social science researchers who need access, funding, and legitimacy. These researchers, in turn, have a reciprocal responsibility to make their findings, theories, and recommendations more practical and accessible to HO practitioners. For understandable reasons, the relationship between these two groups has a history tainted by skepticism and mistrust. Nonetheless, without movements toward reconciliation, neither group stands to gain much insight or improvement. And without improvement, the world's crisis-affected communities will be the ones who continue to suffer most.

REFERENCES

1. H. Slim, The Continuing Metamorphosis of the Humanitarian Professional: Some New Colours for an Endangered Chameleon, *Disasters, 19*:2, 1995.

2. S. George, Food, Famine, and Service Delivery in Times of Emergency, Chapter 3 in *Ill Fares the Land: Essays on Food, Hunger, and Power*, Penguin Press, London, 1990.
3. M. Lipsky, *Street-Level Bureaucracy: Dilemmas of the Individual in Public Services*, Russell Sage Foundation, New York, 1980.
4. J. Hyndman, *Managing Displacement: Refugees and the Politics of Humanitarianism*, University of Minnesota Press, Minneapolis, 2000.
5. L. Festinger, *A Theory of Cognitive Dissonance*, Stanford University Press, Stanford, 1957.
6. P. Bruckner, *The Tears of the White Man*, translated from French by W. R. Beer, Free Press, New York, 1986.
7. A. O. Hirschman, *Exit, Voice, and Loyalty: Responses to Decline in Firms, Organizations, and States*, Harvard University Press, Cambridge, 1970.
8. W. R. Scott, *Institutions and Organizations*, Sage, London, 1995.
9. W. Powell and P. DiMaggio (eds.), *The New Institutionalism in Organizational Analysis*, University of Chicago Press, Chicago, 1991.
10. E. Schein, *Organizational Culture and Leadership*, Jossey-Bass, San Francisco, 1985.
11. M. Kets de Vries and D. Miller, Leadership Styles and Organizational Cultures: The Shaping of Neurotic Organizations, in *Organizations On the Couch: Clinical Perspectives on Organizational Behavior and Change*, Kets de Vries, Manfred, and Associates (eds.), Jossey-Bass, San Francisco, 1991.
12. H. Abravanel, Mediatory Myths in the Service of Organizational Ideology, in *Organizational Symbolism*, L. Pondy, P. J. Frost, G. Morgan, and T. Dandridge (eds.), JAI Press, Greenwich, Connecticut, 1983.
13. T. Scheid-Cook, Mitigating Organizational Contradictions: The Role of Mediatory Myths, *Journal of Applied Behavioral Science, 24*:2, 1988.

34

Training for Humanitarian Assistance

Kevin M. Cahill

International humanitarian assistance is a professional discipline influenced, appropriately, as are the professions of medicine or nursing, by the loftiest ideals of civilized society. To help one's fellow human beings alleviate hunger and pain, give succor to the starving and homeless, unite ruptured families and re-build destroyed societies are the noble goals of humanitarian assistance. But the sheer scope and extent of the human calamities that follow conflicts and disasters make most individual efforts in such situations touching but ineffectual. Unless humanitarian assistance is carefully planned, coordinated, and delivered, with under-standing and sensitivity, it often produces more harm and pain to individual victims and fragile communities; it also endangers and frustrates the very donors who wish to help.

One of the reasons for so much failure in the attempt to do good is a lack of training in the fundamentals of humanitarian assistance. Good will, or the desire to share in human tragedy, is simply not an adequate foundation. If timely and effective help is to be delivered, all participants must develop a common language, and this depends on a universally accepted basic standard of training.

Assistance workers must understand how complex humanitarian crises develop and what are the potential roles for, and skills required, when, as strangers, they become involved in traumatized communities where the normal supportive services of society have collapsed, when entire populations become vulnerable dependents. Those who presume to offer help in such situations must be taught to appreciate the early warning signs of impending disasters so that prevention as well as reaction becomes part of their approach. They must learn from previous catastrophes how to devise the most efficient, rapid, and flexible response to each challenge, no two of which are identical.

There are basic tenets, however, common to all disaster relief efforts. One must learn to be vigilant against the known dangers of inappropriate aid, to preserve, even in the midst of chaos, an equanimity, a humility and respect that are the hallmarks of true professionals in every discipline. Humanitarian workers must learn to develop, and utilize, accurate tools to measure the extent of needs, and to evaluate the efficacy of aid programs. They must also learn to use a new, universally accepted vocabulary so they can coordinate their efforts with other international agencies and especially with local authorities and leaders. They must properly plan programs so they can eventually leave and end their support without adding insult to existing injury.

Many factors mandate a change in the way humanitarian assistance workers should be trained. International relief efforts are now "big business" with profound diplomatic, military, political, and economic implications. In 2000, billions of dollars were spent on humanitarian assistance. Yet, there were no widely agreed upon training programs to certify the multiple actors in this critical discipline.

The International Diploma in Humanitarian Assistance (IDHA) is a product of the loss of innocence that followed the Somalia debacle in the early 1990s. It reflects a new and profound appreciation of the dangers aid workers face and can create. My interest in the levels of training offered by different agencies was sharpened when I was asked to care for a young woman who had just been raped in Somalia in 1992. She had been sent into anarchy, armed with a pleasant two-day orientation program, and was led to believe that, somehow, if she caressed the starving babies the problems of Somalia would be solved. No one told her that when societies collapse, people rob and murder and rape.

As I looked further I discovered that even the largest international aid organizations offered mostly in-house courses of differing durations and quality. None offered a university diploma that could become part of a person's educational resume, a very useful credential as one moves on, changing jobs. The IDHA fills that essential need.

Young volunteers, as well as seasoned professionals, now frequently move from local voluntary organizations, to national governmental services, to the agencies and divisions of the United Nations, and back and forth. This movement of skills and personnel among organizations is both desirable and inevitable; it promotes cross-fertilization and should be encouraged.

However, this very mobility makes it imperative that there be a common foundation, an acceptable basic minimum standard of training. Brief orientation courses for humanitarian volunteers are no longer adequate. There is a role for year-long Master's degree training courses for the committed professional, but such programs are hardly suitable for preparing large numbers of people urgently needed to serve in humanitarian crises, particularly in conflicts and disasters. Just as one would not consider sending a soldier into battle without basic military training, so also one must insist upon an adequate level of preparedness before permitting any involvement in complex humanitarian emergencies.

The Center for International Health and Cooperation (CIHC) developed a widely accepted curriculum that offers the necessary practical, thorough grounding in the fundamentals required for international humanitarian assistance. The IDHA course was developed after extensive consultation with colleagues from leading agencies involved in humanitarian work: the United Nations, the International Federation of the Red Cross, and the International Committee of the Red Cross, governmental and non-governmental voluntary organizations, and university-based experts.

An indispensable ingredient in making the IDHA program unique was the involvement of academia. It was critical that prestigious universities acknowledge practical humanitarian assistance training as a legitimate scholarly discipline worthy of an International Diploma. A careful, thoughtful curriculum, based on solid field experience, as well as academic analyses and research studies, should now replace the vague, emotion-laden ideologic approach that characterized so many previous training programs.

Humanitarian crises cry out for an immediate response. The affected communities have obvious basic needs that must be met. Acute emergencies frequently become chronic situations and thus require a response that is capable of evolving from life-saving aid to rehabilitation and development.

Humanitarian crises can often be predicted and may be preventable, or their impact minimized, with appropriate foresight and planning. Social, cultural, political, and economic forces influence crises and one must learn to determine these and other critical factors such as the local levels of health education, and existing social service traditions. Health concerns in humanitarian crises are not limited to the control of communicable diseases, the provision of food and water, the treatment of malnutrition and other medical and surgical problems. One must also be aware of the severe psychological stresses that result from and follow torture, rape, and the displacement from the security of family and neighborhood. Thus, a course designed to prepare for an appropriate "humanitarian response" must have its foundation in a multi-disciplinary approach involving and integrating personnel from a variety of backgrounds including health, mental health, logistics, management, engineering, agriculture, communications, education, conflict resolution, advocacy, international law, economics, politics, and diplomacy.

The IDHA course is purposefully intensive. It was constructed to simulate a humanitarian crisis, with long days of hard work and a forced intimacy of shared meals and dormitory accommodations. Fourteen hours a day, six days a week for a full month, candidates participate in seminars and meetings absorbing the thoughts and experiences of an expert faculty, all of whom have had extensive field experience in conflicts or disasters. Theory must be welded with experience if one is to train people for real crises. A remarkable cadre of men and women, who have lived through the hells of Somalia and Rwanda, of Liberia, Bosnia, and Chechnya, have joined in teaching the courses.

In complex humanitarian emergencies it is often difficult to identify any single paramount feature; transport, housing, sanitation, and security are as essential, for example, in a health program as are efforts toward diagnosis, immunization, and therapy. Throughout, the IDHA course fosters an appreciation of the myriad facets in humanitarian crises. The program encourages those who intend to provide help to do so with respect for the basic rights and dignity of those affected by such crises. The course, and the diploma, promote cooperation and dialogue among the critical triad, the international, governmental, and non-governmental agencies, on which international humanitarian assistance depends.

The IDHA program is rooted in an academic structure which can establish and maintain standards, support research, evaluate interventions, and identify examples of good practice. The evolving discipline of humanitarian assistance must develop an essential institutional memory that should enable operating agencies to avoid the most egregious failures and errors of earlier programs.

The curriculum approaches humanitarian assistance by devoting the first week to disaster preparedness, identifying those economic and political forces that make nations vulnerable to collapse. The second week considers the emergency response. The third week is spent defining the steps necessary to rehabilitate fractured societies. In the fourth week candidates reflect on exit strategies and, where possible, on how to assure the critical transition from emergency relief to local development. Finally, the candidates are challenged by various forms of assessment to satisfy academic criteria for a university diploma.

Throughout the course there is an emphasis on specificity—on exact definitions, methods of quantification, and assessment, exact measurement of effectiveness—for without these tools only words and emotions prevail. It is easy to stress the need for training but it is equally essential to recognize the obstacles to learning, the inherent prejudices of institutions, and individuals even in times of great humanitarian need. Lectures and seminars on politics or lack of political will, on basic human rights, ethical issues, and codes of conduct are integral parts of the humanitarian puzzle and they must be addressed, and debated, in an academic setting.

Regardless of the candidate's background or aspirations, the IDHA curriculum prepares humanitarian assistance workers to understand how political, climatic, and agricultural forces influence a crisis, and how logistics and supplies are essential elements in every undertaking. Adequate supplies, appropriate and thorough planning and efficient application are obviously a better approach than feeble, haphazard attempts to quell a crisis.

Throughout the course, there is an emphasis on those most affected in humanitarian crises, on children, too often the victims of preventable disease, too often lost or orphaned, frequently traumatized by seeing the violent deaths of family, even being forced themselves into conflict. Lecturers train the IDHA candidates in how best to help reunite families lost in a massive flood of refugees, how to help victims come to terms with the stress of national or clan collapse, personal injury and family loss.

The curriculum is all-embracing, recognizing, for example, the important role and limitations of the military during a humanitarian crisis. There is a continuous effort to promote coordination among the multiple actors that influence a humanitarian crisis. Individuals and organizations, each with their own viewpoints, interests, and even selfish agendas, must be encouraged, or even forced, to cooperate if overwhelming problems are to be resolved.

The IDHA course content indicates the complexity of international charity. How to assure funding for humanitarian efforts, how to eliminate the wasteful, and demeaning "begging bowl" approach for each crisis, and how to divide a finite fiscal pie so that all parts of the humanitarian triad can continue to contribute are essential topics for discussion. The role of the media—for good or for ill—is also studied. In Rwanda and the former Yugoslavia, for example, the perverse use of the radio helped promote, and even justify, horrible genocidal acts. Yet without media attention—

the "CNN factor"—international leaders can, and do, conveniently ignore obvious famine and oppression.

The Presidents of Fordham University in New York, the University of Geneva in Switzerland, the Royal College of Surgeons in Ireland and the CIHC are the signatories of the diploma. Several universities, including the University of Geneva, now offer up to 40 percent credit toward a Master's degree to any candidate who has successfully completed the IDHA. Further information on the curriculum and application process can be obtained from the following Web site: www.cihc.org or www.idha.ch.

35

An Attempt at a Legal Remedy: The Convention on the Safety of United Nations and Associated Personnel

M.-Christiane Bourloyannis-Vrailas*

As soon as attacks against United Nations personnel started taking on alarming proportions, proposals were put forward for a legal response to the host country's deficiency in fulfilling its duty to ensure the safety of such personnel. The concept of an international convention on the issue emerged in 1992. By the end of 1993, the UN General Assembly (GA) decided to entrust the elaboration of such a text to an ad hoc committee open to all member States.[1] On 9 December 1994, the GA adopted, by resolution 49/59, the Convention on the Safety of United Nations and Associated Personnel (hereafter: "the Convention"). This instrument addresses the issue of the safety of UN and associated personnel from two perspectives: (a) certain fundamental obligations of States and protected personnel; and (b) a mechanism to ensure that those who have attacked such personnel are brought to justice. Before proceeding to a brief overview of the main provisions under each aspect, it is necessary to take a closer look at the crucial issue of the scope of the Convention.[2]

THE SCOPE OF THE CONVENTION

Personnel Protected by the Convention

The Convention applies in respect of two categories of persons: "UN personnel" and "associated personnel." The former are defined as follows in article 1(a):

---

*The views expressed here are solely those of the author and do not necessarily represent those of the United Nations.

[1] GA Res. 48/37.

[2] The present analysis of the Convention is based in part on the following two articles by the author: "The Convention on the Safety of United Nations and Associated Personnel", 44 *International and Comparative Law Quarterly* 560 (1995) and "Crimes Against United Nations and Associated Personnel" in *Substantive and Procedural Aspects of International Criminal Law: The Experience of International and National Courts*, vol. I (Gabrielle Kirk McDonald and Olivia Swaak-Goldman, eds., 2000) 333.

(i) Persons engaged or deployed by the Secretary-General of the United Nations as members of the military, police or civilian components of a United Nations operation;

(ii) Other officials and experts on mission of the United Nations or its specialized agencies or the International Atomic Energy Agency who are present in an official capacity in the area where a United Nations operation is being conducted.

Coverage of personnel in a particular area of activity is contingent on the deployment therein of a "United Nations operation" within the meaning of the Convention. Thus, the latter would not be applicable with respect to UN High Commissioner for Refugees (UNHCR) personnel in Guinea, where there is no UN operation as defined in this instrument. And yet, in September 2000, one such staff member was killed and another was abducted in that country.[3] However, where such deployment has taken place, *all* personnel of the UN system of organizations are covered. For instance, the Convention would be applicable in Sierra Leone to both peacekeepers of the United Nations Mission in Sierra Leone (UNAMSIL) and relief workers of UNHCR. Indeed, to have drawn a distinction between persons participating in a given operation and other personnel of the UN system present in the same place but under different mandates would have resulted in unwarranted inequality of treatment. Both face the same risk, since it is rather unlikely that potential attackers would make such subtle distinctions between persons working for the UN system.

Yet, a strict interpretation of the terms "in the area" might still lead to discrimination. Let us take the cases of the murder in East Timor of a peacekeeper of the United Nations Transitional Administration in East Timor (UNTAET)[4] and the murder of three UNHCR staff in West Timor.[5] Obviously all four were present on the island in the context of the same conflict. Technically, however, West Timor is not part of UNTAET's area of deployment and the Convention's provisions for the punishment of criminals would thus not be applicable to those who murdered the relief workers.

Most post-cold war UN operations have been complex and multidimensional enterprises, involving also persons not strictly speaking part of the operation but who perform functions directly related to such operations and therefore face risks similar to those confronting "United Nations personnel" as defined in the Convention. Consequently, it was felt that such "associated personnel" also deserved coverage under this instrument. Three categories of persons fall under the definition of this term in article 1(b), when carrying out activities "in support of the fulfilment of the mandate of a United Nations operation." First, persons "assigned by a Government or an intergovernmental organization with the agreement of the competent organ of the United Nations." This would be, for instance, the case of Kosovo Force (KFOR) personnel who, inter alia, have the mandate to support the work of the United Nations Interim Administration Mission in Kosovo (UNMIK). Second, civilian contractors and any other person "engaged by the Secretary-General of the United Nations or by a

---

[3] *See* UN Press Release, Daily Highlights of 18 September 2000.
[4] *See* UN Press Release, Daily Highlights of 3 August 2000.
[5] *See* UN Press Release, Daily Highlights of 6 September 2000.

specialized agency or by the International Atomic Energy Agency." And finally, persons "deployed by a humanitarian non-governmental organization or agency under an agreement with the Secretary-General of the United Nations or with a specialized agency or with the International Atomic Energy Agency."

Operations to Which the Convention Applies

The above definitions of "United Nations personnel" and "associated personnel" both make reference to a "United Nations operation." This term is defined in article 1(c) by two elements. First, the operation must be "established by the competent organ of the United Nations in accordance with the Charter of the United Nations and conducted under United Nations authority and control." This wording has given rise to some puzzlement.[6] Indeed, an operation *established* as a subsidiary organ of the UN is normally under UN "*command* and control": this is the term of art used to designate "the political direction and exclusive operational command of the United Nations."[7] The expression "*authority* and control," on the other hand, could be interpreted by some as applying also to operations undertaken by Member States under their command and control in accordance with an "authorization" of the Security Council. However, such operations are not *established* by a UN organ and therefore would not qualify as "United Nations operations" under the Convention. Nevertheless, persons participating in national or multinational operations authorized by the Security Council may, in certain instances, qualify as associated personnel "assigned by a Government...with the agreement of the competent organ of the United Nations" if they perform their functions in support of a separate *UN* operation; they would then fall within the Convention's scope. As mentioned above, this would be, for instance, the case of KFOR personnel. There is a second component in the definition of a UN operation. Indeed, the Convention applies only:

> (i) Where the operation is for the purpose of maintaining or restoring international peace and security; or
> (ii) Where the Security Council or the General Assembly has declared, for the purposes of this Convention, that there exists an exceptional risk to the safety of the personnel participating in the operation.

Thus, although personnel may be working under similarly hazardous conditions, it is the purpose of their mandate that will determine whether the Convention is automatically applicable to them, or whether a prior declaration to that effect is required. It is particularly bewildering that UNHCR relief workers are not automatically covered. The Secretary-General, as well as the executive heads of all the organizations of the UN system, had called for equal protection for all UN personnel

---

[6] *See, e.g.,* Daphna Shraga, "The United Nations as an Actor Bound by International Humanitarian Law," in *The United Nations and International Humanitarian Law* 317, 335-336 (Luigi Condorelli, Anne-Marie La Rosa and Sylvie Scherrer, eds., 1996); and Claude Emanuelli, "La Convention sur la sécurité du personnel des Nations Unies et du personnel associé: des rayons et des ombres," 99 *Revue Générale de Droit International Public* 849, 867 (1995).

[7] Shraga, *supra* note 6, at 335-336.

while the Convention was being negotiated. But others argued that the Convention's criminal law provisions should apply only in very exceptional circumstances, when the host country was unable to offer protection and redress. Hence the above solution, presented as a compromise, but in fact more of a victory for the restrictive approach. First of all, declarations of risk under subparagraph (ii) would most likely be made in the wake of serious attacks which themselves would not be covered by the Convention. Moreover, in the two years the Convention has been in force, no such declaration has been made, although there have been clear opportunities for doing so.

To remedy this flaw, the Secretary-General has advocated the adoption of a protocol extending the automatic applicability of the Convention to all UN operations. He further proposed extending it to all humanitarian intergovernmental and non-governmental organizations present in a UN area of operation but not necessarily linked to it, "provided they carry out humanitarian relief activities in a neutral, impartial and non-discriminatory manner"; a more extreme option was to dispense with the requirement of presence in a UN area of operation. Alternatively, the Secretary-General suggested that he be empowered to make declarations of risk so as to trigger the applicability of the Convention. Pending the adoption of a protocol, he submitted for consideration three measures to strengthen the existing regime of the Convention: a procedure whereby he would recommend to the GA or the Security Council that they make declarations of risk; his designation as the "certifying authority" for the purpose of attesting to the status of a victim of an attack as "UN or associated personnel" within the meaning of the Convention, or to the existence of a declaration of risk, or to the existence of an agreement between the UN and a non-governmental organization, where such certification would assist national authorities in bringing to justice persons who have attacked protected personnel; and the incorporation of the Convention's key provisions in status-of-forces or status of mission agreements concluded with host countries.[8] By resolution 55/175 of 19 December 2000, the GA decided that the above proposals of the Secretary-General shall be considered in its Sixth (Legal) Committee in the fall of 2001.

There is one more issue related to the Convention's scope that deserves mention. It was clear, from the start of the negotiations on its text, that attacks against persons otherwise falling under the above definitions of protected personnel should not *as such* be criminalized in one specific instance, namely, when UN forces are engaged in combat. This situation is indeed regulated by international humanitarian law which treats all opponents equally; upsetting this balance could undermine compliance with such law.[9] Article 2(2) thus circumscribing the Convention's scope of application reads as follows:

> This Convention shall not apply to a United Nations operation authorized by the Security Council as an enforcement action under Chapter VII of the Charter of the United Nations in which any of the personnel are engaged as

[8] *See Scope of Legal Protection under the Convention on the Safety of United Nations and Associated Personnel—Report of the Secretary-General*, UN Doc. A/55/637, paras. 2 and 20-33 (2000).

[9] *See* Evan T. Bloom, "Protecting Peacekeepers: The Convention on the Safety of United Nations and Associated Personnel", 89 *American Journal of International Law* 621, 625 (1995).

combatants against organized armed forces and to which the law of international armed conflict applies.

This language is not devoid of ambiguities, which will complicate the judge's determination in a concrete case as to whether an attack on UN or associated personnel constituted a crime or not. Commentators have, for instance, reached different conclusions as to the applicability of the Convention to UN operations in Bosnia and Herzegovina and in Somalia on the basis of this provision.[10] One may also wonder as to the purpose of the inclusion of the phrase "and to which the law of international armed conflict applies." Is it simply stating the obvious—this is the law that applies in that case—or does it imply that there are situations in which the law of *internal* armed conflict would apply to UN personnel engaged in combat? The second interpretation would be somewhat perplexing for those—including the author—who believe that, even if a UN operation is undertaken in the context of an *internal* armed conflict, the law applicable in case it engages in combat is the law of *international* armed conflict. The question further arises as to the legal consequences of the use of force in self-defense by a UN operation which is not an enforcement action under Chapter VII, such as a classical peacekeeping operation. Where, by such use of force, peacekeepers become in fact combatants, the law of armed conflict applies. Yet, under the terms of the above exclusion clause, persons who attack in these circumstances UN personnel while respecting the rules of international humanitarian law would be characterized as criminals for the purposes of the Convention.

FUNDAMENTAL OBLIGATIONS OF STATES AND PROTECTED PERSONNEL

Obligations of States

A core provision of the Convention is article 7, which embodies three basic principles concerning the safety of UN and associated personnel:

- the obligation not to make UN and associated personnel, as well as their equipment and premises, the object of attack, or of any action that prevents such personnel from discharging their mandate. Incidentally, this prohibition is drafted in the passive voice and could be interpreted as applying not only to States, but also to individuals or to groups of individuals;
- the obligation of States, and particularly host States, to take all appropriate measures to ensure the safety of UN and associated personnel; and
- the obligation of States to cooperate with the UN and with one another in the implementation of the Convention. Such cooperation is required particularly where the host State is unable itself to take the necessary action. How this would translate in practice remains to be seen, however. Indeed, a number of

---

[10]*Contrast* Bloom, *ibid.*, *with* Emanuelli, *supra* note 6, at 873-874.

legal questions arise in these circumstances, such as the modalities for apprehending in the territory of the host State a person who has allegedly attacked
protected personnel and transferring him or her for trial to another State.

The Convention addresses the question of the privileges and immunities enjoyed
by UN and associated personnel primarily in an indirect manner. Indeed, article 4
requires the host State and the UN to "conclude as soon as possible an agreement on
the status of the United Nations operation and all personnel engaged in the operation
including, *inter alia,* provisions on privileges and immunities for military and police
components of the operation." The focus on speedy conclusion of such agreements
can be explained by the serious difficulties the UN was experiencing, at the time,
in their negotiation. But article 4 does not resolve the question of what specific
privileges and immunities apply in the absence of an agreement between the UN and
the host country, especially with regard to personnel outside the scope of the 1946
Convention on the Privileges and Immunities of the United Nations— in particular,
military and police personnel of UN operations—or in situations where the
host State is not a party thereto. Nevertheless, one aspect of this issue is dealt
with in specific terms in the Convention. Article 8, as well not specifically
addressed to States and therefore arguably binding also individuals and groups
of persons, reads:

> Except as otherwise provided in an applicable status-of-forces agreement, if
> United Nations or associated personnel are captured or detained in the course of
> the performance of their duties and their identification has been established, they
> shall not be subjected to interrogation and they shall be promptly released and
> returned to United Nations or other appropriate authorities. Pending their release
> such personnel shall be treated in accordance with universally recognized
> standards of human rights and the principles and spirit of the Geneva Conventions
> of 1949.

A further obligation of States Parties is contained in article 19, which requires
them to disseminate the Convention as widely as possible and, in particular, to
include the study thereof in their programs of military instruction. The duty of
dissemination also applies to "relevant provisions of international humanitarian
law," which underlines the fact that they are pertinent to the protection of UN and
associated personnel. For instance, knowledge of the principles and spirit of the
Geneva Conventions of 1949 is necessary to be able to implement the above-
mentioned obligation under article 8 regarding treatment of captured or detained
UN personnel.

Obligations of UN and Associated Personnel

Two main provisions address the obligations of protected personnel. Article 3
deals with the issue of their identification. It lays down different rules for military and
police components of a UN operation and for civilian personnel. The former, in
accordance with well-established rules, are required to bear distinctive identification.

As for the latter, they are to be appropriately identified unless the Secretary-General decides otherwise for safety reasons. The same rules also apply to the respective means of transportation of the two categories of personnel. This differentiation, however, concerns only exterior markings: *all* personnel are required to carry appropriate identification documents. They would thus be able, at any time, to show evidence of their special status, which could prove important for their safety. This may be the case, for instance, if UN or associated personnel are captured or otherwise apprehended by persons unaware of their identity.

Article 6 reminds UN and associated personnel that they must (a) respect host States' laws and regulations and (b) act strictly within their mandate, that is "refrain from any action or activity incompatible with the impartial and international nature of their duties." The Secretary-General has to take all appropriate measures to ensure that UN and associated personnel abide by these rules.

BRINGING OFFENDERS TO JUSTICE

The Convention applies with respect to the following crimes set out in article 9: (a) a murder, kidnapping or other attack upon the person or liberty of any United Nations or associated personnel; (b) a violent attack upon the official premises, the private accommodation or the means of transportation of any protected personnel likely to endanger his or her person or liberty. Moreover, threats and attempts to commit any of these acts also constitute crimes. So does participation as an accomplice, including in "organizing or ordering others to commit" an attack on United Nations or associated personnel. This is a recognition of the fact that, in the "context in which this Convention will be invoked, there will often be occasions on which attacks are ordered by superior authorities, both military and political."[11]

Like a number of other multilateral instruments adopted for ensuring that perpetrators of crimes of international concern, such as terrorism, are held accountable for their actions, the Convention is based on the principle *aut dedere aut iudicare* (extradite or prosecute) embodied in article 14. It follows closely their provisions for the practical implementation of this principle. Under the terms of the Convention, States parties have the obligation to make the crimes defined therein punishable under domestic law "by appropriate penalties which shall take into account their grave nature" (article 9(2)). The following States are required to establish their jurisdiction over such a crime: the State where it was committed, the State of registration in case it was committed on board a ship or aircraft, and the State of nationality of the alleged offender (article 10(1)). The Convention also gives the following States the option to establish their jurisdiction over a crime: the State of habitual residence of a stateless alleged offender; the State of nationality of the victim; and, where the crime was committed in an attempt to compel a State to do or abstain from doing any act, the targeted State (article 10(2)). Moreover, each State must establish its jurisdiction over

---

[11]Bloom, *supra* note 9, at 626.

a crime under the Convention in case it does not extradite an alleged offender present in its territory to any of the above States that have established their jurisdiction on the basis of their connection with the crime (article 10(4)). This ensures that, if a State chooses not to extradite, it can implement the alternative obligation of submitting the case to its competent authorities for the purpose of prosecution.

Rules are also provided for the implementation of the extradition option. Thus, to the extent that the crimes set out in the Convention are not extraditable offences in any extradition treaty existing between States parties, they shall be deemed to be included therein. States also undertake to include them as extraditable offences in extradition treaties to be concluded in the future. Those States that make extradition conditional on the existence of a treaty may choose to consider the Convention as a legal basis for extradition, subject to domestic laws; States that do not must recognize the crimes in the Convention as extraditable offences between themselves, subject to domestic laws (article15).

The Convention further provides that States shall cooperate for the prevention and punishment of crimes against UN and associated personnel, in particular through exchange of information (articles 11, 12 and 13(2)). They are also required to afford one another "the greatest measure of assistance" in connection with relevant criminal proceedings, including assistance in obtaining evidence (article 16(1)).

CONCLUSION

The adoption of a legal instrument was obviously never intended to provide a comprehensive solution for the protection of UN and associated personnel. Many more aspects of this complex issue are analyzed in this book. It is, however, appropriate to wonder whether the Convention has at all contributed to enhancing the safety of such personnel. This instrument has only been in force since 15 January 1999, as the pace of ratifications was initially rather slow. Moreover, just fifty-two States, less than a third of UN members, are parties to the Convention at present.[12] A momentum appears to be building up, however, since 23 of these States became parties in the course of the last 15 months. But while the majority of State parties are troop contributors, only one is currently a host to what appears to qualify as a "UN operation" within the meaning of the Convention.[13]

Although this instrument does not impose obligations exclusively upon host States, they naturally have a pivotal role to play in its implementation. One can thus hardly evaluate the Convention's impact given the above statistics. But is it only a matter of ratifications? To what extent can the Convention really make a difference?

---

[12] As of 23 May 2001, the following States were parties to the Convention: Albania, Argentina, Australia, Austria, Azerbaijan, Bangladesh, Belarus, Botswana, Brazil, Bulgaria, Chile, Costa Rica, Croatia, Czech Republic, Denmark, Ecuador, Fiji, Finland, France, Germany, Greece, Guinea, Hungary, Iceland, Italy, Jamaica, Japan, Lesotho, Libyan Arab Jamahiriya, Liechtenstein, Lithuania, Monaco, Nepal, New Zealand, Norway, Panama, Philippines, Poland, Portugal, Republic of Korea, Romania, Senegal, Singapore, Slovakia, Spain, Sweden, Tunisia, Turkmenistan, Ukraine, United Kingdom, Uruguay and Uzbekistan.

[13] Croatia is a host to the United Nations Mission of Observers in Prevlaka (UNMOP).

States have a duty to protect UN personnel on their territory irrespective of whether they are parties to the Convention or not. Nevertheless, the adoption of an instrument which elaborates on what this entails is certainly a welcome development. In addition, by establishing that the principle *aut dedere aut iudicare* shall apply in respect of crimes against UN and associated personnel, the Convention makes clear that such crimes are of concern to all States; indeed, all States have an interest in ensuring that the perpetrators of attacks against persons who act on behalf of the international community are brought to justice.

The current definition of protected personnel, as discussed above, constitutes, however, a major shortcoming. It is to be hoped that States will agree to follow the Secretary-General's recommendation for comprehensive coverage. The Convention, moreover, does not offer specific guidance in the situations it was meant primarily to address, namely, when the host State is not ensuring adequate protection. The obligation of other States under these circumstances to cooperate with each other and with the UN in implementing the Convention is phrased in very general terms. Furthermore, despite their political significance, the practical impact of the Convention's criminal law provisions may be somewhat limited—at least in the short term—where attacks on protected personnel occur in the context of an internal armed conflict. The well-established mechanism based on the principle *aut dedere aut iudicare* is indeed useful in denying a safe haven to criminals who travel as a matter of course, such as terrorists. But a person attacking UN or associated personnel is not as likely to leave the country where the operation is being conducted, particularly when actively involved in a protracted conflict. If the host State is unable or unwilling to exercise its jurisdiction over such crimes, the offender may escape prosecution.

The above critical remarks notwithstanding, it is certainly too early to pass a definite judgement on the Convention. One can only hope that where the Convention will become applicable, States will implement its provisions in good faith. This will certainly contribute to providing a more secure environment for UN and associated personnel.

36

A Call for an Accountability Campaign

Arthur C. Helton *

Over the past decade, the world has witnessed a growing number of complex humanitarian emergencies that have created an unprecedented number of refugees and internally displaced persons. Terms such as "ethnic cleansing," "failed states," and "humanitarian intervention" have entered the lexicon. Basic concepts of national sovereignty and human rights are juxtaposed in new, dynamic relationships.

In this era, burgeoning humanitarian needs have been accompanied by a new willingness on the part of the international community to become involved with conflicts inside of states. While the state may no longer be opaque, it is far from transparent. And while we now may look into the inner workings of a state for a variety of purposes, whether we then reach in to make changes for humanitarian reasons depends largely on notions of morality and legitimacy as well as capacity and proportionality, all of which may engender controversy. The international responses to circumstances involving forced displacement provide an important context for evolving humanitarian involvements inside of states in crisis, including the deployment of humanitarian aid workers.

These new trends have produced new casualties. One of the harsh outcomes associated with the deployment of humanitarian workers in the midst of conflict has been the abuse of aid workers. Humanitarian agencies are often targeted now by one or more of the sides in a conflict, or they become targets merely because of their resources and relative wealth.

There have been many notorious recent incidents. In September 2000, three staff members of the United Nations High Commissioner for Refugees were brutally murdered in Atambua, West Timor. In October 1999, two workers with UNICEF and the World Food Programme were killed in Burundi. The International Committee of the Red Cross (ICRC) had six staff savagely killed in Chechnya in late 1996. In April 2001, six ICRC workers were shot and hacked to death in the northeast of the Democratic Republic of Congo, and an assault on the Médecins

*The assistance of Eliana Jacobs, Research Associate at the Council on Foreign Relations, in the preparation of this chapter is gratefully acknowledged. The chapter is based on a section in Mr. Helton's forthcoming book, *The Price of Indifference: Refugees and Humanitarian Action in the New Century*, to be published by Oxford University Press in 2002.

Sans Frontières (MSF) compound in Mogadishu, Somalia, resulted in the death of twelve Somalis, including compound guards.

The trends, moreover, are ominous. Many aid workers have been killed, assaulted, or kidnapped with impunity over the past decade. While there is no comprehensive archive, an ad hoc compilation shows that in 1998, 48 civilian relief workers died and, after a brief downturn in 1999, a like number perished in 2000 [1]. In September 2000, the UN stated that a total of 198 of their civilian workers in the field had been killed since 1992 [2].

The exact dimension of the problem, whether abuses of aid workers are increasing or not, was not clear to Austen Davis of MSF-Holland, when we spoke in Amsterdam in 2000. He was unconvinced that the incidents are increasing, but this is distinctly a minority view. Marion Harroff-Tavel, with whom I spoke later at the ICRC in Geneva, believes that incidents are increasing, in part because of the changing nature of conflict. Armed conflict is increasingly intrastate in character, and the combatants have proliferated in unstructured ways. In one instance of internal conflict in central Africa, ICRC had 32 "interlocutors" to whom to relate, she said, "Criminality, drugs and light weapons now move from conflict to conflict."

On occasion, in some venues such as Somalia or Chechnya, even the ICRC has had to arrange for armed escorts, despite a general policy to the contrary. Harroff-Tavel's passion on this issue was perhaps informed to some degree by the fact that when we spoke in August 2000, two ICRC delegates were being held for ransom in Georgia along with their driver. While they were later released, ICRC suspended its operations in the remote Georgian province adjoining Chechnya until appropriate security arrangements could be made.

Humanitarian workers traditionally accept the sacrifice of personal comfort and safety in order to help others. Aid agencies are thus often embarrassed in some sense to champion their own security. But the result is an outcome deeply disruptive of the efforts to provide assistance in countries roiled with conflict and crisis. Access by agencies to minister to vulnerable populations can be effectively blocked by attacks on aid workers, which are tantamount to attacks on the system of humanitarian assistance itself. The international community must deal with this problem directly and robustly.

The current efforts to address it have been largely relegated to providing equipment—armored vehicles, helmets, flak jackets—and training. Most large operating humanitarian agencies now have ex-military security advisors on staff. In February 2000, a full-time UN security coordinator was appointed to address the problem [3]. But equipment and training are not sufficient. The international community must ensure that there is an adequate legal framework to hold accountable those who kill or abuse humanitarian workers.

As elaborated in the immediately preceding chapter, a United Nations treaty that entered into force in January 1999 provides universal jurisdiction to bring to trial offenders who have assaulted or murdered aid workers, and enjoins a duty on the part of signatory countries to prevent such abuses from occurring in the future. As of March 2001, 50 states had become party to this treaty [4]. While a good start, the UN safety convention leaves uncovered certain aid workers who are not associated with the United Nations, and there is a gap where the UN has undertaken peace enforcement activities and become itself a party to the conflict. Coverage in this circumstance is left to the province of humanitarian law and the 1949 Geneva Conventions. Some have called for an additional protocol to the safety treaty to extend coverage more broadly.

The International Criminal Court, established by a multilateral UN treaty which 139 states have signed as of February 2001, could provide another mechanism to safeguard humanitarian aid workers when it becomes operational [5]. But limitations on the jurisdiction of the Court to "widespread or systematic" infractions of international law in the nature of crimes against humanity could preclude protection of individual abuses of aid workers [5, Art. 7(1)]. The Court would have authority to remedy war crimes committed in the context of "armed conflict not of an international character" (as opposed to riots, sporadic acts of violence, or similar acts) [5, Art. 8(2)(c) and (d)]. That the Court's jurisdiction would extend only to crimes against humanity and war crimes committed as a matter of "policy" could also be held to limit its protection in relation to humanitarian workers [5, Art. 8(1)].

But the real challenge is beyond legal mechanisms. What is needed is an international political campaign to bring such offenders to justice. The United Nations Security Council now recognizes the crucial role played by humanitarian workers in complex emergencies. On several occasions recently, Security Council resolutions have cited the responsibilities to protect aid workers and to bring to justice those who commit offenses against them.

For example, in 1998, the Security Council addressed the situation of insecurity in relation to the conflict concerning Abkhazia in the Gali region of Georgia, expressing deep concern "for the refugees and displaced persons returning to the region, for aid workers and for the personnel of the United Nations Observer Mission in Georgia (UNOMIG) and of the Collective Peacekeeping Forces of the Commonwealth of Independent States (CIS peacekeeping force)." The Council called upon "the parties" to ensure the safety and freedom of movement of all United Nations personnel, the CIS peacekeeping force and "international humanitarian organizations" [6]. Likewise, in 2000, the President of the Security Council underscored the need for a robust effort to protect aid workers in connection with recent emergencies in Africa:

> The Security Council underlines the importance of safe and unhindered access, in accordance with international law, of humanitarian personnel to civilians in armed conflict, including refugees and internally displaced persons, and the protection of humanitarian assistance to them, and recalls the responsibility of all parties to conflict to ensure the safety and security of such personnel. The Council condemns recent acts of deliberate violence in Africa against humanitarian personnel [7].

After the grisly murder of UNHCR staff in West Timor in September 2000, the Security Council insisted that the Indonesian authorities ensure the safety and security of humanitarian workers and stressed that "those responsible for the attacks on international personnel" be brought to justice [8].

But resolutions are not sufficient; the basic problem is impunity. Concerted efforts must be undertaken, including providing appropriate political and diplomatic incentives or disincentives in order to ensure that those who perpetrate offenses against aid workers are arrested, and either tried in a court of law or extradited to stand trial. This is a crucial adjunct to new efforts to assist vulnerable populations in the midst of conflict [9].

Information is often a prerequisite to action. That there is no comprehensive archive cataloging the abuses perpetrated against aid workers is the starting point for an accountability campaign. A systematic archive, ideally electronic, would inform all stakeholders of the dimensions and trends relating to the problem. The ReliefWeb web site would be an obvious candidate for this purpose, particularly its new advocacy site that is currently being developed [10]. But other hosts should be considered as well.

For a campaign to be effective, information must be compiled, analyzed, and promoted. Aid worker casualties would be an important element of a report on the state of humanitarianism that should be published by NGO consortia in cooperation with international organizations. The advocacy targets should be, in the first instance, the governmental authorities in whose jurisdictions abuses occur. Where those authorities are unwilling or unable to provide redress, the international community, taken in the widest sense to mean governments, international organizations, NGOs, and civil society more generally, should step in to provide a remedy.

If the international community is to find workable approaches to address humanitarian needs within countries that are riven by crisis and war, much more has to be done to ensure that aid workers, this essential channel of access to humanitarian assistance, are protected. This is not just a plea to not harm the helpers; it is a recognition that the basic strategy of providing humanitarian aid in situations of internal strife and crisis depends upon achieving this measure of human security.

REFERENCES

1. *Chronology of United Nations and Humanitarian Aid Workers Killed in 2000*, compiled by Dennis King, UNICEF Office of Emergency Programmes, 15 January, 2001, available at <www.reliefweb.int/library/documents/2001/chronology_15jan.htm>. Numbers for 1998 and 1999 obtained privately from Dennis King.
2. U.N. Staff Protest Killing of Co-Workers, *Deutsche Presse-Agentur*, 21 September, 2000.
3. Robert Holloway, Full-Time UN Security Coordinator to Protect Aid Workers, *Agence France Presse*, 9 February, 2000.
4. *Convention on the Safety of United Nations and Associated Personnel*, adopted by resolution 49/59 of the General Assembly dated 9 December, 1994, entry into force 15 January, 1999, U.N. Doc. A-49/742.
5. *Rome Statute of the International Criminal Court*, available at <www.un.org/law/icc/statute.htm>, visited on 29 March, 2001.
6. *Security Council Resolution 1150 on the situation in Georgia*, adopted on 30 January, 1998. U.N. Doc. S/RES/1150 (1998), Sect. 9.

7. *Statement by the President of the Security Council*, U.N. Doc. S/PRST/2000/1, 13 January, 2000.

8. *Security Council Resolution 1319 on the situation in East Timor*, adopted on 8 September, 2000, U.N. Doc. S/RES/1319 (2000), Sect. 2

9. See, *Report of the Secretary-General to the Security Council on the protection of civilians in armed conflict*, U.N. Doc. S/2001/331, 30 March, 2001.

10. See <www.reliefweb.int>.

Voice

SOME PRINCIPLES OF SELF HEALING
Yael Danieli

Viewing trauma treatment and training from a long-term, including intergenerational, perspective, elsewhere I have introduced extensively [1, 2] the following general principles of self-healing, designed to help protectors and providers to recognize, contain, and heal their emotional reactions to trauma, and thought that they may benefit the readers of this volume as well:

A. To recognize one's reactions:
1. Develop awareness of somatic signals of distress—one's chart of warning signs of potential reactions, like sleeplessness, headaches, perspiration.
2. Try to find words to name accurately and to articulate one's inner experiences and feelings. As Bettelheim commented, "what cannot be talked about can also not be put to rest; and if it is not, the wounds continue to fester from generation to generation" [3, p. 166].

B. To contain one's reactions:
1. Identify one's personal level of comfort in order to build openness, tolerance and readiness to hear **anything.**
2. Knowing that every emotion has a beginning, a middle and an end, learn to attenuate one's fear of being overwhelmed by its intensity to try to feel its full life-cycle without resorting to defensive reactions.

C. To heal and grow:
1. Accept that nothing will ever be the same.
2. When one feels wounded, one should take time, accurately diagnose, sooth and heal before being "emotionally fit" again to continue to work.
3. Seek consultation or therapy for previously unexplored areas triggered by patients' stories.
4. Any one of the affective reactions (i.e., grief, mourning, rage) may interact with old, unworked through experiences of the therapists. Protectors and providers will thus be able to use their professional work purposefully for their own growth.
5. Establish a network of people to create a "holding environment" [4] within which one can share one's trauma-related work.
6. Protectors and providers should provide themselves with avocational avenues for creative and relaxing self-expression in order to regenerate energies.

379

Being kind to oneself and feeling free to have fun and joy is not a frivolity in this field but a necessity without which one cannot fulfill one's professional obligations, one's professional contract.

REFERENCES

1. B. Smith, I. Agger, Y. Danieli, and L. Weisaeth, Emotional Responses of International Humanitarian Aid Workers: The Contribution of Non-Governmental Organizations, in *International Responses to Traumatic Stress,* Y. Danieli, N. S. Rodley, and L. Weisaeth (eds.), Baywood, Amityville, New York, pp. 397-423, 1996.
2. Y. Danieli, Countertransference, Trauma and Training, in *Countertransference in the Treatment of PTSD,* J. P. Wilson and J. D. Lindy, The Guilford Press, New York, pp. 368-388, 1994.
3. B. Bettelheim, Afterword, in C. Vegh (ed.), *I Didn't Say Goodbye,* E. P. Dutton, New York, 1979.
4. D. W. Winnicott, *The Maturational Processes and the Facilitating Environment,* Hogarth Press, London, 1965.

Conclusion

Yael Danieli

The chapters and voices in this book point clearly to a crisis facing our international institutions, both intergovernmental and non-governmental, and the media who seek to alleviate and report human suffering throughout the world. All too often, the world loses sight of the costs, notwithstanding the accomplishments, borne by international protectors and providers sharing the front lines and the back hills. This should not be a silent crisis: the media, the governing bodies and management of these institutions, and states must do everything possible to mitigate the increasing vulnerability and danger faced by, and their detrimental effects upon, these interveners and, consequently, on their work on behalf of victims.

Lamenting that representatives of the United Nations, relief agencies, and the media are no longer given protection by warring parties, as befits their impartial status, is understandable. But it is unrealistic to expect that this alarming trend will be significantly reversed. In today's world, there are likely to be attacks on more tents with red crosses on the roof and on vehicles with the UN letters on the side. We need to examine carefully and revise personnel policies that have not kept up with increasingly volatile situations where the Geneva Conventions provide no protection.

While it is clearly desirable to have more states ratify and honor the Convention on the Safety of United Nations and Associated Personnel, and to support the Secretary-General's suggestion for the adoption of a protocol extending the automatic applicability of the Convention to all UN operations, this would be of only limited value. States already have the obligation to protect those personnel on their territories whether they are a party to the Convention or not. As noted in chapter 35, the Convention does not offer specific guidelines as to what must be done when the host state fails to provide protection; the obligation of other states to cooperate with the UN and others to implement it is phrased in very general terms. Further, the Convention's scope does not extend to most NGO humanitarian workers and the media, a fact that should be revisited in this context or elsewhere. In his 30 March 2001 report to the Security Council on the protection of civilians in armed conflict (S/2001/331), the Secretary-General advocated creating a culture of protection. While his call is aimed at civilian populations, its recommendations also cover obtaining safe and meaningful access to vulnerable populations [1]. A crucial task ahead is thus to create additional safety and security systems that maximize political and legal pressure on behalf of protectors and providers and the media. The single most important initiative that can be taken is to bring pressure to bear on host states to live up to their commitments.

Arthur Helton (chapter 36) suggests that the real challenge is to go beyond legal mechanisms, and that what is needed is an international political campaign to bring offenders to justice. The issue of impunity, or near impunity, must be addressed. This will clearly not be an easy task. Between 1992 and 2000 only three people from the 177 incidents involving the violent death of UN personnel were brought to justice. The short sentences handed down by a Jakarta court for the brutal killings in September 2000 of three UNHCR staff members poignantly demonstrate the parody of justice that at time characterizes such trials. Only the muscle of UN Member States, exercised through incentives and disincentives, can send a strong message to governments and other groups who endanger protectors and providers that they will be held accountable. The creation of a database cataloguing the abuses perpetrated against aid workers, comparable to that on the media compiled by the Committee to Protect Journalists, would be a beginning.

No organization can take its continued relevance for granted if it fails to protect and care for the very agents it dispatches to troubled lands. The war against armed conflict, poverty, famine, HIV/AIDS, and all other ills that afflict humanity cannot be waged, let alone won, if the workers for peace and relief are themselves potential casualties. While recent attention by the General Assembly and the Security Council to the safety and support of international workers is a welcome development, it is insufficient. The issue needs to be mainstreamed into the agendas of both bodies. An initial step would be for them to sponsor jointly a day in the margins of each General Assembly devoted to creating the political, legal and financial bases for enhancing staff security and for a meaningful implementation of the recommendations in this book.

Faced with this crisis, over the past few years a broad array of responses has emerged. The book organized them in a threefold format: before, during, and after missions.

BEFORE THE MISSION

A critical element of any mission is recruitment, staffing and assignment. Authors who comment, posit the best situation to be having regular staff, pre-trained in hazardous area operations, reasonably rested, in manager Arès' words, "so that their minds and bodies can recuperate" (having been rotated within the organization between hazardous duty and less threatening and stressful tasks), motivated, and having personal and professional matters in hand so that they can leave quickly. In fact, this rarely happens. The sheer magnitude and pressure of the emergency ("do something and do it fast"), perhaps as well for competitive reasons, usually require that regular professional staff be supplemented by staff recruited expressly for the mission, and on (renewable) short-term contracts. Frequently, these are drawn from the ranks of the "career" complex emergency corps (chapter 22), with all the problems that may entail. At the other extreme, desperate for staff, recruiters resort to the dangerous practice of sending "someone really green . . . but often it is these people who are most motivated to go" (chapter 6). In fact, most recruitment requires a combination of all three: the young and enthusiastic, the well-trained regular staff, and the pros on the circuit who go from emergency to emergency. To meet the complex needs of this diverse staff, proper assignments, as much training as possible, and the creation of a solid support network are required.

The significance of the fit between the individual's personality and the place and nature of the assignment was driven home to me in Rwanda when I was asked to evaluate a young man who had been placed "on a back hill" where he was all alone after the workday, and "became utterly depressed and nonfunctioning." Had he been placed in a team, his breakdown would probably have been averted. In the context of peacekeeping, research (chapter 2) has shown that being single and having a lower educational level are risk factors for developing PTSD symptoms. More attention should be given to this important dimension (chapters 18, 25).

Effective pre-mission training must begin with instilling awareness of the need for security and psychosocial support in the culture of organizations. Patched together, ad hoc and solely programmatic efforts will have only minimal impact. Security and support must be integrated, both structurally and functionally, into the mainstream of pre-mission operations: mission planning, staffing, and budgeting. But for this to happen, states, governing bodies, and senior management must be committed to the change in the organizational culture that will make authentic, comprehensive support—both for physical safety and mental health—possible (chapters 4, 22). A sound psychosocial support system begins with the recruitment of appropriately trained mental health professionals, with expertise, for example, in trauma, gender (chapter 7) and family issues, and their full integration into the organization's work program. Medical briefing, information about food safety and common diseases, including HIV/AIDS, and traumatic stress are essential components of preparation (chapter 6).

This inevitably raises the question of resources. Here, hard choices must be made, and adhered to. Funding for training, safety, and support must be built not only into budgets of missions, but into the regular, continuing administrative budgets of organizations. This is beginning to happen, but often reluctantly; resources for staff support remain scarce when compared with the guaranteed line items for other functions. And, there is even greater resistance to addressing concerns about staff mental health and well-being than confronting their physical safety and security. When the budget reviews, and cuts, come, it is unacceptable, if not irresponsible, to look at the line items for security and support measures as places where cuts can be made.

Ideally, teams should never be sent into the field until a satisfactory level of security can be assured. Adequate security and risk training should be a pre-condition for UN, NGO, or media going into a high-risk area, as well as for locally recruited, staff. In reality, this is hard to do since emergencies demand rapid response. But, the higher the level of advance preparation and training, the lower the risk of a security-related disaster. It is essential that decision-makers understand this simple, yet vital, fact, and act (and budget) accordingly.

DURING THE MISSION

Staff on mission in hazardous areas must be cared for and trained to understand their (external as well as internal) environment and to care for themselves. Security concerns should be addressed forthrightly. The media, humanitarian, and human rights workers must circulate widely among those in need, and they do not have the luxury of moving in heavily armed groups, or spending most of their time in fortified compounds, so such basics as suitably equipped vehicles, flak jackets, emergency equipment, and the like must be routine (chapter 9). As Kris Hurlburt (chapter 15) observes: "A sound security system is the best prevention in terms of both physical and psychological safety." Perhaps even more important is educating the workers on-site about ways to minimize all risks and avoid those which can be avoided. This may be complicated by the fact that, as several authors noted—especially those in the media, some writing about themselves—work in hazardous areas seems to attract people who are not only less averse to risk, but even welcome it, as well as bringing out risky behaviors in those who, in their usual environments, would be more cautious [2]. Given that a plurality of deaths among aid workers occurs in the first ninety days (chapter 16) and that, among peacekeepers, negative appraisal of mission predicts PTSD symptoms (chapter 2), special attention must be paid in the initial period of service.

Staff must be made aware of basic provisions, such as what the U.S. Peace Corps (chapter 14) terms an appropriate cultural lifestyle (respectful of local norms), as well as defensive driving, movement in groups, and avoidance of conflict situations. As in the pre-mission stage, education is required about the nature of stress, how to recognize post traumatic stress reactions, and related behaviors (see chapters 24, 29, 30, 31), and what assistance is available. Supervisors should be alert for signs of stress, as denial may inhibit effective self-care, and also be aware that frequently those who need help most are those most reluctant to seek it (chapter 21). Human rights education focusing on their behavior toward the local population, particularly victims, and on preserving their own moral integrity, is necessary (chapter 2) [2].

The overwhelming importance of maintaining open communication on all levels came through in most contributions. Research (chapter 24) found that limited communication with the outside world was a stressor, and that poor communication with clients and coworkers is associated with burnout. Social factors such as access to communications with family and friends appear particularly important. As Kris Hurlburt (chapter 15) noted: ". . . the development of communications technology has proven the single, most effective support for expatriates worldwide." Data have clearly shown the importance of open communication within units or teams (chapters 17, 20, 22) and between leaders and soldiers (chapter 2). Even reaching out to an attacker may create a sense of safety (chapter 12). Effective communications between headquarters and the field are essential to making sound security decisions based on reliable information (chapter 5), whereas lack of such communication has proven both demoralizing and dangerous.

Caring for humanitarian workers and the media during missions must include psychosocial support, which should be immediately available to them as well as to family members, especially if things go wrong. This book may facilitate the expansion of a worldwide network of counselors for these groups. Several organizations report the use of peer support networks made up of volunteer staff who receive appropriate training, and operate under the supervision of professionally trained counselors. This has the advantage of being relatively low-cost, as compared to recruiting a larger number of professionals. Another simple support strategy is a "buddy system" (chapter 20).

Again, the importance of senior level support of readily accessible stress management and counseling programs cannot be overemphasized. It must be clear and accepted policy—especially by senior management who determine promotions and future assignments—that no stigma be attached to seeking psychological support. Where critical incident debriefing is required, providers must be available as quickly as possible: MSF-Holland's stringent goal is within 24 hours (chapter 17), WFP's is 72 (chapter 4). A UN manager, Kathleen Cravero, calls for respect for individual differences, as healing and the pace of healing are uniquely individual, perhaps also culturally determined. Indeed, research has shown (chapter 32) that some individuals are more likely to benefit from help at a later date.

Recreation facilities, properly planned and budgeted for; mandatory R&R, and emergency and compassionate leave arrangements are all necessary elements of a well thought out support system. Out of dedication and guilt, staff may press to put off leisure or leave while people are dying. The on-site supervisor, frequently overwhelmed by the needs of the victims, may agree. Giving in to these behaviors is deleterious, both for the aid workers and, ultimately, for those they are dedicated to helping. As Søren Jessen-Petersen states (chapter 3): "only when staff are safe, healthy and psychologically prepared can they be expected to protect and support" the victims.

AFTER THE MISSION: COPING WITH THE AFTERMATH

Every author addressing the return home commented on the "conspiracy of silence" [4, 5] or "homecoming stress" [6] returnees experience far too often following missions. As with many trauma victims, providers and protectors find that friends, colleagues, and even their families back home find little time for or interest in listening to and discussing their mission experiences. These reactions often force them to conclude that no one could really understand unless they had been through the same experiences. Both intrapsychically and interpersonally, though seemingly protective, silence is profoundly destructive, for it attests to the inability of the individual, family, society, community, and nation to integrate trauma. This prevalence of a conspiracy of silence stands in sharp contrast to the widespread findings that social support is among the most important factors in coping with traumatic stress [7].

Although some steps have been taken to improve the situation (chapter 11), compassionate, (multi)culturally-sensitive response to death of employees should replace the "solidly litigation-oriented" culture (chapter 6).

Throughout the book, there is repeated and enthusiastic emphasis on the need for debriefing following critical incidents or service in a hazardous area. In their comprehensive review of psychological debriefing, Raphael and Ursano (chapter 32), however, caution that the growth of the debriefing movement has been based on perceptions of need and of helpfulness in the absence of critical examination and empirical evidence, and appeal for more research that recognizes the complexity of recovery from trauma.

To compensate for their shared sense of alienation and to address job insecurity, several organizations (chapters 14, 17, 20, 30) have developed networks of alumni/alumnae groups that give continued psychosocial support and assistance with career development. Chapter 34 describes an international training course in humanitarian assistance which provides a university diploma that becomes part of the person's educational resume, a useful credential as he or she changes jobs. As stress reactions can occur long after missions, medical and psychological support should be available for some time after contracts end.

NATIONAL STAFF

National staff do not receive the security and support afforded their international colleagues, including remuneration and insurance, nor are they as respected for their credentials, experience, and knowledge of local culture (chapters 1, 8, 13, 19, 22, 23). Most of all, when missions leave or evacuate, they stay, often in danger to themselves and their families. Indeed, international protectors and providers report feeling outrage, incompleteness, and guilt when locally-recruited colleagues and their families are left to this fate.

Some parallels exist between nationally recruited staff, freelance journalists and stringers, short-term professionals, and reservists in military units. They tend not to be treated equally to their counterparts, or fairly; they may feel and, in fact, are left out of some arrangements and benefits. These gaps should be addressed.

CONTINUING RESEARCH

The book underscores consistently the need for continuing empirical research. UNHCR (chapter 3) calls for a research component "to document the work done, monitor trends and guide further development of stress and management strategy." The pioneering studies by Lopes Cardozo and Salama (chapter 24) on humanitarian aid workers, Feinstein (chapter 27) and Newman (chapter 28) on journalists, in addition to the numerous studies reviewed by Weerts et al. (chapter 2) on peacekeepers, should be replicated widely and built upon systematically and creatively.

A serious research need that must be addressed is that, while up to 75 percent of military peacekeepers come from developing countries, almost all available research is on troops from developed countries. Also, there is little research on civilian police and military observers. Each country should develop a database with ongoing registration of relevant medical, psychological and social data of its military personnel. Finally, as most studies are retrospective and PTSD-focused, they should be expanded.

The WHO proposal (chapter 6) that the Inter-Agency Standing Committee set up a reference group on the occupational health of humanitarian workers, in its broadest sense, from behavior and environment related risks to those related to violence, could be the umbrella group to coordinate broad-based research, in consultation with NGO and academic experts such as is done in this volume.

THE QUESTION OF RESOURCES

At the end of the day, after all the horror stories, all the revelations of gaps in security and psychosocial support, and all of the statements that we must do better, if only to ensure the retention of staff, the fundamental question of resources remains: how can they be made both adequate and sustainable?

Peacekeeping budgets submitted by the Secretary-General should contain adequate, assured funding for security and support components. Often, psychosocial care (at least for troops from developed countries) is provided by their governments (chapter 1). The real problem lies in the funding of organizations that provide humanitarian workers, both those in the UN system and NGOs. For NGOs, who frequently receive their funding from governments and private sources, the imperative is to build security and support costs into the budget, at all stages, and keep them there.

For the UN system, there is a clear need to enhance the coordinating and clearinghouse role of the UN Security Coordinator (UNSECOORD). It is impossible, at current funding and staffing levels, for UNSECOORD to do an acceptable job on behalf of tens of thousands of UN staff in more than 150 duty stations. Depending on voluntary contributions is a necessary interim measure; however, it is unreasonable to expect UN staff to rely on an uncertain flow of resources for their safety. There have been some encouraging steps in this regard in the 2001 budget, but these are only the beginning. Member States of the UN must recognize and act on their obligation to support and protect those they ask to aid, often at great risk, the world's victims. As UN Secretary-General Kofi Annan stated (A/55/494): "There is no question that good security requires adequate and predictable funding. There should be nothing discretionary about the financing of staff security: it is neither a luxury nor a perk. It is something we owe those who are willing to serve humanity under the most challenging of circumstances."

A FINAL WORD

This book covers experiential reflections from the ground, between field and headquarters, organizational and management views at and from headquarters, and the perspectives of governing bodies. This multilayered approach creates a book rich in both concept and detail that seeks to address comprehensively, both structurally and functionally, the many facets of a complex set of issues and needs. The volume reveals how the authors view, understand, and conceptualize the concerns of the main groups of international protectors and providers—peacekeepers, humanitarian aid workers, human rights defenders, and the media—and places the findings within a long-term multidimensional, multidisciplinary, integrative framework [3].

Participants' responses to being asked to contribute to the book ranged from gratitude for the opportunity to share and reflect on their experiences to dismissing the effort to focus on the protectors and providers, rather than on the victims, as preposterous or obscene ("What do I matter in the face of a million dead?"). Some sanitized their experiences when they put them on paper, fearing that their criticisms of organizational practices, or recounting their problem and need for help, would invite stigma and endanger their careers, sadly demonstrating how far we still have to go to change organizational cultures in order to provide proper support for their staff (chapter 10).

Many of the support programs described in the chapters are significant responses to eloquent statements of need. However, a substantial number of people—many of whom contributed their voices to this volume—expressed dissatisfaction with the security and care they had received, which challenges the often glowing reports of the programs described. In this sense, the book portrays an almost ideal picture of a select few rather than reflecting the wider reality.

Organizations, too, suffer from cumulative stress without realizing it or taking it into account. In fact, many internal ruptures of organizations, on personal or functional bases, are perhaps a repetition of the rupture of trauma and the neglect to attend to the need for healing from it. Walkup's analysis of organizational response to its members' exposure to trauma (chapter 33) shows how this contributes to their rigidity and inability to change while deluding themselves into thinking that they are doing everything right. While in the short term they may feel that they are saving costs, or at least saving face, in the long run the cumulative impact is much larger.

International organizations must recognize, for their workers and for themselves, the potential effects of (massive, intense, and often unrelenting) exposure to trauma, and establish policies, budgets, and programs to be integrated into their cultures and streamlined through guidelines and practices informed by experience and research. To do so, they have to keep alive ongoing dynamic dialogues among all layers of involvement. This continued exchange with protectors and providers on the ground and upon reentry will ensure that these policies and programs are not taken for granted and do not become stale.

However, even though the wide gap between need and solutions exists, the information in this book provides many building blocks for the future. The book's power is that what on the surface seem to be disparate groups of people—peacekeepers, humanitarian workers, human rights defenders, and the media—face similar problems and respond similarly to direct and vicarious exposure to trauma. Together in the same book, they can learn from each other, and make their individual cases stronger.

Given the deep, underlying causes of today's conflicts and the weak capacity for peace and development in the most affected countries, it would be unrealistic to conceive of a world with no war, suffering, or interveners. It is, however, within the realm of possibilities to conceive of a world where conflict prevention could play a more prominent role in the international peace agenda. It is our hope that the forceful voices this book projects will not only help improve the performance of international protectors and providers in the face of adversity, but strengthen our collective resolve to make conflict prevention an indispensable element of that peace agenda. A serious examination of history, a required discipline for our understanding, teaches us that most often crises can be anticipated and be either prevented or prepared for. It should go beyond analyses of current political and socioeconomic trends, to studying multigenerational legacies of trauma [2]. If this book about international protectors and providers contributes to a broader and stronger partnership for conflict prevention and the pursuit of human security, then it will have succeeded, and hopefully may not have to be written again.

I had two dreams in creating this book. The first was to assemble a body of policy and program recommendations based on the bedrock of experience articulated in authentic voices and systematic research rather than on only ad hoc, short-term emergency responses to crises. The second was to build a place where protectors and providers will feel at home: (their experiences) articulated, heard, acknowledged, comforted, understood, no longer lonely in their moral and other confusion and pain, appreciated and cared for. Only then will international organizations be truly humanized. Sometimes I symbolically visualized the voices in the book as forming a tapestry to give warmth and enrich that home. Many of the contributors to the book shared my dreams. I fervently hope that we have succeeded in conveying the profound sense of satisfaction with serving, the unabiding commitment to helping those in need, and the need and obligation to support protectors and providers and their families so they can better serve humanity.

REFERENCES

1. S. Chesterman (ed.), *Civilians in War*, Lynne Rienner Publishers, Inc. Boulder, Colorado, 2001.
2. B. Smith, I. Agger, Y. Danieli, and L. Weisaeth, Emotional Responses of International Humanitarian Aid Workers: The Contribution of Non-Governmental Organizations, in *International Responses to Traumatic Stress*, Y. Danieli, N. S. Rodley, and L. Weisaeth (eds.), Baywood, Amityville, New York, pp. 397-423, 1996.
3. Y. Danieli, E. Stamatopoulou, and C. J. Dias (eds.), *The Universal Declaration of Human Rights: Fifty Years and Beyond,* Baywood, Amityville, New York, 1999.
4. Y. Danieli, Confronting the Unimaginable: Psychotherapists' Reactions to Victims of the Nazi Holocaust, in *Human Adaptation to Extreme Stress: From the Holocaust to Vietnam*, J. P. Wilson, Z. Harel, and B. Kahana (eds.), Plenum Press, New York, pp. 219-238, 1996.

5. Y. Danieli (ed.), *International Handbook of Multigenerational Legacies of Trauma*, Plenum/Kluwers, New York, 1998.
6. D. R. Johnson, H. Lubin, R. Rosenheck, A. Fontana, S. Southwick, and D. Charney, The Impact of the Homecoming Reception on the Development of Posttraumatic Stress Disorder: The West Haven Homecoming Stress Scale (WHHSS), *Journal of Traumatic Stress, 10*:2, pp. 259-277, 1997.
7. C. B. Eriksson, H. V. Kemp, R. Gorsuch, S. Hoke, and D. W. Foy, Trauma Exposure and PTSD Symptoms in International Relief and Development Personnel, *Journal of Traumatic Stress, 14*:1, pp. 205-212, 2001.

Epilogue

Kenzo Oshima
Under-Secretary-General for Humanitarian Affairs and
Emergency Relief Co-ordinator

In the Millennium Declaration of 8 September 2000 the 189 Member States of the United Nations undertook "to expand and strengthen the protection of civilians in complex emergencies, in conformity with international law." The pledge is a bold one: many serious constraints stand in the way of its fulfillment; equally, there are grounds for cautious optimism. So, too, are there practical measures that can be taken. As the various chapters of this book have emphasized, one crucial prerequisite for the enhanced protection of civilians is the creation of a legal and political environment in which the humanitarian workers, peacekeepers, and the media—the providers and protectors referred to in the title of the book—can do their jobs in conditions of greater security.

The creation of such an environment is sorely needed. The last decade has witnessed a sorry litany of wars and human catastrophes that have transformed both the scale and the nature of the tasks facing the international community. In this period alone there have been more than a hundred armed conflicts, claiming the lives of millions of civilians and displacing many more from their homes. Of these conflicts only seven have been between states. Typically, these internal wars have been accompanied by a blurring of the lines between combatants and non-combatants, whereby the targeting of civilians has become a deliberate end, and no longer the side effect, of armed confrontation. Today's warfare takes place in cities and in villages: civilians and aid workers have become preferred targets, the propagation of terror is now a premeditated tactic, and the physical elimination or mass displacement of certain categories of populations (defined by race, social origin, or geography) has evolved into an overarching strategy of warmongers. In conflicts today, between 75 percent and 90 percent of casualties are civilians. Breaches of human rights and humanitarian law, including mutilation, rape, forced displacement, denial of the right to food and medicines, diversion of aid, and attacks on medical personnel and hospitals have become the means of achieving objectives. The deliberate targeting of civilians has been central to the military strategy of one or more of the combatants: genocide in Rwanda, "ethnic cleansing" in former Yugoslavia, anarchy in Somalia, and mass mutilation in Sierra Leone, to list only the most egregious.

Here and elsewhere, the lion's share of expanding and strengthening the protection of civilians has been taken on by the international humanitarian community, working for the most part in the absence of a peace process or peacekeeping operation. Peacekeepers go where they are mandated under specific resolutions, with concrete areas of responsibility and rules of engagement, and often for limited periods of time. Humanitarians, on the other hand, are usually the first on the scene and often stay when others leave. In Sierra Leone, for example, humanitarian concerns are being addressed in conjunction with a peacekeeping operation, whereas in neighboring Liberia and Guinea a humanitarian effort is dealing with the spillover effects from Sierra Leone as well as deteriorating internal strife, but in the absence of peacekeeping. In Afghanistan, a protracted conflict where the peace process is stalled and the fighting continues, humanitarian aid workers are attempting to provide emergency relief alongside development activities and institution building. Even when the emergency has failed to reach the media limelight, as in Georgia, or the post-conflict situation still requires attention as in Tajikistan, humanitarian aid workers are there.

The changed nature of conflict has in turn transformed the international community's task. In addition to becoming more complex, protecting and providing has become vastly more dangerous. Increasingly, aid workers and peacekeepers operate in an intensely politicized climate wrought with uncertainty and insecurity. In internal wars where civilians are targeted, those providing succor have all too often found themselves also in the line of fire. The traditional shields of neutrality and impartiality offer, all too often, no defense. The impact of this change is brought home by some of the personal accounts in this book, which tell a harrowing tale of the vulnerability of the aid providers. Since 1992, 198 civilian personnel have lost their lives in the service of the United Nations. In the last seven years, 240 UN civilian staff were taken hostage or kidnapped. Delegates of the Red Cross movement, NGO workers, and the media have been similarly exposed. A far greater number sustained profound personal psychological scars in the course of doing their jobs.

In brief, while the need to be present at the front line has never been greater, the perils of being there have never been more acute.

What then can be done? While the changes in the environment of humanitarian action and peacekeeping run deep, a number of steps can be taken by the international community: the threats that have been noted in the preceding chapters represent serious, though not insuperable, challenges. As this book has shown, there are a number of areas where real improvements can be made at the operational level to enhance staff security and address the devastating impact of post-traumatic stress.

At the global level, a good start would be to bring pressure to bear on host states to live up to their commitments. From the perspective of the humanitarian workers, peacekeepers, and the media, this is perhaps the single most crucial area for improvement. The formal recognition by all UN Member States that the protection of civilians in armed conflict is a responsibility of the Security Council was a positive first step; however, the reality in today's world is that the majority of States still define security more in terms of their sovereignty and territorial integrity than in terms of the rights and welfare of their civilian populations. This is particularly true, as is very often the case, when states are not in de facto control of parts of their territory or when civilians fleeing persecution seek refuge across their borders.

The concept of protection implies the primary responsibilities of Member States engaged in armed conflict to safeguard international humanitarian and human rights law. However, in practice this is an area where governments have been frequently unwilling or unable to live up to their commitments. The delivery of humanitarian goods is often seen as political by one or more of the warring parties; consequently, relief workers themselves are often viewed as partial, biased one way or the other. A broadening of the scope of humanitarian action implies a concomitant broadening of the traditional state-based views of security as control and defense of territory. We talk more and more of the importance of "human security:" we must step up our activities to realize a world where human security—the freedom from fear, from hunger, from poverty, from violence—takes precedence over a purely strategic conception, in both the words and deeds of Governments and in the reality on the ground.

All too often, however, the threats come not only from states but from those they are fighting: from so-called "non-state actors." In conditions of state collapse or the breakdown of government institutions, the reality on the ground is frequently that the state is unable or unwilling to provide a sufficient measure of protection. The combatants in such conflicts are often "free-lance" or "entrepreneurial," motivated largely by economic goals, the struggle for control over the exploitation of natural resources such as diamonds being but one of many examples. Such combatants are increasingly inclined to view international protectors and providers as a tempting economic opportunity. Thus, the very concept of humanitarian space often falls victim to localized fragmented interests or the individual ambitions of a particular commander or warlord. In Liberia, we have seen that the control and exploitation of diamonds, timber, and other raw materials has been a principal objective of the warring parties. In Afghanistan and elsewhere, those who profit from internal mayhem tend to have external collaborators profiting from the arms and drug trades. The plunder of natural resources in Cambodia and Sierra Leone could not have occurred in the absence of criminal profiteers and external markets.

If the obstacles posed to the provision of relief to the suffering are to be surmounted, there is no circumventing the need for a broad-based humanitarian dialogue in which non-state actors are included. Affected states, however, are often inclined to view any form of dialogue with non-state actors as an infringement of their sovereignty, especially when those same non-state actors are armed groups in de facto control of part of their territory. Dialogue is often seen as tacit acknowledgment of legitimacy, by which insurgents and rebels achieve recognition "by the back door." It is important that the international community understands, recognizes, and supports the imperative of maintaining a dialogue free from political constraints, and that states accept that such dialogue is not an infringement on their sovereignty.

Several chapters in this book have highlighted the glaring prevalence of impunity despite an agreed upon international legal regime. Aid workers, peacekeepers, and the media can be better protected by strengthening the legal regime, which is meaningless without greater accountability on the part of states and non-state actors alike. There can be little doubt that the climate of impunity has permitted, if not encouraged, aggression toward international protectors and providers. Between 1992 and 2000 only three of the 177 cases involving the violent death of UN personnel have been brought to justice. In May 2001, a Jakarta court handed down light sentences to six men in connection with the brutal killings on 6 September 2000 of three staff members of UNHCR in West Timor. The Secretary-General expressed shock, stating that this constituted a blow to the international community's efforts to ensure the safety and security of humanitarian personnel, and a wholly unacceptable response to the ultimate sacrifice which our three colleagues made. Putting an end to impunity is, undoubtedly, one of the most fundamental requirements for generating new beginnings and effective peace-building following conflicts; it is also vital if we are to limit the targeting of aid workers and peacekeepers.

There are also actions that we must take internally to enhance the safety of our staff. Aside from the Secretary-General's special measures to strengthen staff security, outlined earlier in this book, we must apply pressure for a clear demarcation of duties and clear mandates in complex emergencies, both within the aid community and within the wider international community. We must be wary of situations where, in lieu of political action, humanitarianism has become the default option. This is perilous, since "passing the buck" can have the practical effect of placing humanitarian workers in harm's way, alone and exposed where, in fact, robust measures are called for. We also need to be clear as to who does what on the ground: there are aspects of protection, like the identification and separation of armed elements from the civilian population or the clearance of mines and unexplored ordnance, that are the responsibility of police and soldiers rather than aid workers. Other protection activities, like those undertaken by the ICRC, the High Commissioner for Human Rights or UNHCR in support of prisoners of war, refugees and other vulnerable groups, should remain their prerogative.

Lastly, far from the front line, it is imperative to raise awareness in donor countries of these crises and their impacts. At present, media interest in humanitarian crises and the challenges faced by humanitarian aid workers tends to be fitful and short-term. The media have the potential to play a much greater role in drawing attention to the plight of civilian populations. They can raise the needed public awareness of the inherent risks and limits to humanitarian action and peacekeeping. The United Nations with its partners must therefore be more proactive in drawing media attention to emergencies, as well as to the risks and concerns of protectors and providers on the ground. Public pressure to do something in the face of complex emergencies, in turn, will ultimately translate into pressure on governments to safeguard humanitarian space.

Ultimately, all these recommendations point in one direction: broadening the dialogue. This book is an important step in doing just that. Involving all relevant actors in a humanitarian dialogue: the United Nations as well as individual Member States, governmental parties to conflicts as well as non-state actors, the media as well as the general public, civil society as well as the corporate sector, is a pressing task. Only in this way will we be able to construct the global partnership that is required, today more than ever, for the promotion of peace and security and the alleviation of human suffering.

In the final analysis, greater security can only translate into greater effectiveness. One indisputable lesson of the tragedies of the last decade is that we cannot afford to do nothing. The costs of inaction, both to those who provide and protect and to those in need of such assistance, have never been greater. Our message to Member States must be clear and unequivocal: "Enough is enough. We work to save lives on behalf of everyone. We cannot tolerate failure to honor security obligations to our staff." The UN and its partners are working urgently to increase dramatically the protection of staff and to ensure adequate post-traumatic support is available to them. Any measures taken, however, will be inadequate if the Governments concerned do not give their own whole-hearted and practical commitment to ensuring the security of humanitarian personnel and their fellow international protectors and providers.

About the Editor

DR. YAEL DANIELI is a clinical psychologist in private practice, a victimologist, traumatologist, and the Director of the Group Project for Holocaust Survivors and their Children, which she co-founded in 1975 in the New York City area. She has done extensive psychotherapeutic work with survivors and children of survivors on individual, family, group and community bases; studied post-war responses and attitudes toward them, and the impact these and the Holocaust had on their lives; lectured widely and published in numerous books and journals, translated into at least 8 languages, around the world on these findings and on optimal care and training for this and other victim/survivor populations, and received several awards for her work. Most recently, she has served as consultant to South Africa's Truth and Reconciliation Commission and the Rwandan government on reparations for victims, and is leading ongoing Project (Promoting a Dialogue: "Democracy Cannot Be Built with the Hands of Broken Souls") in Bosnia and Herzegovina. Her books are *International Responses to Traumatic Stress. . .* ; *The Universal Declaration of Human Rights: Fifty Years and Beyond* (Baywood) both published for and on behalf of the United Nations; and *International Handbook of Multigenerational Legacies of Trauma* (Plenum/Kluwer). She is Director of Psychological Services for the Center for Rehabilitation of Torture Victims, and Adjunct Associate Professor of Medicine, Seton Hall University School of Graduate Education, New Jersey.

A Founding Director of The International Society for Traumatic Stress Studies, Dr. Danieli was its (1988-1989) President. The Initial Report of her Presidential Task Force on Curriculum, Education, and Training for professionals working with victim/survivors was adopted by the United Nations (E/AC.57/1990/NGO.3). Currently she co-chairs the ISTSS's Task Force on International Trauma Training

Dr. Danieli has been the Senior Representative to the United Nations of the World Federation for Mental Health and of the International Society for Traumatic Stress Studies. A Founding Member of WFMH's Scientific Committee on the Mental Health Needs of Victims, and Chair, she has been active in developing, promoting, adapting and implementing the United Nations *Declaration of Basic Principles of Justice for Victims of Crime and Abuse of Power* (A/RES/40/34) and all subsequent UN victims-related work, including their right to reparation (E/CN.4/Sub.2/1996/17) and their role of in the International Criminal Court.

She has served as Consultant to the UN Crime Prevention and Criminal Justice Branch and on the Board of its International Scientific and Professional Advisory

Council; a consultant to UNICEF, the Office of the UN High Commissioner for Human Rights and various governments on trauma and victim/survivors' rights and care. In the U.S., she has consulted for the National Institute of Mental Health, the Federal Bureau of Investigation, Associated Press and CNN.

Concurrent with a variety of clinical activities, during 1970-1977 she taught Psychology at Brooklyn College, and John Jay College for Criminal Justice, of the City University of New York, and in the 1980s at the National Institute for the Psychotherapies. Before arriving in the United States, where she earned her Doctorate in Psychology at New York University (1981), she was a Sergeant in the Israeli Armed Forces, earned degrees, taught and wrote in music, philosophy and psychology.

Contributors

AMY B. ADLER is the lead scientist at the U.S. Army Medical Research Unit-Europe in Heidelberg, Germany. Her operational experience includes assignments to Kosovo, Bosnia, Hungary, and Croatia, and she has published extensively on military deployment issues. She is a graduate of Brown University and holds M.A. and Ph.D. degrees from the University of Kansas in psychology.

ALASTAIR AGER is Director of the Centre for International Health Studies and Professor of Applied Psychology at Queen Margaret University College, Edinburgh, Scotland. He is a Board Member of the Antares Foundation, Amsterdam, a Research Associate of the Refugee Studies Centre, University of Oxford, and an Honorary Consultant Psychologist with the Rivers Centre, Edinburgh Primary Healthcare Trust. He has published over 50 works, including the edited *Refugees: Perspectives on the Experience of Forced Migration* (1999, London: Cassell). He has worked with a number of inter-governmental and non-governmental agencies, with field experience across southern Africa, south Asia, the Caribbean, and eastern Europe.

GIELT ALGRA studied political science at the Free University of Amsterdam. He served as President of the Dutch conscripts union, and of the European council of Conscripts Organisations (ECCO). He works at the Veterans' Institute in Doorn, in the Netherlands (VI), doing research on Dutch peacekeeping veterans.

PAUL E. ARÈS, a Canadian, joined the UN World Food Programme in 1991, where he was Chief of Resources and then Chief of Programming before becoming WFP Regional Manager for West Africa in 1997. Since July 2000, he is on loan from WFP as Associate Director to the United Nations Development Group Office in New York. Earlier in his career, he studied opera and promoted bilingualism and French-Canadian culture. He was also involved in the restoration of historical buildings and sites, was Director of the Property Program for Heritage Canada, and was a Deputy Director in the International Programs Branch at Agriculture Canada.

MILAGROS BACAREZA completed both her undergraduate and medical degrees at the University of Santo Tomas in Manila, Philippines. She completed a post-graduate internship at the same university followed by residency training in psychiatry at the National Center for Mental Health. A Filipino psychiatrist, Dr. Bacareza has worked with refugees, disaster survivors, and other vulnerable persons in the Philippines, Myanmar, and Papua New Guinea.

OMAR BAKHET is the Director of the Emergency Response Division of the United Nations Development Programme.

MARTIN BARBER is Chief of the UN Mine Action Service in New York. He holds a Ph.D. in Sociology. From 1975 to 1981 he served with UNHCR in Southeast Asia. In 1981 he was appointed Director of the British Refugee Council. In 1988 he joined the UN Office for Coordination of Assistance to Afghanistan, becoming Humanitarian Coordinator in 1995. From 1996 to 1998 he served as Deputy SRSG in Bosnia and Herzegovina, and from 1998 to 2000 as Chief of Policy in the Officer for Coordination of Humanitarian Affairs in New York. Mr. Barber is married with two sons.

M. CHERIF BASSIOUNI is Professor of Law and President, International Human Rights Law Institute, DePaul University College of Law; President, International Association of Penal Law; President, International Institute of Higher Studies in Criminal Sciences; Chairman, Drafting Committee of the United Nations Diplomatic Conference on the Establishment of an International Criminal Court; Former Chairman, United Nations Commission of Experts Established Pursuant to Security Council Resolution 780 (1992) to Investigate Violations of International Humanitarian Law in the former Yugoslavia.

BILL BERKELEY is the author of *The Graves Are Not Yet Full—Race, Tribe and Power in the Heart of Africa.* He has been an editorial writer at *The New York Times,* and for more than a decade he reported on African affairs for *The Atlantic Monthly, The New Republic, The New York Times Magazine,* and *The Washington Post.*

CATHERINE A. BERTINI is the Executive Director of the World Food Programme. Appointed in 1992, she was the first American woman to head a UN organization and the first woman to lead WFP. Previously, Bertini worked in the U.S. Government, in the Departments of Agriculture and Health and Human Services. Born in Syracuse, New York, she graduated from State University of New York at Albany. Her numerous awards include honorary doctorates from the State University of New York and McGill University in Montreal, Canada. She is married to international photographer Thomas Haskell.

M.-CHRISTIANE BOURLOYANNIS-VRAILAS, Research Fellow, Marangopoulos Foundation for Human Rights, Athens, Greece; former Legal Officer, Codification Division, UN Office of Legal Affairs. Over her 12-year service with the UN, she was a member of the Secretariat of various legal bodies, including the Sixth Committee of the General Assembly, International Law Commission, Ad Hoc Committee on the Elaboration of an International Convention dealing with the Safety and Security of UN and Associated Personnel, Ad Hoc Committee on International Terrorism, and Rome Conference on the Establishment of an International Criminal Court. Author of several articles on legal aspects of the work of the UN and international criminal law.

HILARY BOWER is a field information officer for the World Health Organization's Emergency and Humanitarian Action Department and spends the majority of her time traveling in countries of complex emergency. In the past two years she has worked in Kosovo, Ethiopia, Somalia, South Sudan, Eritrea, Sierra Leone,

Guinea, Liberia, Iraq, Angola, and the Democratic Republic of the Congo. Previously she was a freelance journalist specializing in health, science, and medicine for British national daily newspapers, monthly magazines, and medical journals and, for a period, editor of health features with the *Guardian* newspaper.

INGE BRAMSEN, Ph.D., is working as a researcher and university lecturer at the department of medical psychology of the VU Medical Center, Amsterdam, The Netherlands. In 1995, she finished her thesis on the long-term psychological adjustment of World War II survivors in the Netherlands. She has continued her research in the field of traumatic stress until the present time.

SHIRLEY N. BROWNELL is Chief of the Publications Service in the United Nations Department of Public Information. Born in Liberia and educated in England and the United States, she studied journalism and international relations. She has worked as a reporter, editor, and media analyst in her 23 years at the United Nations, having also served as Spokeswoman for the President of the 54th session of the General Assembly in 1999-2000. She was injured in an ambush while on a peace-keeping mission in Somalia in 1993.

KEVIN M. CAHILL, M.D., is president of the Center for International Health and Cooperation. He holds professional academic appointments in tropical medicine as well as in international affairs. He is the author of many books and articles on these topics. He is a senior consultant to the United Nations health services and to numerous governments.

IAN D. CAMPBELL, a physician, is the International Health Programme Consultant of The Salvation Army International Headquarters based in London, United Kingdom. Since 1990 this task included facilitation of participatory design and evaluation of home- and community-based approaches to a range of health issues, often resourced by hospitals or clinic systems. Prior to this role, he was the Chief Medical Officer at the Salvation Army Chikankata Hospital in rural Zambia, from 1983.

SHARON CAPELING-ALAKIJA has been Executive Co-ordinator of the United Nations Volunteers program since January 1998. Prior to that, she was Director of the Office of Evaluation and Strategic Planning at the United Nations Development Programme (1994-1997), and Director of the United Nations Development Fund for Women (1989-1994). She received her degree in education from the University of Saskatchewan, and began her career as a volunteer with CUSO (formerly Canadian University Service Overseas).

CARL A. CASTRO is a Major in the U.S. Army and Commander of the U.S. Army Medical Research Unit–Europe in Heidelberg, Germany. In addition to serving in multiple deployments to Bosnia and Kosovo, he has been chief and program manager of several different medical research programs. He is a graduate of Wichita State University and holds an M.A. and Ph.D. in psychology from the University of Colorado. He is the author of over 60 scientific publications.

CHRIS CRAMER, based in CNN world headquarters in Atlanta, is president of CNN International Networks, responsible for the CNN News Group's rapidly expanding news networks and Web sites outside of the United States, currently totaling 23. Since joining CNN, he has introduced 70 hours of new programming each week and, in September 1997, launched "regionalization," that led to creating five separately scheduled English language international CNN channels throughout the world. Before joining CNN in 1996, he was the head of newsgathering for the British Broadcasting Corporation. Cramer is Honorary Chairman of Newscoverage Unlimited, and author of the book *Hostage*.

KATHLEEN CRAVERO became Deputy Executive Director of the Joint United Nations Programme on HIV/AIDS (UNAIDS) on 1 March 2000, on secondment from UNICEF. She assists in overall management of the UNAIDS Secretariat, as well as having direct responsibility for the External Relations and Programme Support Departments. Among her responsibilities are cosponsor relations, UNAIDS governance structures, resource mobilization, and liaison with NGOs and the private sector. She has been UN Resident Coordinator in Burundi, and has represented UNICEF in Uganda and Chad. Ms. Cravero has a doctorate in Political Sciences (Fordham University) and a Masters in Public Health (Columbia University).

MAAIKE DE VRIES has been working during the last four years at the University Medical Centre St. Radboud, Nijmegen, The Netherlands, Department of Medical Psychology. She conducted several studies on health symptoms in (ex-)servicemen who were deployed in the 1992-93 peace operation UNTAC. In 1996 she got her degree (cum laude) in Health Sciences at Maastricht University, The Netherlands.

MARIE DIMOND joined the United Nations in 1994. After serving in Somalia, southern Sudan and Burundi, she joined UNDP's Emergency Response Division in New York in 2000. From 1991 to 1993 she also served as a Peace Corps Volunteer in Namibia. She holds a B.A. degree in Political Science and French from Boston University.

ANJA J. E. DIRKZWAGER, M.A., is a Ph.D. student at the department of medical psychology of the VU Medical Center, Amsterdam, The Netherlands. She is studying the long-term psychological adjustment of elderly World War II veterans and peacekeeping veterans and their families.

SUE DOWNIE of the Department of Politics, Monash University, Melbourne, Australia, is a former Asia correspondent who has written widely on peacekeeping, and is completing *Inside Peacekeeping: The UN in Cambodia and East Timor* and a doctoral thesis on peacekeeping and peacebuilding.

JOHN FAWCETT is Director of Staff Support Services for World Vision International based in Monrovia, California. Between 1993 and 1996 he worked for WVI in Cambodia where he was responsible for the development of support services for 60 international and 350 local staff. Since 1996 he has been located at the WVI international coordinating office. He has led emergency support interventions in Sierra Leone, Northeast India, Cambodia, Lebanon, and Kosovo. He is also a leading trainer in field security management in NGO environments and has considerable experience in stress and trauma management in war zones.

ANTHONY FEINSTEIN obtained his medical degree in South Africa and completed his postgraduate training in Psychiatry at the Royal Free Hospital in London. Thereafter, he undertook his Ph.D. through the University of London and the Institute of Neurology, Queen Square. He is currently an Associate Professor of

Psychiatry at the University of Toronto and Director of the Neuropsychiatry Program at Sunnybrook and Women's College Health Science Center. His research interests are the neuropsychiatry of multiple sclerosis and traumatic brain injury, and coping with life-threatening stressors. He also studied mental health in post-apartheid Namibia on a Guggenheim Fellowship.

ERIK FLAPPER is senior partner with the Antares Foundation, Amsterdam, The Netherlands. He has a background in physiotherapy and education and has specialized in treatment of clients with psychosomatic complaints and symptoms of burnout related to traumatic incidents or life events. He has been active for six years in the Psycho Social Care and Trauma Unit of Médecins Sans Frontières–Holland, as a field consultant, trainer, and trauma specialist. He has conducted field consultations, debriefings, and workshops on trauma prevention and stress management for international and national NGOs in Africa (Rwanda, Burundi, Somalia, Democratic Republic of Congo), South America, the Balkans, and the former Soviet republics.

ROBERT M. FRANK, a founder of Newscoverage Unlimited, is based in Montreal, where he has, since 1999, reported freelance for *The New York Times*. He began his career in television news with the Canadian Broadcasting Corporation, hosted a radio current affairs morning show on Baffin Island, and later worked as a spokesman for several large organizations.

JOSHUA FRIEDMAN, a winner of the Pulitzer Prize in international reporting, covers wars and humanitarian disasters for *Newsday*. He is a former chairman of the Committee to Protect Journalists and teaches international reporting at Columbia University Graduate School of Journalism.

ELIZABETH D. GIBBONS' career in social development and humanitarian affairs has spanned more than 20 years, 17 of which have been spent with the United Nations Children's Fund (UNICEF). Between assignments in New York City, she lived and worked in Togo, Kenya, Zimbabwe, Angola, and Madagascar before being appointed in 1992 to head UNICEF's office in Port-au-Prince, Haiti, where she stayed for more than four years. Now UNICEF's Representative to Guatemala and Belize, Ms. Gibbons holds degrees from Smith College and Columbia University; she is the author of Sanctions in Haiti: Human Rights and Democracy under Assault.

MARIANA GOETZ is an Associate Legal Officer at the International Criminal Tribunal for Rwanda. She studied law at King's College, London University. After completing a Master's in International Law at the London School of Economics in 1996, she worked in Brussels, first as an intern at the European Commission Humanitarian Office, then for an NGO "No Peace Without Justice," campaigning for the establishment of an International Criminal Court. She joined the Rwanda Tribunal in August 1999.

WILLIAM D. HAGLUND was Chief Medical Investigator of the King County Medical Examiner's Office. In 1995 he became Senior Forensic Advisor for the United Nations International Criminal Tribunals (Rwanda and the former Yugoslavia). Now Director of the International Forensic Program for Physicians for Human Rights, he has conducted forensic investigations worldwide. He teaches investigators through the Washington State Criminal Justice Training Commission.

He has served on the Board of Directors of the National Association of Medical Examiners, is a past president of the Washington State Coroner's Association, and is a fellow of the American Academy of Forensic Sciences.

RON HAVIV's images of the first killings of Bosnian civilians in the civil war of the former Yugoslavia, warned the world of the horrors to come. Since the onset of conflict in the Balkans, he has continually photographed the ongoing strife in this turbulent region, committed to the necessity of keeping our attention focused on the emotional consequences of these bloody ethnic wars. Widely published by magazines throughout the world, his photographs have earned him several World Press and Overseas Press Club awards and the Leica Medal of Excellence. *Blood and Honey: A Balkan War Journal* is his first book.

REINHART HELMKE's career with the United Nations system began in Brazil in 1973 and led him across the world in different capacities with the International Labor Organization, UN Development Programme, International Atomic Energy Agency, and the UN. Since 1994 he has been Executive Director of the UN Office for Project Services, the only entirely self-financing entity in the UN system, handling a worldwide project portfolio of $3.7 billion. A German citizen, he holds a degree in economics and finance, with a specialization in foreign trade. He is a director of Social Accountability International and the Bonn International Conversion Center.

ARTHUR C. HELTON is Program Director of Peace and Conflict, and Senior Fellow for Refugee Studies and Preventive Action at the Council on Foreign Relations. Previously, Mr. Helton founded and then directed the Open Society Institute's Forced Migration Projects, as well as the Refugee Project at the Lawyer's Committee for Human Rights. Mr. Helton has taught courses on migration and forced displacement at the New York University School of Law, and at the Central European University (Budapest). He also teaches a course on refugee law and policy at the Columbia Law School begun in the fall of 2001.

NOELEEN HEYZER is the Executive Director of the United Nations Development Fund for Women (UNIFEM). Born in Singapore, Dr. Heyzer received her Ph.D. in the Social Sciences from the University of Cambridge, England, and was a Research Fellow at the Institute for Development Studies, Sussex, England. Since her arrival in 1994, Dr. Heyzer has doubled UNIFEM's annual resource base while augmenting strategic partnerships between women's groups, governments, and bilateral donors globally. With programs in 130 nations, UNIFEM is dedicated to expanding women's economic capacities and promoting women's human rights and their participation in governance.

KRIS HURLBURT has worked for the International Federation of Red Cross and Red Crescent Societies since 1993, managing its social welfare program in post-war Croatia, coordinating relief and development efforts in Asia when based in Geneva, Switzerland; and pioneering psychosocial services in Kosovo. In the United States she spent 12 years as a child abuse specialist, conducting investigations, advocacy, and training and worked under a U.S. Department of Justice grant implementing missing and exploited children's programs. She participated in the development of several not-for-profit organizations and co-founded a critical incident debriefing team. She holds a Master's degree in Counseling Psychology.

SØREN JESSEN-PETERSEN has been the Assistant High Commissioner for Refugees since January 1998, supervising the Regional Bureaus and the Division of Operational Support. Previously, he served as Director of the UNHCR Liaison Office at UN Headquarters in New York (1994-1998); the High Commissioner's Special Envoy to the former Yugoslavia (1995-1996); Chef de Cabinet of the High Commissioner (1990-1993), and Director of External Relations (1992-1994). In 1989, Mr. Jessen-Petersen was seconded from UNHCR to be Special Advisor to the UN Under-Secretary-General for Political Affairs. Other assignments include Executive Secretary of the Intergovernmental Conference on Asylum-Seekers and Refugees in Europe (1985), and Executive Secretary of the Second International Conference on Assistance to Refugees in Africa (ICARA II) from 1983 to 1984.

NILS ARNE KASTBERG is presently Director of the Office of Emergency Programmes in UNICEF, New York. As part of his duties, he coordinates emergency programmes; advises the Executive Director on policy and strategy matters; supports her in mobilizing UNICEF corporate response for complex emergencies; and liaises with the other UN agencies on emergencies. Previously, he worked in different agencies, representing Sweden and the United Nations, and served in various countries in Africa, Asia, Latin America, and prior to his present position, in Bosnia and Herzegovina. He obtained his education in Sweden, the United Kingdom, and the United States.

BEN KIERNAN is the A. Whitney Griswold Professor of History and Director of the Genocide Studies Program at Yale University, and Convenor of the Yale East Timor Project. He is the author of *How Pol Pot Came to Power* (1985), *The Pol Pot Regime* (1996), and other works on Southeast Asia and genocide, and was founding Director of the Cambodian Genocide Program, 1994-1999.

ELIZABETH KRAMER has been working as a public affairs specialist for the Peace Corps New York regional office since 1999, having worked in print and radio journalism and communications since 1985. From 1991 to 1994 she served as a Peace Corps volunteer in the Federal Islamic Republic of the Comoros, working as a communications specialist in an environmental program. She worked as a communications officer at the United Nations Environment Programme (1994-1995) and for UNICEF's Nairobi-based Operation Lifeline Sudan, its Burundi office, and covering the eastern and southern Africa regions (1995-1999).

XAVIER LEUS, M.D., M.P.H., M.S. (Sloan Fellow) is presently the Director for Emergency and Humanitarian Action at the World Health Organization (WHO), with a mission, through a concerted effort across WHO, to increase the capacity and self-reliance of countries in the prevention of disasters, preparation for emergencies, mitigation of their health consequences, and the creation of a synergy between emergency action and sustainable development. A medical epidemiologist, he has worked in international health over the past 20 years, both in development cooperation and health coordination as well as in humanitarian assistance, or the development of cross-border health programs.

BARBARA LOPES CARDOZO, M.D., M.P.H., holds a Medical degree from the University of Amsterdam, a Master's degree in Public Health from Tulane University, and a specialization in Psychiatry from Louisiana State University. She is a founding member of Doctors Without Borders—Holland. She worked as a medical coordinator for the United Nations High Commissioner for Refugees in 1996. Currently, she is the mental health expert at the International Emergency and Refugee Health branch of the U.S. Centers for Disease Control in Atlanta, Georgia, focusing on mental health and psychosocial issues in complex emergencies.

YOUSSEF MAHMOUD is Director of the Africa Division in the United Nations Department of Political Affairs in New York. Prior to this assignment, he served with the UN Transitional Authority in Cambodia (UNTAC) and, subsequently, as Head of the Office of the Under-Secretary-General for Political Affairs and Senior Advisor to several Special Envoys of the Secretary-General for Central Africa. He received his Ph.D. in Linguistics from Georgetown University and taught at the University of Tunis, Tunisia, before joining the United Nations in 1981.

BEN MAJEKODUNMI completed his university education in law and politics in the United Kingdom, Portugal, and France. He first joined the United Nations in 1994 with the High Commissioner for Refugees in Geneva. From 1994 to 1996 he worked with the Office of the High Commissioner for Human Rights' (OHCHR) field operation to Rwanda. In 1997 he joined UNICEF, working first with the Country Office in Burundi and moving, in 1998, to UNICEF's International Child Development Center in Florence. He re-joined OHCHR in 1999 and is currently based in Geneva.

SONIA MARGALLO, a Filipino psychologist, obtained a Bachelor of Science in Elementary Education at Far Eastern University in Manila, Philippines. She completed graduate studies in social psychology at Ateneo de Manila University and pursued a doctorate in clinical psychology at the University of the Philippines. Ms. Margallo has worked with refugees and displaced persons for many years in the Philippines, Hong Kong, Cambodia, Myanmar, and Indonesia.

IAN MARTIN was Special Representative of the Secretary-General for the East Timor Popular Consultation and head of the United Nations Mission in East Timor (UNAMET) in 1999. He has worked for the UN or other international organizations in Haiti, Rwanda, and Bosnia, and is currently Deputy Special Representative of the Secretary General in the UN Mission in Ethiopia and Eritrea. He was Secretary General of Amnesty International 1986-92.

GERALD MARTONE is the Director of Emergency Response at the International Rescue Committee's Headquarters in New York. In this role, he is responsible for implementing emergency start-up operations and concluding assessments in response to complex humanitarian emergencies. During the past eight years at IRC, he has overseen the start-up of programs in Burundi, Liberia, Kosovo, Chechnya, Ingushetia, DR Congo, Bas Congo, Sierra Leone, Congo-Brazzaville, Rwanda, East Timor, West Timor, Guinea-Bissau, Northern Uganda, Albania, Macedonia, Angola, and Ethiopia.

PETRA MICZAIKA is the Head of the World Food Programme (WFP) Staff Counseling Unit. She holds degrees in pharmacology and psychology and worked in the psychopharmacological research of depression. After raising her children, she trained in Bioenergetic Analysis and pursued a career as a psychotherapist. She has worked for WFP since 1995.

BO MILLS, Consultant in Stress Management and Psychosexual Medicine, worked as a surgeon in the war zone in north Sri Lanka in the mid-1980s and took part in many interviews with war correspondents at that time. Working in Psychosexual Medicine naturally led to a special interest in the impact of trauma on partners and families. He is Guest Editor for the British Association of Sexual and Relationship Therapy, has been Clinical Tutor at the Maudsley Hospital, Consultant to the Body Shop International in Stress Management, and Fellow of the Royal Society of Medicine. Dr. Mills has lectured widely in the United Kingdom and internationally on stress management and the impact of stress on families.

JEAN-GUY MORISSET, Staff Counselor, United Nations Secretariat, has managed the employee assistance program of the United Nations Secretariat since 1988, serving staff and families of all United Nations Organizations at Headquarters New York. His activities have included mission readiness training and emergency support following Swissair 111 and helicopter crashes in Haiti and Mongolia. He had previously served with the Canadian University Service Overseas in Burundi and with the Canadian International Development Agency in Haiti. He has degrees in Philosophy and in Psychology from the University of Ottawa and is a member of the Ordre des Psychologues du Québec.

KATHLEEN NADER, D.S.W., has worked both nationally and internationally since 1974 to provide psychotherapy, consultations, training, and specialized interventions for children, adults, families, and communities exposed to war, other violence, disaster, treatment for catastrophic illness, and severe accidents. Dr. Nader has written and contributed to a variety of publications, screening instruments, and videotapes regarding childhood trauma.

ELIZABETH NEUFFER is a reporter for the *Boston Globe*. As a foreign correspondent, she has reported on conflicts in the Middle East, Europe, and Africa. She is the author of *The Key to My Neighbor's House: Searching for Justice in Bosnia and Rwanda,* which tells the story of the two war crimes tribunals and the victims who look to them for justice.

ELANA NEWMAN, Assistant Professor of Psychology at the University of Tulsa, is a clinical psychologist who studies the meaning, aftermath, and assessment of psychological trauma and Post Traumatic Stress Disorder (PTSD). Recent research projects examine: 1) how media professionals are affected by covering traumatic events; 2) research ethics; and 3) the health costs of PTSD. Currently she serves as editor of *Traumatic Stresspoints,* the newsletter for the International Society of Traumatic Stress Studies, and on the Executive Board for the Dart Center for Journalism and Trauma.

CLÉMENTINE OLIVIER is a lawyer specializing in International Criminal Law and Humanitarian Law. She has a Diplôme D'Etudes Approfondies in Public International Law from the University of Paris II, France, and a Master's of

International Human Rights Law from the University of Essex, Great Britain. She has worked as an expatriate for Handicap International (HI) from 1994 to 1997 as a Head of Mission in the field in Rwanda, former Yugoslavia, and Tanzania. She then worked at HI's Headquarters in Lyon, France, both as a lawyer and as the Desk Officer for programs in the Middle East until 1999.

MICHAEL D. O'NEILL has been Coordinator for Volunteer Safety and Overseas Security for the U.S. Peace Corps since 1998. In this capacity he has conducted research, developed training resources, formulated policy recommendations, and coordinated the efforts of the intra-agency Volunteer Safety Council to support Peace Corps staff and volunteers in their efforts to address safety risks and mitigate crises. His overseas work included Peace Corps Volunteer, Project Coordinator (Sierra Leone, 1978-82; 1982-88); Regional Relief Administrator, Red Cross (Sierra Leone, 1991-92; Ethiopia, 1993). He earned a BSSW from St. Louis University and a M.Sc. in International Rural Development Planning from the University of Guelph in Ontario, Canada.

JOHN OWEN is the European Director of The Freedom Forum, an international journalism foundation with headquarters in the United States. He created the London office in 1996. In addition to organizing journalism programs and events in London, he also oversees Forum activities in Central and Eastern Europe, the Balkans, and former Soviet Union. Before joining The Freedom Forum, he was chief of foreign bureaus for CBC Television News and London Bureau Chief. He spent 20 years with the CBC and headed CBC Television News for five years as its chief news editor based in Toronto. Prior to his CBC career, he worked in radio and television news in Milwaukee, Wisconsin, and Rochester, New York. He received a BA from DePauw University and an MA from Indiana University.

SHEILA M. PLATT is a social worker who has spent 15 years working with organizations wishing to develop comprehensive support and training for staff exposed by their work to both physical and psychological hazard. She has consulted to the United Nations, including UNHCR, UNICEF, UNDP, and UNEP, as well as to international and national NGOs, News and Human Rights organizations. Based in New York, she currently holds the position of Director for External Affairs for Community and Family Services International (CFSI). Her MSW is from Catholic University, Washington, D.C.

ALISON RADER is the consultant for community development in relation to HIV/AIDS and health issues working with The Salvation Army International Headquarters. Since 1988 she has been intensively involved in participatory design and evaluation at local and organizational levels, and has facilitated process analysis of the link of care to change in relation to the impact of HIV/AIDS on local communities and within organizations.

BEVERLEY RAPHAEL is Director of the Centre for Mental Health for NSW and Emeritus Professor in Psychiatry from the University of Queensland. She also holds professorial appointments at The University of NSW and The University of Sydney. She has a long-term interest in prevention in mental health, with special reference to child and adolescent mental health, family issues, and issues affecting consumers in mental health care systems, and in a public health approach to mental health. She has been involved in the development of Aboriginal Mental Health Policy and contributed in the field of trauma, grief, and disasters.

PAUL REES of Centurion Risk Assessment Services Ltd. (United Kingdom) (former Royal Marine Commando) was asked, in 1995, to devise a one-day pilot course for BBC staff heading to volatile areas. Since then, the training has developed into a practical five-day course that aims to raise awareness of the hidden dangers faced by journalists, camera crews, and aid workers working in the field. Centurion now trains the staff of many other international broadcasters, as well as charity workers, for whom Hostile Environments training has become mandatory for staff heading to volatile regions.

DIANA RUSSLER is Deputy Security Coordinator for the United Nations. She received her License-es-Lettres (Linguistics) from Université de Brazzaville, Congo, and her Master of Arts in International Relations and Political Science from New York University. She joined the United Nations secretariat in 1978 as a political officer in the Department of Political Affairs, Trusteeship and Decolonization. She has also worked in the Department of Administration and Management, has been Secretary of the Committee on Contracts, and Administrative Officer of the Advisory Committee on Administrative and Budgetary Questions.

PETER SALAMA, M.B.B.S., M.P.H., is a medical epidemiologist with the International Emergency and Refugee Health Branch at the U.S. Centers for Disease Control and Prevention. He trained as a physician in Australia and was a medical officer with MSF. A Fulbright and Harkness scholar in international health policy, he holds a Masters of Public Health in International Health from Harvard University where he taught a course on Health and Human Rights. His last position was as Medical Co-coordinator for Emergency Programs for the largest Irish NGO, Concern. He has led numerous health assessments and programs in refugee and emergency settings.

MINNA SCHRAG is a retired litigation partner in the Proskauer Rose law firm in New York, and a former Assistant United States Attorney. In 1994 and 1995 she was a senior trial attorney at the International Criminal Tribunal for the former Yugoslavia in The Hague. She served on the United States delegation in the negotiations for establishing the International Criminal Court, is a board member of the International Center for Transitional Justice, and has spoken and written widely about international criminal justice issues.

WINNIFRED SIMON is a senior partner with the Antares Foundation, Amsterdam, The Netherlands. She has a background in clinical psychology, philosophy, and education. For over eight years she has been the head of the Psycho Social Care and Trauma Unit of Médecins Sans Frontières–Holland. She has been responsible for training, crisis intervention, and counseling throughout the whole organization. She has set up and supervised a multidisciplinary unit and team of trauma-prevention specialists and facilitated and organized support structures for other MSF organizations. She has conducted numerous field consultations for international and national NGOs in Africa, Southeast Asia, South America, the Balkans, and the former Soviet republics.

SUSANNAH M. SIRKIN has been Deputy Director of Physicians for Human Rights (PHR) since joining in 1987. PHR, an organization that uses science to promote international health by protecting human rights, was a co-recipient of the 1997 Nobel Peace Prize because of its role in founding the International Campaign to Ban Landmines. She has organized medical human rights investigations to dozens of countries, including PHR's International Criminal Tribunal exhumations of mass graves in the former Yugoslavia and Rwanda. Sirkin graduated from Mount Holyoke College and received her Master of Education degree at Boston University.

BARBARA SMITH is the Vice President for Overseas Programs at the International Rescue Committee. She is responsible for 9,000 local and national staff in 28 country programs serving refugees with an annual budget of $100,000,000. Beginning in 1979, she worked in 10 different IRC and ICRC emergency and long-term programs before joining IRC's headquarters in 1994. She has a BS in Nursing from St. Louis University and a PH.D. in Clinical Psychology from Washington University.

FRANK SMYTH is a freelance journalist and a contributor to *Crimes of War: What the Public Should Know,* edited by Roy Gutman and David Rieff. He has covered El Salvador, Guatemala, Iraq, Rwanda, Eritrea, Ethiopia, and Colombia. He has reported for CBS News, consulted for Human Rights Watch and Amnesty International, and written for *The Nation, The New Republic, Jane's Intelligence Review, Foreign Affairs, The Washington Post, The New York Times,* and *The Wall Street Journal.* His clips are posted at www.franksmyth.com.

ANDREW SPEARMAN is a journalist and a photographer, now working as media and information officer with GOAL.

SHASHI THAROOR is Interim Head of the Department of Public Information at the United Nations, where he was previously Director of Communications and Special Projects in the Office of the Secretary-General. During his 23-year UN career, he has served the UN High Commissioner for Refugees in Europe and Southeast Asia and led the team in New York responsible for peacekeeping operations in the former Yugoslavia. He is the award-winning author of five books, including two novels; a sixth, *Riot: A Novel,* was published in the fall of 2001. He completed his Ph.D. at the Fletcher School of Law and Diplomacy at Tufts University.

GORDON J. TURNBULL, Consultant Psychiatrist and Clinical Director of Trauma Services at Ticehurst, previously served in the Royal Air Force and was deployed to the Gulf War as RAF Psychiatric Adviser in the Field. He was responsible for psychological debriefing of British POWs and released British hostages from Lebanon in 1991. His main interests are evaluation and treatment of traumatic stress reactions and development of the special interest group within the International Society for Traumatic Stress Studies to improve awareness of the impact of trauma on peacekeepers, aid workers, and newsgatherers.

ROBERT J. URSANO, Professor and Chairman, Department of Psychiatry and Professor of Neuroscience, Uniformed Services University of the Health Sciences, Bethesda, Maryland, was educated at the University of Notre Dame, Notre Dame, Indiana, and Yale University School of Medicine, New Haven, Connecticut. He was the first Chairman of the American Psychiatric Association Committee on Psychiatric

Aspects of Disaster (1996-2000). He recently received the Lifetime Achievement Award of the International Society of Traumatic Stress Studies. Author of numerous publications on trauma and disasters, he has received many professional honors and recognition for his research/clinical work, and is an often sought international speaker.

REINOUD VAN DEN BERKHOF, B.C. is co-head of the Psycho Social Care Unit of Médecins Sans Frontières–Holland. He graduated from the Royal Dutch Naval Academy in Den Helder, as well as from two Professional Universities in The Netherlands on Human Resource Management and Policy specializing in counseling and coaching. A retired Naval Officer, he had a long history in naval/military management, teaching, and psychological rapid interventions in the Royal Dutch Navy, the Royal Dutch Marine Corps and in the field for Médecins Sans Frontières–Holland. Holland in field stress management and critical incidents.

HENK M. VAN DER PLOEG, Ph.D., is professor in medical psychology at the VU Medical Center, Amsterdam, The Netherlands. He has conducted studies on medical consumption and long-term psychological adjustment of different populations of survivors of traumatic incidents and their families.

PIET VAN GELDER is co-head of the Psycho Social Care Unit of Médecins Sans Frontières–Holland. He studied Child and Adult Education at the University of Amsterdam, The Netherlands, with specialities in Conflict Science, Psychotherapy, and Social Philosophy. He worked extensively in management, teaching, and on MSF Holland psychic rapid interventions in the field regarding field stress management and critical incidents.

TINEKE VAN PIETERSOM is a senior partner with the Antares Foundation, Amsterdam, The Netherlands. Her background is in education, law, and health management. She has held management positions within international humanitarian organizations for over 15 years, in the field and at headquarters, has set up management training for field directors and was responsible for coaching field managers. She carried out field assessments, monitoring missions, and project evaluations for international and national NGOs in the Middle East, Horn of Africa, West Africa, the Balkans, and the former Soviet Republics.

MARK WALKUP works for the U.S. Department of State's Bureau of Population, Refugees, and Migration, where he seeks to integrate research and evaluation into humanitarian policy, program design, and strategic planning. He holds a Ph.D. in political science from the University of Florida. Based on his studies of refugees and those who help them, his dissertation, Policy and Behavior in Humanitarian Organizations: The Institutional Origins of Operational Dysfunction (Ann Arbor, University Microfilms International, 1997) articulates the origins and effects of the peculiar organizational culture of humanitarian organizations.

JOS M. P. WEERTS, M.D., studied medicine at the Catholic University at Nijmegen, The Netherlands, with specialized training in psychiatry and epidemiology. He is the Head of the Centre for Expertise and Research of the National Institute for Veterans in The Netherlands.

STEVAN WEINE is author of *When History is a Nightmare: Lives and Memories of Ethnic Cleansing in Bosnia-Herzegovina* (Rutgers University Press, 1999) and Associate Professor of Psychiatry at the University of Illinois at Chicago.

WENDY WHITE is a military psychiatrist with the Canadian Forces. After completing her medical degree at the University of British Columbia, she worked as a medical officer at Canadian Forces Base Esquimalt for six years. She completed her degree in psychiatry at the University of Calgary and has been stationed at Edmonton Garrison for four years. Lieutenant Colonel White is currently the clinical director of the recently opened Operational Trauma and Stress Support Center which, in conjunction with four "sister clinics" across Canada, cares for Canadian Forces personnel suffering from deployment-related stress.

AD ZIJLMANS studied clinical psychology at the University of Tilburg. Since 1996 he has worked at the Individual Psychological Support Division of the Royal Netherlands Army. His work concentrates on the subject of personnel care and psychological support measures before, during, and after deployment in peacekeeping operations.

Index